WRITING AND LITERACY
IN CHINESE, KOREAN AND JAPANESE

STUDIES IN WRITTEN LANGUAGE AND LITERACY

AIM AND SCOPE

The aim of this series is to advance insight into the multifaceted character of written language, with special emphasis on its uses in different social and cultural settings. It combines interest in sociolinguistic and psycholinguistic accounts of the acquisition and transmission of literacy. The series focusses on descriptive and theoretical reports in areas such as language codification, cognitive models of written language use, written language acquisition in children and adults, the development and implementation of literacy campaigns, and literacy as a social marker relating to gender, ethnicity, and class. The series is intended to be multi-disciplinary, combining insights from linguistics, psychology, sociology, education, anthropology, and philosophy.

Volume 3

Insup Taylor and M. Martin Taylor
Writing and Literacy in Chinese, Korean and Japanese

WRITING AND LITERACY IN CHINESE, KOREAN AND JAPANESE

INSUP TAYLOR

and

M. MARTIN TAYLOR

JOHN BENJAMINS PUBLISHING COMPANY
AMSTERDAM/PHILADELPHIA

TM The paper used in this publication meets the minimum requirements of American National Standard for Information Sciences — Permanence of Paper for Printed Library Materials, ANSI Z39.48-1984.

Library of Congress Cataloging-in-Publication Data

Taylor, Insup.
    Writing and literacy in Chinese, Korean, and Japanese / Insup Taylor, and M. Martin Taylor.
        p.   cm. -- (Studies in written language and literacy, ISSN 0929-7324 ; v. 3)
    Includes bibliographical references and index.
        1. Chinese language. 2. Chinese language--Writing. 3. Korean language. 4. Korean language--Writing. 5. Japanese language. 6. Japanese language--Writing. 7. Literacy. I. Taylor, Martin M. II. Title. III. Series.
PL1171.T37   1995
306.4'4'0951--dc20   95-43614
ISBN 90 272 1794 7 (Eur.) / 1-55619-319-X (US) (alk. paper)   CIP

John Benjamins Publishing Co. • P.O.Box 75577 • 1070 AN Amsterdam • The Netherlands
John Benjamins North America • P.O.Box 27519 • Philadelphia PA 19118-0519 • USA

For 金基梅 (Kim Ki-mae),
I wrote this book for both of us.

About the Authors

Insup Taylor was educated in S. Korea and the USA. She obtained her B.A. in psychology at the Seoul National University, and her M.A. and Ph.D. also in psychology, specializing in psycholinguistics, at the Johns Hopkins University, Baltimore, Maryland. She is involved in a comparative literacy project at the McLuhan Program in Culture and Technology, and is a member of the Association for Korean Studies in Canada, University of Toronto. A multilingual, she is responsible for the content of the present book, and is the "I" of its text and dedication.

She is the author of numerous papers in psycholinguistics as well as the following books:

Introduction to Psycholinguistics (Holt, Rinehart and Winston, 1976)

The Psychology of Reading (with M. M. Taylor, Academic Press, 1983)

Psycholinguistics: Learning and Using Language (with M. M. Taylor, Prentice Hall, 1990)

Scripts and Literacy: Reading and Learning to Read Alphabets, Syllabaries, and Characters (edited with D. R. Olson; Kluwer Academic, 1995)

M. M. Taylor obtained his B.A.Sc. in engineering physics at University of Toronto, M.S.E. in industrial engineering and Ph.D. in psychology at Johns Hopkins University. He edited *The Structure of Multimodal Dialogue, I* and *II*, with F. Néel and D.G. Bouwhuis. He also co-authored *The Psychology of Reading* and *Psycholinguistics* with Insup Taylor, and has published many papers in perceptual and cognitive psychology as well as in psycholinguistics and computer science.

Besides collaborating on both the content and the writing of the book, he made possible its preparation on a computer.

Table of Contents

Part II: Korean

Part III: Japanese

Preface

Chinese, Koreans and Japanese have a long and rich cultural history. In recent years they have achieved, or are in the process of achieving, spectacular economic success. Among them, the Japanese were the first to become an economic power and are now an undisputed economic superpower. South Korea, together with Taiwan, Hong Kong, and Singapore is one of the "four little dragons of Asia." The People's Republic of China (PRC) is transforming its command economy into a market economy at a breakneck pace and may become a major economic power in the near future. Already, measured in purchasing power parity, China is the third largest economy in the world, after the United States and Japan. Among the peoples considered in this book, North Koreans alone cling to a command economy with an uncertain future.

The Chinese, the Koreans, the Japanese use individually unique and fascinating writing systems. All of them use Chinese characters, which have a long history (3400 years, perhaps longer) and a huge number of users (over a quarter of the world's population). To supplement, and in some cases to supplant, Chinese characters, these peoples use a variety of unique and interesting phonetic writing systems, some of them syllabaries and some of them alphabets.

For each writing system or script we describe how it originated and developed, how it relates to its spoken language, how it is learned or taught, how it is used in daily life, how it can be computerized, and how it relates to the literacy, education, and culture of its users, past and present. Some of the issues are straightforward, while others are controversial. Two of the most controversial issues, with far-reaching implications, are how Chinese characters differ from phonetic writing systems, and whether they should be retained or abolished in each of the three East Asian languages. Rather than probing a few narrow topics in depth, we try to cover a wide range of topics to provide an overall picture of scripts and literacy in Chinese, Korean, and Japanese. The discussion is based on personal observations, literature research, and psychologists' experiments.

The book is intended for people from various backgrounds, such as the general public or academics, business people or government officials, students or educators, computer scientists, psychologists, or linguists. It is more for the general public and students than for scholars on East Asia.

The book explains and discusses all the scripts used in Chinese, Korean, and Japanese, often in relation to each other and in comparison with the English alphabet. It also describes literacy associated with these scripts, in a historical, cultural, and educational context. Readers will learn a great deal about various scripts and literacy, some exotic, some familiar, some simple, some complex, but all fascinating.

Toronto 1995

Acknowledgements

I am grateful to the funding agencies and individuals who helped in writing this book. The International Development of Research Centre (IDRC) of Canada funded the McLuhan–Nanjing Cooperative Project on Literacy. The fund enabled me to travel to the People's Republic of China in the fall of 1989 for a firsthand look at reading instruction in kindergartens and primary schools. Prof. Lu Lezhen of Nanjing Normal University worked tirelessly to make the trip to China a success. The IDRC also enabled me to visit in 1990 the Department of East Asian Studies of the University of Hawaii. Unfortunately, the project could not continue because of budgetary retrenchment.

Dr. Forrester R. Pitts, professor emeritus of University of Hawaii, read the early draft of the MS. With his knowledge of all four languages — Chinese, Japanese, Korean, and English — he was an invaluable critic of the book. Dr. Danny D. Steinberg of Surugadai University, as usual supported the project.

On Chinese, helpful comments came from Prof. Zhang Zhi of Beijing Foreign Studies University, Prof. Rumjahn Hoosain of University of Hong Kong, Prof. Wayne Schlepp and Ms. Shuning Sciban of University of Toronto, Ms. Jinwen Steinberg of University of California at Los Angeles, and Ms Dawn Gardham of DCIEM.

On Japanese, among the students in my comparative literacy class, Dr. Ryuko Kubota, Zhang Zhujiang, and Mariko Haneda acted as a sounding board for my ideas.

On Korean, Prof. Noh Myong-wan of Seoul Teachers' College and Prof. Park Kwon-saeng of Daegu University supplied textbooks on the Korean language. Professors Lee Ki-moon and Shim Jae-kee of Seoul National University made valuable corrections and comments. At the University of Toronto, two visiting professors, Shim Jae-rong and Ko Heung-do, and Dr. Kim Young Gon helped in many ways, big and small.

I could not have written this book without the well-stocked and ever-expanding Cheng Yutung East Asian Library of University of Toronto. I particularly thank Ms. Kim Yong-hyŏn and Ms. Kim Chin Sun for their help, both as librarians and friends.

I thank the director of the McLuhan Program, Prof. Derrick de Kerckhove, and also Ms. Kathryn Carveth, for their support for the project on comparative literacy and for the book.

Finally, I thank Dr. Ludo Verhoeven, the editor of the series, *Studies in Written Language and Literacy*, and the editors at John Benjamins, Yola de Lusenet and Kees Vaes, for their work on the book.

1

Introduction

The scientific or literary well-being of a community is to be estimated not so much by its possessing a few men of great knowledge as its having many of competent knowledge.

Horace Mann 1867: 315

We will not collapse tomorrow from a lack of adequate literacy skills, but we may find that year by year, we continue to fall behind in international competitiveness, and that society becomes more divided between those who are skilled and those who are not.

Venezky et al. 1987: 53

How do the Chinese, Koreans, and Japanese write and read, and how have they, through their long, intertwined histories? This book, *Writing and Literacy in Chinese, Korean, and Japanese*, tries to answer these questions from a cultural perspective. This introductory chapter considers several preliminary topics as background: How the three East Asian peoples relate to each other; some linguistic units and terms necessary for discussing writing systems; how writing systems began in human history, and how they relate to each other and to literacy. Finally, it discusses how the rest of the book is organized.

Chinese, Koreans, and Japanese

The three East Asian peoples—Chinese, Koreans, and Japanese—are closely enough related to be discussed within one book. They are related geographically, historically, culturally, and racially. In particular, they are today the only peoples in the world who use Chinese characters, either alone or along with phonetic scripts.

How Many Chinese, Koreans, and Japanese?

This book is more about the Chinese, Korean, and Japanese peoples and how they write and read than it is about the nations of China, Japan, and Korea. The distinction between peoples and nations is significant. Chinese live not only in the People's Republic of China (PRC) in the mainland of Asia but also in many other parts of the world. Their number is huge: close to 1.2 billion with an annual rate of increase of over

1% in the PRC (8% of the population belong to one of 55 different ethnic minorities); 21 million in Taiwan (the Republic of China), and 5.6 million in Hong Kong. The Chinese also form two-thirds of the Singaporean population of 2.8 million, one-third of the Malaysian population of 18.8 million, and 3% of the Indonesian population of 197.2 million. Many Chinese live in such other Southeast Asian nations as Thailand and Vietnam. In North America (United States of America and Canada) and Australia, they may form a small minority, but even so they number a few millions. Overseas Chinese outside the PRC and Taiwan are estimated to number 34 millions. Chinese and their descendants, wherever they may live, interest us, as long as they speak Chinese and use Chinese characters, whether exclusively or along with other languages and scripts.

(Almost all the population figures and land areas cited here and elsewhere in the book are estimates for July 1993 taken from the *World Factbook* 1993. According to the 1990 census in the PRC, the population was 1,133,682,501, an increase of 12.45% since the 1982 census.)

The population of Korea is 67 million: two-thirds live in South Korea and one-third in North Korea. Virtually all are of Korean stock, except some Chinese in S. Korea. About 5 million ethnic Koreans and their descendants live in different parts of the world, such as China (2 million), North America (1.5 million), and Japan (0.7 million).

Japan has close to 125 million people and an annual growth rate of 0.3%. The overwhelming majority, 99.4%, are Japanese, and only 0.6% are others, mostly Koreans. Many Japanese and their descendants live in South American countries, but some of them are going back, with temporary work permits, to a newly prosperous Japan. Only about a quarter million ethnic Japanese live outside Japan, mostly in S. and N. America, some temporarily.

The Chinese, Koreans, and Japanese living in different parts of the world together make up one-quarter of the world population of 5.7 billion. All over the world, where there are sizable numbers of these peoples, there are schools and mass media in their languages.

How are the Three Peoples Related?

As the sketch map in Figure 1-1 shows, the Chinese, the Koreans, and the Japanese live in territories that differ markedly in size and characteristics but are geographic neighbors. China is a part of the great Eurasian continent and is itself a giant; Korea is a small peninsula that juts southeastward out of this continent; and Japan is a chain of islands in the Pacific Ocean forming an arc east of Korea. Two Chinese provinces in the northeast (former Manchuria) border N. Korea. Otherwise, China is separated from Korea by the Yellow Sea, and Korea from Japan by the Sea of Japan. But these separations are short; so, for example, one can fly between Tokyo, the capital of Japan, and Seoul, the capital of S. Korea, in only two hours. These geographic conditions have had a profound influence on the history and culture of the three peoples. As they say, the geography of a nation is its destiny.

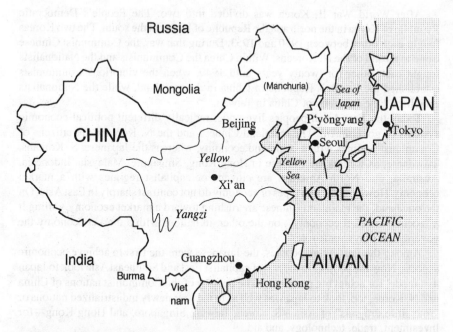

Figure 1-1. East Asia (not to scale) showing the geographic relations among the areas covered in this book: China, Korea, Japan, and Taiwan. Guangzhou is known also as Canton, and Yangzi (River) as Yangtze.

Over a long history that stretches back thousands of years, the three peoples have had close relations, sometimes amicable and at other times hostile. In antiquity successive waves of Chinese refugees settled in northern Korea, and the Chinese Han dynasty established a few administrative units there. In the 13th century the Mongol ruler of China, Kublai Khan, forced the Koreans to assist in two abortive attempts to invade Japan. In the other direction, in the late 16th century, a Japanese warlord invaded Korea, with the aim of overthrowing the Chinese Ming dynasty. His death put an end to the Japanese aggression.

Near the end of the 19th century, Japan invaded China with the aim of severing Korea's dependence on China and of dominating Korea. As booty of war, Japan secured what it coveted, and as a bonus it took Taiwan from China. In the first half of the 20th century, Japan took Korea as a colony in 1910, set up a puppet regime in Manchuria (now the northeast of China) in 1932, and engulfed much of China in a full-scale war in 1937. All of these gains had to be given up in 1945 when Japan was defeated in World War II. Today the Japanese aspire to become an economic rather than a military power.

After World War II, Korea was divided into two: The People's Democratic Republic of Korea in the north and the Republic of Korea in the south. The two Koreas fought each other between 1950 and 1953. During that war, the Communist Chinese came to the aid of the N. Koreans. Within China the Communists and the Nationalists fought each other for twenty years until 1949, when the victorious Communists established the People's Republic of China in the mainland, while the Nationalists established the Republic of China in Taiwan.

Today the East Asian peoples live under radically different political-economic systems of government. The mainland Chinese and the N. Koreans are citizens of Communist regimes with a command economy, whereas the Japanese, S. Koreans, Taiwanese, as well as the Chinese in Hong Kong, Singapore, Malaysia, Indonesia, Australia, and North America, are citizens of capitalist regimes with a market economy. However, the two types of economy do not contrast sharply in East Asia: On the one hand, the mainland Chinese are rushing toward a market economy, calling it a "socialist market economy"; on the other, in nations with a market economy the government plays some role.

Among the East Asian peoples, the Japanese were the first to achieve economic success. Now the peoples in the rest of capitalist East and Southeast Asia look to Japan as a model for achieving prosperity. The peoples of the Communist nations of China and N. Korea, too, look to Japan, as well as to the four newly industrialized nations or "four little dragons" of Asia—S. Korea, Taiwan, Singapore, and Hong Kong—for investment, trade, technology, and aid.

The three peoples of East Asia share a rich and ancient cultural heritage. In antiquity the Chinese created Chinese characters, Confucianism, a civil service with an examination system, paper, and silk; before the West they invented printing, the compass, gunpowder, and porcelain. Between 300 BC and AD 1700, China was one of the most advanced countries in the world, and its culture was avidly borrowed by the Koreans, and through them the Japanese. China's power has declined precipitously over the last few centuries, but its cultural influence on the Koreans and Japanese has not been extinguished. These East Asians still share many Chinese cultural practices, such as those related to eating: chopsticks, soy-bean paste, soy sauce, and beancurd (*doufu* in Chinese, *tubu* in Korean, and *tōfu* in Japanese). Most relevant to this book, these three peoples share thousands of Chinese words and characters, and perhaps a vestige of Confucian ethics.

Most Chinese, Koreans, and Japanese belong to the same race, Mongoloid. The peoples in the southern extremes of China and of Japan and Taiwan may have some Austronesian or Malayo-Polynesian features, having darker skin and being shorter than Mongoloids. Throughout their long history, especially in times of war and turmoil, the three peoples have migrated from and to China, Korea, and Japan. Anyway, they cannot be easily distinguished from their physical appearance alone, any more than English, French, and Germans can be.

What Chinese, Koreans, and Japanese do not share is language.

Linguistic Units and Terms

In this book we learn about writing systems and how they are read. To do so we must relate writing systems to the spoken languages they represent, and to discuss languages, we cannot avoid using some linguistic units and terms. I describe here a bare minimum of terms that are absolutely necessary for this book. For those who wish to know more about language and its use, the bibliography lists books on linguistics (description of units and structure of language) (e.g., Akmajian et al., 1984; Crystal 1987) and also on psycholinguistics (description of how people learn and use language; Steinberg 1993; Taylor and Taylor 1990).

Languages of the World

Today several thousand different languages are spoken in the world. Some languages are spoken by many people and others by only a few. Together, the four languages in which we are interested—Chinese, Korean, Japanese, and English—are learned and used by a huge number of people, almost half of the world. The speakers of the three East Asian languages together make up one-quarter of the world's population. English is spoken as a first language by over 365 million people in different parts of the world. Nations with over million English speakers include: Great Britain (58 million), United States of America (258 million), Canada (28 million; a minority speak French as a first language), Australia (18 million) and New Zealand (3 million). Furthermore English is an official language in many other parts of the world, including the Indian sub-continent, Africa, and Asia (e.g., Hong Kong and Singapore). And many people in much of the world, including East Asia, learn English, which is the main international language of diplomacy, commerce, science, and technology.

The languages of the world can be grouped into a number of families, based on their historical relations and their linguistic similarities (e.g., Ruhlen 1987). Chinese belongs to the Sino-Tibetan language family, whereas Japanese and Korean—which have similar syntax—are thought to belong to the Altaic language family. In its sounds Japanese differs from Korean, and shows some affinity also with the Malayo-Polynesian family. The differences in speech sounds and native words among Chinese, Japanese, and Korean are large enough for them to be mutually unintelligible. In writing, however, the users of the three languages can communicate to some degree because they share many Chinese words and characters (see fig. 1-4 below).

Languages may differ enough to be mutually unintelligible; you as an English speaker listening to a Chinese, Japanese, or Korean talk, have no idea what the talk is about; for all you know it might be nothing but gibberish. And yet all languages share certain elements, units, and structures. Language consists of meaningless speech sounds, which are organized into meaningful small units such as words, which are grouped into phrases, which are sequenced to form sentences. A group of sentences is organized into a discourse, which can be a story, a conversation, a passage of written text, or an article in a newspaper.

Phonemes and Syllables

Two of the units of speech sounds described by linguists are the phoneme and the syllable. What is a phoneme? Given the word *dog*, you can divide it into three letters, and thereby into three phonemes, because in this case one letter codes one phoneme. But letters do not always match phonemes. Given the word *photograph,* you can divide it into ten letters, but count only eight phonemes, because each *ph* codes one phoneme /f/. (Following linguistic convention, the symbol for a phoneme is written between two slashes, whereas a letter or letter group used as an example is written in italics.)

Obviously, the 26 English letters are too few to represent all the English phonemes, of which there are about 40. The discrepancy between the two numbers arises because some English phonemes, such as the sounds in *THis* and *THin*, are not represented by their own unique letters. Korean uses 24 letters and their compounds to represent about 30 phonemes, some of which are similar to English phonemes and some not. (The number of phonemes of a language may be counted slightly differently by different linguists, depending partly on whether non-standard or ambiguous sounds are included.)

Linguists use special letters or phonetic symbols to express all the phonemes of the English language and other languages of the world. In this book I will use only those letters that are found in the English alphabet and so are familiar to my readers. There is not much point in using phonetic symbols (e.g., θ in *THink* and ð in *THis*), which are unfamiliar to non-linguists, and which moreover are not available on a normal keyboard. Most importantly, if certain phonemes of a foreign language have no equivalents in your native language, the phonetic symbols for them do not help you to pronounce the foreign phonemes correctly. For example, the two English phonemes just cited are not found in many languages of the world, and are poorly pronounced by non-native English speakers, with or without the benefits of their phonetic symbols. The sound of *THis* may be pronounced something like /z/ by Japanese and like /d/ by Koreans.

Getting back to the definition of phonemes, the phoneme is defined quite independently of letters, for various reasons. The relation between a phoneme and a letter in an alphabet is not necessarily one-to-one. Many languages in the world do not have a script at all. Even if a language does have a script, it may be not an alphabet, in which one letter represents one phoneme, but a syllabary, in which one written sign represents a syllable. Or a script may not directly represent sound. But all languages have phonemes.

One technical description of the phoneme goes like this. A phoneme has little meaning by itself, but changing a phoneme can turn one word into another. *Pit* and *bit* are two different English words, and therefore /p/ and /b/ are two different phonemes. By contrast, if you pronounced *pit* in a normal manner with a puff of air (which can be felt on the back of your hand), or without a puff of air (like some foreigners speaking English), you spoke the same word, not two different words. English ignores the presence or absence of the puff of air in distinguishing phonemes, but in some languages this puff would change a word into another word, and the two versions of /p/ would be different phonemes. To put it in another way, in any given language, similar speech sounds are regarded as belonging to the same phoneme, as long as they do not cause changes in word meaning. Defined in this way, the number of phonemes varies across languages, but most have between 20 and 37 (Maddieson 1984).

Some phonemes are called consonants, and some are called vowels. Consonants are produced by obstructing the air flow through the throat and mouth, whereas vowels are produced by letting the air flow freely. The ways in which the air flow is obstructed distinguish the variety of consonants. The three consonants /p, t, k/ are called stop consonants, because the air flow is stopped and then released. They are called also voiceless, because the vocal folds or chords do not vibrate in pronouncing them; the three voiceless stops contrast to the voiced stops /b, d, g/. Three consonants /m, n/ and the last sound in *soNG* are called nasals, because in pronouncing them the nasal cavity is open while the air flow through the mouth is blocked. Because the sound -*ng* is used in Chinese, Korean, Japanese, and English, it would be convenient to have a special phonetic symbol for it. We will use N, instead of its conventional phonetic symbol /ŋ/, which not only is unfamiliar but also is unavailable on a normal keyboard. (N is used in the Machine Readable Phonetic Alphabet, which avoids unfamiliar phonetic symbols.)

The vowels, such as /a, e, i, o, u/, are pronounced by molding the cavities of the mouth and throat into different shapes and sizes with the tongue and the lips while leaving the vocal tract unobstructed, thus changing the sound. A sequence of two vowels pronounced like one vowel is called a diphthong.

A sound unit larger than a phoneme is a syllable. A syllable has one strong energetic sound, typically a vowel or diphthong, surrounded by consonants. Spoken language consists of a series of syllables, with occasional pauses between them. Syllables come in various lengths and structures, as shown in Table 1-1.

Different languages allow different syllable structures: English uses all the structures listed in Table 1-1; Korean uses the first five; Chinese uses the first four; and Japanese uses only the first two (the third and fourth may be used if the final consonant is N). Languages differ also in the number of different kinds of syllables they use: about 110 in Japanese; 400 in Chinese; 2,000 in Korean; and several thousand in English.

Table 1-1. Some Syllable Structures

Structure	English Word
V	a
CV	go
VC	at
CVC	get
CVCC	lend
CCVC	glad
CCVCC	blend
CCCVCCC	strengths
CCVCCCC	twelfths

V = vowel; CV = consonant–vowel;
CVC = consonant–vowel–consonant

Morphemes and Words

Let us now move from small sound units, the phoneme and the syllable, to small meaning units, the morpheme and the word. A morpheme is the smallest meaning-bearing unit. Morphemes can be words by themselves, called "free morphemes," such as *kind* and *love*. Some morphemes are word parts called prefixes and suffixes, such as *un-* and *-ly*. Prefixes and suffixes are called "bound morphemes," because they are always bound into words, as in *UNkind, kindLY, UNkindLY*. In the four languages we discuss, a word usually consists of one or two morphemes, as in (1); occasionally a word consists of three or four morphemes, as in (2); and rarely a word consists of five or six morphemes, as in (3).

 1. establish, establish-ment
 2. establish-ment-arian, establish-ment-arian-ism
 3. dis-establish-ment-arian-ism, anti-dis-establish-ment-arian-ism

Words of a language can be broadly classified as either content words, which have substantive meanings, or grammatical morphemes, which have mainly grammatical functions. Chinese, Japanese, Korean, and English are similar in their content words, which are nouns, verbs, adjectives, and some adverbs, roughly speaking. In any language, one can usually get the main message by attending only to the sequence of the content words. You can do so in this English sentence, in which the content words are in uppercase letters. A Japanese speaker can do so in the Japanese version of the same sentence, whose content words are ordered: MOTHER, CAT, BISCUIT, GIVE.

 the MOTHER GIVEs BISCUITs to a CAT.
 HAHA ga NEKO ni BISKETTO o YARu.

The languages are dissimilar in their grammatical morphemes, which are written in lowercase letters in the above English and Japanese sentences. English grammatical morphemes are function words (e.g., prepositions, articles) and inflectional endings (e.g., plural noun or third-person verb *-s*). Instead of English function words, Japanese (and also Korean) has postpositions (*ga, ni, o*) after nouns and verb or adjective endings (*-u*), while Chinese has "empty words" such as particles, all of which can be explained better in Parts I, II, and III than here.

Words in a sentence are ordered, and word order can differ among languages. For example, the basic word order is "subject-verb-object" in English and Chinese, but "subject-object-verb" in Japanese and Korean. The word order and the use of grammatical morphemes are specified by the syntactic rules of each language.

In this section I have introduced some linguistic terms necessary for the book. The terms that will keep recurring are: *phoneme, consonant, stop consonant, voiceless, voiced, nasal, vowel, syllable, morpheme, prefix, suffix, word, content word, grammatical morpheme, function word, and syntax*. In the course of the book, a few more linguistic terms may appear and be defined. All are listed in the glossary.

The four major linguistic units—phoneme, syllable, morpheme, and word—are each the basis of a different kind of writing system, as we shall see in the next section.

Writing Systems of the World

How and where did writing begin? What varieties of writing systems are there and how do they relate to each other? Answers to these questions provide some background to studying individual writing systems and the scripts of our interest, Chinese, Korean, Japanese, and English. What is written here is necessarily a brief sketch of the topic. Those who wish to learn more about it may read some of the books cited here and in the bibliographies for this chapter as well as for the three main parts of this book (e.g., Coulmas 1989; Gelb 1963; Jensen 1970).

Writing represents, to some extent, a spoken language in visual form. Writing systems and scripts differ in their origins, in the linguistic units they code or represent, in the shapes of their signs, in the number of signs they require, in the rules relating shapes to sounds or meanings, and so on. Yet most, by no means all, of them are interrelated.

How did Writing Begin?

Long before there was a written language, people used markings on objects to record events, identify owners, or invoke magic. From the Stone Ages down to modern times, simple geometric designs have been put on objects of daily use, such as pots and weapons. Potters' marks are found on pottery from ancient Egypt, and masons' marks are found on ancient buildings in Anatolia, Turkey. Some such marks are triangles, arcs, diamonds, and vertical or horizontal lines. Some of these record-keeping symbols may have been the forerunners of writing. Clay tablets about 5000 years old, impressed with signs for units of grain or land measure, animal enumeration, and other economic items, have been found in the regions of present-day Iran, Iraq, and Syria (Schmandt-Besserat 1981). Geometric marks have been found on pots used in China 6000 years ago (Part I).

A full writing system is not just a collection of objects or symbols but can represent almost everything a spoken language can. Such writing systems were developed relatively recently in human history, no earlier than 5000 years ago. Full writing systems are roughly categorized into two major types, those that **primarily** represent meaning units and those that **primarily** represent sound units.

Of the systems based on meaning, we can think of international graphic signs, each of which might represent a short message. Since a graphic sign is not tied with any particular language or linguistic unit, it can be used by speakers of any language. But such signs are often ambiguous and can be misunderstood. A drawing of an umbrella ⌂ on a package could stand for various messages, such as "This package contains umbrellas," "The content of this package should not be exposed to rain," and simply "Keep dry." Some cultures — such as tribes living in a desert or rain forest — may never have seen an umbrella.

To express a slightly more complex message, a few graphic signs are needed, and they have to be put in some order. A sequence of signs can be even more ambiguous and prone to misunderstanding than single signs, as the following anecdote shows.

Proctor & Gamble have a well-known advertisement for laundry detergent. The ad shows a pile of dirty clothes on the left, a box of Tide in the middle, and clean folded clothes on the right. It worked well in North America and Europe but not in Arabic-speaking countries. The problem, it turns out, was that Arabic readers viewed the ad from right to left, in the same direction they read text.

A full system based on graphic signs would be impractical, because it would need too many different, and often ambiguous and incomprehensible, signs. It will not be discussed further in this book.

Among the meaning-based writings, this book is concerned only with logographs (logo = word; graph = written symbol) that represent primarily the meanings, and secondarily the sounds, of words or morphemes. Consider two logographs, the Arabic numeral 10 and the Chinese character 十. While the meaning of these two logographs remains more or less the same, the sounds associated with, or assigned to, them vary across different languages, and even across dialects, in case of Chinese. To list only a few sample sounds: 10 is *Zehn* in German, *dix* in French, *ten* in English; 十 is *shi* in Mandarin Chinese, *sip* in Korean, *jū, tō, so, jutt-, jitt-* in Japanese.

By contrast, a phonetic script primarily represents sounds, and through a string of sound-letters, the meaning, of a word. Phonetic scripts are distinguished between syllabaries and alphabets. In a syllabary one graph or sign, in principle, represents one syllable. Of several syllabaries used today by different peoples in different parts of the world—such as Vai used in Liberia, Africa, and Cree/Ojibway in northern Canada—this book is concerned only with a syllabary used by the Japanese. In an alphabet one letter, in principle, represents one phoneme. Today alphabets are by far the most popular scripts in the world. Of many alphabets, this book is concerned with Korean and English. Actually, Korean is better described as an alphabetic syllabary.

As we shall see in this section and in the rest of the book, the distinctions among the categories of scripts are real but not clearcut, and hence the words "primarily" and "in principle" modify "represents" in all the above definitions. In Part I, we explore fully the controversies surrounding this topic.

Before proceeding with further discussion of individual writing systems and scripts, let us pause to consider how the terms "writing system" and "script" relate to one another. The two may differ subtly: "writing system" may refer to a type of system such as alphabet, syllabary, and logography. Or it may refer to a set of different scripts used to represent one language, in expressions such as the "Japanese writing system," which consists of a set of logographs and two forms of a syllabary. "Script" may then refer to an individual form of some type of writing system, such as the Roman alphabet, the Greek alphabet, or the Cyrillic alphabet (used in Russia) under the writing system "alphabet." The term script may refer also to a style of writing, such as the "clerical" and "cursive" script styles of Chinese characters (table 3-1). These differences between various terms are not always clearcut and are observed loosely rather than slavishly in this and other books on writing systems and scripts.

Development of Writing Systems

In antiquity three important writing systems emerged, apparently independently, in Sumeria, Egypt, and China. Let us consider the first two of these writing systems, as preparation for discussing the Chinese system in Part I of the book.

The Sumerian system was used in Mesopotamia (modern Iraq) between 3300 BC and AD 75. It seems to have served mainly to keep records of commercial transactions and tax collections. It developed from pictographs to cuneiform (wedge-shaped) in at least four stages, as shown in Figure 1-2.

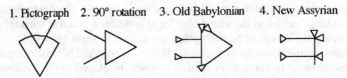

1. Pictograph   2. 90° rotation   3. Old Babylonian   4. New Assyrian

Figure 1-2. Development of Sumerian cuneiform: A pictograph for "ox" shown in four stages of its development into an abstract cuneiform symbol

1. To show that the tax was in the form of an ox, a scribe drew a picture of an ox on a clay tablet. At first, clay tablets were small enough to be held in the palm of one hand.

2. As the tablets became larger in order to record more information, the scribe found writing easier if the tablets—and the symbols on them—were turned sideways. With the 90-degree turns and also with the elimination of curves, many signs lost their resemblance to objects.

3. The scribe used a blunter instrument that could simply be pressed on the clay tablet. The resulting wedge-shaped impressions or cuneiforms kept some remote resemblance to the original pictographs.

4. Any lingering attempts to maintain pictographs yielded to abstract symbols.

For some concepts that were complex or hard to picture, composite signs were possible: "to eat" = "bread + mouth." Words have sounds as well as meanings. The word *may*, which could not be pictorially represented, was represented by the sign for *fish*, since the two shared the same sound. Signs were created first for one-syllable words, and then two one-syllable signs were joined for two-syllable words. The Sumerian cuneiform was adopted in antiquity by a few other languages such as Akkadian (the eastern Semitic language of Assyria and Babylonia), but it now has no descendants (fig. 1-3 below).

Around 3100 BC the Egyptians developed a writing system that was used for over three millennia, until AD 400. They may have possibly been inspired by the Sumerian writing but did not borrow it, for right from the beginning the signs in the two systems differed clearly. By around 500 BC, the Egyptian system consisted of hieroglyphs (sacred inscriptions on stone) for public display, and two cursive systems, hieratic and demotic, for everyday practical use. In its developed form, the Egyptian system had hundreds of signs for words and syllables.

Some signs represented pictures of objects, such as a circle with a center dot representing the sun. Some other signs coded the consonantal frame of a word— e.g., ▽ codes *nb*, pronounced as *neb* ('basket'); it could be used to write other unpicturable words with the sound of *nb*, such as *nib* and *nob*. When the combination of word signs with sound signs created a wealth of words with the same consonantal frame, there emerged "determinatives," each of which indicated or delimited the conceptual sphere to which a word belongs. For example, the determinative for "seated goddess" added to the sound sign for *st* indicates a goddess's name.

So, among the Egyptian hieroglyphs some served as signs for words, some for determinatives, and some for consonantal frames of words. This last category may have been taken up in subsequent writing systems developed in the Mediterranean region.

Relations Among Writing Systems and Scripts

How and when did the Semitic writing begin and develop? Different authors have different answers, which do not concern us. Our main concern is to show, as simply as possible, how the Phoenician script, the ancestor of most alphabets used today, emerged.

Figure 1-3 shows the historical interrelationships among the major scripts of the world: the Sumerian cuneiform with no modern descendants; the Semitic scripts and their many descendants; Chinese characters and their few descendants; and the independently created script in Korea, which has no descendant. The figure is intended mainly to show where the four scripts of our interest— Chinese, Korean, Japanese, and English—fit in; it is not intended to include all the scripts that did or do exist.

The Proto-Semitic system developed in the vast Semitic area extending from Sinai to northern Syria in the middle of the second millennium BC, under the influence of the Egyptian system, according to Gelb (1952). Of the various Semitic attempts to create a new writing, the one created in Byblos was by far the most successful. Byblos (near modern Beirut, Lebanon) was an ancient seaport and one of the cultural centers of the Phoenicians, who had extensive contacts with Egypt in the third millennium BC. This script was the ancestor to the all-important Phoenician and Aramaic scripts.

The Phoenician script had a handful of letters, which were no longer pictographs but were simple linear symbols, some of which resembled *k*, +, *I*, *o*, *L*. These symbols represented consonants but not vowels. But the lack of vowel letters did not pose a serious problem in the Semitic (Phoenician; Hebrew) and Hamitic (Egyptian; Arabic) writings, because in these languages consonants are used for the roots of words, while vowels are used for grammatical inflections such as verb tense. By analogy, consider the English *sing-sang-sung*.

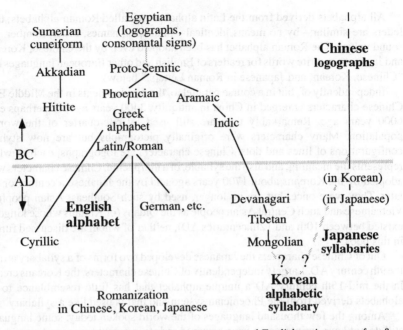

Figure 1-3. Where do the Chinese, Korean, Japanese, and English scripts come from?

As shown in Figure 1-3 the Aramaic script was the ancestor of the Indic script (e.g., Gauer 1984; Gelb 1952). One of the most important descendants of the Indic script is Devanagari, which is the script for Sanskrit literature and for the Hindi language; as such it is the most widely used script in India today. One of the characteristics of the scripts derived from the Indic script is that a consonant sign includes the inherent vowel /a/ as its value; that is, a letter is read as a syllable "consonant + /a/."

The Indic script is the ancestor to the Tibetan script, which in turn is the ancestor of the Mongolian script called Paspa, which was used for 100 years in the Middle Ages. Paspa is hypothesized by some scholars as the model for the Korean phonetic script. If this hypothesis were proven correct, then all the alphabets of the world could be traced back to one source, but it has not been so proven (Part II).

Between the 8th and 11th centuries BC the Phoenician consonantal alphabet was augmented by the Greeks, who created letters for vowels. In the Greek language, which is a member of the Indo-European language family, vowels are as important as consonants, unlike in Semitic Phoenician. The Greek alphabet in turn is the source of the Cyrillic alphabet used in Russia and some other East European nations. It is also the source of the Latin alphabet, which led to most of the contemporary European alphabets, including Spanish, French, Finnish, German, Polish, and English.

All alphabets derived from the Latin alphabet are called Roman alphabets; their letters are similar—by no means identical—in shapes, names, order, number, and sound values. The Roman alphabet has been adopted even by the Chinese, Koreans, and Japanese to write words for readers of English and other European languages (see "Chinese, Korean, and Japanese in Roman Letters," below).

Independently of, but in a course parallel to, the developments in the Middle East, Chinese characters emerged in China in antiquity, 3400 years ago, or perhaps even 6000 years ago. Remarkably they are still used by one-quarter of the world's population. Many characters were originally pictographs but are now stylized configurations of lines and dots. Chinese characters are logographs, each of which represents the meaning, and also the syllable, of a morpheme. Chinese characters were adopted by the Koreans about 1700 years ago and by the Japanese a century or two later. They were once, but are no longer, used by such Southeast Asian people as Vietnamese and such Central Asian people as the Qidans (or Khitans whose kingdom existed between 10th and 12th centuries AD), neither of whom are discussed further in this book.

Out of Chinese characters the Japanese developed two forms of a syllabary around the 9th century AD. Largely independently of Chinese characters, the Koreans created in the mid-15th century AD a unique alphabet that has little resemblance to the alphabets derived from the Phoenician system and that is used like a syllabary.

Among the few thousand languages of the world spoken today, some languages still do not have scripts, some have acquired scripts in recent times, and some are in the process of acquiring scripts. Scripts created in modern times tend to be phonetic, strongly influenced by the Western scripts. Consider the Amerindian Cree script, a syllabary, invented by a Christian missionary in Canada in the 19th century. With slight modification, the Cree syllabary has been adopted by some other Amerindians such as Ojibway and Inuit (Eskimo) in Canada.

If one looks at only the descendants of the Sumerian system or the Egyptian system, writing systems seem to have developed first from pictographs to logographs, and from logographs into two types of phonetic scripts, syllabaries first and alphabets next. One might be tempted to describe this sequence as a progression from primitive or less developed to more developed scripts. But look at Chinese characters and their descendants. Chinese characters indeed began as pictographs and logographs, but have remained as logographs for thousands of years. Who now use these "primitive" scripts? The Chinese, whose past civilisation was the most glorious in the world, the Japanese, whose economy today is one of the strongest in the world, and the South Koreans, whose economy is one of the most dynamic in the world. The Japanese developed a syllabary out of Chinese characters but have not "progressed" to an alphabet. Why have logographic Chinese characters been used by so many people for so long, if there is a natural progression of pictograph–logograph–syllabary–alphabet? A good question, which is explored in this book.

Scripts and Literacy

About the writing systems and scripts of the world there are many good books, several of which are listed in the bibliographies for this chapter as well as for Parts I, II, and III. But on the question of how writing systems are used—learned, written, and read—there are few books for the general public and students. This book deals with this important topic.

People learn and use scripts to acquire and disseminate information; they become literate. Obviously, different degrees of literacy are required, depending on the quantity and quality of information acquired and acquirable. For convenience of discussion, let us recognize four levels of literacy, as defined by levels of reading and other skills, and of education, which usually go hand in hand with literacy. Let us consider illiteracy, limited literacy, and high-level literacy briefly and the most useful functional literacy in some depth.

Illiteracy. People of certain age—say, 15 or older—can read and write nothing or no more than a few vital pieces of information, such as their names and addresses. They have had little or no primary school education. Or they have not practised reading and writing since finishing primary school years before.

Limited literacy. In developing nations, birth rates and infant mortality are substantially reduced when mothers have some schooling to read simple instructions for hygiene and birth control, and to help children with their early lessons. In China, peasants may learn 1,000 out of 3,500 common characters so that they can read very simple materials ("Degrees of Literacy Using Characters" in chap. 10).

High-level literacy. People can read almost any contemporary reading materials, including specialized or technical ones; some may write manuals and articles or books. Such people often have a university education.

Functional literacy. People can read such everyday reading materials as newspapers and manuals, and also can fill in forms and write memos or simple letters. In addition, they have basic numeracy skills. In a highly industrialized society where computers are ubiquitous, one hears the phrase "computer literacy." In today's world where English is the preeminent international language, non-English speakers' skill in that language can be useful.

A declaration adopted in 1987 by the International Seminar on Literacy in Industrialized Countries stated:

> Literacy is more than the ability to read, write, and compute. The demands
> created by advancing technology require increased levels of knowledge, skills
> and understanding to achieve basic literacy. [Velis 1990: 132]

Normally the phrase "literate people" refer to people who have attained functional literacy. A society can be described as one with a high rate of literacy or mass literacy if most of its citizens have attained functional literacy. American educator, Horace Mann, 125 years ago said (1867: 315): "The scientific or literary well-being of a community is to be estimated not so much by its possessing a few men of great knowledge as its having many of competent knowledge."

To function adequately in an industrialized society, people need at least functional literacy. Even to apply for a menial job, a person should be able to read a job description and fill in an application form. In the workplace, workers have to deal with manuals, memos, and other kinds of critically important written information. Those who stay at home do not escape written information, as almost everything they buy, including packaged food, comes with written information.

The concept of functional literacy seems to have originated in the United States, where it was equated, at various times between the 1940s and the 1960s, with a 3rd-grade education, a 5th-grade education, an 8th-grade education, and eventually a 12th-grade education. Did a person with a 3rd-grade education in the 1940s read as well as someone with a 12th-grade education in the 1960s? Perhaps so. More likely, the educational level required for functional literacy rises as a society becomes industrialized and complex.

In the 1970s functional literacy was tested for reading skills needed to survive and function in an industrialized society. One test, the "Adult Performance Level Project," was conducted by the University of Texas, funded by the Office of Education. People were asked to read road maps, insurance policies, product labels, pay statements, and the like. The test required considerable knowledge about the world and skills beyond document reading (Venezky et al. 1987).

Today it appears that not all American workers are well educated and literate. One reads in newspapers headlines such as "Lack of literacy plagues adult Americans": In a four-year federal study of literacy nearly half of the 191 million adult U.S. citizens are not proficient enough in English to write a letter about a billing error, or to calculate the length of a bus trip from a schedule (*The Globe and Mail*, Sept. 7, 1993; supplied by the New York Times Service). By contrast, Japan equips almost all its citizens with 9 years of rigorous primary and secondary education, and has built its economic success by relying on these literate workers.

Can literacy rates be compared among nations? Only tenuously. There are no universal definitions and standards of literacy, and not all nations measure or estimate literacy rates. UNESCO (1991) defines literates as people—15 years old or older—who can read and write a short simple statement about everyday life. By this definition, most industrial nations (e.g., Japan, S. Korea, Canada) have a literacy rate above 95%, while some underdeveloped nations (e.g., Sierra Leone, Somalia, Nepal) have less than 50% literacy. There is a correlation between GNP per capita (in US$ 1991) and literacy rate: the higher the GNP the higher the literacy rate. China's literacy rate is given as 73% (84%, according to China's own 1990 census).

Is a high literacy rate among its citizens necessary and sufficient for the economic success of a country? The answer must be "yes" to the necessary condition, when we look at Japan and other industrial nations. But the answer must be "no" to the question of whether a high literacy rate is sufficient for economic success. Compare the two Koreas: South Korea, with a market economy and multi-party democracy, has a high rate of literacy and a dynamic economy, whereas North Korea, with a command economy and a totalitarian regime, has a high rate of literacy but a dismal economy. Obviously, political-economic policies have something to do with economic success.

Is it easier to attain a high literacy rate with one script than with another? Let us compare first the same script, used in two somewhat different ways. Both English speakers and Finnish speakers use the Roman alphabet. But English is notorious for its irregular spelling and pronunciation: think how the letter *a* is pronounced in words such as *about, farm, fat, fall, face, fare, feat, instead, boat, oar, learn*; think how the sound /f/ is spelled in words such as *fall, enough, photo*. By contrast, Finnish spelling and pronunciation are highly regular, and are mastered rapidly, faster than English spelling and pronunciation (Kyostio 1980).

Now consider logographs, Chinese characters. Both the Japanese and the Koreans use about 2,000 characters, many of them the same. But the characters used in Japan are a lot harder to master than those used in Korea mainly because of their multiple readings.

While we are considering Chinese characters, let us ask one more question: Is it possible to attain a high rate of literacy using these complex and numerous characters? Yes, it is. Using them, people in Taiwan have attained a high rate of literacy, while people in mainland China have not yet attained such a high rate. Taiwan and the mainland differ in their political-economic-social systems and the educational systems, as well as in the size of the land and the population. All of these factors may affect the literacy rate.

When scripts and literacy are viewed from a historical perspective, the rate of literacy has increased dramatically over the last few decades, sometimes using the same scripts and at other times using reformed scripts. This phenomenon has happened in all the East Asian nations, as described in this book, as well as in other industrialized nations of the world. It again demonstrates that political-economic-social factors affect the literacy rate of citizens of a nation. So does the fact that literacy rates in the United States vary greatly among different ethnic groups, who tend to belong to different socio-economic groups.

Lest you may conclude that literacy is affected only by political-economic-social factors, let me point out that the Japanese and the Koreans would have been unlikely to have achieved their present high rate of literacy, if they had not invented phonetic scripts to supplement Chinese characters. Phonetic scripts are critical for the Japanese and the Koreans to write their native words and grammatical morphemes. As well, scripts in East Asia have long been, and continue to be, streamlined, standardized, and rationalized in attempts to make their learning and use ever more easy.

So literacy is affected by political-economic-social factors as well as by scripts. This book touches on the former only in passing without getting deeply involved with them. (For those who are interested, several books are listed in the bibliography.) It describes Chinese, Korean, and Japanese scripts, often in comparison with the English script, and discusses their learning and use in the past and the present, especially in the present.

Chinese, Korean, and Japanese Scripts

Let us have a preview of the scripts we learn about. The Chinese normally use only logographic Chinese characters, called Hanzi, but for special purposes they also have phonetic scripts—a Roman alphabet called Pinyin in the mainland and a sort of a syllabary called Zhuyinfuhao in Taiwan. The Japanese use Chinese characters, called Kanji, along with phonetic scripts, two forms of a syllabary, called Hiragana and Katakana. The Koreans use an alphabetic syllabary, called Han'gŭl, along with some Chinese characters, called Hancha. And English-speakers use a Roman alphabet that has upper- and lower-case letters.

Figure 1-4 shows the same sentence "I go to school everyday" written in two forms of English, three Chinese, three Japanese, and two Korean scripts. The foreign writings may look, well, foreign to you; they will become familiar as you read this book.

English
Upper- and lower-case: I go to school every day.
All upper-case: I GO TO SCHOOL EVERY DAY.

Chinese
Hanzi: 每天 我 去学 校
Pinyin: Mei tian wo qu xue xiao.
Zhuyinfuhao: ㄇㄟ ㄊㄧㄢ ㄨㄛ ㄑㄨ ㄒㄩㄝ ㄒㄧㄠ

Japanese
Kanji and Hiragana: 私 は 毎日学校 へ行く
ll Hiragana: わた し は まいに ゙ち が ゙っこ ゙うべいく
All Katakana: ワタシ ハマイ ニチガ ッコウヘイク

Korean
Han'gŭl with Hancha: 나 는 毎日 學校 에 간다
All Han'gŭl: 나 는 매일 학교에 간다

Figure 1-4. The same sentence written in English, Chinese, Japanese, and Korean scripts

The simple sentence "I go to school every day" written in characters, or characters mixed with phonetic letters, will be understood by speakers of Chinese, Japanese, or Korean, because some of the words and their characters are the same or synonymous across the three languages and their scripts. The same sentence written in a phonetic script of any one of the three languages would not be understood by anyone but speakers of that language. Needless to say, the same is true of spoken sentences. The longer and more complex a Chinese text, the harder it is for a Japanese or Korean to understand because of differences in syntax as well as in the words. We will discuss all these differences and similarities as we go through this book.

About This Book

This book deals with the diverse writing systems and scripts used by Chinese, Koreans, and Japanese in comparison with the system used by English speakers. For each writing system or script I describe how it: originated and developed; relates to its spoken language; is learned or taught; is used in daily life; can be computerized; and relates to the literacy and culture of its users. Some topics are straightforward, while others are controversial. Two most controversial questions, with far-reaching implications, are whether logographic Chinese characters differ from phonetic scripts, and whether they should be retained or abolished in each of the three countries.

Chinese, Korean, and Japanese in Roman Letters

The Chinese, Koreans, and Japanese, of course, have their own writing systems, which are unfamiliar to most readers of this book. So I have to write their words in a writing system familiar to the readers, the Roman alphabet, specifically the English alphabet. There have been various attempts at romanizing Chinese, Korean, and Japanese, which are discussed in Parts I, II, and III, respectively.

Meanwhile, here is a brief guide to reading Chinese, Korean, and Japanese words in Roman letters. Of several romanization systems developed for each of the three languages one system has been adopted as a standard: Pinyin for Chinese, Hepburn for Japanese, and McCune-Reischauer (M-R) for Korean. For Japanese the Hepburn system, though not the standard, is commonly used for foreigners. Because the sound systems of Chinese and Japanese are simple, Pinyin and Hepburn are simple, whereas the M-R system is complex, reflecting the rich variety of sounds of the Korean language.

The five basic vowels in the Chinese, Korean, and Japanese romanizations are pronounced as in Italian, German, or Spanish:

- *a* as in *father* but short
- *e* as in *end*
- *i* as in *eel* but short
- *o* as in *oh* but short
- *u* as in *rude* but short

The basic vowels are modified with special marks:

- *ü* in Chinese is like *yu*; it is the same as its German origin
- *ŏ* in Korean is like *uh* or the *o* in *bottle*
- *ŭ* in Korean is between the *oo* in *foot* and the *i* in *bit*
- *ō* in Japanese is *o* held long
- *ū* in Japanese is *u* held long

As a rule only one sound is associated with one vowel letter. However, the Chinese Pinyin *i* has three sounds, *ee*, *r*, and *uh*, while *e* has the sounds of *eh* and *uh*, depending on context. In Korean, certain sequence of two vowel letters represents one vowel sound, as *ae* in *mae* ('whip') is pronounced like *a* in *bat*, but in Japanese *ae* in *mae* ('front') is pronounced in two syllables as *ma* and then *e* .

Consonant letters are pronounced roughly like the English letters in their most common or regular sounds, as in words such as *bib, church, did, fief, gag, hip, jam, kit, lip, mom, nun, pop, ran, sit, ship, tip, zip*. In contrast to English, which distinguishes only the voiceless stop /k/ from the voiced stop /g/, Korean distinguishes three kinds of stops — *k, k', kk* (in the M-R romanization), which are hard for English speakers to discriminate in listening, let alone to pronounce correctly. They will be explained in Part II. Briefly, *k* is like the English /g/ or /k/, depending on phonetic context; *k'* is usually like the English /k/; and *kk* is like French *q* in *quoi*. Chinese Pinyin uses three Roman letters in unusual ways: *c* like *ts* in *cats*, *q* like *ch* in *church*, and *x* like *ss* in *sissy*. The Roman letters *q* and *x* are not used for Japanese and Korean; *l* at the beginning of a word occurs in Chinese but not in Japanese and Korean. In some words syllable breaks have to be indicated, using an apostrophe ('): *kan'i* (CVC + V) vs *kani* (CV + CV).

Some Chinese, Korean, and Japanese words appearing in the book are technical or semi-technical terms, such as Hanzi, Hancha, and Kanji each of which means "Chinese character(s)" in Chinese, Korean, and Japanese, respectively. Many others are ordinary non-technical words, such as *doufu, tubu,* and *tōfu,* ('beancurd') in Chinese, Korean, and Japanese, respectively. The technical terms are in Roman font and their initial letters are capitalized, while ordinary words are in italics. The two types need to be distinguished for the reader's convenience: The technical terms, because of their importance and recurrence, must stand out from ordinary words, so that the reader can remember them. They are listed also in the glossary.

How the Book is Organized

Apart from this introductory chapter, the book consists of three parts: Part I on Chinese contains 9 chapters (chaps. 2–10); Part II on Korean contains 6 chapters (chaps. 11–16); and Part III on Japanese contains 8 chapters (chaps. 17–24). Each of Parts I, II, and III begins with an introduction to the nation and its people and a chapter describing the language covered in that part. The rest of the chapters in each part deal with scripts and literacy, sometimes similarly and sometimes differently among the three parts.

Part I on Chinese contains several chapters on Chinese characters: How they began and evolved, how they are structured and classified, and how many there are, and so on. Part I has a substantial chapter on the reform of spoken and written Chinese, which is an urgent and important problem. It also has one chapter on learning to read and write characters, and another chapter on the history of education and literacy. Part I contains two chapters that deal with topics that concern not only Chinese but also Korean and Japanese: Logography vs phonetic scripts, and text writing conventions in East Asia.

Part II on Korean needs a few more chapters on the use of Chinese characters. Though the Koreans borrowed characters from the Chinese, they use characters somewhat differently from the Chinese. More importantly, they supplement characters with their own phonetic script, an alphabet used like a syllabary. The Korean phonetic script deserves extensive coverage, both because it is the major script of South Korea and the sole script of North Korea, and because it is indigenous, unique, ingenious, and effective. Part II asks questions such as how this phonetic script was created, how it is structured, how it is used, and how it is learned. Not to be overlooked is the fact that over the past few decades North Korea and South Korea have taken somewhat different policies on education and scripts. As in Part I, Part II has a chapter on learning to read and write the Korean scripts, as well as a chapter on history of literacy and education.

Part III on Japanese needs yet a few more chapters on Chinese characters. The Japanese use characters in a more complex way than do the Chinese and the Koreans. They also created two forms of a simple syllabary out of characters, which are used along with characters. The way these three scripts are used is complex yet interesting. Part III contains one substantial chapter on the Japanese educational system, which is of great interest to us all because of its success in turning out literate workers. To these well-educated workers and managers, Japan owes her spectacular economic success. As Japan publishes a prodigious quantity of books and research data, including many on its language and writing system, I was able to use a great deal of resource material.

Parts I, II, and III discuss some research on how people recognize, read, and write characters and other graphs, words, and sentences. Emphasis is on word recognition, which seems to be most affected by types of scripts. Out of the masses of research data available, mostly in technical journals, often in Japanese, I select a small amount for its relevance, interest, and comprehensibility.

The one-page Postface drives home the core message of the book.

Finally let me say a few words on bibliographies. I have learned the things I write about in this book partly through my own observations, experiences, and experiments, but mostly through reading books and research written by other authors. On any topic I cull information from many sources, digest it, and express it in my own words. Thus, it is often difficult to attribute a piece of information to any particular author. Besides, to fill this non-technical text with numerous references would constantly disrupt the narrative flow. To show my debt to the authors and at the same time to recommend some books to the readers, I list, often at the beginning of a section or chapter, a few authors as general sources of my information. Of course, my citation of authors is specific when their words, information, numbers, figures, and tables are more or less directly quoted. It is specific also when their experimental findings are reported, however briefly.

Each of the three Parts—Part I on Chinese, II on Korean, and III on Japanese—as well as this introductory chapter, ends with a bibliography that has brief descriptions or comments on most books. I try to include in bibliographies as many English language books as possible. Inevitably some of the referenced books are in Chinese, Korean, and Japanese. I hope that this book will be read by speakers of English as well as of these East Asian languages!

Bibliography for Introduction

Akmajian, Adrian, Demers, Richard A. and Harnish, Robert, M. *Linguistics: An introduction to language and communication.* Cambridge, Mass: MIT Press, 1984 (2nd ed.) It describes linguistic terms used in this book as well as many other terms and concepts.

Claiborne, R. *The birth of writing.* New York: Time-Life Books, 1974. The book focuses on the birth of writing in Sumeria, Egypt, and China several thousand years ago. Its pictures, often in color, are a joy to look at.

Corterell, Arthur. *East Asia: from Chinese dominance to the rise of the Pacific Rim.* London: John Murray, 1993. It is readable and informative.

Coulmas, Florian. *The writing systems of the world.* New York: Basil Blackwell, 1989. It describes many scripts of the world in relation to the languages they represent.

Crystal, David. *The Cambridge encyclopedia of language.* New York: Cambridge University Press, 1987. It describes, using many pictures, interesting facts about languages of the world.

Davidson, James Dale and Rees-Mogg, Lord William. *The great reckoning: How the world will change in the depression of the 1990s.* New York: General, 1992. It predicts that the end of this millennium will see a major shift from the mechanical world to that of electronics and information, and from U.S.A. to Japan.

Diringer, David. *The alphabet: A key to history of mankind.* New York: Funk and Wagnalls, 1968. It describes, in two volumes with many figures, wealth of information about the alphabet.

Fairbank, John K., Reischauer, Edwin O., and Craig, Albert M. *East Asia: Tradition and transformation.* Boston: Houghton Mifflin, 1973. It is a comprehensive and authoritative history of China, Japan, Korea, and Vietnam. But since its publication in 1973, how dramatically things have changed in East Asia!

Gaur, A. *A history of writing.* London: British Library, 1984.

Gelb, I. J. *A study of writing.* Chicago: University of Chicago Press, 1952. This small but classic book traces the origin and spread of writing systems.

Globe and Mail/Economist *Report on Business. The world in 1993* and *The world in 1994.* Both issues predict robust economy for East Asia.

Jensen, H. *Sign, symbol and script.* London: George Allen and Unwin, 1970. The book is full of pictures of the variety of writing systems used in the world.

Kyostio, O. K. Is learning to read easy in a language in which the grapheme-phoneme correspondences are regular? In J. F. Kavanagh, and R. L. Venezky (Eds.), *Orthography, reading and dyslexia.* Baltimore: University Park Press, 1980.

Maddieson, I. *Patterns of sounds.* New York: Cambridge University Press, 1984. It surveys the sound patterns of the languages of the world.

Mann, Horace. *Lectures and annual report on education.* Cambridge, MA: Harvard University Press, 1967.

Moseley, Christopher. *Atlas of the world languages.* UK: Routledge, 1994. It counts 6,500 languages in the world, 2,000 of which have less than 1,000 speakers and are likely to die out in the next 50 to 100 years.

Naveh, Joseph. The origin of the Greek alphabet. In D. de Kerckhove and C. J. Lumsden (Eds.) *The alphabet and the brain: The lateralization of writing.* Berlin: Springer-Verlag, 1988.

Nishida R. *Sekai no moji (Writings of the world)* Tokyo: Daishukan, 1981. Its detailed descriptions of scripts used in Asia are useful. It has many figures.

Overholt, William H. *The rise of China: How economic reform is creating a new superpower.* New York: Norton, 1994. It marshalls data supporting the book's theme that China is becoming an economic superpower.

Perkins, D. H. *China: Asia's next economic giant?*, Seattle: University of Washington, 1986. The book predicted that China would be the next economic giant. Seen in 1995, its prediction seems to be turning out to be correct.

Rassekh, Shapour. *Perspectives on literacy: a selected world bibliography*. Paris: UNESCO 1991. It has a brief comment on each of many books written, mostly in English, on literacy.

Ruhlen, M. *A guide to the languages of the world* (vol. 1, *Classification*). California: Stanford University Press, 1987. It is an ambitious book that surveys thousands of languages of the world, but its information on the numbers of speakers of major languages is outdated.

Schmandt-Besserat, D. Decipherment of the earliest tablets. *Science*, 1981, *211*, 283-284.

Steinberg, Danny D. *An introduction to psycholinguistics*. UK: Longman, 1993. It has three parts: I. first language; 2. language and mind; and 3. second language.

Steinberg, David I. *The Republic of Korea: Economic transformation and social change*. Boulder: Westview Press, 1989. It tracks S. Korea's recent rapid and remarkable economic growth and social change.

Taylor, Insup with Taylor, M. M. *Psycholinguistics: Learning and using language*. Englewood Cliffs, N. J.: Prentice Hall, 1990. This introductory text for college students explains phonemes, syllables, morphemes, words, sentences, and discourses, and then reviews some experiments on processing them. It also has chapters on language acquisition and one chapter on bilingualism.

UNESCO. *Statistical yearbook*. Paris 1991. It compares levels of education, literacy, publication, and culture of many member nations of UN.

Velis, J. P. *Through a glass darkly: Functional illiteracy in industrialized countries*. Paris: UNESCO 1990.

Venezky, Richard L., Kaestle, Carl F., and Sum, Andrew M. *The subtle danger: Reflections on the literacy abilities of America's young adults*. Center for the Assessment of Educational Progress, Educational Testing Service Report No. 16-CAEP-01. Jan 1987.

World factbook 1993. Prepared annually by the Central Intelligence Agency for the use of the US Government officials, it provides up-to-date information on land areas, population, economy, literacy rates, and other pieces of information, of close to 200 nations of the world. It may be purchased in photocopy, magnetic tape, or diskettes. National Technical Information Service 5285 Port Royal Road, Springfield, VA 22161.

Part I

Chinese

The Chinese script is so wonderfully well adapted to the linguistic condition of China that it is indispensable; the day the Chinese discard it they will surrender the very foundation of their culture.

B. Karlgren (1923: 41)

The Chinese language, especially in its written form, has always been one of the most powerful symbols of this cultural unity.

J. Norman (1988: 1)

Writing is not equivalent to culture; it is only a means of conveying culture. We value the traditional culture, and we therefore also value the Chinese characters that convey traditional culture. But we value even more highly the creation of a modern culture of the present and the future, the creation of a Chinese Pinyin orthography [romanization] suited to conveying a modern culture .... The two kinds of writing will coexist and will both be used, each having its own place, each being used to its utmost advantage.

Language Reform Association of the PRC (1981)

China and Chinese

Mainland China is officially called "Zhonghua Renmin Gongheguo" ('The People's Republic of China' or PRC). We will call it simply China. It occupies the whole of central east Asia, stretching from the Pacific coast as far west as the Pamir mountains in central Asia (map, fig. 1-1). Its territory—9,596,960 sq km—is vast enough to cover all of western Europe; it is slightly larger than the United States but smaller than Canada. The vast land mass of China dwarfs its two eastern neighbors: Korea, a small peninsula, and Japan, a chain of islands in the Pacific Ocean.

China is an ancient nation, rich in history and unique in culture. The historian Spence (1990: 7) observes, "In the year AD 1600, the empire of China was the largest and most sophisticated of all the unified realms on earth." For hundreds of years China exerted a powerful cultural influence over its neighbors: Mongolia in the north, Korea and Japan in the east, and Vietnam in the south. Chinese words still permeate the vocabularies of neighboring nations, and Chinese characters are still used in some of them, especially in Japan and Korea. (Chinese characters were officially abandoned by the Vietnamese in the 1940s; they were abandoned by the North Koreans in 1949 but are now taught once more in secondary schools.) It is not for nothing that the Chinese call their nation *Zhongguo* ('Middle kingdom'), the center of the universe. Today China may no longer be considered the center of the universe, but it still remains the center of our attention.

The population of China constitutes one-fifth of the world population of 5.7 billion. In the July 1990 census it was 1,133,682,501; by July 1993 it had increased to nearly 1.2 billion. With an annual increase of 1.1% it is projected to reach 1.3 billion by the year 2000. Modern Chinese distinguish themselves from other ethnic groups in China by calling themselves the "sons and daughters of Han." The Han dynasty created a stable and unified empire over 2000 years ago. Most people in China are Han, but 8%, or 91 million, belong to the 55 different non-Han ethnic minorities, such as Uygurs, Mongols, Tibetans, and Koreans. The Han and most of the non-Han peoples are Mongoloid, but the Uygurs are Turkic.

Most ethnic Chinese are citizens of the People's Republic of China (PRC) on the mainland of Asia. The PRC has a Communist government with a "socialist market economy," a mixture of a command and market economy. Millions of ethnic Chinese live outside the PRC: 21.1 million in Taiwan (the Republic of China), 5.6 million in Hong Kong (which will join the PRC in 1997), 2.8 million (along with other ethnic minorities) in Singapore, 6.0 million in Malaysia (one-third of the population), and 6.6 million in Indonesia (3% of the population). Also many Chinese, a few millions, live overseas in the United States, Canada, Australia, and other parts of the world. Many of them speak Chinese, albeit in different dialects and along with the languages of their adopted countries. Chinese is indisputably the language with the largest number of native speakers in the world.

During its long and continuous history as a nation, China has seen glories and miseries, peace and wars, dynasties and republics. Table Part I-1 shows some major dynasties and republics during which significant events related to scripts and literacy occurred; these events will be elaborated throughout this Part I.

Table Part I-1. Scripts and Literacy in Some Chinese Dynasties or Republics

Dynasty/Republic	Year	Script and Literacy
Shang/Yin	c. 1750–1040 BC	Oracle bone script
Zhou	c. 1100–256 BC	Confucian classics
Qin	221–206 BC	Standardization of characters
Han	206 BC–AD 220	Shuowen Jiezi (1); paper invented
Sui	589–618	Civil service exam began
Tang	618–907	Woodblock printing
Song	960–1279	Printing industry; Neo-Confucianism
Yuan (Mongols)	1279–1368	Civil service exam suspended
Ming	1368–1644	Exam restored; romanization by missionaries
Qing (Manchus)	1644–1912	Kangxi Dictionary; exam abolished
Republic, Nationalist	1912–1948	Vernacular language; Zhuyinfuhao (2)
People's Republic	1949–present	Characters simplified; Pinyin (3); Putonghua (4)

Notes: (1) Shuowen Jieji ('Explanations of Simple Characters and Analysis of Composite Characters') is the first major study of characters.
(2) Zhuyinfuhao ('National/Mandarin Phonetic Symbols') is a phonetic script now used in Taiwan to give the sounds of characters.
(3) Pinyin is the romanization adopted by the PRC.
(4) Putonghua ('Common speech') is standard Chinese promoted by the PRC.
The dates for dynasties are as given by Fairbank (1992: 24; 31).

Spoken Chinese

Presented here is a quick sketch of spoken Chinese to give you a glimpse of what the Chinese language is like, and how it differs from the three other languages of our interest: Japanese, Korean, and English. The discussion is based on books such as Norman (1988), Ramsey (1987), and the *Encyclopedic Dictionary of Chinese Linguistics (Zhongguo Yuyanxue Dacidian* 1991*)*.

Typically, spoken language is described in terms of its speech sounds, its morphemes and words, and its sentences. To understand the technical aspects of any discussion of spoken language, readers should recall or re-acquaint themselves with the linguistic terms introduced in Chapter 1, such as phoneme, consonant, stop consonant, vowel, syllable, morpheme, and syntax.

Standard Language and "Dialects"

What is called "the Chinese language" actually consists of seven major dialects: Mandarin (the northern), Yue (includes Cantonese), Wu (includes Shanghainese), Xiang, Gan, Kejia, and Min. Speakers of one dialect, such as Mandarin, cannot readily communicate with the speakers of other dialects, such as Cantonese. The degree of difference among the Chinese dialects is sometimes compared to that among the Romance languages of the Indo-European language family, such as French, Spanish, Italian, Romanian, and Portuguese.

Mutually unintelligible though the dialects may be, the Chinese are loath to call them "different languages." Chinese see themselves as one unified nation of one ethnic group, the Han people, under one central government, speaking one language, Chinese. Respecting the wish of the Chinese people, I will henceforth use the term "dialect," but often in quotation marks to hint at their mutual unintelligibility.

Of the several major Chinese "dialects," the one with the greatest number of speakers—over 700 million or two-thirds of the Han population—is Mandarin, so called because it was the language spoken by central government officials, *mandarins*. The word comes from the Portuguese word *mandar* ('to command'). The number of people who speak Mandarin is nearly twice as many as the number of people who speak English as their first language in the whole world ("Languages of the World" in chap. 1).

The area where Mandarin is spoken is vast, covering three-quarters of China, north and southwest of the Yangzi River (map, fig. 1-1). The open plains of the north allow easy transportation and communication, and hence speech in this area is relatively uniform. By contrast, there are several mutually unintelligible "dialects" in a small area in the southeast, which is dotted with mountains and rivers and where travel is difficult. Within this small area, two sharply divergent forms of speech may occur only a few kilometers apart, as reflected in such Chinese sayings as, "A language changes when you cross a mountain," or "At a distance of 100 *li* people cannot understand each other." (100 *li* represents, loosely, a day's march; more precisely, 1 *li* = 0.5 km or 0.3 mile).

Mandarin itself has four subgroups, which are as mutually intelligible as are the various dialects of English. One of them, the northern Mandarin spoken in and around the capital Beijing, is designated by the People's Republic of China as Putonghua ('common speech' or "standard language"). Putonghua is used in government business, on the national TV and radio, and is taught in schools throughout China. Mandarin, under the name of *guoyu* ('national language'), is spoken also in Taipei, the capital of Taiwan, and under the name of *huayu* ('Chinese language') in Singapore, but not as much in Hong Kong or in North America, where Cantonese predominates. Almost all of the examples of Chinese syllables, morphemes, words, and sentences used in this book are in Putonghua/Mandarin.

Differences among dialects in any language tend to be greatest in sounds, then in words, and least in sentence structure. Chinese is no exception. When dialects differ in their sound systems, their words are bound to sound different, and the dialects then become mutually unintelligible, despite having similar sentence structures. Korean and Japanese have highly similar sentence structures, but because they differ in sound system and native vocabulary, they are mutually unintelligible.

Getting back to the Chinese "dialects," Mandarin does not have the initial sound *ng-*, but Cantonese and Shanghainese do; Mandarin does not have the final consonants *-k, -t, -p, -m*, but Cantonese does. Chinese words in various "dialects" sound even more different when pronounced with their tones (pitches that can rise or fall; table 2-2 in the next section), because Mandarin uses only four tones while Cantonese uses nine. Also the stop consonants, *b, d, g,* though written using the same Roman letters, are pronounced somewhat differently in Mandarin and Shanghainese. The five words in Table 2-1 sound similar in Shanghainese and Cantonese but quite different in Mandarin.

Such differences in pronunciation are typical, so it is no wonder that speakers of Mandarin and Cantonese or Shanghainese cannot readily communicate. Cantonese retains the old Chinese sound system better than does Mandarin, and Chinese words borrowed by Koreans in early history are closer in sound to Cantonese than to Mandarin. For example, the Korean sounds of the last two words in Table 2-1, 'ten' and 'nation', are *sip* (*sap* in Cantonese) and *kuk* (*kwok*, in Cantonese).

Table 2-1. Morphemes in Three Chinese "Dialects"

Meaning	Mandarin	Shanghai	Cantonese
I	wo	ngu	ngo
tooth	ya	nga	nga
happiness	fu	foq	fuk
ten	shi	sa	sap
nation	guo	go	kwok

So much for the differences among the Chinese "dialects." Let us turn to some similarities among them. All Chinese "dialects" share a common ancestor, Ancient Chinese, and belong to a language family called Sino-Tibetan. They have many linguistic features in common, such as having tones, simple syllable structures, monosyllabic morphemes, and non-inflecting words. In our discussion of the Chinese language, details of linguistic features that differ among the various "dialects" are largely, though not entirely, ignored.

Sound System

Traditionally, Chinese speech is analyzed into syllables. The Chinese syllable is an easily accessible unit, because one syllable represents one morpheme (word or word part), and is represented by one Chinese character. (Exceptions will be described later.) Ask a Chinese speaker to divide an utterance into small segments, he or she is likely to dissect it into a series of syllables rather than into words or phonemes. The phoneme as a phonetic unit is so alien to Chinese speakers that even literate adults have difficulty segmenting a word into phonemes (Read et al. 1986). By contrast, literate English-speakers have no trouble segmenting simple words such as *dog* and *desk* into three and four phonemes, respectively.

Let us re-examine the Chinese version of the sentence "I go to school everyday" shown in Figure 1-4, analyzing it this time into individual syllable–morphemes (for illustration, a dot divides two syllable–morphemes that form a compound word, and initial consonants are capitalized).

Mei.Tian wo Qu Xue.Xiao ('Every day I go [to] school').

Each of the syllables in this sentence is represented by one Chinese character:

每天 我 去学校

Again traditionally, the Chinese syllable is described in terms of an initial, a final, and a tone. There are 21 or 22 different initials, consonants such as *b, q, m, x*, as written in Pinyin, the official Chinese romanization. The stop consonants *p, t, k* are aspirated, (i.e., pronounced with a puff of air, like English /p, t, k/ at the initial position of words) as in *pin, tin, kin*, whereas the other stop consonants *b, d, g* are usually voiceless and unaspirated, almost like English /p, t, k/ in *spin, sting, skin*.

The final is the remainder of the syllable, namely, a simple vowel (*a, e, i, o, u*) or a complex or compound vowel that combines two or three of the simple vowels (e.g., *ei, iao*), and sometimes a final consonant, which may be *n, ng*, or *r*. (Some linguists do not consider -*r* as a final consonant. In Cantonese, the final consonants can include *p, t, k, m* as well.) Words starting with *y-* or *w-*, two semi-vowels, are considered to have finals with no initials. There are 38 or 39 different finals.

Mandarin uses four syllable structures (here, a dot divides a syllable into an initial and a final):

> V (vowel) — *a, ai*
> CV (consonant–vowel) — *d.a, d.ao*
> VC (vowel–consonant) — *ang, ian*
> CVC (consonant–vowel–consonant) — *zh.ang, d.ian*

Chinese has no consonant clusters. In Pinyin, three of the initial single consonants are transcribed as pairs of Roman letters—*ch* as in *chow* aspirated; *sh* as in *show,* and *zh* as in *urchin* unaspirated. The only final consonants in CVCs are *-n, -ng,* and possibly *-r.*

Altogether, Mandarin uses only about 400 different syllables (401 according to C.-M. Cheng 1982; 398–418 according to DeFrancis 1984). By comparison, English uses several thousand different syllables including such complex ones as *strengths,* which has the structure CCCVCCC, and *twelfths* (CCVCCCC). Because of the large differences between the sound systems of Mandarin and English, some well-known English names and words sound strange when transcribed into Mandarin: *Shashibiya* ('Shakespeare'), *sanmingzhi* ('sandwich'), and *Makesi* ('Marx'). When the tones are added to the words, they sound even further removed from their original English forms (also "Foreign Loan Words," below).

Chinese is a tone language: Tone or pitch variations differentiate the meanings of morphemes that have the same syllable. All Chinese "dialects" have tones, though the numbers of tones vary. Cantonese has nine (not described further) and Mandarin four. The four Mandarin tones are: level high, rising, fall–rise, and falling. Table 2-2 shows four different meanings of the same morpheme–syllable *ma* in four tones.

The use of tones is hard to explain to speakers of English or other languages that do not use them. As the distinguished Swedish Sinologue, Karlgren (1923:21), describes, the even tone is like an ordinary, unemotional statement *yes;* the quickly and directly rising tone is like the inquiring *yes?* (what do you want?); the slowly and

Table 2-2. Four Tones of the Morpheme ma *in Mandarin*

Morpheme	Tone	Meaning
mā	level high (1st tone)	mother
má	rising (2nd tone)	hemp
mǎ	fall–rise (3rd tone)	horse
mà	falling (4th tone)	to scold

brokenly rising tone is like a doubtful, hesitant *yes;* and the falling tone is like a triumphant *yes!* (there you are!). But, remember, the Chinese tones signal meanings rather than a speaker's mood or attitude. A changed tone in Chinese is as significant as a changed sound in English words, say between *log* and *dog* or between *log* and *leg.*

The 400 different syllables multiplied by four tones yield 1,600 possible tone syllables, of which about 1,300 actually occur, because not every syllable is used in all the four tones. The Chinese dictionary, *Cihai* (1979), which defines 14,872 characters, provides as an appendix a comprehensive list of 1,359 Chinese tone syllables. But the dictionary includes a few characters each pronounced in two tone syllables, such as the English loan word *yingchi* ('inch'), tone syllables found in a "dialect" such as *ngu,* as well as a few characters each pronounced in a single consonant (*n*) or two consonants (*hn*). These atypical tone syllables may be rarely used. So we settle on the convenient round number of 1,300 tone syllables.

Unless tones are specially needed to make a point, they are not indicated in this book, for convenience in typing.

Morphemes: Words or Word Parts

The smallest meaningful unit of a language is a morpheme, which can be either free or bound. A free morpheme can be used by itself as a word (e.g., *kind*), whereas a bound morpheme is used only as an attachment to another morpheme, such as the prefix *un-* before, or the suffix *-ly* after, a morpheme, as in *un-kind-ly*. Here are two Chinese free morphemes, *yi* ('one') and *si* ('four'). Add to them the prefix *di-* and we have the ordinal numerals *di-yi, di-si* ('first', 'fourth'). Similarly, a suffix added to the end of morphemes can turn a noun into an adjective, as in *heping–heping-de* ('peace'–'peaceful'). (The hyphen is not used in Chinese to separate morphemes in a word but is inserted here for illustration.)

A language typically does not have enough words and morphemes to represent all the concepts—objects, events, and ideas—that people want to talk about. To deal with this situation, most words represent more than one meaning, some related but some not. In English the word *bright* can be used figuratively for a smart person as well as literally to describe sunshine. The English noun *head* has several related meanings: head of a body, head of an organization, head on top of beer, and so on. The English noun *palm* has two quite unrelated meanings: of a hand or a type of tree. The first meaning then begets related meanings such as "a length of the hand" and "to hide in the hand," while the second meaning begets meanings such as "symbol of victory" and "victory."

Chinese, too, has morphemes with multiple meanings: *sheng* ('life, living') means also 'to be born' and 'raw, uncooked'; *tian* ('heaven') means also 'day', 'season', 'weather', 'natural', 'innate', 'imperial'. Which of these meanings is intended can be discerned from the meanings of other characters in a compound word: *tiansheng* ('innate nature') but *jintian* ('now day' = 'today'). Inevitably, some morphemes describing physical properties of objects come to be used figuratively to describe abstract qualities, as does *zhong* ('heavy') in *zhongyao* ('important') and *ming* ('bright') in *mingliang* for bright sunshine or *congming* for a bright person.

In English, a morpheme can have one or more syllables: *man, wa.ter, long.ev.i.ty*. In Chinese, one morpheme is almost always one syllable long: *ren, shui, shou* ('man', 'water', 'longevity'). There are a few exceptions to the general pattern of "one morpheme = one syllable": the diminutive or endearing suffix *-r* in *guanr* ('petty official'), has no vowel and is sub-syllabic (smaller than a syllable), while *yingchi* ('inch' from English) is one morpheme in two syllables.

To Chinese people, the morpheme is a more familiar unit than is the word because of the way Chinese is written: one morpheme is represented by one Chinese character (with a few exceptions), and spaces are left between morpheme–characters rather than between words that may consist of more than one morpheme–character. In Beijing you see posters in romanized Chinese, Pinyin, written with syllable–morphemes either all connected or all separated (Zhou 1991: 20):

ZHONGGUOGONGSHANGYINHANG (phrase unit), or
ZHONG GUO GONG SHANG YIN HANG (syllable–morpheme unit), but not
ZHONGGUO GONGSHANG YINHANG (word unit)
In the syllable–morpheme–character unit the same phrase is written as

中 国 工 商 银 行

('middle nation industry commerce silver row' or "Chinese Industrial and Commercial Bank").

Chinese who are accustomed to character writing have little sense of "word." In Hong Kong middle school students were not proficient in segmenting a text into word units (Hoosain 1991). In English writing, of course, spaces are left between words rather than between morphemes:

master's unkindly words, and not "master' s un kind ly word s."

The Chinese language has a term for individual syllable–morpheme–characters, namely, 字 *zi*. The very word for Chinese character, Hanzi, contains it (*Han* = Chinese; *zi* = character or characters). The length of a manuscript is typically counted in characters. Only recently, under Western influence, has Chinese adopted a term for word, namely, *ci*. If a Chinese wants to ask what the word *tanke* ('tank') means, he is likely to say, "*tan (and) ke*, these two *zi*, what do they mean?"

So, in Chinese (with some exceptions), one morpheme = one syllable = one character. Many single morphemes are used as words, especially in casual speech:

> *Wo zhi mai bi. Shu wo bu mai*   (I just buy [a] pen. [A] Book I [do] not buy),

or

> *Wo zhi mai bi, bu mai shu*   (I just buy [a] pen, [I do] not buy [a] book).

(The words in [ ] are needed in English but not in Chinese.)

In a computer count of 6,321 Chinese written words, one-third were one-character words (Suen 1986), and one-character words can be considered one-morpheme and one-syllable words as well. But the one-morpheme words are used frequently in casual speech, accounting for two-thirds of the words actually used. In another survey of written texts, among the 800,000 characters examined, all of the 29 most frequent words and 76 of the 84 most frequent words were one-character–morpheme words (Wu and Liu 1988).

Not only in Chinese but also in English and other languages, the shorter a word the more frequently it tends to be used; or to put it in another way, a frequently used word tends to be short. This relation between frequency and length is pervasive and is called "Zipf's Law" in honor of the scientist who discovered it. People appear to want to expend as little effort as possible to convey a message by saying or writing *TV* rather than *television* and *car* rather than *automobile*.

Most Chinese words, two-thirds of the 6,321 common words in Suen's (1986) count, have two character–morpheme–syllables, while about 5% have three and four character–morpheme–syllables. The words we have just read about, *zhongguo* ('middle nation' or "China") and *yinhang* ('silver row' or "bank"), are good examples of two-morpheme–syllable words. Examples of three- and four-morpheme–syllable words are: *dongwuyuan* ('moving' + 'thing' = 'animal'; 'animal' + 'garden' = 'zoo') and *dongwuxuede* ('animal' + 'learn' = 'zoology' + '-cal' = 'zoological'). Multi-morpheme–syllable words tend to occur in formal speech and writing. In English, too, people tend to use one-morpheme–syllable words (e.g., *tree*) in casual speech and multi-morpheme–syllable words (e.g., *botanical*) in formal speech and writing.

Many Chinese morphemes and words, along with the characters that represent them, were borrowed by the Koreans and the Japanese over a period of 1500 years, especially in their early history. In modern times many words have been coined, on a

Chinese model in characters, by the Japanese for Western concepts, and many of these words were then borrowed by the Chinese and the Koreans. Chinese morphemes and words—whether they are used in Chinese, Korean, or Japanese—are represented well in Chinese characters. Obviously the topic of Chinese morphemes and words is important to this book, and is further discussed in the next few sections.

Two-Morpheme Words

As we have seen, some Chinese words consist of single morphemes, but the majority, two-thirds of them, consist of two morphemes. Two-morpheme words are constructed variously by repeating the same or similar morpheme, by attaching a bound morpheme as a suffix or prefix to a free morpheme, or by joining two free morphemes. Let us take up each kind in turn.

Reduplications are formed by merely repeating the same morpheme, as in *renren* ('person person' = 'everyone'), *haohao* ('good good' = 'very good', emphasis), and *zouzou* ('walk walk' = 'walk a little'). Many Chinese kinship terms have reduplicated morphemes, as in *mama, baba, gege, meimei* ('mother', 'father', 'elder brother', 'younger sister'). They resemble "baby words" in English and other languages, such as *papa, mama, dindin, tata.*

Some Chinese words have the form "morpheme + prefix or suffix." The prefix *di-*, for example, turns cardinal numerals into ordinal numerals, as in *yi, di-yi; er, di-er* ('one', first'; 'two', 'second'). This useful prefix has been adopted into Japanese and Korean. The suffix 子 *-zi* is attached to many nouns that name concrete objects, as in *bi-zi, dao-zi, shi-zi, mao-zi* ('nose', 'knife', 'lion', 'hat'). The suffix *-r* is the only Chinese morpheme that is less than a syllable long. Attached optionally to many nouns and a few verbs it adds a familiar, diminutive, and sometimes pejorative flavor, as in *mar, guanr, wanr* ('little horse', 'petty official', 'to play'). It is like *-y* in English *horsey, doggy, dolly.*

In borrowing Chinese morphemes and words, Koreans and Japanese sometimes include the suffixes, as in *maozi, shizi* ('hat', 'lion'), which are in Korean *moja, saja* and in Japanese *bōshi, shishi.* The Chinese suffix *-r*, which appeared after the Koreans and the Japanese borrowed most Chinese words, are not included in Japanese and Korean words, so that the Chinese *mar* ('horsey') and *guanr* ('petty official') are in Korean *ma, kuan* and in Japanese *ba, kan.*

Two or more free morphemes can be joined to form a compound word, as in English *plain-clothes-man.* Chinese compound words parallel Chinese sentences in syntactic construction. For example, a compound can have a subject + verb construction, as in *Di zhen* ('[The] earth quake[s]'), which becomes the noun *dizhen* ('earthquake'), and *Tou teng* ('[My] head ache[s]'), which becomes the noun *touteng* ('headache'). Table 2-3 shows the syntactic relations of these and other compound words. The syntactic method of compounding is simple and straightforward in Chinese, because Chinese sentences tend not to contain the equivalents of the English inflections and function words shown in square brackets [ ].

Many Chinese compound words are formed by joining two synonyms, as in *meili* ('beautiful + exquisite' = 'beautiful'), *daolu* ('way + road' = 'road'). The practice of joining two synonyms into a word crept into Chinese-based pidgin English, in words

Table 2-3. Syntactic Relations of Compound Words

Syntactic Relation	Compound Word	Meaning
subject + verb	dizhen	earth + quake = earthquake
adjective + noun	daren	big + person = adult
verb + object	sharen	kill + person = homicide

such as *look-see*. In some other compound words, two antonyms are joined, as in *daxiao* ('large + small' = 'size') and *duoshao* ('much + few' = 'quantity'). In still other compound words, two morphemes with contrasting meanings are joined, as in *weiji* ('danger + opportunity' = 'crisis'). This particular compound word contains a lot of wisdom and is often cited in the West as well.

Instead of joining two or more morphemes into a word, one or more morphemes can be eliminated from a multi-morpheme idiom to create a word, as in *jingji* ('control + save' = 'economy') from the Chinese classical idiom *jingshi jimin* ('control the world to save the people'). This word was first used by Japanese and has since been adopted by Chinese and Koreans. When a few morphemes are eliminated from a phrase, the meaning of the resulting word can be puzzling: *dongxi* ('east, west' = 'thing') comes from "things produced in the four directions (east, west, south, and north) or various areas."

Some two-morpheme words have amusing origins. Take the word *maodun* ('lance + shield' = 'contradiction'). A merchant was selling lances and shields, saying, "This is the ultimate lance; it can pierce any shield. And this is the ultimate shield; it can stop any lance." A man asked him, "Can your lance pierce your shield, or can your shield stop your lance?"

In many examples cited here and elsewhere, the meanings of the component morphemes contribute to the meaning of the compound word. But not so in some compound words: *(luo)huasheng* ('to drop, flower, live/raw' means 'peanut'), *mashang* ('horse, above' means 'at once', and the playful word *mamahuhu* ('horse, horse, tiger, tiger' means 'of no importance').

Many of the reasonable and a few of the unreasonable Chinese words cited in this section — e.g., *dizhen* ('earthquake'), *maozi* ('hat'), *weiji* ('crisis'), *maodun* ('contradiction'), *luohuasheng* ('peanut') — are used in Japanese and Korean with the same meaning, written in the same characters, but with somewhat changed sounds. For example, Chinese *maodun* is *mosun* in Korean and *mujun* in Japanese.

Why Compound Words?

Since each monosyllabic morpheme is meaningful by itself, why are two morphemes joined to make a compound word? In particular, why are two synonyms joined in one compound word? Isn't repeating a morpheme a waste of time and energy for a speaker and writer? Yes, but it helps a listener, since each morpheme by itself may be ambiguous, but one meaning in each morpheme supports and emphasizes the appropriate meaning of the other. Joining two or more morphemes, even if they have the same or similar meanings, in a two-syllable word is a reasonable way to reduce, though by no means to eliminate, many homophones, morphemes that share the same tone syllable. (In English, *rite, write, wright, right* are homophones.)

One way to reduce ambiguity is to add noun-marking suffixes, such as *-zi* as in *maozi* ('hat'), to certain morphemes to indicate that the morphemes are nouns and that the nouns name common objects. Another way is to join two morphemes. For example, *yi* (falling tone) by itself has various meanings ('meaning', 'contemplate', 'clothe', 'different', 'wing', 'city', 'translate', 'post', 'righteousness', etc.); so has *si* (level tone) ('meaning', 'thought', 'this', 'servant', 'private', 'control' etc.). If *yi* and *si* are joined in *yisi*, the compound is far less ambiguous: "Meaning + meaning" makes sense, but other joinings such as "wing + private" work less well. But even two-morpheme–syllable compound words can occasionally be homophonic. A dictionary of homophones lists as many as 18 words—e.g., "different opinion," "different meaning"—all pronounced *yiyi* (both falling tones).

Chinese is full of homophones. The mere existence of a dictionary of homophones, such as *Tongyinci Cidian* (1989) containing 6,000 sets of homophones, attests to this observation. Over 85% of all tone syllables have homophones, according to my count in the Chinese dictionary *Cihai*. Why? Many centuries ago the final consonants *-p, -t, -k* were dropped from syllable structures, and *-m* was merged with *-n*. Consequently, many morphemes with different meanings came to have the same syllable. For example, if one morpheme was "fut," another "fuk," the third "fup," and the fourth "fu," the four morphemes became homophones having the same "fu" syllable when the final consonants were dropped.

The syllable most notable for its many homophones, nearly 200 in a 50,000-character dictionary, is *yi*. *Cihai*, which defines 14,872 characters, has 149 characters with the sound *yi* (falling tone). Even in a much smaller 4,200-character dictionary, this tone syllable still has 38 different meanings. Homophones do not pose a big problem, according to DeFrancis (1984), who points out that all these 38 *yi* morphemes, with the exceptions of three or four, are fixed parts of multi-syllabic expressions with no life of their own. Why is *yi* used mostly in multi-syllabic expressions? Precisely because it is so ambiguous by itself. In spite of that, some homophonic monosyllables are used as words. For example, *ba* (level tone) by itself is used as eight different words, such as 'eight,' 'fence,' and 'scar'.

English, too, has homophones but not so many as does Chinese. The largest set of homophones has four (or five) words: *right, write, rite, wright; heir, air, ere, (eyre), err.* As English homophones can be differentiated by spelling, so can Chinese homophones be differentiated by their characters, as we shall see.

Homophones in speech are ambiguous and can cause misunderstanding or incomprehension. Listeners can often use context to clarify the meaning or sound of an ambiguous word, but to do so costs time and effort, if ever so slightly. And in some cases the use of context requires certain skills.[1] Besides, context can be non-existent, brief, neutral, or too complex. Even in the context of a sentence and discourse, homophones can be ambiguous. When asked, "How did the students in your class do at the exam?" A teacher might answer,

---

[1]In an experiment, in the sentence *The bat flew out of the tree*, some English-speaking American children read *bat* as a baseball bat rather than a flying animal, even though it violates the context (Mason et al. 1979).

Quan bu ji ge,

which could mean either "All passed" or "All failed." The Chinese sentence

Wo dai biao

has two meanings: "I have a watch with me" and "I represent someone."

Compound words increased over time to reduce the ambiguity caused by homophonic monosyllable morphemes. They increased also to coin words and phrases for new concepts, such as *dongwuyuan* ('zoo') and *dongwuxuede* ('zoological'), as culture became complex. Finally, they result from an influx of foreign words, which cannot easily be expressed in single Chinese morphemes, partly because foreign words have to be explained while being translated, and partly because foreign words themselves tend to consist of more than one morpheme, as shown in the next section.

Foreign Loan Words

Even the Middle Kingdom could not escape from an influx of foreign concepts. In the first century AD, Buddhism came to China from India, bringing with it some Indian words, such as *bud,* now *fotuo* ('Buddha').

In modern times many European words and concepts have come to China and have been assimilated into Chinese. They are treated in four ways. In the first, sound-based way, the sound sequence of an European word is segmented into syllables, which are then replaced by similar sounding Chinese syllables with no regard to meaning, as in *Jianada* ('add, take, big' = 'Canada') and *sanmingzhi* ('three, bright, govern' = 'sandwich'). Meaningless sound-based words tend to be used for foreign words whose meanings are obscure. As you can see, the fact that these words are sound based do not guarantee that they faithfully transcribe the sounds of the original European words. Could English speakers recognize Chinese–English words such as *Jianada* and *sanmingzhi?*

In the second, meaning-based way, once the meaning of a foreign word is known, two or three Chinese morphemes are chosen to express that meaning, as *dianhua* ('electricity, speak' = 'telephone') and *zixingche* ('self, go, wheel' = 'bicycle'). (The word for telephone was coined by the Japanese and adopted by the Chinese.) The Chinese words are not necessarily direct translations of the Greek or Latin origins of the English words (*telephone* = 'far voice' and *bicycle* = 'two wheels'). Initially the Chinese tended to transcribe the sounds of European words, as in *telephone* transcribed as *delüfeng,* but recently they have tended to represent the concepts rather than the foreign words for those concepts. This tendency is perhaps salutary, as it avoids distorting—mercilessly!—the sound of an European word, on the one hand, and as it takes advantage of Chinese characters that are well suited to represent meanings, on the other.

The third kind of Chinese rendition of an European word is a hybrid, in which one part of a Chinese translation is sound-based and another part is meaning-based: *jiuba* (*jiu* 'wine' + character with the sound *ba* = 'bar') and *pijiu* (character with the sound *pi* + 'wine' = 'beer').

The fourth kind is based simultaneously on meaning and sound. Chinese syllables are so chosen that they reflect the meaning as well as the sound of a foreign word, as in, *kekou-kele* ('tasty and enjoyable' for 'Coca-Cola'). This felicitous name was the prize winner at a public contest held in 1930 when Coca-Cola began marketing its soft drink in China. The linguist Y.-R. Chao coined a playful Chinese name for *ma(r)tini* ('horse kick you'). The newly coined Chinese words for AIDS is *aisi* ('love death'). In China, when I had a seal or chop sign made for my name *Taylor,* naturally I chose two Chinese characters that approximate the sounds of my name and at the same time have nice meanings: *tailu* ('great/exalted/serene way'). However, to my disappointment, the second character carved on the seal turns out to be *lei* 勒 ('to restrain'), which, being a Chinese surname, is the standard for *Taylor.*

In the late 19th and early 20th centuries, the Japanese were the first among East Asian peoples to accept Western concepts. They coined words for these concepts on a Chinese model, using Chinese characters. Many of their words were readily borrowed into Chinese, and form a very large proportion of the loan words used in modern Chinese, though they may not be perceived as loan words (Gao and Liu 1958). There are three kinds of Chinese words that come from Japanese. In the first kind, the Japanese found words in Chinese classics and slightly modified them. For example, the word *wenhua* ('culture') comes from the classic phrase, *wenzhijiaohua* ('writing, govern, educate, transform'), meaning roughly "govern and lead the people through learning and arts rather than through military force," and the word *wenming* ('civilization') comes from the classic phrase *wenliguangming,* meaning roughly "the nature of things become clear." The second kind of coined words includes purely Japanese words, such as *langren* ('floating person' = 'masterless samurai') and *wutai* ('dance, platform' = 'theatrical stage'). The third kind includes new words coined by Japanese for new concepts without resorting to Chinese classics, such as *kexue* ('branches, learning' = 'science') and *dienhua* ('electricity, speak' = 'telephone'). These modern Japanese words—numbering several hundreds—have been adopted not only by Chinese but also by Koreans.

Full Words, Empty Words, and Classifiers

Chinese words are traditionally divided into two major classes: full words and empty words. Full words include nouns, verbs, adjectives, and adverbs as they would be classified in many languages such as English, Japanese, and Korean. In Chinese, apart from the full–empty classification, boundaries among word classes are not clearcut, so that some words can function, without changing their forms, as nouns, verbs, adjectives, or adverbs, depending on context. For example, the morpheme *shang* can be used as a noun 'top', as a verb 'to mount', as an adjective 'superior', as a preposition, 'on', or as an adverb 'upward'. Its antonym *xia* can be used similarly but with opposite meanings, such as 'bottom' and 'descend'. Under these circumstances, some dictionaries do not bother to mention the word classes of words.

Still, let us consider nouns, verbs, and adjectives. In a traditional grammar, a noun is defined notionally as the name of an object or concept. A noun can also be defined functionally, by its role in a sentence: In

Xiao ren bu da haizi ('[A] Small person [does] not hit [a] child'),

ren ('person') functions as the subject and *haizi* ('child') as the object, and so both are nouns. Further, the noun *ren* is modified by an adjective *xiao* ('small'), and the noun *hai* has the noun-marking suffix -*zi*. Notionally, verbs describe actions or relationships. Functionally, verbs relate the subject and the object in a sentence, as *da* ('hit') does in the above sentence.

Full words—nouns, verbs, adjectives, and adverbs—have the following characteristics: They form an open class, by including a large and unspecifiable number of members; they are of low or medium frequency; and they have tones. Above all, they have semantic content so that even a single item can be used as a sentence or utterance, as in "Come," "Slowly," "Good!" or "Fire!"

By contrast, empty words have the following characteristics: They include prefixes, suffixes, and particles whose functions are more grammatical than semantic; they form a closed class, by including a fixed and limited number of members; they are of high frequency; some of them may not have tones; they are not always obligatory, i.e., they can be deleted without the result being ungrammatical; and they have little semantic content so that a single item by itself cannot be used as a sentence or utterance. For examples of empty words, see the suffix -*men* in the next paragraph and also some particles in "Sentence Structures."

Chinese words, whether full or empty, do not change their forms or inflect. A Chinese noun does not change its form for number and gender, and a Chinese verb does not change its form for tense, number, and person. The lack of inflection in Chinese has important implications for writing Chinese. One invariant morpheme can be conveniently represented by one invariant character: the same morpheme–character *ren* 人 is used for "person, person's, persons', persons"; and the same morpheme–character *qu* 去 for "go, goes, gone, went, going." The same morpheme–character *wo* 我 is used for "I, my, me, mine" though for "my" the particle -*de* may be used optionally, as in *wo(de)*; also an optional plural suffix -*men* is used only for persons, *wo-men, ta-men* ('I + -*men*' = 'we', 'he + -*men*' = 'they'), in which -*men* does not change its form for different words.

In contrast to Chinese, Korean and Japanese verbs and adjectives require constantly changing endings. For example, *go* in Japanese has many forms, such as *iku, ikimasu, ikimashita, ike,* and *ikō*. In Korean and Japanese sentences, nouns must be followed by rather meaningless grammatical items called postpositions, as described in "Sentence Structures." These grammatical items are not convenient for writing in logographic Chinese characters. Consequently Koreans and Japanese were compelled to create phonetic scripts to supplement characters.

In English, a noun takes the plural suffix -*s* (e.g., *dog* vs *dogs*). Some mass nouns use classifiers of sorts, as in *two cups of coffee* and *three sheets of paper*. Note that the English "classifiers" also take the plural suffix -*s*. By contrast, a Chinese noun does not change its form for plurality, but if necessary it can express plurality by using the expression,

numeral + classifier + noun, as in
shi-BEI jiu ('ten-CUP wine'),
shi-WAN fan ('ten-BOWL rice'),
shi-PI ma ('ten-HEAD horse').

Chinese classifiers change according to the nature or shapes of the objects counted and give us a glimpse into the way Chinese classify objects in the world. For example, *zhang* ('sheet') is used for counting objects having flat surface, such as beds, papers, and tables, while *tiao* ('stripe') is used for counting long objects, such as rivers, ropes, and streets. But classifiers are not always logical. For example, *tiao* is also used inexplicably for counting diverse objects and concepts that appear to have nothing much in common: aprons, fishes, dogs, ideas. Among domestic animals, cows are counted with *tou* ('head'), horses with *pi* ('animal'), pigs with *kou* ('mouth'), and dogs with *tiao* ('stripe'). Then there is the handy general-purpose classifier *ge* ('piece') that can be used for ears, people, melons, steamed buns, baskets, houses, doors, islands, weeks, mountains, and so on. Classifiers have crept into Chinese-based pidgin English in expressions such as "two fella man" or "two piece man."

Classifiers sometimes differentiate noun homophones. For example, *shan* (level tone) can be 'mountain' or 'shirt'. With appropriate classifiers the two morphemes are distinguished: *shi-ZUO shan* ('ten site mountain') vs *shi-JIAN shan* ('ten article shirt').

Because of their occasional arbitrariness, the use of about 200 classifiers is difficult to master for foreigners learning Chinese. Ethnic Chinese children in Britain, having difficulty choosing appropriate classifiers for various objects, would use the general-purpose classifier, *ge* ('piece') in its Cantonese version (Wong 1992). A good English–Chinese dictionary helpfully tells you which nouns call for which classifiers.

The use of "numeral + classifier + noun" has been borrowed by the Japanese and the Koreans.

Sentence Structures

Words in a sentence play syntactic roles: a noun plays the role of the subject or object, a verb or adjective the predicate, and an adjective or adverb the modifier. These roles can be signalled in various languages by the order of words, by grammatical morphemes, and/or by the inflections of the words.

In a Chinese sentence, word order plays an important role, since empty (grammatical) words are not always included, and since words do not inflect. The basic word order in a Chinese sentence is "subject–verb–object," as in an English sentence. Change the order of the subject and the object, and the meaning of the sentence changes: In Chinese,

   Gou yao ren ('Dog bite man')

differs from

   Ren yao gou ('Man bite dog'),

as it does in English.

By contrast, in Japanese (and Korean) the type of postposition used after a noun indicates whether the noun functions as the subject (takes *ga*) or the object (takes *o*) of a sentence, and so the positions of the two nouns can be exchanged, as in

   Man ga *dog* o *bite/ Dog* o *man* ga *bite*.

In Latin, too, the order of the two nouns can be exchanged, because a noun as an object has a different ending from the same noun as a subject.

   Homo canem mordet

conveys, though with a different emphasis, essentially the same message as

Canem homo mordet ('Man bites dog'),
but both are different from
Canis hominem mordet ('Dog bites man').

So far, the cited sentences are statements. To turn a Chinese statement into a question, the word order stays unchanged, but the question particle *ma* is added at the end, as in:

Ni mang→Ni mang ma? ('You [are] busy'→'[Are] you busy?')

Another way to ask a question is to present the listener with a choice, as in

Ni mang bu mang? ('You busy not busy?').

The answer to either form of the question might be

Mang ('[I am] busy') or *Bu mang* ('[I am] not busy').

Chinese has wh-question words, such as *shui, shenme, zenme, nar* ('who, what, how, where'). A question word occupies the same position in a sentence as the word it replaces, as in

Ta shi Wang tongzhi→Ta shi shui? ('He/She is comrade Wang→He/She is who?').

Other kinds of questions are:

Ni yao shenme? ('You want what? = What do you want?') and

Ni yao shenme ma? ('Do you want something?').

To make an exclamation, attach an exclamatory particle instead of a question particle at the end of a statement, as in

Shi ni a! ('[It] is you!').

For a negative sentence, a verb or adjective can be negated by the adverb *bu,* as in the above sentence *Bu mang.* Or, it can be negated by *meiyou* ('not have'), as in

You jiu ma? Meiyou ('Have [you] wine *ma?*' 'Not have').

Commands can be a verb alone or subject + verb, as in

Lai! Ni lai! ('Come! You come!').

Negative commands are made with *buyao* ('not want' or 'need not'), as in

Ni buyao lai! ('You need not come = Don't come!').

Since a Chinese verb does not change its form for person, number, or tense, an act can be located in time by words such as "yesterday" and "tomorrow" or by context, as in

Ta pengyou zuotian ma wo ('He/His friend yesterday scold I/me')

for "His friend yesterday scolded me." Verbs in sentences take a variety of particles, i.e., empty words, to indicate "aspect," the duration or completion of a reported event relative to other events. For example, *le* indicates completed action, as in

Ta qunian si le ('S/he died last year'),

while *zai* indicates duration, as in

Wo zai jieshi Hanzi ('I am explaining Chinese characters').

A Chinese sentence often involves a topic (what the sentence is about) and a comment on the topic. The topic comes first in the sentence, and is often followed by a pause in speech. Here the topic is followed by a comma, for illustration.

Zhege shu, yezi da ('This piece tree, leaf big')

The topic, unlike the subject, need not have a direct semantic relation with the verb. The subject, and even the object, of a sentence can be omitted, producing a sentence that might be considered ungrammatical in written English. One can ask,

> *Jiu he bu he?* ('Wine drink not drink?)

or "[As for] wine, [do you] drink [it] or not?"

As compared with their English translations, the Chinese sentences cited above omit some empty (grammatical) words and even some full words. The following two sentences are found in volume 1 of the first grade textbook used in China:

> *Taiyang da, diqiu xiao* ('Sun big, earth small') and

> *Youle dian, duo fangbian* ('Have electricity, many convenience').

Such sentences lack function words such as *the, is, but, if, then, you, there are* used in English. The two clauses of "Have electricity, many convenience" lack even the subjects, which would add nothing to the meaning of the sentence. A Chinese sentence is lean, like a telegram in English. Though lean, Chinese sentences usually convey their messages unambiguously, because the missing items are either inconsequential or predictable from context.

Finally, a few words on respectful and humble speech, which is simple when compared with the elaborate system of Korean and Japanese. It is simple because it relies on a choice of words rather than on changing verb forms. For the English *you* there is a choice between ordinary *ni* and respectful *nin*. A noun can be modified by *gao* or *gui*, ('noble' or 'worthy') or *gaogui*. "What is your *xing* ('name')?" can be asked in one of two ways,

> *Ni xing?* or *Nin gui xing?*

One's own things are modified by words such as *zhuo* ('unskillful') as in *zhuozhu* ('my humble written work'), and *yu* ('foolish') as in *yujian* ('my humble opinion').

Now that we have some notion of what the Chinese language is like, we are ready to see how it is written using Chinese characters.

3

Chinese Characters: Hanzi

Among the few writing systems in use before 1,000 BC, Chinese is the only one still used, and it is used by a huge number of people, one quarter of the world population. In this and subsequent chapters we ask many questions about Chinese characters, which are called Hanzi ('Han/Chinese graphs'). When did Chinese characters begin and how have they evolved? How are they shaped? How many are there? How are their meanings and sounds represented? How do they differ from alphabets or syllabaries? After addressing such questions, we then ask, How are Chinese characters learned? How are they used in reading and writing? How are they computerized? How do they affect the spread of literacy?

For answers to these questions, I consulted many books, such as Gao (1987), Ma (1993), Qiu (1988;1989), as well as countless research articles cited in the text. I also consulted the *Encyclopedic Dictionary of Chinese Linguistics (Zhongguo Yuyanxue Dacidian* 1991). This dictionary is organized by major topics in linguistics, and its first topic is writing, attesting to the importance of writing in China. (In a Western book in linguistics, the topic of writing tends to be either relegated to the end or ignored.) In the end I develop my own views of Chinese characters and their influence on reading and literacy.

Let us begin our study by searching for the beginning of Chinese characters.

Beginning of Characters

The origin of Chinese characters is shrouded in the mist of legend.

> Long, long ago, in the golden age, there was a dragon horse which came up out of the Yellow River with curious symbols traced upon its back, and revealed them to Fu-hi (the first of China's legendary primeval emperors). This potentate copied them and thus acquired the mystical characters, which later became the skeleton of I King [*I Ching* or *Yijing; Book of Changes*], the Canon of Changes, one of the Five Canons [Confucian classics]. And under the third primeval emperor, Huang-ti [Huang Di], the minister Ts'ang Kie proceeded further along the path of invention and fashioned the first primitive characters, by copying footmarks of birds made in the sand. [Karlgren 1923: 32]

A less fanciful account links the origin of Chinese characters to signs used in farming communities of the Yangshao culture in neolithic times, around 5000–3000 BC. This culture developed in the middle and lower reaches of the Yellow River in northeast China, the cradle of Chinese civilization, and produced painted pottery and stone implements. In the 1950s at the neolithic village of Banpo (now in the city of Xi'an) many pieces of potsherds were unearthed, bearing over 100 incised signs, singly, with no context. The simple, non-pictorial or linear signs, could have been numerals or names of clans identifying either potters or owners of the pots (fig. 3-1a).

Pottery	Bone	Modern	Meaning
(a)			one
			two
		五	five
(b)		五	five
		日	sun
(c)		日	sun
		火	fire
		山	mountain

Figure 3-1. Signs on neolithic pottery in China. (a) Banpo signs, Yangshao culture; (b) Liuwan signs, Yangshao culture; (c) Dawenkou signs

Some of the signs have corresponding forms in later "(oracle) bone characters" in the Shang dynasty, to be described shortly. Some of the pots bore simple pictures of such animals as fish and frog, which resemble early bone picture characters.

More potsherds bearing signs were excavated in Jiangzhai, another site of Yangshao culture. The signs are by and large similar to those found in Banpo, but a few join two simple signs. Still more potsherds bearing signs were found in Liuwan. Some signs, such as numerals, are similar to those found in Banpo, and a few signs for objects already resemble bone characters, or even present-day Chinese characters (fig. 3-1b).

Another neolithic culture, Dawenkou, lasted over 2000 years, between 4500 and 2300 BC in the present Shandong Province. Its signs—not many are known—have a strong pictorial appearance. The most complex Dawenkou sign is a three-character composite of "sun, fire (or cloud), mountain" found on a 5000-year-old pot (fig. 3-1c). Each of the three constituent characters had a corresponding form in the bone script. A composite of two characters, either "the sun over fire" ('hot' or 'heat') or "the sun over the horizon" ('dawn'), exists in the modern script. Still another neolithic culture, Longshan (3000–2200 BC), lasted 800 years around Shandong. It produced black pottery with potters' signs, and used divination and metallurgy. These neolithic signs are considered by some scholars to be forerunners of Chinese characters.

The neolithic culture was succeeded by the legendary three dynasties of ancient China: Xia (c. 2200–1750 BC), Shang (c. 1750–1040 BC), and Zhou (c. 1100–256 BC), according to chronicles compiled during the Zhou period or shortly thereafter. There is also material evidence for their existence: Zhou was known directly from its own written records; Shang became known in the late 19th century through its oracle bones bearing writing; and Xia became known only in the mid-20th century through the large palaces excavated at its possible capital, Erlitou (not far from modern Luoyang on the Yellow River). The Shang dynasty had about 30 kings and seven successive capitals. Its early period was centered around nearby Zhengzhou, one of its capitals. This culture had bronze and pottery objects bearing signs, a few of which are recognizable in the modern characters for 'big', 'sword',' fish', and so on.

Evolution of Script Styles

A large set of Chinese characters used in text appeared about 3400 years ago in the late Shang dynasty. Since then, Chinese characters have been used continuously, albeit changing their script styles. The changes have been brought about partly by the uses to which characters are put, and partly by the kinds of writing materials available—bone, bronze, bamboo, wood, stone, silk, and paper—as well as by writing implements such as chisel, knife, brush, and pen. By and large, the shapes of characters have been simplified and stylized for convenience of writing. Of the several script styles, Table 3-1 (partly based on Qiu 1988: 28) shows eight that are important for our discussion: clan-name bronze, oracle bone, Zhou bronze, small seal, clerical, standard, semi-cursive, and cursive.

According to Qiu (1988; 1989), changes in script styles depend on mutual influence between two contrasting styles: an elaborate orthodox form for formal writing and a simple popular form for informal writing. An orthodox script gradually changes under the influence of a popular script, absorbing some of its elements. This way, a popular script plays a leading role in the evolution of script styles.

During the Shang dynasty the orthodox form was the bronze script (*jinwen*). Early bronze characters represented clan names, which were carefully written with a brush and carved into the clay mould used in casting ritual bronze vessels. The clan-name bronze characters were decorative and pictorial, containing round shapes, lines of varying thickness, and filled forms. In Table 3-1, they are far more pictographic than are the bone characters that appeared around the same time.

Table 3-1. Evolution of Script Styles of Chinese Characters

Old Scripts						Modern Scripts		
bronze clan-name	oracle bone	Zhou bronze	small seal	clerical	standard	semi-cursive	cursive	simplified

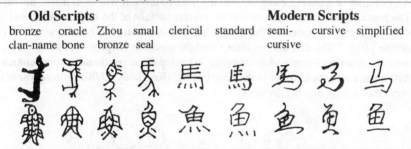

The popular form during the Shang dynasty was the oracle-bone script (*jiaguwen*), whose characters were incised with a knife on hard bones and shells. The material to be written was not just a few isolated characters but a brief text containing a number of characters. And writing was done frequently. For faster and easier writing, characters became simpler and less pictorial than bronze characters when the round shapes became angular, lines became uniformly thin, and outlines were no longer filled.

Some later bronze characters in the Zhou period, in turn, became simple under the influence of the bone characters and came to resemble them, as can be seen in Table 3-1. A bronze object of the early 9th century BC contained a long text containing as many as 500 characters.

When we move on to the oracle bone characters, we are blessed with abundant samples. Legends have grown around the exciting story of how their existence came to be known. According to one legend, in 1899 a Beijing scholar Wang Yirong was taking medicine, which contained an ingredient called "dragon bones," actually ancient animal bones. On these bones Wang and his friend Liu E saw inscriptions that resembled Chinese characters. So the two bought up the bones in apothecaries in Beijing.

In 1903, after Wang's death, Liu introduced the inscribed bones to the world by publishing a book on them. Eventually scholars and merchants traced the source of the bones to the royal graves at Xiaotun in Anyang county, Henan Province, which lies north of the Yellow River, and which was the last capital of the Shang dynasty. In its last period (14th–11th century BC), when Anyang was its capical, the Shang dynasty was called the Yin dynasty.

Subsequently, in the early 20th century, numerous excavations at the Anyang sites uncovered over 175,000 pieces of bones and shells, bearing over 4,500 different characters. Of these, only about one-fifth have descendants in small-seal characters and thus can be identified. Several hundred more can be recognized by analyzing their components. But the remaining two-thirds await decipherment. The bones and shells bearing inscriptions are called oracle bones because they were used for divination.

First, a diviner polished a piece of oxen bone or turtle shell and bored rows of shaped hollows into its back or inner surface (fig. 3-2a). At the moment of divination, he announced a king's "charge" (topic of divination), while applying a hot rod to one hollow after another. The charge, often stated in a positive and negative mode, concerns events such as planting crops, military campaigns, and religious ceremonies. An example of a charge might be, "In the next 10 days, it will rain; it will not rain." The heat caused cracks to appear on the reverse surface of the bone or shell, and the shape of a crack induced by the shaped hollows is captured in the character ┣ ('to divine') (fig. 3-2b). The diviner interpreted the cracks as auspicious, inauspicious, or neutral. Often, a charge and an outcome, occasionally a verification, were engraved with a knife into the exterior of the bone or shell (Keightley 1978). Writing was at the service of a king and his diviners.

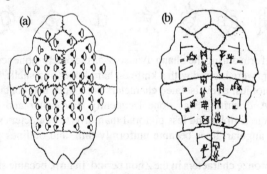

Figure 3-2. Oracle bones used during the Shang/Yin dynasty (1750–1040 BC): (a) turtle interior shell with hollows bored in preparation for divination; (b) turtle exterior shell with ┣ shaped cracks and incised characters

Oracle-bone characters were either regular or irregular in size and shape, and were arranged either neatly or higgledy-piggledy on bones and shells. Some characters were written in mirror reversals. They were written vertically, a column of text moving usually from right to left (which became the traditional writing direction), but sometimes left to right. They became more regular in shape and arrangement in a few hundred years of use.

After the fall of the Shang/Yin dynasty the use of oracle-bone divination largely but not entirely died out. In the 1950s, in Zhouyuan (Shaanxi Province), which was the capital of three Zhou kings, pieces of bones—some bearing a few characters—were discovered. Some character-bearing bones were made during the last period of the Yin dynasty, while others were made during the early Western Zhou dynasty that followed the Yin. The characters of the two periods were by and large similar, but with some differences.

The Western Zhou dynasty was followed by the Eastern Zhou dynasty, which is conventionally divided into two periods: Spring and Autumn (771–484 BC) and Warring States (403–221 BC). During the Warring States, Chinese society underwent rapid change, and the hereditary ruling class, aristocrats, lost power to newly rising classes. In losing their power, the aristocrats lost also their monopoly of writing, which came to be used more and more by non-aristocrats. With this trend, a variety of popular script styles developed in the different warring states. Among the states, it was Qin in the west who inherited the Western Zhou's writing tradition, which was called the great-seal script (*dazhuan*). This orthodox writing style was conservative and was little affected by the various popular writing styles used in the eastern six states.

When Qin unified the warring states in the 3rd century BC, its first emperor standardized the varied shapes of characters that were used there. He had his minister standardize them as a small-seal script (*xiaozhuan*), by simplifying the traditional Qin script, i.e., the great-seal script, and suppressing variant forms used in other states. Small-seal characters were uniform in size and also in stroke thickness. Though stylized, some characters retained faint traces of their pictographic origins (table 3-1). They were used mainly for inscriptions on stones and formal engravings. (This first emperor also standardized coins, weights, measurements, and enlarged the Great Wall, which was further enlarged during the Ming dynasty and still stands today.)

Thanks to the Qin emperor's standardization, Chinese characters have since been seen as a glue that unifies the various Chinese peoples who speak diverse "dialects." The Qin emperor was the first ruler who could read, and started the tradition that learning to read should be part of the emperor's training. The small-seal script represents the last stage of old Chinese writing. Today it is used only on seals or chop signs used as signatures by Chinese, Japanese, and Koreans.

Some simplified seal characters of the late Warring States evolved into a clerical script (*lishu*). The clerical script, so called because it was used by official clerks, was the popular form in the Qin period, whose orthodox form was the small-seal script. Many pieces of bamboo strips bearing early clerical characters were unearthed from Qin tombs in the 1970s. The clerical script makes writing easier, by abandoning the effort to draw pictures of objects, by straightening circles and semi-circles into lines, and by simplifying complex components (table 3-1). It is the watershed that divides the old, heavily pictographic characters from the modern, stylized characters.

The modified clerical script became the orthodox form of writing during the Han dynasty (206 BC–AD 220), as the demands for official documents grew. As for writing implements, silk and paper replaced the cumbersome wood and bamboo strips, and the brush was used to full advantage. The clerical script is used today as an art form in calligraphy.

The clerical script began to change into the standard script (*kaishu*) during the latter part of the Han dynasty, and in that form became dominant with the advent of printing technology in the late Tang (618–907) and early Song (960–1279) dynasties. Characters in the standard script appear less formal and easier to write than those in the clerical script (table 3-1). They are prevalent today.

In handwriting characters, or English letters for that matter, writers want to gain speed and ease by taking short cuts. They may join a series of four dots into a single line, omit a few strokes, join a few adjacent strokes, and round sharp edges, and so on. So there developed a shorthand version of the clerical and standard scripts, a highly cursive "grass script" (*caoshu*), described as "dance of the brush." There are a variety of this script, but *jiancao* ('modern cursive') is the most common (table 3-1). Because of the drastic simplifications and distortions, cursive characters are not easy for untrained readers to decipher. Yet, some prestige was associated with writing in an illegible hand: Some people believed themselves dishonored if they wrote legibly (rather like physicians in the West). There also developed a semi-cursive "running script" (*xingshu*), whose shapes are moderately simplified and are legible (table 3-1; also fig. 3-4b, below). The standard and the semi-cursive scripts had become the two prevalent scripts by the Tang dynasty; they are still so today.

In present China many standard characters have been simplified (table 3-1; chap. 8). Some simplified characters, now considered orthodox or official, are none other than their popular versions used in the past.

Chinese Calligraphy

The variety of Chinese script styles described in the preceding section developed side by side with Chinese calligraphy, the ancient and venerated art of beautiful handwriting. Characters with their complex and varied shapes have great potential as aesthetic objects. Chinese calligraphy, revered as the mother of all visual arts, is still practised and appreciated not only by the Chinese but also by the Koreans and the Japanese. It is practised not only by artists but also by every literate person. In the days of imperial China, when bureaucrats were recruited through civil service examinations, a candidate could not pass without a good hand, regardless of his mastery of the Confucian classics and the prescribed essay form ("The Civil Service Examination System" in chap. 10).

Calligraphic characters are usually written on white paper using a brush dipped in black ink. The ink for calligraphic writing comes from an inkstick, which is soot mixed with glue made into a hard cake. An inkstick is rubbed against an ink stone that has been wetted with a few drops of water. The inkstick is moved around against the wet stone to release the ink, which is prepared freshly for each use. A modern brush has a bamboo handle with a conical, tapered tip of animal hair. Some brushes are thick and some thin to suit different purposes. The writing brush is as old as the script. Even in the Shang/Yin dynasty it had its pictograph 聿 — a hand holding a brush vertically. The brush, ink, ink stone, and paper are called the Four Treasures or Four Friends of a Scholar. Figure 3-3 shows the tools of calligraphy and a person using them.

Chinese calligraphy is said to induce in its practitioners a state of mental peace and quiet. A calligrapher should perform his or her art in a peaceful and quiet environment with a minimum of distraction and disturbance. Traditionally a calligrapher writes while sitting on the floor, moving the fingers, wrist, arm, and shoulder, and controlling the respiration so as not to disturb mental concentration and the flow of the physical movement of writing. "If the heart is right, then the brush will be right," said the master calligrapher Lu Shihua.

The instruments of writing—the brush, the ink, and the paper—were critical in fashioning the shapes of characters in calligraphy. A writing brush made with stiff yet elastic hair

Figure 3-3. Calligraphy tools in use. The calligrapher is Ms Kim Chin Sun. (photograph by the authors)

flattens out when pressed down, twists when turned, and projects its point when raised up. The brush requires swift execution, as ink spreads on absorbent paper if it lingers too long. It can produce strokes of varying thickness and dryness.

Training in Chinese calligraphy, and also in its appreciation, takes time. A trained calligrapher executes each stroke in one move, never retracing or retouching the once-drawn stroke. The force of the brush applied to paper can be heavy or light, prolonged or swift, bold or delicate, and so on, in an infinite range of rhythmic variations. To capture the poetry of Chinese calligraphy I can only quote the great Tang calligrapher Sun Ch'ien-li:

> Sometimes a stroke may look heavy like dark hanging clouds; sometimes as light as a cicada's wings. Sometimes a light tilting of the tip of the brush makes a stroke flow like a spring; or deliberate "stay" of the brush gives another stroke the preponderance of a mountain. Sometimes its delicate beauty reminds one of the new moon emerging from the horizon; sometimes it is resplendent like an array of stars in the sky.... Heart and hand in perfect co-ordination. [in Ch'en Chi-mai 1966]

Elsewhere he rhapsodizes:

> Of the wonders of *shufa* (art of writing) I have seen many and many a one. Here a drop of crystal dew hangs its ear on the tip of a needle; there, the rumbling of thunder hails down a shower of stones. I have seen flocks of queen-swans floating on their stately wings, or a frantic stampede rushing off at terrific speed. Sometimes in the lines a flaming phoenix dances a lordly dance, or a sinuous serpent wriggles in speckled fright. And I have seen sunken peaks plunging headlong down the precipices, or a person clinging on a dry vine while the whole silent valley yawns below. [p 198]

As shown in Figure 3-4, a calligraphic work of art can be displayed on all sorts of objects, such as a teacup and a brush holder (a), a scroll (b) or a rock (c). Scrolls that carry characters—idiomatic phrases or lines of a poem or prose—written by master calligraphers are highly treasured. Written characters can stand alone, as on these objects, or they may accompany paintings, done in the same manner as in writing.

(a)

(b)

(c)

Figure 3-4. Objects bearing samples of calligraphy (photographs by the authors)
  (a) A cup bearing the character dao *('the way') written by former Japanese Prime Minister Nakasone, and a wooden brush holder bearing old style Korean Han'gŭl (chap. 13).*
  (b) A scroll bearing a text written by a master Korean calligrapher on the occasion of my departure for the United States for graduate study. The text loosely translated: "As treasures of mountains and rivers must be brought out, so must be beauty in a person by learning."
  (c) A rock bearing the first clause of Confucius's saying: "A man of benevolence never worries; a man of wisdom is never in two minds; a man of courage is never afraid." [Analects; "Confucianism and Confucian Classics" in chap. 10]. *The character* 仁 *('benevolence') happens to be the first of my own two character name, Insup.*

Six Categories of Characters

Characters were invented not by a single individual at one particular time, despite what legends may say, but have evolved over thousands of years of continued use by a huge number of people. Still, characters are not simply a collection of unrelated arbitrary symbols. By examining a large number of characters it is possible to discern certain principles used in creating them and to group them into six categories.

The first significant attempt to examine characters was made by the lexicographer Xu Shen in the Han dynasty 2000 years ago. In the book titled *Shuowen Jiezi* (*'Explanations of Simple Characters and Analysis of Composite Characters'*), Xu Shen examined the shapes, meanings, and sounds of 9,353 small-seal characters (plus hundreds of great-seal characters and other characters used during the time of the Warring States). He wrote the explanations in the clerical script.

He first divided all characters into two broad categories: simple characters called *wen* and composites of two or more *wen* called *zi*. Hence the title of his work. He then divided the characters into six categories, as shown in Table 3-2 along with examples: pictographs, indicators, meaning composites, semantic–phonetic composites, mutually defining characters, and phonetic loans.

Table 3-2. The Six Categories of Characters Described by Xu Shen (AD 121)

Category	Example			
	Bone	**Modern**	**Sound**	**Meaning**
Pictograph	⊙	日	rì	sun
	☽	月	yuè	moon
Indicator	⌣	上	shàng	above
	⌢	下	xià	below
Meaning composite	日 月		rì, yuè	sun, moon
	明		míng	bright
Phonetic loan	⬚ ------------		wan	scorpion
	萬		wàn	ten thousand
Semantic–phonetic	女 馬		nü, mǎ	woman, horse
	媽		mǎ	mother
Mutually defining	*(ambiguously defined by Xu Shen; see text)*			

Pictographs are drawings of objects, such as 山 ('mountain'), originally three peaks of a mountain. Because of stylistic changes over the years the pictographic origins have been all but lost in modern characters.

Indicators (called also ideographs) symbolically represent relational concepts that cannot easily be depicted by pictures. For example, the characters for the concepts "above" and "below" use a horizontal line with a short bar above 上 and below it 下 respectively. This category in Chinese is called *zhishi* ('indicate', 'affairs'), which Karlgren (1923) translated as "indicators." The alternative label for this category, "ideograph," is not only a poor translation of the Chinese term but also is applied by some people for Chinese characters of all categories, as discussed in "Logographic Characters vs Phonetic Scripts" (chap. 6).

Two or more—usually up to four—indicators or pictographs may join to form a meaning composite. For example, the two pictographs, one for "sun" and the other for "moon," join in the character for "bright" 明. Or one character for "person" 人 and another for "mountain" 山 join to make "hermit" 仙 .

In the categories described so far, a shape (character) is directly linked to its meaning (morpheme) without any reference to its sound. In the following two categories, phonetic loans and semantic–phonetic composites, the sounds of characters are taken into consideration.

Phonetic loans are seen in the two characters, one for "scorpion" and the other for "ten thousand," which shared the same sound in archaic Chinese. Because it was far easier to draw the picture of a "scorpion"—two claws sprouting from its body and a curved tail—than "ten thousand," the character for the former was used for the latter (which is now used in a simplified form; "scorpion" now has another character). Phonetic loans are common for numerals for large numbers, such as this example, as well as for empty (grammatical) morphemes, which, having little concrete meanings, are not suited for pictographic or meaning representation.

In a semantic–phonetic composite (also called a phonetic compound), a sound-cuing phonetic component (or a phonetic) and a meaning-conveying semantic component (or a signific) are joined. For example, in the composite character "mother," pronounced *ma* and shown in Table 3-2, the left character supplies its semantic component, "woman," while the right character supplies its phonetic *ma*.

The category called "mutually defining" (*zhuanzhu*) ('turn, comment') was so ambiguously defined by Xu Shen that it has been interpreted widely differently by later scholars. In one interpretation, one character is used to represent two words of the same or similar meaning, and in different sounds. For example, 樂 means 'music' with the sound *yue*, and means 'pleasure' with the sound *le*. (It is used in a simplified form in China.) This category applies to only a few characters anyway (table 3-4, below).

Most characters examined by Xu were semantic–phonetic composites. How were they created? Widespread use of phonetic loans produced many homophonic characters; that is, several different morphemes, if they had the same sound, came to be written with the same character. To give a distinct shape to each of several homophonic characters, a semantic component was added to a phonetic loan. For example, the character for "work" 工 with the sound of *gōng* was used to write many morphemes such as 'red', 'river', 'attack', 'sky', which in earlier days sounded like *gōng*. To differentiate various meanings, a different semantic component was added to each of many characters that shared the same phonetic, as shown in Table 3-3 (repeated later as table 5-1 with explanations). There is no rule as to the position a phonetic or semantic component occupies in a character: it can occupy the top, left, bottom, right, outer, or inner positions of a character.

Table 3-3. Various Tone Syllables that Use the Phonetic Component 工 *(gōng)*

Hanzi	Sound	Semantic	Meaning	Hanzi	Sound	Semantic	Meaning
功	gōng	strength	merit	虹	hóng	insect	rainbow
訌	hòng	speak	mischief	缸	gāng	vessel	pottery
貢	gòng	shell	tribute	空	kōng	cave	hole, sky
項	xiàng	head	neck	恐	kǒng	mind	frighten
江	jiāng	water	river	汞	gǒng	water	mercury
邛	qióng	walled city	place name	杠	gàng	tree	flagstaff

Five of the six categories were found even in the oracle-bone characters, suggesting that these characters were at an advanced stage of development. But the relative proportions of the six categories changed over time, as shown in Table 3-4. The oracle-bone characters were used in the 14th–13th centuries BC, *Shuowen Jiezi* was written in the early 2nd century AD, and *Tang Yin (Tang Rhyming*, a pronunciation dictionary*)* in the mid-8th century AD. In Table 3-4 (based on Xu Yizhi 1991), the exact proportions (which differ slightly in Woon 1987) are not as important as their changes over time. The most dramatic changes are the decreased proportion of pictographs and the increased proportion of semantic–phonetic composites. Joining semantic and phonetic components is a favored method of creating new characters in China. In modern times, the character for the technical concept 'oxygen' has been created by joining the semantic component "air" with the phonetic component *yang*.

Table 3-4. Proportions of the Six Categories in Three Different Texts (and Times)

Text	Picto-graph	Indi-cator	Meaning composite	Phonet. loan	Semantic–phonetic	Mutual defin.	No. of charact.
Oracle	23.9	1.7	34.3	11.2	28.9	0	1,155
Shuowen	3.8	1.3	12.3	1.2	81.2	0.07	9,475
Tang Yin	2.5	0.4	3.1	2.5	90.0	1.5	24,235

Now that some semantic components have been eliminated in simplifying over 2,000 characters in China ("Simplifed Characters" in chap. 8), what proportion of characters used today are semantic–phonetic composites? Between 80–90% in various counts or estimates (Zhou 1978; Zhu 1987; *Zhongguo Yuyanxue Dacidian* or *Encyclopedic Dictionary of Chinese Linguistics* 1991). So, for long time, the great majority of characters have been semantic–phonetic composites.

In Table 3-4, we note that the number of characters has also increased over time, even allowing for the fact that only about one-third (those deciphered?) of the available oracle-bone characters were examined, and for the fact that the 4,500 different characters excavated may not represent all the different ones used at the time.

Number of Characters

How many characters are used today? This question has no definite answer. A Chinese character is a logograph. It represents a morpheme, and hence there should be as many characters as there are morphemes in a language. Think of morphemes representing all the objects, events, and ideas, i.e., concepts, that we talk about in our lives: "fire," "water," "tree," "love," "hate," and so on. And new morphemes are needed for new concepts, such as *laser, quasar,* and *neutrino.* When one is dealing with such a large number of items, one cannot be precise and specific about how many there are. As the number of morphemes is large and unspecifiable, so is the number of Chinese characters that represent morphemes.

Since the first Qin emperor standardized characters over 2200 years ago, there have been several significant efforts to collect, organize, and explain them. Three of these efforts were as follows. The first was in AD 121 when the lexicographer Xu Shen collected and explained 9,353 characters in the *Shuowen Jiezi* (*'Explanations of Simple Characters and Analysis of Composite Characters'*). The second was in AD 1716 when 30 scholars under the Qing emperor Kangxi collected and defined 47,035 characters in the *Kangxi Dictionary.* The third was in the 1980's when the Chinese Character Analysis Group in Taiwan collected and coded some 74,000 characters, of which 49,300 are standard and 24,700 are variants (Huang and Huang 1989). Variants are different forms of standard characters, having the same meanings and sounds as their standard versions. For example, the character for *xue* ('learning') has several forms, three of which are: standard 學, variant 斆 and simplified 学.

So, the number of characters has kept increasing over the few thousand years they have existed. Why? On the one hand, more and more variants of standard characters appear, as do new concepts that need new characters; on the other, characters used in ancient texts but no longer used are kept in a large dictionary. However, of this huge number of characters, most are of complex shapes and seldom used. They are "monstrosities of no practical use," to borrow Wieger's (1915) words.

In 1975 the National Publication Bureau of China conducted a large-scale count of how many different characters are used in various fields of endeavour, such as science and newspapers. The bureau counted a total of 24,213,955 characters to learn that only a little over 6,000 different characters are used. Table 3-5 (based on Tajima 1989: 233) shows the numbers of characters used in five different fields; the total at the bottom of the table shows the means for all ten fields examined.

Table 3-5. Number of Characters Used in Different Fields

Field	% Accounted	Characters
Science/	99.0	2,246
Technology	99.9	3,917
	100	5,712
Newspaper/	99.0	2,072
Communication	99.9	3,404
	100	5,078
Politics	99.0	1,785
	99.9	2,966
	100	4,356
Arts/	99.0	2,178
Literature	99.9	3,204
	100	3,965
Machine/	99.0	1,238
Engineering	99.9	1,861
	100	2,626
	99.0	1,904
Mean of the	99.9	3,070
five fields	100	4,347
All	99.0	2,400
ten fields	99.9	3,839
	100	6,876

A neat pattern can be found in general publications: 1,000 most common characters account for 90% of characters used, and each additional 1,400 characters account for additional 9%, .09%, and .009%. So, 2,400 characters account for 99%; 3,800 characters account for 99.9%; and 5,200 characters account for 99.99% (based on Zhou 1987).

Today a typical typesetting tray of a printing press contains a few thousand different characters. In a study done by the Institute of Psychology of the Academy of Sciences in the 1960s, the average college-educated Chinese person, who is not an expert in Chinese literature or history, knew between 3,500 and 4,000 characters. The four-volume edition of *The Collected Works of Mao Zedong* contains only about 3,000 different characters.

In 1988 the Committee for the Writing of the National Language published the "Lists of modern Chinese characters for everyday use," which included a primary list of 2,500 characters and a secondary list containing an additional 1,000 characters. These lists are not prescriptions; rather they are guidelines for teaching and using characters. Armed with the 3,500 common characters a reader may need to use a dictionary only occasionally. In Taiwan the Ministry of Education and the Normal University of Taiwan published in 1982 and 1984 a set of 4,808 most frequently used characters, 6,341 next most frequently used ones, and 18,480 rarely used ones.

For our own discussion let us settle on some nice round numbers of characters for convenience:

- 50,000 in a large dictionary
- 6,000 for high-level, scholarly literacy
- 3,500 for common use or functional literacy
- 2,000 for limited literacy

Remember, the use of 3,500 characters means the use of 3,500 **morphemes**; it does not mean the use of only 3,500 words, because one morpheme is used in many different words as the first, second, third, or fourth character, as shown in Figure 3-5. The character used as an example in the figure appears as the last morpheme in the words for almost all scholarly disciplines, such as mathematics, physics, economics, linguistics, chemistry; in such uses it is considered a suffix.

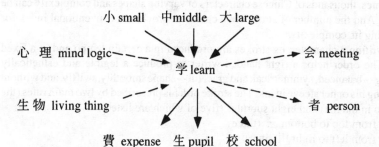

Figure 3-5. Examples of compound words that contain the character for "learn(ing)." Arrows indicate the directions in which characters are combined: small/ middle/ large + learn = primary/ middle/ university education; learn + school = school; small + learn + school = primary school. Mind + logic = mental state; mind + logic + learn = psychology; learn + person = scholar; mind + logic + learn + person = psychologist.

In one count made in Taiwan, the number of characters in daily use was 4,532, but the number of words was 40,032 (Liu et al. 1975). To calculate from these figures, each character should occur, on average, in nine different words, but actually some characters occur in many words while some others occur in only a few. In a survey of 800,000 characters used in a variety of texts, each of the 120 most frequent characters occurs on average in 126 different words, and each of the next 120 most frequent characters in 77 words (Wu and Liu 1988). So, each common character is used as a constituent of many different words.

Shapes of Characters

Consider the shapes of the familiar English letters such as *I, i, g, H, x, E, O*: they are formed by arranging between one and four elements, each of which is a line, a curve, a circle, or a dot. The sizes, and sometimes the shapes, of letters distinguish upper- from lower-case letters. Because the English alphabet has only 26 upper- and 26 lower-case letters, a letter can afford to be simply shaped and still be reasonably discriminable from other letters.

Chinese characters, like English letters, are formed by arranging dots and lines. But Chinese characters use more varied dots and lines, and more of them to build shapes more complex than the English letters. Lines in characters can be vertical, diagonal, and horizontal; they can be straight, gently curved, or with a hook. Modern characters do not use semi-circles or circles. These building blocks of Chinese characters are called strokes, and each stroke is written in one movement of a brush or pen. One stroke is usually a single line or dot, but it can involve a curved shape, as in 乙 . It can involve an angle so that the character for "mouth" 口 for example has 3 rather than 4 strokes, as the top horizontal line and the right-side vertical line form one angle stroke. The number of different strokes has been estimated to be between 8 and 30. Remember, a stroke is strictly a building block of a shape of a Chinese character; it neither codes any sound nor represents any meaning.

By assembling a set of different strokes, sometimes by repeating the same stroke a few times, thousands of Chinese characters of varying shapes and complexity can be formed. And the number of strokes in a character provides a conventional index for measuring its complexity.

In writing a character, its strokes are produced in a certain tempo and in a fixed order. The order helps a right-handed writer to produce a legible and esthetically pleasing — balanced, symmetrical, and graceful — shape smoothly, swiftly, and without smudging his or her sleeve in ink. The stroke order is prescribed by two main rules (the first two in the list) and eight subrules (five of which are listed):

- from top to bottom 三 (three)
- from left to right 川 (river)
- a horizontal before a vertical stroke 十 (ten)
- from a central stroke to a left and then a right stroke 山 (mountain)
- an outer shell before an inner component 同 (same)
- draw last a vertical center line that penetrates a character 中 (middle)
- draw last a horizontal line that penetrates a character 母 (mother)

As always with such sets of rules there are some minor exceptions. The stroke order for writing characters is illustrated often in dictionaries and textbooks (see fig. 9-2).

Because of their large number, Chinese characters need to have complex shapes if they are to be discriminated from each other. Among the 3,500 characters designated for common use and listed in *Hanzi Xinxi Zidian (A Dictionary of Chinese Character Information* 1988), the simplest two have 1 stroke each, and the most complex has 24 strokes; the majority have between 6 and 13 strokes; and only fourteen characters have between 20 and 24 strokes, as shown in Figure 3-6. The most common stroke number

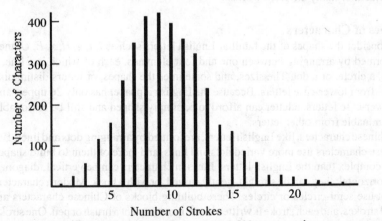

Figure 3-6. Distribution of stroke numbers among 3,500 common characters

is 9. The most complex character, found in a large
dictionary that defines over 30,000 characters,
has 64 strokes (table 3-6).

Even common characters are complex in shape,
compared to the English letters, which range in
complexity from 1 stroke (*I*) to 3 or 4 strokes (*E*),
with the average being 2 strokes. Characters are
also more complex than Japanese Hiragana, a
syllabary, which has 75 differently shaped signs.
The simplest Hiragana sign 〈 has one stroke,
while the most complex (ぽhas 6 strokes.

More complex characters tend to be composites
of a few simple characters. In Table 3-6 the
character for "grove" consists of two slim "tree" characters, and the character for
"forest" consists of three small "tree" characters. The complex character with 29
strokes, too, has two tiny "tree" characters on the top. (Its simplified shape lost "tree"
characters and has 8 strokes.) Note that the shapes of individual simple characters
change somewhat when they form components of a composite character. The most
complex character, with 64 strokes, consists of four copies of the "dragon" character,
each with 16 strokes, arranged in a 2 x 2 square, i.e., two in the top row and two
underneath it. Mercifully, such a monstrously complex character is rarely, if ever, used.
The character for "dragon" itself has been simplified and now has only 5 strokes. Each
character—whether simple, complex, or composite—fits into a shape of roughly the
same size, which might be a square, a rectangle, or a triangle.

Japanese psychologists do much research on the nature of characters. Among the
common characters used in Japan, frequently used ones tend to be simpler than
infrequently used ones (Kawai 1966). Thus the simplest 一 ('one') is the most
frequently used; the moderately complex 実 ('fruit' or 'real', 8 strokes) is less
frequently used; and the most complex character studied, with 18 strokes, is least
frequently used. In another Japanese study of over 2,000 common characters,
complexity ranges from 1 to 29 strokes, and the simpler a character the more frequently
it tends to be used (Miyajima 1978).

What accounts for this relation between characters' complexity and frequency of
use? Some frequently used characters are moderately simplified in Japan. For
example, the character for 'fruit' or 'real' with 8 strokes is a simplified version of its
original 14-stroke form. This character is simplified in China too, but slightly
differently. Also over the long history of use, increasingly complex characters have
been created to represent increasingly rare and esoteric meanings. For example, the
character for insect has 6 strokes. But each of the numerous characters for different
species of insect contains the semantic component "insect" plus additional strokes. So
the character for louse has 7 strokes, for glow worm 16, for big caterpillar 19, and short-
legged spider, 27.

The relation between complexity and frequency of use found in characters is found
between length and frequency of use in words in Chinese, English and other languages,
as pointed out in "Morphemes: Words and Word Parts" (in chap. 2).

Table 3-6. Characters of Varying Complexity

Hanzi	Stroke	Meaning
一	1	one
木	4	tree
林	8	grove
森	12	forest
龍	16	dragon
鬱	29	melancholy
龖龖	64	talk too much

Complex vs Simple Characters

Chinese characters vary enormously in complexity. Are complex characters more difficult to learn, read, and recognize than simple ones? To answer this question properly we have to resort to experiments rather than to intuition.

To compare complex characters with simple ones, researchers have to ensure that the two types of characters are equal or similar in frequency of use or occurrence. Given two characters of equal complexity, 行 ('go') and 汗 ('sweat'), the first occurs in text far more frequently than the latter, and tends to be more familiar to a reader. (Frequency, which can be objectively tabulated, and familiarity, which is a subjective perception, are intimately related but are not identical.) The more familiar a verbal item the faster and more accurately it tends to be recognized, whether the item is spoken or written, or whether it is written in English letters or Chinese characters. Because of the importance of frequency, there are books that tabulate words and characters according to their frequencies of occurrence (e.g., Francis and Kucera 1982 for English words; Liu et al. 1975 for Chinese words and characters used in Taiwan; *A Dictionary of Chinese Character Information* 1988 in China).

The results of observations and experiments on complexity are mixed and inconclusive: (1) some show that complex characters are read or learned faster or more accurately than simple ones; (2) some show the reverse; (3) and some show that complexity has no effect. Let us consider them in order.

Complex characters are easier than simple ones. The Japanese educator Ishii (1988) observed that, given the three characters and one Japanese phonetic sign shown in Table 3-7, Japanese preschoolers learned the meanings and sounds of the complex characters faster than the simple ones; they learned the simple phonetic sign slowest. Characters' meanings rather than their shape complexity must have been a factor: the character for, 'dove' is complex but has a concrete meaning, whereas the simple phonetic sign for *ku* has no obvious meaning.

Table 3-7. Complex and Simple Graphs

Graph	鳩	鳥	九	ク
Sound in Japanese	hato	tori	ku	ku
Meaning	dove	bird	nine	(none or ambiguous)
Stroke number	13	11	2	2

Japanese psychologists do much research on how characters are read aloud, recognized, and learned. Kawai (1966) tested Japanese adults reading 160 simple (e.g., 王 'king' 4 strokes) and 160 complex (e.g., 鼻 'nose' 13 strokes) single characters of similar frequency, selected from among the 3,328 characters used in Japan. Kawai used a complexity index of his own device, which was slightly more elaborate than the customary index of stroke counting. For example, he gave a point to a corner or angle so that 人 has a complexity index of 3, even though conventionally it has only 2 strokes. The adults had to give the meaning of each character and its two pronunciations (in Japan each character tends to have two or more quite different sounds; chap. 18).

The Japanese adults made fewer errors on the more complex than on the less complex characters, when both types of characters were similar in frequency of use. Frequency had its own effect: The higher the frequency, the more correctly the characters were read. Similarly, when Japanese adults were required to associate a word to a nonsense figure, the more complex figures were learned faster than the less complex ones.

One expects that at least in writing, simpler characters should be more correctly written than complex ones. But unexpectedly, schoolchildren in Hong Kong wrote a complex character 健 with 10 strokes more correctly than a simple one 仁 with only 4 strokes (reported in Leong 1972).

Simpler characters are easier than complex ones. Japanese kindergarteners learned the correct sounds of four simple characters with an average of 4 strokes (e.g., 冬 'winter'; 5 strokes) faster than those of complex ones with an average of 10 strokes (星 'star'; 9 strokes) (Ozawa and Nomura 1981). The time to pronounce was also faster for the simpler characters than for the complex ones. When Chinese adults had to decide whether a character was real or fake, their response was slower to a complex character than to a simple one (Leong et al. 1987). This task, called "lexical decision," is far removed from normal reading in that readers examine a character far more closely than they would in normal reading. Be that as it may, it is a popular experimental procedure on word recognition.

Complexity has no effect. Four decades ago the Chinese psychologist Ai (1950) observed:

> It is my finding as well as that of Professor Chai Loh-Sen, in different laboratories at different times, that when characters are produced for recognition, it does not matter whether they are simple or complex in form, or whether they contain too many strokes or only a few, because the subjects [readers] perceive them as a whole. [p. 212]

More recently, in recognizing, there was no marked difference between simple and complex characters (in Fan et al. 1987). In reading aloud, latency to pronounce was about the same for simple and complex characters, if the characters were of high frequency, but it was somewhat slower for complex characters, if the characters were of low frequency (Leong et al. 1987). Again, the effect of frequency was much greater than the effect of complexity.

In Japan, in Steinberg and Oka's (1978) study, when 3- and 4-year old preschoolers learned to read aloud 42 Kanji words that varied in complexity from 3 strokes (e.g., 川 'river') to 16 strokes (薬 'medicine'), their correct scores did not relate to the stroke number. That is, even the most complex Kanji tested was learned as fast as the simplest one. Fukuzawa (1968) studied close to 400 schoolchildren (3rd–7th grades) learning to read characters. The most influential factor was familiarity, and then frequency of occurrence, but complexity had no effect. That is, the more frequent and familiar the characters, the faster they were learned, regardless of their complexity.

In a large-scale Japanese survey of primary and middle school students' reading and writing performance, complexity and "regularity" of characters had no relation with reading aloud; that is, complex and irregularly shaped characters were read as well as simple and regular ones. (Regularity refers to symmetry and balance of a shape:

車 is regular, whereas 応 is irregular, as rated by Japanese students in a separate study; in Kaiho and Nomura 1983: 142).

The results of these observations and experiments are consistent on the potent effect of familiarity and frequency, but inconsistent on the effect of complexity, perhaps because different researchers used different indexes of complexity and different degrees of separation between complex and simple characters. Most researchers, except Steinberg and Oka, dichotomized characters' complexity into complex and simple categories when in fact it varies in degrees. Readers' tasks also differed. Performance was measured for speed or accuracy, or for both; it was measured for pronunciation alone or along with meaning. None of these experiments compared the same characters in their complex and simplified versions. What these observations and experiments do show us is that the difficulty of learning and reading a character is not related to its shape complexity in any obvious and straightforward manner. Why not?

Since a character, if it is familiar, is recognized not necessarily stroke by stroke but as a whole pattern, what matters is not so much the complexity but the distinctiveness of characters. Distinctiveness, in turn, depends largely on the outer contour and the density pattern of strokes within the character, not on its number of strokes per se. Even two or three extremely simple characters, if they differ only in minor details, can be confused with each other, as between 土 ('earth') and 士 ('expert'), and among 己 ('self'), 已 ('already') and 巳.[1] So are two moderately complex characters, as between 栽 ('plant') and 裁 ('judge'). And it is not only the visual patterns but also the concepts represented by characters that determine the difficulty of characters. So, a preschooler may learn the relatively complex character for "dove" (table 3-7), assuming that she has seen a dove, more easily than the simple character (4 strokes) 心 ('mind').

One expects to find benefits from simple shapes of characters at least in writing them by hand. Yet, as mentioned, a complex character can be written more accurately than a simple but non-distinctive shape with a few strokes. But by and large, a simpler character with few details is easier to write than a complex one, because it can be recalled more accurately than a complex shape, and because it has a fewer strokes to write one by one.

Any advantages in writing simple characters over complex ones almost disappear in one form of word processing. On a computer a writer can call for, or output, a desired character by typing in its sound in a phonetic script. Here, there is no need to recall a shape, and there is no stroke-by-stroke writing. Instead, the ease of discrimination among characters is important. But writing on a computer or even on a mechanical typewriter is still a distant dream for most people in China, who have no choice but write characters by hand ("Computerizing Chinese Characters" in chap. 8). Word processors are more common in Singapore, Taiwan, Japan, and S. Korea than in China.

---

[1] This character is used in the Chinese calendar system or zodiac, which arranges years in a cycle of 12, with each year symbolized by a different animal, such as rat, ox, or snake. This character designates the 6th year, which is snake. Each cycle of 12 is further associated with one of the Five Phases (Table 10–2) to create a 60-year cycle.

For readers, too, an excessively complex character poses a problem, as they may have difficulty recognizing its intricate and complex internal detail. Consider the character 圞 ;it has 27 strokes, and its inner detail is 龘. I sometimes use a magnifying glass to see such complex inner detail on a printed page. Even on a computer, character complexity matters to some degree. Characters are represented on the computer screen as a pattern of dots, called pixels. In software a Chinese character may be put into a block of 24 x 24 pixels or more, whereas a simpler English letter can be put into a shape as few as 5 pixels high. (More pixels need more computer memory.) So, to be as easily discriminated, a character on a computer screen must be about three times as high as an alphabetic letter, taking 10 times the area. The above 27-stroke character appears on my computer screen as a black square object whose inner detail I cannot perceive. Fortunately, its inner detail has been simplified drastically in China and moderately in Japan.

Excessively complex characters, say those over 21 strokes, should be either simplified or eliminated from lists of characters designated for common use. As part of a large-scale reform of the writing system, in China over 2,000 common characters have been simplified, some drastically but not necessarily judiciously (chap. 8). What is needed are experiments that compare the difficulty of complex characters to their simplified versions used in China, under conditions in which other factors (e.g., frequency, familiarity, concreteness–abstractness of meaning) are adequately controlled.

4

Meaning Representation
in Characters

The logographic Chinese characters represent the meanings of morphemes. They do so as pictographs, indicators, meaning composites, or semantic components in semantic–phonetic composites, as we saw in the last chapter (table 3-2). (Characters can represent sounds also, as pointed out, and is discussed in the next chapter.) Let us first discuss these four categories of characters in some more detail. Then we shall see that characters, because they represent meanings of morphemes, are highly effective in compound words, idioms, abbreviations, and personal names. They are even credited with magical qualities.

Pictographs and Indicators

A pictograph is originally a drawing of a concrete and simple object, such as a tree or a mountain. Obviously a pictograph is not easy to make for such an abstract and complex concept (object, event, or idea) as nation, loyalty, or love. Pictographs, especially of complex objects, are not easy to draw and so tend to be simplified and stylized over time until they bear little resemblance to the objects depicted.

Only a small proportion of modern characters are pictographs. Even in these, because of stylization, the objects depicted can be discerned only when pointed out. Can you tell what objects the following eight characters represent?

日 月 山 石 水 火 田 土

The pictographic origin of the first three characters has been already pointed out, whether you remember or not. The characters represent "sun," "moon," "mountain," "stone," "water," "fire," "field," "earth." For the objects these characters represent, see Figure 9-2. Although you seldom can determine the object represented by a pictograph, once you are told about the relation between the two, you are likely to remember it well. In this sense, pictographs have mnemonic values, which can be exploited in teaching characters.

Indicators tend to represent relational concepts. In Table 3-2, the concepts "above" and "below" were represented by two characters, one with a short bar above, and the other below, a line. The three characters for numerals "one," "two," and "three" are appropriately one horizontal bar, two horizontal bars, and three horizontal bars, respectively.

A meaning composite is created by joining two or more indicators or pictographs to represent one meaning, as the characters for moon and sun are joined to make the character "bright." The morpheme "bright" can be used in Chinese, as in English, literally to describe a bright object such as the sunlight but also figuratively to describe a bright person. Occasionally, a meaning composite is made of one character repeated:

the character "tree" repeated twice is "grove" and repeated thrice is "forest," as was shown earlier in Table 3-6.

Characters created in Japan tend to be meaning composites. For example, 峠 *tōge* ('mountain pass') consists of one pictograph "mountain" and two indicators "above" and "below." Meaning composites can represent concrete concepts (e.g., 仙 'person + mountain' = 'hermit') as well as abstract ones (信 ' person + word' = trust').

Semantic Components and Radicals

Most Chinese characters used today are semantic–phonetic composites. In a semantic–phonetic composite, a semantic component cues the semantic field—e.g., person, mouth, body, tree, insect, and water—to which the meaning of a composite character belongs, rather than its exact meaning, while a phonetic component cues the sound of a composite character (chap. 5). For example, the semantic component "tree" is found in numerous characters that once had something to do with tree or wood, such as 柱 *zhu* ('pillar'), 橋 *qiao* ('bridge', now used in a simplified version), and 枕 *zhentou* ('pillow'; *tou* is a noun suffix). All these characters share the visual component 木, called a radical. A radical is usually, though not always, the same as a semantic component, and the two terms are often used interchangeably. Strictly speaking, radicals (*bushou* 'section heads') are classifiers of characters based on shape, whereas semantic components (*yifu* 'meaning indicators') are cues to meaning. A semantic component is almost always a radical, but a radical may not be a semantic component.

Even when radicals are semantic components, the classification of characters using them is not expected to be always semantically sensible; after all, characters have evolved over thousands of years of use, rather than having been set down at a single moment by a committee of scientists. Examined today, we would still find many radicals reasonable but some now seem unreasonable. Consider the radical "tree/wood." In old days wood was used for such objects as pillars, bridges, and pillows, and so it was appropriate in these characters. Figure 4-1 shows an old wooden pillow.

Today, of course, the objects represented by the radical "tree" are not necessarily made with wood: a pillow tends to be a cloth bag stuffed with straw, foam, or down, and a bridge tends to be made of stone, concrete, or steel. Some people do use the

Figure 4-1. The character for 'pillow' has the semantic component for "wood." This antique wooden pillow consists of two identical parts that can be opened for use or shut for portability; it is ingeniously carved using one piece of wood, with no nails or glue. It is an ideal pillow for a hot summer day, because its holes allow air to circulate. (photograph by the authors)

radical "stone" or "metal" in the character "bridge." Also, the original shapes of certain radicals are no longer retained in some characters, such as 球 ('ball'), whose radical was originally 玉 ('round thing').

Consider another radical 虫 ('insect'): It occurs reasonably in numerous characters that represent different species of insects, such as louse, flea, mosquito, but it occurs less obviously in the characters for snake and crab, perhaps because a snake slithers and a crab crawls like an insect. Most puzzling is the occurrence of the radical "insect" in the character 虹 ('rainbow'). But we are not short of conjectures: The wings of some insects have rainbow colors (suggested by Prof. F. R. Pitts); a rainbow is long, slender, and curved like a worm (by Wang Y.-H.). The rainbow character in the oracle-bone script was a picture of a curved snake with a head at each end, as in ancient times a rainbow was regarded as a living thing.

Here are some anecdotes involving radical/semantics. The Japanese army in China during the Sino–Japanese War in the 1940s called themselves *kōgun (huangjun* in Chinese) 皇軍 ('imperial army'). To express their dislike of the Japanese army, the Chinese added the radical "insect" to the character "imperial," turning it into 蝗, which still is pronounced *huang* but means "locust." The Japanese, on the other hand, added the radical "beast" to two characters, one for America and one for England, during WWII.

The semantic components/radicals reflect the categories of objects and events the Chinese see in the world. They could number only four—nature, flora, fauna, and man—in which case they would be too broad to be informative; they could number in the thousands, in which case they would be too complicated visually and too precise semantically. In AD 121 the lexicographer Xu used 540 radicals to classify 9,353 characters, but the 18th century *Kangxi Dictionary* used only 214 radicals to classify 47,035 characters. In China, where many characters have been simplified, sometimes by eliminating their radicals, the number of radicals is fewer than 200. Whatever their number, radicals are unevenly distributed among characters: The most common radical "grass" occurs in 2,149 characters, while the least common radical "perverse" occurs in only 6 of 50,000 characters (Huang and Huang 1989).

The radicals of the *Kangxi Dictionary*, numbered 1 to 214, are used to classify characters in many other dictionaries. Suppose we are seeking the simple 女. We look for it among the radicals with three strokes, finding it to be number 38, where it is given the sound *nü* and the meaning "woman." Now instead we may look for 好, a meaning composite that consists of two radicals, each with three strokes. The numbers of the left radical and the right radical are 38 and 39, respectively. As there is no way of deciding under which of the two radicals the composite character is listed, we try one and then the other.

How do readers of characters respond to radicals? As with many other questions concerning characters, Japanese psychologists try to answer the question through research. Kaiho (1975) prepared four lists of character pairs:

1. same radical with similar meanings: 鉄 銅   (iron, copper)
2. different radical, similar meanings: 軒 門   (eaves, door)
3. same radical, different meanings: 塩 坂   (salt, slope)
4. different radicals, different meanings: 鉄 塩   (iron, salt)

Japanese students had to decide quickly whether characters in a pair belonged to the same semantic category. There was no difference in time to decide between the characters that shared the same radical (1 and 3) and the ones that had different radicals (2 and 4). So, in rapidly recognizing familiar characters, people do not seem to rely on radicals. Under these conditions, they recognize a character as a whole pattern, without decomposing it into its components. However, in another experiment where time was not pressing, Japanese readers used radicals in reading less familiar characters (Morioka 1980).

Readers can use a semantic component only to the extent that the whole character's meaning has something to do with mouth, tree, water, and so on. Furthermore, the cues contained in semantic components are not always reliable, as we have seen. Still, the meaning-cuing function of semantic components is greater than the sound-cuing function of phonetic components (Zhu 1987; chap. 5). Also the number of radicals, around 200, is easier to remember and use than the number of phonetics, over 1,000.

Users of characters should learn and memorize the radicals, as dictionaries of characters and words tend to be organized by radicals. For word processing on a computer, characters tend to be organized in at least two different lists: the first list contains the most frequently used characters arranged according to their sounds, and the second list contains the less frequent characters arranged according to their radicals ("Computerizing Chinese Characters" in chap. 8).

Users of characters should be aware of some other aspects of radicals. Some radicals, such as "mouth," are used by themselves as independent characters, but others, such as "grass," are not. Some radicals change their forms in different composite characters: the radical "water" comes in three forms, two of which appear in 汞 ('mercury'; the bottom component is the radical) and 江 ('river'; the left component is the radical). A radical can occupy any position within a character: left or right, top or bottom, inside or outside. But the majority occupy the left or the top (Hoosain 1991). Characters tend to be written from top to bottom and from left to right ("Shapes of Characters" in chap. 3). Writers may put the most significant element of a character first, and over time this tendency might lead the radical to migrate to the top left.

Characters Tell Stories

English letters, such as *a* and *b*, now merely indicate sounds, and then only inconsistently; but in their earliest forms these two letters were pictographs, which came to represent the initial sounds of the Semitic words *alef* ('ox') and *beta* ('house'). These two words were joined to form the word we now know as *alphabet*.

Compared with the now meaningless and workaday phonetic letters, some Chinese characters have interesting origins, which can be elaborated into stories. These stories give us an intriguing glimpse into the way Chinese people lived and viewed the world in ancient times. They might be learned when characters are learned; if not, they are readily found in any good book on Chinese characters (e.g., Li L.-Y. 1992 and Ma 1993). Let us sample some characters that have interesting stories. The characters are listed in old pictographs — most in the oracle-bone script — and contemporary standard script. Some of them are used in simplified shapes in China (for one example, see the characters for 'child'.)

术→木 *mu* ('tree') shows a trunk and two leafless branches of a tree. The bottom half of the character may be hanging branches or the roots of a tree. As shown in Table 3-6, the character doubles to represent "forest" and triples to represent "dense forest." It joins with the character for "person" to represent "rest," as shown below. 末 *mo* ('last' or 'top') shows a tree in which the top is marked with a horizontal stroke, while 本 *ben* ('source' or 'origin') shows a tree in which the root is marked with a horizontal stroke.

ʔ→人 *ren* ('person') shows a person in a profile, standing upright with arms hanging down. In another interpretation a person is marching with two legs. The character, often in a slender form, appears in many composite characters: with a tree 休 *xiu* ('rest'), a person resting against a tree; with a mountain 仙 *xian* ('hermit' or 'immortal'), a person secluded in a mountain; and with a dog 伏 *fu* ('lie prostrate'). 北 *bei* ('north') shows two persons standing back to back for "the direction toward which people turn their backs." In China the icy winter winds from Siberia and the yellow spring sandstorms from the deserts of Mongolia come from the north. To protect themselves, people turned their backs on them. The house gate, the emperor's throne, and all important ceremonial sites face south.

ʮ→兒 *er* ('child') consists of a child's head sitting on the character for "person." The head shows two tufts of hair above the ears, characteristic of a child's hair style to this day. Alternately, the top is open, showing an immature skull in which its two halves are not yet closed. In the simplified form used in China 儿 the child's head vanishes!

井→井 *jing* ('a well') represents eight square lots of fields, divided among eight families, reserving the middle square with a well in it for public use. In ancient China eight families formed a village and cultivated a well-field in common for the purpose of taxation. Alternately, the character is a pictograph of a well with a square opening. Sometimes a well has a center dot, which may represent a bucket that brings water up from the well.

門→門 *men* and 閂 *shuan* ('door' and 'bolting') show that the ancient Chinese had folding doors that could be bolted with a bar. The simplified forms now used in China no longer depict the door. 開 *kai* ('open') shows the bar on the door removed with two hands.

⼷→貝 *bei* ('shell', 'valuable') shows that cowrie shells were used as currency in antiquity. Their supply did not meet the demand and so copies of shells were made out of bone. In bone shells, only a few horizontal strokes were filled across the surface to mimic the mouth wrinkles of a real shell, as depicted in the pictograph. 貧 *pin* ('poverty') consists of the valuables in the form of shells (the bottom component), which is partitioned (the top component). In China the family property was divided equally among male offspring, and so in a family with many sons poverty followed the partition of the property.

卜→卜 *bu* ('divination') is a pictograph of a crack appearing on an ox bone or turtle shell when heat is applied on its reverse side. This technique was used in divination in the Yin period (chap. 3). 占 *zhan* ('to consult a diviner') has the character for 'mouth' underneath 'divination'.

肀→筆 *bi* ('brush', 'pen') began as a pictograph showing a hand holding a brush vertically. This character existed in the oracle-bone script, suggesting that some kind of brush was used over 3400 years ago. During the Zhou dynasty this character was crowned with the radical for 'bamboo'. In the several brushes preserved from the late Zhou dynasty, the shaft is usually made of bamboo, and the head is made of animal hairs of various kinds. In the simplified form, the character's "hand" and "brush" are replaced by the character for "hair."

㚻→女 *nü* ('woman') shows a woman squatting down with the arms crossed in front of her body. The "woman" character appears in many compound characters with favorable meanings, such as 安 *an* ('peace'), which shows a woman under a roof. But some characters containing the "woman" have such undesirable meanings as "jealousy," "slave," and "sly."

㝅→家 *jia* ('house') shows a pig under a roof; in the old days pigs and dogs lived around and in the house of a peasant. The street-cleaning and privy-emptying tasks were left to these two animals.

The interpretions of characters are occasionally ambiguous or controversial: witness the two or more possible interpretations for some characters. About 2000 years ago the lexicographer Xu Shen misinterpreted the pictographic origins of some characters, especially because he was not aware of the oracle-bone script. For example, he explained the character for earth 土 *tu* as two layers of soil through which a plant pushes upwards. The oracle-bone and bronze character, however, has the form ⚆ , which shows an altar with a wooden sacred pole on it representing the god. The earth was a divinity in ancient China, and in front of the pole offerings for the god of the soil were laid (Karlgren 1923). Yet another interpretation says that the archaic character simply depicts a mound of earth on the ground.

These stories—whether authentic or fabricated, and realistic or fanciful—make characters come alive and at the same time serve as excellent mnemonics for remembering them. A mnemonic is an art or trick used in memorizing a seemingly meaningless or complex item, or in memorizing a large number of items. (Example : I memorized the name in English of the fish *splake* by asssociating it with "splash in a lake.") The thousands of Chinese characters do not form a collection of totally arbitrary graphs, but neither are they systematically related to each other. The use of mnemonics is bound to help in learning Chinese characters (chap. 9).

> The more I could tell them [my Swedish students] about the construction and early forms of the characters, the easier it was for them to understand and remember them [characters]. The very best was when I could also tell them something about the world from which the characters were drawn. [Lindqvist 1991: preface]

Referring to Chinese characters that tell stories, Glahn (1973: 16) observed, "Such a language is already half way to poetry." I would add, "And to psychology and anthropology."

Compound Words and Idioms

One or more individual characters, because they represent meanings, combine to form an effective compound word, idiom, or aphorism. In *daren* 大 人('big + person = adult'), each character contributes its meaning to the meaning of the compound. Here are a few more examples of compound words.

中 国 *zhongguo* ('middle + nation = China') (the second character is a simplified form)

中 国人 *zhongguoren* ('China + person = Chinese')

動物 *dongwu* ('move + thing = animal')

動物園 *dongwuyuan* ('animal + garden = zoo'; the first and the last characters, shown here in their original forms, are simplified in China)

Some technical terms are far easier to understand in Chinese characters than in English, because the individual characters that make up a Chinese technical compound word tend to be familiar to Chinese speakers, whereas the Greco–Latin roots that make up a technical word in English are often unfamiliar to English speakers. Modern technical terms are often coined originally in the West and then are translated into Chinese. In translation, they appear to be explained using familiar morphemes.

dermatology	*pike* ('skin, branch/section')
gynocology	*fuke* ('women, branch/section')
helicopter	*zhisheng feiji* ('straight, rising, flying, machine')
microbiology	*weishengwuxue* ('tiny, living, thing, study')
ophthalamology	*yanke* ('eye, branch/section')
psychology	*xinlixue* ('mind, logic, study')
telescope	*wangyuanjing* ('view, distance, mirror')

Users of characters who encounter these terms for the first time may be able to guess their meanings. Even young children aged 4–6 can infer the meaning of a compound word from the one familiar character it contains. For example, the character *dou* 斗 ('fight') helped the children to infer the meaning of a two-character word such as *douzheng* ('struggle') (cited in Fan et al. 1987).

There are, however, atypical cases in which individual characters making up a compound word do not in any obvious way contribute to the compound word's meaning: *(luo)huasheng* ('to drop, flower + life/ raw' = 'peanut'). The meanings of characters are ignored in transcribing foreign words whose meanings are unknown: 三明 治 *sanmingzhi* ('three, bright, govern' for 'sandwich'). Some compound words may appear puzzling, until their stories are told. Examples are *maodun* ('lance + shield = contradiction') and *dongxi* ('east, west = thing') ("Two-Morpheme Words" in chap. 2).

Countless compound words in characters, some coined in China and some in Japan, are used by Chinese, Koreans, and Japanese, but with different sounds. The Chinese words *dongwu* ('animal') and *dongwuyuan* ('zoo'), for example, use the same characters but are pronounced as *tongmul* and *tongmulwŏn* in Korean and *dōbutsu* and *dōbutsuen* in Japanese.

Our discussion can smoothly move from the topic of Chinese compound words, each of which typically consists of two morpheme–characters, to the topic of Chinese idioms, each of which typically consists of four morpheme–characters. In English an idiom consists of two or more words that are often used as a whole unit for their figurative meaning, as is *wash one's hands of (something)* for "give up responsibility" or *kick the bucket* for "to die." An aphorism tends to be a brief sentence conveying a piece of wisdom, such as *Time is money.*

A Chinese idiom or aphorism, called *chengyu* ('established words'), typically consists of four characters and is in a terse classical or literary style, with few empty grammatical morphemes (see "Literary vs Vernacular Language" in chap. 8). Chinese people, whether they are educated or not, and whether they are speaking or writing, are fond of using idiomatic phrases, which are vivid, apt, wise, and earthy in expressions. The origins of these idioms can be sometimes traced to incidents in Chinese history or to lines in classic poetry or prose. Not that ordinary Chinese users, any more than English users, are aware of the origins of the idioms they use everyday.

Here are several Chinese idioms, chosen from dictionaries of idioms for their popularity, vividness, and/or interesting origins.

The idiom *wo xin chang dan* ('lie down on firewood and lick a gall bladder' or "to achieve a goal, one endures great privations and sufferings"). In ancient China, there were two nations called Wu and Yue that fought each other for 20 years. In one battle the king of Wu was defeated. His son, in order not to forget his father's defeat, subjected himself to physical pain by sleeping on a pile of wood. He finally defeated the king of Yue, who, to remind himself of the bitterness of the defeat, hung in his room a gall bladder, which he licked everyday. Eventually he defeated his enemy again.

The idiom *hua long dian jing* ('to a picture of a dragon add the eyes' or "the whole becomes alive with the addition of a small detail"). Once upon a time a painter drew a picture of a dragon on a temple wall. As a final touch, he added the eyes to the dragon, whereupon the dragon broke through the wall and flew away. One can say also "it lacks *hua long dian jing*," meaning it lacks a critical detail.

Sometimes an idiomatic phrase is lifted out of a poem or passage and cannot be fully understood until its source is known. For example, *ying cheng san ren* ('to have a shadow for the third man') means "being happy in solitude." It is taken from the following poem by the great Tang poet, Li Bo.

Among flowers, with a kettle of wine, I fill my cup in solitude and have no companion. I lift the cup and invite the bright moon. My shadow becomes the third man of the company.

The idiom *sai weng shi ma* ('the old man near the border who lost his horse') is about a person's misfortune turning into a fortune, and vice versa. The phrase comes from a famous anecdote in the 2,000 year-old philosophical book, *Huainanzi*.

Once upon a time there was an old man who lived near a fort in the north and owned a horse. One day the horse ran away to a northern barbarian nation. His neighbors pitied him. But the old man told them to wait and see if this misfortune could not lead to something good. And, indeed, one day the horse returned accompanied by a beautiful Mongol horse. The neighbors congratulated him. "Don't be rash," said the old man, "this may yet bring misfortune." Sure enough, shortly afterwards his son was thrown off the new horse and became a cripple. When the neighbors condoled with him, the old man answered: "Who knows if this misfortune will not turn out happily?" Soon the Huns invaded the district, and all its young men were called up. Nine out of ten of these men were killed. The cripple, of course, stayed at home, and so the old man until death had a son to support him. [Karlgren 1923: 90–91, with slight changes in wording]

The idiom *zhao san mu si* ('morning three evening four') means "to trick a gullible person with crafty words" or "to play fast and loose with words." Once upon a time there was a man who raised many monkeys and worried about the cost of feeding them. One day he said to his monkeys, "From now on I will give each of you three acorns in the morning and four in the evening. How about that?" The monkeys complained, "Only three acorns in the morning? That's not enough!" Thereupon the man said, "How about four acorns in the morning and three in the evening?" The monkeys were well satisfied.

The idiom *wu shi bu xiao bai bu* ('fifty steps laugh hundred steps' or "don't quibble about minor details" or "the pot calling the kettle black"). In a homily to a king the sage Mencius (c. 372–289 BC) asked: "In a battlefield, one soldier took one hundred steps backward, while another soldier took only fifty steps backward. The latter laughed at the former, saying 'You are a coward, running so far away.' Do you think his criticism is fair?" The king replied, "No, both of them fled. Whether by one hundred steps or fifty makes no difference."

The idiom *meng mu duan ji* ('Mencius's mother cuts a loom' or "Complete the task you have begun"). The sage Mencius studied away from home in his youth. One day he came home without completing his study. His mother cut the cloth she was weaving, to show her son that a work not completed is useless.

One favorite device used in idioms is hyperbole, as in *jiu chi rou lin* ('wine lake meat forest' or "feast with abundant wine and meat.") The idiom originally described two evil emperors of ancient China who spent days and nights indulged in drinking wine, eating meat, and dallying with women. Naturally the two were resented by their subjects.

Some idioms do not require long explanations: *yi xin sheng an gui* ('A doubting mind lets a devil appear in the dark'); *ku jin gan lai* ('When bitterness exhausts, sweetness comes'); *da qi wan cheng* ('A big vessel takes a long time to complete' or "Great talents mature late").

Countless Chinese idiomatic phrases have drifted into the Korean and Japanese languages and cultures, with the same characters and meanings but with different sounds. For example, *da qi wan cheng* ("great talents mature late") is *tai ki ban sei* in Japanese and *tae ki man sŏng* in Korean. Chinese idioms are taught in schools in China, Japan and Korea. They are collected and explained in many dictionaries in each of the three languages.

Characters for Abbreviations

The names of institutions, if they are long, tend to be abbreviated for convenience. In English the common method of abbreviating a name consisting of several words is to pick the initial sound or letter of each word to form an acronym, such as *United*

States of America–USA and *Federal Bureau of Investigation–FBI.* The trouble is, it is difficult to know what some infrequently used acronyms, such as *NAFTA* and *OECD,* stand for. The acronym *AAA* is not only meaningless but also ambiguous in that it can stand for many organizations such as "American Automobile Association," "Amateur Athletic Association," "Agricultural Adjustment Administration," which actually exist; or "Association of American Anthropologists/ Accountants/ Astronauts," which might exist. The American Medical Association encourages people to use its full name to avoid confusion with the "American Motorcycle/ Marketing/ Mining Association."

An effective method of abbreviation is available in Chinese, thanks to its logographic characters. Many names of frequently mentioned places and institutions are abbreviated by retaining only a few key morphemes, which can be the initial, the middle, or the last morpheme. In Table 4-1 the capitalized parts are retained in abbreviations.

Table 4-1. Abbreviations Using Characters

Original	Meaning	Abbreviation
beiJING shi	Beijing City	京
BEIjing DAxue	Beijing University	北大
ZHONGguo GONGchandang	Chinese Communist Party	中共
NEIMENGgu zizhiqu	Inner Mongolian Autonomous District	内蒙

Because the key morphemes are chosen for their meanings rather than for their sounds, Chinese abbreviations written in characters are by and large unambiguous. Also care is taken to ensure that the morphemes retained for one abbreviated name are distinct from those retained for other abbreviated names. For example, from *Beijing city* ('north, capital, city'), the character for "capital" is retained, and from *Beijing Daxue* ('north, capital, large, learning'), the characters for "north" and "large" are retained. Abbreviations patterned on Chinese models are used widely in Korean and Japanese.

Chinese Numerals

Chinese numerals are simple, especially when written. The characters for one, two, and three, are represented appropriately by one horizontal bar, two horizontal bars, and three horizontal bars, respectively. By now you should be familiar with the character for "ten" that resembles the plus sign ╋. Table 4-2, column 2, lists the Chinese numerals 1 to 10. These ten Chinese numerals and their characters, because of their usefulness and simplicity, are among the first items learned by children in nations that use Chinese characters.

The numerals between ten and twenty are formed by adding an appropriate numeral to ten: eleven is "ten-one," and "seventeen" is "ten-seven." Twenty, and higher multiples of

Table 4-2. Chinese Numerals

Arabic	Chinese	Character
1	yi	一
2	er	二
3	san	三
4	si	四
5	wu	五
6	liu	六
7	qi	七
8	ba	八
9	jiu	九
10	shi	十
17	shiqi	十七
20	ershi	二十
23	ershisan	二十三
777	qibaiqishiqi	七百七十七

ten up to one hundred are expressed as "two-ten," "three-ten," and so on. Writing these numerals are also simple, as shown in Table 4-2, column 3. Higher numerals are: *bai* ('hundred'), *qian* ('thousand'), *wan* ('ten thousand'), *baiwan* ('hundred ten-thousand' = 'million'), and so on. However, Chinese numerals, like Roman numerals, are not convenient for arithmetic, for which Arabic numerals are used.

The characters for one to ten numerals are simply shaped, but they have complex versions as a safeguard against forgery for use on banknotes, receipts, pawn tickets, and other important documents. Examples are 壹 'one'; 貳 'two'; 參 'three'; 伍 'five'; 拾 'ten'. For zero, either the character 零 *ling* or the Arabic 0 can be used. Cardinal numerals can be turned into ordinal numerals by adding the prefix *di-*, as described in "Two-Morpheme Words" (in chap. 2).

In any language, numerals are handy in fixed phrases, idioms, or slogans. Examples from English are: the seven deadly sins, the seven wonders of the world, and the ten commandments; idioms such as *at sixes and sevens* (confused), and proverbs such as *A stitch in time saves nine*.

The Chinese are particularly fond of using numerals in this way. From Confucianism, we find phrases such as: the Five Virtues, the Three Bonds, the Five Cardinal Relations, the Five Classics, and the Four Books (chap. 10). In Mao Zedong's days, the Chinese people were content to own "Four Musts": a bicycle, a radio, a watch, and a sewing machine. Now in Deng Xiaoping's prosperous world, the Chinese people want the "Eight Bigs": a color TV, a refrigerator, a stereo, a camera, a motorcycle, a suit of furniture, a washing machine, and an electric fan. A long distance is described as "a thousand *li*" (*li* is a distance measure). Many divergent schools of thought are described as "a hundred schools of thought." "Long live!" is *Wansui!* ('May you live for ten-thousand years' or "hip hip hurrah"). Chinese expressions such as *qian xin wan ku* ('one thousand labors and ten thousand pains' or "prodigious effort"), *cheng yi jing bai* ('punish one to warn hundred'), and *jiu si yi sheng* ('nine death, one life' or "a narrow escape") are much more colorful and forceful than their English counterparts.

Chinese numerals are used also in Korean and Japanese, sometimes by themselves and sometimes along with native numerals (chaps. 11 and 17). Chinese phrases and idioms containing numerals are also popular in Korean and Japanese. For example, Chinese *Wansui!* ('May you live ten-thousand years!') is *Banzai!* in Japanese and *Manse!* in Korean.

Chinese Personal Names

Chinese names are intimately related to the meanings represented by Chinese characters. Before walking into such esoteric territory, let us take a moment to consider Western names.

A person in most parts of the world has a compound name consisting of a family name or surname and a given name. In the West the use of surnames began 2500 years ago among the ruling class of the Roman Empire; it declined during the 5th century when the Roman empire fell; but it revived in the 9th century among the upper class in Italy. It was not until the 18th century that the use of surnames became popularized among the general public (Shimamura 1977).

Some surnames, such as *Taylor* and *Baker,* began as labels for trades; others, such as *London,* were place names; others were masters' names given to their servants; and still others were simplified versions of complex names, as the Slavic *Jakobslevinsky* becoming the English *Jacobs.* Because of large-scale movements of peoples from culture to culture and place to place throughout history, one can find a huge variety of surnames in the West, especially in North America. Under such circumstances, as Taylors we do not feel any affinity whatever to numerous other Taylors, unless they are close relatives.

Chinese naming practices and their attitudes toward names are quite different from those in the West. A Chinese name typically consists of three syllables written in three morpheme–characters, one for the family name and two for the given name, in the order "family name–given name," as in *Mao Zedong.* Occasionally, a given name may consist of only a single syllable–character, as in *Wang Zhi* and a surname may have two syllable-characters, as in *Ouyang Zhi.* In Pinyin romanization, the "family name–given name" order is preserved, and neither the family name nor the given name is written with a hyphen. (In another romanization system, the Wade–Giles, a hyphen is used, as in Mao Tse-tung.) But even in Pinyin the initials of Zedong is Z.-D. to reflect that it is written in two characters for two syllables.

According to legend, all Chinese are ultimately descended from a common ancestor, the legendary Yellow Emperor, Huang Di, who lived 4500 years ago. The emperor had 25 sons, and gave distinct names to 14 of them. The characters for some of these and other family names of antiquity contain the radical "woman," reflecting the matriarchy of the time. Take 姜 *Jiang,* which is a meaning composite, 羊 "sheep" over 女 "woman," denoting a clan of shepherds led by a woman (Pan 1990). It is one of the old and powerful family names whose ancestor is believed to have been a non-Han leader who was defeated by the Yellow Emperor.

Legends aside, names have been used in China for more than 2500 years, perhaps longer than in any other part of the world. In the Zhou times nobles had a clan name based on common descent from a distant, perhaps mythical ancestor; the clan name defined the set of people one should not marry. They also had a local family name that did not always indicate kinship connection. The modern system of patrilineal surnames seem to have begun when the Qing dynasty unified the nation and made efforts to register the entire population. Thereafter the hodgepodge of names by which people had been called came to be classed as surnames, now uniformly called *xing,* to be passed down to patrilineal descendants. These surnames came to be considered a sign of kinship connection (Ebrey 1990).

As for the number of different surnames, about 3,700 are mentioned in the classical literature and 6,000 in a handbook published by the Chinese Post Office. Today only a limited number, around 400, is commonly used, as indicated by the phrase "the hundred surnames," meaning "all the citizens." This number of surnames is extremely small for over one billion Chinese people. A quarter of the Chinese population are named *Wang, Li, Zhang,* or *Liu. Wang* (*Wong* in Cantonese) in particular is very common. Moreover, some surnames share the same sound and must be distinguished by Chinese characters. For example, a person named Li has to specify which of several characters with the sound *li* represents his or her name, "Wo xing Li, mu zi Li" (My surname is Li, tree 木 child 子 Li 李).

Some Chinese surnames were once official titles or ranks; others were place names, the province or district of birth; and still others were royal family names bestowed by the emperor on loyal ministers and barbarian chieftains. Some non-Chinese "barbarians," in order to enhance their social acceptability, have adopted Chinese names.

The Chinese take their surnames very seriously. They shun marriage between people of the same surname. They even take their surname systems to wherever in the world they may emigrate. Witness the numerous same-surname associations that spring up wherever overseas Chinese settle. Chinese immigrants in the United States are mostly *Wong* in Stockton, *Fong* in Sacramento, *Hom* in San Diego, and *Tang* in Phoenix, because most Chinese immigrants tend to come from the two southern coastal regions, Fujian and Guangdong, where the villages were single-surname settlements. Many lineages can trace their ancestry as far back as 20 or 25 generations.

A given name typically consists of two morpheme–syllable–characters, which are selected with care. For boys, the characters selected may have such desirable meanings as "nobility" and "bravery," while those selected for girls may have the meanings of "chastity" and "obedience." No parents would use characters with such bad meanings as "death" and "sickness," though they do use playfully deprecatory "milk names" such as *Goushi* ('dog food') and *Shazi* ('fool') to ward off ghosts or evil spirits. A milk name is given to a boy or girl at birth and is used by his or her relatives and neighbors. On first going to school a "book name" is given to a child to be used by his or her school mates and teachers.

The Chinese traditional attitude of valuing boys and devaluing girls is reflected in some girls' names, whose characters mean "invite/welcome younger brother." Sometimes given names are numerals such as "eleven" and "twenty six," reflecting the order of birth among brothers and male cousins within the same generation.

Sometimes characters are selected according to principles based on Chinese philosophy. Across succeeding generations — grandfather, father, self, son, grandson — one of the two characters for a given name is selected from the five characters or their radicals that represent the Five Phases — wood, fire, earth, metal, water — that rotate in a fixed order in myriad phenomena of the universe (table 10-2).

On the other hand, within the same generation, brothers or male cousins, or sisters, may share one of the two characters of a given name. For example, the three famous sisters in recent Chinese history had the surname Song (Soong) and the following given names that share the last character -*ling: Ailing (Eye-ling)* ('kindness, age'), was married to H.H. Kong (K'ung), a direct descendant of Confucius and a prominent banker; she later served in several capacities in the nationalist government; *Qingling (Ch'ing-ling)* ('felicity, age'), was married to Sun Yat-sen, the leader of the republican revolution, who is revered as the father of modern China; as a widow she became the vice chairperson of the People's Republic of China; Wellesley-educated *Meiling (May-ling)* ('beautiful, age') was married to Chiang Kai-shek, the generalissimo and president of the Republic of China or Taiwan.

The Chinese observed certain taboos with names. The characters used in an emperor's name could not be used either during his reign or for the rest of the dynasty. All literate people had to know the name in order to avoid using it. The character of the given name of Confucius was avoided by Confucians for centuries. Chinese, even now, may avoid also the characters used for their own grandparents, parents, close relatives, teachers, and other respected people.

In place of the English Mr., Mrs., Miss, and Ms, the Chinese in the Communist mainland use the handy, though now somewhat anachronistic, *tongzhi* ('comrade') that can be applied to the name of anybody, from Chairman Mao to peasant Zhang. Other titles, which are politically neutral, are: the respectful *laoshi* ('old, teacher',"sir") or *xiansheng* ('teacher' or "Mr., gentleman") and *furen* ('madam'). The names come before the titles, as in *Zhang laoshi/ furen/ tongzhi.* However, *xiao* ('small' or 'young') precedes a surname, as in *xiao Zhang.*

Chinese naming practices, and even some names, have been adopted by Koreans since the 7th century (chap. 15); certain aspects of Chinese naming practices have been adopted by the Japanese as well (chap. 21). The names of Koreans and Japanese, like those of Chinese, are typically written in Chinese characters.

Magical Quality of Characters

Chinese characters are not just signs with which to write and read; they are imbued with magical, mystical quality and power, and hence are objects of reverence. Chinese characters can bring good or bad luck to their users or foretell future events. In antiquity they were used in divination and cast on bronze vessels used for important rites ("Beginning of Characters" in chap. 3). Characters acquire such quality and power through the meanings they represent.

In traditional China written words were so venerated that nothing with writing on it could simply be thrown away but had to be ritually burned. In later part of the Qing dynasty one foreign observer wrote:

> They [the Chinese] literally worship their letters [characters]. When letters were invented, they say, heaven rejoiced and hell trembled. Not for any consideration will they tread on a piece of lettered paper; and to foster this reverence, literary associations employ agents to go about the street, collect waste paper, and burn it on an altar with the solemnity of a sacrifice. [Smith 1983: 82]

These altars, known as "pagodas for cherishing the written word," could be found in virtually every city, town, and village in traditional China. Today, alas, Chinese newspapers, if not used for wrapping fish and as toilet paper, are thrown away or recycled, as are newspapers in other scripts.

In China, and in Korea and Japan as well, certain characters with felicitous meanings—e.g. 福 ('fortune') 寿 ('longevity'; the character is slightly differently simplified in China), 富 ('wealth,') and 貴 ('nobility')—decorate many common objects, from fabrics to fans, and from bowls to boxes. Well-known couplets may decorate pillars and posts in a house to bring good luck. Scrolls and objects bearing characters in calligraphy adorn many houses, including my own (fig. 3-4). Brand names of certain merchandise, such as wines and cigarettes, use characters with nice meanings like "crane" and "upright." Personal names also use characters with good meanings (see "Chinese Personal Names," above). Some people are concerned that the characters in their given names do not have good shapes and want to change them to other characters, in a belief that the character shapes influence people's fates. In Japan, people do not mind if their names in characters are read with wrong sound, but they do mind if their names are written in their wrong characters.

Chinese write, not speak, their prayers. To bring about good fortune or ward off ill-fortune, some Chinese use a magic writing for spells. The writing is done in distorted or embellished characters, which can be in any of the several script styles, such as seal, clerical, and standard. The characters have to be written on an appropritely colored paper, with a sacred seal stamped on. The writing is burned by a Daoist priest in a rite with chanting and dancing.

The Chinese observe certain taboos with names, and those who use taboo or even suggestive characters were punished in the days of imperial China. One scholar who in his dictionary criticized the *Kangxi Dictionary* and printed in full the taboo Qing emperors' temple names (assigned after their death) was executed, and 21 of his family were enslaved (Fairbank 1992: 159). Another Qing official was imprisoned for selecting a classical phrase for the provincial civil service examinations that contained two characters that would have been similar in appearance to those of the emperor's reign title, if the top portions had been cut off. These "topless" characters were interpreted as expressing the wish that the emperor would be decapitated. The offending official died in prison, and his body was dismembered. During the Qing period an official could be degraded for miswriting a single character in a memorial to the throne (Smith 1983: 82).

Certain characters with bad meanings, and even ones sharing their sounds with undesirable characters, tend to be avoided. Chinese avoid cutting pears to share among friends, because "cutting pear" *likai* has the same sound as "to part, separate." Japanese tend to shy away from using the numeral four in numbering floors in a building, because the characters for "four" and "death" happen to have the same sound, *shi*. Similarly, Chinese people in Taiwan and Hong Kong shun the number 4, whose sound and the sound of the character "death" share the syllable though not the tone.

To the users of characters, 文 *wen* ('writing' or 'written word'; originally 'pattern') has extraordinary significance. "*Wen* means ... by extension its influence in thought, morality, persuasion, and culture" (Fairbank 1992: 69). The character appears in the compound words for "literature" 文学 *wenxue* ('writing, learning'), for "literati" 文人 *wenren* ('writing, person'), for "culture" 文化 *wenhua*, ('transform by writing') and even in the word for "civilization" 文明 *wenming* ('to make brilliant by writing'). Such words, found in classic Chinese literature, have been given new or modified meanings by the Japanese in modern times. For example, the word *wenhua* ('culture') comes from the classic phrase, *wenzhijiaohua* ('writing, govern, educate, transform'), meaning roughly "govern and lead the people through learning and arts rather than through military force," and the word *wenming* ('civilization') comes from the classic phrase *wenliguangming*, meaning roughly "the nature of things become clear." These useful words have since been brought into Chinese and Korean.

Characters Understood Across Times and Places

The fact that Chinese characters represent primarily meanings and secondarily sounds has some advantages beside differentiating homophones. Characters enable speakers of different "dialects" and eras to communicate, because the meanings of characters remain more or less the same while their pronunciations vary across "dialects" and over time.

In Figure 4-2a you see a poem written 1200 years ago by the noted Tang poet Du Fu (712–770) who, having lost his position in government, left the capital and became for many years a wanderer.

> Over the emerald green river glint the brilliant gulls
> On the blue mountains, blaze the red flowers
> Yet another spring has passed me by
> When will come the day of my return?

In Figure 4-2b you see a passage, Confucius's (552–479 BC) famous saying, written 2500 years ago.[1]

> Confucius said: At fifteen I set my mind on learning. At thirty I had formed my character. At forty I had no more perplexities. At fifty I knew the will of heaven. At sixty nothing that I heard disturbed me. At seventy I could let my thought wander without trespassing the moral law.

The literate readers of Du Fu's days may have read aloud the two texts in middle Chinese, those of Confucius's days in old Chinese, and those of modern days in one of seven "dialects" such as Mandarin and Cantonese. But all educated Chinese readers understand and appreciate these old masterpieces. So can Japanese and Korean readers, even though their languages differ from Chinese. Readers need some instruction in

何　今　山　江
日　春　青　碧
是　看　花　鳥
歸　又　欲　逾
年　過　然　白

七　十　三　子
十　而　十　曰
而　知　而　吾
從　天　立　十
心　命　四　有
所　六　十　五
欲　十　而　而
不　而　不　志
踰　耳　惑　于
矩　順　五　學

Figure 4-2. Ancient texts written vertically: (a, above) a poem by Du Fu; (b, right) a saying of Confucius.

reading the classics, which differ from modern vernacular texts ("Literary vs Vernacular Language" in chap. 8). This remarkable ability is possible because the logographic Chinese characters have maintained, more or less, their visual forms and meanings while their sounds have undergone big or small changes over time and across regions ("Assigning Syllables to Characters" in chap. 5).

Can a literate English speaker easily read a passage from *Beowulf* written in vernacular language 1000 years ago? Try it yourself. Read *ae* as in *glad*. To be fair to modern readers, *th* as in *think* and *this*, is used instead of the old, obsolete letter for it. Bars over some vowels are omitted.

---

[1] This saying was included even in a book entitled *How to be a Good Communist*, which became staple reading for Communists cadres in the 1940s and 1950s.

tha com of more   under misthleothum
Grendel gongan; Godes yrre baer;
mynte se manscatha   manna cynnes
sumne besyrwan   in sele tham hean.
Wod under wolcnum   to paes the he winreced,
goldsele gumena   gearwost wisse
faettum, fahne.

[from *Beowulf*, lines 710–713; Alexander 1973]

Here is a close translation:

Then came out of the moorlands   beneath the mist-slopes
Grendel stalking; he bore God's ire;
The evil one meant   of human kind
Someone to snare   in the high hall.
He went on under the clouds   till their wine-hall,
The gold-hall of men   he could clearly make out plated in gold.

Now try this extract from *Canterbury Tales* by Chaucer, written only 600 years ago

And specially from every shires ende
Of Engelond to Caunterbury they wende,
The hooly blisful martir for to seke,
That hem hath holpen whan that they were seeke.
[from General Prologue, *Canterbury Tales*]

I cannot make any sense out of *Beowulf,* though I can read it aloud if inaccurately;
by contrast, I can make some, though not full, sense out of the Confucian saying shown
in Figure 4-2b, though I cannot read it aloud in Chinese. Chaucer's work is almost
readable; even so, some words, especially content words, have changed their sounds
in 600 years, and these changes are sometimes reflected in spelling changes, as in
soote, which is now spelled *sweet*.

Certain 2500-year old Chinese classics, written in logographic characters, are
more accessible to educated Chinese readers than 1000-year old English classics,
written in phonetic scripts, are to educated English speakers.

5

Sound Representation by Characters

Characters represent the meanings of morphemes, and this fact has various ramifications, as considered in the preceding chapter. Now we have to tackle the dry but necessary issue of how characters represent sounds. Suppose you encounter a new character and want to find out its sound. What recourse do you have? Does a character itself hold clues to its sound apart from through its meaning? If so, how reliably?

Assigning Syllables to Characters

The letters of a phonetic script, such as an alphabet, attempt to code the sounds of a language directly. For example, each of the three letters codes its sound in words such as *tan* and *ant* or even in non-words such as "nat." Knowing the sounds of all the 26 letters of the English alphabet, you can more or less sound out most words and even non-words.

True, English spelling codes the sounds of words imperfectly, partly because it has not changed as fast and extensively as have the sounds of English speech in the various dialects across the world over time. Still it codes sounds better than Chinese characters do. Regularly spelled words such as *met*, *net*, and *pet* are pronounced as they are spelled. But even irregularly spelled words such as *laugh* and *hasten* contain some sound clues so that a learner can pronounce them approximately. Even irregular letter–sound relations follow some patterns. For example, -*gh* at the end of a syllable is either /f/ or has no sound (*enough*, *neighbor*), while at the initial position of a syllable it is /g/ (*ghost*, *aghast*). No other sounds are represented by this letter sequence in standard English. Most other phonetic scripts, be they syllabaries or alphabets, reflect rather faithfully the contemporary sounds of the languages they represent. For example, the Japanese syllabary signs か and き represent the Japanese syllables *ka* and *ki* respectively, in whatever words they occur.

In contrast to a phonetic letter or sign that directly **codes** the sound of a phoneme or syllable, a logographic Chinese character represents primarily the meaning of a morpheme, through which—secondarily or indirectly—its sound. A (tone) syllable is **assigned to** a character: No part of a Chinese character—unless it contains a phonetic component—codes a phoneme, syllable, or tone. Consider the now familiar character 十: As an unanalyzed whole pattern it represents the morpheme "ten"; this morpheme in Mandarin Chinese has the sound *shi* with a rising tone; and hence, this tone syllable is assigned to the character in question. None of the character's components—the horizontal stroke, the vertical stroke, or the arrangement of the two as a cross—codes *sh*, *i*, or the rising tone. Because strokes and their arrangement in a character do not indicate the character's sound, entirely different sets of strokes and their arrangements can have exactly the same tone syllable, as do 十, 石 , 食 , 時, ('ten', 'stone', 'eat' 'time') and many others. If the tones are disregarded, even more characters have the sound of *shi* (fig. 5-1).

Conversely, a variety of sounds can be assigned to one character at different times and in different "dialects" and languages. For example, the following diverse sounds are assigned to the character 十 ('ten'): *shi* in Mandarin; *sap* in Cantonese; *sip* in Korean; and *jū, jitt-, jutt-, to-, tō, so* in Japanese, all the while maintaining the same meaning. The fact that two or more characters have the same tone syllable in Mandarin does not guarantee that they will have the same sound in other "dialects" and languages. The character 石 ('stone'), like 十, is pronounced *shi* in Mandarin but is *shek* in Cantonese; *sŏk* in Korean; and *seki, sett-, shaku, -jaku, shatt-,* and *ishi* in Japanese.

Even within one "dialect" or language, one character can have two or more unrelated sounds. In Mandarin, occasionally a character has two sounds and two or more meanings, as does 行 *hang* ('row') and *xing* ('go'). Of about 8,000 characters examined, 90% have only one sound, while remaining 10% have between two and five sounds, mostly two (*Hanzi Xinxi Zidian* or *A Dictionary of Chinese Character Information* 1988).

According to the Chinese linguist Li Rong (1987), at one time the character for "cancer" and the character for "inflammation" shared the same sound, *yan*. This fact is inconvenient: Being told by your physician that you have *yan*, you would be desperate to know whether you have cancer or mere inflammation. So in 1962 when a committee of linguists were compiling a dictionary, it decided to assign a new sound, *ai*, to the character for "cancer." This sort of arbitrary assignment of a new, quite different sound to an old character is not lightly undertaken. Nevertheless, it highlights the fact that nothing in a character codes its sound.

The sounds of Mandarin, like those of other languages, have changed over time. In particular, between 4th and 12th centuries AD, the sounds /p/, /t/, and /k/ disappeared from the finals of syllables, and /m/ and /n/ merged into /n/. These and other changes are reflected in the sounds assigned to characters. For example, 家 (a pig under a roof for 'house' or 'specialist') was pronounced as *kɔ* (as in *call*) in BC, as *ka* in AD 500, as *kia* in the 17th century, and as *jia* in modern Mandarin, while the shape has remained the same for the past 2000 years since the day of the clerical script, and its meaning has remained the same for over 3000 years since the day of the oracle-bone script (Karlgren 1923). It is read as *ka* in modern Korean, as it was in AD 500 in China. As usual, it has multiple sounds in Japanese, four (*ka, -ga, ke, -ge*) Chinese-based and two (*ie, ya*) native. One particular character 生 has no fewer than 12 officially sanctioned different sounds in Japanese; including "unofficial" ones, it is said to have 100 different sounds!

You may ask, To find the sound of a character, do I have no other recourse than to ask someone or to look it up in a dictionary? Yes and no.

Phonetic Components

Most characters are semantic–phonetic composites. A phonetic is often but not always an independent character with its own meaning and tone syllable, which can become a part of a composite to which it imparts its sound. For example, 工 (perhaps an ancient carpenter's tool) as an independent character represents the morpheme "work" and the tone syllable *gōng*; it becomes a phonetic in many semantic–phonetic composites.

How useful is a phonetic in giving an accurate tone syllable of a character? Karlgren (1962: 44) observed, "It is only in rare instances that a phonetic retains its original function after a sound evolution of many centuries." By contrast, Woon (1987: 183) insists, "After two thousand years of sound variation, the phonetic is still effective in most of these cases." Who is right?

Under the phonetic *gōng*, the 2000-year old classic *"Explanations of Simple Characters and Analysis of Composite Characters"* lists 20 characters, one of which has two different sounds (reproduced in Woon 1987: 182). Of these 21 tone syllables only four (19%) have the same tone syllable as the phonetic; the remaining 17 have 10 different tone syllables. Table 5-1 lists these 10 plus one that has the identical tone syllable as the phonetic. Under the same phonetic, Wieger (1915) lists 30 characters, of which only four (13%) have the same tone syllable as the phonetic.

Table 5-1. Various Tone Syllables that Use the Phonetic Component 工 *(gōng)*

Hanzi	Sound	Semantic	Meaning	Hanzi	Sound	Semantic	Meaning
功	gōng	strength	merit	虹	hóng	insect	rainbow
訌	hòng	speak	mischief	缸	gāng	vessel	pottery
貢	gòng	shell	tribute	空	kōng	cave	hole, sky
項	xiàng	head	neck	恐	kǒng	mind	frighten
江	jiāng	water	river	汞	gǒng	water	mercury
邛	qióng	walled city	place name	杠	gàng	tree	flagstaff

Table 5-2 lists two other "unspecific" phonetics that are associated with varied tone syllables (based on Li Xiuqin 1990). The two syllabes *dui* (fall tone) and *tui* (fall) in Table 5-2 are similar enough, one might say. The sound of a character is either correct or wrong: a phonetic that indicates a similar but not exact sound is not good enough to determine the correct tone syllable. In other languages "similar" may be good enough, but not in Chinese. In English, if mono-morphemic but multi-syllabic words such as *vegetable* and *potato* are pronounced with minor errors as "begetable" or "potaato," they are unlikely to be confused with other words. The situation is different in Chinese, which uses only about 400 differ-ent simple syllables or 1,300 different tone syllables. Furthermore, almost all morphemes are monosyllabic. The syllables of many characters sound the same or similar, with or without phonetics. For example, several other characters (e.g., 弓 'bow', 宮 'palace', 公 'public') have the tone syllable *gong* (level tone), each of which also serves as a phonetic. So, in Chinese, slight pronunciation errors can yield valid tone syllables with meanings quite different from the intended one.

Table 5-2. Varied Tone Syllables with the Phonetic Components dui *and* ye

Syllable	Tone	Syllable	Tone
dui	fall	ye	fall–rise
tui	fall	yi	rise
rui	fall	chi	rise
shui	fall	shi	level
shuo	level	di	fall
tuo	level	ta	level
zhuo	level	tuo	level
yue	fall		

Let us consider studies that examined a large set of characters. The Chinese linguist Zhou (1978) examined about 8,000 characters of the *New Chinese Dictionary* (1971 edition) and found that in 39% of the characters the phonetics and the characters containing them had the same syllables, if tones were disregarded. This disregard of the tones seems unreasonable, considering the fact that Chinese morphemes can change meanings solely because of changed tones, as in *mai* (fall–rise tone) ('buy') and *mai* (falling tone) ('sell') (see also the four meanings of *ma* in four tones in table 2-2).

In another study that did consider the tones, the psychologist Zhu (1987) examined 6,335 characters commonly used today (the entire sample of characters in a published frequency count) and found that only 18.5% of phonetics were specific, i.e., the phonetics predicted the tone syllables of the characters in which they occurred. The specific phonetics tended to occur among infrequently used characters, thus not helping beginners who need to find the sounds of even frequent characters. Phonetics that indicate the tone syllables of characters correctly in only one of five cases cannot be considered as effective sound indicators. Why is a phonetic so unspecific? After the clerical script style (*lishu*) was adopted over 2000 years ago (table 3-1), the structure of Chinese characters has remained relatively unchanged, while the Chinese sounds have changed extensively. Thus, the sound of a phonetic is no longer the same in different phonetic–semantic composites. Even at the beginning, the phonetic and the composite that contained it were not always exact homophones but shared merely either the initial or the final of a syllable; now after many centuries of sound changes, the two are in many cases even less similar.

Should a reader routinely use a phonetic to discover the sound of a new character? Not really. First, about 10–20% of characters do not contain phonetics (80–90% are semantic–phonetic composites). Second, phonetics are numerous—858 (Wieger 1915) or 1,348 (Zhou 1978)—and their sounds have to be learned individually; about 1,300 shape–sound associations may well be too numerous for a reader to remember securely and recall readily. (By comparison, radicals number around 200.) Third, a reader cannot be sure which phonetics are specific in which characters. At any rate, unlike *gong* (level tone) that occurs in 20 to 30 characters, most phonetics occur in only a few of the 6,000 common characters. Lastly, it is not always clear which component of a character is a phonetic and which a semantic, as the same simple character can be used for either component and in an unspecified position—top, bottom, left, right, outside, or inside—of a character. For example, 工 , which serves as a phonetic in Table 5-1, also serves as a semantic in many characters, including some of the ones in which it is also a phonetic. When I saw a composite with the character for 'horse' as its right component, I was confident that it had the sound *ma*, in analogy with the composite for 'mother' in Table 3-2, but its sound turned out to be *feng*.

A phonetic may not help beginners to discover the sound of a new character, but when many individual characters are arranged in a list by phonetics to reveal a pattern of differences and similarities of sounds, as in table 5-1, phonetics seem to help in remembering the sounds of the characters. But characters should be learned in context of sentences and passages, not in a list.

Do phonetics help in "naming" (pronouncing) phonetic–semantic composites? In Seidenberg's experiment (1985), naming was faster and errors fewer for phonetic–semantic composites compared with non-composites, but only for less familiar characters and not for familiar ones. To name a character, the readers appeared to have relied on its whole shape if the character is familiar but on its phonetic if the character is less familiar. But their reliance on phonetics did not prevent them from making naming errors, as might be expected from the unreliability of phonetics. In Zhu's experiment (1987), phonetic–semantic composites having sounds identical to their phonetics were named faster than those composites having sounds different from their phonetics. Again, phonetics had effects on less familiar characters but not with familiar ones.

Phonetics may help oral reading only to a limited degree. At the same time, they may induce writing errors. People tend to make substitution errors when an error and a target share a phonetic. They may write a wrong character that has the same sound and similar shape to the target, both in Chinese (Wong 1992) and in Japanese (chap. 22).

So, readers who want to sound out a character do not use a phonetic if the character is familiar, but they may use a phonetic if it is unfamiliar or less familiar, perhaps out of desperation. But in doing so they are bound to make some errors because phonetics are not reliable.

Phonetic Loans and Fanqie

There are ways to be taught the sound of a new character without having it spoken to you; you can be taught it from other known characters, using phonetic loans and Fanqie ('cut and join').

In a phonetic loan, the sound of one character is indicated by the sound of another character homophonic to it. Suppose you want to know the sound of the character 目 ('eye'); a book tells you that the character 木 *mu'* ('tree'), which you already know, happens to possess the required tone syllable. To give an example from English, suppose you want to know the sound of *wright;* a book might tell you that it has the same sound as *rite* assuming that you already know the latter. Because of the abundance of homophones in Chinese, phonetic loaning can be used for most characters. About 15% of characters have no homophones in the list of tone syllables provided in the Chinese dictionary *Cihai.* But phonetic loaning presupposes knowledge of many characters and so is not much help to beginners. Also a phonetic loan may be less frequent and more complex than the character whose sound has to be determined.

Another method of indicating the sound of a character is Fanqie ('cut and join'): the sound of one character is indicated using the sounds of two other characters. Suppose you want to indicate the sound of one character *lao* (fall–rise tone). You need two other characters, one beginning with *l-* and the other ending in *-ao* in the following manner:

老 = 里 + 好   *lao = l(i) + (h)ao*.

The tone of the to-be-pronounced character should be, but is not always, the same as that of the second character.

Fanqie follows the Chinese phonological tradition of dividing a syllable into initial and final (see "Sound System" in chap. 2). It was used in *Qieyun* (AD 601), the authoritative rhyming and pronouncing dictionary of 12,000 characters. (There were earlier rhyme dictionaries, which have not been preserved.) Fanqie indicates the sounds of a Chinese character more reliably than its phonetic component does. For example, "to roar" is *hou*, which is shown as *h(u)* + *(m)ou* by Fanqie, but the sound of its phonetic is *kou*. Fanqie, though reliable, is cumbersome. Furthermore, it presupposes knowledge of many characters, and so is not much help to beginning learners of characters. Fanqie is not widely used today.

To arrange words in a dictionary in a traditional way, firstly arrange the words by tones, and then within each of the tones, according to the finals, grouping words that rhyme; and then within each rhyme group, arrange the words according to their initial consonants. In such a dictionary you can find only a word whose sound you already know. It may be useful in looking for characters that rhyme or for ascertaining the meaning of a compound word whose first member is of known sound. But you cannot use such a dictionary to find out how to pronounce a word you do not know, as you can with an English dictionary.

Homophonic, Polyphonic, or Unpronounced Characters

Within one "dialect," each Chinese character usually is pronounced the same way in different linguistic contexts. But some characters have more than one sound, depending on context. For example, 行 is pronounced as *hang* in the word *yinhang* ('silver row' = "bank"), where its meaning is "row, line" but as *xing* ('go') in words such as *xingjin* ('go, progress' or "march"). As pointed out earlier, about 10% of characters have multiple sounds, usually two sounds, but a few have four or five sounds.

A small number of characters, 235 out of 13,464 entries in one dictionary, have no known sounds, perhaps because their old sounds have been forgotten from long disuse (Huang and Huang 1989). Such characters can exist, because nothing in them indicate sounds. They do have meanings, and can be written but not spoken. Their existence shows clearly the difference between a phonetic script and logography.

As already pointed out, the spoken Chinese language has many homophones, which are discussed here again because of the vital role Chinese characters play in distinguishing them. How many characters share one tone syllable? Since there are about 1,300 different tone syllables in Mandarin Chinese, a true phonetic script, a syllabary, would require only 1,300 graphs. But there are as many as 50,000 characters, of which about 3,500 are basic characters. The Chinese dictionary *Cihai* defines 14,872 characters, but only 1,359 tone syllables. In it, each tone syllable is represented by 11 different characters on average. Of the 1,359 tone syllables, 199 (14.6%)—for example, *bai* (rising tone, 'white') and *gu* (rising tone, 'bone')—have no homophones, while a few have over 100 homophones. In particular, *yi* (falling tone) represents 149 different morphemes (e.g., 'meaning', 'contemplate', 'bosom', 'different', 'wing', 'righteousness').

By contrast, the largest set of homophones in English has four (or five) words: *heir, air, (eyre), ere, err;* the same is true among native Korean and Japanese words.

Whichever count we use, we have to conclude that the Chinese language abounds in homophonic syllables. One syllable can be associated with several morphemes, but each of the homophones is written with its own unique character. The notorious *yi* may have 38 or 200 homophones, depending on the size of the dictionary examined, but each of these numerous homophones has its own unique character, thus differentiating the meanings.

Homophones are inconvenient not only in speech but also in remembering, writing, and reading. They cause misunderstanding and comprehension failure in speech, as we have seen in "Why Compound Words?" (in chap. 2). In everyday communication, you may see people augmenting their speech by writing characters on paper, on the palms of their hands, in the air, or citing a well-known phrase or name in which the target syllable–character is a part (e.g.,"the same *en* as in Zhou Enlai"). If a surname with homophones is a composite character, its components can be listed, as in "tree over child" for *Li* 李 .

Homophones cause writing errors. In one study of ethnic Chinese children learning characters in Britain, 26 out of 60 writing errors were caused by homophones (Wong 1992). For example, instead of writing *sangning* ('new', 'year') a student may write *sangning* ('born' or 'raw', 'year'), not differentiating the two characters with the same Cantonese sound, *sang*, with two different meanings. In Japanese studies, too, errors in writing Chinese characters are often homophonic substitutions (chap. 22).

Homophones adversely affect memory. In Chinese, as in English, short-term memory seems to be largely phonetic. In one experiment, Chinese readers were asked to read lists of characters aloud and then write down what they could recall. One list contained 24 characters with no homophones, while the other list contained 12 pairs of homophones (Zhang and Simon 1985). All the characters were selected from Chinese surnames, among which it was possible to find the required number of characters without homophones. The readers could recall on average 7 surnames that have no homophones, compared to only 5.33 surnames that have homophones.

To output an individual Chinese character on a word processor, one typically inputs its sound in a phonetic script, and the computer displays the target on its screen. If the character has numerous homophones, the computer displays them, batch by batch, from the most common to the least common. The writer has to choose the target among these homophonic possibilities. Needless to say, this process takes time and effort, and there are various schemes to simplify it ("Computerizing Chinese Characters" in chap. 8).

Homophones adversely affect also sentence comprehension, whether in English or Chinese. In judging whether a sentence was grammatical or not, response times depended on the degree of sound similarity among characters making up the sentence: the times were faster for phonetically varied sentences than for phonetically same or similar ones (Tzeng et al. 1977). To recall items soon after seeing or hearing them involves short-term memory, which tends to process verbal information in acoustic form. To understand a written or heard sentence, too, its words are retained in short-term memory until they are related to each other to sort out who does what to whom. So the same or similar sounding verbal items can get confused in short-term memory, adversely affecting their memory or understanding.

In Chinese it is possible to compose a whole paragraph that consists of a string of homophones, as in the following oft-quoted example.

> Shi shi shi shi shi shi, shi shi, shi shi shi shi. Shi shi shi shi shi shi shi shi shi,
> shi shi shi shi shi, shi shi, shi shi shi shi shi. Shi shi shi shi shi, shi shi shi shi, shi
> shi shi shi shi shi. Shi shi shi shi shi shi, shi shi shi shi. Shi shi shi, shi shi shi shi
> shi shi. Shi shi shi, shi shi shi shi shi shi shi. Shi shi shi shi shi shi shi shi
> shi shi shi shi shi. Shi shi shi shi.

To quote my Chinese colleague Zhang Zhi, who provided this passage,"When we Chinese hear this passage, we feel like being lost in the clouds."

When spoken, the passage, even with tone variations, is difficult to understand. When written as in Figure 5-1, this passage consisting of nothing but repetitions of *shi* transforms itself to a passage consisting of many different characters, and thanks to these varied characters the passage becomes decipherable and translatable into English.

「 石室詩士施氏，嗜獅，誓食十獅。氏時時適市視獅十時，適十獅適市，是時，適

施氏適市。氏視是十獅，恃失勢，使是十獅逝世。氏拾是十獅屍，適石室。石室

溼，氏使侍拭石室。石室試，氏始試食是十獅屍。食時始識是十獅屍實十石獅屍。

試釋是事。」

Figure 5-1. A passage consisting of homophones of shi

> A poet named Shi lived in a stone house and liked to eat lion flesh and he vowed
> to eat ten of them. He used to go to the market in search of lions and one day
> chanced to see ten of them there. Shi killed the lions with arrows and picked
> up their bodies carrying them back to his stone house. His house was dripping
> with water so he requested that his servants proceed to dry it. Then he began
> to try to eat the bodies of the ten lions. It was only then he realized that these
> were in fact ten lions made of stone. Try to explain the riddle.

Here is a conclusion to this chapter on how characters represent sounds. Throughout this book I describe Chinese characters as logographs that represent morphemes, their meanings primarily and directly and their sounds secondarily and indirectly. Although characters can indicate sounds by means of phonetic components, phonetic loans, and Fanqie ('cut and join'), these means are either inadequate or cumbersome, or both. Precisely because characters contain few reliable, simple, and direct clues to their sounds, several true phonetic scripts have been created to indicate the sounds of characters. One such script is Pinyin, the Roman alphabet, in China; another is Zhuyinfuhao or the National/Mandarin Phonetic Symbols, a script that is halfway between an alphabet and a syllabary, now used in Taiwan; two forms of Kana, a syllabary, in Japan; Han'gŭl, an alphabet used like a syllabary, in Korea. These phonetic scripts will be described in appropriate places.

So, to find out the exact sound of a new character, you ask someone or look up a dictionary that gives its sounds in a phonetic script. That is how I learn the sounds of characters in Chinese, Japanese, and Korean. Most people I polled — be they Chinese, Japanese, or Koreans — do the same.

6

Logographic Characters vs Phonetic Scripts

Now that we have learned much about Chinese characters, we can tackle the controversial questions of whether and how logographic characters and phonetic scripts differ, and how their differences affect thinking and doing science. These questions, while they relate to writing systems in general, relate closely to Chinese characters. Some old material is reviewed here and new material is introduced in order to address these questions.

Logography, Alphabet, and Syllabary

Consider a familiar phonetic script, such as the English alphabet. An English letter represents directly, though not always consistently, a small sound unit, the phoneme, and indirectly a meaning unit: A few letters, meaningless in themselves but arranged in a certain sequence, represent the sound of a word, and through the sound sequence the meaning of the word. The sequence of sounds is critical. So, the English letters *t, e, n*, arranged in that order, represents the word *ten;* if the three letters are arranged in the reverse order, it represents another word *net*; and if two of the three letters are re-used, we have *tenet,* which includes the meaning of neither *ten* nor *net.* In fact, *ten* can occur in countless words, such as *tendon, tendency, tender, tenancy, tension,* lending its sound but not its meaning. On the other hand, the word *ten* partly changes its form and sound but keeps its meaning in a few related words, such as in *teen* and *sixteen.*

Since a language uses only a limited inventory of around 30 speech sounds or phonemes, an alphabet will require only about 30 letters, or 60 if they come in upper- and lower-case forms. Such a small number of letters can have simple shapes without being confused with each other. With an alphabet it is possible to determine the probable sound of a string of letters, without knowing the string's meaning. For example, you can pronounce an unfamiliar word such as *tetradynamous* without knowing its meaning;[1] you can pronounce even a meaningless word such as "tetenete."

Now consider another kind of phonetic script, a syllabary, in which one sign represents one syllable. In the Japanese Kana syllabary, each sign represents one syllable, and there are about 110 signs to represent that many syllables of the Japanese language. (For many details of Kana, see Part III.) For example, the Kana sign カ represents the syllable *ka* and has no meaning by itself. But the logographic Chinese character 加, from which this Kana sign was derived, represents the syllable *ka* and also the morpheme 'add'. Kana signs, because of their small number, can afford to be far simpler in shapes than the characters from which they were derived.

[1]Having four long and two short stamens, as a cruciferous flower.

Kana form a true phonetic script. The Kana sign ニ represents the syllable *ni* and ク represents *ku*. Each of the two syllables is meaningless or ambiguous by itself, but when the two are put together, *niku* ('meat') is meaningful; the two signs in a reverse order form a different word, *kuni* ('nation'). In the word *sayonara* ('goodbye'), each of the four syllable signs さ よ な ら contributes to the word only its sound and not its meaning. A string of Kana—whether familiar, unfamiliar, or even nonsense (e.g. に く こ る *nikukoru*)—can be pronounced by any Kana reader, even by a preschooler.

Consider now Chinese characters, which are called ideographs by some people and logographs by others. I prefer the label logograph (one graph represents one word) to ideograph (one graph represents one idea). An "idea" does not refer to any particular linguistic unit, meaning, or sound ("Writing Systems of the World" in chap. 1). Moreover, "ideograph" is used by some people to refer to one of the six categories of Chinese characters ("Six Categories of Characters" in chap. 3). By contrast *logograph* simply means that a graph, a written sign, represents the linguistic unit, the word— actually the morpheme. A morpheme represents the smallest meaningful linguistic unit, which can be a word or a word part; at the same time, it has a sound associated with it. An eminent scholar of the Japanese writing system, Sir George Sansom, clearly distinguished the two terms, and Miller (1986) heartily concurred:

> The unit in Chinese writing is a symbol which, through a curious but pardonable confusion of thought, is usually styled an ideograph, but is much more accurately described as a logograph. It is a symbol which represents a word, as contrasted with symbols which, like the letters of an alphabet or syllabary, represent sounds or combinations of sounds. [1928: 2]

With a logograph, it is possible for people to know its meaning without knowing its sound. Literate speakers of Mandarin, Cantonese, Korean, and Japanese all know the meaning of the character 十, though they may know its sound only in their own language or "dialect." Given the word formed by the pair of characters 凸凹 you may from its shape be able to guess its meaning ('convex–concave') but you will not be able to guess its sound. I myself did not know its Chinese sound but knew its Japanese sound, *dekoboko*, by means of which I could output the pair on my computer. I now know its Chinese sound *tuyao*, Korean sound *ch'ŏlyo*, and another Japanese sound *totsuō*. Try to guess the meanings or the sounds of the following three characters, 一, 二, 三. On the other hand, even an expert reader of characters has no clue as to the sound of a nonsense character such as 米. In this respect, logographs differ from the letters and signs of phonetic scripts, which people can read aloud without knowing their meanings, as described earlier.

The fact that one Chinese character represents one morpheme has far-reaching consequences for the Chinese writing system. The system requires thousands of characters to represent the numerous morphemes of a language, and many of these characters must have complex shapes in order that they can be discriminated from each other. And the large quantity and complexity of characters affect the way people learn and use them, as we shall see. Table 6-1 compares in number and complexity the logographic characters to the letters of the English alphabet and the signs of the two forms of the Japanese syllabary.

Table 6-1. Logography vs Phonetic Script: Number and Shapes of Graphs

	Characters	English Alphabet	Japanese Syllabary
Number*	3,500, or	26 lower-case	110 Hiragana
	6,000, or	26 upper-case	over 110 Katakana
	50,000		
	large and	small and closed	moderately small
	open-ended		and closed
Complexity	1–24 strokes	1–4 strokes	1–6 strokes
	(smaller set)		
	or 1–64		
	(full set)		

*In China 3,500 characters are required for functional literacy and 6,000 for high-level literacy; 50,000 are defined in a large dictionary. In Japan and S. Korea about 2,000 characters are designated for common use.

Some scholars assert that Chinese characters are best characterized as a syllabary rather than "ideographs" (DeFrancis 1984; Horodeck 1987, whose research is discussed in Part III). Woon (1987: 271) calls the Chinese system "a sort of phonetic script." Such an assertion may have been necessary to counter the opposite extreme view, which asserts that logographs represent solely meanings but not sounds, or that logographs represent meanings always clearly. Characters indeed represent the sounds, in addition to the meanings, of morphemes; conversely, a string of correctly sequenced alphabetic letters or syllabary signs indeed represent the meaning of a word. But logographs and phonetic scripts differ in the manner and efficacy of representing the meanings and sounds of morphemes, as discussed in this chapter and also throughout this book.

The Chinese writing system cannot be characterized as a phonetic script, a syllabary. Why not? The definition of a syllabary is that one graph, in principle, represents or codes the sound of one syllable. In the case of a Chinese character, a sound is **assigned** to it: this sound is usually one tone syllable in Chinese, one syllable without a tone in Korean, and one-to-five syllables in Japanese. For example, 志 ('aspiration') is *zhi* (falling tone) in Mandarin, *chi* (no tone) in Korean, and in Japanese it may be *ji* (no tone) or *kokorozashi*. Note that in Japanese this character has two quite different sounds, one of which has five syllables. While the sound changes, the meaning of this character remains constant across the three languages.

If each character's function were to represent a syllable, the Chinese writing system would require only around 400 characters to represent the 400 different syllables, or 1,300 characters to represent the 1,300 different tone syllables, of the Chinese language. In fact, the number of characters is variously estimated to be 3,500 (for functional literacy), 6,000 (for high-level literacy), or 50,000 (total available; see "Number of Characters" in Chapter 3). The numbers are not only large but also varied and open-ended. If only 400 or 1,300 characters were used, their shapes need not be complex to be discriminated from each other, but in fact they are complex, and also vary enormously in complexity, ranging from 1 to 24 strokes in a small set, or even to 64 strokes in a full set (fig. 3-6 and table 3-6).

If characters are best described as a syllabary, why did the Chinese feel the need to devise a true phonetic script, a Roman alphabet called Pinyin, and a sort of syllabary called Zhuyinfuhao? Why were the Japanese compelled to devise the syllabary Kana, and the Koreans the alphabetic syllabary Han'gŭl, when they already had the Chinese characters? One important use of these phonetic scripts is to give—directly, simply, and precisely—the sounds of logographic characters in Chinese, Japanese, and Korean. Without a phonetic script it is difficult to learn and remember the sounds of Hanzi. Ethnic Chinese learning Cantonese in Britain and the United States even devise their own romanizations based on the English alphabet, to annotate the sounds of Hanzi (Wong 1992).

One test of a phonetic script is that a word—be it familiar, unfamiliar, or nonsense—can be sounded out. Even English spelling, which is notorious for its irregularity, gives some clue to the sounds of unfamiliar words and nonsense words. By contrast, a Chinese character can be sounded out easily when familiar but not so easily or not at all when unfamiliar. True, many characters contain sound-cuing phonetic components, but they are not only numerous but also unreliable, in that in only one case out of five does a phonetic give the correct tone syllable of its character (chap. 5).

In special cases, such as in transcribing foreign words whose meanings are unknown or not fully understood, characters are used as if they were syllable signs, i.e., they are chosen for their sounds and not for their meanings, as in 三明治 *sanmingzhi* ('three, bright, govern' = 'sandwich'). There are many characters with the sound of *san, ming*, or *zhi*, out of which these three have been chosen arbitrarily.

As for meaning representation, each logograph by itself represents the meaning of a morpheme, though it can join another logograph to form a compound word. In contrast, in a phonetic script, be it an alphabet or syllabary, the meaning of a morpheme emerges when two or more letters or signs are sequenced in a particular order, as we have seen.

In short, a logographic character represents directly or primarily the meaning, and indirectly or secondarily the sound, of a morpheme. Almost every character represents at least one meaning and sometimes a few extended meanings. But a character may have many different sounds across times and "dialects" or languages, or a character may share the same sound with many other characters. A few characters even have no known sound, though they still have meaning. In their long, long history, Chinese characters have undergone changes in their number, shapes, sounds, and meanings. Yet their fundamental logographic nature remains the same.

The truth, as usual, may lie between the two extreme views, one asserting that a character's function is to represent a syllable and the other asserting that it is to represent only meaning, or that its representation of meaning is perfect. The middle ground espoused in this book is that logographic characters and phonetic scripts have some shared features. Nevertheless, the differences between the two types of writing systems are real enough to have consequences, some of which—such as the number and complexity of graphs—have been pointed out in this section, and some of which are explored in the next section, which describes some research on the question.

Logographs vs Phonetic Graphs: Research

In reading a text such as this book, readers use several subskills, such as: recognizing individual words; relating the recognized words to each other — to sort out who does what to whom, for example — in order to comprehend a sentence; relating sentences to each other to comprehend a paragraph — to sort out which is the topic sentence and which supporting sentences, for example; and ultimately extracting the gist of a paragraph, chapter, or book. During the comprehension process, readers may differentiate important information from less important, and attend more to the former. And they process linguistic information in short-term memory in a phonetic form (Taylor and Taylor 1983: 393–94).

For the past few decades psychologists, usually in North America and Japan, have carried out numerous experiments to compare reading processes in logographs and phonetic scripts. In whatever script people may read, they appear to use similar comprehension processes for large linguistic units, such as sentences and paragraphs. But they appear to recognize individual words somewhat differently in different types of writing systems. Thus, this book discusses word recognition in some depth but text comprehension only in passing.

What does it mean to recognize a word? In reading a text, readers recognize words, at least some critical words. Seeing the word *mountain*, they recognize it as a word they know by matching it with a representation they have stored in memory so that they can extract various pieces of information about the word — e.g., its sound, meaning, and word class. If they are reading a sentence, such as "This mountain is rocky and dangerous," "This mountain of paper is just one tax law," or "Don't make a mountain out of a molehill," they use this information about the word to understand the sentence.

As shown in the following body of research, the extraction of meaning and sound is similar in some ways and different in others between logographic Chinese characters and words in phonetic scripts. Let us start with a few preliminary words about how psychologists do experiments. Since skilled readers recognize a word effortlessly and rapidly, in a fraction of a second, and without being aware of how they do it, psychologists usually devise seemingly contrived experimental procedures. They ask people to do unnatural tasks, and measure how accurately and quickly the tasks are performed. The people studied in an experiment are called subjects, and adult subjects are often university students because of their easy availability to experimenters. Sometimes the performance of adult subjects is compared to that of children.

What do experiments show us about word recognition? The meanings of words are responded to faster in logographs than in phonetic scripts. Most interestingly, the meanings of logographs are responded to even when they should not be; in other words, a logograph represents the meaning of a morpheme so directly and compellingly that readers cannot help but respond to it. Logographs that have been studied include Arabic numerals and Chinese characters.

Two psychologists tested English readers' responses to a pair of numerals written either in English letters or in Arabic numerals (Besner and Coltheart 1979). Consider the pair *four* vs *nine* or 4 vs 9. Note that the two number names have the same length in English spelling. The readers' task was to judge which of the two numerals in each pair was physically larger. On the Arabic numeral pairs, response times were slower if a smaller number was printed physically larger (4 vs 9). Also, the larger the separation between the values of the two numerals in each pair the longer was the response time (the pair 1 vs 2 has a smaller separation of values than does the pair 4 vs 9). Obviously the readers responded to the meanings of the Arabic numerals, even though their task was to judge the physical sizes of the written numerals. On the English numeral names, however, the subjects took about the same time to judge all types of numeral pairs. The unavoidable response to the meanings of test words was found only with logographic Arabic numerals but not with phonetically spelled English numeral names. Furthermore, the readers took much longer to judge the size of the English numeral names than the Arabic numerals.

A similar experiment was carried out with Chinese speakers, who judged pairs of numerals in Chinese characters (Tzeng and Wang 1983). One of the characters was printed physically larger than the other (e.g., 四 'four' was printed larger than 九 'nine'), and subjects were asked to judge which was physically larger. The Chinese subjects' responses to the characters was similar to the English readers' responses to the Arabic numerals in the above experiment.

Readers of the English word *mountain* can recognize it by identifying its letter sequence, which can be matched to its sound sequence, through which its meaning can be retrieved from memory. This kind of recognition process might be used by beginning readers, especially by those who are taught by a phonics method, which teaches children letter–sound relations so that they can sound out any printed words, be they familiar, unfamiliar, or nonsense. As readers encounter *mountain* repeatedly through years of reading they may eventually recognize it as a whole pattern, without first analyzing it into a letter–sound sequence.

These two major routes to recognizing words—whole-word vs letter–sound sequence—can be demonstrated. In one experiment, Grades II, IV, VI schoolchildren and college students were asked to judge whether a set of English words belonged to animal or non-animal categories (Samuels et al. 1978). Words varied in length from three to six letters (e.g., *hog, pony, whale, cattle*). The younger the children, the more slowly they judged the words. Further, the young children's judging times increased as the word length increased, suggesting that they recognized words as letter sequences. But college students' judging times were more or less the same, independent of word length, suggesting that they recognized a word as a whole pattern, regardless of its length. Note that the longest test words were reasonably common and short, as compared with words such as *arachnophobia* and *tachistoscope*, for which even college students are less likely to use whole-word recognition.

Logographic Chinese characters and phonetic English words appear to be learned in a different manner. In a cross-cultural study, Stevenson and Stigler (1992) compared the ability of first graders in Beijing and in Chicago to read words. The Chicago children were over-represented at the top and bottom groups; that is, some could read words above their grade level, and others below it, suggesting that English-speaking children who catch on how to break down words by sound can read new words not yet taught, whereas those who do not acquire this decoding ability tend to be poor readers. Once they can sound out new words, they can understand the meanings of these words, which are likely to be in their oral vocabulary. By contrast most Beijing children read

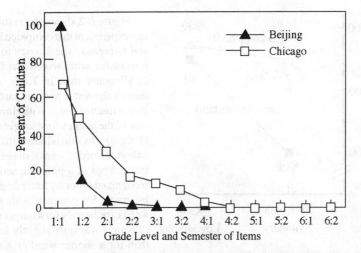

Figure 6-1. Chinese and American first graders' ability to read words at and above different grade levels (Stevenson and Stigler 1992: 47; with permission)

at their grade level: they can read words already taught but not those not yet taught, because they cannot sound out new words in Chinese characters. Figure 6-1 shows the two different patterns of word reading by Chinese and American first graders.

If the character 山 means 'mountain' and is given the sound *shan* (in Mandarin) or *yama* (in one of several Japanese sounds associated with it), then a reader has to recognize it as a whole pattern; there is no point in decomposing it into a series of strokes, which would represent neither its sound sequence nor its meaning. In learning simple characters, each character as a whole pattern is associated with its tone syllable and morpheme. But characters that are composites of two or more simple characters (e.g., 仙 'person + mountain' ='hermit') may be analyzed into components, each of which is often a simple character that is learned as a whole pattern.

So, a logographic Chinese character, or a component that makes up a composite character, is recognized as a whole pattern, whereas an English word may be recognized as a whole pattern or as a sequence of letter–sounds, depending on, among other things, its familiarity to a reader.

Because logographs represent the meanings of morphemes directly and their sounds indirectly, while phonetic letters do the reverse, people indeed get the meanings of morphemes faster from logographs than from phonetic signs; conversely, they read aloud, or pronounce, words in phonetic signs faster than in logographs. The time differences are minute but are found consistently in psychologists' laboratory experiments. Experimenters sometimes measure "pronunciation latency": how quickly people can start pronouncing a word after it is flashed on a screen. They often use Japanese words as test materials, because the same word can be written either in logographic characters, Kanji, or the phonetic syllabary, Kana. There are two forms of Kana, curvaceous Hiragana and angular Katakana.

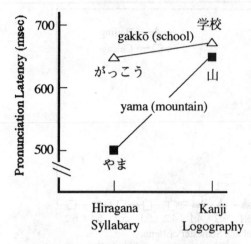

Figure 6-2. Hiragana syllable signs are pronounced faster than Kanji logographs for the same words (Kaiho and Nomura 1983; translated from Japanese; permission requested)

Figure 6-2 shows the results of one experiment that compared Kanji and Hiragana. The latency to pronounce the same words was faster in Hiragana than in Kanji, even though the test words are customarily written in Kanji. With Hiragana words, the latency for a longer word (4 signs) was much longer than for a shorter word (2 signs), suggesting that a word in a phonetic script is recognized letter by letter or graph by graph. By contrast, with Kanji words, the latency for a longer word (2 Kanji) was only slightly longer than for a shorter word (1 Kanji), suggesting that a familiar Kanji word, whether it has one or two Kanji, is recognized as one visual–meaning unit. Note also the very short latency required to pronounce a 2-graph Hiragana word, as compared with the same word in 1 Kanji.

Saito (1981) prepared two-morpheme Sino-Japanese compound words in four ways:

1. Kanji–Kanji
2. Kanji–Kana
3. Kana–Kanji
4. Kana–Kana

Normally, a compound word is written in form 1, and occasionally in form 4, but hardly ever in forms 2 or 3. The time taken by Saito's subjects to read them aloud was, from fastest to slowest: 4, 3, 2, 1. However, in a comprehension test, subjects read silently a sentence containing a blank and then a test word, and judged whether the word fitted in the blank. The response time for this task was the reverse, from fastest to slowest: 1, 2, 3, and 4 (see also "Why Keep Kanji?" in chap. 21).

Hiragana is a phonetic script that directly codes the sound of a word, whereas Kanji is a logograph that represents the sound of a word indirectly through its meaning. Korean Han'gŭl is also a phonetic script and similar experiments give similar results. Korean college students read aloud two-morpheme compound words faster in Han'gŭl than in Hancha (the Korean term for Chinese characters). Moreover, they read aloud the Han'gŭl words uniformly fast, with no error, but read aloud the familiar Hancha words at varying speeds, making some errors (Simpson and Kang 1994).

Another study compared short-term memory of Chinese words and English words presented to Chinese and American subjects, respectively (Turnage and McGinnies 1973). The words were presented either orally or visually. The subjects were asked to indicate the serial order of the test words in a booklet by marking their order from memory. The Chinese subjects did better when the words were presented visually rather than orally, but the American subjects did better when the words were presented orally rather than visually. A visual code seems to be involved more in remembering Chinese characters than in remembering English words. In recalling Japanese words, either immediately after seeing the words or after some delay, 2-Kanji words were better recalled than the same words in Hiragana (Yokoyama et al. 1991).

Let us make a brief foray into how the brain processes logographic Kanji and phonetic Kana. The brain, specially its outer covering called the cortex, allows human beings to speak, read, and do many other mental activities. The cortex is divided into two hemispheres, the left and the right. Of the two, it is the left hemisphere that is mostly though not exclusively involved in language processing, whether language is spoken or written, and whether it is Chinese or English. When the cortex is damaged— whether by stroke, tumor, or wound—speech and reading can be impaired. The type of reading impairment associated with particular damage allows researchers to identify, if roughly, the area(s) in the cortex involved in a particular aspect of reading and writing.

After reviewing the literature on reading impairment caused by brain damage, Paradis and his associates (1985: 194–5) conclude that the left hemisphere is involved in processing both logographic Kanji and phonetic Kana, but within the left hemisphere, the areas involved in Kanji and Kana processing seem to differ: "Oral reading, and kana processing in particular, depend on a preserved left temporal area [which processes temporal, acoustic information], whereas reading comprehension and kanji processing depend on a preserved left parieto–occipital area [which processes language and visual information]." They further conclude: "The visual route [whole-word recognition] is more common for reading kanji and the phonological route for reading kana (at least for visually unfamiliar kana words)."

The classification of script symbols into logographs and phonetic signs, like most classifications—e.g., between adults and children, between the rich and the poor— does not have a sharp boundary. Logographs have some characteristics of phonetic signs, and vice versa. When Chinese readers see a familiar logographic character they respond to both its tone syllable and meaning; when English readers see a familiar short word they recognize it as a whole pattern, without analyzing it into a letter–sound sequence. Nevertheless, differences between these two major types of writing systems are real enough to influence word recognition, as the experiments described here.

Figure 6-3 summarizes the differences in word recognition between the logographic Chinese characters and two phonetic scripts, the English alphabet and Korean Han'gŭl.

Alphabet vs Logography for Science

The benefits of writing to civilization are incalculable. Writing enables humans to record natural phenomena and commercial transactions and to transmit culture and knowledge across space and time. It is one of the most important ways people acquire the information that allows them to function as useful members in an industrial society. People should be able to reap these benefits of writing no matter what kind of writing system—alphabet, syllabary, or logography—they use.

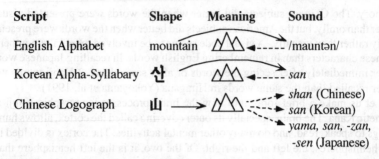

Figure 6-3. Word recognition: Phonetic script vs logography. A written morpheme's meaning can be obtained indirectly through its letter–sound relation in a phonetic script, whereas it is obtained directly from its graphic shape in a logograph. On the other hand, pronunciation is direct in phonetic scripts but indirect in logographs.

Yet, some scholars claim that logical thinking and abstract science are possible only for users of an alphabet but not for users of logographs. McLuhan (1962: 47; 49) observed: "Cultures can rise far above civilization artistically but without the phonetic alphabet they remain tribal, as do the Chinese and the Japanese." "By the meaningless sign linked to the meaningless sound we have built the shape and meaning of Western man." Havelock (1974) attributes the ascendency of Greek analytic thought to the introduction of vowels into the alphabet. (The original script invented by Semitic peoples consisted only of consonants and a few semi-vowels, but vowels were not critical in their scripts; chap. 1.) "The Greeks did not just invent an alphabet; they invented literacy and the literate basis of modern thought" (p. 44). "It is no accident that the pre-alphabetic cultures of the world were also in a large sense the pre-scientific cultures, pre-philosophical and pre-literary" (p. 50).

McLuhan's and Havelock's extravagant claims on the power of the alphabet are taken up and expanded by Logan (1986). "The alphabet ... has contributed to the development of codified law, monotheism, abstract science, deductive logic, and individualism, each a unique contribution of Western thought" (p. 18). As a corollary, the use of logographic Chinese characters is said to have contributed to the failure of abstract thought and science to develop in East Asia, in particular in China.

Logan then makes some sweeping generalizations, such as those shown in Table 6-2. These dichotomies are inaccurate, simplistic, and dangerous. Take, for example, the right–left brain and nonlinear–linear dichotomies for East–West. Whether one speaks Chinese or English, or whether one reads in logographic characters or in a phonetic script, one has to arrange sounds and written signs linearly in a sequence. See what happens if the three words in the Chinese sentence, *Gou yao ren*, are re-ordered as *Ren yao gou*: The first says and means "Dog bite man" and the second says and means "Man bite dog." The difference is just as in English.

Table 6-2. Alleged Differences between East and West

East	West
right-brain oriented	left-brain oriented
nonlinear	linear
decentralized	centralized
craft	technology
relativity	absolutism

Also in comprehending a sentence and eventually a text, the meanings recognized in individual characters must be related to each other (to sort out who does what to whom, for example), and even in Chinese text this relating appears to be done by way of phonetic coding in short-term memory (e.g., Tzeng et al. 1977). All languages are mostly, though not exclusively, processed in the left hemisphere, which specializes in sequential, temporal, and phonetic processing.

Anyone who claims that science is possible only with an alphabet but not with logographs should have an adequate knowledge of Chinese characters and Chinese civilization. How much does Logan know about characters? Here are some excerpts from his book; judge their accuracy for yourself, in the light of what you have read so far.

> Chinese writing has evolved so little from its pictographic origin that contemporary Chinese are able to read texts 3,500 years old.... All Chinese words are monosyllabic. There are no prefixes, no suffixes, only single-syllable words.... There are 2,365 different Mandarin words, each with its own unique pictogram or character, that are all pronounced *shih* . [p. 32–33] The Chinese ideogram "retraces the meaning" of a word graphically. [p. 59] The Chinese writing system, basically unchanged from its original form, is still purely pictographic. [1986: 30]

To blame the use of logographic Chinese characters for the failure of abstract science to develop, one has to assume that reasoning and problem solving can be done only through writing, and that Chinese characters are not suited to abstract or analytic thinking. These assumptions are questionable. Science is conducted through observation, experimentation, mathematical models, and quantitative analysis of data. The first two processes depend marginally on language, spoken or written, and the third and fourth processes depend on mathematics, a universal language.

During or after scientific observation, language becomes useful in recording and communicating the results. Chinese characters are no better and no worse than an alphabet for this purpose. Some Chinese characters represent abstract concepts, such Confucian virtues as "benevolence,""loyalty," and "filial piety." Some characters are analyzable into semantic and phonetic components, and every character is analyzed into a correct sequence of strokes in writing. If new Western concept such as atom, laser, and software have to be adopted, Chinese words in characters are coined, usually combining existing characters.

Perhaps the greatest authority on Chinese civilization is Joseph Needham, the originator of the monumental 28-volume work *Science and Civilization in China* (1954–). Needham documents numerous scientific and technological advances the Chinese made long before the West. The five best-known Chinese inventions are writing, paper, gunpowder, compass, and printing. There are many other, less well-known inventions and discoveries: iron and steel metallurgy, the drive belt, the chain drive, irrigation systems, metal-barrel cannons, rockets, porcelain, silk, stirrups, wheel barrow, deep drilling, pound-locks on canals, fore-and-aft sailing, the sternpost rudder, the paddle-wheel boat, quantitative cartography, immunization techniques (variolation), seismographs, and the systematic exploration of the chemical and pharmaceutical properties of a great variety of substances, acupuncture, herbal medicine, forensic medicine, fingerprinting... That's not all: the Chinese made astronomical observations of novae and supernovae, comets, eclipses, sun spots, and other heavenly phenomena.

The Chinese produced these achievements while using logographic Chinese characters. Their achievements were notable for their practical rather than theoretical importance, and also for being made before the Middle Ages. Since then the Chinese have fallen behind the Westerners in science and technology. They had to borrow even the word for science, *kexue,* from the Japanese, who coined it on a Chinese model in the 1870's. In the West, the dark Middle Ages were followed by the Reformation and Renaissance, which spurred experimentation, inductive reasoning, and the mathematical approach to all natural phenomena. By contrast, Chinese social and economic life moved straight from feudalism to bureaucratism.

The Chinese thought about science and technology differently from Westerners. They developed mathematics early in their history, but more as a tool of science than for its own sake. At any rate between the mid-13th and the 16th century, they did not produce mathematical innovations. This failure has been blamed on the use of the Chinese abacus and not on the use of Chinese characters. The abacus was remarkably efficient as a calculator but was limited to a dozen or so digits in a linear array and so was useless for advanced algebra (Sivin 1973).

As Sivin (1990) points out, in Europe since classical times the various sciences were part of a single structure that included all systematic rational knowledge. And the natural sciences were subsumed under the overarching structure of natural philosophy. By contrast, in China the sciences tended to develop independently of each other, rarely responding directly to contemporary philosophic innovations. The sciences reflected the concerns of the tiny literate elite and their cosmologies, while technology was a matter of craft tradition, passed down privately from father to son or from master to apprentice. It was on these mainly oral and manual traditions rather than on cumulative science, recorded in writing, that the technological preeminence of China was built. Chinese scientists were aware of their increasing ability to predict, but lacked the conviction that eventually all phenomena would yield their ultimate secrets.

Sivin blames also political, social, and economic factors for the loss of the early Chinese technological preeminence.

> Some of the reasons for the reversal in technological preeminence are internal
> to China: centuries of disastrous fiscal and other administrative policies, the
> remorseless pressure of increasing population, and a large measure of social
> stability and cultural homogeneity that left traditional values and forms
> practically unchallenged as the creativity behind them was sapped by intellectual
> orthodoxies. [1990: 166]

I would blame also the traditional Chinese world views and the civil service examination system, which are the topics of Chapter 10. Meanwhile, I point out here that the East Asians were once too poor and backward to worry about abstract science but are now wealthy enough to do so. They see science and technology as the main route to economic advancement, for an individual as well as for a nation. They value education in these fields more than in social sciences and humanities, and do so more than do the Westerners. At recent international contests in math and science, East

Asians usually score higher than Europeans and North Americans. For example, at the 36th annual International Mathematical Olympiad held in Toronto, Canada, in July 1995, the Chinese team were the top scorers with four gold medalists. Of the 6 highest scorers from Canada, four had East Asian names.

The four Tigers of Asia (Hong Kong, Singapore, S. Korea, and Taiwan), not to mention Japan, are plowing billions of dollars earned selling cars and computer parts into their technical universities and research institutes. Many East Asian scientists who have received advanced degrees in N. America and Europe are returning to these universities and institutes. For example, Yuan T. Lee, a Nobel Prize winning chemist, has returned to Taiwan to run Academia Sinica, a collection of 21 research institutes. The ambitious goal of East Asians is not only to catch up with the West but also to surpass the West eventually. "The scientific breakthroughs of the 21st century—and the market opportunities that follow—may be born on the Pacific Rim" (Nash with Guest 1994). The East Asians are making these advances while using Chinese characters.

Needham pleads with the West for better appreciation of the Chinese achievements.

> There is a commonly received idea that the ideographic language was a powerful inhibiting factor to the development of modern science in China.... This is grossly over-rated.... The Chinese language at present day is found to be no impediment by the scientists of the contemporary culture. [1963: 137]

Effects of Scripts and Literacy on Cognition

East Asians and Westerners may perform certain mental tasks somewhat differently, probably because of differences in educational tradition, and not necessarily because of differences in scripts *per se*. In Chinese education in bygone days, learning the cultural heritage such as the Confucian classics was valued more than original thinking. This tradition was entrenched in the 1300-year old civil-service examination, which tested mainly memorized knowledge of the classics (chap. 10). As a residue of this tradition, even in modern times, teaching in schools in East Asia tends to emphasize drill in basic skills and memorization of information rather than original thinking. Perhaps as a consequence of such teaching, students in Taiwan, from Grade II to college age, scored lower than American students of similar age on the Torrance test of creative thinking: idea fluency, originality, and flexibility (Liu and Hsu 1974; Paschal et al. 1980). On creative thinking, Taiwanese college students scored lower not only than American students but also than Taiwanese senior high school students. On the other hand, Taiwanese students scored higher than American students on verbal memory (Huang and Liu 1978).

Mathematics requires problem-solving skills, and is the foundation on which almost every branch of science is built. The modern language of mathematics is more or less universal. Who does well in mathematics and why? Over the past 10 years, in three repeated cross-cultural comparisons of the mathematical abilities of school-children from Taiwan, Japan, and the United States, children from Taiwan and Japan far outperformed those from the United States (Stevenson et al. 1993). At the 1991 international competitions of mathematics and science, again it was the students from

S. Korea and Taiwan who scored the highest among the testees from competing nations that included the United States and Canada. In mathematics, Asian children even in the United States usually score higher than other ethnic groups (Flaugher 1971). The high math and science skills of East Asian students everywhere may be attributable to factors such as hard work, strong motivation, and parents' encouragement; they may be attributable also to effective teaching and respect for learning in Taiwan, Japan, and S. Korea.

Some scholars—e.g., Goody and Watt (1968); Havelock (1974)—claim that a particular type of script, i.e., an alphabet, promotes abstract concepts, analytic reasoning, new ways of categorizing, a logical approach to language, and so on. As Scribner and Cole (1981: 7) rightly pointed out: "It is striking that the scholars who offer these claims for specific changes in psychological processes present no direct evidence that individuals in literate societies do, in fact, process information about the world differently from those in societies without literacy."

Scribner and Cole themselves carried out an extensive study—through a variety of cognitive and linguistic tests—on the effect of different types of literacy on mental functioning among the Vai of Liberia, Africa. They studied four types of literates among Vai speakers: children who receive formal schooling using English; children and adults who learn a Vai syllabary (which has over 200 simple graphs), which they use not for text reading but for writing letters among themselves; children who learn to read aloud and memorize, without necessarily understanding, the Qur'an (Koran; the scripture of Islam); and children who learn the Arabic language and alphabet. Literacy activities in three of the four types of literacy—Vai, Qur'an, Arabic—are restricted in that they are associated with neither formal schooling nor text reading. Only English is associated with years of formal schooling; it is also the official language, the language of commerce and government. In English but not in other languages, reading materials such as newspapers, magazines, and books are available.

Here are some major findings. Formal schooling with instruction in English increased the Vai people's ability to provide a verbal explanation of the principles involved in performing various tasks. Schooled individuals, more than non-schooled ones, gave task-oriented and informative justifications; they more often made use of class and attribute names. For example, given a set of similar problems, the schooled individuals tended first to classify problems and then to find a general solution for each class, whereas non-schooled individuals tended to seek a solution to each problem separately. Speaking English never substituted for schooling variables, and on verbalization measures, school, not English reading scores, was the best predictor.

The effect of non-schooled literacy was found on those tasks that Scribner and Cole adapted to mirror specific literacy practices. For example, Vai-script literates consistently outperformed other types of literates when talking about good or bad sentences. It turned out that letter writing and instruction in the Vai script puts much emphasis on "correct Vai." Qur'an literacy had an effect on memory, in particular on incremental recall. On no tasks did all non-literates perform at lower levels than all literates.

It is schooling, and not a type of script or literacy, that contributes to the development of logical thinking. Scripts and literacy may influence reading and cognition only for lower-level, specific tasks.

To conclude this chapter, logographic Chinese characters differ from phonetic scripts in several characteristics: the linguistic units they represent; how they represent meanings and sounds; in the number of written symbols or graphs; and in the complexity of the shapes of these graphs. Such physical and linguistic differences affect word recognition—reading aloud is faster in a phonetic than logographic script, but meaning extraction is faster in a logographic than phonetic script. In teaching word recognition using an alphabet, phonics can be, though need not be, used, whereas simple Chinese characters are commonly taught by whole shape. The users of Chinese characters and the Japanese syllabary are aware of, and can manipulate, the syllable unit but do not attend to phonemes as units, whereas the users of an alphabet eventually become aware of phonemes. Apart from such differences in word recognition, types of scripts do not seem to influence greatly how people read text, think, or do science.

7

Text Writing in Chinese, Korean, and Japanese

So far we have learned mainly about individual Chinese characters and words, and occasionally their arrangement in a phrase or sentence. Now we learn about how these items are arranged in a text, in which writing direction, punctuation, spacing, and paragraphing are important. These conventions, or lack of them, began originally in Chinese and were adopted into Korean and Japanese. They have been largely Westernized in all three languages since the early 20th century, and are the same in outline, though not in detail, among the three languages. The text writing conventions are described here in Part I and will not be repeated in Parts II and III.

Writing Directions: Vertical vs Horizontal

More than 3000 years ago, brief texts on oracle bones were written vertically, columns moving either from right to left or left to right. Ever since, Chinese text has been traditionally written vertically from the top to bottom of a page, with the columns moving from right to left (figs. 7-4 and 4-2ab); books accordingly open at the right-hand cover, rather than at the left-hand cover as English books do. Apparently, this writing direction was convenient in ancient times when a book was a scroll: the right hand wrote characters vertically, while the left hand unrolled a scroll a little at a time.

For the past few decades, however, there has been a movement to change the writing direction from vertical to horizontal. Since 1956, China's leading newspaper, *The People's Daily*, has been printed in a horizontal direction, left to right. But its page may contain occasional vertical texts, perhaps for a flexible use of paper space or to attract the attention of readers. Most textbooks and government documents are written horizontally. For a Chinese text written horizontally see Figure 5-1.

Koreans and Japanese used the Chinese vertical direction in the past. Today Koreans use usually the Western horizontal direction and occasionally the traditional vertical direction, while Japanese use both directions equally often. Figure 7-1a shows a Korean text written horizontally, while figure 7-1b shows a Japanese text written vertically.

In Japan, most books, textbooks, newspapers, and magazines are still written in the vertical direction, which is considered formal. However, modern technical texts tend to be written horizontally in the Western manner, in order better to accomodate Arabic numerals, mathematical and chemical formulas, and European words. Even in one copy of a newspaper, some sections, usually political–economic sections, tend to be written vertically, while some other sections, such as entertainment and lifestyle, tend to use a horizontal direction.

Which direction is better for reading? Left-to-right horizontal writing and reading should have advantages over vertical writing and reading for the following reasons.

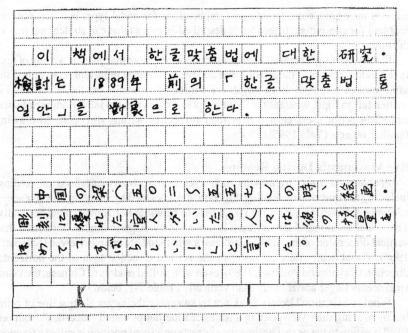

Figure 7-1. Two East Asian texts prepared on half of a standard manuscript sheet: (a) Korean text written horizontally, using mainly Western punctuation marks and Arabic numerals; (b) Japanese text written vertically (turn the page sideways), using mainly East Asian punctuation marks and Chinese numerals.

The Korean text says: In this book the object of research and examination of Han'gŭl spelling is the pre-1989 "unified rules of Han'gŭl spelling."

The Japanese text says: During the time of China's Ryō (502–557), there was an official who excelled in painting and sculpture. Everybody exclaimed "Excellent!" in praise of his talent.

1. Right-handed writers can avoid smudging the part already written or their elbows.
2. Right-handed writers can see what has been written so far.
3. Writers can accommodate the writing direction of the letters of the Roman alphabet and Arabic numerals.
4. The visual field is wider horizontally than vertically.
5. The jump of the eye is easier to make horizontally than vertically.

An aside: Writing in China, as well as in Korea and Japan, is done usually with the right hand; writing with the left hand is strongly discouraged, so that even left handers will write with the right hand, though they may do other tasks with their left hands.

In commercial printing, the font types for vertical writing and horizontal writing are not interchangeable, because vertical fonts are made slightly wider than high, and horizontal fonts slightly higher than wide, to compensate for the optical illusion created by the barlike lines of text on the page (Unger 1987). Such typographical niceties may have considerable cost implications for metal type, but they pose no problem for computers, if the font is described as curves that can stretch one way or the other.

Finally, writing directions have consequences for more than just the writing of text. In the Indian continent the Hindi script and the Urdu script represent more or less the same spoken language. Both scripts are written horizontally, but the Hindi script is written left to right, whereas the Urdu script is written right to left. Hindi script users and Urdu script users carried over their respective writing directions to drawing familiar objects (Vaid 1995).

Eye Movements During Reading

People read a text by moving their eyes over it. Many questions on reading, including the question on reading direction, are answered by studying how a reader's eyes move. Research shows the visual field to be wider horizontally than vertically: The visual scanning of the newborn is more widely dispersed in the horizontal than vertical dimension of the field, regardless of what kind of figure is viewed (Salapatek 1968); visual acuity falls off faster in the vertical direction than in the horizontal direction (Rayner and Pollatsek 1989); even with skilled readers of Chinese, the visual span seems larger horizontally than vertically (Table 7-1, below).

What is a fixation? People read, not by sweeping their eyes along a line of print, but by moving their viewpoint in a series of little jumps called "saccades" from one fixed position to the next. The time the eye rests on a fixed position is called a fixation. You can easily see the effect—just watch a reader's eyes. As one reads, a target word is brought into the "fovea" by a saccadic jump.[1] The eyes then fixate on the word for about a quarter of a second, during which time the image of the object is more or less stationary upon the retina. It is mainly during the fixation that a reader acquires information on the fixated word. At the end of the fixation, the eyes jump to the next target word. On average, 90% of reading time is spent in fixations. Although the eyes generally move forward in the left-to-right direction (in English), they occasionally jump back, or regress, to fixate on words insufficiently perceived earlier. So the best strategy of a speed reader is to reduce the number of fixations or equivalently to have long saccades. Figure 7-2 shows how fixations are distributed and how long each fixation lasts in an example of typical English reading.

In a study that compared the eye movements of readers of 14 different scripts written in various directions, the direction did not greatly affect reading (Gray 1956). One reads best in one's accustomed direction, be it vertical or horizontal, left to right or right to left. But the study may not have ensured that the readers' skill, which also affects reading performance, was "equal" in the 14 writing systems.

More recently in Hong Kong, Grade I Chinese children named four colors and their character labels better in a vertical than horizontal arrangement, but by Grade V, the vertical advantage disappeared, perhaps because by then the children have had

---

[1]The fovea is the tiny central part of the retina—a screen of photosensitive neural receptors lining the eyeball—where vision is sharpest.

Regular   bouts   of   aerobic   exercise   may   also   help
● ●   ●   ● ○   ● ○   ● ●
36 37   38   39 42   40 43   41 44
212 75   312   260 271   188 350   215 221

spark   a   brainstorm   of   creative   thinking
●   ● ○ ●   ●   ●
45   46 50 47   48   49
266   277 179 120   219   266

Figure 7-2. Part of a series of eye-movement fixation points when one college student read a piece of English text. Filled dots represent the placement of forward fixations, open dots the placement of regressions. Numbers indicate: (above) sequence number of the fixation, (below) fixation duration in milliseconds. (Taylor and Taylor 1990, fig. 5-1, adapted from Rayner and Pollatsek 1989, fig. 4-1; by permission)

extensive experience in horizontal reading (Chen and Chen 1988). In the same study, reading easy Chinese prose for comprehension, horizontal was faster than vertical reading, perhaps for two reasons: The visual field is wider horizontally than vertically, and the jump of the eye is easier to make horizontally than vertically. There was no difference in comprehension between the two reading directions. Another study on eye movements also concludes that Chinese readers today are more at home with horizontal than vertical text (Sun et al. 1985).

Because Japanese writing uses both vertical and horizontal directions, it is a suitable system for comparing the relative advantages of the two, with reading habit reasonably equated. In one study a Japanese research team asked a large number of students to read, silently and for comprehension, easy texts written either horizontally or vertically (Satō 1958). Both middle-school and high-school students read faster vertically than horizontally. However, the high-school students showed a smaller difference between the two directions than did the middle-school students. In their patterns of eye movements, university students did not show any difference between the two directions. As the students advanced in levels of school, they showed less and less difference between horizontal and vertical directions, presumably because they became more practised in horizontal reading.

Table 7-1 shows that skilled Chinese read faster horizontally than vertically, and that horizontally they read as fast as English readers (data of Sun et al. 1985). Had the reading material used for the two directions been similar in difficulty, the differences between the two in reading rates might have been smaller than those shown in Table 7-1. The text for the vertical direction was a poem, written in a classical language, handwritten with brush (calligraphy) in a semi-cursive script style, whereas for the horizontal direction, it was expository prose written in a vernacular language

Table 7-1. Reading Span and Rates in Chinese and English

	Chinese		English
	Vertical	Horizontal	Horizontal
No of Hanzi*	1.2	2.6	
No of Words	0.8	1.7	1.8
Fix (sec)	0.29	0.26	0.27
WPM	170	390	380

*The number of characters or words perceived in one fixation, the fixation duration in seconds (Fix), and words read per minute (WPM)

and printed in a standard script style. (For the script styles, see Table 3-1; for the classic vs vernacular language, see chap. 8.)

Still, one reads best in the direction to which one is accustomed, but if the effect of reading habit is eliminated, reading is more efficient in the horizontal than vertical direction.

Figure 7-3 shows that the English phrase *mountain range* requires 13 letters and a space between two words, when written vertically (the first column); the same phrase requires only two logographic characters in Chinese, Korean, and Japanese (second column); it requires two Korean Han'gŭl syllable blocks (third column); and it requires five Hiragana syllabary signs (fourth column). In the three East Asian

English Alphabet	Chinese Hanzi	Korean Han'gŭl	Japanese Hiragana
m o u n t a i n r a n g e	山 脈	산 맥	さ ん み ゃ く

Figure 7-3. Vertically arranged 'mountain range' in four scripts

languages, the two words for "mountain" and "range" join firmly to become a compound word, with no extra space between them.

With alphabetic letters a vertical arrangement is a long thin string of letters, and so readers are likely to underuse their horizontal visual field. At the same time, in one fixation they may not be able to perceive a whole word consisting of several letters. In Tinker's (1955) study, English readers initially read vertically arranged English 50% slower than horizontally arranged text, and still after 4 weeks of practice their reading speed was 22% slower than for the horizontal text. Even very long practice may not overcome the inherent disadvantage of writing English vertically. By contrast, practised readers of Chinese characters, alone or mixed with syllable signs as in Japanese and Korean, should be able to use both vertical and horizontal visual fields efficiently.

The two writing directions affect the kinds of punctuation marks and numerals used in East Asian texts, as we discuss in the next section.

Punctuation Marks and Spacing

Punctuation marks make reading easier by indicating the boundaries of linguistic and thought units, such as sentences and clauses. They also indicate in the text special items, like quoted remarks and book titles. In the West, punctuation marks became reasonably standard and obligatory in the Middle Ages. In the East, for a long time, Chinese writers, as well as the Korean and Japanese writers who followed them, were indifferent to punctuation marks, as can be seen in Confucius's saying in Figure 4-2b, and in the exam answer (Figure 7-4). They began to use punctuation marks only several decades ago. Even now their use is not as consistent and regular as in the West.

In English and many other languages using the Roman alphabet a written sentence is clearly marked by two devices: the first letter of the sentence is capitalized, and the end of the sentence is marked by a period. Chinese characters and other East Asian scripts do not have counterparts to the English upper-case and lower-case distinctions. And the traditional writing did not use a period. Without these two devices the end of an East Asian sentence could be recognized only with effort, using clues such as the character 也 (*ye* in Chinese; *ya* in Korean; and *ya* or *nari* in Japanese) for a statement, or other characters for questions, exclamations, and so on. But these clues did not stand out in text; nor were they used regularly or consistently. So they could not be relied on as indicators of where to break the text, and classical texts were often subject to a variety of readings, requiring commentaries.

Figure 7-4 shows a traditional Chinese text containing 5 occurrences of the character *ye* that might mark the end of a statement (if you can spot them) but no punctuation marks whatever. This text is written, in fine calligraphy, as an answer to a question from an emperor at a civil service examination (chap. 10), and so the characters referring to the emperor are raised above the rest of the text, while those referring to the writer, "Your humble servant," are written small and a little to the right (at the head of the first—right-hand—column).

Under Western influence, punctuation marks—some Western and some Eastern—are now used in Chinese, Korean, and Japanese writings, as shown in Figures 7-1ab and 5-1. Two punctuation marks—question (?) and exclamation (!)—are the same in the West and in East Asia. In horizontal writing, the East has adopted many Western marks, such as semicolon (;), colon (:), period (.), comma (,), single and double quotation marks (') and ("), dash (—), and parentheses ( ).

Some East Asian marks, which tend to be used in vertical writing, differ from the Western ones in form though not in function: a period

Figure 7-4. An answer in a civil service exam

is a tiny circle; a comma is slanted toward the right; single and double quotation marks are single and double angle brackets, respectively; underscoring is done by a series of heavy dots or East Asian commas; omission is a string of six dots (......); *em*-dash is tilde (~) in Korean and Japanese; a book title is enclosed in «» in Chinese, sometimes in Korean too.

Some marks unique to East Asia include an open square for a missing or unclear character (found sometimes in an ancient text), a symbol for a repeated item (often in Japanese), and a center dot (·). The center dot separates two or more juxtaposed items, as in Marx · Engels (Marx and Engels). It is used also for dates, as in "the 8 · 15 Liberation" (the August 15th, 1945, when Korea was liberated from Japanese rule). It can be used in Japanese and Korean to separate two components of a Western name, as in Abraham · Lincoln. To separate items in a list, the East Asian comma can be also used.

In a horizontal text the East Asians tend to use the Western marks, along with Arabic numerals, and in a vertical direction the East Asian marks, along with Chinese numerals. Note the phrase "tend to"; occasionally horizontal texts have East Asian marks (figs. 5-1, 7-1, and 20-1).

With a change of writing direction from vertical to horizontal, there is a rotation by 90 degrees of some punctuation marks and special symbols, such as the tilde ~ for *em*-dash and the short bar used for a lengthened vowel in Japanese Katakana (one form of a syllabary) words. The set of dots for underscoring is placed on the right side of target graphs or words in vertical writing but over or under the targets in horizontal writing.

In a Chinese text, characters are written separate from each other, and no extra space is left between words. Since each word can consist of from one to several morpheme–characters, there is nothing in the visual appearance of the text to indicate word boundaries. In a text written in Pinyin (the Roman alphabet for writing Chinese), spaces can be left either between syllable–morphemes or between phrases, but not between words. The phrase in characters, 中 国 工 商 銀行 ('middle nation industry commerce silver row' or "Chinese Industrial and Commercial Bank"), is written in Pinyin with syllable–morphemes either all connected or all separated, as in

ZHONGGUOGONGSHANGYINHANG (phrase unit), or

ZHONG GUO GONG SHANG YIN HANG (syllable–morpheme unit)
   but not as

ZHONGGUO GONGSHANG YINHANG (word unit) (Zhou 1991: 20).

The important question is, which kind of spacing—between morpheme–syllables or between words—is easier for reading? In Taiwan, psychologists investigated this question and found that spaces between words made the sentence hard to read (Liu et al. 1974). The result may be explained partly by reading habit: Chinese readers are accustomed to reading with spaces between characters and not between words. It may also be explained partly by the fact that individual characters are strong units in their own right; after all, packed in each character are three kinds of important information: shape, meaning, and tone syllable. When two or more characters join to form a compound word, each character contributes its information package to the word ("Compound Words and Idioms" in chap. 4).

Within a Japanese sentence, words, phrases, and even clauses tend not to be separated by extra spaces, because alternations between Kanji (Chinese characters) and Hiragana (one form of Japanese syllabary) can mark their boundaries; that is, one phrase tends to consist of one content word (e.g., noun, verb) in one or two Kanji plus a grammatical morpheme (a postposition after a noun or a verb ending) in Hiragana. Occasionally a long phrase or clause in Hiragana may not contain any Kanji, in which case the lack of adequate spacing impedes reading. All-Hiragana texts for young children and romanized texts for foreigners leave spaces between words and phrases, precisely because they contain few or no Chinese characters to mark the content words (Part III).

Koreans use some Chinese characters but use mostly a phonetic script called Han'gŭl, whose letters are arranged in syllable blocks. When characters are used they may be enclosed in parentheses. Syllable blocks, like Chinese characters, are written separate from each other, but in contrast to a Chinese or Japanese text, extra spaces are left between phrases in a Korean text, as specified by spelling rules (fig. 7-1a, above). In romanized texts spaces are left even between a noun and a postposition (chap. 14).

In preparing a manuscript for publication, East Asian authors (when they do not use word processors) write on a manuscript sheet containing 20 rows of 20 or 25 columns, making 400 or 500 cells. Generally, each cell is occupied by one written symbol or graph — be it a Chinese character, a Japanese syllabary sign, a Korean syllable block, an uppercase letter of the Roman alphabet, or a punctuation mark; but each cell is occupied by two written symbols when they are lowercase letters of the Roman alphabet, single digit Arabic numerals, or a series of six dots for an unfinished sentence. So, it is easy to count the number of graphs on each page and hence to find the length of a text by counting the number of 400- or 500-character pages. As illustrated in Figure 7-1ab, above, a manuscript sheet provides ample space for corrections and revisions.

Prose and Paragraph Structure

This section does not attempt to trace the 3000-year history of Chinese prose writing; rather it is limited to asking whether the structure of a Chinese essay differs fundamentally from that of a Western essay.

In European languages, prose began to be developed as a form of writing, with the paragraph as a unit of prose, only in the Middle Ages. Until the 19th century, paragraphs tended to be long, running one or more pages. In the 20th century, they tend to be short, especially in newspapers and advertisements, perhaps reflecting the presumed short attention span of contemporary readers. Certainly, a long paragraph taxes a reader's short-term memory, which integrates and distills the information in a paragraph centered around a topic sentence.

A paragraph may consist of only one sentence, but it usually consists of several sentences. Visually, the beginning of a paragraph is indented or is preceded by an extra line space, or both. A paragraph has an internal structure, consisting of a topic sentence and several sentences that support — e.g., elaborate, illustrate, analyze, and summarize — the topic. Ideally, it should contain only relevant sentences and no irrelevant ones.

The topic sentence, if it is included, can appear anywhere in a paragraph. But it is most effective if it is explicit, prominently placed at the beginning, and well supported by all the sentences in the paragraph. It is the most useful information to keep alive in short-term memory, because it is needed to comprehend the other information in the paragraph, and ultimately is used in summing up the entire passage. Then the topic sentence can serve as a cue for retrieving the other information in the paragraph and passage.

In Imperial China, since the 15th century, a candidate at the civil-service exam (chap. 10) was required to write his essay in a rigid format called eight-legged essay *(baguwen)*. He was given a question from the Confucian classics as a topic, on which he wrote a short essay (200–300 words) in a set form of eight sections or parts, each with strict requirements even as to the number of characters or words, with no room left for innovation. The eight parts consist of (Lai Ming 1964: 314):

1. a gist of the essay in two sentences; like a news headline
2. expansion of part 1
3. introduction of the main part
4. and 5. contrasting aspects of the topic
6. body of the composition
7. continuation of part 6
8. conclusion.

The eight-legged essay was one of many forms of writing literary language, and was used only for the civil service exam, not for other purposes. It probably did not much influence modern Chinese essay writing, because the exam was abolished in 1905, and the literary language was replaced by a vernacular language in the early 20th century (chaps. 8 and 10).

The traditional structure of prose writing in China, and also in Korean and Japanese, is said to consists of four steps:

1. *qi*: Present an argument.
2. *cheng*: Develop or elucidate it.
3. *zhuan*: Turn the idea to a subtheme or to another view point.
4. *jie*: Conclude.

One would think that steps 1, 2, and 4 are required in any well-written exposition. Step 3 could be optional: A simple topic may not require it, while a complex topic may require it, even repeatedly.

The Western paragraph structure has been adopted in East Asian writing in modern times. A paragraph begins with an indentation by one character or graph in Korean and Japanese (fig. 7-1) or by two characters in Chinese. Paragraphs tend to be long. In a recent book on the correct writing of the Korean language, I found some pages without any paragraph break. Such very long paragraphs seldom occur in recent English writings.

Some Western scholars claim that paragraphing differs between the West and the East even today. For example, Kaplan (1966: 10) characterizes Chinese and Korean writing as "indirect." A paragraph develops

> "turning and turning in a widening gyre." The circles or gyres turn around the
> subject and show it from a variety of tangential views, but the subject is never

looked at directly. Things are developed in terms of what they are not, rather than in terms of what they are.

Kaplan further claims that English essays by four Chinese students he examined resemble the format of the eight-legged essay (described above). They lack unity and coherence.

Other Western researchers claim that writing by Koreans and Japanese lack a statement of purpose (Eggington 1987), or that a purpose exists but its introduction is delayed (Hinds 1990). A Japanese rhetorician, Tayama (1983: 23) writes:

> [Western] paragraphs differ from Japanese paragraphs. In European languages, the most important information comes at the beginning [of a paragraph], as shown in figure A (an upside down triangle, with its base at the top and its apex at the bottom). The rest [of the paragraph] is an enlargement of, supplement to, and filling in [that information]. By contrast, a Japanese paragraph does not put the important information at its beginning. Initially the [important] information appears in dribs and drabs. As the paragraph progresses, more and more important information appears, and the end is the most important. And the end is valuable. A reverberation or trailing feeling lingers on. (A Japanese paragraph structure is illustrated by a rightside up triangle.)

Tayama goes on to claim that this Japanese structure (a light and soft beginning that builds up to a heavy ending) is found also in the structure of a Japanese sentence, essay, and book. However, the above paragraph by Tayama himself does not support his claim in that it is more Western than "Japanese" in structure. In translating it into English from Japanese, I was more struck by its omission of linguistic items (enclosed in square brackets) than by its so-called Japanese structure.

Other researchers find no fundamental structural differences in essays written by East Asians and Westerners (Kubota 1992; Mohan and Lo 1985; Taylor and Tingguang 1991). An effective paragraph structure, characterized at the beginning of this section, has evolved to help a writer organize his or her thoughts and convey them effectively to the readers. To the extent that writers everywhere have the same goals, they are likely to use similar paragraph structures in whatever scripts and languages they may write. More than 2000 years ago Confucius said, "The purpose of writing essays is to express one's opinions clearly" (Lai Ming 1964: 318).

Let us end this section with a model paragraph from the *Liji (Record of Rites)*, one of the Five Confucian classics (chap. 10) compiled more than 2200 years ago. (*Li* means 'rites' or 'code of behavior'.)

> The princes of today are greedy in their search after material goods. They indulge themselves in pleasure and neglect their duties and carry themselves with a proud air. They take all they can from the people and invade the territory of good rulers against the will of the people, and they go out to get what they want without regard for what is right. This is the way of the modern rulers, while that was the way of the ancient rulers whom I [Confucius] just spoke of. The rulers of today do not follow *li*. [Lin 1938: 217]

8
Reforming Spoken and Written Chinese

Reform of spoken and written language may be nowhere more urgent than in modern China. Because Chinese characters are numerous and complex in shape, and do not indicate sounds well, they are hard to master and inconvenient to look up in a dictionary. A text is sometimes written in a classical literary style that is removed from everyday speech. The language itself has several mutually unintelligible "dialects" that hamper oral communication. These problems are serious and pressing.

As early as the third century BC, the first Qin emperor standardized the Chinese characters ("Evolution of Script Styles" in chap. 3). But subsequent imperial governments paid little attention to the problems of language and scripts, except that the Ming and the Qing governments (14th to the early 20th centuries AD) promoted *guanhua* ('speech of officials') among bureaucrats who spoke different "dialects."

In the 20th century the two republics, Nationalist and subsequently Communist, have paid much more attention to language and script reform. Reform is closely tied to three aspirations of the Chinese people: nationalism (one standard language for one unified nation); modernization (the use of a modern vernacular style instead of a classic literary style of writing; the time and effort needed to master characters should be used instead to learn modern science); and populism (a literary style of writing is enjoyed only by a small elite group, whereas a vernacular style is closer to the speech of the masses; numerous and complex characters can be mastered only by a small group of privileged people and not by the masses).

Language and script reform could involve:
- adopting and promoting a national standard language;
- replacing a classic literary style with a vernacular style of writing;
- deciding whether and how to simplify characters;
- limiting the number of characters for common use and school instruction;
- devising a phonetic script and then deciding whether to use it as an auxiliary script or as the only script.

How these problems are solved bear on how well children are educated in schools and how widely literacy is spread through the nation. Let us take them up one by one. For this chapter I consulted authors such as Norman (1988), Ramsey (1987), Seybolt and Chiang (1978), and Zhou (1987) as well as many others cited in the text.

Mandarin and Putonghua (Common Speech)

In the vast territory of China, there are seven mutually unintelligible major "dialects" and over 50 different ethnic minority languages (chap. 2 "Spoken Chinese"). With such a diverse set of "dialects" and languages, it is difficult to unify the nation or to adopt a single phonetic writing system. Accordingly, various central governments have sporadically tried to adopt and promote a form of standard language. The motto is, "national unity through linguistic unification." For over 600 years, while the capital was usually in Beijing, the speech based on the Beijing "dialect" or Mandarin has been the accepted lingua franca for communication among bureaucrats from different regions speaking mutually unintelligible "dialects."

In 1912, soon after the new republic was founded, its ministry of education held a conference to discuss issues such as establishing a standard national pronunciation for characters and adopting a set of phonetic symbols to represent the sounds of characters. After three months of wrangling between the northern Mandarin faction and the southern non-Mandarin faction, the conference recommended that the sounds of Mandarin become the national standard. The republic viewed China as one nation inhabited by one people speaking one language. Its language policy was to achieve a single *guoyu* ('national language') at the expense of the ethnic minority languages spoken by the Tibetans, Mongols, and other groups, as well as the "dialects" spoken by the Han Chinese in Guangzhou (Canton), Shanghai, and other regions. *Guoyu* was to be used as a means of official communication and also for instruction in schools. To assuage opponents' apprehension, the proponents of linguistic unification had to allow that anyone may speak the national language, but nobody had to speak it. In time, the National Language Unification Commission was formed, and in 1932 the commission published "A glossary of frequently used characters in national pronunciation," whose sounds were based on the speech of Beijing.

Opposing the view of China as a unitary nation were the liberals and leftists, who viewed China as a multi-national state made up of many ethnic minorities, of which the Han Chinese was only one. They wanted to allow speakers of different "dialects" and ethnic minorities to keep their own languages. A national language would be an addition to, rather than a replacement for, other forms of speech.

In 1949 the People's Republic of China was founded, with its capital still in Beijing. It set up a committee for language and writing reform, called since 1954 "the Committee for Chinese Writing Reform" under the State Council, the highest administrative organ of China. In 1956 the State Council published a document called "Direction with respect to the promotion of the common speech," which reads in part as follows:

> The foundation for the unification of the Chinese language is already in existence. It is Putonghua, which has as its standard pronunciation the Peking [Beijing] pronunciation, as its basic dialect the Northern dialect, and as its grammatical model the exemplary literary works written in the modern colloquial language.

Putonghua was a form of speech that was popular among merchants near the end of the Qing dynasty (1644–1912). It was close to Mandarin but retained elements of various "dialects"; today it still incorporates elements from other "dialects" as well as from the speech of workers and peasants. Although its pronunciation and vocabulary are codified in semi-official dictionaries, Putonghua is rarely spoken in its standardized form outside the region of Beijing. Non-Han ethnic minorities such as Tibetans and Mongols keep their own languages but learn Putonghua in the upper levels of schools.

The Chinese in Taiwan and Singapore also use Putonghua, though it is called *guoyu* ('national language') in Taiwan and *huayu* ('the language of Han people') in Singapore. In China itself, the term *hanyu* seems to be gaining currency, especially in academic writings, at the expense of a purely functional designation like *Putonghua* ('common speech'), which lacks any specific reference to the Chinese either as an ethnic or cultural entitiy.

In China since 1956 there have been several directives on the use of Putonghua in schools. The 1990 directive stipulates that by the year 2000 Putonghua should be the language of teaching in primary schools in cities and in key schools in rural areas ("Instruction of and in Putonghua" in chap. 9). The general public is exposed to spoken Putonghua via film, radio, TV, and public announcements over loud speakers. Radios and TV sets are now available throughout the nation, even in rural communities. TV and radio stations not only broadcast in Putonghua but also give lessons in it. The public is exposed also to materials, such as newspapers and government documents, written in it. In big cities like Shanghai and Guangzhou (Canton), people may speak their local "dialects" at home but use Putonghua for educational and official functions.

Thanks to their exposure to this variety of spoken and written materials, educated Chinese from all parts of the country learn, or rather pick up, enough Putonghua to get by. In most regions, including southern cities, retail store and sales personnel may understand, if not speak, it. This salutary state is a far cry from pre-revolutionary China, where outsiders who did not know the local "dialect" could quickly find themselves hopelessly lost.

All in all, the campaign for Putonghua has been more successful among the youth than among older adults, among the educated than the uneducated, in the north than in the south, in urban than in rural areas, and in listening skills than in speaking skills.

Literary vs Vernacular Language

One of the objectives of language and script reform is to move from a classic literary style of writing, called *wenyan* ('literary language') to a simple, vernacular style of everyday speech, called *baihua* ('plain speech' or 'vernacular language'). To roughly distinguish the two, the literary language can be understood only when read, while the vernacular language can be understood even in listening. The vernacular movement in China is analogous to one that occurred about 500 years ago in Renaissance Europe, when the dead Latin language was replaced as a literary medium by the living local languages, such as Italian and French.

Chinese prose and poetry were written in a classic literary style for a few thousand years. It was first established as the written language in the Zhou dynasty (1100–256 BC), then standardized and consolidated in the Qin dynasty (221–206 BC) and the Han dynasty (206 BC–AD 220). It lasted into the early 20th century. It is in the classic literary language that the important and influential texts were written for centuries: the Confucian classics, which had an enormous influence on traditional China (chap. 10); the laws and documents of the central government; and poems, prose, and idioms. Thus the literary language enjoyed prestige akin to that enjoyed by Classical Arabic in Islamic countries.

In China the written language was never a transcription of the spoken language; even at the beginning it may have been a stylistically refined version of a spoken language. With the passage of time the written language and the spoken language have separated widely, as the former has changed little while the latter has changed much. The classic literary language differs substantially from the present vernacular language in speech sounds, syntax, words, and expressions. In particular, its words tend to be of single morpheme–syllables with many homophones, whereas many words used in the modern vernacular have two morpheme–syllables ("Why Compound Words?" in chap. 2). The literary language does not use as many empty (grammatical) morphemes or sentence subjects, as does the vernacular language. The meanings of some of the literary words and expressions are no longer the same as those used today. Its allusions are often obscure.

A text written in the literary language is terse and elliptic, sometimes to the point of being cryptic. Many idiomatic phrases in the literary language can be understood only after several words have been filled in. One of Confucius's sayings,

jun jun chen chen fu fu zi zi ('rule rule minister minister father father son son') is paraphrased as "Let the ruler rule as he should; let the minister be a minister as he should; let the father act as a father should; and let the son act as a son should." You have seen more examples of the literary style in "Compound Words and Idioms" (in chap. 4) as well as in Figure 5-1 (a paragraph consisting of repetitions of the syllable *shi*) and Figure 4-2ab (Du Fu's poem and Confucius's saying).

Chinese poetry written in the literary style exploits to its advantage the ambiguous word classes and the lack of inflection in the language. It uses rhymes and parallelism. The following two lines are taken from an eight-line poem by the great Tang dynasty poet, Li Bo (712–770). The lines are laconic yet evocative.

> green tree   hear sing bird
> blue pagoda   see dance person

Nothing is said about who hears the singing bird or sees the dancing person. Does it matter? In each line, the first two words set the stage, where the action depicted in the last three words takes place.

Those who value the literary language find it elegant, economic, and evocative, but for those who oppose it, the language is elitist, cryptic, and stilted. One aspect of language and script reform is to replace the literary style with a vernacular style of writing that reflects modern everyday speech and so is familiar to readers. As well, the vernacular style contains many two-morpheme words and empty (grammatical) words, thus reducing the chance of misunderstanding. All in all, it is more comprehensible to ordinary people than is the classic literary style. (For Koreans and Japanese, the classic literary language is more understandable than is the modern vernacular language, precisely because the former does not contain too many grammatical morphemes that are unique to Chinese. As well, many Chinese words and idioms in Korean and Japanese come from the classical literature.)

The vernacular style, which also kept changing, came into use as a literary form gradually over hundreds of years. Beginning in the Later/Eastern Han dynasty (AD 25–220) Buddhist works, which were translations and paraphrases of Indian originals, began to have a vernacular flavor. During the Tang (618–907) and Song dynasties (960–1279) some dramas, fantastic tales, and novels were written in the vernacular. During the Mongol rule in the Yuan dynasty (1279–1368), when the civil service exams were suspended, educated Chinese turned to the writing of novels and plays, often in the vernacular. During the Ming and Qing dynasties (the 14th to the early 20th centuries) some novels and Christian missionary tracts were written in it (see "Books and Publications" in chap. 10).

But it was in the early 20th century that the use of the vernacular began to spread widely. From 1918, one influential magazine *New Youth,* co-edited by six professors of Beijing University, published entirely in the vernacular, which was later to be called *guoyu* ('national language'). One of its editors, Hu Shi, experimented with writing poems in the vernacular, a collection of which was published in 1920.

The vernacular movement was part of the May 4th Movement, which was a student-led crusade for nationalism, modernization, and democracy, indeed for a new China. The May 4th demonstration of 1919 saw a large group of university students assembled at—where else?—Tiananmen Square to protest against the Versailles treaty, which transferred Germany's Shandong concessions to Japan.[1] The students then marched toward the foreign-legation quarter, handing out broadsheets to the watching citizens, calling on them to join in the protest. These broadsheets, as well as many periodicals and newspapers of that heady period, were written in the vernacular.

The motto of the vernacular movement said, "A dead language cannot produce a living literature." More specifically, the movement demanded:

• a new writing style to go with modern thought;
• plain, simple, and expressive literature of the people in place of the stereotyped and cryptic classicism;
• emancipation of the individual by destroying the written language that had been the repository of Confucian morality and Daoist superstition.

In 1920, in a bow to the reform movement, the ministry of education of the republic stipulated that schoolchildren in the first two grades should be taught exclusively in the vernacular. Two years later textbooks at all levels of schools were written in it. Today the modern vernacular is the language taught in all Chinese primary and secondary schools, both in mainland China and Taiwan, and is used in writing of all types, such as literary, journalistic, administrative, technical, and personal. It represents Putonghua, but is by no means identical to the spoken standard. In the West, too, written language is not necessarily the same as spoken language, because written language tends to be more structured and explicit than spoken language to compensate for the lack of situational context and listeners' feedback.

The literary language has not entirely been replaced by the vernacular. It can still be found occasionally in political slogans, such as *Baihua qifang, baijia zhengming*

---

[1]Tiananmen Square is named after the Tianan (Heavenly Peace) Gate, which was once the south gate of the Imperial City. It was rebuilt and expanded after the founding of the PRC to accommodate gatherings of five hundred thousand people. This is the place where the huge pro-democracy demonstration was held in June 1989.

('[Let a] hundred flower[s] bloom [and let a] hundred school[s] [of] thought contend'), which had an ancient origin but re-appeared during a brief political–cultural thaw in May–June, 1957. Idioms and lines of poetry and prose written in the literary style tend to creep into other material written basically in the vernacular. In randomly selected pages of a political magazine, every page contained words and phrases taken from classical Chinese (Li and Thompson 1982). Because of its appearance in contemporary writing as well as its importance in its own right, the classical literary language is taught as a subject in schools not only in China and Taiwan but also in Japan and Korea.

The literary language depends on Chinese characters for its existence, because prose or poetry that consists of arrangements of monosyllabic morphemes, many of which are homophones, is unlikely to be fully understood in a phonetic script.

Rationalizing the Chinese Writing System

Chinese characters have advantages, some discussed already and some to be discussed further in Parts II and III. At the same time, they have three obvious disadvantages: they are numerous, complex in shape, and deficient in sound indication. They are often said to be difficult to learn and use. The next few sections discuss how these three disadvantages of characters can be ameliorated, though not eliminated.

As the first approach to rationalizing the writing system, a reasonable number of characters must be designated for school instruction and common use, as is done in S. Korea and Japan, where this number is about 2,000. Admittedly, limiting the number of characters for daily use will not be easy in Chinese, where the names of places and people alone require a few thousand different characters, and where there is no phonetic script that can be used in text along with characters as in Korean and Japanese. Even if the number of characters were to be limited, it would still have to be far larger than in Korean and Japanese. The Chinese need characters to represent all their words and morphemes, whereas the Koreans and the Japanese use characters mainly to represent words adopted from Chinese and not necessarily their native words.

In "Number of Characters" (in chap. 3) we settled on the following nice round numbers of characters:

- 50,000 in a large dictionary
- 6,000 for scholarly, high-level literacy
- 3,500 for functional literacy and school instruction
- 2,000 for limited literacy

What is critical for mass literacy in China is to choose the characters in the last two lists with utmost care, after extensive research, and then to adhere to them closely. The lists need to be revised from time to time to reflect changes in the use of characters. Students of the Chinese classics may continue to learn many characters beyond this list, much as students of English classics learn to read Anglo-Saxon or Latin. Remember, even 2,000 characters can generate thousands of multi-character compound words, and complex characters not in the list can be replaced by compound words.

In the second approach to rationalizing the writing system, complex characters are made simpler by reducing their number of strokes. Among the several objectives of language and script reform, this kind of simplification has already been implemented, as it was deemed, mistakenly, to be a non-controversial and conservative part of an overall reform. Yet, as discussed in "Complex vs Simple Characters" (in chap. 3), there is no strong evidence to show that moderately complex characters are more difficult to read than their simplified versions.

Let us trace the chronology of simplification policies. For long time, writers unofficially simplified some characters to save effort and time. The following discussion is about official attempts to use simplified characters in all reading material. In 1935 the Nationalist government published a table of simplified characters but did not promote it. Even now the government in Taiwan, in the interest of maintaining traditional culture, shuns the use of simplified characters.

The People's Republic of China has taken a different path. In 1956 the Committee for Chinese Writing Reform published a list of 29 characters to be abolished and 486 characters to be simplified. In 1964 it published "A comprehensive list of [2,238] simplified characters" to supersede the much shorter list of 1956. The 2,238 officially simplified characters represent about two-thirds of the 3,500 characters needed for functional literacy. This definitive list of simplified characters was distributed widely around the country. In 1977 the Committee re-issued the definitive list along with an appendix containing a list of 200 additional simplified characters, but in 1978 it withdrew the appendix in face of widespread resistance from the population. So soon after the traumatic Cultural Revolution, the population yearned for stability. So, for the time being there is no more simplification, and the 1964 list of 2,238 simplified characters stands. The simplified characters are taught in schools and used in government publications as well as in popular newspapers and magazines.

Among the nations that use Chinese characters, China has performed the most drastic simplification. The characters simplified in China are used also in Singapore. In Taiwan, Hong Kong, and South Korea simplified characters (not necessarily simplified in the same manner as in China) may not be used in printing, though they may be used in handwriting and calligraphy. In Japan a few hundred characters have been moderately simplified. Some of the simplified characters are identical to their Chinese counterparts, but some are quite different, as shown in Table 8-1 (the numbers come from a Japanese source; Hayashi 1982). Sadly, some of the characters so drastically simplified in China are no longer recognizable to overseas Chinese or to Japanese or Koreans who use characters in their original shapes.

Table 8-1. Characters Simplified in China and Japan

Country	Number	Example		
		Original	China	Japan
in China and Japan	440			
different		廣	广	広
same		學	学	学
in China only	670	電	电	電
in Japan only	70	佛	佛	仏

Simplifying Character Shapes

Character shapes have been simplified in a variety of ways, such as selecting simpler, shorthand versions of complex characters, replacing complex characters with simple ones that share the same sounds, eliminating parts—semantic or phonetic components, inner details—of characters, or letting one or a few strokes stand for a complex component of a character. Generally, the simpler forms adopted had been already used in old literature or by the masses as shorthand forms. This trend is one more example of an orthodox or official script taking elements of a popular script ("Evolution of Script Styles" in chap. 3). In the examples of simplified characters shown in Table 8-2, some simplifications are judicious but some are not.

In Table 8-2, the first five rows are concerned with the sounds of characters.

Row 1. In a meaning composite containing three semantic components ('speak', 'edge', 'mind'), two components, including the most critical, 'mind', are replaced by a phonetic, *ren*, even though its tone is wrong. The remaining semantic component for 'speak' is simplified.

Row 2. The phonetic *mian* is retained but the radical 'wheat plant' is deleted from the character meaning 'flour', 'wheat', or 'noodle'. Now two different morphemes, 'noodle' and 'face', share not only the same sound but also the same shape.

Table 8-2. Original Complex Characters and their Simplified Shapes

	Complex Character	Sound	Morpheme	Simplified Character
1.	認	rèn	recognize	认
2.	麵	mìan	flour	面
3.	鬬	dòu	fight	斗
4.	戰	zhàn	war	战
5.	撲	pū	pounce	扑
6.	難	nán	difficult	难
7.	衆	zhòng	multitude	众
8.	淚	lèi	tear	泪
9.	家	jia	house	宀
10.	廠	chǎng	factory	厂
11.	萬	wàn	ten thousand	万
12.	門	mén	door	门

Row 3. A simple character replaces the original complex character, because it happens to have the same sound as the complex one. Actually, the simple character is pronounced as *dou* (falling tone) for 'fight' but as *dou* (fall–rise) for its original meaning 'funnel' or 'quantity measure'. The pictographic origin of the outer shape of the complex character—two hands fighting—is lost.

Row 4. A complex phonetic is replaced by a simple phonetic.

Row 5. Of two homophones with similar meanings, the simpler one is retained. The next four rows are concerned with semantic components or radicals.

Row 6. The complex radical is simplified.

Row 7. This archaic form resurrected is not only simple but also introduces a semantic component, namely the character 'person' tripled.

Row 8. The simplified character for 'tears' is now a meaning composite ('water' + 'eye'); the only appropriate semantic component in the original was 'water'.

Row 9. The original character for 'house' contains a pig under a roof for the reason given in "Characters Tell Stories" (in chap. 4). The new one replaces a pig with a person. But this character is one of many simplified unofficially by the general public.

The next three characters are concerned with shapes.

Row 10. The inner detail is unceremoniously gutted, leaving only a hollow outer shell. Unfortunately, some other characters have been simplified in the same manner and have similar shapes. See the middle character in the first row in Table 8-1.

Row 11. The shorthand version of the original is adopted.

Row 12. The cursive form of the original is adopted. But the pictographic origin of the original is lost ("Characters Tell Stories" in chap. 4).

In an inconsistent and confusing simplification, a semantic or phonetic component is replaced by its cursive form, and the simplified component is used in some but not all characters that contain it. For example, as an independent character 言 *yan* ('speech') with seven strokes is simple enough to escape simplification. But as a radical, it has been simplified to two flowing strokes, as in the character for 'recognize' in *Row 1*. Moreover, the simplified radical is used only when it occurs as the left component of a character (which is most common) and not when it occurs as the bottom, top, or right component. Now a Chinese reader has to learn two shapes of one radical. The same is true of other radicals, such as 金 *jin* ('metal') and 食 *shi* ('food').

Simplification by means of phonetic loaning sacrifices one of the advantages of characters, namely, that characters distinguish morphemes with the same sound. Simplification sacrifices pictographic quality, which has a mnemonic value for some characters. It sacrifices meaning-cuing semantic components and sound-cuing phonetics in some characters. And such simplification methods are applied inconsistently, i.e., to some characters but not to others.

If the semantic, phonetic, and visual advantages of characters are to be sacrificed in order to represent the sounds of characters and simplify their shapes, then why not adopt a phonetic script in the first place? All the Chinese sounds can be expressed using a proper phonetic script with 27 letters, like Pinyin, or with 37 symbols, like Zhuyinfuhao ("Roman Letters and Phonetic Symbols," below). Or Mandarin/Putonghua could be written using a syllabary of 1,300 signs for its 1,300 tone syllables. These phonetic letters or signs, since their numbers are not large, need not be as complex in shape as characters.

In China many people succumbed to a mania for creating their own unofficial, idiosyncratically simplified characters, such as *Row 9*, thus contributing to confusion. And simple characters have not completely replaced their original complex versions; on the contrary, original characters are increasingly used in the more conservative era since the Cultural-Revolution. The original characters, because they are used in prosperous Taiwan and Hong Kong, lend an aura of prestige and sophistication. A deluxe edition of Mao Zedong's poetry is written in them, as are most classical texts. In calligraphy, too, for esthetic effects original characters are preferred to some drastically simplified ones. They may appear on shop signs and merchandise packages. Now *The People's Daily* publishes its overseas edition in the original characters.

Because of the increasing popularity and importance of the original complex characters, some literate Chinese learn characters in both simple and complex forms. They learn the simple characters and then their complex versions, whereas before the simplification the complex characters were learned first. But many ordinary people in China itself know only the simplified characters.

One of the advantages of logographic characters is that characters can be recognized even among peoples who speak different languages because of the relatively unchanging shapes and meanings of characters in the face of changing sounds. This advantage has been diminished by the drastic changes caused by the simplification of over 2,000 common characters in China but not in Japan and South Korea. For economic reasons the Chinese want to have close contacts with the Japanese and the South Koreans, and some Chinese study the Japanese language. So it makes little sense to diminish the ability of Chinese to communicate with their potential economic partners. In writing this book, I used word processing software for English in conjunction with Japanese. The Japanese part of the software enabled me to write Chinese characters, but the differences in the shapes of some common characters used in China and Japan presented a problem to me. I solved the problem in two ways. One was to use original characters where possible (with a warning that they are used in simplified forms in China), and the other was to draw by hand some simplified characters that are needed for illustration, as was done for Table 8-2.

Regretably, the large-scale script reform, with its far-reaching consequences, was implemented with much debate but without thorough research on its method and effect. Are the sounds and meanings of characters learned by children and recognized by adults faster in their simplified than in their original forms? Research shows no unequivocal advantage of simple characters over complex ones in reading and remembering, or even in writing ("Complex vs Simple Characters" in chap. 3). Apparently, a simple character with too few strokes does not form a distinct enough shape. How should characters be simplified, drastically as in China or moderately as in Japan? How about using characters in original shapes in printing but in simplified shapes in handwriting, as is done in Taiwan, Hong Kong, and S. Korea?

I may lament the fact that the Chinese have not done as effective a job as they could have in simplifying characters, but I do not oppose their attempts at simplification. On the contrary, I assert that there is no need for any characters to be so complex as to contain over, say, 21 strokes, especially if only 3,500 common characters are used. Remember, great complexity is needed only to ensure that infrequent characters can be discriminated from 50,000 others.

If characters are to be simplified, ideally there should be research on how to do it to best effect for writing, reading, and learning. Furthermore, this research should be done cooperatively among the peoples who use characters in different parts of the world. Judiciously simplified characters should retain the following components or qualities:

1. meaning-bearing semantic components and sound-cuing phonetic components;
2. visual discriminability;
3. esthetic quality (e.g., balance, symmetry);

4. similarity to the original shapes.

In carrying out reform of the language and script in China, one solid experiment would be better than 100 armchair debates!

Roman Letters and Phonetic Symbols

A good script should represent adequately both meaning and sound. As a logograph a Chinese character represents the meaning of a morpheme better than its sound. As described in "Sound Representation by Characters" (chap. 5), Chinese characters are not good at indicating sounds: phonetic components are numerous and unreliable, phonetic loans are confusing, and Fanqie ('cut and join') is cumbersome. These indicators of sounds can be used only by people who already have some knowledge of characters, and so do not help beginners who need them most. What is needed is a small set of phonetic symbols that represent the Chinese sounds directly, precisely, reliably, and simply. Because the inventory of sounds of a language is far smaller (a few dozens) than that of morphemes (many thousands), a set of true phonetic symbols can be small, and the symbols in a small set can afford to be simply shaped.

Devising a set of phonetic symbols for the Chinese language has turned out to be highly emotional and controversial, fraught with many problems. Should there be seven different sets to represent the seven different "dialects"? If only one set is to be devised, which "dialect" should it represent? Should it be a syllabary or an alphabet? If an alphabet, should it be the English (Roman), the Russian (Cyrillic), or some other alphabet? Should it be based on the sounds of English, German, French, or Russian? Should tones be represented, and if so, how? Most controversial of all, should a set of phonetic symbols supplement or supplant Chinese characters for general writing?

Over the past few hundred years, and especially in the past few decades, there have been many attempts at developing an alphabet for Chinese, first by foreigners and then by the Chinese themselves. European Christian missionaries who came to China in the 16th and 17th centuries were the first to write Chinese using the letters of a Roman alphabet. Among them, *A Guidance to Chinese Romanized Spelling* (c. 1605) by the Italian Jesuit Matteo Ricci was adopted by foreign clergy in China. In 1625 the French missionary N. Trigault wrote the book *Aids to the Ear and the Eye of Western Scholars* using a Roman alphabet to transcribe Chinese characters.

In the 19th century, Christian missionaries devised a number of Roman transcriptions for writing Chinese "dialects," and some of them, like those for the Amoy "dialect," were used widely among Chinese Christian converts. Many books, including the Bible, were published in it. Some overseas Chinese still use the alphabet for Amoy when corresponding with their families in China. (Amoy, now called Xiamen, is a major port in Fujian Province in southern China.)

Turning to Chinese efforts at devising phonetic scripts, there had been at least twenty by the end of the imperial era in the early 20th century, some based on Chinese characters, some on shorthand symbols, and some on a Roman alphabet. In 1918 the government promulgated Zhuyinfuhao (National/Mandarin Phonetic Symbols), a set of 37 symbols fashioned out of Chinese characters. Table 8-3 shows 14 of the 37 symbols along with their Pinyin equivalents. Each symbol of this phonetic system represents the initial or final sound of a Chinese syllable; the initial is used like an initial consonant in an alphabet but the final is used like a vowel sequence or a vowel with a final consonant, which may only be *-n, -ng, -r.* The system has contributed to promoting Mandarin as the national language. It is still used in Taiwan as an aid to pronunciation, but because of its difference from a Roman alphabet it is not convenient for foreigners.

Table 8-3. Zhuyinfuhao and Pinyin

Initial		Final	
Zhuyin	Pinyin	Zhuyin	Pinyin
ㄅ	b	ㄚ	a
ㄆ	p	ㄛ	o
ㄇ	m	ㄟ	ei
ㄈ	f	ㄩ	ü
ㄑ	q	一	i
ㄊ	t	ㄦ	er
ㄋ	n	ㄡ	ou

In 1928 a national romanization, a true alphabet, devised by Chao and other Chinese linguists was promulgated as a second form of phonetic script. But because of its complex system of tone marking, the national romanization has never gained popularity.

In the early 20th century a group of Chinese linguists, in consultation with Russian linguists, devised a Latinized new script in the former Soviet Union, mainly to promote literacy among Chinese workers living in the Soviet Far East. Though devised in the Soviet Union, it used a Latin or Roman alphabet rather than a Cyrillic alphabet. The alphabet appeared to be based on several northern "dialects" and was read by individual Chinese according to his or her own "dialect." It did not mark tones. Though the Latinized script ceased to be used in the Soviet Far East after 1936 when the Chinese there were repatriated, it attracted many supporters in China itself, especially among leftist intellectuals such as the influential writer Lu Xun. In 1938 schools were set up in certain Communist-controlled areas in China to instruct peasants and soldiers in the new alphabet, and subsequently a newspaper and textbooks were published in it. This alphabet was looked upon as a powerful weapon in the fight against illiteracy but not as a replacement for Chinese characters.

How did the Communist leaders view a phonetic script? In 1936 Mao Zedong said in an interview with the American journalist Edgar Snow in Yan'an:

> We believe Latinization is a good instrument with which to overcome illiteracy. Chinese characters are so difficult to learn that even the best system of rudimentary characters, or simplified teaching, does not equip the people with a really efficient and rich vocabulary. *Sooner or later, we believe, we will have to abandon characters altogether if we are to create a new social culture in which the masses fully participate.* [1968: 446, Snow's emphasis]

In 1951 Mao re-asserted: "The written language must be reformed; we must proceed in the direction of phonetization being taken by all languages of the world." But later, Communist leaders became more cautious, judging from Premier Zhou Enlai's remarks to a former French minister of education:

> In the 1950's, we tried to romanize the writing. But all those who had received an education, and whose services we absolutely needed to expand education, were firmly attached to the ideograms. They were already so numerous, and we had so many things to upset, that we have put off the reform until later. [Peyrfitte 1973: 153]

Pinyin vs Wade–Giles Romanization

Today one of the best known romanization systems for Chinese is Wade–Giles. In 1867 Sir Thomas F. Wade (Secretary of the British Consulate in Beijing) wrote *A Mandarin Language Reader* using a Roman alphabet of his own devising, which was later modified by Herbert A. Giles (British Consul) for his Chinese–English dictionary published in 1912. The Wade–Giles system was intended for international use, and so was based not only on English but also on French and German sounds. It was used widely for several decades, until it was officially supplanted by a new Roman alphabet called Pinyin in the late 20th century in the PRC, though not in Taiwan. It is still used in the library catalogue systems in the West.

In 1958 the People's Republic of China promulgated Pinyin ('spell sound' or phonetic spelling), mainly to write the sounds of Putonghua ('common speech'), which they were promoting. Pinyin uses the 26 letters of the English alphabet plus *ü*, which is pronounced as in German. It is based largely on the Latinized new script that had been devised by the Chinese linguists in the former Soviet Union. Reflecting the choices made by these linguists, the Pinyin uses three "leftover" letters to represent Mandarin sounds that lack handy equivalents in the Latin alphabet: *c* represents *ts* in *its*, *q* represents *ch* in *chip*, and *x* represents *ss* in *sissy*. Initially these unfamiliar letter–sound relations are confusing to readers of English and other Roman alphabets, but before long they become familiar, thanks to their consistent letter–sound relations.

Pinyin vowel letters have more or less consistent sound values, those of Italian or Spanish, with some variations that depend on phonetic context. Pinyin spelling normally does not mark tones, except in new words for children, for "dialect" speakers, or for non-Chinese speakers. It leaves spaces between syllable–morphemes rather than between words, as in character writing; thus, *dian hua* and not *dianhua* ('telephone'). However, in this book, as in many other English-language books on Chinese, spaces are left usually between words rather than between syllable–morphemes.

On January 1, 1979, Pinyin was adopted as the official romanization in China and has since been used by the New China News Agency, the principal source of official news for journalists and diplomats. It has been adopted by the United Nations and other international agencies as well as by academic communities, though not in library systems in the West. It is also sometimes used as a phonetic script to call out characters on a computer ("Computerizing Chinese Characters," below) and to write Chinese words in this book for readers of English. The Wade–Giles and other spellings are kept only for a handful of names of Chinese places and people well known in that spelling, such as Chiang Kai-shek (Jiang Jieshi).

Table 8-4 lists the initials and some finals that differ between the two romanizing systems, Pinyin and Wade–Giles. Some initials and finals—e.g., those in *a, ha, liao, mai, nan, seng*—are the same in the two, but some differ. By and large, Pinyin represents the Chinese sounds better than the Wade–Giles system, and does so with fewer extra marks. It can be seen on road signs, store fronts, and other public places, but it is not used in text such as letters, documents, newspapers, and books. It is put to specialized uses: Teaching the sounds of Chinese characters to foreigners as well as to Chinese children (chap. 9 "Learning Hanzi, Pinyin, and Putonghua"); writing

Chinese names and words for foreign publications; telegraphy, indexing, and so on. Pinyin is particularly useful for input to a word processor, as described in the next section.

Unfortunately, today at least three different romanization systems are still used, confusing the users. In many publications we still see some Chinese names spelled in the Wade–Giles system: *Mao Zedong (Mao Tse-tung), Kangxi (Kang-Hsi)* and *Qin (Ch'in)* (Wade–Giles spelling in parentheses). Place names on maps and gazetteers are sometimes spelled in the former Post Office system (in parentheses), which tries to approximate the local pronunciation: *Beijing (Peking), Xiamen (Amoy),* and *Xianggang (Hong Kong).*

Table 8-4. Romanization: The Initials and Some Finals that Differ in Pinyin and Wade–Giles

Initials		Some Finals	
Pinyin	Wade–Giles	Pinyin	Wade–Giles
b	p	-ie	-ieh
c	ts', tz'	ye	yeh
ch	ch'	er	erh
d	t	you	yu
g	k	yong	yung
j	ch	-ong	-ung
k	k'	-ian	-ien
p	p'	-iong	-iung
q	ch'	yan	yen
r	j	yi	i
t	t'		
x	hs		
z	ts, tz		
zh	ch		

Computerizing Chinese Characters

We live in an age of information and computers. Word processing on a personal computer using a phonetic script is commonplace in the West, and is spreading in such East Asian nations as Japan, S. Korea, and Taiwan. It makes writing easier, faster, and better for the users, who can write as fast as they think, and also can store and edit what they write. Its output is a clean printout. Word processing can be used not only for writing text but also for many other, ever expanding uses, such as electronic mail, electronic shopping, educational programs, bulletin boards, and desk-top publishing.

Compared to the few dozens of letters in an alphabet, Chinese characters are numerous, have complex shapes, and have changeable pronunciations across "dialects." Can they be used in a computer? Yes, they can, but only after much effort and expense to develop hardware and software. Even then, word processing in Chinese is not as efficient as in English. The following description is based on various sources—Liu (1991), Yin (1991), and Zhou (1991) in one edited book—as well as on Huang and Huang (1989).

Every computer system has its character set(s). A "character" is a member of a finite set that is used for expressing or controlling information. Characters are classified into graphic characters and control characters. Control characters are used in giving commands to a computer and are somewhat standardized internationally. Graphic characters can be defined by users. They have visual representations, and have concepts, names or readings, fields of uses, shapes, and codes. Graphic characters might be Arabic numerals, alphabetic letters, and Chinese characters.

The English character set, using ASCII (American Standard Code for Information Interchange) includes letters, numerals, punctuation marks, and control characters, 128 characters in all. It is a small and closed set. For example, the concept of "two" can be represented by the shape 2, the letter string *two*, or an ASCII code. The control character that marks the end of a line of text has no shape but might have the code 012.

By contrast, a Chinese character set is large and open-ended. In addition to the standard numerals, punctuation marks, and control characters, the set includes several thousand graphic characters. The Code of Chinese Graphic Characters for Information Interchange includes a primary set of 6,763 common Chinese characters and a supplementary set of 14,276 Chinese characters for special users. The primary set is further divided into a first level of 3,755 common Chinese characters arranged in the order of their Pinyin sounds, and a second level of 3,008 less common Chinese characters (whose sounds may not be known to a user) arranged according to 180 radicals. The Chinese character shapes in the primary set are simplified characters, but their original complex forms and variant forms are cross referenced. In addition to the Chinese characters, phonetic scripts — Pinyin (used in China) and Zhuyinfuhao (used in Taiwan) — have to be stored.

The shape of a character is stored in a computer in some manner that allows it to be printed or displayed on the screen, together with some label by which the user calls up the shape, using some kind of input method, typically a keyboard. There are basically two types of Chinese input methods, one type based on the shapes of the characters (Character-Code), and the other based on the sounds of characters, usually using Pinyin (Pinyin-to-Character Conversion). Each has several variations in the detail of how it works.

The Pinyin-input method allows you to call out a character by entering its sound in Pinyin. Here is how one particular Pinyin-input method works. Suppose you type in *zhong* , which has several homophonic characters, such as 中 and 忠. The computer will display in a character-generation box all the characters pronounced as *zhong*, several at a time. You view the first set looking for the desired character, the target. If you do not find it in the first set, you enter tabs to view the subsequent sets until you find the target. When you find it, you select it for entry in the text, close the character-generation box, and go on to the next character. The characters are usually arranged according to their frequency of occurrence, so that the target is likely to be found earlier rather than later. Also characters once chosen can be programmed to reappear as the first choice when the same sound is entered again.

Pinyin input is convenient, provided that you know Putonghua ('common speech'). You need to remember only the 27 Pinyin letters and their sounds. Calling up a character from a computer consumes less time and effort than does writing it stroke by stroke. You can call out characters even if you cannot recall their correct shapes. But the Pinyin-input method cannot be used by Chinese who do not speak Putonghua well, or by Japanese or Koreans. The latter can, however, use their own phonetic scripts.

One big problem with the phonetic input of Chinese is how to deal with the abundant homophones, those different morphemes and words that share the same sound. Even though a computer can display several homophonic characters from which the writer chooses a target, the process is time consuming and requires the user to have considerable knowledge about the use of Chinese characters.

There are ways to minimize the choosing process. One way is to differentiate the phonetic spellings of homophones according to their meanings. In one scheme the homophones with the sound of *feng* are spelled variously as follows: *feng* ('wind'), *fengs* ('summit'); *s* is the first letter of *shan*, 'mountain'); *fengss* ('to sew', *ss* represents *si*, 'silk'), *fengd* ('to seal'; *d* represents *dongci*, 'verb') and so on. To memorize many different, sometimes arbitrary, quasi-phonetic spellings for each of hundreds of syllables would not be easy for an ordinary user. Understandably, such a cumbersome scheme is not widely used. However, different spellings of a handful of very common empty (grammatical) words might save input time even for the casual user. For example, three empty words all with the sound of *de* might be spelled variously: the adjective suffix 的 as -*d*, the adverb suffix 地 as -*di*, the verb particle 待 as -*de*.

Two-thirds of the words in Chinese are compounds consisting of two syllable–morphemes. For such words, a better method of dealing with homophones might be to enter not one syllable at a time but word by word, or even phrase by phrase, because the larger or longer the linguistic unit, the less ambiguous it becomes. For example, to input *zhongguo* 中国 , if you enter *zhong* and *guo* separately, you will get several homophonic characters for each of these two syllables, as shown above for *zhong*. But if you enter the two-syllable-morpheme word, you will probably get the right characters immediately without choosing, because *zhongguo* has few homophones.

Pinyin-to-Character conversion based on words or phrases, even without indicating tones, is said to be 90% accurate in obtaining the correct characters. The accuracy rate improves to 95% when tones are marked on certain ambiguous words. In some experiments it improves to 97% when the translation to characters is based on even larger linguistic units, such as sentence or paragraphs. Entering by a sentence unit requires artificial intelligence techniques to specify the context in which a particular syllable is to be matched with a particular character. The word unit, on the other hand, requires that a large vocabulary list be stored in a computer. At present, Pinyin-to-Character Conversion is usually based on the word unit, and occasionally on the syllable unit.

One-third of the words of Chinese are monosyllabic, especially the frequent words, and some of them have many homophones. To differentiate these words the phonetic input can be modified to allow tones. But tone marking, whether using diacritic marks or numerals over, before, or after syllables (table 2-2), takes time, and so is usually omitted in phonetic input. In one scheme the most frequently occurring monosyllabic word is left without tone marking, while less frequent words are marked with tones. For example, at least four words have the sound *wo*, but only one of them occurs very frequently. So tone is not marked for *wo* ('I, me') but is marked for the other words. The same solution—mark tones only on infrequent members of a homophone set— can be applied if necessary to two-syllable words.

Some monosyllabic homophones have not only the same sounds but also the same tones, though they have different characters. How can they be dealt with? One scheme is differential spelling, suggested above for the three common empty words with the sound of *de*, which might be spelled differentially as -*d*, -*di*, and -*de*. In a similar way the homophonic monosyllabic word *you* might be spelled variously as *you* ('have'), *yeu* ('from'), and *iu* ('again').

An alternative to a sound-to-character conversion is a Character Code, which decomposes a character into various components. This method is tedious but is necessary, if you are copying a Chinese text or if you do not know the Putonghua/ Mandarin sounds of Chinese characters. There are several character codes, two of the most common being based on radicals and strokes. A radical system may use between 100 and 200 radicals, several of which are arranged on each input key. Out of the several radicals on each key, one is chosen depending on a second key, such as the shift and the option. To input 調, you type in the sequence of radicals 言冂 土 口. An efficient radical system should have a small yet sufficient keyboard and require only a few keystrokes, fewer than five, per Chinese character.

A Chinese character is made up of a number of strokes and can be assembled with a sequence of strokes. Stroke codes are simple in conception, but a code can be long. As the techniques of handwriting recognition are developed, a Chinese character, rather than being analyzed into a sequence of components and strokes, is input directly as a handwritten shape, bypassing a keyboard.

For typing Chinese characters into my English text, I use an alphabetic input that represents the sounds, but my phonetic input is based not on Pinyin (that represents the characters' Chinese sounds) but on Japanese Kana (and the characters' Japanese sounds). Since I am interested in comparing the use of Chinese characters by the Chinese, the Japanese, and the Koreans, my procedure enlightens me about differences and similarities in the shapes, sounds, and meanings of Chinese characters used by these three peoples of East Asia. I can use this procedure precisely because Chinese characters used by the three peoples are the same in shapes and meanings, even though they are not in sounds. But even the shapes are not always the same, as Table 8-1 shows, because the Chinese use many drastically simplified characters while the Japanese use some moderately simplified ones. The Japanese software I use, *SweetJAM* (1992), includes JIS (Japan Industrial Standard) character sets 1 and 2, but not 3, which would include the simplified Chinese characters used in China.

The product of word processing is usually characters printed on papers or displayed on a computer screen. Because many Chinese characters have complex shapes, programmers often display them in a block of 24 x 24 pixels (dots) or more, whereas English letters are legible when displayed 7 pixels high. Even with 24 x 24 pixels, an excessively complex Chinese character, say one with over 25 strokes, shows up on the screen only as a dark object whose inner detail cannot be easily perceived, as pointed out in "Complex vs Simple Characters" (in chap. 3). The problem is an issue for the writer who might not be able to see whether the correct character has been selected, but it is not an issue when the character is printed, since printing is normally done at a much higher resolution.

Computers can be used for typesetting and editing Chinese newspapers and for Chinese language instruction; they can be used for compiling Chinese dictionaries, Chinese classical literature, Chinese telephone directories, and other documents. Computerization of Chinese characters is improving and spreading.

Pinyin Complements Characters

Should Pinyin or some other phonetic script replace Chinese characters, and if so, when? This question touches the very soul of Chinese culture itself. To use a phonetic script as the sole script means nothing less than abandoning the Chinese characters that have lasted for several thousand years. To quote the distinguished Swedish Sinologue, Karlgren:

> If China does not abandon its peculiar script in favour of our alphabetic writing, this is not due to any stupid or obdurate conservatism. The Chinese script is so wonderfully well adapted to the linguistic conditions of China that it is indispensable; .... [1923: 41]

Another Western student of Chinese said:

> Yet, there are those both in China and in the West as well who believe that it is only a matter of time before the characters must give way to a simpler system of writing. If they are right, that day would bring easier access to literacy for China's citizens, as well as increased internationalization of China's culture. But, ... these advantages would be at a cultural cost far higher than the present generation of Chinese would ever be willing to pay. [Ramsey, 1987: 154]

Chinese themselves are divided: The well-known writer Lu Xun pronounced: "Shall we sacrifice ourselves for the ideographs, or shall we sacrifice the ideographs for ourselves? All but the insane can answer this immediately" (quoted in Huang and Huang 1989: 87). He advocated using Latin alphabets, different ones for different "dialects." Huang and Huang themselves, two computer scientists in Taiwan and the United States, are vehemently opposed to the elimination of characters in favor of an alphabet:

> Any attempt to turn the Chinese into an alphabetical language is doomed to failure. Five thousand years of continuous usage can not be wiped out overnight by a small group of mad men. Romanization is a dead end waste of time. [1989: 43]

Language reformers in China assert:

> Writing is not equivalent to culture; it is only a means of conveying culture. We value traditional culture, and we therefore also value the Chinese characters that convey the traditional culture. But we value even more highly the creation of a modern culture of the present and the future, the creation of a Chinese Pinyin orthography suited to conveying a modern culture .... The two kinds of writing will coexist and will both be used, each having its own place, each being used to its utmost advantage. [Language Reform Association 1981]

A national conference on language and scripts was convened in Beijing in 1986. As my Chinese colleague Zhang Zhi wryly observed, "in some ways the greatest achievement of the conference was that it passed over in silence the issues of alphabetization and the elimination of Chinese characters."

Before closing this chapter, let us be reminded of the suitability and advantages of Chinese characters to the Chinese. Consider their suitability. Since Chinese morphemes do not inflect, they can be conveniently represented by characters whose shapes need not change. One Chinese morpheme in one syllable is conveniently represented by one character. Single characters representing non-inflecting and monosyllabic morphemes can be joined, without a change in shape, to form a multi-morpheme–syllable–character compound word or idiom.

Now consider the advantages. Chinese characters differentiate the abundant Chinese homophones; they also allow communication among peoples who speak mutually unintelligible "dialects," thus unifying the huge number of Chinese speakers in the mainland as well as overseas. They allow some degree of communication even among speakers of unrelated languages, such as Chinese and Japanese or Korean. (In shopping in Toronto's Chinatown, where Cantonese is spoken, I rely on written labels, Chinese characters and Arabic numerals, to learn about sales, prices, and other vital information.) Those who know characters and the classic literary language have access to classical literature as old as 3000 years. Had they not been useful and effective, Chinese characters could not have been used continuously for thousands of years by so many people, especially in the face of the effort and time involved in learning them.

Chinese characters, Hanzi, are unique and picturesque; they are useful as well, once you have learned enough of them. Is their antiquity, picturesqueness, suitability, and usefulness great enough to justify a few years of learning? I would say yes, provided that characters are simplified judiciously and limited to about 3,500 for functional literacy, or even to about 2,000 for limited literacy. Anyway, it is the present policy of the People's Republic of China and also of the Taiwan government to retain Hanzi. Since Hanzi do not indicate sounds well, their use must be supplemented by the use of a good phonetic script, such as Pinyin, as an auxiliary script. So, for now and in the foreseeable future, Hanzi and Pinyin will coexist, each serving its own function.

9

Learning Hanzi, Pinyin, and Putonghua

Chinese characters, Hanzi, are numerous, have complex shapes, and do not indicate sounds adequately. Yet they are learned and used extensively by about one quarter of the world's population in several parts of the world: China, Taiwan, Hong Kong, Singapore, Japan, and Korea as well as by overseas Chinese in Southeast Asia, North and South America, Europe, and Australia. In these different places, characters are learned in some ways similarly and in others differently.

Simple characters like pictographs or indicators are usually learned early, each as a whole pattern. Composite characters tend to be learned later, by analyzing each composite into a phonetic component and one or more semantic components. Learning to write characters usually accompanies learning to read them. Characters are learned batch by batch. It is easy to learn the first few batches, which contain only a few hundred characters representing common concepts, but it is difficult to master a few thousand. The number of characters learned in primary school varies considerably in different nations, from none in Korea to almost 2,800 in China. The nations differ also in how they use phonetic scripts as an aid to teaching the sounds of characters.

Chinese characters, like letters in Western nations, are normally introduced to children at school, but occasionally they are taught to preschoolers at home or in kindergarten.

Should Preschoolers be Taught to Read?

Preschoolers can be taught to read either by their own parents at home or by teachers in kindergartens. You might well ask, Should children be taught reading so early? If so, how should they be taught? Preschool reading or early reading is a highly controversial issue everywhere in the world. Some parents and educators object to early reading. They argue that young children should have a carefree childhood, and that reading can be taught at school, where there are teachers trained and paid to do the teaching. The overwhelming majority of children learn to read at school, and some of them become great writers, thinkers, scientists, and so on.

Some other parents and educators argue that young children have sufficient intelligence, time, and especially desire, to learn to read, and that once the children learn to read, they can read to learn. And book reading and acquisition of knowledge can accelerate children's intellectual development. To quote myself, "Reading is the magic key that unlocks the door to the wonderland of stories and information" (Taylor and Taylor 1983: 397). So, if children are ready and eager, by all means provide them with the magic key.

Throughout history, probably since the beginning of writing, a few children have been taught to read as preschoolers, even as young as age 2. Some early readers have become great scholars and writers. Here are the names of several early readers of European languages in modern times: Jonathan Swift, Thomas Hobbes, Charles Dickens, Ralph Waldo Emerson, Voltaire, John Stuart Mill, and Jean Paul Sartre (Smethurst 1975).

In China for centuries young boys born into scholarly or wealthy families began learning to read and write at home, informally, sometimes taught by women. The children would later enrol in formal studies with a tutor. In the great novel *A Dream of Red Mansions*, which describes life in the mid-Qing dynasty (1644–1911), one finds a passage: "Even before Pao-yu [Baoyu] started school, when he was hardly four years old, she [his elder sister who became an imperial consort] taught him to recite several texts and to recognize several thousand characters" (Yang and Yang 1978: 253, v 1). Hu Shi (1891–1962), the scholar and writer whom we encountered earlier, had learned over a thousand characters by the age of four ("Literary vs Vernacular Language" in chap. 8).

So my response to the controversy is as follows. If preschoolers show interest in letters and written words, as many do, why not encourage them? On the other hand, if they show no interest or even have an aversion to regular lessons in reading, why force them? Similarly, if parents believe in early reading and have the time and patience to give regular lessons to their children, why shouldn't they go ahead with the lessons? But if parents do not believe in early reading and have little time and patience with regular lessons, why should they be forced into giving the lessons? What any parents can do, regardless of their beliefs, is to provide models for their children by being readers themselves, by reading to the children, or by having reading materials around the house. Reading story books to children is perhaps the best way to interest them in reading. It is pleasurable for parents, too.

The benefits of early reading have been well documented in many parts of the world. In an American study, early readers tended to be brighter than non-early readers and far better readers in later school years than their equally bright classmates who did not learn to read early (Durkin 1966). In a Japanese survey, the earlier the parents — usually mothers — began to read to the children, the more fluently the children read at age 5 (Sugiyama and Saito 1973). In a Canadian study, almost all early preschool readers had stories read to them daily (Patel and Patterson 1982). In Ontario, Canada, grade 9 students who were read to as preschoolers outperformed others on a province-wide test of reading and writing (*The Globe and Mail*, 25 Oct. 1994). In Israel, schoolchildren in early grades who were read stories became better readers than those who received special attention but had no stories read to them (Feitelson 1988).

If parents and other caregivers take on the task of teaching preschoolers, what method should they use? I should think any reasonable method will succeed, if the children are eager to learn, and if their parent-teachers shower them with attention and encouragement. Two thousand years ago the Roman schoolmaster Quintilian said: "Very young children can acquire reading, provided it is made easy and gentle and pleasant." Still, let us compare a few different methods to see whether some methods are more effective than others.

How Hanzi are Taught to Preschoolers

In imperial China, small boys in elite households learned more than 1,000 characters at home in less than a year, before they enrolled in formal studies with a tutor. Their primers could be the 13th century *Trimetrical Characters*, which organizes hundreds of characters into three-character couplets, or the 10th century *Hundred Family Names*, which is a list of about 440 Chinese surnames.

A most famous elementary text, both for reciting and for calligraphy, was the *Thousand-Character Essay (Qianziwen)*, which was used for over 1400 years until the 20th century, not only in China but also in Korea and Japan. It is said that its author was provided by his emperor with 1,000 individual characters and was asked to compose them into an essay. He managed to do so within a single day, ingeniously using all the one thousand characters without repetition. His hair turned white from the mental exertion, and so the essay is called also the "white-headed essay." The essay deals with such lofty topics as nature and morality. The 1,000 characters are organized into 250 four-character couplets. To paraphrase the first three couplets:

> The sky above is black and the earth below is yellow. The universe is wide and limitless. The sun sets in the west and the moon tilts when full.

As a preschooler I myself learned characters using the *Thousand-Character Essay* as the text and with my grandfather as the instructor. Consider the very first character: I learned its meaning (e.g., Korean *hanŭl* 'sky') given first and the sound (Sino-Korean sound *chŏn*) given after the meaning, as *hanŭl chŏn*. (For "Sino-Korean," see chap. 11.) I can still recite the first phrase by heart: *hanŭlchŏn ttaji kamulhyŏn nuruhwang* ('sky' *chŏn*, 'earth' *ji*, 'black' *hyŏn*, 'yellow' *hwang*). In retrospect, I would say that this method of learning characters is not efficient. The 1,000 characters may have been chosen and arranged to tell a story, but the story is all but lost to young children who are learning a handful of characters in each lesson. Also the content of the story, even of each phrase, is too erudite for young children to comprehend. Indeed, it was not expected that young children would understand the meaning of the text; rather, it was expected that the meaning would present itself after the children had recited the text hundreds of times. In short, the material is not very meaningful or interesting for preschoolers, and to learn it is nothing but rote memory.

Let us consider a few more modern teaching methods. In order to prepare children for reading texts, they can be taught as many characters as possible in a short time, using a method called "systematic learning" or "concentrated character recognition." This method teaches characters systematically, making full use of the visual, semantic, and phonetic relations among them. Since 80–90% of the common characters are composed of sound-cuing phonetics and meaning-cuing semantic components, once one basic character is learned, its components can ease the learning of many other characters that share either a phonetic or semantic component. A number of characters are taught in a group if they interrelate either phonetically or semantically, regardless of their complexity in shape and meaning.

In Japan the educator Ishii (1977: 30; 1988) advocates using the systematic method to teach as many as 1,000 characters or Kanji to preschoolers as young as age 3. He also teaches multi-character compound words in groups that share the same character and have related meanings.

If an adult teaches these words in Kanji [鳩 'dove', 鶴 'crane', 蟻 'ant', and 蝶 'butterfly'], children will quickly understand that a dove and a crane belong together [sharing the semantic component 'bird'], and an ant and a butterfly group together [sharing the semantic component 'insect'], and that 'bird' and 'insect' are the two superordinate concepts. In this way, children develop the understanding of abstract concepts via concrete objects.

Apparently, Ishii's systematic method was practised in the 1980's in 500 (out of 50,000) nursery schools and kindergartens in Japan, and very occasionally in China and South Korea.

Ishii is so intent on teaching related characters that he pays little attention to the fact that the meanings of some characters taught are unfamiliar, abstract, and irrelevant to preschoolers, and that some of the characters are exceptionally complex. In fact, in Japan names of animals such as butterfly that would require complex characters tend instead to be written in a Japanese phonetic script ("How to Use Kana" in chap. 19).

Another method, "character labels for objects," emphasizes that preschoolers should be taught character labels for common objects and actions (e.g., Steinberg and Xi 1989). Their program of instruction has four stages.

1. *Familiarization*: Children become familiar with character labels attached to objects around the house, such as *yizi* 椅子 ('chair').
2. *Recognizing words*: They match written words with spoken words.
3. *Recognizing phrases and short sentences* : They use some of the words already learned.
4. *Reading books*: They read a group of connected sentences in books that are geared to their intellectual and linguistic levels.

Teaching, which lasts about 15 minutes per day, is done through much play and many games. Writing is not emphasized, but children who want to write are helped. After one year's instruction, toddlers aged two or three have learned the characters for a few hundred words. They grow up reading many books and reading at higher grade levels than their age mates in primary school. The same method has been used in teaching a group of children in nursery schools.

An eclectic method might be devised by combining the good points from Steinberg's object-label method and from Ishii's systematic method: One might teach preschoolers character labels for familiar objects, but in doing so, group the objects in such a way that their character labels share some components. For example, in one lesson, teach the labels for those household objects found in a room that contain the radical "tree" 木, such as 椅子 *yizi* 'chair', *zhuozi* 'table', *shugui* 'bookcase', and *yigui* 'wardrobe'. 木 ('tree') is a pictograph whose origin could be pointed out ("Characters Tell Stories" in chap. 4); and the second character in two of the four labels is the noun-marking suffix -*zi* 子. The two- or three-character labels for electric gadgets around the house—telephone, television, fan, light, refrigerator, battery, computer—contain as their first character "electricity" and could all be learned together. Such a systematic method should become more helpful as more characters are learned.

This eclectic method is a suggestion. Another eclectic method that has been used adopts the method of labelling common objects with character names. It has been used to prepare a set of textbooks for 3-, 4-, and 5-year-olds (Xu 1992). Familiar words, such as *baba* ('papa') and *mama,* are repeated several times in different sentences making up a simple story on a tape read aloud in Putonghua by an actor. While the tape is being played, the preschoolers try to point with their finger at each word as it is read. Their pointing, or recognition of characters, gradually improves, as words and stories are repeated. The idea is to get the children to "pick up" or acquire characters as informally and painlessly as they pick up speech. According to its advocate, thousands of preschoolers in China are acquiring characters by this method.

All the different methods described claim success in turning preschoolers into readers, suggesting that there is no single royal road to teaching reading, and that learning a few hundred characters is not difficult. The few hundred characters learned by preschoolers, impressive though they are, provide only an initiation into the long road to full literacy. There are a few thousand more characters to be learned, and they have to be written and understood as well as read.

In China, characters can be, and often are, taught informally at home by family members, but as a rule they are not formally taught in kindergartens, which lack trained teachers and adequate textbooks. At home, Pinyin, the Roman alphabet for Chinese, tends not to be taught, perhaps because many adults are themselves not familiar either with the script or with how to use it in teaching.

How Reading is Taught in School

Teachers of Chinese characters, Hanzi, can try any of the various methods described above. They might also explain the six categories of characters: pictograph, indicator, meaning composite, semantic–phonetic composite, phonetic loan, and mutually defining (table 3-2). In Ai's (1950) old study, beginners who were taught by a method based on the six categories scored three times higher than the control group, who were taught by a method that did not pay any attention to the categories. They scored higher than the control group whether they were tested immediately after learning or three months later. Some contemporary textbooks of characters now explain the six categories, especially pictographs (see fig. 9-2 later).

Nowadays, Hanzi tend to be taught by means of the phonetic script, Pinyin, which is needed to indicate the sounds of logographic characters directly, simply, and precisely. In China in 1989 I was fortunate enough to have an opportunity to visit several grade-one classrooms in Shanghai, Nanjing, and Beijing. Each class was large, having about 50 children, all neatly dressed and well behaved, as shown in Figure 9-1. The class is learning Pinyin.

Reading is typically taught using a series of graded textbooks. There used to be one standard series nation-wide, but since 1993 different series have been allowed, as long as they are inspected and approved by the authority. The primary school series published in 1989 and revised slightly in 1991 by the People's Education Publisher consists of twelve volumes, two for each of the six grades. The following description is based on the 1989 edition. The number of Hanzi to be learned over the six years is 2,834, of which over 2,000 are learned in the first three grades, as shown in Table 9-1. In the lower grades children tend to learn a large number of Hanzi so that in the upper grades they can concentrate on reading passages. A similar number of Hanzi is learned in primary schools in Hong Kong and Taiwan, as shown also in Table 9-1.

Figure 9-1. A Grade I class of 50 girls and boys learn Pinyin at a school in Shanghai, the People's Republic of China. Photograph by the author (1989)

The contents of textbooks progress from small to large linguistic units. Volume I-1 (Grade I-volume 1) starts with a few wordless pictures. Then it gives lessons in Pinyin, vowels alone first, and then with consonant initials. Next, individual letters are formed into syllables, as in: *x-i-a→xia*. Whenever individual letters represent morphemes with concrete meanings, pictures illustrate these meanings. For example, *é* (rising tone) is illustrated with a picture of a swan. The lessons progress from Vs (vowels) to VVs, CVs (consonant–vowels), VCs, CVCs, and finally two-syllable–morpheme words, such as *xue xiao* ('school'). Pinyin syllables, even within one word, are separated by a space, as in character writing, and their tones are marked. There is no need to learn the names of consonant letters, since their names are more or less their sounds, such as "bo" for *b* and "mo" for *m*, unlike the English "eitch" for *h*.

Volume I-1 carries Hanzi—the numerals one to ten annotated with Pinyin—for the first time on its page 28. Figure 9-2 shows one of the early lessons in Hanzi. Each Hanzi is accompanied by its pictographic origin and a picture of the object it represents, its Pinyin, an example of its use in a two syllable–morpheme word, and the order of writing its strokes. Hanzi for each lesson appear to be chosen because they occur in a common context, not because of their relation in shape or sound.

The first sentence in Hanzi, annotated with Pinyin, appears on page 53 of volume I-1. One

Table 9-1. Number of New Hanzi Learned in Each Grade

Grade	China	H.K.	Taiwan
I	571	460	407
II	825	500	506
III	672	530	450
IV	295	590	554
V	252	260	459
VI	219	260	386
Total	2,834	2,600	2,762

5 **6**

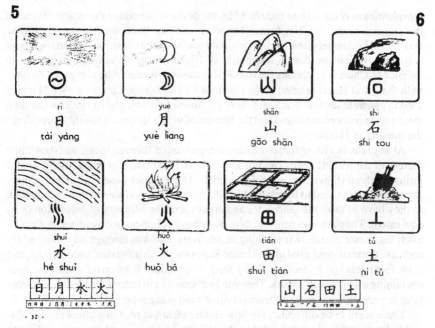

Figure 9-2. The pictographic nature of some Hanzi is exploited in early teaching (Lessons 5 and 6 of "Recognizing Hanzi," pages 32–33 from volume I-1 used in China. People's Educational Publications, 1989)

early sentence says: "The people of the entire nation passionately love the Communist Party." A few brief stories end this thin (116 pages) volume. Some Hanzi are still annotated with Pinyin in volume II–1 (1991 edition). All the Hanzi learned are listed at the end of each volume with Pinyin annotation.

In Taiwan, too, schoolchildren learn first a phonetic script, Zhuyinfuhao (table 8-3), and then Hanzi annotated with it. Hanzi, which are not simplified as they are in China, start to appear in volume I-2. They are taught from the beginning in sentences, rather than as individual words. Writing is taught along with reading.

Millions of ethnic Chinese live in nations where Chinese is not the official language, or if it is, not the only one. Where there are sizable numbers of ethnic Chinese, supplementary schools teach the Chinese language. In Europe and North America, the Chinese spoken is often Cantonese, and Hanzi are taught without romanization. In such a situation, the children may annotate Hanzi with a romanization they devise on their own based on the English letters with which they are familiar (Wong 1992). Chinese characters do not indicate sounds adequately, and the so-called sound-indicating devices—phonetic loans, phonetic components, and Fanqie (chap. 5)—are not much help to beginners.

DeFrancis (1984) describes Chinese textbooks as being "of low quality," pointing out that literary morphemes such as *zu* ('foot') and *mu* ('eye') are used instead of their spoken forms *jiao* ('foot') and *yanjing* ('eye, clear' = 'eye'). The choice of literary morphemes may have been motivated by the desire to introduce the simpler forms at the expense of the familiar forms. He points out that the content level of Chinese textbooks is extremely low, introducing only one-sixth the content contained in Soviet textbooks, which introduce a vocabulary of 10,000 words in the first four grades. In defence of Chinese textbooks the 10,000 Russian words cannot be compared directly with the 2,363 Hanzi learned in the first four Chinese grades, because each Hanzi is used to generate several words (fig. 3-5). A Chinese psychologist Ai (1950) examined three sets of readers and found that the number of words learned is roughly three times the number of Hanzi.

At any rate, in a recent cross-cultural comparison of Taiwan, Japan, and the United States, all the reading textbooks introduce about 7,000 different words by the end of primary school (Stevenson and Stigler 1992). The textbooks used in Taiwan, China, Japan, and Korea tend to be relatively uniform in quality and size within each nation, as they have to meet the guidelines and approval of the Ministry of Education or its equivalent. They are inexpensive, thin, paperback volumes, two volumes per grade. Such textbooks ensure that teaching is relatively uniform throughout a nation. By contrast, the textbooks used in the United States vary with publisher, state, school, and even from teacher to teacher. They tend to be thick, hard-cover volumes, each containing a whole year's work. They can be distracting in format, and redundant from year to year. Not surprisingly teachers often omit some topics.

There seem to be differences in how children learn to read in a phonetic alphabet and in logographic characters: American children in Chicago who caught on how to break down English words by sound could read new words not yet taught, while those who did not do so read below their grade level; by contrast, Chinese children in Beijing could read most words taught but few words not yet taught (Stevenson and Stigler 1992). As shown in Figure 9-3, most first graders in Beijing read at their grade level, whereas some first graders in Chicago read above and some below their grade level.

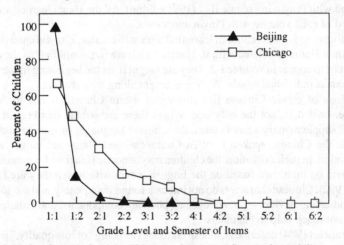

Figure 9-3 (also shown as fig. 6-1). Chinese and American first graders' ability to read words at and above different grade levels (Stevenson and Stigler 1992: 47; with permission)

In the same study, the percentages of poor readers—Grade V children who read only at Grade III level—were 12% for Chinese, 21% for Japanese (Sendai), and 31% for American. Such results may reflect the relative efficiency of teaching, the quality of textbooks, the time spent on learning, and the children's motivation. For example, the number of hours per week spent in learning-oriented activities—school, homework, reading—was higher for the Chinese and Japanese children than for the American children. Do they also reflect the relative complexity of the scripts learned?

Research on the Use of Pinyin

Although reading instruction is now more or less uniform throughout China, some variation was at one time allowed in primary schools attached to "normal universities" (teachers' colleges). Various teaching methods and scripts were tried, including Hanzi without Pinyin; Pinyin first and then Hanzi; Pinyin along with Hanzi; Pinyin in syllable units; Pinyin in letter sequences or spelling; writing along with reading; reading without writing, and so on. In one kindergarten I visited in Beijing in 1989, computers were used to teach reading. However, there seems to have been no systematic comparison of different methods and scripts that would allow educators to pick the most effective.

One large-scale study was carried out to assess the effectiveness of Pinyin in reading instruction (reported in Wang Y.-H. 1989). It studied six first-grade classes in one city and two counties of Heilongjiang Province in northeastern China. Each class contained between 36 and 44 boys and girls, most of whom were aged 7, with some 6 or 8. Among these, 25% had attended preschool programs, such as kindergartens. When the experiment began, some of the children already knew some Hanzi: 29% recognized 1–50 Hanzi; 11% 51–100 Hanzi; and 3% recognized more than 100 Hanzi. In the second year of the experiment, a class of 46 boys and girls from a farming community was added. Of these 46, only one could recognize 10 or more Hanzi.

Pinyin was taught in the first 6–8 weeks of Grade I. Then the children learned to read and write in the following order: (1) lessons and stories written only in Pinyin; (2) materials written in Hanzi annotated with Pinyin; (3) materials written only in Hanzi, with a few difficult ones being annotated with Pinyin. Each week two class periods were devoted to Hanzi recognition and writing through analysis. The children also wrote compositions about given pictures and topics, initially in Pinyin and eventually in Hanzi. They learned to write Hanzi first in pencil, then in pen, and finally in brush. Putonghua was used in the four language skills—listening, speaking, reading, and writing—from the first day of school. In the second grade, speaking classes were held once every week.

The following results were obtained in the first year of the study. Within a few weeks, 80% of the children could recognize Pinyin syllables by sight, and could read between 340 and 500 Pinyin words. In pronunciation accuracy, reading speed, and comprehension, they exceeded the level of skill achieved by the regular (no Pinyin) second-grade classes in the same schools. Through extensive reading and writing, they could recognize 1,000 different Hanzi. The amount of composition produced in Pinyin by the first graders in the experiment approached that produced in Hanzi by the regular third graders. However, their word usage and writing speed lagged behind those of the regular third-grade classes. In the second year, the children in the study could read in Hanzi at the 4th-grade level. They were eager to buy, borrow, and read books and newspapers, according to their parents, teachers, and social workers. (They seem to have received a lot of attention from adults.)

The Pinyin study was pronounced a resounding success, and Pinyin-based reading instruction, described in the preceding section, has been adopted throughout China since 1987. The Pinyin study may have had clear results, but it used inadequate procedures in having a study group but no proper control group. The performance of the so-called experimental group was compared to the so-called regular group, which presumably received little attention during the study. The superior performance by the study group might have been attributable to certain phenomena well-known in psychological experiments: Often the experimental group performs well due partly to the extra attention paid to it, partly to the "Hawthorne Effect" (people change their behaviors when they know that they are being observed), and partly to the "experimenter effect" (experimenters' expectations are reflected in the results of experiments). Much attention can translate also into superior teaching materials, teachers, parents' involvement, and so on.

Considering the importance of Pinyin as a teaching aid, what is needed is another experiment in which a proper control group and an experimental group differ only in the use of Pinyin, but not in such other conditions as teachers' qualifications and expectations of educators and parents.

Instruction of and in Putonghua

Hanzi can be pronounced in Putonghua ('common speech') or in any of the six other major "dialects," but in schools only the Putonghua sounds are supposed to be taught. The teaching of Putonghua is important in its own right as a means to facilitate oral communication among speakers of mutually unintelligible "dialects." Primary school is an ideal place to advance the national goal of promoting Putonghua. Even in the Pinyin study described in the preceding section, Putonghua was used for the study group from the first day of school, and speaking classes in it were held once every week.

Ideally, schoolchildren learn Putonghua through immersion, i.e., by learning all school subjects in it. On the first day of school the children may hear their own "dialect" but gradually, over a period of months, they hear more and more words and phrases in Putonghua, until at the end of the first year they hear only Putonghua. They are sometimes given classes in spoken Putonghua. The children become Putonghua speakers fairly rapidly, conversing in it on almost any school subject, though they may retain local "accents."

However, most of these children gradually lose their ability to speak Putonghua after they leave school, because the people around them speak a local "dialect." But we may assume that this loss is probably only partial. Skill in Putonghua may be revived and brought close to its former level with some practice, when the need arises. (I am speaking from my personal experience with Japanese and Korean, which I cannot speak fluently while living in Canada but regain during a short stay in Japan or Korea. And I learned Japanese through immersion at school, just as "dialect"-speaking Chinese schoolchildren learn Putonghua.)

To use Putonghua as the sole medium of school instruction, there would have to be enough Putonghua-speaking teachers to go around, but this apparently is not yet the case, especially in rural areas. Teachers of language and literature are required to use Putonghua, but most of them cannot do so fluently, and teachers of other subjects, such as mathematics, are not even required to use it. Teachers usually resort to their own "dialects" to read aloud or to explain the material in the texts, which are written in Hanzi based on Putonghua vocabulary and grammar. The teaching of Putonghua might benefit from a greater emphasis on training the teachers.

In the proud and arrogant city of Guangzhou (Canton) where Cantonese reigns supreme, only half of schools use Putonghua as a medium of teaching, and in the surrounding areas outside the city, some primary and middle schools do not use it at all, complained the *People's Daily* (1992, March 1). Cantonese is the predominant language spoken by ethnic Chinese overseas, and is taught to children in Chinese schools. Mandarin/Putonghua is occasionally taught partly because of its importance and partly because of the increasing number of its speakers among Chinese emigrants.

The People's Republic of China (PRC) has 55 ethnic minorities, such as Uygur, Mongols, Tibetans, and Koreans. Almost all ethnic minorities, 53, posses their own languages, and half of the 53 posess their own scripts as well. The law governing the languages and scripts in the ethnic autonomous regions stipulates that:

> In a school where most students belong to an ethnic minority group, it can use textbooks in the group's script, and teaching must be done in the group's language. However, the group's primary and secondary schools must provide classes in the Chinese language and must spread Putonghua that is used nation-wide.

Since 1956 there have been several directives on the use of Putonghua in schools. The 1990 directive stipulates that by the year 2000 Putonghua should be the language of teaching in all primary schools in cities and in key schools in rural areas. This goal is to be met in two stages: In the first stage, Putonghua should be used in classrooms and assemblies; in the second stage, it should be used everywhere in school. As more and more children are educated in Putonghua, and more and more adults are exposed to the radio and TV that are broadcast in it, Putonghua is likely to spread ever more widely throughout China.

Primary and Secondary School

Since most reading instruction takes place in primary and secondary schools, let us look at these schools, first in the PRC and then briefly in Taiwan. In the PRC the State Commission for Education takes charge of planning all educational undertakings and coordinates education among different sectors. It sets successive 5-year plans. In 1986 it promulgated the "Compulsory Education Law," setting a goal of giving all children 9 years of primary education by the year 2000.

Today Chinese children typically have 6 years of primary school and 6 years of secondary school. They start primary school at age 6, or in some rural areas, at age 7. In the past few decades there has been a tremendous increase in the number of primary schools and in the number of schoolchildren. In 1952 the rate of enrollment in primary school was around 50%, but in 1992 it reached 98%.

In primary school, the most important subject is the Chinese language, i.e., reading, speaking, composition, and handwriting. It takes up more than one-third of the class periods. Slightly more class time is allotted for the Chinese language in rural than in urban areas: in Grade I, urban children take 8 reading classes per week, while rural children take 10 classes. In Grade VI, both groups of children take 6 reading classes per week. The next most important subject is mathematics, which takes up one-quarter of the class periods. The subject of ideology and moral education is given 1 class per week in every grade. Foreign languages may be taught in the upper levels of schools in some urban areas, 3 classes per week. Labor takes up 1 class per week in the upper three grades (*Chūgoku Nenkan*, or *China Yearbook* 1991, 1992).

Secondary school in the PRC usually lasts 6 years (3 years of middle and 3 years of high school). High school is divided into a vocational stream and a general academic stream. In both middle and high schools, the three most important subjects are the Chinese language including classics, several branches of mathematics, and foreign languages, which can be English, Russian, Japanese, or others. Politics is a school subject, and labor skills take up a few weeks of a school year. In 1992, nearly 80% of primary school graduates entered middle school, and 40% of middle school graduates entered high school. By contrast, in S. Korea and Japan, almost all primary school graduates advance to middle school, and most middle-school graduates to high school.

The impressive statistical data notwithstanding, not all is well in primary and secondary education in China. The official rate of primary school enrollment, 98%, masks the fact that millions of schoolchildren, especially females in poor rural areas, drop out of school. There is a growing resistance to universal primary education among parents and employers seeking cheap labor for their farms and enterprises. Moreover, primary education is unequal in quality in different regions and social classes. On the one hand, some schools in backward rural areas are "mini-schools" that have only three or four grades; on the other, some schools in big urban centers are private schools that offer enriched education.

Let us have an intimate look at one mini school in Shaanxi Province, housed in four caves—one for teachers and three for children—hollowed out of porous loess, as described by Jan Wong for *The Globe and Mail* (July 14, 1992). This no-name mini school has three teachers instructing 70 pupils of four grades: pre-schoolers (aged 5 or 6), first graders, second graders, and third graders (aged 9 to 13). This school, along with thousands of others in poor rural areas, lacks many things, such as electricity, central heating, running water, flag pole, and library.

Here are a few important activities selected from a daily schedule of the no-name school. Time is approximate, as there is no school bell.

9 a.m. Sprinkle water on dirt floors to keep down the dust. Play.
9:40 a.m. Combined class, language or math. For example, 10 third graders study a 1000-year-old Song dynasty poem. After ordering one pupil to recite the poem, the teacher turns to 11 second-graders to teach addition.
2:00 p.m. Calligraphy.
2:40 p.m. Nature, ideology (e.g., "Following in Marx's Footsteps"), morals, music, sports, or art
4:40 p.m. Sweep class rooms, and go home.

Because there are only three teachers for four grades, one grade is often left alone for self study, which is spent chanting their lessons in unison. The children do homework, usually lots of copying Hanzi. When the children reach fourth grade, they will transfer to a bigger school in the next village. Many are unlikely to finish.

Now let us look at private, elite schools in big cities like Beijing. In a socialist nation like China, newly well-to-do families send their children to such schools, in spite of steep fees, reflecting the fact that public education is underfunded and neglected. Private schools offer extras that are not available in the public system, such as computers, language labs, and electronic musical instruments. They also have lower student–teacher ratios and put less emphasis on political ideology than do public schools. Private education is available in hundreds of primary schools and some in secondary schools and also in universities. Some secondary schools specialize in preparing students for the national entrance exams to universities. Private education is expanding at a breakneck pace, and there is a waiting list for it.

As privileged as are private schools, apparently they are not as comfortable as key schools that cater to the children of top-level Communist Party cadres. Key schools were restored in the late 1970s when the devastating Cultural Revolution was over, in order to quickly produce trained personnel. Schools were instructed to identify gifted children early, through screening examinations, and to give them special consideration by providing them with the best teachers and facilities.

Briefly, in Taiwan the duration of compulsory education was 9 years until 1994, when it was extended to 12 years (6 years of primary school, 3 years of middle school, and 3 years of high school). In schools the two most important subjects are Chinese language and math, followed by English and computer. Since 1993, even at primary schools English and computer have been offered as elective subjects, along with abacus, calligraphy, and choral singing. Computer has been offered as an elective subject in high school since 1973. In securing good jobs and social advancement a university education counts a great deal. So commercial cram schools proliferate to prepare middle school graduates for entrance examinations to good high schools, and high school graduates to good universities. A plan is afoot to abolish the entrance exams to high schools.

Back to the PRC, in 1992, public expenditure on education was 1.5% of GNP, compared with around 4% in S. Korea and Japan, and 7% in Canada (UNESCO 1994). Thanks to the extremely low expenditure, public school teachers in China are not only paid low salaries but also are not always paid on time. Not surprisingly teachers are leaving in droves for more lucrative jobs. In an article entitled "The impoverished education," the Chinese authors Zeng and colleagues say:

> The extremely inferior educational quality of the Chinese people and the enormous size of its total population is one of the root causes underlying the poverty and backwardness of China today. This is also a critical factor holding China back in the future world-wide competition in high technology in various areas. [Zeng et al, 1990: 18].

To end the chapter on a positive note, China is transforming itself rapidly and profoundly in many areas, and its education no doubt will improve along with its economic and social improvement.

10

History of Education and Literacy in China

Chinese people posessed written signs as early as 3400 years ago, possibly earlier in neolithic times. They produced books and established schools more than 3000 years ago. They invented paper 2000 years ago and wood-block printing 1300 years ago. Thus they had a solid headstart in education and literacy over other peoples of the world. Yet today, the quality and quantity of education and literacy in China lag behind Japan, Korea, Taiwan, Singapore, and Hong Kong. What has happened?

In search of answers to the question we study the history of education and literacy in China, which is interesting not only in its own right but also in illuminating factors other than the writing system that affect a nation's literacy.

Confucianism and Confucian Classics

To discuss the education and literacy of the Chinese, as well as of the Koreans and the Japanese, we must start with Confucianism, which, as the official ideology of many governments over the centuries, shaped education, literacy, indeed the whole outlook on life, of these peoples. In its long history, Confucianism has produced a mass of literature, which was learned by generations of scholars in preparation for a series of civil service examinations in imperial China.

Confucianism is derived from the teachings of Confucius (Kong Fuzi, 551–479 BC), who was born in Qufu, Shandong Province, during the feudal Zhou period. He held minor official positions but mostly was shunned by various principalities. In his later years he devoted his time to teaching his diciples. He said of himself that he was not a saint but that he was tireless in learning and in teaching other people. He focused on the problems of this world, with little concern for spirits and the afterlife.

Confucianism is a set of ethical codes that tell people how to live together in harmony. Subjects must be loyal to their ruler, a son must respect his father, and a wife must obey her husband (called the "Three Bonds"); a younger brother must defer to his older brother, and a friend must be trustworthy to a friend (called, together with the Three Bonds, the "Five Cardinal Relations"). To maintain these harmonious human relations, a person must cultivate such virtues as filial piety, uprightness, loyalty, trustworthiness, and, above all, benevolence, to become a superior human being. The study of the Confucian classics and observance of rites helped people to achieve this ideal state. Ironically, Confucius, who preached harmonious human relations, had a wife who ran away from him, apparently because of his fastidiousness about food. For three successive generations, the Master, his son, and his grandson were either divorced or separated from their wives (Lin 1938).

Confucian learning is encapsulated in the "Five (Confucian) Classics," which are said to have been edited, commented on, or taught by Confucius himself. The Five

Classics are as follows, from the earliest and most important to the latest and least important.

1. *Book of Poetry (Shiji* or *Shijing)* contains 305 poems dating from the Shang/Yin and early Zhou periods 3000 years ago to the Warring States 2200 years ago. Some are folk songs, some are verses of songs sung at court, and some are ritual hymns. Confucius edited the book and referred to it often in the *Analects* (described below). He said to his disciples, "Why don't you people study *Poetry? Poetry* will stimulate your imagination, help you to be more observant of things, more understanding of others and more moderate in your opinion... " (Lai Ming 1964: 24).

2. *Book of Documents* or *Book of History (Shujing* or *Shangshu)* contains declarations and speeches of rulers from legendary times thousands of years ago to the early Zhou dynasty, a utopian period of Chinese history with an enlightened government and contented populace. The speeches are believed to have been taken down by officials exactly as the rulers spoke them. The latest event referred to took place in 626 BC.

3. *Book of Changes* or *Book of Divination (Yijing* or *I Ching)* is a diviner's handbook that is a work of ancient but mixed age. It centers around eight trigrams, each of which consists of three lines, broken (representing Yin) or unbroken (representing Yang). The trigrams combine in various ways to produce 64 hexagrams, each of which has a name and an explanatory text. For example, the 55th hexagram is *feng* ('abundance' or 'fullness') and its main description, and the ancient commentary on it, say as follows.

> Abundance has success. The king attains abundance. Be not sad. Be like the sun at midday.

> When the sun stands at midday, it begins to set; when the moon is full it begins to wane. The fullness and emptiness of heaven and earth wane and wax in the course of time. How much truer is this of men, or of spirits and gods!
> [Spence 1990: 101–102]

The *Book of Changes* is more than a diviners' manual; it has supplied many concepts and terms to Chinese philosophical and cosmological thoughts for a long time. (Four of the Eight Trigrams are used in the four corners of the S. Korean national flag, whose center has the Yin–Yang symbol.)

4. *Spring and Autumn Annals (Chunqiu)* is a brief record of major events between the 8th and the 5th century BC in the feudal state of Lu where Confucius was born. It was compiled by Confucius.

5. *Record of Rites (Liji)* compiled in the 2nd century BC, is a detailed codification of moral and social rites. The correct observation of the rite is a moral as well as social duty in Confucianism.

Confucianism in its long history has gone through some changes, though its core concepts may have remained constant. The period between the 11th and 12th centuries AD in the Song dynasty was a time of especially great philosophical ferment when "a hundred schools of thought" contended. Born in this climate was Neo-Confucianism, which not only re-asserted the ancient principles and wisdom of Confucius but also buttressed them with cosmological and metaphysical speculations inspired or challenged by Buddhism and Daoism.

One philosopher, Zhou Dunyi (1017–1073), wrote *An Explanation of the Diagram of the Supreme Ultimate,* in which he expounded the Supreme Ultimate (*Taiji*), as well as the doctrines of Yin–Yang and the Five Phases ("Chinese World Views," below). He gave a central place to the *Book of Changes.* Another leading Neo-Confucian, Zhu Xi (1130–1200), provided a broad philosophical view of the universe and the individual's place in it. He also selected from the mass of classical literature dating from the Zhou period the "Four Books" as the central canon. The Four Books, which were studied before the Five Classics, became the standard texts for Chinese and Korean education for the next 600 years. The Four Books, in the sequence put by Zhu Xi, are:

1. *Great Learning* (*Daxue*) consists of two chapters taken from the *Record of Rites.* It aims at educating a ruler to be virtuous and at reinvigorating the people.

2. *Analects* (*Lunyu*) consists largely of Confucius's answers to his disciples' questions, prefaced by the phrase "Confucius said." It reflects his lofty moral ideal. Here are a few gems from it (Lau 1979):

> A man of benevolence never worries; a man of wisdom is never in two minds; a man of courage is never afraid.
>
> Shall I tell you what it is to know? To say you know when you know, and to say you do not when you do not, that is knowledge.
>
> Do not impose on others what you yourself do not desire.
>
> Not to mend one's ways when one has erred is to err indeed.
>
> The gentleman is devoted to principle but not inflexible in small matters.
>
> The gentleman is troubled by his own lack of ability, not by the failure of others to appreciate him.

3. *Mencius (Mengzi)* contains Mencius's (390–305 BC) sayings and deeds recorded by his disciples. Mencius was a supporter and developer of Confucianism. In his view, all human beings are born with goodness and may retain it by practising benevolence and justice.

4. *Doctrine of the Mean* (*Zhongyong*) written by the Master's grandson, comprises Confucius's thoughts about man's relationship to himself and to his fellow men.

Neo-Confucianism stressed the concept that a man fulfills himself by playing his allotted role in a rigidly hierachical and man-centered society. It stressed, more strongly than did any earlier form of Confucianism, authoritarian hierarchical relationships within a family, a society, and a state. In addition to observing the Three Bonds and the Five Cardinal Relations, described at the beginning of this section, a female has to observe the Three Obediences: to her father before marriage, to her husband after marriage, and to her son as a widow. (A widow is discouraged from remarrying. A woman without a husband or son is nobody!)

Neo-Confucianism was adopted as the state ideology in China during the Ming dynasty (1368–1644) and the Qing dynasty (1644–1912), in Korea during the Chosŏn kingdom (1392–1910), and in Japan during the Tokugawa Shōgunate (1603–1867). In these Neo-Confucian societies, people were ranked in a hierarchy of four classes: mandarins, artisans, farmers, and then merchants, who were stigmatized as unscrupulous and parasitic. Below the four classes were the "degraded people," who included slaves, prostitutes, and butchers.

In the mid-18th century, during the Qing dynasty, some Confucian scholars rejected the speculative Neo-Confucianism of the Song dynasty, and adopted a new method of inquiry called *kaozheng xue* ('evidential research'), which searched for evidence in books, events, and observable phenomena. This scholarship provided Confucian scholars a respectable alternative to service in the Manchu government, which sometimes persecuted Chinese scholars. One *kaozheng* scholar analyzed the chronology and linguistic structures of part of the Confucian classic of historical documents, proving that several sections of this work were a later forgery. Such analysis took the sheen off the Confucian classics on which generations of state exam questions had been based.

Confucianism has had both a positive and negative influence over the Chinese, Koreans, and Japanese for hundreds of years. It has fostered respect for learning because of the long tradition in which bureaucrats were recruited through state exams that tested knowledge of the Confucian classics ("The Civil-Service Examination System," next section). It has fostered obedience to authority figures—emperor, employer, father, older brother, husband—and thereby promoted a veneer of social harmony. But if any of these authority figures lacked or was deficient in the Confucian virtues, the subjects, the children, the wives (a wealthy man could afford several wives), or the younger brothers suffered.

Confucianism can be faulted for fostering male chauvinism, authoritarianism, rigidly hierarchical human relations, and conservativism (traditionalism and hide-bound views of the world); it can be faulted also for stifling individualism, adventurism, imagination, critical thinking, and originality in thoughts and actions. In short, Confucianism stands in the way of democracy and progress. The East Asians have achieved economic success in a market economy not because of Confucianism, as asserted by some pundits (e.g., Elegant 1990; Kim 1992), but in spite of it. They succeed because their governments adopt judicious economic policies, and because they are prepared to work hard to make money. Living in overcrowded regions that often have few natural resources, good education and hard work are their main means to get ahead.

The Neo-Confucian outlook on life, in a much diluted form, still seems to permeate East Asians, who are ambivalent toward Confucianism. They may reject some of its anachronistic concepts while accepting some of its useful teachings. The birthplace of Confucius, Qufu in Shandong Province, receives visitors and puts on ceremonies, and universities hold conferences on Confucianism. Chinese and S. Korean philosophers are having a second look at Confucian humanistic idealism.

The Civil-Service Examination System

In their long existence, the Confucian classics—the Five Classics and the Four Books—have received much commentary by Confucian scholars, and have swollen to a massive body of literature, containing some 500,000 characters. Generations of scholars studied and memorized it in preparation for a series of civil service examinations. The long and arduous study of Confucian literature promoted scholarly literacy among a tiny upper crust of males while preventing the spread of functional literacy among the masses.

The exam system had a long history, with occasional disruptions. As early as the late Zhou dynasty (1100–256 BC) the tradition of the scholar–statesman was established. At first, only members of the nobility were scholar-statesmen, but later a new class, a bureaucracy, developed between the nobility and the peasants. In 136 BC an emperor of the Han dynasty recruited some lower-ranking bureaucrats through examinations on the Confucian classics, but the examinations were on a limited scale.

The institutionalized civil-service examination system was begun by the first emperor of the Sui dynasty, Wen Di (reigned AD 589–604). Its Chinese name is *keju* ('branch', 'raise/select', or "selection of talented personnel through examinations in various branches"). It was expanded during the Tang (618–907) dynasty, without dominating the process of recruiting officials. The exam system was firmly institutionalized during the Song (960–1279) dynasty, which added the palace examination to the system. Whereas the mid-Tang civil service had obtained about 15% of its officials from examinations, the Song obtained 30% (Fairbank 1992: 54). The exam system was abolished for part of the Yuan (Mongol) dynasty (1279–1368) but was restored in 1315. It was refined in the next dynasty, Ming (1368–1644), and continued several hundred more years becoming progressively more complex, until it was finally abolished in 1905 near the end of the last dynasty of China, Qing (1644–1912).

This section does not begin to describe the candidates' extreme stress nor the administrators' logistical headache associated with the examination system, appropriately called "examination hell" (Miyazaki 1963). At its fully developed stage in the latter half of the 19th century it involved a sequence of several exams in ascending order of importance and difficulty. The series was necessary, in order to reduce the number of candidates progressively.

At the first-stage, local level, candidates who passed a series of 3 or 4 examinations were awarded the lowest degree *shengyuan* ('licentiates' or government students), which qualified them for the next-level exam but not for office holding. Nominally the exams were for admittance to national schools, which, however, were ineffective as teaching institutions.

At the next level, the civil service exam proper, in a sequence of three, was held in a permanent examination compound in the capital of each province. The compound, isolated from the outside world by a high wall, was overseen by soldiers stationed in watch towers. It was a honeycomb of thousands of tiny cells, each of which was occupied by a single candidate during a two-night, three-day exam. These cells were in worse conditions than today's prison cells, having neither beds nor toilet facilities. Servants replenished water supplies and removed human waste. Successful candidates were awarded the degree *juren* ('recommended/selected men') and accredited as permanent members of officialdom. Figure 10-1a shows a portion of an examination compound.

The candidates, who were now *juren*, went to the imperial capital Beijing for a metropolitan exam, which also lasted a few days and took place in an exam compound. The metropolitan exam was historically the heart of the exam system, the provincial one being preparatory and a next-level one being a re-exam. If successful there they became *gongshi* ('presented scholars'), and went to the palace for a final test before the emperor or his proxy. The emperor bestowed the degrees of *jinshi* ('advanced

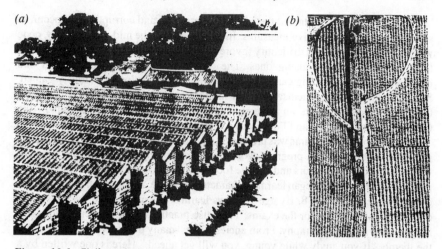

Figure 10-1. Civil service examination: (a) cells in a provincial exam compound, Qing period; (b) an undershirt covered with the Confucian classics for cribbing, unknown period

scholars') on 200–300 candidates, and ranked a few of the highest scorers in order of excellence for appointment. The top-ranking scholar was given the title *zhuangyuan* ('grand scholar'), the first scholar in the empire, and was appointed the first-class Compiler in the Hanlin Academy (AD 754–1911), which was the highest academic center and also a reservoire of future high officials. Some grand scholars became prime ministers. Table 10-1 summarizes the exam system in the late Qing period (based on Miyazaki 1963).

The examinations tested mainly knowledge of the Confucian classics. Since the 15th century the ability to compose a formal essay called the "eight-legged essay" (chap. 7) on a quote from the Confucian classics was essential to success at the exam, along with poetry composition and skilled calligraphy to write them. Only very occasionally, and briefly, were other subjects also tested. For example, in the mid-8th century during the Tang dynasty, Daoists were tested on Daoist texts; in the mid-11th century, during the Song dynasty, the reformer Wang Anshi introduced to the exam technical and scientific subjects; and in the mid-19th century during the brief reign of the Taiping (see below), candidates were tested on the Chinese translation of the Bible. Normally, exams in such technical skills as law, medicine, and mathematics led only to low positions. Exams in military branches paralled those in civilian branches, but they were never regarded highly.

Table 10-1. Civil Service Examination in the Qing Period

Level of Exam	Degree	Success Rate
Local	*shengyuan*	varied regionally; 1 to 10 out of 10
Provincial	*juren*	1 in 100 *shengyuan* ('licentiates')
Metropolitan	*gongshi*	1 in 30 *juren* ('selected men')
Palace	*jinshi*	most *gongshi*; 1 in 3,000 licentiates

The exam system contained the seeds of corruption, and corruption did occur, in spite of elaborate preventive measures. In one scheme in the mid-19th century, code words allowed examiners to identify favored candidates, whose poor papers could be then replaced with promising ones. The offending examiners were caught and beheaded, and the cheating candidates lost all the qualifications previously gained. Some candidates armed themselves with miniature copies of the Confucian classics. One candidate even wore an undershirt covered with some 500,000 Hanzi—the Confucian Five Classics and Four Books with commentaries (fig. 10-1b).

Preparation for the exams was protracted and arduous. It is said to have begun with pre-natal conditioning: A pregnant woman wishing for a gifted son would sit erect; would avoid clashing colors and strange food; and would hear poetry and the classics read aloud. Boys age 3 began learning characters at home, and began the study of the classics at school at age 8. By age 15, boys learned and memorized the Confucian classics, in preparation for the exams. They also practised writing poems and eight-legged essays, and calligraphy. From ancient times, many poems were composed on the theme, "If you study while young, you will get ahead." Here is one written by a Song emperor (Miyazaki 1963: 17).

> To enrich your family, no need to buy good land:
> Books hold a thousand measures of grain.
> For an easy life, no need to build a mansion:
> In books are found houses of gold....
> A boy who wants to become a somebody
> Devotes himself to the classics, faces the window, and read.

Competition at the exams was fierce, and became more so with the passage of time. In the Tang dynasty, the average candidate for higher level exams was in his mid-20's, but in the Song dynasty he was in his mid-30's. Many candidates tried repeatedly, some eventually succeeding at the exams in their 50's. There is a story about the old age of a successful candidate. In the Song dynasty, at a palace exam the emperor noticed among the new *jinshi* a white-haired old man, who turned out to be 73 years old and single. The emperor in sympathy gave him a beautiful palace lady as wife. Some of the wits of the day quickly made fun of him, "The groom telling the bride his age: Fifty years ago, twenty three."

What were the rewards for successful candidates? To become an official was the most lucrative as well as honorable thing to do in imperial China. The lowest degree holders, *shengyuan*, became gentry and literati, who wore distinct attire and enjoyed exemption from labor service and corporal punishment. Some holders of the highest degree *jinshi* obtained official positions, and some continued to study in the Hanlin Academy. A few years of officeholding enabled a scholar to make enough money from salary, perquisites, and perhaps graft, to repay the costs incurred in obtaining the position, and still to retain a surplus to invest in land and in his children's education.

The exams were in theory open to people from all socio-economic backgrounds except the "degraded classes," and some candidates were indeed from families with no record of civil-service status. But only a small minority, sons of elite families, could afford the time and money to study for the exams. And some men were allowed to inherit or purchase official posts, bypassing the exams.

Women were barred by law from taking the exams, with the following exceptions. During the mid-7th and early 8th centuries the female ruler and emperor Wu Zetian allowed women to obtain highest degrees, *jinshi*, at the civil service exam if they were successful at poetry exams. During the brief reign (1853–1864) of the Taiping ("Heavenly Kingdom," a rebel band based in Nanjing), exams were based on Chinese translations of the Bible, and women were allowed to sit for their own exams and to hold offices in the bureaucracy. (The leader of this band, Hong Xiuquan, failed the lowest-level exam four times. No wonder he became a rebel!)

Throughout its existence, the civil-service exam system was criticized for various reasons (e.g., Nivion 1963). In the mid-18th century the exams were attacked as sterile exercises that failed to select the finest scholars for office. (But would the finest scholars necessarily make the best bureaucrats?) As well, the number of available openings did not rise in proportion to the rise in population, and worse, passing the exams did not always lead to positions in the bureaucracy. Understandably, swelling numbers of educated men affected by these inadequacies were frustrated and disillusioned. In 1898 the Qing emperor Guangxu issued a series of edicts to begin what is called the "hundred days' reforms." In the exam system he ordered, among other things, that candidates should be graded for questions related to governmental problems instead of calligraphy, composition of a rigid eight-legged essay, and poetry. Unfortunately, his efforts were thwarted by his aunt, the formidable and hidebound dowager empress Ci Xi (Ts'u Hsi).

The exam system had positive and negative consequences. In its early years, Sui, Tang, and Song emperors could use the exam system to suppress the power of the hereditory aristocracy and to establish in its place an imperial autocracy. It was convenient for any emperor to have a bureaucracy that was educated in one standard Confucian curriculum, especially one that emphasized obedience to him. The examination system was at least more democratic than the earlier system, which had recruited bureaucrats from aristocratic families. It promoted reading and writing, and fostered respect for learning. But it did not promote functional literacy among the masses. Nor did it foster science and technology ("Chinese World Views," below). The products of the examination system were cultured dilettanti rather than men of sound judgment, useful skills, and decisive action. The fault lies not so much in the exam system itself but in the kind of learning that was required for it.

The Chinese civil-service examination system was adopted lock, stock, and barrel by the Koreans between the 10th and early 20th centuries (chap. 16) and by the Vietnamese between the 11th and early 20th centuries. Its principles, but not its content, were copied even by some European countries, such as Prussia in the 1690s. In the 19th century it influenced the mode of the civil service exams in India and United Kingdom. Today, in many countries bureaucrats are recruited through civil service exams.

Though the exam system was abolished in China some decades ago, its influence is still discernible in the entrance exams to the most prestigious university in each nation of East Asia: Beijing University in China, Seoul National University in South Korea, and Tokyo University in Japan. The entrance exams to these universities are intensely competitive, but admission to each university is a passport to good positions in government, industry, and academia. Some candidates who fail the entrance exam at the first try will repeat it year after year. As a bow to the 20th century, the university entrance exams test knowledge not so much of the Confucian classics as of reading and writing in the native language and in English, and in mathematics, social sciences, and physical sciences. But memorization, rather than analysis, of information still plays an important part in studying for the written exams.

Chinese World Views

For centuries the Chinese world views were colored by the "three great traditions" of Confucianism, Daoism, and Buddhism, which in turn were colored by the doctrines of Yin–Yang and the Five Phases (*wuxing*). These world views may be still held, but not as strongly as in the past. They, along with the civil service exams, may be responsible for the failure of modern science to develop in China, rather than the use of Chinese characters, as asserted by some Western scholars ("Alphabet vs Logography for Science" in chap. 6).

Confucianism favors past over present, orthodoxy and conformity over original and heterodox thinking, the study of human relations and classic texts over the probing of nature. These Confucian attitudes do not foster science. Needham, in his multi-volume opus on Chinese civilization (1954–), blames the *Book of Changes*, one of the Five Confucian Classics, for inhibiting the development of science in China.

Confucianism had an inhibiting influence on the development of science in another, indirect yet potent, way through the civil-service examination system that tested mainly knowledge of the Confucian classics. Think about it: For 1300 years the best minds in China were devoting their brains, time, and energy to learning and memorizing the archaic Confucian classics. What might have happened, had all these talents devoted their energies and time to the pursuit of science!

Another great tradition, Daoism, originated in antiquity. It is said to have begun by legendary Huang Di ('Yellow Emperor'), who lived 4500 years ago, and then was given a new direction by Laozi (604 BC). What is Dao? It means literally a way or path, and philosophically the truth or reality. As a way of life, Dao preaches simplicity, spontaneity, tranquility, weakness, and above all, non-action (*wuwei*). Non-action means taking no action that is contrary to Nature.

> The Tao [Dao] of Heaven operates mysteriously and secretly; it has no fixed shape; it follows no definite rules; it is so great that you can never come to the end of it; it is so deep that you can never fathom it. [*Huainanzi*, a philosophical text written in 139 BC by a Han dynasty prince who was a devout Daoist; Ronan/Needham 1978: 298]

The Daoist philosophy is embodied in a small classic called the *Laozi* or *Daodejing* (*Classic of the Way and its Virtue*), which is believed to have been written by Laozi in the 6th century BC. According to Chan (1963: 136), no one can hope to understand Chinese philosophy, religion, government, art, medicine — or even cooking — without appreciating the profound philosophy taught in this little book. To quote from the *Classic of the Way and its Virtue* (Chan 1963: 162):

> There is no calamity greater than lavish desires.
> There is no greater guilt than discontentment.

And there is no greater disaster than greed.
He who is contented with contentment is always contented.

The pursuit of Tao is to decrease day after day.
It is to decrease and further decrease until one reaches the point of taking no action.
No action is undertaken, and yet nothing is left undone.

These Daoists' teachings contain gems of wisdom. But they seem to advocate people to be in tune with nature without actively probing it. They teach, "Do not seek to probe the workings of nature, and all things will then flourish of themselves." They do not advocate that people use the powers of reason and logic.

While Daoism as a philosophy was developing, another Daoist movement, led by practitioners of the occult, searched for immortality on earth through divination and magic. This movement, in its search for elixirs or so-called "immortality pills," fostered alchemy, and then pharmacology and chemistry. The alchemists contributed to the technology of porcelain, dyes, alloys, and eventually to other Chinese inventions such as gunpowder. Many of the Daoists' achievements are described by Needham as "proto-science" rather than "pseudo-science."

The Chinese were influenced also by Buddhism, which came to China from India during the Han dynasty (206 BC–AD 22). Buddhism is concerned with finding principles regulating the incessant reincarnation in the *samsara* (the endless series of births, deaths, and re-births) and eternal emancipation from the *samsara* in the final attainment of *nirvana* ('blown out' in Sanskrit; a mental state in which all desires and illusions are extinguished). One Buddhist sect, Chan (Japanese Zen), developed in China around the 6th and 7th centuries AD under the influence of Daoism. (The term *Chan* is the Chinese transcription of Sanskrit *dhyana*, a type of meditation.) Chan Buddhism considers meditation, and not the study of texts or chanting, as the best means of attaining a spontaneous intuition of one's own Buddha nature. Meditation is intense and prolonged, and enlightenment may come either gradually or suddenly. Chan Buddhism views the visible world and existence as illusory and transitory. It has had a salutary effect on painting and poetry but has not fostered science.

Confucianism and Daoism absorbed the Chinese doctrine of Yin–Yang, which originated in antiquity and was summarized in the *Book of Documents*, one of the Five Confucian Classics. The Yin–Yang doctrine has touched every aspect of Chinese civilization, whether it be cosmology, metaphysics, medicine, government, history, art, or even cooking. According to the doctrine, all things and events are products of two opposite yet complementary forces: Yin which is negative, passive, weak, and destructive; and Yang, which is positive, active, strong, and constructive. In the well-known symbol of Yin–Yang, a circle is divided into two halves by a curved line ☯. (This symbol can be found in the center of the S. Korean national flag.) The two forces complement each other, as a male does a female, or grow out of each other, as day does out of night and vice versa. The Yin and Yang components never become completely separated, but at each stage, in any given fragment, only one is manifested. This splitting and re-splitting of two factors, with one dominent and one recessive, has parallels in modern scientific thinking of the West, e.g., in genetics, according to Needham.

The doctrine of the Five Phases (wood, fire, earth, metal, water) elaborates the Yin–Yang doctrine and at the same time adds the important concept of rotation, i.e., that things succeed one another as the Five Phases take their turns: wood produces fire, fire earth, earth metal, metal water, and water wood. The Five Phases were believed to lie behind every substance and every process. Things behaved in particular ways not necessarily because of the prior actions of other things, but primarily because their position in the ever-changing cyclical universe organized by the fivefold correlations. Table 10-2 gives a few of the myriad phenomena that are thought to correlate with the Five Phases.

Table 10-2. Some of the Phenomena Correlated with the Five Phases

Five Phases	wood	fire	earth	metal	water
Five Cardinal Points	east	south	center	west	north
Five Planets	Jupiter	Mars	Saturn	Venus	Mercury
Five Senses	eye	tongue	mouth	nose	ear
Five Colors	azure	red	yellow	white	black
Five Weekdays	Thursday	Tuesday	Saturday	Friday	Wednesday

The fivefold classificatory scheme was so entrenched that it was not revised even when the sixth planet, Uranus, was discovered. Today, of course, we know that nine planets—including Earth, Neptune, and Pluto—orbit around the Sun. Classification is not explanation. Consider the Five Colors. Why are these five chosen, and why are they arranged in that order? Modern physiology recognizes three unique primary hues or colors: red, green, and blue, which combine to produce other colors. White light, seen as white, is a mixture of all three, and is not considered a separate color.

The doctrines of Yin–Yang and the Five Phases, which have been absorbed by Confucians and Daoists, became the repository of pseudo-explanations of natural phenomena and human affairs; they became no more than a "giant filing system," to borrow Needham's word, that led to all concepts being stylized so that they fitted into the system. They even provided a philosophical underpinning—superfluous and useless though it may be—of the Korean phonetic script (chap. 13). The doctrine of the Five Phases is observed in selecting characters for given names in China and Korea (chaps. 4 and 15), and is incorporated in the 60-year cycle calendrical system (footnote 1 in chap. 3) still used by some East Asians.

In early history, these Chinese world views may have been neutral toward science and technology, but when they were held for too long and too deeply, almost to the exclusion of new ideas from outside, they may have come to inhibit it. Correlative thought based on the Five Phases gained unusual currency and dominated thinking for an unusually long time in China because of the centripetally organized Chinese state and society, according to Fairbank (1992: 65). In his book, *China in the Sixteenth Century*, the Jesuit missionary Matteo Ricci (1552–1610) observed:

> The study of mathematics and that of medicine are held in low esteem, because they are not fostered by honors as is the study of philosophy, to which students are attracted by the hope of glory and the rewards attached to it. [tr. Gallagher 1942: 32]

To conclude, it was the Chinese world views and not Chinese characters that influenced how the Chinese did, or did not do, science in the past. Anyway, Chinese technology, if not abstract science, was well developed before the Middle Ages, as can be seen in the next section.

Invention of Paper and Printing

Printing and paper are essential if literacy is to spread widely, though they are not enough in themselves, as we have just seen. The Chinese invented paper 1900 years ago and wood-block printing 1300 years ago, long before the West. Several examples of early papers that date back to the reign of Wu Di (140–87 BC) of the Han dynasty have been found.[1] This early paper was coarse and was probably intended for wrapping rather than for writing. A better quality paper is believed to have been made by an eunuch official, Cai Lun, who presented his new paper at the Han court in AD 105, the date normally associated with the Chinese invention of paper. Paper was made from inexpensive materials such as tree barks, scraps of hemp and flax, wornout fishnets, and rags (Twitchett 1983).

Because paper was relatively cheap to mass produce and was convenient to carry around and write on, its use spread quickly and widely. The earliest Chinese documents written on paper, discovered in the dry sands of Inner Mongolia and Xinjiang, date from the 2nd century AD. By the 4th century paper had virtually replaced the ancient writing materials, namely the silk roll and strips of wood or bamboo. In the 6th century, paper products and paper-making technology were introduced to Korea, and from there to Japan. In 751 there was a Chinese–Arab war, in which the Chinese were defeated. The Chinese prisoners of this war introduced paper to the Arabs in the region of Samarkand, and in the 11th century the Arabs introduced it to Europeans.

Chinese printing began early, though its precise origins remain obscure. Long before the Han dynasty (206 BC–220 AD) the Chinese used seals to sign documents (fig. 18-2 shows a seal from AD 57). In the 6th century they used large seals carved from hardwood to reduplicate Daoist charms, and small wooden stamps to replicate images of the Buddha, some of which have survived in the arid northwestern regions of Gansu Province and Xinjiang. The larger images appear to have been made in much the same way as a rubbing from a stone inscription: Paper was laid over the inked surface of a wooden block and rubbed over with a brush to take an impression.

Printing using wood blocks was invented during the Tang dynasty (AD 618–907). The oldest surviving example, of a printed Buddhist charm, is preserved in a stone pagoda at Pulguksa temple in Kyŏngju, S. Korea. The document is likely to be older than the temple and the pagoda, which were completed in 751. For wood-block printing a smooth wood block was covered by a page of written manuscript, face down, and then a skilled woodcarver cut away all the wood except where the ink showed a character. Wood-block printing in China had many advantages. A page printed in this

---

[1]Around 1500 BC Egyptians made papyrus from papyrus-reed and used it for writing. The English word *paper* comes from *papyrus*. However, it is the Chinese who invented paper proper, papyrus being made quite differently.

way could easily accommodate both illustrations and text in a variety of script styles, sizes of characters, and colors. The block was made from a hard, close-grained wood, and could take a great many impressions—as many as 30,000—before it wore away. Then the block could be planed down and re-used. The blocks could be stored so that the book could remain "in print" indefinitely. Wood-block printing required something abundant in China, namely cheap labor and raw materials (paper, wood, ink).

The Song dynasty (960–1279) saw a great flowering of wood-block printing and the development of a true printing industry. The style, calligraphy, and technique of the Song printers set standards for the printers of later times. Even today one of the most common Chinese typefaces is called "Old Song." The entire Buddhist scripture, the *Tripitaka*, was completed between 971 and 983 using 130,000 printing blocks.[2] Daoists, too, had their canon printed in the 11th century, from 83,198 blocks. At the capital Kaifeng, a special court for printing was established to house this vast store of printing blocks. Besides these huge projects backed by the state and religion, local officials, even private individuals, undertook the printing of a wide variety of books such as handbooks on medicine, botany, and agriculture. During this period, printed books began to displace manuscript copies, contributing greatly to the spread of literacy. "Printed matter was the life-blood of the expanding Song educated elite" (Fairbank 1992: 94). Confucian texts became available in a greater quantity and variety than ever before, thus widening the circle of potential competitors for the civil-service exams. Exam questions and answers were also printed and sold. In succeeding dynasties, large quantities of cheap books of popular literature and on other topics were produced for the mass market.

In wood-block printing, a whole page is engraved on a single wood block, which can be used only for one particular book, until it is planed smooth and re-engraved. By contrast, with movable type, which is appropriately called *huozi* ('living character'), each character is engraved by itself on an individual block, as a piece of type that can be used repeatedly for different books. The major problem with Chinese movable type is the huge and unspecifiable number of characters, which number several thousands counting only the common ones, compared to the 26 upper- and 26 lower-case letters of the English alphabet ("Number of Characters" in chap. 3). To set a page of type, a compositor sat between two huge revolving tables divided into a framework of separate compartments for the type. One table contained the common characters, and the other the less common ones, all arranged according to their rhymes. To compose a page of a book, the compositor selected each individual type block from its compartment on the table and placed it into a wooden form to assemble it into columns, then wedged it tight with bamboo wedges. The composed page of type was then laid face up and inked, and an impression taken. After all the desired copies had been printed, the type was broken up and redistributed into its proper compartments on the revolving table.

---

[2]The *Tripitaka* is a collection of Buddhist scriptures, originally recorded from oral traditions in the 1st century BC. It is divided into three parts or Pitakas: Sutra consists of sermons; Vinaya, the rules of the Buddhist order; and Abhidharma, a treatise on philosophy and psychology.

Ceramic movable type was invented in China in the mid-11th century, but there was little economic incentive to perfect it. It was fragile and held the ink poorly. Ceramic type, and also wood type, which had to be cut individually, could not be made to accurate dimensions. Metal movable type made from copper and lead was used in China during the late 15th and 16th centuries, but it was expensive, for it was cut individually, not cast, as it was in Korea. The cast bronze type developed in Korea in the 13th century was adopted in China in the late 17th and early 18th centuries.

Typesetting using movable type remained a problem, and the simple, inexpensive, and convenient wood-block printing was still common during the Ming and Qing dynasties. In the 19th century Western printing technique was adapted to Chinese printing and publishing.

Books and Publications

Just as Chinese characters have a long history, so do Chinese books. In ancient books, characters were incised or written on bamboo or wood strips, each bearing a line of text. The strips were strung together with ropes on their tops and bottoms. The picture of a bamboo book is captured in the character for the "book" 冊 *ce,* which is found even among oracle-bone characters dating back 3400 years ago. Such books were heavy and bulky. The ropes disintegrated over time, and the ancient books have not been well preserved. Still, in the early 20th century, hundreds of pieces of wooden and bamboo strips produced during the Warring States (403–221 BC), Qin dynasty (221–206 BC), and Han dynasty (206 BC–220 AD) were discovered. They bore characters in the clerical script.

A later form of book was a scroll. To produce such a book, individual sheets of silk or paper, each roughly 12 inches by 18 inches, were marked out in faint columns, and the text was copied on to them. The completed sheets were then pasted together end to end to form a continuous scroll. One scroll commonly contained the text of one chapter of a book, and ten scrolls were bundled together in a cloth wrapper for convenience of storage. The scroll books were extremely inconvenient to use: for one thing, a reader could not easily look back or jump ahead in the text; for another, a scroll was bulky to store and easily damaged. The oldest extant copy of a silk scroll book, excavated in the 1970s, dates back to 168 BC.

Two alternative forms of book, accordion-fold and fascicle, replaced the scroll form during the 10th century. In accordion-fold, a long continuous text was folded in a series of accordion folds so that it could easily be opened at any given place. In fascicle, each double page was printed on one side of a single sheet, which was folded down in the middle, with the fore-edge left uncut. The doubled sheets were then sewn together at the inner margin to form a fascicle protected by a cover of heavy paper (Twitchett 1983).

Now let us consider some important books that have been written over the long history of Chinese literature. Some texts of the Confucian classics were written during the Zhou dynasty (1100–256 BC), but of these, many were lost in the first Qin emperor's infamous "burning of the books" in the early 3rd century BC. The books that escaped the burning were in such utilitarian fields as medicine, horticulture, and divination, including the *Book of Changes*. During the Han dynasty some of the lost Confucian texts were reconstructed from the memories of scholars.

In the Han dynasty, books that interpreted classical texts and history flourished. In particular, *Historical Records (Shiji)* by the first great historian Sima Qian (145–86 BC) became a model for later histories. It deals with the 2597-year history of China from the legendary Emperor Huang Di to Emperor Wu Di of the Han dynasty, mostly through the lives of leading personages. *The Yellow Emperor's Compendium of Corporeal Healing*, compiled in the 2nd century BC, was one of the greatest classics of Chinese medicine. It became the foundation of Chinese medical thought over the subsequent 2000 years. Also during the Han dynasty the first comprehensive book that explains and analyzes characters, *Shuowen Jiezi*, appeared ("Six Categories of Characters" in chap. 3). Apparently there were bookshops in the later Han capital city of Luoyang centuries before the emergence of printing proper.

The Tang dynasty (618–907) is called the "golden age of literature," especially of poetry. A selection of poems from the best known poets, titled *300 Poems from the Tang Dynasty*, has been used as a school text for centuries and has been translated into English. We sampled a few Tang poems earlier (e.g., fig. 4-2). Some Tang emperors were themselves poets (a tradition extended by Chairman Mao Zedong), promoted literature, built libraries, and made many copies of rare works of literature. Manuscript copies of texts, popular poems, rubbings of stone inscriptions, and model essays for the state exams were on sale in the markets of big cities.

In the Song dynasty (960–1279) the state undertook massive printing projects to produce standard editions of commentaries on the Confucian canon, histories, encyclopedias, dictionaries, and literary anthologies. By the late Ming dynasty in the 16th century works of philosophy, poetry, history, and moral exhortation were printed and distributed, and the wealthy could maintain extensive private libraries.

Turning to novels and dramas, such books were read mainly for entertainment by non-scholars and scholars alike, in contrast to the Confucian classics that were studied mainly by scholars to prepare for the civil-service exams. According to the writer Lu Xun (1959: 415), the best thing scholars of the Song dynasty did was to compile a 500-volume *Taiping Miscellany*, which collected stories from the Han dynasty to the beginning of the Song dynasty. It included some Tang prose romances, whose plots became more elaborate and whose language more polished than ever before. The stories in *Taiping Miscellany* were in the vernacular rather than literary language— "a tremendous change in the history of Chinese fiction." During the Mongol rule in the Yuan dynasty (1279–1368), when the state exams were suspended, educated Chinese turned to the writing of novels and plays, in the vernacular language.

Among the many novels, several described below have become popular classics, and have been translated into English, not to mention into Korean and Japanese. Mao Zedong remembered vividly the pleasure he had derived as a boy from reading great Chinese novels like these. These novels, written in colloquial language, if mixed with literal language to varying degrees, contributed to the development of this type of language as an artistic medium. Let us begin with "the four great amazing novels of the Ming dynasty."

The Romance of Three Kingdoms is based on some historical characters and events of the three competing kingdoms that followed the downfall of the Han dynasty in AD 220. It was probably compiled by a number of anonymous authors and editors over several generations. The earliest extant version dates from the early 16th century. This epic story paints a vast canvas encompassing the length and breadth of China over a century of political and military turmoil. It is full of battles and intrigues, centered around the themes of brotherhood, loyalty, ambition, and revenge. It is the source of many Chinese operas.

The next great novel *Water Margin*—also translated as *All Men are Brothers* or *Outlaws of the Marsh*—deals with the adventure of a historical figure and his band of outlaws who lived in marshes. Like Robin Hood and his band in England, the chivalrous outlaws defended the poor and the persecuted, often in conflict with the government. The story had been a popular legend since the Song dynasty. It was the first great Chinese novel to be written entirely in the vernacular.

In the 16th century China's most beloved novel of religious quest and picaresque adventure, *Journey to the West* or *Monkey*, was published. As with other pieces of fiction written earlier, this story grew by degrees into a legend between the end of the Tang and Yuan dynasties, until it was gathered together into one long novel by Wu Cheng'en (1500–1582). The story is about a pious but helpless and plodding monk who undertakes a long and treacherous journey to India in search of Buddhist scriptures, accompanied by three disciples, mischievous Monkey, greedy Pigsy, and quiet Sandy (water imp). Thanks to Monkey who is endowed with magical powers, the journey is filled with grotesque incidents and fantastic episodes.

> Through all the comedy and satire shine what we might call a Taoist [Daoist] amusement at human absurdities, a Buddhist critique of greed and materialism, and a Confucian appreciation for moderation in all things. [Ropp 1990: 323]

In 1610 another of China's greatest novels, *Jin Ping Mei* ('*Gold–Vase–Plum*', from the names of the three main female characters) or *Golden Lotus* (the name of one of the five consorts of the protagonist) was published anonymously. It describes in detail the many sexual exploits of a licentious and unscrupulous young man of wealth and status. He finally dies of sexual overexertion. The publication of the book has been banned from time to time, especially in the People's Republic of China, because of its pornographic passages. (One English translation has those passages in Latin.) According to legend, the author of *Golden Lotus* presented the book to his enemy, the Prime Minister Yan Shifan, coating the top of each page with poison. Yan dropped dead after he had wet his thumb to turn the final page. Its pornographic flavor notwithstanding, the novel is invaluable in providing us a window into the daily lives of ordinary people of the late Ming dynasty, when economy was expanding, and society was changing rapidly. The novel's characterization of women shows much psychological insight.

In the 18th century in the Qing dynasty (1644–1912) the great, perhaps the greatest, Chinese novel *Hong Lou Meng* by Cao Xueqin appeared in manuscript. It has been translated into English variously as *The Dream of the Red Chamber*, *A Dream of Red Mansions*, and *The Story of Stone*. The story takes place in a wealthy extended family during Emperor Qianlong's reign, depicting meticulously its every aspect like an encyclopedia: Buddhism, Daoism, and Confucianism, family ritual, festivals, customs, food, clothing, and so on. There is now in Beijing a theme park that recreates some famous scenes from this novel.[3]

On the surface the story is about a doomed love story. Teenage Jia Baoyu is handsome, intelligent, and sensitive, but is idle and indifferent to classical studies. He grows up happily surrounded by adoring women folk, relatives as well as servants, and ruled by his autocratic but benevolent grandmother. Among the young relatives, there is beautiful and sensitive Black Jade. Jia and Black Jade come to love each other. But because Black Jade is frail and without wealth, Jia is tricked by his parents into marrying a wealthier and stronger girl. The grief-stricken Black Jade dies on Jia's wedding day, thus changing his attitude to life for good. At the novel's end, Jia, though he has just passed a civil-service exam, disappears and is lost to his family. Pervading the novel are the undertones of transitoriness of the material world and melancholy, as may be suggested by the two verses that end different parts of the book in different translations, *A Dream of Red Mansions* (Yang and Yang 1978: 586, v. 3) and *The Story of Stone* (Hawkes 1986: 16, v. 5).

A tale of grief is told,	All is insubstantial, doomed to pass,
Fantasy most melancholy.	As moonlight mirrored in the water,
Since all live in a dream,	Or flowers reflected in a glass.
Why laugh at others' folly?	

During the Qing dynasty, three monumental reference books were published by a group of scholars under the patronage of Emperors Kangxi, his son Yongzheng and grandson Qianlong. One is the *Kangxi Dictionary*, a comprehensive and authoritative dictionary that defined 47,035 Chinese characters. Another is the enormous encyclopedia, the *Complete Collection of Illustrations and Writings of Ancient and Modern Times* published in 1728. It assembled all the finest past writings on natural phenomena, geography, history, literature, and government. Containing 10,040 volumes, it is one of the largest classified reference works in the world. The third monumental work is *Four Treasuries*, a complete anthology of famous works in four areas: classics, history, philosophy, and miscellaneous literary. Comprised of 79,000 volumes, it is one of the great achievements of Chinese bibiliography. On the other hand, Emperor Qianlong destroyed a few thousands of "unacceptable" books that expressed heretical views toward his Manchu dynasty. It is said that the Manchu emperors undertook these large-scale literary works to keep Chinese intellectuals occupied and to deflect them from criticising the Manchu. At any rate, traditionally, to be responsible and to maintain control over writings was part of a Chinese emperor's prerogative as well as his duty.

In the early 19th century, Christian missionaries introduced Western printing technology into China, and published Christian texts in Chinese. Preliminary Chinese translations of the Bible had been finished in the 1820s, and revisions circulated widely by 1850. Special editions of the Bible, in romanization, were used in the "dialect" areas of the southeast. In the 1860s and 1870s Western missionaries and scholars wrote or translated into Chinese several works in mathematics, science, and

---

[3]When I asked my Chinese colleague Zhang Zhi whether he had read *Hong Lou Meng*, he replied, "That's an inappropriate question; an appropriate question should be, 'How many times have you read it?'" He read it five times. Mao Zedong told his niece that he read it several times.

technology. Chinese themselves translated many Western works, fiction and non-fiction. One Chinese translated as many as 171 English and French works of fiction. These translated works were popular and influenced Chinese novelists of the time.

In the late 19th century, the technology of the printing press and the spread of a new urban readership spurred the growth of magazines and newspapers, which in turn contributed to an ever increasing number of readers. Still, the total readership of newspapers at that time has been estimated to be only between 2 and 4 million, one percent of China's population. By the mid-1930s readership of the papers had increased to between 20 and 30 million, still a tiny proportion of the huge population (Fairbank 1992). The newspapers and magazines exposed their readers to political views and ads for health and beauty products. In the early 20th century, as part of the May 4th Movement, several journals were published with names that reflect the excitement of the time, such as *The Dawn, Young China, New Society, The New Women*.

The most influential journal was *New Youth*, which led an all-out attack on the vestiges of Confucianism and urged the use of the vernacular in place of the literary style ("Literary vs Vernacular Language" in chap. 8). Its founder Chen Duxiu called for doing away with the cliche-ridden and grandiose literature of classicism and for creating a fresh and honest literature of realism. It was for this journal that the noted writer Lu Xun wrote his "Diary of a madman," which is considered one of the best Chinese short stories. It published a special issue on Henrik Ibsen, thus introducing Western-style plays to China. In 1921 the first literary association in China, The Society of Literary Studies, was founded.

Today the publishing industry in the People's Republic of China is controlled by the Newspaper and Publication Bureau, under the State Council. According to a decree issued in 1983 by the State Council, "The basic task of the publishing industry is to propagate Marxism–Leninism and Mao Zedong's thoughts, to spread scientific-technological and cultural knowledge useful for economic and social development, and to enrich the people's spiritual–cultural life."

In 1992 China published 6,345 magazines and over 2,000 newspapers. The most authoritative newspaper, with the largest circulation, is *The People's Daily (Renmin Ribao)*, the organ of the Central Committee of the Communist Party of China. There are a handful of newpapers and magazines in English, such as *The China Daily*. Newspaper readership is still small: In 1988–1990 it was estimated to be 30 per 1,000 people, compared to 632 in Hong Kong (highest among the nations of the world) and 587 in Japan (second highest). The number of book titles published has steadily increased in the past few decades: it was 13,692 in 1952; 31,784 in 1982; and 92,910 in 1992, for over one billion Chinese people. (Japan, with 125 million people, published 48,053 titles in 1993.)

In 1993 some important books were published. The year was the centennial of Mao Zedong's birth, and a spate of books on Mao were published, including *Mao Zedong's Merits and Faults, Right and Wrong* by his former secretary. In that year the third volume of the *Selected Works of Deng Xiaoping* was also published. As well, all the 74 volumes of the *Great Chinese Encyclopaedia* were finally published after 15 years of work.

China's publishing industry is currently in trouble. Squeezed by inflation and shrinking subsidies, publishers are under pressure to make money. Books that sell are *kungfu* adventure tales, soft-pornography pulp novels, and fortune-telling manuals. Authors of serious books, instead of receiving advances, have to first put up enough cash to cover publishing costs. So, many books in science and technology are not going to be written, or if they are written they are not going to be published. But according to the 8th 5-year plan, over 1000 titles in scholarly and technical fields are to be published between 1991 and 1995 with a subsidy.

Taiwan, with over 21 million people, has its own publishing industry. In 1992 it published 12,418 titles, a tenfold increase from a decade ago. It published 4,204 magazines and 294 newspapers. The number of its public libraries has also increased phenomenally, from 20 in 1951 to 310 in 1991.

In China itself, the oldest libraries could be the 3400-year old "archives" or the "stack rooms" of animal bones and tortoise shells that bore records of divination (chap. 3). Nearly every dynasty, starting with Han, sponsored the collecting of books in state libraries. During the Ming dynasty, its first emperor founded many libraries in provincial capitals and large cities. A library set up by a private indvidual in Zhejiang Province in 1566 is still extant. During the Qing dynasty, duplicates of all the books in the Imperial Library were maintained in the magnificent library of the Hanlin Academy, the nation's highest institution of learning.

On the other hand, Emperor Qianlong destroyed a few thousand "heretical" books. As a refuge from the literary inquisitions, some Confucian scholars pursued pure scholarship and antiquarian research, *kaozheng xue* ('evidential research'; see "Confucianism and Confucian Classics," above). They were supported by an interlocking infrastructure of book dealers and publishers, library owners, and teachers. Many merchants became patrons of *kaozheng* scholarship and accumulated large libraries that they put at the scholars' disposal.

By the mid-20th century, libraries were built in most provinces and big cities. Many Chinese classic books, including rare antiques, along with new books and foreign books, are now housed in the Beijing National Library, one of the largest libraries in the world. Its predecessor, the Capital Library, was opened in 1912.

History of Literacy

Chinese characters have existed for 3400 years, if not longer. But in antiquity only a handful of specialists used them. For example, in the Shang/Yin dynasty, diviners recorded the particulars of divination using oracle-bone characters. In the 3rd century BC, the Qin dynasty, which enacted many laws, had clerks to handle official documents. In the Han dynasty, which followed Qin, the use of documents grew, and along with it, the stylized clerical script became the prevailing form of writing. The Han dynasty established the tradition of learning the Confucian classics as the highest level of literacy. Subsequently, for over 1,000 years, literacy was enjoyed by a tiny group of privileged men who could afford the time and money to study the Confucian classics, usually for the civil service exam.

During the Song dynasty (960–1279), with the expansion of trade, there arose a merchant class who could read and write material pertinent to their business affairs, though not the Confucian classics. This class broadened still more widely during the late Ming and early Qing dynasties, as local schools developed, printing expanded, and vernacular literature became popular. In 1792, during the Qing dynasty, when the full version of the great novel *The Dream of the Red Chamber* was published, it became an immediate success. The historian Spence observes:

> One may speculate that the novel's wide readership was composed of men and women from the upper class, of under-employed scholars, and also of those with some education who lived and worked as merchants and traders in the flourishing cities of the largely peaceful mid-Qing world. [1990: 109]

In the middle and late 19th century, 30–45% of the men but only 2–10% of women attained some degree of literacy. In a large survey made during the Republic era in the 1930s by John L. Buck, 45% of all males over the age of 7 had received schooling and 30% were considered literate. There were great disparities between or among regions (higher literacy in urban than rural regions), sexes (higher among males than females), occupations (higher among scholars and merchants than peasants), and income levels (higher among the rich than the poor) (Rawski 1979).

In Qing China, men attended school for several years and studied the Confucian classics, at least at an elementary level, but many abandoned their studies for want of funds or lack of academic ability. They became merchants, artisans, shopkeepers, landlords, well-to-do peasants, and monks. They probably could read and write a thousand or more characters, enough for their business activities. Many of these men, though they themselves were not scholars, aspired to educate one or more of their sons for the civil-service exams. There were also some men who had brief schooling, in rural winter schools, urban short-term schools, and the like. They probably learned only a limited number of characters, enabling some to keep simple accounts and to cope with the transactions involved in their daily lives.

Even before the founding of the People's Republic of China in 1949, Communist leaders launched a mass education movement to teach reading to illiterate adults, especially in the rural areas. They developed a flexible program that responded to local demands for specific kinds of knowledge, improvising teaching materials and using the local supply of limited literates as teachers. Teaching could be conducted at night or in any spare time, and lessons could be taught by "little teachers," namely schoolchildren. Instead of a textbook, a teacher would write characters to be copied and learned by students.

Mao Zedong instructed educators, sensibly, to search out in each village the characters locally needed to record work points and to write down the names of people, places, implements, and so on. He thought 200 to 300 characters would do; then another few hundred would be sufficient to handle matters beyond the village; and so on, until 1,500 were learned. Knowledge of even this limited number of characters can be useful.

In the early 20th century, during World War I, in an effort to educate the large number of Chinese laborers working in France, one of the leaders of the mass education movement, James Yen (Yan Yangchu), compiled a 1,000-character vocabulary, called "The People's Thousand Character Lessons," to be learned in 4 months, given an hour's study a day. He also published a periodical, *The Chinese*

Workers' Weekly, which used only those thousand characters. With the aid of literate staff, he wrote numerous letters home for these laborers. In China these brief and simple letters from France were read and reread aloud to the villagers. One surviving letter ran as follows:

> For the inspection of my elder brother. I have come many ten thousand *li* since I saw you. I am doing well and you need not have anxiety about me. I am earning three francs per day, but as living is expensive I cannot send money home yet. As to my quarrelling with you, that day at Yaowan, before I left, forget it! I did unworthily. Please take care of our parents and when I return in three or five years, I will bring enough money to help support them the rest of their days. [Spence 1990: 292]

Since the establishment of the People's Republic of China in 1949, an ever-growing number of children receive primary education, and hence are literate to some degree. But by no means all school-age children receive education and attain functional literacy, as described in the following section (also chap. 9).

Degrees of Literacy Using Characters

There is a range of literacy using any script, and this is particularly true of Chinese characters. Remember, a large dictionary lists 50,000 characters. How many of these characters does one have to know to be considered literate? The answer to the question depends on what kinds of literacy activities one wishes to engage in. The range of literacy in China, as in elsewhere, might be classified into four categories: scholarly, functional, limited, and illiterate, as described in "Scripts and Literacy" (in chap. 1).

Scholarly literacy. In imperial China a tiny group of male scholars studied the Confucian classics, histories, and other literary texts that had been handed down for centuries. They could read texts written in the literary style, and also write poems and formal essays. Such scholars probably knew several thousand characters, some of which were found only in the classic literature. Some of them passed the civil service exams, and some did not. Even today, when there are no civil-service exams, any society needs a small group of classical scholars and authors.

Functional literacy. People can read such everyday reading materials as newspapers and manuals, and also can fill in forms and write memos or simple letters. In addition, they have basic numeracy skills; and some can use a computer.... A society can be described as one with a high rate of literacy or mass literacy if most of its citizens have attained functional literacy.... To function adequately in an industrial society, people need at least functional literacy.... Industrialized nations try to equip their citizens with functional literacy through 9 years—6 years of primary and 3 years of middle school— of universal and compulsory education.

To be functionally literate a Chinese person may have to know about 3,500 common characters ("Number of Characters" in chap. 3). This number should be adequate for reading various kinds of modern popular texts, such as educational materials, newspapers, and magazines. Recall that primary school teaches about 2,800 characters (table 9-1); middle school might teach about 700 additional characters as well as consolidating knowledge of the characters already learned. Functionally literate Chinese must be able to read these characters and write most of them; they may have to know some characters both in their simplified versions and in their original complex shapes; they also must keep using the characters constantly, lest they forget some. Additionally, they should have some skills in Putonghua ('common speech') and Pinyin. As with most functional literates everywhere, they should have basic numeracy skills as well.

The proportions of the Chinese population who have attained different levels of education and literacy are shown in Table 10-3 (based on *Zhongguo Renkou Nianjian* or *Almanac of China's Population* 1992).

Table 10-3. Educational Levels and Literacy Rates in the PRC

Educational Level	1982	1990
college/university	0.98	2.07
high school	11.15	11.98
middle school	26.53	33.05
primary school	32.68	37.24
(semi-)illiteracy	28.66	15.48
total population	1,008,175,288	1,133,682,501

If functional literacy requires at least primary education, then in 1990 around 84% of people in China had it; if in addition it requires middle-school education, then only around 47% of people had it. (Semi-)illiteracy will be defined shortly. Those who fall between functional literacy and (semi-)illiteracy may have limited literacy.

Limited literacy. In November 1953 the Committee for Eradication of Illiteracy established, for the first time, the degrees of literacy for three social classes: 2,000 common characters for workers and officials; 1,500 for urban dwellers; and 1,000 for peasants. In 1956 "The Decision on the Eradication of Illiteracy," which was jointly promulgated by the Communist Party of China and the State Council, stipulated that workers and peasants learn 2,000 characters and 1,500 characters, respectively. With these many characters the workers and peasants could, at a very simple level, read printed materials, keep accounts, write notes, and make calculations with the aid of an abacus. The same stipulation was reiterated in 1978. Recall that in the early 20th century James Yen compiled a 1,000-character vocabulary and published *The Chinese Workers' Weekly* using only those thousand characters.

Illiteracy and semi-illiteracy. In 1953 the Committee for Eradication of Illiteracy defined "illiterates" (*wenmang*, 'writing, blind') as people, at a specified age, who know fewer than 500 characters, and "semi-illiterates" (*banwenmang,* 'semi-, writing, blind') as those who know more than 500 characters but do not meet the standards set for their social class. This definition has been consistently used ever since. The specified age was "12 or older" in the 1982 census and "15 or older" in the 1990 census. The percentage of illiterates and semi-illiterates does not change much whether age 12 or 15 is used, according to Prof. J. Lamontagne who analyzed the 1982 data for the various age groups (personal communication 1993). The rate of illiteracy and semi-illiteracy was 15.5% in the 1990 census.

As shown in Figure 10-2, there is a good correlation between the rate of illiteracy and the ages of people. Illiterates tend to be found among old people, females, and in rural areas in China, and in Taiwan.

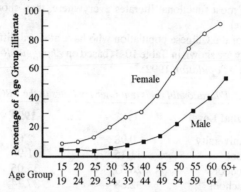

Figure 10-2. Rate of illiteracy and semi-illiteracy among different age groups of males and females according to the 1990 census in the People's Republic of China

In the 1990 census, about 8% of China's population belonged to 55 ethnic minorities (e.g., Tibetans, Mongols, and Koreans). They tend to have high rates of illiteracy. The 2 million ethnic Koreans in the Korean autonomous region in northeast China are an exception in having a low rate of illiteracy, indeed a lower rate than the Han Chinese. They learn Korean and a phonetic script, Han'gŭl (chap. 13); they also learn Putonghua and Hanzi.

Characters, once learned, must be used often. The injunction "use it or lose it" applies more to knowledge of the numerous and complex Chinese characters than to knowledge of the 26 simple letters of the English alphabet. Chinese peasants who do not use their limited literacy skill often enough are liable to lapse back into illiteracy. Such relapsed illiterates may number millions. One may ask why Chinese peasants might not use characters often enough. Perhaps knowledge of thousands of characters is an unnecessary luxury for them, until they start using sophisticated farm implements, fertilizers, and management methods that come with written instructions.

At the plenum of the Central Committee in late 1988 and in the National People's Congress of early 1989, one of the problems discussed was illiteracy, along with such other problems as labor unrest, graft, and rapid population growth. The 5-year literacy target is to raise the rate of literacy among people aged between 15 and 40 to 85% in rural areas and 90% in urban areas. The state bureau estimated that, despite the one-child policy, 20 million babies would be born each year for at least the next eight years. At this rate, by the year 2000 China's population would explode to 1.3 billion! Feeding them is a daunting task; so is educating them.

Can mass literacy be achieved using Chinese characters? The answer must be a resounding "yes." Look at the steadily decreasing rate of illiteracy in China itself over the past few decades: 38.1% of the total population in 1964; 28.66% in 1982; and 15.48% in 1990. Look at also the low rates of illiteracy (2.8%) among young (age 25–29) males (fig. 10-2). In Taiwan, where only Chinese characters are used, the rate of illiteracy in 1991 among males aged between 25 and 29 was extremely low, 0.14%. In Japan and South Korea, where about 2,000 Chinese characters are used along with phonetic scripts, the rate of illiteracy is negligible. Such high rates of literacy have been achieved in these nations even though (or perhaps because) they use the original complex characters rather than the drastically simplified ones used in China. (In Korea, Chinese characters are taught late and used sparingly in text; so they are not well mastered; the major script in Korea is Han'gŭl.)

A 9-year period of compulsory and free education is only a goal to be attained in China, but it exists in practice in Taiwan, in Japan, and almost in S. Korea and N. Korea. The rate of participation in compulsory education in these nations is close to 100%. That is, almost all children go to primary and middle schools and graduate from them. The territories of these nations are small, permitting easy communication; their peasant populations are small and not so isolated from the cities. In case of Taiwan, most of the population is bilingual in the local "dialect" and Mandarin, making it easy to promote literacy in a writing system based on the standard language, Mandarin. In the PRC, Putonghua ('common speech') has not yet penetrated every corner of China, despite the government's best effort ("Instruction of and in Putonghua" in chap. 9).

So, someday the Chinese people may achieve mass literacy, when their political and socio-economic conditions improve; conversely, when the Chinese people are better educated and more literate, they may improve their socio-economic conditions. But, remember, mass literacy is necessary but not sufficient for economic success (chap. 1).

Traditional and Pre-1949 Education

In remote antiquity, in the Shang and Zhou dynasties, it is said that there were state and local schools, and Confucius (551–479 BC) is said to have studied in one of them. Confucius himself is credited with opening a private school at his birthplace Lu, now the city of Qufu in Shandong Province. According to the *Historical Records*, he taught the *Book of Poetry*, the *Book of History*, rites, and music. His disciples, who came from both noble and common families, were said to have numbered 3,000, a handful of whom became well enough known for their names to go down in history.

In 124 BC during the Han dynasty the Grand Academy (*Taixue*) was founded with a small number of students, and by the mid-2nd century AD it boasted 30,000 students, presumably not resident all at once. The academy taught the Five Classics, and was a training ground for high officials. There were also official provincial schools. Though Confucian learning declined during the period of disunity following the fall of the Han dynasty, there were some independent Confucian scholars who taught in the provinces, attracting many students.

The reunited and centralized empires of the Sui (589–618) and Tang (618–907) dynasties, requiring large numbers of officials with a common training, revived the official school system. The Grand Academy of the Han dynasty was re-established as one of the five Directorates. In the mid-8th century, this State Academy Direcorate (*Guozijian*) at the capital Chang'an (modern Xi'an) consisted of six schools with over 2,000 enrolled students. Three of the Directorate's six schools taught mainly the Confucian classics to prepare the students for the civil-service exams, while the three other schools taught such practical subjects as mathematics, law, and calligraphy. There were also official provincial schools, as in the Han dynasty.

During the Tang dynasty, there were private schools, where the students' goal was not limited to passing the civil srvice exam but included as well the pursuit of knowledge under renowned scholars. At one time there was even a college for Daoism. In AD 740 the Hanlin Academy ('Forest of Pens'), the main preserve of Confucian ideology, was founded at the imperial court. It became the top institution for high-ranking officials, scholars, and literati for more than a thousand years, until the end of the Qing dynasty in 1911. Tang education attracted students from Korea and Japan.

During the Northern Song dynasty (960–1125) small boys were taught to read and write at home and then went to school around age 8. In the 1020s the government began to encourage the establishment of schools by awarding them land endowments as well as printed books. Recall that the Northern Song was the first society in the world with printed books ("Invention of Paper and Printing," above). By the early 1100s the state school system had 1.5 million acres of land, which could provide a living for some 200,000 students (Fairbank 1992).

In the late Ming and early Qing dynasties, early education took place in a clan school where boys of one clan were taught by a live-in tutor hired by the clan. A clan or lineage organization was based on family descent through the male line. It often held a large amount of land that provided income for support of its own school. Pupils who showed academic promise at clan schools were admitted to advanced schools or academies, where they studied the Confucian classics in preparation for the civil service exams. These academies, located mostly in but some outside cities, numbered in the thousands. The less talented students at clan schools were encouraged to turn to trade or farming. Through this educational system, the males of the upper socio-economic class were well educated. Sons of families of modest means also received elementary education at village schools for two to four years before entering a trade or craft. The schools were run in the homes of teachers, who were often degree-holding scholars, or in nearby temples. During these last two dynasties, the national educational system — the university in the capital and schools in other localities — declined, and school examinations served merely as preliminary exams to qualify for the civil service examination.

Near the end of the 19th century, progressive Chinese thinkers clamored for modern, Western education emphasizing science, mathematics, and foreign languages, in place of the traditional education emphasizing the Confucian classics. Some students went abroad to Japan, the United States, and Europe to absorb modern ideas. "The Hundred Days of Reform" of 1898, backed by Emperor Guangxu, proposed sweeping reforms in education and in the civil service exam, but they were only partially carried out. Finally, in 1905 the 1300-year-old imperial examination system was abolished.

Christian missionaries helped to usher modern, Western, and Christian, education into China. Throughout the 19th century, European powers forced the Qing government to open one Chinese port after another — eventually 48 — for trading. In these ports, called "treaty ports," the traders enjoyed the benefit of extraterritoriality (immunity from Chinese law). With the opening of each new treaty port, the number of mission schools increased steadily. Often run by an individual missionary or by a few teachers, these schools prepared young Chinese for English-speaking jobs in the treaty ports and as missionary assistants. They offered basic education to poor Chinese, both boys and girls, who otherwise would have received none. China's first two women doctors were mission-school graduates.

In January 1912 the Republic of China was founded. Recognizing the importance of modernizing education, it established the Ministry of Education and doubled the number of primary schools in China over the next ten years. By 1937, when the war with Japan broke out, there were nearly 300,000 modern elementary and secondary schools throughout China. However, these schools fell far short of the goals of universal education, equality of opportunity, and instruction in practical skills. Until the end of WWII in 1945 the number of schools and students continued to grow, but so did the population and its unschooled segment.

In Women Ignorance is Virtue

Let us take a moment to consider women's education or non-education, before moving on to the next section on education in the People's Republic of China. After all, women make up half the population of a nation, or "women hold up half the sky," as Mao Zedong put it.

Before historically reviewing women's education, we consider one unusual and interesting script, *woman's script (nüshu* or *nüzi)*, used over a millennium exclusively by women in Jiangyong county of Hunan province. The script, a syllabary, represented the local "dialect" of the Chinese language, and had about 2000 signs, 800 of which were commonly used in writing letters to women friends, diaries, poems, and songs. The origin of the script is a mystery, and its signs do not resemble Chinese characters. The use of the script declined in the 1950s when education opened up to women.

Women's education was ignored in Confucian China, where the motto was, "Value men and devalue women." A son is forever a part of the Chinese patrilineal line, but a daughter is a mere transient to be married off to another family. So why would a Chinese family invest money in educating women? Women were barred by law from taking the civil service exams and so did not need rigorous study in the Confucian classics. The attitude toward female education was, "In a woman ignorance is a virtue." In *A Dream of Red Mansions* (Yang and Yang 1978: 53, v. 1), which depicts the mid-Qing life, we read:

> When he became head of the family, however, in the belief that "an unaccomplished woman is a virtuous woman," he simply had her [his daughter] taught enough to read a few books such as the *Four Books for Girls* and *Biographies of Martyred Women...* while devoting her main attention to weaving and household tasks. That was why he gave her the name Li Wan ['plain silk'] and the courtesy name Kung-tsai ['palace seamstress'].

One Chinese woman scholar of note was Ban Zhao (c 50–112 AD) whose father was enlightened enough to teach her to read and write, along with her brothers. She wrote *The History of the Han Dynasty (Han Shu)*, which was begun with her historian brother Ban Gu and then completed by her alone after his death. In spite of her own intellectual achievement, in her book *Lessons for Women (Nüjie)* she counselled women of her time to be content with their lowly positions in a male-dominated society.

Imperial China boasts at least one empress, Wu Zetian (625–705), who wielded autocratic power for half a century, first through her husband, the third Tang emperor, then through the emperor's young successors, and finally for 15 years alone as an emperor of a newly declared dynasty. Another powerful woman ruler was Empress Dowager Ci Xi (1835–1908), who as a regent for her son and later her nephew Pu Yi, the last emperor, became a powerful figure for half a century in the dying days of the Qing dynasty.

During the Tang dynasty, some courtesans in the city pleasure quarters were well trained in poetry and music, the better to charm their educated male patrons. Some women of good family also learned from their parents or brothers to write classical poetry. Of the more than 50,000 poems in the anthology, the *Complete Tang Poems*, 600 were written by women. In particular, there were five Song sisters who were well educated, and, interestingly, remained single. The first sister wrote *Women's Analects* (*Nü Lunyu*), and the second sister wrote a commentary on it. Their works were read widely by women for 1000 years. The second sister also held a high official position in the palace for many years. Unfortunately, only a few of the five sisters' poems have survived.

The greatest female poet is considered to be Li Qingzhao (1084–c 1151) of the Song period. She was born to a wealthy scholar-official family and also was married to a scholar. She had a gift for depicting the genuine feeling of a woman in response to the vicissitudes of life. Of the many poems she wrote, about 50 have survived.

Some literate female members gave their male offspring informal lessons in Chinese characters before the boys entered more formal school. For example, the elder sister of the protagonist of *A Dream of Red Mansions* taught her younger brother, hardly 4-years old, to recognize several thousand characters. There is a saying in present-day Kerala, India, "If you teach a man you teach one person; if you teach a woman you teach a whole family."

In late Ming, in the 17th century, women's education was championed by some social thinkers, who argued that educating women would enhance the general life of a society by bringing improvements in morals, child rearing, and household management. Too bad that these thinkers were not listened to! In the 18th century certain thinkers again vigorously advocated the education of women. Several women did achieve prominence as poets, as described above, but the long and arduous study required for the Confucian classics or the rigorous research demanded by *kaozheng xue* ('evidential research') ensured that women would remain outside the intellectual elite.

Because of such negative attitudes toward women's education, in the early 20th century only about 1 to 10% of women, depending on the region, were literate. In John L. Buck's large survey of rural areas in the 1930s, only about 2% of the female population over age 7 had ever attended school, and only half of these were considered literate. But the southern coastal province of Guandong, which has been the main source of Chinese emigration for centuries, had a much higher literacy rate, judging from the 1896 census for Hawaii, according to which 25% of the Chinese female immigrants were literate (Rawski 1979). Even as late as 1909, only around 13,000 girls were enrolled in schools in the whole of China, and a few hundred more overseas, mainly in Japan. The first women's institution of higher education, Ginling College, was opened in Nanjing in 1915 by a Christian mission, and the first female students were admitted to Beijing University in 1920. Once educated, some women became critical of China's arranged marriages, restricted family life, and especially of the cruel practice of footbinding.[4]

Today women in China in theory have equal opportunity for education and employment. Yet the traditional attitude toward women's education prevails, though in a diluted form. The rate of school enrollment is lower for girls than boys, especially in the higher levels of schools. Furthermore, the dropout rate is much higher for girls than boys. In China, there are 86 female students to 100 male students, and they receive on average 3.6 years of schooling, giving a "female education index" of 67. Measured in this index, China ranks below France (99.7), Canada (99.4), South Korea (86.2), Hong Kong (82.6), Singapore (78.4), though above India (50.4), Pakistan (27.6), and Chad (21.0), among selected countries (prepared by the Population Action International; reported in *The Globe and Mail*, 31 Jan 1994). Consequently, in both mainland China and Taiwan most illiterates and semi-illiterates are females in rural areas, especially among the elderly (fig. 10-2).

Education: Ideology and Post-secondary

In October 1949 the People's Republic of China, a Communist regime, was founded. Its educational philosophy is to instill socialist ideology into the masses as well as to instruct them in practical skills. In place of the harmony, hierachy, and obedience of Confucian ideology, the Communists promote self-assertiveness, struggle, and rejection of the past. Between ideological correctness and academic excellence, or between red and expert, which is more important? As one is emphasized at the expense of the other, there arises a tension, which in turn causes a great deal of turmoil in the educational system.

Soon after its founding, the Communist regime copied the former Soviet Union's model of education, which stressed the specialized training of scientific and technical personnel. It also tried, perhaps vainly, to create intellectuals out of workers and peasants. The regime and its chairman Mao Zedong were distrustful of "intellectuals," the 5 million or so people with high school or college education under the former regime. And in 1956 Mao launched the hundred flowers campaign, "Let a hundred flowers bloom; let a hundred schools of thought contend." But in 1957, shocked and angry at the outburst of criticism of the regime from the intellectuals, Mao launched the Anti-Rightist Campaign, sacking from jobs a large number of "rightists," meaning intellectuals with skills. According to Fairbank, the year 1957 was the first of China's "twenty lost years" during which patriotic talents were not allowed to help the nation's

---

[4]For hundreds of years until the early 20th century, it was fashionable for Chinese women to have tiny bound feet, no larger than three inches, which allowed women to "erotically" waddle but not to walk properly, and certainly not to run. Footbinding began to spread during the Song dynasty, first among dancers and courtesans.

development. The "ten lost years" that characterize the Cultural Revolution was only a continuation of what began in 1957.

The Great Proletarian Cultural Revolution convulsed the whole of China for ten years from 1966 to 1976, when Mao died. Its stated objective was to combat elitism, revisionism, and the bourgeois mentality of the bureaucracy. It ravaged Chinese education: Schools and colleges were reduced to shambles, with buildings closed for years, students deployed as Red Guards or reassigned to the remote countryside, administrators and teachers were humiliated or dismissed, and no new books and materials were produced.

Waking up from the bad dream of the Cultural Revolution, the government under the pragmatic paramount leader Deng Xiaoping, set the goal of four modernizations in agriculture, industry, defence, and science-technology. It planned to restore the shattered schools and universities, to make them places where intellectual and scientific research could flourish. Toward this end, a number of key schools and lower-track technical colleges were established, and a crash program to train a large number of scientific research workers was introduced.

As part of a program to increase the number of trained teachers and researchers, since 1978 thousands of students and scholars have been sent to many developed nations, especially to the United States, some sponsored by the Chinese government and some privately funded. The number of students from China on US campuses alone rose sharply from 14,000 in 1985–1986, to 30,000 in 1987–1988 (Pepper 1990). By 1994 as many as a quarter million Chinese students and scholars had traveled abroad to study or conduct research.

Unfortunately for China, not all of these overseas-trained students and scholars, especially younger ones, have returned to China. After the pro-democracy demonstration at Tiananmen Square in June 1989, the Chinese government tried to restrict the travel of young university graduates out of the country, on the one hand, and to plead with the overseas students to return home with offers of good positions, on the other. Other changes prompted by the Tiananmen Incident included a revival of ideological penetration and work–study programs for university students, and strict control of teachers and their political attitudes. Since 1993 these measures have begun to be relaxed. Still fewer than one in five (one in three, according to the PRC) Chinese students are reported to return from studies abroad.

Since primary and secondary schools have been described already (in chap. 9), let us look at post-secondary education. Different categories are available, from comprehensive universities to specialized universities, and from regular 4-year universities to short-term professional colleges. When national college entrance examinations, which were discontinued during the Cultural Revolution, were reinstituted in the late 1970s, the 3-day nation-wide exam attracted millions of candidates, but only one in 20 passed it. Some candidates were recent graduates of secondary schools, and some were taking the test for the second time. Such fierce competition was reminiscent of the civil-service examinations of bygone days (chap. 10). Not only the test scores at the exam but also political evaluation and recommendation were considered for admission to a college.

In the 1990 census, only 2.1% of the total population of the PRC were college graduates, compared to over 30%–40% in North America. (highest in the world). In 1992 only 15% of high school graduates entered post-secondary institutions. Between 1978 and 1994, enrollment more than tripled to 2.5 million, which is still a drop in the ocean of 1.2 billion people in China. The increase has been mainly in specialized or vocational programs at the expense of pure academics. The majority of university students study science, engineering, agriculture, and medicine, and only a minority study liberal arts and law. (The same trend is found in Taiwan, where over 40% of high school graduates enter post-secondary institutions.)

The Communist leaders under Mao Zedong were suspicious of intellectuals, calling them "the rightists," and mistreated them. Recall the "hundred flowers campaign" in 1956 and the Cultural Revolution between 1966 and 1976. Today when China's socialist market economy is developing at a breakneck pace, its rulers still fear the effect of teaching their citizens how to think. They are reluctant to foster genuine universities. According to the dean of education at Hong Kong University, Cheng Kai-ming, "China doesn't really have universities in the Western sense of the term, with a culture of liberalism and critical thinking. But they need them if they want to innovate and grow." The quote is found in an article by Brauchli (1994), appropriately titled "Mao's thought still hangs over education."

University education used to be free in China. As a repayment for the free education, graduates were required to accept jobs chosen for them by the state. No longer. As more and more young people see a university degree as the route to success, costs are rising faster than government education spending. As one way to meet this financial crunch, some universities have gone into side businesses, such as consulting and publishing; as another way, universities charge tuition fees to students. In the fall of 1994, students entering three dozen or so top-rated universities had to pay annual fees that were the equivalent of half a year's income for an average urban wage earner. Eventually, tuition will be charged at all of China's over 1,000 universities. Now that the students shoulder some (20% by 1996) of their higher education cost, when they graduate they can choose careers and jobs on their own instead of taking those selected by the state.

In an article entitled "The impoverished education," Zeng et al (1990: 21) conclude that "We are confronted by a serious brain drain, lowered income for the intellectuals, and the devaluation of higher learning under the impact of commercialization." If all goes well, China's modernization effort in education will eventually bear fruit.

Part I: Summary and Conclusions

There is a huge number of Chinese speakers: about one billion in mainland China and 54 million more in Taiwan, Hong Kong, and other parts of the world. They speak seven major Chinese "dialects," which may be mutually unintelligible but still share basic linguistic features. Of the seven "dialects," the one spoken in the region around the capital Beijing has been designated as the official standard, called Mandarin or Putonghua ('common speech').

Putonghua uses only about 400 different syllables, each of which can be pronounced in one of four tones. The number of different tone syllables actually used in the language is about 1,300, each of which is associated with one morpheme. Chinese morphemes do not change their forms or inflect for different grammatical functions. A single Chinese morpheme–syllable can be a word, but more often two or more morpheme–syllables join to form a compound word, partly to minimize the ambiguity of the many monosyllabic homophones.

One Chinese morpheme is represented by one Chinese character. About 50,000 characters may be available to represent the many morphemes of the Chinese language, but most of them are hardly ever seen. About 6,000 characters may be sufficient for scholarly literacy, 3,500 characters for functional literacy, and 1,000–2,000 characters for limited literacy, as each character can be used and re-used in many different words. The thousands of characters have complex shapes to make them discriminable from each other. The range of complexity, as measured in stroke number, is large: from 1 to 64 in a full set, and 1 to 24 among the 3,500 common characters.

Characters are traditionally grouped into six categories based on their origin, construction, and use: pictographs, indicators, meaning composites, mutually defining, semantic–phonetic composites, and phonetic loans. Most characters commonly used today are semantic–phonetic composites, in which there are two components, one of which cues, if unreliably, its tone syllable and the other its semantic field. Many characters may have originated 3400 (or possibly 6000) years ago as pictographs, but their pictographic origins have been all but lost in the stylized characters that have evolved from them.

Chinese characters have some good points. They are suited to represent the Chinese language, because Chinese morphemes are one syllable long and do not change their forms, and because the Chinese language does not require a variety of grammatical morphemes that either have little meanings or change forms constantly. Characters are also useful: they differentiate homophones, which are abundant in Chinese; they readily combine to create compound words and idioms; they produce meaningful and unambiguous abbreviations; above all, they can be read across different times and "dialects." Thanks to the last point, Chinese speakers all over the world feel that they are unified as the Han people, and that they have access to the vast storehouse of knowledge written in characters that has accumulated over thousands of years.

Chinese characters are logographs, each of which represents directly the meaning and indirectly the sound of a morpheme. The meaning is extracted faster from a logograph than from a word in a phonetic script; conversely, the sound is extracted faster from a word in a phonetic script than from a logograph. Such differences in word recognition are small but are consistently found in experiments. Beyond word recognition, in comprehending sentences and paragraphs, the differences between the two types of writing systems seem to decrease.

Chinese characters have disadvantages too. Because characters are numerous, complex in shape, and deficient in sound indication, they take time and effort to master. They are inconvenient for dictionary compiling and consulting, typesetting, typing, and word processing. As part of language and writing reform, 3,500 characters have been designated for common use, over 2,000 characters have been simplified, vernacular language has replaced literary language, and Putonghua has been adopted as a standard language. Also a Roman alphabet called Pinyin has been adopted to indicate the sounds of characters directly and precisely.

Viewed from a historical perspective, the Chinese can boast 3400 years of continuous use of the same, albeit modified, writing system. The Chinese wrote primitive books 3000 years ago, invented paper 2000 years ago and printing 1300 years ago. But they cannot boast an equally glorious history of mass education and literacy. For 1300 years, until the early 20th century, education meant studying the Confucian classics in preparation for the civil service examination. The exam, by testing knowledge of the difficult yet impractical Confucian classics rather than of contemporary practical learning, promoted scholarly literacy among a small elite group of males but hindered the spread of functional literacy among the masses.

In China today most school-age children go to primary school, where they learn about 2,800 characters, initially through Pinyin. They learn characters batch by batch, beginning with pictographs and indicators and then moving on to more complex meaning composites and semantic–phonetic composites. They learn to recognize each simple character as a whole pattern, but in writing they analyze it into a series of strokes. A similar number of characters is taught in primary school in Taiwan and Hong Kong.

China's illiteracy rate has been steadily declining in the past few decades, but it— 15% in the 1990 census—is still not low enough for a nation aspiring to become industrialized. But the use of characters cannot be blamed, because Taiwan has achieved a high rate of literacy using characters in their original complex shapes. A nation's economic and political policies have something to do with its rate of literacy. For example, in China, educational spending is low, and there are urban–rural disparities in primary education. Anyway a high literacy rate may be a prerequisite for, but is not a guarantee of, economic and political progress.

The use of characters cannot be blamed, as it sometimes is, for the failure of modern abstract science to develop in China. Rather, blame the Chinese world views—centered around Confucianism, Daoism, Buddhism, Yin–Yang, and Five Phases—that were not sympathetic to probing nature and original thinking. Blame also the civil-service examination system that siphoned off, for 1300 years, the best talents of the land. With these obstacles mostly gone, the Chinese in different parts of the world are poised to develop science and technology.

Characters have been continuously used for over 3400 years by the Chinese; they have been used for over 1700 years by the Koreans and over 1500 years by the Japanese as well. Their continued use is debated but seems assured for the foreseeable future.

Bibliography for Part I

In English or French
The authors' own romanized spellings are used when available.

Ai J. W. A report on psychological studies of the Chinese language in the past three decades. *Journal of Genetic Psychology*, 1950, *76*, 207–220.

Alexander, Michael. *Beowulf.* Penguin Classics, 1973.

Besner, B. and Coltheart, M. Ideographic and alphabetic processing in skilled reading of English. *Neuropsychologia*, 1979, *17*, 467–472.

Brauchli, Marcus. Mao's thought still hangs over education. 1994 Dow Jones & Co. Inc., reproduced in *The Globe and Mail*, Nov. 15, 1994.

Chan Wing-Tsit. *A source book in Chinese philosophy.* Princeton, N.J.: Princeton University Press, 1963. It is an authoritative source book on Confucianism, Daoism, Buddhism, and other Chinese philosophies.

Chao Y.-R. *A grammar of spoken Chinese.* Berkeley: University of California Press, 1968. It is a comprehensive and authoritative book on the topic.

Ch'en Chi-ma. *Chinese calligraphers and their art.* Melbourne: Melbourne University Press, 1966.

Chen H. C. and Chen M. J. Directional scanning in Chinese reading. In I. M. Liu, H. C. Chen, and M. J. Chen (Eds.), *Cognitive aspects of the Chinese language.* Hong Kong: Asian Research Service, 1988.

Cheng Chao-Ming. Computational analysis of present-day Mandarin. *Journal of Chinese Linguistics*, 1982, *10*, 281–358.

Chinese Academy of Social Sciences. *Information China* (3 volumes). Oxford: Pergamon Press 1989. A comprehensive and authoritative reference source on China.

DeFrancis, John. *The Chinese language: Fact and fantasy.* Honolulu: University of Hawaii Press, 1984. It is written to debunk many misconceptions Westerners have about the Chinese language and characters.

de Kerckhove, Derrick and Lumsden, Charles J. (Eds.) *The alphabet and the brain: The lateralization of writing.* Berlin: Springer-Verlag, 1988. It has several articles relevant to Chapter 10 of this book.

Durkin, D. *Children who read early.* New York: Teachers College, Columbia University, 1966.

Ebrey, Patricia. Women, marriage, and family in Chinese history. See Ropp (Ed.) 1990.

Eggington, W. G. Written academic discourse in Korean: Implications for effective communication. In U. Connor and R. B. Kaplan (Eds.) *Writing across languages: Analysis of L2 text.* Reading, MA: Addison-Wesley, 1987.

Elegant, Robert. *Pacific destiny: Inside Asia today.* New York: Crown, 1990. It is a readable introduction to Pacific-Rim nations: China, Japan, Korea, Hong Kong, Taiwan, Singapore, Vietnam, Malaysia, Indonesia, Philippines, Thailand, and Australia. It captures the dynamics of change occurring in these regions.

Fairbank, John King. *China: A new history.* Cambridge, Mass: Harvard University Press, 1992. The famous historian brings history of China from its neolithic days to its troubled present, including the Tiananmen Uprising. It is concise yet comprehensive, and authoritative yet readable.

Fan Liu, Tong Lequan, and Song Jun. The characteristics of Chinese language and learning to read and write. In D. Wagner (Ed.) *The future of literacy in a changing world.* New York: Pergamon 1987.

Feitelson, D. *Facts and fads in beginning reading: A cross-language perspective.* NJ: Ablex, 1988.

Flaugher, R. L. *Patterns of test performance by high school students of four ethnic identities.* Princeton, N. J.: Educational Testing Service, 1971.

Francis, W. N. and Kucera, H. *Frequency analysis of English usage.* Boston: Houghton Mifflin, 1982.

Glahn, E. Chinese writing through four millennia. In A. Toynbee (Ed.), *Half the world*. New York: Holt, Rinehart and Winston, 1973. This edited book describes the cultures of China, Japan, Korea, and Vietnam in many pictures, some in color.

Goody, J. and Watt, I. The consequences of literacy. In J. Goody (Ed.) *Literacy in traditional societies*. Cambridge: Cambridge University Press, 1968.

Gray, W. S. *The teaching of reading and wrting: An international survey*. Paris: UNESCO, 1956.

Havelock, E. A. *Origins of Western literacy: four lectures delivered at the Ontario Institute for Studies in Education*. Toronto: OISE, 1976.

Hawkes, David. See Cao Xueqin.

Hayashi Ooki (chief Ed.). *Tosetsu nihongo (The Japanese language in graphs)*. Tokyo: Kakukawa, 1982.

Hayhoe, Ruth (Ed.) *Education and modernization: The Chinese experience*. New York/Oxford: Pergamon 1992. The volume combines historical perspectives on Chinese education with a thematic analysis of a range of contemporary issues.

Hinds, John. Inductive, deductive, quasi-inductive: Expository writing in Japanese, Korean, Chinese, and Thai. In U. Connor an A.M. Johns (Eds.) *Coherence in writing: Research and pedagogical perspective*. Alexandria, VA: TESOL, 1990.

Hook, Brian (Ed.) and Twitchett, Denis (Consulting Ed.) *Cambridge encyclopedia of China*. Cambridge, England: Cambridge University Press, 1991.

Hoosain, Rumjahn. *Psycholinguistic implications for linguistic relativity: A case study of Chinese*. Hillsdale, N. J.: Lawrence Erlbaum, 1991. It reports and discusses many experiments done on Chinese characters. It is useful though technical.

Horodeck, Richard Alan. *The role of sound in reading and writing Kanji*. Cornell University Ph. D. thesis, 1987.

Huang, Jack K. T. and Huang, Timothy D. *An introduction to Chinese, Japanese, and Korean computing*. Singapore: World Scientific, 1989. It provides some useful statistical information on Chinese characters, and describes Chinese computing in detail but Japanese and Korean computing only in passing.

Kaplan, R. B. Cultural thought patterns in inter-cultural education. *Language Learning*, 1966, *16*, 1–20.

Karlgren, Bernard. *Sound and symbol in Chinese*. London: Oxford University Press, 1923 (also Hong Kong University Press, 1962). It is a delightful little book about the Chinese language and characters. As the first Sinologue to reconstruct old and middle Chinese sounds, Karlgren often provides historical background to some contemporary phenomena. Interestingly, he perpetuated some of the myths that DeFrancis tries to debunk.

Keightley, David N. *Sources of Shang history: The oracle-bone inscription of bronze age China*. Berkeley: University of California 1978. A useful book on the oracle-bone inscription.

Kratochvil, Paul. *The Chinese language today*. London: Hutchinson University Library, 1968. It discusses phonemes, morphemes, words, idioms, and sentences of modern Mandarin Chinese. The book is more suited for linguists than for the general public.

Kubota Ryuko. *Contrastive rhetoric of Japanese and English: A critical approach*. Ph.D. thesis, Department of Education, University of Toronto, 1992.

Lai Ming. *A history of Chinese literature*. London: Cassell, 1964. It gives a history of Chinese literature spanning over 3000 years, from Yin dynasty to the mid-20th century.

Lamontagne, Jacques. Personal communication on Chinese illiteracy. May 1, 1993.

Lau D. C. *Confucius: The analects*. Middlesex, England: Penguin Books, 1979. A good English introduction to Confucius.

Leong C. K. Hong Kong. In J. Downing (Ed.) *Comparative reading: Cross-national studies of behaviors and processes in reading and writing*. New York: Macmillan, 1973.

Leong C. K., Cheng P.-W., and Mulcahy, R. Automatic processing of morphemic orthography by mature readers. *Language and Speech*, 1987, *30*, 181–197.

Li N. Charles and Thompson, Sandra A. The gulf between spoken and written language: A case study in Chinese. In Deborah Tannes (Ed.) *Spoken and written language: Exploring orality and literacy*. Norwood, N.J.: Ablex Publishing, 1982.

Li N. Charles and Thompson, Sandra A. *Mandarin Chinese: A functional reference grammar*. Berkeley: University of California Press, 1981 (cloth); 1987 (paper). It is a useful reference book on Mandarin grammar.

Li Xiuqin. *Evolution de l'ecriture chinoise*. Beijing: Shang wu yin shu guan, 1990. (in French)

Lin Yutang. *The wisdom of Confucius*. New York: Random House, 1938. It gives a biography of Confucius as well as samples of his sayings.

Lindqvist, Cecilia. *China: Empire of living symbols*. New York: Addison-Wesley 1989. (translated from Swedish by J. Tate, 1991). This interesting book illuminates Chinese culture through a set of Chinese characters. It has many pictures.

Liu In-mau. A survey of memorization requirement in Taipei primary and secondary schools. Unpublished manuscript, 1984.

Liu In-mau and Hsu M. Measuring creative thinking in Taiwan by the Torrance Test. *Testing and guidance*, 1974, *2*, 108–109.

Liu Yongquan. Difficulties in Chinese information processing and ways to their solution. In V.H. Mair and Y.-Q. Liu (Eds.) *Characters and computers*. Amsterdam: IOS Press, 1991.

Logan, Robert, K. *The alphabet effect: The impact of the phonetic alphabet on the development of Western civilization*. New York: William Morrow, 1986. It claims that the alphabet has contributed to the development of the Western civilization.

Lu Xun. *A brief history of Chinese fiction*. Peking: Foreign Language Press, 1959. The noted writer discusses the well-known Chinese popular novels from a historical perspective.

Mason, J. M., Kniseley, E., and Kendall, J. Effects of polysemous words on sentence comprehension. *Reading Research Quarterly*, 1979, *15*, 49–65.

McLuhan, Marshall. *The Gutenberg galaxy: The making of typographical man*. Toronto: University of Toronto Press, 1962.

Miller, Roy Andrew. *Nihongo: In defence of Japanese*. London: Athlone Press 1986. It is a set of essays that defend the Japanese language against misconceptions.

Miyazaki Ichisada (translated from Japanese by Schirokauer, Conrad). *China's examination hell: the civil service examinations of Imperial China*. New Haven: Yale University Press, 1963/1981. A slim but informative book on the exam system in its last, most complex phase in the Qing dynasty. See also its Japanese original, below .

Mohan B. and Lo W. Academic writing and Chinese students: Transfer and developmental facts. *TESOL Quarterly* 1985, *19* (3), 515–534.

Nash, Madeleine, with Guest, Robert. Tigers in the lab: Asian-born, US-trained researchers are headed home to challenge the technological supremacy of the West. Science section, *Time*, 1994, Nov 21.

Needham, Joseph. *Science and civilization in China*. Cambridge: Cambridge University Press, 1954–?. This multi-volume work (projected to be 28) describes Chinese achievements in science and technology. It is more for scholars and researchers than the general public. See Ronan, and also Temple, below.

Needham, Joseph. Poverties and triumphs of the Chinese scientific tradition. In Crombie, A. C. (Ed.), *Scientific change*. London: Heinemann, 1963.

Nivion, David S. The criteria of excellence. In J. M. Menzel (Ed.) *The civil service: Career open to talents?* Boston: Heath, 1963.

Norman, Jerry. *Chinese*. New York: Cambridge University Press, 1988. It is strong on history and dialects of the Chinese language; it has one chapter on writing. Though intended for linguists, it is readable for non-linguists.

O'Neill, Hugh B. *Companion to Chinese history*. New York: Facts on File Publications, 1987. Nearly 1,000 entries on events, people, places, and organizations that have shaped Chinese history are presented alphabetically and concisely.

Pan, Lynn. *Sons of the Yellow Emperor: The story of the overseas Chinese*. London: Mandarin, 1990. This absorbing book describes the Chinese diaspora that stretches all over the world for several centuries.

Paradis, Michel, Hagiwara Hiroko, and Hildebrandt, Nancy. *Neurolinguistic aspects of the Japanese writing system*. New York: Academic Press, 1984. It reviews the literature on the effects of brain damage on reading Kanji and Kana, and concludes that the visual route is more common for reading Kanji and the phonetic route for reading Kana.

Paschal, B. J., Kuo Y.-Y., and Schurr, K. T. Creative thinking in Indiana and Taiwan college students. Paper read at the 5th Conference of the International Association of Cross-cultural Psychology, 1980.

Patel, P. G. and Patterson, P. Preconscious reading acquisition: Psycholinguistic development, IQ, and home background. *First Language*, 1982, *3*, 139–153.

Pepper, Suzanne. *China's education reform in the 1980s*. Berkley, Calif: Institute of East Asian Studies, University of California at Berkley, 1990.

Peyrfitte, Alain. *Quand la Chine s'eveillera ... le monde tremblera*. Paris, 1973. (in French)

Ramsey, S. Robert. *The languages of China*. N.J.: Princeton University Press, 1987. It gives a readable and detailed account of the dialects of the Chinese language and several important ethnic minority languages in China. The book describes also the writing systems of these languages.

Rawski, Evelyn Sakakida. *Education and popular literacy in Ch'ing China*. Ann Arbor: The University of Michigan Press, 1979. It presents evidence that during the 18th and 19th centuries a wide variety of educational opportunities provided many ordinary Chinese, who did not aspire to master the Confusian classics, with functional or limited literacy.

Rayner, Keith and Pollatsek, Alexander. *The psychology of reading*. Englewood Cliffs, N. J.: Prentice Hall, 1989. It describes many experiments on reading, especially on eye movements.

Read, C., Zhang Y.-F., Nie H.-Y., and Ding B.-Q. The ability to manipulate speech sounds depends on knowing alphabetic writing. *Cognition*, 1986, *24*, 31–44.

Republic of China yearbook. Taipei, Taiwan: Kwang Hwa Publishing company, 1993.

Ricci, Matteo. (tr. Gallagher, Louis J.) *China in the sixteenth century: The journals of Matthew Ricci, 1583–1610*. New York: Random House, 1942. It introduced China to the West.

Ronan, Colin A./Needham, J. *The shorter science & civilization in China: I*. New York: Cambridge University Press 1978. It is Needham's volumes 1 and 2 made easy for the general public.

Ropp, Paul S. The distinctive art of Chinese fiction. See Ropp (Ed.) 1990.

Ropp, Paul S. (Ed.) *Heritage of China: Contemporary perspectives on Chinese civilization*. Berkely: University of California Press, 1990. It has chapters on such topics as philosophy, political orgnization, and art.

Salapatek, P. Visual scanning of geometric figures by th human newborn. *Journal of Comparative & Physiological Psychology*, 1968, *66*, 247–258.

Samuels, S. J., LaBerge, D., and Bremer, C. D. Units of word recognition: Evidence of developmental change. *Journal of Verbal Learning and Verbal Behavior*. 1978, *17*, 714–720.

Sansom, George. *An historical grammar of Japan*. Oxford: Clarendon Press, 1928.

Scribner, S. and Cole, M. *The psychology of literacy*. Cambridge, Mass.: Harvard University Press, 1981. It reports the findings of several experiments done in Liberia, Africa, comparing consequencies of literacy in different scripts and schooling.

Seidenberg, M. S. The time course of phonological code activation in two writing systems. *Cognition*, 1985, *19*, 1–30.

Seybolt, P.J. and Chiang G. K.-K. *Language reform in China (documents and commentary)*. White Plains, New York: M.E. Sharpe, 1978–1979.

Simpson, Greg, B. and Kang Hyewon. The flexibile use of phonological information in word recogntion in Korean. *Journal of Memory and Language*, 1994, *33*, 319–331.

Sivin, Nathan. In Nakayama Shigeru and Sivin, Nathan (Eds.) *Chinese Science: Exploration of an ancient tradition*. MIT Press, 1973.

Sivin, Nathan. Science and medicine in Chinese history. See Ropp (Ed.) 1990.

Smethurst, W. *Teaching young children to read at home.* New York: McGraw-Hill, 1975. It describes some great thinkers and writers who learned to read early at home.

Smith, Richard J. *China's cultural heritage: The Ch'ing dynasty, 1644–1912.* Boulder, Colorado: Westview Press, 1983. It covers such topics as language, thought, art, literature, religion, and social activities.

Snow, Edgar. *Red star over China.* New York: Grove Press, 1968.

Spence, Jonathan D. *The search for modern China.* New York: W.W. Norton, 1990. It gives a colorful and detailed history of China between the Ming dynasty and the present Communist regime.

Statistical Yearbook of the Republic of China. Taipei, Taiwan: Directorate-General of Budget, Accounting, and Statistics, 1991–1992.

Stevenson, Harold, Chuansheng Chen, and Shin-Ying Lee. Mathematics achievement of Chinese, Japanese, and American children: Ten years later. *Science,* 1993, *259,* 53–58.

Stevenson, Harold and Stigler, James W. *The learning gap: Why our schools are failing and what we can learn from Japanese and Chinese education.* New York: Summit Books 1992. It describes a large-scale, longitudinal, cross-cultural study of mathematical and reading achievements of schoolchildren in the United States, China, and Japan.

Suen C.-Y. *Computational studies of the most frequent Chinese words and sounds.* Singapore: World Scientific 1986.

Sun F.C., Morita, M., and Stark, L. W. Comparative patterns of reading eye movement in Chinese and English. *Perception & Psychophysics,* 1985, *37,* 502–506.

Taylor, G. and Tingguang C. Linguistic, cultural, and subcultural issues in contrastive discourse analysis. *Applied Linguistics,* 1991, *12* (3), 319–336.

Taylor, Insup and Taylor, M. M. *The psychology of reading,* New York: Academic Press, 1983. It covers topics such as eye movements, word recognition, sentence and text reading, and reading instruction, mostly in English but some in East Asian languages.

Temple, Robert. *The genius of China: 3,000 years of science, discovery, and invention.* New York: Simon & Schuster, 1986. It is a distillation of Needham's multi-volume work. It has many pictures and drawings, some in color.

Tinker, M. A. Perceptual and oculomotor efficiency in reading materials in vertical and horizontal arrangement. *American Journal of Psychology,* 1955, *68,* 444–449.

Tu Wei-ming. The Confucian tradition in Chinese history. See Ropp (Ed.) 1990.

Turnage, T. W. and McGinnies, E. A cross-cultural comparison of the effects of presentation mode and meaningfulness on short-term recall. *American Journal of Psychology,* 1973, *86,* 369–381.

Twitchett, Denis Crispin. *Printing and publishing in medieval China.* London: The Wynkyn de Worde Society, 1983. The volume, thin (94 pages) though it is, covers in detail the subject matter stated in the title. Its many illustrations are useful. It even has a two-page section on Korean printing.

Tzeng O. J. L., Hung D. L., and Wang W. S.-Y. Speech recoding in reading Chinese characters. *Journal of Experimental Psychology: Human Learning and Memory,* 1977, *3,* 621–630.

Tzeng O. J. L. and Wang W. S.-Y. The first two R's. *American Scientist,* 1983, *71,* 238–243.

UNESCO. *Statistical yearbook.* Paris, 1991 and 1994.

Unger, J. Marshall. *The fifth generation fallacy: Why Japan is betting its future on artificial intelligence.* New York: Oxford University Press, 1987. It points out that the complex Japanese writing system is incompatible with computer technology and the Fifth Generation (AI) Project.

Vaid, Jyotsna. Script directionality affects nonlinguistic performance: evidence from Hindi and Urdu. In I. Taylor and D. R. Olson (Eds.) *Scripts and literacy: Reading and learning to read alphabets, syllabaries and characters.* The Netherlands: Kluwer Academic, 1995.

Wang Yuehua. Beyond character recognition. Unpublished manuscript, Ontario Institute of Studies in Education, 1989, Toronto.

Wieger, L.S.J. (translated by Davrout, S. J.) *Chinese characters: Their origin, etymology, history, classification and signification. A thorough study from Chinese documents.* New York: Dover, 1915/1965. The long title describes aptly this reference book.

Wong Lornita Yuen-Fan. *Education of Chinese children in Britain and the USA*. Multilingual Matters Ltd, UK: Clevedon, 1992.

Woon Wee-lee. *Chinese writing: Its origin and evolution*. Hong Kong: Joint Publishing 1987. It provides a good introduction to the origin and evolution of Chinese characters, using many sample characters and pictures.

Wu Jei-Tun and Liu In-Mao. A data base system about the psychological features of Chinese characters and words. In I.-M. Liu, H.-C. Chen, and M.-J. Chen (Eds.) *Cognitive aspects of the Chinese language*. Hong Kong: Asian Research Service, 1988 (vol. 1).

Yang Hsien-yi and Yang, Gladys (translators). *A dream of red mansions*. (See Cao Xueqin.) Beijing: Foreign Language Press, 1978. 3 volumes.

Yin Binyong. Pinyin-to-Chinese character computer conversion systems and the realization of digraphia in China. In V. H. Mair and Y.-Q. Liu (Eds.) *Characters and computers*. Amsterdam: IOS Press, 1991.

Zeng Qiang, Chen Yuejin, Tang Zhihui, and Liu Xiguang. "The impoverished education. *Shijie Jingji Daobao* (*World Economic Herald*), no. 426, (Jan 16, 1989); reprinted in English in *Chinese Education*, 1990, Summer, vol. 23, No. 2, 18–21.

Zhang G. and Simon, H. A. STM capacity for Chinese words and idioms: Chunking and acoustical loop hypothesis. *Memory and Cognition*, 1985, *13*, 193–201.

Zhang Zhi. The use of Chinese characters in mainland China. Unpublished manuscript.

Zhou Youguang. Intrinsic features of Chinese language as applied in word processing on computers. In V. H. Mair and Y.-Q. Liu (Eds.) *Characters and computers*. Amsterdam: IOS Press, 1991.

Zou Yuliang (Ed.) *Education in contemporary China*. Hunan Education Publishing House 1990. A comprehensive survey of educational policies and practices in the People's Republic of China.

In Chinese (or Japanese). Some articles have English abstracts or summaries.

Chūgoku nenkan (China yearbook). Research Center on China. Tokyo: Daishūkan 1992, 1993, and 1994. (in Japanese)

Chūgoku sōran (China survey). Tokyo: Kasumiyamakai 1993 and 1994. Comprehensive and up-to-date survey of all aspects of modern China. (in Japanese)

Cihai (A grand dictionary of Chinese words). Shanghai: Shanghai Dictionary Press, 1986 (a compact version of 1979 edition). This authoritative dictionary defines 14,872 charactrers and 91,706 words. It lists 1,360 tone syllables as an appendix. Its 1989 edition has three volumes.

Dong Kun. *Hanzi fazhan shihua (History of development of Chinese characters)*. Beijing: Shang wu yin shu guan, 1981.

Fukuzawa S. Developmental study on the factors of the difficulty in reading Kanji. *Science of Reading*, 1968, *11*, 16–21. (in Japanese)

Gao Ming. *Guwenzi leibian (Characters of old scripts classified)*. Beijing: Zhonghua Shufang, 1980. It lists Hanzi in bone, bronze, small-seal, and other scripts.

Gao Ming. *Zhongguo guwenzixue tonglun (Study of Chinese old scripts)*. Beijing: Wenwu Publisher, 1987. It gives a comprehensive description, with many pictures, of the oracle-bone script and bronze script.

Gao Mingkai and Liu Zhengtan. (translated into Japanese by Katsuyuki Torii). *The study of loan-words in the modern Chinese language*. The Institute of Oriental and Occidental Studies, Kansai University, 1988. It examines 1,500 loan words in Chinese, including Sino-Japanese words coined by Japanesee.

Hanzi xinxi zidian (A dictionary of Chinese character information). Beijing: Science Publishing Co. 1988. One of its appendices is a list of 2,500 common characters and additional 1,000 characters organized by stroke numbers.

Huang J. T. and Liu I. M. Paired-associate learning proficiency as a function of frequency count, meaningfulness, and imagery value in Chinese two-character ideograms. *Chinese Psychological Journal*, 1978, *20*, 5–17.

Ishii Isao. *Nihongo no zaihakken (Re-discovery of the Japanese language)*, Tokyo: Nihon kyōmun, 1988 (in Japanese). It contains essays on the Japanese language and writing, as well as the Ishii method of teaching Chinese characters to preschoolers.

Kaiho Hiroyuki. The process of extracting meaning information from Kanji. *Tokushima University Report*, 1975, *24*, 1–7. (in Japanese)

Kaiho Hiroyuki and Nomura Yukimasa. *Kanjijōho no shori no shinrigaku (Psychology of Kanji information processing)*. Tokyo: Kyōiku, 1983 (in Japanese). It reports and discusses many experiments done on Kanji (Chinese characters used in Japan) and Kana (Japanese syllabary). It is useful though technical.

Kawai Y. Physical complexity of the Chinese letters and learing to read them. *Japanese Journal of Educational Psychology*, 1966, *14*, 129–138 (in Japanese).

Kim Il-gon. *Tōajia no keizai hatten to jukyo bunka (East Asia's economic development and Confucian culture)*. Tokyo: Daishūkan 1992. It attributes East Asians' economic success to Confucian culture. (in Japanese)

Li Leyi. *Hanzi yanbian wubai li (Evolution of Chinese characters: 500 examples)*. Beijing: Shang wu yin shu guan, 1992. It traces the pictographic origins of 500 characters, which are shown in their seven different script styles as well as simplified shapes, if available.

Li Rong. Chinese characters: their changes and future. In M. Hashimoto and others. In *Kanji minzoku no ketsudan (Decision of peoples who use Chinese characters)*. Tokyo: Daishukan shōten, 1987. (in Japanese)

Liu In-Mao., Chuang C. J., and Wang S. C. *Frequency count of 40,000 Chinese words*. Taiwan: Luck Books Company, 1975.

Liu In- Mao, Yeh J.-S., Wang L.-H., and Chang Y.-K. Effects of arranging Chinese words as units on reading eficiency. *Journal of Chinese Psychology*, 1974, *16*, 25-32.

Liu Yuan, et al. *Xiandai hanyu changyongci cipin cidian (Dictionary of usage frequency of modern Chinese words)*. Beijing: Yuhang Publishing, 1990.

Liu Zhengtan, Mai Yonggan, and Shi Youwei. *Hanyu wailaici cidian (A dictionary of loan words and hybrid words in Chinese)*. Shanghai: Dictionary publisher, 1984. Over 10,000 loan words are examined.

Ma Rusen. *Yinxu jiagu wen yinlun (Introduction to oracle-bone characters in Yin ruins)*. Changchun: Dongbei Normal University Press, 1993. It describes the bone characters used in the Yin dynasty, and touches on the pottery marks used in neolithic cultures.

Meng Shu, Re Bing, Han Cheng, and Qin Gong (compiled). *Tongyinci cidian (A dictionary of homophones)*. Guangxi Minzu Publisher, 1989. It lists thousands of homophones.

Miyazaki Ichisada. *Kakyo: Chūgoku no shiken zigoku (Selection of talents through examination in various branches: China's examination hell)*. Tokyo: Chūko Shinsho, 1963/1994. The book, slim though it is, describes fully the complexity of the exam system in its last stage. It includes a few telling pictures. (in Japanese)

Miyajima Tatsuo. Stroke number of new character (Kanji) shapes. *Keiryo Kokugogaku* (Measurements on the Japanese Language). 1978, 11-17. (in Japanese)

Morioka Yusan. Theory on character shape. *The National Language and National Literature*, 1968, *45*, 8–26. (in Japanese)

Nomura Yukimasa. The information processing of Kanji, Kana script: The effects of data-driven and conceptually driven processing of reading. *The Japanese Journal of Psychology*, 1981, *51*, 327–334. (in Japanese)

Ozawa Atsuo and Nomura Yukimasa. The effect of discrimination and understanding processes on kindergarteners' reading of Kanji and Kana. *Educational Psychological Research*, 1981, *29*, 199–206. (in Japanese)

Okada Tamaki and Kida Akiyoshi. *Chūkai Senjimon (Ten-thousand-character essay explained)*. Tokyo: Iwanami shōten, 1984. (in Japanese)

Qiu Xigui. *Wenzixue gaiyao (An outline of character study)*. Beijing: Shang wu yin shu guan, 1988. It describes and theorizes how Chinese characters began and evolved.

Qiu Xigui. An orthodox style and a popular style in Yin–Zhou characters. In *Chūgoku kobunji to in-shū bunka (Chinese old characters and Yin–Zhou culture)*. Tokyo: Tōhō shoten 1989. A symposium with Li Xueqin, Higuchi Takayasu, et al.

Saito Hirofumi. Use of graphemic and phonemic encoding in reading Kanji and Kana. *The Japanese Journal of Psychology*, 1981, *52*, 266–273. (in Japanese)

Satō Yasumasa. Typeface and printing. In *Kotoba no kōgaku (Language engineering)*. v. 6 *Kotoba no kagaku (Science of language)*. Tokyo: Nakayama Shoten, 1958. (in Japanese)

Shimamura Shūji. *Sekai no namae (Names of the world)*. Tokyo: Kōdansha, 1977 (in Japanese). The book classifies personal names used in the world according to religious and cultural blocks.

Steinberg, D. D. and Oka Naoki. Learning to read Kanji is easier than learning individual Kana. *The Japanese Journal of Psychology*, 1978, *49*, 15–21. (in Japanese)

Steinberg, D. D. and Xi J. *Liangsui youer keyuedu (Two-year-olds can read: Teach your child to read)*, Tianjin, China: Tianjin People's Publishing House,1989. This little book describes the procedures taken to teach 2-year olds to read a few hundred characters.

Sugiyama Y. and Saito T. Variables of parent reading in relation to social traits of kindergarten pupils. *Science of Reading*, 1973, *15*, 121–130. (in Japanese)

Tajima Kazuo. Computer and Kanji. In Satō Kiyoji (Ed.) *Lectures on Kanji (Kanji Kōza)*, vol. 11, *Kanji and the problems of the national language*. Tokyo: Meiji Shoten, 1989. (in Japanese) See also Part III.

Tayama Shigehiko. *Nihon no shūjigaku (Japanese rhetoric)*. Tokyo: Misuzu Shobo, 1983.

Xu Dejiang. Teaching Chinese characters to preschoolers. Seminar given at East Asian Studies, University of Toronto, November 1992.

Xu Yizhi. *Zhongguo wenzi jiegou shuohui (Explanation of structure of Chinese characters)*. Taiwan: Shang wu yin shu guan, 1991.

Yokoyama Shoichi, Imai Motoi, and Furukawa Satoshi. The effect of orthography and imagery on recall of stimuli items which were read aloud. *Journal of Japanese Psychology*, 1991, *61*, 409–412.

Zhang Ruifan. (Ed.) *Zhongguo jiaoyushi yanjiu (Research on Chinese Educational history) (volume on pre-Qin)*. Shanghai: Huadong Normal University Press, 1991.

Zhongguo dabaike quanshu (Complete Encyclopedia Sinica), volume on language and writing. Beijing: Encyclopedia Publisher, 1988.

Zhongguo renkou nianjian (Almanac of China's population). Beijing: Population Research Institute, 1992.

Zhongguo tongji nianjian (Statistical yearbook of China). Beijing: Statistical yearbook publisher, 1993.

Zhongguo yuyanxue dacidian (Encyclopedic dictionary of Chinese linguistics). Beijing: Jiangsi Educational Publisher, 1991/1992. Information is organized by topics, such as writing system (the first topic) and phonology.

Zhou Youguang. Problems of efficiency of modern Hanzi phonetics. *Zhongguo Yuwen*, 3rd period, 1978.

Zhou Youguang. Chinese characters in China: their reform and education. In M. Hashimoto and others. In *Kanji minzoku no ketsudan (Decision of peoples who use Chinese characters)*. Tokyo: Daishukan shōten, 1987. (in Japanese)

Zhu Y. P. Analysis of cueing functions of the phonetic in modern Chinese. Unpublished paper, East China Normal University, 1987.

Part II

Korean

Because our language differs from the Chinese language, my poor people cannot express their thoughts in Chinese writing. In my pity for them I create 28 letters, which all can easily learn and use in their daily lives.

King Sejong, in the preface to his new Korean phonetic script, 1446

The bright can learn the [Korean writing] system in a single morning and even the not-so-bright can do so within ten days.

Chŏng In-ji, in the postface to the explanation of the new phonetic script, 1446

Korea and Koreans

Korea is a small mountainous peninsula that juts southeastward from the huge Asian Continent at the northeast corner of China (map fig. 1-1, chap. 1). Its size, 219,020 sq km, is about the same as England or as Japan's main island, Honshu. At the north end of the peninsula, Korea borders on two provinces of China; otherwise, it is separated from China's Shandong peninsula to the west by the 190 km width of the Yellow Sea and from Japan's Tsushima Islands in the southeast by 55 km of the Eastern Sea or the Sea of Japan.

Because of its location Korea has long served as a bridge between China and Japan in more ways than one. For example, before the sea level had risen at the end of the last glacial period around 10,000 BC, people from Siberia in the north and from China in the west came to Korea, and some went on to Japan. In the 13th century, Mongols from northern Asia and China stormed southward into Korea to invade Japan, and in the 16th century the Japanese invaded the peninsula to obtain a base for northward advances to China. More importantly, early Chinese culture—e.g., Confucianism, Chinese texts, Chinese characters, Chinese words, Sinified Buddhism—went to Japan after first having been absorbed by Korea.

Korean history can be traced back several thousand years to neolithic settlements. By about the 4th century BC the Han tribe established Old Chosŏn in northern Korea. (The Korean Han is written in a different character 韓 from that for the Han Chinese 漢.) *Chosŏn* means "morning fresh" and is one name for Korea. In 194 BC Old Chosŏn became Wiman Chosŏn when it was overthrown by the leader of a group of Chinese refugees, Wiman. In 108 BC Wiman Chosŏn itself was overthrown by the armies of the Chinese Han dynasty, which installed in northern Korea four administrative units or commanderies, one of which lasted as late as AD 313.

Meanwhile, the deposed Korean Han tribe migrated south to the Han River basin in the middle of the peninsula and split into three federations, two of which developed into kingdoms in the first century BC: Silla in the southeast and Paekche in the southwest. A third kingdom, Koguryŏ, which included part of Manchuria (now the northeast of China), emerged in the north. In 668 Silla unified the three kingdoms, but in 918 Unified Silla itself was replaced by the Koryŏ kingdom, which is the source of the name *Korea*. Koryŏ, in turn, was replaced in 1392 by the Chosŏn kingdom, which ruled until Korea was annexed by Japan in 1910.

In 1945, at the end of World War II, Korea was liberated from Japanese rule and was divided into two along the 38th parallel. In territory N. Korea (120,540 sq km) is larger than S. Korea (98,480 sq km), but in population (22.6 million) it is only about the half the size of S. Korea (44.6 million). Both are populated by the same homogeneous ethnic group, the Koreans.

In 1948 two nations were established: the Democratic People's Republic of Korea (DPRK) in the north and the Republic of Korea in the south. The two have taken radically different political and economic paths. N. Korea in 1995 has the dubious distinction of being one of the few Communist countries left in the world. Its command economy, as in all the former and present Communist nations, has been weak, even dismal. By contrast, capitalist S. Korea has been industrializing at a dizzying speed and is now counted among the four newly industrialized nations or "four little dragons of Asia," along with Taiwan, Singapore, and Hong Kong. Its per capita GNP (gross national product) is many times larger than that of N. Korea.

In spite of their differences in political and economic systems, South and North Korea share a common history (up to 1945) and many customs; most relevant to this book, the two share a language and scripts. Both have achieved a high rate of mass literacy. So if you wonder whether mass literacy is a sufficient condition for a nation's prosperity, just compare the two Koreas.

Table Part II-1 lists important events related to scripts and literacy that occurred during Korean history. These events will be elaborated in the rest of Part II.

Table Part II-1. Scripts and Literacy in Korean Kingdoms and Republics

Kingdom/Republic	Year	Script and Literacy
Wiman Chosŏn	194–108 BC	A few Chinese characters arrive
Han commanderies	108–AD 313	More characters arrive
Three kingdoms		Characters begin to be used
Koguryŏ	37 BC–AD 668	A stele bearing characters erected
Paekche	18 BC–AD 660	Characters transmitted to Japan
Silla	57 BC–AD 668	Chinese words adopted
Unified Silla	668–935	Many Chinese words adopted
Koryŏ	918–1392	Civil service examination; printing; surviving history books
Chosŏn	1392–1910	Phonetic script Han'gŭl invented; heavy use of characters persists
(Japanese rule)	1910–1945	Use of Korean and Han'gŭl suppressed
Republic of Korea	1948–present	Universal primary education; high rate of literacy; limited use of characters
DPRK (N. Korea)	1948–present	Universal primary education; high rate of literacy; characters taught but not used

11

Korean Language

The Korean language is spoken by 67 million S. and N. Koreans, as well as by some of the 5 million overseas Koreans. Its linguistic family relations are uncertain, but it may belong to the Altaic language family, along with Japanese. It differs greatly from Chinese, which belongs to the Sino-Tibetan family, and from English, which belongs to the Indo-European family. Similarities and differences in sounds, words, and sentences among the four languages will become apparent as you read on.

Broadly, the Korean language is divided into six dialects: two northern, one central, two southern, and one in Cheju Island off the southern tip. The dialects differ most clearly in their speech sounds. Because of its geographical isolation, the dialect of Cheju Island differs most strikingly from the other dialects. For example, for "Stay and come back," Cheju islanders say *sittang orang,* while people from Seoul say *ittaga onŏra.* Today, however, thanks to the spread of education and the mobility of people, the young Cheju islanders are largely bilingual, speaking both their dialect and standard Korean.

The following description of the Korean language is based on the central dialect in S. Korea, in particular the variety spoken today by the educated class in the capital of S. Korea, Seoul. N. Korea has designated the speech of its capital city, P'yŏngyang, as its "cultured speech," which is by and large the same as the standard language of S. Korea but has some of its own specific words and phrases.

As in Part I on Chinese, Part II begins with a quick description of Korean speech sounds, words, and sentences, to prepare readers for the study of the Korean writing system.

Speech Sounds and Syllables

A few preliminary words are necessary before describing the Korean speech sounds. It is difficult, almost impossible, to discuss speech sounds without using some linguistic terms, such as phoneme, consonant, stop, voiceless, voiced, vowel, diphthong, and syllable. These terms were explained in "Phonemes and Syllables" (chap. 1).

Korean words come in three kinds: native; Sino-Korean (S-K; Chinese words that were adopted into Korean long ago); and foreign loan words, mostly from European languages.[1] The individual sounds and syllable structures used for the three kinds of Korean words differ somewhat. The sound system described in this section is for native words, unless indicated otherwise; the sound structures of S-K words and European words will be described in separate sections.

---

[1] For historically similar reasons, English has a like division among native Anglo-Saxon words, words derived from Norman French long ago, and foreign loan words assimilated into English. As we will see, the same kind of division also occurs in Japanese (chap. 17).

The Korean sound system uses 31 phonemes: 19 consonants—*k, kk, n, t, tt, r, m, p, pp, s, ss, o (-ng), ch, tch, ch', k', t', p', h;* 10 vowels—*a, o, u, ŭ, ŏ, i, e, ae, oi, ui;* and 2 semi vowels—*y, w* (in *ya, yŏ...wa, wŏ...*). In describing Korean phonemes, I shun the international phonetic symbols, because they are unfamiliar to most readers, and because they alone, unaccompanied by extensive training, do not help readers pronounce the Korean sounds correctly. I use instead the McCune–Reischauer romanization system (chaps. 1 and 14), which the readers of this book would normally use to read Korean words.

Some Korean phonemes are close to English phonemes, which are written between slashes, as in /m/ and /n/ to distinguish them from the letters *m* and *n*, but others differ from English. English distinguishes two kinds of stop consonants, the voiceless /p, t, k/ and their voiced counterparts /b, d, g/. By contrast, Korean stops are all voiceless but are contrasted between aspirated and unaspirated or between tense and lax. Say /p/ in *pot* (aspirated) and then in *spot* (unaspirated): A puff of breath, which you can feel on the back of your hand, accompanies the aspirated consonant but not the unaspirated one. A tense consonant is produced with great muscle tension, by tightening up the throat. The Korean sound *kk*, for example, sounds like French *q* in *quoi?* A lax consonant does not involve great muscle tension.

The place of articulation refers to the speech organs involved in producing a sound. Bilabial: the two lips closely approach or touch each other. Alveolar: the tongue touches the gum above the upper teeth. Sibilant: affricative (friction through a narrowed air passage) produced on the hard palate. Velar: the back part of the tongue is raised toward the velum or soft palate.

Some Korean sounds change in certain phonetic contexts. The top row of Table 11-1 shows *p* or *b, t* or *d, ch* or *j,* and *k* or *g:* the lax stops change from voiceless to voiced in certain phonetic contexts, such as -*k*- changing to -*g*- between two vowels, as in *mŏkja* ('Let's eat') and *mŏgŏra* ('Do eat'). Other examples of phonetic changes are: *b* before *m* becomes like *m,* as *sibman* ('ten, ten thousand') becomes like "simman," just as in English *give me* is sometimes pronounced as "gimme." The consonants *t* and *t'* become like *j* and *ch',* respectively, before the vowel *i,* as in *kuti* ('firmly') becoming "kuji," and *kat'i* ('together') becoming "kach'i," just as in English *Tuesday* is often pronounced as "chewsday." These changes in sounds are usually not reflected in Korean spelling.

Rich as is the inventory of Korean consonants, it does not have the two English *th*- sounds found in *THis* and *THink*. It lacks also /f/ and /v/. Korean uses -*r*- only at the medial position and -*l* only at the final position of a syllable; neither of the two sounds occurs at the initial position. In S. Korea, the initial *l*- in Chinese words is

Table 11-1. Korean Stop Consonants

Manner of Articulation	Place of Articulation			
	Bilabial	Alveolar	Sibilant	Velar
lax	p or b	t or d	ch or j	k or g
aspirated	p'	t'	ch'	k'
tense	pp	tt	tch	kk

pronounced either as *n-* in *noin* (*laoren* in Chinese; 'old person') or as a vowel in *iron* (*lilun* in Chinese; 'theory'). The initial *r-* and *l-* in European words may be pronounced as *r-*, such as *radio* and *lady,* which become *radio* and *reidi*.

Koreans obviously can pronounce the initial *r-*, since they do so with European words. North Koreans use it even for S-K words, as a matter of linguistic policy, so that the Chinese word *laoren* ('old person') is pronounced as *roin* in N. Korea, rather than the S. Korean *noin*. How the initial *r-* is pronounced is one of several examples of policy differences between the two Koreas in linguistic matters, even though they use basically the same language, Korean. Anyway, Koreans, like Chinese and Japanese, tend to have trouble distinguishing /l/ and /r/ in European speech.

Korean has 10 vowels, and vowel length is phonemic: two words with the same sound can have different meanings solely because of differences in vowel length (symbolized with :), as in *pam vs pa:m* ('night' vs 'chestnut') and *nun vs nu:n* ('eye' vs 'snow'). In some words the longer version of a short vowel merely expresses emphasis, as in *on chong'il* vs *o:n chong'il* ('all day long' vs 'a:ll day long'). Vowel length, however, is not readily perceived by Koreans under age about 40, perhaps because it is not indicated in writing. (Vowel length is also phonemic in Japanese, where it is perceived well, perhaps because it is indicated in writing.)

The Korean language uses six basic syllable structures, two without final consonants and four with them, as shown in Table 11-2.

A two-consonant cluster, -CC, occurs only in the final position, but not in the initial position, of a syllable, and when it does, one of the two consonants—the one enclosed in ( ) in Table 11-2—is silent in an isolated word but is pronounced when it is followed by a vowel, as in *anjŏ*(verb + ending) and *kapsi* (noun + postposition). Korean does not use more complex syllable structures, such as the English CCVCC (e.g., *blend)* or CCCVCCC *(strengths)*.

How many different syllables are used in Korean? The number is hard to specify precisely, but is around 2,000 ("Han'gŭl Syllable Blocks" in chap. 13). There are far more Korean syllables than Japanese (about 110) or Chinese (about 400, or 1300 with tones) but fewer than English (several thousands). The many phonemes and syllables of the Korean language enable its speakers to approximate foreign sounds easily, but makes it difficult for foreigners to pronounce Korean correctly. They also complicate writing Korean in a Roman alphabet, requiring special marks and apostrophes to distinguish their rich variety, as in the sample words you see in this book.

Table 11-2. Korean Syllable Structures

Syllable Structure	Sound	Meaning
V (vowel)	i	tooth
CV (consonant–vowel)	na	I
VC (vowel–consonant)	al	egg
CVC (consonant–vowel–consonant)	tal	moon
VCC	an(j) [ŏ]	sit [!]
CVCC	kap(s)	price

Korean Native Words

As already mentioned, the Korean language has three kinds of words: native Korean, Sino-Korean, and foreign, mostly European. The three kinds differ not only in their origins but also in their forms and uses.

Korean native morphemes have been used by Koreans throughout their long history. Some morphemes are monosyllabic, as are all the entries in Table 11-2, but most contain two or more syllables: *param, tokkebi,* and *susukkekki* ('wind', 'ghost', and 'riddle'), which contain two, three, and four syllables, respectively. Monosyllabic morphemes make up only 3% of the native vocabulary, but they are mostly basic, common words that are much used (Kim Chong-t'aek 1992). By contrast, Chinese morphemes are typically one syllable, as pointed out in Chapter 2. For example, the Korean *tokkebi* and *susukkekki* are in Chinese *gui* and *mi*, respectively.

Single native morphemes can be by themselves words, but some morphemes join to form compound words, as they do in Chinese or English. So *hae* ('sun') can be used alone or as a part of compound words such as *haetpit* ('sunlight'), *haedoji* ('sunrise'), or *haebaragi* ('sun, longing = sunflower'). In fact many Korean words seem to be compound words, which can be translated into one morpheme in Japanese, English, and Chinese. Table 11-3 shows some examples.

Some native compound words consist of one morpheme repeated. Repetition may express emphasis, as in *mallang* ('soft') →*mallangmallang hada* ('very soft'); it can mean "every," as in *kot* ('place') → *kotkot mada* ('everywhere'); it may be used to describe a state or appearance, as in *ttungttung* ('obese'); or it may be onomatopoeic (imitation of a sound)—a dog barks *mŏngmŏng* ('bowwow'). Exact duplication is found in Chinese and Japanese compound words as well (chaps. 2 and 17, respectively). In English, the members of a pair often differ in a minor way, as in *bowwow, dingdong, higgledy piggledy*.

In spite of its rich sound system, Korean has occasional homophones (two or more words that share the same sound), such as *tari* ('bridge' or 'leg'). The number of words sharing the same sound is only two in most cases; the few exceptions are *pae,* which is shared by three words— 'stomach', 'pear', and 'ship'; and *mal,* which is shared by four words— 'horse', 'unit of quantity' equivalent to about 4 gallons, 'duckweed' plant, and 'speech' (this word, *ma:l,* has a long vowel). It is a good thing that native words do not have many homophones, since they are written in a phonetic script that does not distinguish homophones. By contrast, the Chinese language has many homophones. For example, in a big dictionary there are 200 different morphemes ('meaning', 'different', 'wing', etc.) that share the tone syllable *yi* (falling tone), but they are distinguished when written in Chinese characters (chap. 2).

Table 11-3. Native Words in Two Morphemes

Korean Word	K. Morpheme	English	Japanese	Chinese
nunmul	eye, water	tear	namida	lei
sonkarak	hand, part	finger	yubi	zhi
mulkogi	water, meat	fish	uo	yu
mulkyŏl	water, texture	wave	nami	bo
salkyŏl	flesh, texture	skin	kawa	pi

As in any language, some native words have a few different, sometimes figurative, meanings. Example: *chugŏtta* ('is dead') was originally used only for a once living thing but now can be used for situations such as "strength faded" and "sunlight disappeared." English too has expressions such as "the wind has died down" and "a dream died." The word *param* ('wind') can mean "fast living" or "profligacy." Some words have the same figurative meanings as in English: *ppalgaeng'i* ('red person' = Communist'; *-i* is a suffix for person).

Sino-Korean Words

Sino-Korean (S-K) words can be written in Chinese characters, unlike native words, which cannot. Because S-K words have been used in Korean for so long and so extensively that they form an integral part of the Korean vocabulary; they are not considered to be foreign loan words. S-K words include also numerous words coined by the Japanese for modern, Western concepts. Such words, modelled on Chinese words and meant to be written in Chinese characters, are indistinguishable from Chinese-origin words ("Foreign Loan Words" in chap. 2). Many S-K words are analogous to such obviously French words in English as *bon mot* and *déjà vu,* which educated English speakers use, knowing their French origins. A few S-K words are analogous to such French words in English as *niche* and *chamber,* which have been so assimilated into English, with Anglicized pronunciations, that their French origins are no longer obvious. As more and more S-K words are written in a phonetic script instead of Chinese characters, their S-K origins might become blurred (chap. 15).

One of the earliest S-K words might have been *wang* ('king') adopted in the 1st century AD by the Koguryŏ kingdom, or perhaps earlier, by a king of Wiman Chosŏn (194–108 BC) or even of Old Chosŏn before that. Some Chinese words were adopted in the early 6th century, when the Silla kingdom (57 BC–AD 668) copied China's political institutions and changed the names of the Korean nation and the title of the king from native to S-K words. The Unified Silla kingdom (668–935) adopted many S-K words in reforming its administration, military, and land. In the mid-8th century King Kyŏngdŏk changed the names of many places and official positions from native to S-K words. The study of Confucianism and Chinese literature throughout the subsequent dynastic history increased the use of S-K words.

In pronouncing S-K words Koreans approximate the sounds of Chinese but omit the tones, using a little over 400 of their 2,000 different syllables. In the *New Age Korean Dictionary* (1989), which lists at its end 2,600 common Chinese characters used in Korean, I counted 436 different syllables. The Korean sounds not used for S-K words include: the tense unaspirated stops (table 11-1) *kk, ss, tt, pp, tch* (three exceptions are: *kkik, ssang,* and *ssi*); the complex syllables that contain the final -CCs (e.g., *-lk*); and certain final -Cs (e.g., *-t, -s, -ch, -ch', -t', -p'* after *ka-*).

Since they use only a limited number of different sounds and syllables, many S-K morphemes and words are homophones, i.e., share the same syllable. For example, in the above dictionary, 40 morphemes (e.g., 'four', 'death', 'temple', 'history') share the syllable *sa,* and 40 other morphemes share the syllable *ki* (e.g., 'period', 'record', 'rise', 'some'). Even when two morpheme–syllables are joined in a compound word, many word pairs are homophonic. Sometimes several compound words share the same sound, as does *tonggi* ('winter season', 'same period', 'sibling', 'motive', 'copper vessel', 'young courtesan').

Certain homophonic S-K compound words are supposed to be differentiated by vowel length, as in *chŏn'gi* ('electricity') vs *chŏ:n'gi* ('tale'). But this difference in vowel length is too subtle for ordinary people to notice. Apparently, older people notice it better than young people do, according to Prof. Lee Ki-moon (personal communication 1992). The vowel length is difficult to distinguish in Korean words, be they native or S-K, perhaps because it is not expressed in writing. Vowel length is not so difficult to distinguish in Japanese words, in which it is expressed in writing.

Because Korean, Japanese, and Chinese differ in their sound systems, Chinese words common to all the three languages always differ in sounds even as they maintain the same meanings, as shown in Table 11-4. Ordinary people are not able to guess the exact sound of a word in the other two languages from its sound in one language, though a philologist may. In particular, there is no way for Korean or Japanese speakers to guess the tones of Chinese syllables. However, once the words of the three languages are arranged as in Table 11-4, even untrained people can see similarities among their sound patterns (minus tones) and remember them easily. When spoken, the words in Table 11-4 are usually not mutually intelligible among the three languages, but when written in Chinese characters they are the same.

In the second column the letter *x* in Pinyin sounds like *ss* in *session*, and Chinese words have tones; In the third column, *l-* that begins a Chinese syllable becomes *n-* or a vowel in S. Korea and *r-* in N. Korea. In the fourth column Sino-Japanese words are shown in their On/Chinese readings (chap. 18).

Table 11-4. Chinese Words Adopted by Korean and Japanese

Meaning	Chinese	S-Korean	S-Japanese
loyalty	zhong	ch'ung	chū
east	dong	tong	tō
read, book = reading	dushu	toksŏ	dokusho
horse, fall = fall from a horse	luoma	nakma/rakma	rakuba
mind, logic, study = psychology	xinlixue	simnihak	shinrigaku
move, thing, garden = zoo	dongwuyuan	tongmulwŏn	dōbutsuen

Native Words vs Sino-Korean Words

Native words form the basic vocabulary of Korean. They tend to name common objects, actions, feelings, and human relations, such as *mul* ('water'), *masida* ('to drink'), *kippŭda* ('is happy'), *ajumŏni* ('aunt'), *tokkaebi* ('ghost'). They are written in the Korean phonetic script. By contrast, Sino-Korean words tend to name abstract concepts, technical terms, and institutions: *ch'ung* ('loyalty'), *simnihak* ('mind, logic, study' = 'psychology'), and *pyŏngwŏn* ('sickness, institute' = 'hospital'). The specialized uses of native and S-K words in Korean resemble those of Anglo-Saxon words and Greco–Latinate (including Norman French) words in English. For example, the learned word for "psychology" is available only as a S-K word in Korean and as a Greek-based word in English. However, in English all types of words are written in one script, the English alphabet, whereas in Korean, S-K words can be written in Chinese characters, but native words are always written in a phonetic script.

S-K words for abstract concepts such as "loyalty" and "logic" simply do not have handy native counterparts. The same is true even for some concrete concepts such as "east" and "west." S-K numerals do have native counterparts but are still commonly used because of their versatility ("Numerals and Classifiers," later in this chapter). Some multi-morpheme S-K words can be translated into native equivalents, which, however, are wordy and strained, and so are not used: *pyŏngwŏn* ('sickness, institute' for 'hospital') could conceivably be expressed in native morphemes as "alnŭn i koch'inŭn kot" ('place for healing sick people'). But other S-K words can be, and are, readily translated into native words: the S-K *sŏŏn* ('preparatory word' = 'preface') is the native *mŏrimal* ('head word'). Sometimes a S-K word and its native counterpart are joined in one redundant word, as in *han'ok CHIP* ('Korean-style house house') and *NŭLGŭN noin* ('old old person'). The uppercase in these examples indicate the native part.

Sino-Korean words and their native equivalents sometimes overlap in use but sometimes do not, as Table 11-5 shows.

Table 11-5. Use of S-K Words and Native Words

Meaning	Sino-Korean	Native
father	puch'in ('father, parent'; formal)	abŏji (informal)
child	adong ('child, infant')	ŏrin'i ('young, person'; equivalent)
old person	noin ('old, person'; polite)	nŭlgŭn'i ('old, person'; plain)
spirit	yŏnghon ('spirit, spirit'; Christian)	nŏk(s) (non-Christian; shamanism)
today	kŭm'il ('now, day'; pretentious)	onŭl (informal)
toilet	hwajangsil ('make-up room'; euphemism)	tyutkan ('rear place'; old fashioned)

A few "native" words turn out to be S-K words that have been so Koreanized, with a sound change, that their Chinese origins are no longer recognizable: *chŏ* ('flute') from S-K *chŏk* and *ch'o* ('candle') from S-K *ch'ok*. The word *yŏnmot* is thought to be a native word, but in fact etymologically it consists of a S-K *yŏn* ('pond') + native *mot* ('pond') (Shim 1995). To my surprise, even *kimch'i* ('pickled vegetable'), the well-known native dish, began as a S-K word (Cho 1991). By and large, if a word can be written in characters, it is S-K; if not, it is native. But all words, including S-K words, can be written in the phonetic script. S-K words often are written phonetically in S. Korea and always are in N. Korea, but when they are, some infrequent or homophonic words are not easily recognized (chap. 15).

The contrast between native words and S-K words in the Korean vocabulary is similar, but not identical, to a distinction found in the Japanese vocabulary. In Japanese even native words, if they are content words, tend to be written in characters.

There are more S-K words than native words in Korean dictionaries. Table 11-6 shows the relative proportions of native words, S-K words, and loan words in two large dictionaries and one small one. The two large ones are The *Unabridged Dictionary (of Korean Words)([Chosŏnmal] K'ŭnsajŏn)* (1957) compiled by the Society of Han'gŭl

Studies and the *Great Dictionary of the National Language (Kugŏ Taesajŏn)* compiled by Yi Hŭi-sŭng (1961). The small one was also compiled by the Society of Han'gŭl Studies.

The compilation of the 1957 dictionary started in 1939 but was interrupted in 1940 when the entire editorial team was arrested by the Japanese police. (Korea was under Japanese rule between 1910 and 1945.) The 1961 dictionary was compiled after the liberation of Korea in 1945. The two large dictionaries disagree on the exact percentages but agree that there are more S-K words than native words, and that loan words constitute a small percentage. In the small dictionary, S-K words, while still forming the largest proportion, are only slightly more numerous than native words, suggesting that the less common the word, the more likely it is to be S-K.

Table 11-6 shows the proportions of different word kinds in the dictionaries. In actual use native words are more common than S-K words, especially in informal speech and non-scholarly reading materials. Such a pattern is found in Japanese between native words and Sino-Japanese words, and also in English

Table 11-6. Composition of the Korean Vocabulary

	1957	1961	1960s
No. of Words	164,125	225,203	64,355
Sino-Korean	52.1%	69.3%	45.4%
Native	45.5	24.4	44.5
Foreign Loan	2.4	6.3	3.0
Hybrid			7.1

between Anglo-Saxon words and Greco–Latinate words. For example, in informal chat English speakers tend to use and re-use such simple and short Anglo-Saxon words as *sweat* and *chew* rather than their Latinate versions *perspiration* and *masticate*.

Anyway, now that three decades have passed since the appearance of these Korean dictionaries, we need a new count of the relative proportions of the different kinds of words. A more up-to-date count would probably show that, among common words, native words have increased at the expense of S-K words, and that European words, especially English words, have increased. Let us consider possible reasons for such a new trend.

For hundreds of years native Korean words were considered second-class, and were unceremoniously replaced by Sino-Korean words in educated language whenever possible. However, for the past few decades the South Koreans have been trying to replace S-K words with native words, out of nationalism and a desire to reduce the use of Chinese characters. Two important names, Seoul ('capital city'), the capital of S. Korea, and Han'gŭl ('great letters'), the Korean phonetic script, are native. The N. Koreans also make this effort, although they use the Sino-Korean *Chosŏncha* ('letters of Chosŏn') for Han'gŭl, and their capital has the S-K name *P'yŏngyang*.

Some native words that replace S-K words are old native words that have been resurrected, and some have been coined anew by combining existing native morphemes. In the top three rows of Table 11-7 the native words, which were used until the Chosŏn kingdom (1392–1910), have been almost replaced by their S-K counterparts, whereas the S-K words in the bottom three rows have been replaced by their native counterparts over the past few decades.

Some S-K words are pretentious and should ordinarily be replaced by native words: *kŭm'il* ('now day = today') for native *onŭl*. This pattern is similar to that of

Table 11-7. Native Words and S-K Words Replace Each Other

Native	Sino-Korean	Meaning
moe→	san	mountain
nuri→	sesang	world
ibaji→	konghŏn	contribution
semokkol	←samgakhyŏng	triangle
mŏrimal	←sŏŏn	preface
pogi	←ye	example

Latinate words vs Anglo-Saxon words in English: *masticate* vs *chew*. On the other hand, the S-K *muron* ('no, logic' or "needless to say") becomes wordy in native Korean *mal halkŏt ŏpsi*, and the S-K *am'amni* ('dark, dark, village' or "under cloak of darkness") is not only more concise but is also more expressive than the native *nam i morŭnŭn kaunde* ('while other people are not aware of it'). The kinds of S-K words that should or might be replaced by native words are listed in some handbooks on the Korean language, such as *The Materials for Purifying the National Language* (Ministry of Education 1983).

South and North Korea, though both try to replace S-K words with native words, sometimes go their separate ways. Sometimes S. Korea replaces a S-K word with a native word, while N. Korea does not, and vice versa. Sometimes the two nations adopt or resurrect two different native words to replace the same S-K word (e.g., S. Korean *serossugi* and N. Korean *naeryŏssugi* for S-K *chongsŏ* 'vertical writing'); other times the two select alike (e.g., *serojul* for S-K *chongsŏn* 'vertical line'). Unless both Koreas coordinate their efforts on this problem, the Korean languages used in the two nations will eventually diverge. Koreans fervently hope that this will not happen.

For over 1500 years, S-K words had prestige and dominated native words, but the reverse is now true. Now even some technical terms are native Korean. People's given names, which used to be solidly Sino-Korean, are now occasionally native ("Korean Personal Names" in chap. 15). But in S. Korea the effort to replace S-K words by native words still has a long way to go. For example, in the *Dictionary of Terms for Current Affairs* (Tong'a 1987), 31% of the terms are S-K, including European terms translated into S-K terms, 28% are European (and Japanese), and none are native; the rest, 41%, are hybrids, mostly S-K–European; only a few hybrids include native terms (e.g., English–native–S-K, *sŭrimail sŏm sakŏn* 'Three Mile Island accident').

Many S-K words and phrases have no good native counterpart, and the complete elimination of S-K words may not be possible without impoverishing, or even destroying, the Korean vocabulary.

European (and Japanese) Loan Words

In the 17th century Korea had its first glimpse of Western science and technology, initially by way of Ming China. Korean envoys brought back from China such Western objects as a map of Europe and of the world, a telescope, an alarm clock and books on astronomy and Western culture. Because Western objects and concepts came to Korea via China, they tended to be given S-K words rather than Korean phonetic transcriptions. Thus, *telescope* was not, and still is not, "t'eresŭk'op" but *mangwŏngyŏng,* as in Chinese *wangyuanjing* and Japanese *bōenkyō;* the words use the same three Chinese characters meaning 'view, distance, mirror'. (Originally it was *wŏnjogyŏng,* 'distance, reflect, mirror'.) Even in the early 20th century, Western objects and concepts tended to reach Korea via China or Japan, and were given S-K names, such as *chŏnhwa* ('telephone'), corresponding to Chinese *dienhua* and Japanese *denwa*, written in two Chinese characters meaning 'electricity, speak'.

In recent times Western concepts and words have entered the Korean vocabulary directly and have tended to be phonetically transcribed: *kamera, kŏmp'yut'ŏ, sonata, wotk'a, syamp'ein* ('camera', 'computer', 'sonata', 'vodka', 'champagne'). One is likely to hear a dialogue like the following that is peppered with English loan words (in italics):

onŭl *rŏnch'i* nŭn *pastput* ŭro halka? *haembŏgŭ, saelŏdŭ* wa *k'ŏp'i* ro haji.

The Korean sound system lacks the sounds /f/, /v/, initial /l/, and the *th-* sounds in *think* and *this*. So, the sound /f/, for example, is regularly transcribed as *p'*. Thus *coffee* becomes *k'ŏp'i*, which unfortunately sounds like the native word *k'op'i* ('nose blood') and sometimes tastes like it too! What could be *pastput?* It turns out to be the "transcription" of *fast food*. The Koreans can pronounce and write *hwast huud*, which sounds closer to the original English phrase. So, the above Korean–English sentence means, "Shall we have *fast food* for *lunch?* Let's have *hamburger, salad,* and *coffee.*"

What proportion of the present-day Korean vocabulary is European in origin? I have not found any data on this question, but in the *Dictionary of Terms for Current Affairs* (Tong'a 1987) 28% are European, mostly English, loan words (e.g., *disk'o* for 'disco' and *tallŏ* for 'dollar'). In this dictionary, many European words are translated into S-K or European–S-K hybrid terms (e.g., *tallŏ woegyo* for 'dollar diplomacy'). In the general vocabulary, the proportion of loan words from European languages is likely to be much smaller.

Occasionally a concept appears to have a European word as well as a S-K or native word, but usually the two words name somewhat different concepts: *hotel* for a Western hotel and S-K *yŏ'gwan* for a Korean inn (Japanese *ryokan); pilding* for a Western-style building, usually big and tall, and S-K *kŏnmul* for any edifice, including a temple; *p'aip'u* for a Western pipe, and native *tambaettae* for a Korean pipe, which is a long slender bamboo tube with a small receptacle for tobacco.

After the 36 years of Japanese rule that ended in 1945, inevitably the Japanese language has left its mark on the Korean vocabulary. Some Chinese-based words used by the Japanese have replaced words used earlier by the Koreans (and still used by the Chinese): *ch'ŏlro* ('iron route' or "railroad") became *ch'ŏlto* ('iron road') and *sang'o* ('above noon' or 'ante-meridian') became *ojŏn* ('pre-noon'). Some S-K words for modern concepts, such as *simnihak* ('psychology') and *paekhwajŏm* ('department store'), were coined by the Japanese on a Chinese model and then borrowed by Koreans and Chinese. The Korean native *tyutkan* ('rear place') has been replaced by a S-K word coined by the Japanese, *pyŏnso* ('convenient place = toilet'), which itself is now being replaced by a S-K word coined by Koreans, *hwajangsil* ('make-up room').

Today both S. and N. Koreans use only a few obviously Japanese words, as a result of several decades of concerted effort to eradicate Japanese words from the Korean vocabulary. Thus, Japanese words such as *sakkura, bentō, susi* ('cherry blossom', 'lunch box', *sushi)* have been replaced by Korean *pŏtkkot, tosirak,* and *ch'obap* ('vinegar rice'). But a few Japanese words deeply entrenched in the Korean vocabulary are still being used without the Koreans realizing its Japanese origin. An example is *kudu* from Japanese *kutsu* ('western leather shoes'). Certain Japanese words for uniquely Japanese objects, such as *kimono,* have to be kept.

Numerals and Classifiers

Korean numerals come in two sets, native and Sino-Korean, and are used often with classifiers that indicate the kinds of objects counted, as in Chinese. Native words are available for numbers from 1 to 99, but S-K words can be used for any number at all, from 1 to all the way up to billion, trillion, and so on. Table 11-8 shows the two sets for the numbers from 1 to 10.

Table 11-8. Native and Sino-Korean Numerals

Arabic	Native	Sino-Korean
1	hana	il
2	tul	i
3	set	sam
4	net	sa
5	tasŏt	o
6	yŏsŏt	yuk
7	ilgop	ch'il
8	yŏdŏl(p)	p'al
9	ahop	ku
10	yŏl	sip

The two sets are put to different uses. For example, in talking about time, native numerals are used for marking the time of day, with the S-K time classifier *si* ('o'clock'), whereas the Sino-Korean numerals are used with the S-K time classifier *pun* ('minute') for duration, as shown in Table 11-9. The final sounds of the two Korean numerals enclosed in parentheses are dropped in these uses.

S-K words are used also for days of the month, and the names of the months and years. Their forms do not change, except for *yu(k) wŏl, si(p) wŏl* ('six month' = June, 'ten month' = October), in which the final consonants are dropped.

Some classifiers are native, and some are Sino-Korean. A classifier (native or S-K) is preceded by a numeral (native or S-K) and followed by the native postposition *ŭi* ('of') and a noun (native or S-K), as in:

native numeral + S-K classifier + 'of' + S-K noun: *se(t) KWON ŭi ch'aek* ('three volume of book'), and

native numeral + native classifier + 'of' + native noun: *se(t) MARI ŭi kae* ('three head of dog').

Note that neither the classifier nor the noun is marked for plural number, in contrast to English (e.g., *three bushelS of appleS)*. Cardinals turn into ordinals with the addition of the native suffix *-tchae* to the native numerals, as in *settchae* ('third'), and of the S-K prefix *che-* (Chinese *di-* and Japanese *dai-)* to the S-K numerals, as in *chesam* ('third').

Table 11-9. Native and S-K Numerals and Classifiers

	Korean	Meaning
Native numeral +	han(a) si	1 o'clock
S-K classifier	tu(l) si	2 o'clock
	ilgop si	7 o'clock
S-K numeral +	il pun	1 minute
S-K classifier	i pun	2 minutes
	ch'il pun	7 minutes

As you can see, native words and S-K words, though they can be distinguished in origins and forms, are sometimes inextricably intertwined in use. This is one more reason why it would be difficult to eliminate all S-K words from the Korean language.

Content Words, Grammatical Morphemes, and Sentences

Every language has two major classes of words, content words and grammatical morphemes. In many languages, content words are nouns, verbs, adjectives, and some adverbs. Nouns, which name objects and concepts, form an open class in that they have an unspecifiably large number of members: e.g., *ai, mul, puŏk, k'al* ('child', 'water', 'kitchen', 'knife'). Korean nouns do not change form for number (singular vs plural), gender (feminine vs masculine), or case (e.g., subjective, objective, or possessive). Plural number, if essential, is indicated by numerals with classifiers, as described above.

In a sentence, nouns play specific syntactic roles (e.g., subject and object), which are indicated by postpositions that follow them. Postpositions have syntactic roles but little semantic content. They form one group of grammatical morphemes of the Korean language, while verb or adjective endings form the other group. These Korean grammatical morphemes are quite different from Chinese empty (grammatical) words (chap. 2) and from English function words (chap. 1), but they are similar to Japanese grammatical morphemes (chap. 17). Some postpositions are shown in Table 11-10.

Korean verbs and adjectives change their endings greatly according to sentence type, speech level and style, tense, and so on. For a quick example, the verb *masida* ('to drink') changes to *masinda, masi'nŭnya, masyŏra, masija* for statement, question, command, and suggestion, respectively, all in the present tense, at the plain speech level, and in formal speech. One past tense of *masinda* is *masyŏtta*. We shall see other forms of this verb below. A Korean adjective, if it comes at the end of a clause or sentence, changes its ending in the same way as a verb, except that it does not have forms for command and suggestion. When it modifies a noun it precedes a noun and has the form *-n* or *-ŭn*, as in *ippŭn ai* ('pretty child').

Here is a simple Korean sentence that uses some of the words so far introduced:

ai ka *puŏk* esŏ *mul* ŭl *mashi*nda

('[A] child in [the] kitchen water drink[s]' or "A child drinks water in the kitchen.")

The sentence requires three postpositions: *ka* (subject), *esŏ* (locative), and *ŭl* (objective), which are shown in roman font in the above sentence. The content words are *ai*

Table 11-10. Common Korean Postpositions

Syntactic Role	Postposition	Example
subject	ka (after a vowel)	ai ka
	i (after a consonant)	mul i
possesion (of)	ŭi	ai ŭi
direct object	rŭl (after a vowel)	ai rŭl
	ŭl (after a consonant)	mul ŭl
indirect object (to)	e, ege	ai ege
location (in, at)	e, esŏ	puŏk esŏ
instrument (with)	ro	k'al ro

('child'), *puŏk* ('kitchen'), *mul* ('water') and *masinda* ('drink'). The verb ending for present tense, plain-level, statement is *-(n)da*. Korean does not use grammatical items equivalent to the English articles *the/a* or the third-person verb ending *-s* in *drinkS*.

Thanks to the postpositions that sort out which noun functions as the subject, the direct object, and the location, the word order can be flexible, except that the verb or an adjective always ends a sentence. The flexibility of word order is shown below for the sentence "A child drinks water in the kitchen," from the most to the least natural or common of the six possible order. As the content words are shifted around within a sentence, the relative focus on them also changes slightly.

> ai ka puŏk esŏ mul ŭl masinda
> ai ka mul ŭl puŏk esŏ masinda
> puŏk esŏ ai ka mul ŭl masinda
> mul ŭl puŏk esŏ ai ka masinda
> puŏk esŏ mul ŭl ai ka masinda
> mul ŭl ai ka puŏk esŏ masinda

To change a statement into a question, a negative, a command, or a suggestion you need merely to change the ending of a verb:

Statement: *ai ka puŏk esŏ mul ŭl masiNDA.*
Question: *ai ka puŏk esŏ mul ŭl masiNŬNYA?*
Negative: *ai ka puŏk esŏ mul ŭl masiJI ANNŬNDA.*
Command: *puŏk esŏ mul ŭl masyŎRA.*
Suggestion: *puŏk esŏ mul ŭl masiJA.*

In Korean, a command and a suggestion omit the subject. Even a statement or question may omit the subject and also the object when they are obvious in a context, as in:

mŏgŏ polka? ('Shall [we] try eating [this food]?').

Speech Levels and Honorifics

Every Korean sentence, by its choice of words and verb or adjective endings, indicates whether it is addressed to a superior, equal, or inferior. The following two sentences show how the same content, "(Please) eat [the] rice," is spoken quite differently, depending on the social position of the addressee.

To a superior: *chinji chapsuseyo*.
To an equal or inferior: *pap mŏgŏ*.

The elaborate levels and styles of Korean speech vary according to the relation among the person talked about, the listener, and the speaker. The factors considered are age, social position, familiarity, and gender. There are two basic levels: a polite level for superiors and a plain level for inferiors or equals; each of the two levels is further distinguished between formal and informal styles. These variations in levels and styles are expressed most clearly in verb and adjective endings, as shown in Table 11-11, for the sentences "[I] drink water" and "Please drink water." There are other infrequently used styles, such as the super polite supplication *ch'ukpok ŭl chuOPSOSO* ('Please bless [us]') used in Christian prayers.

Like Korean, Japanese uses speech levels, but Korean has many more special honorific words than does Japanese, as shown in Table 11-12. On the other hand, Japanese has the honorific prefixes *o-* or *go-*, which have no equivalent in Korean.

In Table 11-12, in the first row, the Korean honorific word appears to be derived from its

Table 11-11. Speech Levels and Styles

Level	Style	Sentence Type	Example
Plain	Formal	Statement	mul ŭl masinda
		Command	mul ŭl masyŏra
	Informal	Statement	mul ŭl masyŏ
		Command	mul ŭl masyŏ
Polite	Formal	Statement	mul ŭl masimnida
		Command	mul ŭl masipsio
	Informal	Statement	mul ŭl masyŏyo
		Command	mul ŭl masyŏyo

plain word. In the next three rows, the plain words are native Korean, while the honorific words are Sino-Korean. For the rest, the plain words and their honorific counterparts are unrelated. Korean has also contemptuous words used to humiliate the listener, such as ch'ŏmŏkta ('to eat'; normal mŏkta) and agari ('mouth'; normal ib).

A few words about pronouns. Korean has the plain pronouns for first-person na and second-person nŏ. The third-person pronoun kŭ ('he') or kŭnyŏ ('she') are Western concepts adopted in modern times. A Korean pronoun does not change its form, except that na ('I') changes to nae ('my') in some cases. In talking to, or about, a superior, the speaker does not use the pronoun 'you' or 'he/she' but uses the superior's title or position, as "teacher-nim" and "father-nim," where -nim is an honorific suffix. Again, in talking to a superior, the speaker refers to him/herself by the deferential or humbling chŏ rather than by the plain na used when talking to an equal or inferior. There are also a few different words for 'you', such as tangshin used between spouses, chane used by a male superior to an inferior, and the poetic or archaic kŭdae ('thou'). In a sentence a pronoun, like a noun, takes a postposition to indicate its syntactic role.

In addition to special honorific content words, Korean honorific language uses special grammatical morphemes: the syllable -si- is inserted into a verb ending, as in kada→kaSIda ('go'), and the two alternative postpositions after a subject noun change, as in ka/i→kkesŏ. Speech between husbands and wives tends to be informal, although husbands tend to use plain speech to their wives, whereas wives tend to use polite speech to their husbands. But the gender differences in speech seems to be breaking down in this age of gender equality.

Table 11-12. Plain vs Honorific Words in Korean and Japanese

Kor. Plain	K. Honorific	J. Honorific	Meaning
mal	malssŭm	o-hanashi	speech
nŭlgŭn'i	noin	rōjin	old person
nai	yŏnse	o-tosi	age
chip	taek	o-taku	house/home
pap	chinji	go-han	cooked rice
mŏkta	chapsusida	mesiagaru	eat
chukta	toragasida	nakunaru	pass away
chada	chumusida	o-nemurininaru	sleep

A person's age is an important consideration in the choice of speech style in Korean. Within a family, a mature speaker addresses a sister or brother who is older than him or her by even one year as *ŏnni* ('elder sister') or *hyŏng-nim* ('elder brother'; *-nim* is the same honorific suffix as is used with teacher or father) with an appropriate level of honorific language. Even at school, one addresses someone above oneself by even one grade as *ŏnni* or *hyŏng-nim*. And this younger–older relation lasts throughout a lifetime, even when the younger becomes a superior to the older in professional or social position.

In one comparative study, the Koreans placed great importance on the age differences between the speaker and the listener, whereas the Japanese were more concerned with social roles and familiarity relations (Ogina et al. 1990). Generally, the speech levels and honorific language were found to be more elaborate in Korean than in Japanese.

The elaborate and complex speech levels and honorifics in Korean contrast sharply with their absence in English. An English speaker may show respect or courtesy to a superior or unfamiliar addressee by adding *Sir* or *Ma'am* either to the beginning or to the end of an utterance. The age difference between a speaker and a listener is not important, and students think nothing of addressing their elderly professor by his or her given name.

A foreigner learning Korean may find all these speech levels and styles complicated and confusing. One English-speaking professor of Korean history considers them to be the most difficult aspect of mastering the Korean language. It is reasonably safe to stick to polite speech in speaking to adults and plain speech in speaking to children. Polite speech used to children will make them giggle, while plain speech used to adults will upset them.

12

Hancha: Chinese Characters

Now that we have learned something about the Korean language, we explore, from a historical perspective, how it is written. We learn first about Chinese characters, which came to Korea over 2000 years ago, and then about a phonetic script that was created in the mid-15th century. Then we learn about how the two scripts are used today in S. and N. Korea.

Chinese characters are called Hancha in Korean, which is written using the same two Chinese characters 漢字 as are used for Hanzi in Chinese and for Kanji in Japanese. You may well ask, Having read several chapters on Chinese characters in Part I, do we need more chapters on the topic? Well, "no" and then again "yes." No, we do not have to discuss again questions of the origin, evolution, classification, and logographic nature of Chinese characters. Yes, we need two more chapters, because even though Chinese characters used in Korean and Chinese are similar in meanings, they differ sometimes in shapes and always in sound. The use of Chinese characters is in some ways complicated in Korean, which has three kinds of words—native, Sino-Korean, and European, as well as two kinds of scripts—phonetic and logographic. And Koreans, more persistently and heatedly than Chinese and Japanese, debate the use of Hancha.

Hancha Adoption

In antiquity, whenever there was turmoil in China, waves of Chinese migrated to Korea. One such wave occurred in 194 BC, and its leader Wiman established Wiman Chosŏn in northern Korea. Later, between 108 BC and AD 313, the Chinese Han dynasty established a few administrative units or commanderies in northern Korea. Through these contacts with the Chinese, some Koreans may have been aware of the existence of Chinese characters. A Chinese sword excavated in P'yŏngyang, the present capital of N. Korea, bears a hallmark inscription with a date corresponding to 222 BC. A stone monument with carved characters, regarded as the oldest of its kind in Korea, was erected in AD 85 in the era of Nangnang, the longest lasting Chinese commandery, in today's Pyŏngan Namdo Province in N. Korea.

Between the 3rd and 4th centuries AD, Hancha came to be used among the elite in the three kingdoms: Silla (57 BC–AD 668); Koguryŏ (37 BC–AD 668); and Paekche (18 BC–AD 660). The Koreans were the first non-Chinese to learn and use characters.

In the 4th century AD the Koguryŏ kingdom established national and private schools to teach the Confucian classics, and a history of the kingdom was written in Chinese characters (the history book has not survived). Around this time Koguryŏ embraced Buddhism and wrote its scripture in Hancha. In 414, for its king Kwanggaet'o, it erected a stone stele, which bears 1,800 Hancha, and which still stands in modern

Tongkou in the northeastern part of China, then the capital of Koguryŏ. In the 4th century the Paekche kingdom, too, had its history book written, but the book has not survived. It sent to Japan a sword bearing characters inscribed on both sides. The sword is still preserved in a shrine in Japan. By the 4th or 5th century, Paekche had also sent scholars to Japan as teachers of Chinese characters ("Introduction and Spread of Kanji" in chap. 18).

In the 6th century the Silla kingdom adopted Chinese titles for its kings and had its history written in Chinese characters. Again, the history book has not survived. The Unified Silla (668–935) kingdom, in reforming its administration on a Chinese model, adopted many Sino-Korean words written in Hancha. In particular, in the mid-8th century it changed its native place names into Sino-Korean. By then the sounds of Hancha were modelled on those used in the capital of the Tang dynasty of China, Chang'an (modern Xi'an).

In 958, during the Koryŏ kingdom, a civil-service examination system was established to recruit bureaucrats ("Civil Service Examination" in chap. 16). The exam, modelled closely on the Chinese system, tested primarily knowledge of the Confucian classics and the ability to compose Chinese text. Preparation for the exam promoted the use of Sino-Korean words, which over time replaced some native Korean words. All words, whether S-K or native, were written in Hancha.

During the Chosŏn kingdom (1392–1910), Neo-Confucianism formed the ideological basis of the government and education, while Buddhism was sometimes rejected and sometimes embraced. The civil service exam was maintained. Hancha persisted as a dominant script even after an effective phonetic script was created in the mid-15th century. Even Western concepts, such as "telescope," "science," and "democracy," came to Korea via Japan or China as words written in Hancha.

The use of Hancha began early in Korean history and became deeply entrenched in Korean culture and language. However, in the past few decades the two republics of South and North Korea at one time or another have both tried to abolish Hancha. S. Koreans now use a limited number of Hancha, and N. Koreans learn some Hancha in secondary and post-secondary schools but do not use them in writing texts.

Hancha were used in the past in a complicated way and only by a small group of literati, whereas they are used today in S. Korea by the masses in a rational way, as a supplement to the phonetic script. We shall see that the **manner** of using Hancha, rather than the use of Hancha per se, determines whether literacy is restricted or widespread. We shall also see that the characteristics of a language affects the manner and efficiency with which Chinese characters are used.

Complicated Hancha Use in the Past

Just as the Korean language differs from the Chinese language, so the Korean use of Chinese characters differs from the Chinese. Hancha use might be described as torturously complicated in the past, so much so that it is hard to understand. Even experts do not always agree in their explanations of the phenomenon (e.g., Chang and Chang 1991; Lee Ki-moon 1972; Park Pyŏng-ch'ae 1990). I can only try to suggest the way Hancha were used, without expecting you to follow the detail.

Each Chinese character (shape) is associated with a meaning (morpheme) and a sound (syllable). In borrowing a character, Koreans can pronounce it by approximating its Chinese sound or by using an equivalent native word, and they can ignore or use its meaning, as follows. The Japanese can do the same (chap. 18).

1. Um/Chinese reading (Japanese On reading). Read Hancha using the Chinese sound and preserve its Chinese meaning: 春 ('spring') is *chun* in Chinese and *ch'un* in Sino-Korean Um reading (*shun* in Sino-Japanese On reading). Today, Um reading is the only way Hancha are read in Korean.

2. Hun/Korean reading ('meaning reading'; Japanese Kun reading). Read 春 as *pom*, the native word for 'spring'. Hun reading was practised in the past but is mercifully no longer used, except in learning the meaning and sound of individual Hancha. For example, the Hancha for 'spring' is learned as *pom ch'un*. (In Japan, Kun reading is still practised, and this character is read as *haru*.)

3. Um/Chinese phonetic loan. Read Hancha with the Chinese sound but ignore its Chinese meaning: 五 *o*, used as a verb ending, approximates its Chinese sound *wu* but ignores its Chinese meaning ('five').

4. Hun/Korean phonetic loan. Hancha 加 ('more; add') has the Um/Chinese sound *ka*. But in using it as a part of the verb ending *hadŏni* (roughly 'do so and'), it is given the sound of the native word *-dŏ-* ('more'), though this meaning is irrelevant to the verb ending.

Initially the Koreans used Hancha phonetically (items 3 and 4 above), choosing them for their sounds rather than for their meanings, to transcribe the sounds of native names of people and places. Since there are usually many Hancha with the same sound, one particular Hancha must have been chosen for one sound somewhat arbitrarily, but once chosen it must have been used more or less consistently.

To use Hancha to write a full text, the Koreans faced the problem of the differences in syntax between their language and Chinese. Typically a Korean sentence ends with a verb, and this verb changes its ending, whereas a Chinese sentence has a verb before an object noun, and its verb does not change its form. And a Korean sentence requires postpositions after nouns to indicate their grammatical roles, whereas a Chinese sentence does not. Postpositions have little meaning, and Korean verb or adjective endings vary their forms constantly, making them difficult to write in logographic Hancha, which represent primarily the meanings of morphemes, and which do not change their shapes for grammatical function. Unsuited or not, Hancha had to be used in early times because they were the only script available.

So, how did the Koreans write text using only Hancha? According to some scholars, they wrote in a few different methods, but according to other scholars, they wrote just in one method. The methods differ, depending on which Korean grammatical features — word order and/or grammatical morphemes — were honored, and on how and when they were used. For the sake of simiplicity, we follow the one-method view.

The most popular and enduring method of writing the Korean language using Hancha was called Idu ('cleric reading') or Isŏ ('cleric writing'). Its origin is not clear, but an Idu text written in AD 754 in the Unified Silla period was discovered in 1979. The text, designated as national treasure No. 196, is now kept in a museum in S. Korea (Shim 1993). Idu was used for writing official documents, personal correspondence, contracts, and so on, for hundreds of years during the Koryŏ and Chosŏn kingdoms.

Its use did not diminish even after the phonetic script Han'gŭl was created in the mid-15th century. It was officially discontinued only in 1894, when the Chosŏn kingdom carried out an educational and cultural reform.

Idu used the Korean word order, as shown in Figure 12-1a. As S-K content words were adopted they were written in their own Chinese characters and were given Um/Chinese readings). The native grammatical morphemes posed a problem, which was solved only unsatisfactorily: Hancha for them were chosen sometimes for their meanings and at other times for their sounds; one Hancha could represent a few different but similar sounds; and a few different Hancha might represent the same sound.

Koreans needed not only to write Korean, using Idu, but also to understand Chinese text. To make reading easier by clarifying the relations among clauses, they developed a method called Kugyŏl, which involved inserting native grammatical morphemes into clause boundaries in a Chinese text (fig. 12-1b). These grammatical morphemes were in the past written in Hancha, sometimes using their meanings and sometimes their sounds, but in modern times they are written in Han'gŭl.

(a) Idu: Writing Korean Text		*(b) Kugyŏl: Reading Chinese Text*			
Character	**Meaning**	**Chinese**	**Kugyŏl**	**Modern**	**Meaning**
他	other	父	父	父	husband
人	person	婦	婦	婦	wife
矣	*ŭi* (possessive)	有	隱	ㄴ	*nŭn* (topic)
婦	women-	別	有	有	have
女	folks		別	別	separation
乙	*rŭl* (objective)		為	하	*ha* (verb-
犯	violate		古	ㅗ	*go* ending)
姦	sexually				
為	*ha* (verb-				
在	*gŏ* end-				
乙	*dul* ing)				
良	*lang*				

Figure 12-1. Idu and Kugyŏl. Under "Meaning" the grammatical morphemes are in italics. The text says: (a) If you sexually violate other person's woman folks; (b) Husband and wife have separation.

In Kugyŏl, to make insertion easier in the small spaces between columns of writing, the Hancha for grammatical morphemes were sometimes written small and/or arranged horizontally. About 30 frequently used ones were eventually simplified, by retaining only a fragment or short-hand shape of each original Hancha (fig. 12-2); in a few cases, two simplified Hancha were fused into one, as for *hago* in the last row.

The simplified Hancha for grammatical morphemes were an improvement over the original complex Hancha, in being easy not only to write but also to distinguish from content words. Yet the simplified Hancha were still complicated in that they were used sometimes for their meanings, ignoring their sounds (e.g., *wi* 'do' was read as *ha*) and sometimes for their sounds, ignoring their meanings (e.g., *ko/go* 'old' was used for 'do and' in *hago*).

Some of the simplified Hancha had shapes that are the same or similar to some Katakana syllabary signs now used in Japan, and a few had even the same sounds. The simplified Hancha and Katakana (later Hiragana) both served the same function of expressing grammatical morphemes. It would not be hard to conjecture that the simplified Hancha served as models for Katakana, if they could be proven to have been devised before Kana. Be that as it may, the simplified Hancha have never been trans-

Original	Fragment (Katakana)	Sound Korean	Japanese
為	ソ	ha	so
尼	ヒ	ni	hi
多	タ	ta	ta
古	ロ	ko	ro
加	カ	tŏ	ka
奴	ヌ	ro	nu
伊	イ	i	i
為古	厶	hago	

Figure 12-2. Some simplified Hancha used for grammatical morphemes in Kugyŏl, with related Katakana symbols used in Japan

formed into a full phonetic script in Korean because of its complex sound system and syllable structures, whereas in Japanese the Chinese characters led to a full-fledged phonetic syllabary.

The writing and reading methods described here—Idu, Kugyŏl, and simplified Hancha for native grammatical morphemes—are enough to hint at the difficulty the Koreans faced in using only Hancha to write the Korean language and to read Chinese texts. Needless to say, only a small group of people had the time and patience to learn and use such unwieldy methods of writing and reading. The use of Hancha need not be so complicated, if they are supplemented by a phonetic script, as the next section shows.

Rational Hancha Use in the Present

The greatest difficulty the Koreans faced in using only Hancha to write the their language was that Hancha are ill-suited to writing native grammatical morphemes. (The same difficulty faced the Japanese; Part III.) When a phonetic script was invented, it gradually began to be used for native grammatical morphemes and content words, leaving Hancha only for S-K content words. Figure 12-3 (a part of fig. 1-4 reproduced) shows the same sentence, "I go to school everyday," written in a mixture of Hancha (44%) and Han'gŭl (56%) (top), by writing all the S-K words in Hancha and all the native words—be they content or grammatical—in Han'gŭl, and in Han'gŭl only (bottom).

Today, the proportions of Hancha can vary greatly from text to text, depending on the type of reader, subject matter, author, government policy, and so on. Few Hancha appear in reading materials for young children, or in reading material on light or soft

Han'gŭl with Hancha: 나 는 每日 學校 에 간다
All Han'gŭl: 나 는 매일 학교에 간다

Figure 12-3. The sentence "I go to school every day" in Korean, written in a Hancha–Han'gŭl mixture (top) and in Han'gŭl only (bottom)

subject matters for adults. Some authors favor mixing Hancha and Han'gŭl, while others favor using Han'gŭl only.

Overall the use of Hancha has decreased in the past several decades, as S-K words have been written in Han'gŭl mainly because of government policies (see the next section). Figure 12-4 shows a survey of Hancha use in the newspaper *Chosun Ilbo* between 1920 and 1990. The following tendencies emerge: Headlines used more Hancha than body text; for headlines, a political section and a social section used similar amount of Hancha; for body text, however, the political section used far more Hancha than the social section; for both headlines and body text, the use of Hancha declined over the 70 years surveyed, with the turning point occurring around the year 1950; the social section used no Hancha throughout the 70 years, except a few in 1940.

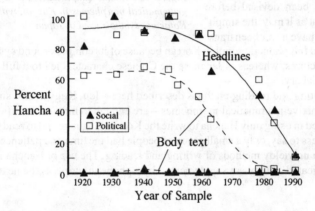

Figure 12-4. A survey of Hancha use in a leading newspaper, Chosun Ilbo, *between 1920 and 1990 (based on data from Yi Sŏk-chu, 1990)*

My own cursory survey of one newspaper, *Hanguk Daily* (6 and 7 May 1994), confirms the current fashion in the use of Hancha. In its editorial, the proportions of Hancha were about 10% in the body of the text but 60% in the headlines. In the same newspaper, a book review column contained only a few Hancha, mostly in the book titles and authors' names. Incidentally, the editorial was written in a vertical direction, while the book review was written in a horizontal direction ("Writing Directions: Vertical vs Horizontal" in chap. 7).

What proportion of Hancha do readers prefer in a text? In a survey conducted by one newspaper in 1962, the readers' order of preference, from greatest to least, was: a text with 25% Hancha (for S-K names of people and places as well as infrequent S-K words); a text with 50% or more Hancha (for almost all S-K words); and a text with no Hancha (An 1983). If such a survey were to be conducted today, when many newspaper readers have had limited instruction and practice in Hancha, a different pattern might emerge. Indeed, in a more recent survey, university students said that they encounter all-Han'gŭl texts most often and read them fastest among texts containing varying proportions of Hancha (Park 1988, in Park and Shon 1990). Some students reported that they could read all-Han'gŭl texts fast but without full comprehension. Many older Koreans who learned Hancha well and are accustomed to reading mixed texts complain that they have difficulty reading all-Han'gŭl texts, prompting some newspapers to switch back to mixed scripts from all-Han'gŭl.

Before closing this section, let me point out a few other facts about the Chinese characters used in Korea. Koreans use Chinese characters in their original shapes, and not in the drastically simplified shapes used in mainland China or the moderately simplified ones used in Japan. In handwriting, however, they may use some moderately simplified Hancha. Koreans have created a handful of characters of their own, though far fewer than the Japanese (tables 18-3 and 18-4). Typically, a made-in-Korea character combines two simple characters, one above or next to the other, to indicate a Korean CVC syllable needed for a native given name. Thus 下 *ha* ('below') is put over 乙 *ŭl* ('B-grade' or 'second') for *hal* (no meaning). Koreans also created a handful of unique Hancha words, such as *yangban* ('both', 'branches'), referring to the civilian and military branches of the ruling gentry class (chap. 16).

Used properly, Hancha need not be ill-suited to write the Korean language; on the contrary, they may even make reading easy and fast by highlighting critical content words in a text (fig. 12-3; also chap. 15). Unfortunately, Hancha are used not to maximum advantage in S. Korea and not at all in N. Korea.

Misguided Attempts to Abolish Hancha

In every nation that uses Chinese characters, there has been a debate on whether characters should be kept or abolished. The Vietnamese officially abolished them in the 1940's in favor of a Roman alphabet that had been in use since the 17th century. The Chinese and the Japanese now and then toy with the idea of abolishing characters in favor of the exclusive use of a Roman alphabet, or occasionally Kana in Japan, but both peoples still live with them. Koreans, too, think of abolishing characters. However, as an altenative script they never think of a Roman alphabet but think of the Korean phonetic script Han'gŭl, because romanizing the Korean sounds is complicated (chap. 14), on the one hand, and Han'gŭl is an effective script (chap. 13), on the other.

S. Korea abolished Hancha in 1970 in favor of the exclusive use of Han'gŭl, only to restore them a few years later. N. Korea in 1949 abolished Hancha, but in the late 1960s revived their teaching, though not their use. Let us trace the chronology of the movement to abolish Hancha in S. Korea.

- In 1948 President Syngman Rhee decreed that all government documents be written in Han'gŭl, though Hancha might be used along with Han'gŭl temporarily.
- In 1950 the Ministry of Education designated 1,200 Hancha for everyday use and 1,000 Hancha for school teaching.
- In 1955 the Ministry of Education decreed that government documents as well as ordinary reading materials—newspapers, magazines, and books—be written in Han'gŭl. But Hancha technical terms, enclosed in parentheses, were permitted.
- In 1957 the Ministry of Education published the 1,300 temporarily restricted Hancha, which were taught in schools between 1963 and 1969.

- In 1968 President Park Chŏng-hi decreed a five-year plan for abolishing Hancha. Later in the same year he shortened it to a two-year plan.
- In 1970, Hancha disappeared from government documents and educational materials, arousing fierce opposition from the public.
- In 1972 the Ministry of Education designated 1,800 Hancha for educational purpose.
- In 1975 textbooks used in secondary schools began to contain Hancha.
- In 1976 the Ministry of Education decided not to teach Hancha in primary school.
- In 1991 the Supreme Court announced 2,854 Hancha permitted for personal names.

Such frequent flip-flops in policy on Hancha use are detrimental to mass literacy. For one thing, they have produced uneven Hancha literacy among different generations of S. Koreans: older generations are comfortable only with Hancha–Han'gŭl mixed texts, shunning Han'gŭl-only texts, whereas younger generations easily read all Han'gŭl texts.

The conditions for abolishing Hancha are particularly favorable in Korea, where Hancha are used only for Sino-Korean words and not for native words, and where the efficient phonetic script Han'gŭl is available. Yet neither South nor North Korea has quite managed to abolish Hancha. Why not?

To abolish Hancha, S-K words must be abolished first. In 1962 the S. Korean government set up the Committee for Exclusive Use of Han'gŭl, which suggested replacing over 14,000 S-K words and other foreign words with native words. But this impracticable suggestion was not taken up seriously. For the past few decades N. Korea too has been replacing many S-K words, leaving only some oft-used, familiar ones. Inevitably two questions arise: which S-K words are common enough to be retained, and which native word should replace a particular S-K word. Regrettably, the two Koreas sometimes disagree on the answers. At any rate, the movement to eliminate S-K words can go only so far, because not all of them can be readily replaced by native words, as discussed in "Native Words vs Sino-Korean Words" (in chap. 11). Imagine Greco–Latinate words such as *telephone* and *encyclopedia* being eliminated overnight from the English language!

Now there seems to be a growing backlash against the Han'gŭl-only policies, spearheaded by such organizations as the Research Institute for Education in the Korean Language and Writing and its organ *Ŏmun Yŏngu (Research on Language and Writing)*. There are books such as *Research on Orthography of the National Language* (Sin 1992) that argues for Hancha–Han'gŭl mixed uses. Some primary schools teach Hancha, if unofficially. Throughout the month of February 1994, the leading newspaper *Chosun Ilbo* carried a series of lessons in Hancha as well as of articles that argued for Hancha use.

To answer the important question of whether Hancha should be kept or abolished, we should consider not only how well they represent a language (chap. 15) but also what alternative script is available to write the language. The alternative script to Hancha in Korea is indisputably the Korean phonetic script, Han'gŭl, which is the topic of our next chapter.

13

Han'gŭl:
Alphabetic Syllabary

Today Hancha is neither the sole nor the major script in Korea; that honor goes to an indigenous phonetic script called Han'gŭl. Let us see how Han'gŭl was created and developed, how it is structured, and how it is learned and used.

Creation and Adoption of Han'gŭl

Inconvenience is the mother of invention. The sheer complexity and inadequacy of using only Hancha to write the Korean language prompted a Korean king to create a novel and efficient phonetic script. This king was Sejong (1398–1450), the fourth in the Chosŏn dynasty. His portrait is shown in Figure 13-1.

The king's noble sentiment is echoed in the original name for Han'gŭl, *Hunmin Chŏng'ŭm ('Correct Sounds to Instruct People')*, or simply *Chŏng'ŭm ('Correct Sounds')*, which is also the title of the document that introduced the new script to the public. The new script was completed in 1443 and promulgated in 1446. It is a short document containing King Sejong's preface and a list of the sounds of the new letters defined in terms of Hancha. In the preface the king observed:

> Because our language differs from the Chinese language, my poor people cannot express their thoughts in Chinese writing. In my pity for them I create 28 letters, which all can learn easily and use in their daily lives.

The king assigned a royal commission to provide a learned commentary on the *Correct Sounds*. The royal commission consisted of seven young scholars, all but one of whom were members of the Academy of Scholars, which was involved in research in many subject areas, including phonology. As part of their phonological research, the

Figure 13-1. King Sejong the Great (1398–1450), the creator of Han'gŭl

Korean scholars studied the languages and scripts of neighboring nations, such as Japanese, Mongolian, Manchurian, and Chinese. Through Buddhist texts some of them were likely to have been familiar with Indian phonetic scripts as well. The scholars' commentary, entitled the *Explanations and Examples of the Correct Sounds*, was published in 1446. It is composed of six sections: the shapes of the letters; initial sounds; medial sounds; final sounds; syllable blocks; and examples of letters in actual use. It concludes with a postface by the head of the commision, Chŏng In-ji. One sentence from Chŏng's postface is the second epigraph to this Part II.

The king, in his effort to popularize the new phonetic script, used it on money, in government documents, in the civil service exams, and in books ("Printing and Publications" in chap. 16). However, the creation of the new script was met not with an enthusiastic welcome but with stiff resistance from the privileged class who were deeply entrenched in Chinese culture. One member of the Academy of Scholars, Ch'oe Malli, presented the king a now famous memorial, listing his reasons for objecting to the new script. According to him, barbarians like Japanese and Mongolians possess their own scripts, but Koreans use splendid Hancha and Chinese text, as well as Idu ('cleric reading', fig. 12-1a) to complement them; there was no need for the new "mean, vulgar, useless" script. Fifty years after the new script was introduced, the regent Yŏnsan'gun (1494–1506), in his fury over the documents written in it that criticized his brutal regime, banned the learning of the script, burned books in it, and punished its users. Apparently, he was not so much against the new script as against the political criticism written in it by people who might not have been able to write using Hancha.

For many years the new script was called *ŏnmun* ('native, vernacular script') vis-à-vis the "true letters," i.e., Chinese characters. It was also called variously "women's letters," "monks' letters," or "children's letters," as it was used mainly by the less privileged. Chŏng'ŭm ('correct sound') has been called Han'gŭl only since 1913. The new name was inspired by the phrase *Han nara mal* ('letters of the Han nation'), which was first used by a pioneer in the study of the Korean language, Chu Si-gyŏng (1876–1914). This name came to be accepted with the publication in 1932 of a journal called *Han'gŭl*, which for many decades has been instrumental in popularizing the script.

The term *Han* has a few different meanings, all felicitous. It means "Korean" in that ancient Korea, before the time of the three kingdoms, was called "Han"; the Chosŏn kingdom was called, briefly between 1897 and 1910, "Taehan Chaeguk" ('Great Han Empire'); and the present S. Korea is called "Taehan Minguk" ('Great Han People's Nation'). As a native morpheme *han* means "one," "great," or "correct." The second word *gŭl* in Han'gŭl is a native word for "letter(s)," "writing," and more broadly "written language."

In N. Korea, which calls itself "Chosŏn Minjujuŭi Inmin Konghwaguk" ('Chosŏn Democratic People's Republic'), Han'gŭl is called "Chosŏncha" ('letters of Chosŏn or Korea') or "Chŏng'ŭm" ('Correct sounds'), the label by which Han'gŭl was promulgated in 1446. Also the creation of Han'gŭl is attributed not to King Sejong but to the Korean people.

In the earlier part of the Japanese occupation (1910–1945) Korean and Han'gŭl were permitted, but in the latter part, between 1938 and 1945, they could no longer be taught at school or used in most publications. Fortunately, the Society of Han'gŭl Studies kept alive the study of Han'gŭl underground so that when Korea was liberated in August 1945, it was ready to launch Han'gŭl as its major script. Today, Han'gŭl is cherished in both North and South Korea. The date it was proclaimed, October 9, is celebrated in S. Korea as Han'gŭl Day, with calligraphy contests and other events.

In the 500 years of use since its promulgation, Han'gŭl has undergone only minor changes. Before learning about them, it is necessary to learn about Han'gŭl, its letters and sounds.

Han'gŭl as an Alphabet

Han'gŭl is first and foremost an alphabet, in which one letter codes one phoneme. But it is not like other well-known alphabets of the world, such as Roman and Cyrilic. As an alphabet Han'gŭl has the following five unique characteristics.

1. The shapes of simple consonant letters suggest the manner in which the letters' sounds are produced by the articulatory organs (table 13-1).
2. Consonant letters and vowel letters are distinctively shaped so that no consonant letter could be taken to be a vowel letter, and vice versa (table 13-2).
3. Simple consonant and vowel letters are used as basic elements to build increasingly complex letters that code consonants and vowels having added articulatory features, such as aspiration and tenseness (table 13-1).
4. The handful of phoneme-coding letters are used as elements in building syllable blocks for a few thousand syllables, which are the actual reading and teaching units (table 13-3).
5. The explanation of the alphabetic letters was originally couched in Chinese philosophy, in particular, the doctrines of Yin–Yang and the Five Phases.

Let us learn more about these characteristics. To represent consonants, Han'gŭl starts with five simple letters for five basic consonants, or the "least severe" sounds as described originally. The fivefold classification of the Korean consonants comes from Chinese phonology and also from the Chinese philosophical doctrine of Five Phases, as discussed below for characteristic 5.

Table 13-1 shows how Han'gŭl consonant letters are formed. The five basic letters are shaped to suggest the shapes of the articulators and places of articulation in pronouncing the sounds they represent: The ㄱ letter for the consonant *k* or *g* depicts the root of the tongue obstructing the throat; the letter ㄴ for the consonant *n* depicts the tongue touching the upper gum; the letter ㅁ for the consonant *m* depicts the closed mouth; the letter ㅅ for the *s* depicts the tongue tip meeting the gum just above the front teeth; and the letter ㅇ for the sound *-ng* (or for the lack of an initial consonant) depicts the opened throat. Then by adding one or two strokes to the five simple consonant letters several related consonant letters are created, as shown also in Table 13-1.

- The stop consonant *t* or *d,* represented by ㄷ, is articulated in the same place in the mouth as *n* represented by ㄴ; its letter is created by adding one stroke above the *n*-letter.

Table 13–1. The Five Basic Consonant Letters, their Articulator Positions, and their Related Letters

Articulators	Basic Old → Modern	Stops (add)	Aspirated (add)	Tense (double)
🗣	ㄱ → ㄱ		─ ㅋ	ㄲ
🗣	ㄴ → ㄴ	─ ㄷ	─ ㅌ	ㄸ
👄	ㅁ → ㅁ	' ' ㅂ	,, ㅂ⌒ㅍ	ㅃ
🗣	ㅿ → ㅅ	─ ㅈ	` ㅊ	ㅆ ㅉ
👁	ㅇ → ㆁ	─ ㆆ ㅎ		

- The stop consonant *p* or *b*, represented by ㅂ, is articulated in the same place as *m* represented by ㅁ; its letter is created by adding two small strokes on top of the *m*-letter.
- The semi-stopped consonant *ch* or *j*, represented by ㅈ, is articulated in the same place as *s*; its letter is created by adding a bar over the *s*-letter.

For the articulatory feature of strong aspiration, another stroke is added:

- inside the *k*-letter ㄱ to create the *k'*-letter ㅋ;
- over the *t*-letter ㄷ to create the *t'*-letter ㅌ;
- under the *p*-letter ㅂ to create the *p'*-letter ㅍ (rotated by 90 degrees).

To represent the articulatory feature of tenseness, one of the *k*-, *t*-, *p*-, *s*-, and *ch*- letters is doubled (5th column in table 13-1 and also 2nd column in table 13-2).

Let us now consider the Korean vowels and their letters. In Chinese phonology, a syllable is divided into two parts: intitial (consonant) and final (medial vowel alone or vowel plus final nasal consonant) (chap. 2). But the Korean scholars went one step further by dividing a syllable into three parts: initial consonant, medial vowel, and final consonant, thus laying the foundation for the creation of an alphabet.

The Han'gŭl vowel letters have different origins and shapes from the consonant letters. In contrast to the consonant letters whose shapes are associated with the articulatory organs and features, vowel letters use a short bar (originally a dot), a horizontal line, and a vertical line, representing respectively heaven (circle), the earth (flat), and a human being (standing upright), the three great powers of the universe or the three germinants of Chinese philosophy. The vowel letters are remarkable not so much for their esoteric philosophical explanations as for their simplicity and versatility. By attaching the short bar as a marker to the two basic lines, one horizontal and the other vertical, 10 basic vowel letters are formed, and then by combining two or more basic vowel letters 11 compound vowel letters are formed.

For easy discrimination among different vowel letters, the short bar should not be too short, as they are in the font used in Table 13-2: in the 4th column, one bar and two bars for *a* and *ya* are discriminable, but in the 5th column, the two are less so in *ae* and *yae*.

Table 13-2. Complete Han'gŭl Letter Array

Consonant			Vowel	
Single	**Doubled**	**Compound**	**Basic**	**Compound**
14	5	12	10	11
k, g ㄱ	kk ㄲ	ㄳ	a ㅏ	ae ㅐ
n ㄴ		ㄵ	ya ㅑ	yae ㅒ
t, d ㄷ	tt ㄸ	ㄶ	ŏ ㅓ	e ㅔ
r, l ㄹ		ㄺ	yŏ ㅕ	ye ㅖ
m ㅁ		ㄻ	o ㅗ	wa ㅘ
p, b ㅂ	pp ㅃ	ㄼ	yo ㅛ	wae ㅙ
s ㅅ	ss ㅆ	ㄽ	u ㅜ	oe ㅚ
(-ng) ㅇ		ㄾ	yu ㅠ	wo ㅝ
ch, j ㅈ	tch ㅉ	ㄿ	ŭ ㅡ	we ㅞ
ch' ㅊ		ㅀ	i ㅣ	wi ㅟ
k' ㅋ		ㅄ		ŭi ㅢ
t' ㅌ				
p' ㅍ				
h ㅎ				

Characteristic 1 (the shapes of the simple consonant letters depict the articulatory organs) may or may not help Han'gŭl learners. But three of the five characteristics — 2 (consonant letters and vowel letters are distinct), 3 (simple letters build compound letters), and 4 (letters build syllable blocks) — can be observed by Han'gŭl users without being taught; they make Han'gŭl a highly systematic script that can be learned and used efficiently.

As for characteristic 5 (a Chinese philosophical perspective) the Korean literati at the time of the creation of Han'gŭl were enamored with Chinese culture. Thus the king and his scholars felt they must justify or rationalize their new script according to Chinese philosophy, in the doctrines of Yin–Yang and the Five Phases (table 10-2), so as to give it authority and legitimacy. However, today not many Koreans understand, much less believe in, these doctrines, into which for thousands of years the myriad phenomena of the universe were fitted willy-nilly. Seen today, the doctrines form more a proto- or pseudo-scientific classificatory scheme than a true explanatory system. Anyway, they have no relevance whatever to learning and using Han'gŭl. I had used Han'gŭl happily in Korea without knowing anything about characteristics 1 and 5; I learned about them only much later in Canada in my literature research while writing articles on Han'gŭl.

How many letters does Han'gŭl have? Table 13-2 lists all the letters of Han'gŭl: 10 basic letters for vowels and 11 compound letters for diphthongs; 14 basic letters for consonants, 5 doubled letters for tense unaspirated consonants, and 12 compound letters for consonant clusters. Each compound consonant letter is used only as the final in a CVCC syllable block. The number of Han'gŭl letters is counted differently in two Koreas: 24 (14 basic consonant letters + 10 basic vowel letters) in S. Korea, but 40 in N. Korea (24 + 5 doubled consonant letters + 11 compound vowel letters).

Among the 14 basic consonant letters, ㅇ has no sound value at the initial position of a syllable block where it acts simply as a place holder, as in 아 for the syllable *a*, but has the sound of -*ng* at the final position of a syllable, as in 앙 *ang* (see "Han'gŭl Syllable Blocks").

The order of Han'gŭl consonant letters is the same in two Koreas, except that the five doubled consonant letters are dispersed in the S. Korean list but are relegated to the end of the N. Korean list:

> *k, kk, n, t, tt, r, m, p, pp, s, ss, o (-ng), ch, tch, ch', k', t', p', h* (S. Korea)
> *k, n, t, r, m, p, s, o (-ng), ch, ch', k', t', p', h, kk, tt, pp, ss, tch* (N. Korea).

It is not clear why in S. Korea *k* and *kk* are next to each other, while *k'* is separated from the two. In N. Korea the order is as listed in Table 13-2, column 1 and then column 2. Anyway the mnemonic for the order is: *ka na ta ra ma ba sa* ..., by adding the sound *a* to each consonant, and disregarding the doubled consonants. The vowel letters are ordered as shown in Table 13-2 in both Koreas. Words in a dictionary are ordered in the order of the 19 consonant letters, and within each consonant, in the order of the 21 vowel letters.

Consonant (C) letters have names, each in two syllables, C*i* + *ŭ*C, as in *niŭn, piŭp, miŭm*, for the letters *n, p*, and *m*, respectively. These names were used in Ch'oe Se-jin's 1527 text for teaching Hancha using Han'gŭl. Originally, the first CV- of each consonant name was represented by one Hancha, and the second -VC by another. Three of the names—*kiyŏk* for the *k*-letter, *siot* for the *s*-letter, and *digŭt* for the *t*-letter—deviate from the C*ŭ*C pattern, perhaps because there were no Hancha with typically patterned sounds for them. In S. Korea, both regular and irregular names are still used, whereas in N. Korea, for easy learning, only the regular C*ŭ*C pattern is used for the names of all the consonant letters.

The C*ŭ*C letter names conveniently include the sound values of the letters once at their initial and once at their final positions. (Compare with the names "eitch" and "double you" for the English letters *h* and *w*). For *siot*, the initial and the final consonants are the same in Han'gŭl, even though the final consonant is written as -*t* when romanized. The name *riŭl* is particularly apt, as this letter is pronounced as *r*- (in N. Korea) at the initial position but as -*l* in the final poisition of a syllable. The names of all Korean vowels are their sounds.

Han'gŭl Syllable Blocks

Han'gŭl is an alphabet, as described so far, yet when it is written its letters are not strung together in a line, as are the letters of the English and other alphabets. A Han'gŭl letter, whether for a consonant or a vowel, is always used in combination with other letters to form a block, which may represent a CV, CVC, or CVCC syllable. For a syllable with no initial consonant, such as *a*, the letter ㅇ with no sound value takes the place of the missing consonant letter, thus ensuring that the syllable is constructed according to the same pattern as a CV syllable, as shown in Table 13-3 (rows 1 and 5). An appropriate label for such a package of Han'gŭl alphabetic letters seems to be "syllable block."

The alphabetic letters are packaged into syllable blocks according to a strict set of rules. First of all, there are two kinds of vowel stroke, horizontal and vertical: The horizontal stroke, which is placed under the initial C- letter, is used for the vowel letters *o, yo, u, ŭ,* etc. (table 13-3, top four rows), while the vertical stroke, which is placed on the right side of the C-, is used for the vowel letters *a, ya, ŏ, i,* etc. (table 13-3, bottom four rows). Then, to add a final consonant to CV-, if -V- has a horizontal stroke, the C-, -V-, and -C letters are arranged vertically; if it has a vertical stroke, C- and -V- are arranged horizontally, and the -C is placed under it. Treat the -CC as if it were a single consonant in adding it to CV-, as shown in Table 13-3. A block thus uses both horizontal and vertical dimensions, having letters

Table 13-3. Han'gŭl Letters Packaged in Syllable Blocks

Alphabet Letter				Syllable Block		
C-	-V-	-C	-CC	Block	Structure	Sound
ㅇ	ㅗ			오	(C)/V	o
ㄱ	ㅛ			교	C/V	kyo
ㄴ	ㅜ	ㄴ		눈	C/V/C	nun
ㅎ	ㅡ		ㄽ	흩	C/V/CC	hŭlt'
ㅇ	ㅏ			아	(C)V	a
ㅂ	ㅏ	ㅇ		뱡 *	CV/C	pyang
ㄸ	ㅣ		ㄹㅂ	뗾	CV/CC	ttŏlp
ㄲ	ㅣ		ㄹㅂ	낄 *	CV/CC	kkilp

*not used in the Korean language.

arranged in rows as well as in columns in a squarish block. The reading order of the letters within a block is systematic and is top to bottom and left to right.

By this packaging method, the 24 alphabetic letters can generate numerous syllable blocks. How many? First, let us create a basic Han'gŭl syllable chart by placing the 10 basic vowel letters in the top row and the 14 basic consonant letters in the leftmost column, as shown in Table 13-4. Each of the 14 C letters combines with each of the 10 V letters to generate a CV syllable block. For example, the *k*-letter combines with each of the 10 vowel letters to produce *ka, kya, kŏ, kyŏ* ...; so does the *n*-letter to produce *na, nya, nŏ, nyŏ* .... Altogether, the chart produces 140 CV blocks.

The basic chart can be expanded to include all 21 vowel letters (10 basic + 11 compound) and all 19 consonant letters (14 basic + 5 double), to produce 399 possible CV syllable blocks. The more complex syllable blocks, CVCs and CVCCs that contain final consonants, can be easily derived from the chart, by placing a final -C or -CC at the bottom of any CV block. For example, the final -*n* is placed under *ka* to derive *kan,* under *na* to derive *nan,* and so on. The number of syllable blocks that can be generated depends on the number of letters involved.

14 basic Cs x 10 basic Vs = 140 CVs
19 (14 + 5 doubled Cs) x 21 (10 + 11 compound Vs) = 399 CVs
399 x 19 Cs = 7,581 CVCs
399 x 31 (19 Cs + 12 compound Cs) = 12,369 CVCs, CVCCs
12,369 + 399 = 12,768

Using all the letters in all possible combinations, as many as 12,768 syllable blocks could be generated, but most of them are not used in the language. As a convenient and quick way to find out how many blocks are actually used, one can count the number of type blocks contained in a printing tray; it turned out to be 2,100 in the case of the newspaper *Chosun Ilbo* in 1981 (An 1983). The director of the Korean Language

Table 13-4. Basic Han'gŭl Chart: 14 Consonant Letters Combined with 10 Vowel Letters to Form 140 Syllable Blocks

Vowels	ㅏ	ㅑ	ㅓ	ㅕ	ㅗ	ㅛ	ㅜ	ㅠ	ㅡ	ㅣ
Consonants	a	ya	ŏ	yŏ	o	yo	u	yu	ŭ	i
ㄱ k, g	가	갸	거	겨	고	교	구	규	그	기
ㄴ n	나	냐	너	녀	노	뇨	누	뉴	느	니
ㄷ t, d	다	댜	더	뎌	도	됴	두	듀	드	디
ㄹ r, l	라	랴	러	려	로	료	루	류	르	리
ㅁ m	마	먀	머	며	모	묘	무	뮤	므	미
ㅂ p, b	바	뱌	버	벼	보	뵤	부	뷰	브	비
ㅅ s, sh	사	샤	서	셔	소	쇼	수	슈	스	시
ㅇ (null)	아	야	어	여	오	요	우	유	으	이
ㅈ ch, j	자	쟈	저	져	조	죠	주	쥬	즈	지
ㅊ ch'	차	챠	처	쳐	초	쵸	추	츄	츠	치
ㅋ k'	카	캬	커	켜	코	쿄	쿠	큐	크	키
ㅌ t'	타	탸	터	텨	토	툐	투	튜	트	티
ㅍ p'	파	퍄	퍼	펴	포	표	푸	퓨	프	피
ㅎ h	하	햐	허	혀	호	효	후	휴	흐	히

Research Society, Hahn (1981), gave 1,950 as the number of different syllables of the Korean language, without specifying how he arrived at it.

One meticulous researcher, Wŏn (1986), took the trouble of making many charts of all possible syllable blocks and of noting those that actually occur in the language. By this method, he arrived at the following figures: Of the 12,768 possible syllable blocks, only 1,832 are used, while the remaining 10,936 are not used. Perusal of his data as well as dictionaries suggest that most, though by no means all, of the possible simple CV blocks are used, whereas some complex CVC blocks and most CVCC blocks are not used. All the blocks in table 13-3, except the two marked with asterisks, are used.

In counting the syllable blocks, Wŏn was the sole judge of the occurrence or non-occurrence of each syllable block in words (not counting archaic ones), no doubt in consultation with a large dictionary. For each "occurring block" he lists a sample word that uses it. In this kind of counting, one is liable to make an error of omission: possibly Wŏn missed some syllable blocks that actually occur. In one Dutch study, literate adult subjects knew only at most 493 of the 713 official Dutch 3-letter words (Bouwhuis 1979). To make doubly sure about non-occurring blocks, Wŏn might have consulted an electronic dictionary, if such a thing had been available. So just to be on the safe side, and to have a nice round number that is easy to remember, let us say that the number of syllable blocks actually used is 2,000, which is inbetween the number of types contained in a typical printing tray (2,100) and the number Wŏn counted (1,832).

In a nutshell, Han'gŭl is an alphabet with a set of 24 (in S. Korea) or 40 (in N. Korea) letters, which are used to build some 12,800 syllable blocks, of which about 2,000 are used. These syllable blocks are the actual units of writing, reading, and teaching.

Varied Complexity of Syllable Blocks

Han'gŭl letters, even including compound and doubled letters, are simply shaped: each letter contains between 1 (ㅇ) and 8 (ㅃ) strokes, the average being 3. They are slightly more complex than English letters, which contain between 1 (*I*) and 3 or 4 (*E*) strokes, or the Japanese Kana signs, which contain between 1 (ㅅ) and 6 (ぼ) strokes. But each Han'gŭl syllable block, which is a package of two or more letters, is naturally complex. Furthermore the syllable blocks are uneven in complexity: The simplest block contains 2 strokes (one stroke for C- and one stroke for -V), as in 기 *ki*, while the most complex block used (that I can think of) 밟 *pa(l)p* ('step on') has 13 strokes. In theory, the most complex block could contain 20 strokes (8 strokes for C-, 5 strokes for -V-, and 7 strokes for -CC), but such a complex block is not needed because its sound is not used in the language. One scholar, Kim Chong-t'aek (1984), has complained about the uneven and "unattractive" appearance of syllable blocks, compared with the even complexity, or rather the simplicity, of alphabetic letters (the next section).

The uneven visual complexity of Han'gŭl syllable blocks should actually help recognition, because the more varied are the visual shapes of graphs, the more easily are they discriminated from one another. This is one reason why a Hancha–Han'gŭl mixed text is easier to read than either an all-Han'gŭl or an all-Hancha text. In English text, a mix of tall letters, short letters, and letters that project below or above the line produce a distinct outer contour or envelope of a word. And some words are short and some long. Try to find *bay* in list 1 and *19th* in list 2:

1. *beg, dog, boy, day, bay, bog, bag*
2. *a, of, book, Reading, 19th, K-mart, Coca-Cola.*

You are likely to find the target among the similarly shaped words in list 1 more slowly than among the dissimilarly shaped words in list 2. (Unfortunately, copy editors often insist that *19th* must be spelled out as *nineteenth*.)

TRY TO READ A SENTENCE IN ALL CAPITALS; YOU FIND IT HARD TO READ EVEN AFTER PRACTICE, BECAUSE THE CONTOURS OF ALL WORDS ARE THE SAME EXCEPT FOR LENGTH. (Again unfortunately, cartoons in English use all capitals.)

Of course many English words, like those in list 1, share the same contours, and so a contour cannot be the sole or major cue for recognizing a word. But contours are used, at least in reading short common words. They are especially useful in recognizing frequently occurring function words (e.g., *the, of, and*). In many cases, readers identify frequent function words only by their contours, which is one reason why they tend to miss misprints in such words when proofreading. (Another reason is that readers tend to skip over predictable or unimportant function words, as shown in fig. 7-2.) Research on English words show that the differences among letter shapes help word recognition (Haber et al. 1981; Taylor and Taylor 1983).

What about the recognition of Han'gŭl syllable blocks? Han'gŭl syllable blocks come in three levels of visual complexity, corresponding roughly to their syllable complexity—CV, CVC, and CVCC—as shown in Table 13-3, above. To demonstrate the advantage of varied complexity over uniform complexity in a discrimination task, I set up two test conditions: In the first condition, Korean readers were asked to recognize and discriminate a target among other syllable blocks of the same complexity, and in the second, they were asked to do the same among other syllable blocks in all three complexity levels (Taylor 1980). The target syllable block could come from any of the three complexity levels. The readers discriminated a target better in the mixed background condition than in the homogeneous background. In normal reading, the ability to discriminate among syllable blocks is an advantage, and the uneven complexity of blocks helps discrimination.

Linear vs Packaged Arrangement and Word Processing

Han'gŭl alphabetic letters are never written in a linear sequence of letters but are always written in their packaged forms as syllable blocks. This packaging feature has remained unchanged since Han'gŭl was created 500 years ago, and remains unique among the alphabets of the world used today. It deserves our close examination.

Could the Han'gŭl alphabetic letters be used in a linear arrangement like English letters? If so, why are not they so used? Figure 13-2 shows one phrase written in three kinds of Han'gŭl arrangements.

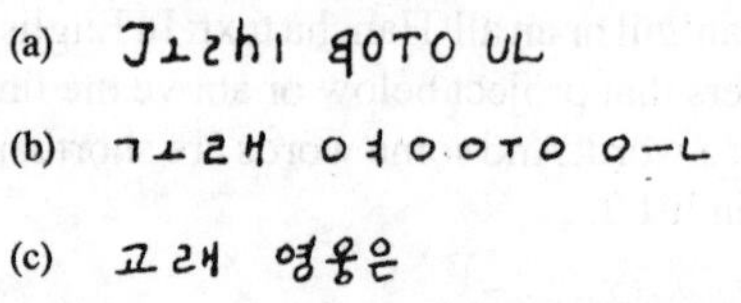

(a)   Јⵏㄹㅏㅣ 웧ㅇㅜㅜㄹ

(b)   ㄱㅗㄹㅐ ㅇㅓ ㅇ.ㅇㅗㅜㅇ ㅇ—ㄴ

(c)   ㄲㄹㅐ 영웧은

Figure 13-2. One Han'gŭl text in two linear arrangements and one packaged arrangement: (a) in 11 pseudo-Roman letters with no initial vowel letters, as suggested by Kim Chong-t'aek (1984); (b) in 13 normal Han'gŭl letters including the customary initial vowel letters; (c) in 5 customary syllable blocks

In Figure 13-2a, why does Kim mercilessly distort Han'gŭl letters in a futile effort to make them look like the letters of the English alphabet? Is he ashamed of them? At any rate, to use pseudo-Roman letters for the Korean sounds will confuse readers familiar with both English and Korean alphabets, as they have to associate one letter shape with two quite different sounds. For example, the English letter *h* has to be read as *a* in Korean, the English letter *T* as *u* in Korean and, the English letter *L* as *n* in Korean.

Kim gives three reasons for favoring the linear arrangement of Han'gŭl letters, one of which is valid and the other two misguided. Leaving the one valid reason—inconvenient typing—for later discussion, here we focus on his two misguided reasons. Kim does not favor syllable blocks because they are varied in visual complexity and are unattractive. He may view varied complexity as unattractive, but others, including myself, may not. More importantly, varied complexity helps recognition of individual syllable blocks, as pointed out in "Varied Complexity of Syllable Blocks." Besides the varied complexity of the blocks, the varied line thickness of letter strokes makes reading easier. A Han'gŭl text is normally in a font type called Myŏng (Ming dynasty) while brief titles are in another font type called

Gothic. Letters and blocks in Myŏng font type, because they have varied thickness of strokes and asymmetrical shapes, are deemed more legible than letters and blocks in Gothic type, which have uniformly thick strokes and symmetrical shapes. The Han'gŭl font type used in this book is close to Myŏng type.

Kim objects to the packaged arrangement for another misguided reason: Two or more words pronounced the same are sometimes spelled differently in syllable blocks. This spelling convention is in fact an advantage, as it differentiates meanings (see "Instruction in Han'gŭl Spelling" in chap. 14).

Contrary to Kim, a packaged arrangement is expected to have advantages over a linear arrangement for the following reasons.

First, packaging shortens the visual appearance of a text. In Figure 13-2, compare the lengths of the different arrangements of the same content. The two forms of linear arrangement, (a) and (b), are more than twice as long as the packaged arrangement (c). A short phrase such as (c) may be recognized within one eye fixation, whereas the same phrase written in a longer string of letters as in (a) and (b) may need two or more. Eye movements during reading, including fixations and visual spans, were described in Chapter 7 in Part I. Remember, the more the fixations the slower the reading.

Second, a packaged arrangement is suitable for both traditional vertical writing and contemporary horizontal writing. Even though the visual span is shorter vertically than horizontally, it is more likely that one can perceive a word in two syllable blocks within one fixation than the same word in several alphabetic letters arranged linearly (see fig. 7-3).

Third, packaging **organizes** letters into syllable blocks. Readers, as they gain skills, tend to read in ever larger linguistic units: letters/phonemes, syllables, words, phrases, clauses, and sentences. (For one experiment that compared letter units to words units, see "Logographs vs Phonetic Graphs: Research" in chap. 6). In a packaged arrangement a series of letters is already organized into a series of syllables so that letter-by-letter processing can be bypassed.

The best and only way to settle the issue is to ask people to read the same material written in two arrangements and compare the distributions of eye fixations, reading time, and accuracy. This experiment has to be done with people who have about the same amount of experience or practice with each of the two arrangements. Here is one modest experiment conducted by me with the help of Saunders (Taylor 1980). We required English-speaking university students, who were unfamiliar with the Korean language and script, to read aloud two kinds of Han'gŭl syllable blocks, CV CV (e.g., *karyu* 가류) and CVC CVC (e.g., *pukkal* 북갈), once in a linear arrangement and once in a packaged arrangement. The students did the task after a 5-minute explanation of how each Han'gŭl letter is pronounced and how the letters are combined into CV and CVC blocks. We measured the times to pronounce the syllables. The experiment was carried out in 18 sessions, each of which lasting 45 minutes, with a one week gap between the 6th and the 7th sessions.

Three of the results are worth reporting. First, pronouncing times decreased over the trial sessions for both sets of materials and both arrangements, from 13 to 3 seconds in the case of the complex CVC CVCs in the packaged arrangement. Second, even though the test material, whether CV CV or CVC CVC, is written in two syllable blocks each, the simpler CV CV blocks were pronounced faster than the more complex CVC CVC blocks in both linear and packaged arrangements, suggesting that each block is analyzed into a series of Cs and Vs in pronouncing, at least by these novice readers. However, the differences between the two sets of material decreased over the 18 sessions, suggesting that with practice a syllable block may be processed as a whole pattern. Third, both sets of syllable blocks were pronounced faster in the linear than packaged arrangement, but over the 18 sessions, the differences between the two arrangements narrowed to the point where they almost disappeared.

To conclude up to this point, Han'gŭl letters are arranged in text not in a linear sequence but in syllable blocks. One block takes up less space than a linear sequence of a few letters, and also organizes a sequence of letter–phonemes into a sequence of syllable–blocks. Each block may come to be recognized as one unit almost as if it were one letter or one Chinese character. Blocks, with their varied complexity, are better for discrimination than are uniformly simple alphabetic letters. All these advantages of a packaged arrangement help readers recognize words and phrases fast and accurately. Finally, Han'gŭl is easier to learn as a set of syllable blocks than as a set of alphabetic letters (chap 14).

The one area in which a linear arrangement could have an advantage over a packaged arrangement is typing, but electronic typing may reduce or eliminate this advantage.

A few kinds of Han'gŭl typewriter, modelled on English typewriters, have been invented in the past few decades. On the simplest keyboard the 24 letters of Han'gŭl, plus several punctuation marks and Arabic numerals, are arranged, one letter per key. A typist could simply type the letters one after another, producing a linearly arranged text like Figure 13-2b, above, which is unfamiliar and difficult to read. If a keyboard is to be used to produce familiar syllable blocks, some complicated procedures are needed, because the shape and size of a consonant letter must be changed slightly, depending on whether the letter is used in a syllable block with a vertical or horizontal vowel letter, or whether it is used as a part of a CV, CVC, or CVCC, as was shown in Table 13-3. And typing has to place the letters of the right shape, so as to form a block.

Matters are easier if the blocks are formed by a computer, which is more flexible than a typewriter in the shapes it creates. A writer should be able to type in a Korean text as a string of alphabetic letters, and let a computer automatically package them into a series of correctly structured and proportioned syllable blocks. Automatic packaging should be possible because alphabetic letters are packaged into syllable blocks in a highly systematic manner.

In 1989 a group of students at Seoul National University developed a multilingual word processor called *HWP (Han'gŭl Word Processor)*, which became an instant hit. The minimum window size is 13 x 13 pixels or dots for a legible Han'gŭl syllable block, compared to 24 x 24 pixels for a Hancha. *HWP* produces a more handsome Korean font than does *LaserKOREAN*, the software I use on a Macintosh, but *HWP* is available only on IBM. It can handle Han'gŭl, Hancha, English, and Japanese scripts. It can handle both contemporary and obsolete Han'gŭl letters (for obsolete letters, see "Changes in Han'gŭl since Its Creation," below).

While on the topic of word processing, the *HWP* software stores also 16,384 Hancha, of which 4,888 belong to level I of the Korean Industrial Standard. It also stores a dictionary of 30,000 Sino-Korean words. The Hancha can be accessed phonetically by Han'gŭl, by their meanings, or by shape, i.e., radicals and strokes. First of all, a writer must know which words are Sino-Korean that can be written in Hancha. If she knows the sound of a S-K word, she can simply input it in Han'gŭl and then press a function key to convert the word into Hancha. When the word has a set of homophones, the writer has to choose the appropriate one. She also has to know how to break up a long Hancha phrase, which is unlikely to be in the dictionary, into smaller units, which probably are. For example, the writer has to break up the 6-Hancha phrase *chayuminjujuŭi* ('free democracy') into *chayu* ('freedom') and *minjujuŭi* ('democracy'). So the inclusion of Hancha words in text may slow down word processing for one writer, but it may help her (many) reader(s) comprehend the text fast and accurately (chap. 15). The *HWP* includes a Han'gŭl spelling check. Today, computers are used widely for writing and typesetting Korean text.

Changes in Han'gŭl Since its Creation

Han'gŭl, as described so far, is the form used today, but it has undergone some changes since its promulgation in 1446. The number of letters has been reduced from 28 to 24, and the letters and blocks have been streamlined and standardized. The changes partly reflect changes in the sound system of spoken Korean and partly are modifications in the writing system itself (based on Kim Jin-p'yŏng 1983). Old and modern styles are illustrated in Figure 13-3

At the time of its creation, when Han'gŭl blocks were printed, often in wood blocks but occasionally in movable type, they had angular, squarish shapes. But soon after, when they began to be written by hand with brush, they lost their squarish appearance. One of the three basic vowel letters, originally a dot, has been changed to a short bar (fig. 13-3a, b).

Near the end of the 15th century, one Han'gŭl letter, ㆆ (representing a stop consonant produced at the throat) disappeared from some books. In 1527, when Ch'oe Se-jin published a popular Hancha text, in which the meaning

Old	Modern	Sound
(a) ·사	사	sa
(b) 영	영	yŏng
(c) ᅀᅵ	지	zi
(d) ᄠᅳᆷ	뜸	ttŭm
(e) ᄃᆞᆰᄉ	닭	talk

Obsolete letters: ㆆ ㅿ ㆁ ㆍ

Figure 13-3. Old and modern Han'gŭl syllable blocks

and the sound of each Hancha was given in Han'gŭl, he did not use this letter. So, the number of Han'gŭl letters had decreased to 27 from the original 28 in the first 50 years.

Twice at the end of the 16th century, Japan invaded Korea, in the war called *Imjinwoeran,* causing much social turmoil. Many type-casting shops were destroyed, many type sets were plundered, and many type-casting workers were taken to Japan as prisoners. Yet people wrote lyrics and poems in Han'gŭl. These were published either as brushwork or in wood-block prints. The size of the consonant letters in syllable blocks shrank, and letters such as ㅅ (which looked like an upside-down V , as in fig. 13-3a) and ㅇ (which was a perfect circle without a top protrusion) became less symmetrical than before. Some complex initial consonant clusters disappeared around this time.

During the 16th and 17th centuries further changes occurred in Han'gŭl. First, left side dots (fig. 13-3a) that used to indicate the high and low tones of the Korean language disappeared, as the tone distinction itself disappeared: e.g., *son* ('guest'), low tone, vs .*son* ('hand'), high tone. Second, between two circle letters—one with a long "handle" or protrusion on the top used only at the final position of a syllable, and the other without a handle used at the initial position of a syllable—the former disappeared, and only the latter has survived to represent both sounds (b). In the font used in this book, only a tiny top protrusion is left in the letter ㅇ. Third, a triangle, the letter for a semi-dental sound /z/, disappeared, as the sound itself disappeared (c). So by the end of the 17th century there were 25 letters, compared with the original 28. Also in the same period, combinations of three consonant letters disappeared (e).

In the 17th century, Han'gŭl was used to write popular stories and poems. It was also widely used in the court by ladies who were in charge of writing royal letters and messages. These script-copying court ladies developed calligraphic forms in regular as well as cursive styles, similar to such script styles for Chinese characters shown in Table 3-1.

In the 18th century, Han'gŭl was once again studied by scholars, and its use spread among the ordinary citizens. One comma-like vowel letter that had represented sometimes *ŭ* and sometimes *o* came to represent *a* (fig. 13-3e); the letter itself lingered on until 1933, when it was eliminated. Since then, the number of Han'gŭl letters has been 24.

Near the end of the 19th century, Korea was aroused by the influence of Western civilization. Many newspapers, magazines, the Bible, and textbooks began to be published in Han'gŭl ("Printing and Publications" in chap. 16). In these publications the final consonant letters used in CVC and CVCC syllable blocks were reduced in size. Toward its end, the Chosŏn kingdom established a Han'gŭl research center with prominent scholars such as Chu Si-gyŏng, who began the use of the label Han'gŭl and laid the ground work for the modern standardized spelling. He also replaced the earlier "*s*-letter + consonant letter" to represent any tense unaspirated stop consonant with a doubling of an appropriate consonant letter (e.g., ㅅㄷ became ㄸ for *tt*).

In the late 19th and early 20th centuries there arose a need to standardize Han'gŭl spelling, which had become confusing, especially in the face of changing spoken Korean. To deal with this and other problems, in 1921 the Society for the Study of the Korean Language, known today as the Society of Han'gŭl Studies, was inaugurated. In 1933, following Chu's basic plan, the Society published the "Guide for the unified Korean spelling," which proved so sensible that it was adopted by both S. and N. Korea, and has since been modified only slightly, as described in "Instruction in Han'gŭl Spelling" (in chap. 14). Also in 1933 a new font type Myŏng(jo) ('Ming dynasty') was developed and used in printing the *Tong'a Daily*. The Myŏng font reflects the influence of brush writing in that its strokes are tapered at the end, compared with uniform thickness of strokes in Gothic font.

The changes in the number of letters, shapes of letters and blocks, and spelling, described here are important improvements over the original. Yet the fundamental characteristics of the original Han'gŭl, those described in the preceding sections and those to be described in the next section of this chapter, remain unchanged.

Was Han'gŭl an Original Creation?

Now that we have learned much about Han'gŭl, we can discuss the question: Was it an original creation, or did it derived from another script? Most writing systems used in the world today are derived, directly or indirectly, from either the proto-Semitic syllabary or the logographic Chinese characters. For example, the English alphabet can trace its ancestry to the proto-Semitic script indirectly via the Roman, Greek, and Phoenician alphabets (fig. 1-2, chap. 1). The Greek alphabet added vowel letters to the Phoenician script; other than that, the letters of related alphabets are similar in their order, number, sound values, shapes, and names. Of course the degree of similarity is close when the derivation is direct, as from the Latin alphabet to the English; it is less so when the derivation is indirect, as from the Greek alphabet to the English. Japanese Kana signs can trace their ancestry directly to Chinese characters. For example, 力 is the left part of the character 加, and the two share the same sound ka.

What about Han'gŭl? Was it derived from any particular existing script? In the mid-15th century, when Han'gŭl was invented, a variety of phonetic writing systems—alphabets and syllabaries—were already in use. And Korean scholars were familiar with the languages and scripts of neighboring nations, especially of China, Japan, Mongolia, Jurchen (Manchus), and India. These scripts must have inspired King Sejong and his scholars to create a phonetic script for Korean. But inspiration aside, was Han'gŭl a newly invented script or was it derived from an existing one?

Let us begin our detective story with Chŏng In-ji's postface to the *Explanations and Examples of Hunmin Chŏng'ŭm* (1446).

> Our Monarch created twenty eight letters .... He named them "The correct sounds to instruct the people." The letters depict the shapes of objects [the speech organs] and resemble the old seal....

All the original documents on and about the new script were in Chinese texts, which have been translated variously into modern Korean and also into English. Here is how Chŏng In-ji's last sentence has been translated.

> While depicting outlines [of the speech organs], these letters imitate the Old Seal. [Ledyard 1966: 358]

> Resembling pictographs, these letters imitate the shapes of the old seal characters. [Ch'oe 1993: 517; English]

> Letters were created to depict objects [the speech organs], and the resulting letters resemble the old seal characters. [Kang 1990: 21; 83; loosely translated from Korean]

The last translation by the Han'gŭl scholar Kang sensibly differentiates between the creating process and the resulting letter shapes. Recall the principles used in creating Han'gŭl, as explicitly stated in the *Explanation and Examples of Hunmin Chŏng'ŭm*: the five basic consonant letters depict the outlines of the speech organs pronouncing the sounds, and other consonant letters are derived from these basic five by adding strokes for added articulatory features (table 13-1). Further, Chŏng In-ji, in his postface to the above document, stated that the new script was "created naturally," i.e., was an original creation, not a copy of any other script.

Different translations arise because of one particular character for a conjunction, which can be translated variously as 'and (so)', 'but', 'that is', 'however', 'yet', 'thus', and so on. The ambiguity with the sentence does not end with its conjunction. Where does the phrase "the old seal" come from, and what does it refer to? The sentence "these letters imitate the old seal" is found in the *Sejong Sillok (King Sejong Chronicle)* of 1443, and the sentence "letter shapes imitate old seal writing" in Ch'oe Malli's 1444 memorial to King Sejong. Of various interpretations, let us consider two of the most plausible ones.

Hypothesis 1. The "old seal," *kochŏn,* is an abbreviation of "(Mong)ko seal signs" or the Mongolian phonetic script, which was used for about 100 years in Mongol and the Yuan (Mongolian) dynasty in China between the 13th and 14th centuries. The script, which was called Paspa (also 'Phags-pa or hPhagspa), was created in the 13th century by the Tibetan monk hPhagspa as a variation on the Tibetan alphabet. The Tibetan alphabet itself was derived from one of the Indic scripts, which can be ultimately traced to the proto-Semitic script (fig. 1-3). The Paspa script began with 41 letters, to which 16 letters were added. It was called also the "square letters" because of the squarish shapes of the letters. Some monuments and documents in Paspa survive (*Zhongguo Minzu Guwenzi* or *The Old Scripts of Chinese Nationalities* 1990).

The first person to suggest the Mongolian model for Han'gŭl was Yi Ik (1682– 1763), a noted scholar of the "practical learning" (chap. 16). He observed that the shapes of the letters of the two scripts were not similar at all but that both were phonetic scripts. Apparently, he was referring to another Mongolian script that is based on the Uygur alphabet, which is still used in Central Asia.

Ledyard (1966), who wrote a Ph.D. thesis on the origin of Han'gŭl, and Hope (1957) before him, provide "evidence" that some Han'gŭl letters were modelled on their "corresponding" Paspa letters. But Ledyard had to resort to some tampering, as follows and as illustrated in Figure 13-4a.

The Han'gŭl *k/g*-letter drops the hanging box of its Paspa counterpart.

The Han'gŭl *r/l*-letter is a straightened version of its Paspa counterpart turned on its right side.

The Han'gŭl *s*-letter has the main outline of its Paspa counterpart.

The Han'gŭl *m*-letter is an enclosure, and its Paspa counterpart is a near enclosure, if with a loop.

Even Ledyard admits that the last case for the *m*-letter is more extreme tampering than he has resorted to so far. The Han'gŭl *t*-letter, according to him, corresponds closely to its Paspa counterpart.

First of all, is such tampering justified? When one alphabet is derived directly from another, the letters of the two alphabets tend to be similar, without tampering, as pointed out at the outset of this section. What about a few unaltered Paspa letters that closely resemble Han'gŭl letters, if their sound values are ignored (fig. 13-4b)? For example, the Paspa letter for /N/ resembles closely the Han'gŭl *r/l*-letter.

(a) 4 Han'gŭl (H) letters resemble altered Paspa (P) letters.

H	P	Sound
ㄱ	귀	g
ㄹ	린	l
ㅅ	자	s
ㅁ	자	m

(b) 5 Han'gŭl letters resemble unaltered Paspa letters.

H	P	Sound H	Sound P
ㄹ	ㄹ	r, l	N
ㅌ	ㅌ	t'	ch
ㄷ	ㄷ	d	e
ㅈ	ㅊ	ch	o
ㅋ	ㅋ	k'	e

(c) Han'gŭl and Paspa syllable blocks differ.

H		P		Sound
이	(C)V	ᅙ	V	i
바	CV	린	C(a)	ba
지	CV	짱	C/V	chi
밍	CV/C	밍	C/V	ming

(d) 5 Han'gŭl letters resemble Roman letters.

Han'gŭl Sound	Han'gŭl Letter	Roman
i	ㅣ	I
t'	ㅌ	E
N	ㅇ	O
u	ㅜ	T
n	ㄴ	L

(e) 6 Han'gŭl letters resemble Hancha.

Han'gŭl Sound	Han'gŭl Letter	Hancha Shape	Hancha Sound
s	ㅅ	人	in
m	ㅁ	口	ku
ŭ	ㅡ	一	il
r, l	ㄹ	己	ki
u	ㅜ	丁	chŏng
a	ㅏ	卜	pok

Figure 13-4. Some Han'gŭl letters compared to Paspa letters, Roman letters, and Hancha

Secondly, the claim that some Han'gŭl letters copied their Paspa counterparts ignores the principles used in creating Han'gŭl, as explicitly stated in the *Explanation and Examples of Hunmin Chŏng'ŭm*: the five basic consonant letters depict the outlines of the speech organs pronouncing the sounds, and other consonants letters are derived from these basic five by adding strokes for added articulatory features (table 13-1). For example, the Han'gŭl *k*-letter depicts the tongue arched to pronounce this consonant, and the *k'*-letter is created by adding a stroke inside the *k*-letter for the added articulatory feature of aspiration. Such articulatory consideration is not evident in the shapes of the Paspa letters.

Without much tampering, and ignoring sounds, only five or six of the 57 Paspa letters resemble Han'gŭl letters (fig. 13-4b). But then, of the 52 upper- and lower-case English letters, five or six resemble Han'gŭl letters (fig. 13-4d). Does such resemblance of some letters mean that Han'gŭl is derived from the Paspa alphabet or the English alphabet? Especially when the resembling letters code quite different sounds? A more likely explanation is that with any two sets of simple shapes a few members of the sets will almost inevitably resemble each other.

In Han'gŭl, vowel letters and consonant letters are distinct in shape, whereas in Paspa they are not. In Figure 13-4b, the two Paspa vowel letters resemble two Han'gŭl consonant letters, and in (c) the Paspa letter for /i/ has no resemblance to its Han'gŭl counterpart. In the Paspa script—as in its direct ancestor, the Tibetan script, and as in its indirect ancestor, the Indic scripts—each consonant letter actually expresses "C + vowel /a/"; if a vowel other than /a/ is required, a diacritic mark can be put over or under each "C + /a/" sign. The Han'gŭl vowel letters have no detectable affinity with the letters of any other script known, declares Ledyard.

Both Han'gŭl and Paspa group a few letters into a syllable block, but they do so differently. In Han'gŭl, within one block two or more letters can be arranged horizontally in one row with another set of two or more letters below them, as in Figure 13-4c (also table 13-3). Because of this packaging method, syllable blocks, whether simple or complex, are similar in overall size. By contrast, the Paspa letters, like letters in most other alphabets, are arranged in a linear sequence, so that a complex syllable CVC is longer than a simple syllable CV, which in turn is longer than V or C. Compare syllable blocks in Han'gŭl and Paspa in Figure 13-4c. Between Han'gŭl and Paspa, because of their differences in letter-packaging and in vowel letters, any hint of resemblance observed in the shapes of some consonant letters disappear in syllable blocks.

What is conceivable is that King Sejong saw in Paspa that it was feasible for simple and squarish geometric shapes to represent consonants. The overall impression of these shapes may have stayed with him when he created the Han'gŭl consonant letters, which were originally squarish (fig. 13-3). On the whole the shapes of the Han'gŭl letters and syllable blocks are simpler than those of Paspa, as can be seen in Figure 13-4abc. Beyond these conjectures, we seem to lack any definitive evidence that the king consciously copied particular Paspa letters for particular Han'gŭl letters.

Hypothesis 2. *Kochŏn* ('old seal') refers to the Chinese great and small seal characters developed during the Qin dynasty over 2000 years ago (table 3-1). The label "seal" derives from the fact that this script style came to be used in seals or chop signs. Some scholars speculate that Chŏng In-ji, in writing the postface to the *Explanations and Examples of Correct Sounds*, had to mention "old seal" to placate the Korean literati who were deeply enamored with Chinese characters and culture (Lee Ki-moon 1972: 56).

Again, let us examine the physical evidence. At the time of the creation of the Correct Sounds, and soon after that, it was necessary to illustrate the sounds of the new letters with the sounds of Chinese characters familiar to literate people. For example, the sound of Han'gŭl letter ㄴ was illustrated with the Hancha 那 *n(a)* because of its initial consonant. Not only are the Han'gŭl letters far simpler than their "sound-matching," or rather "sound-illustrating," characters but also they differ in shape. This observation is even more applicable to old seal characters, which were more complex and pictographic than modern characters. Furthermore, there are numerous characters, all having different shapes, that can illustrate the sound of each Han'gŭl letter. If we ignore sounds and consider only shapes, I can offhand think of only six simple characters—out of 50,000—that resemble certain Han'gŭl letters (fig. 13-4e). A few scholars attempted to force a resemblance between characters and Han'gŭl letters by arbitrarily taking only fragments of Hancha.

Perhaps resemblance should be sought not between Chinese characters and Han'gŭl letters but between the characters and Han'gŭl syllable blocks. A syllable block made up with two or more alphabetic letters is not unlike a phonetic–semantic composite or a meaning composite made up with a few components. Furthermore, a syllable block, like a Chinese character, has more or less the same overall size regardless whether it consists of two or four components. And a syllable block, especially a complex one, sometimes is like a logograph in that one invariant shape by itself represents a unique meaning in whatever context ("Instruction in Han'gŭl Spelling" in chap. 14).

Having pointed out the superficial resemblance between syllable blocks and Chinese characters, now I must point out fundamental differences between the two scripts. First, the constituent letters in a Han'gŭl syllable block code phonemes, and do so reliably, whereas a character's components may approximately represent the semantic field and/or the tone syllable of its morpheme. In experiments, words in Han'gŭl, just like words in any other phonetic script, are read aloud faster than the same words in Hancha (Simpson and Kang 1993; chap. 6). Second, the placing of two or more letters in a syllable block is strictly rule-governed, as described in "Han'gŭl Syllable Blocks," whereas the placing of components in a character is unsystematic in that a semantic or phonetic component can occupy the top, bottom, left, right, center, or outside of a whole character (table 3-3).

In conclusion, in creating Han'gŭl, King Sejong and his scholars appear to owe some debt to other scripts, perhaps to Mongolian Paspa and Chinese characters. But Han'gŭl differs fundamentally from these or any other scripts. Ledyard (1966: 370), who pondered at length the origin of Han'gŭl, concluded, "'Phags-pa [Paspa] contributed none of the things that make this script [Han'gŭl] perhaps the most remarkable in the world." Han'gŭl should be described as a unique creation.

Han'gŭl, an Alphabetic Syllabary

In this final section on Han'gŭl we ponder what should be its appropriate label. An alphabet? A syllabary? A featural system? A logography? Because Han'gŭl has some of all these properties, authors of books on writing systems call it by various names.

Among Western scholars, Coulmas (1989) observes that, of all writing systems invented, the Korean system comes closest to treating distinctive features as the basic units of representation. Sampson (1985) simply calls it a featural system. Diringer (1968) calls it "practically an alphabet," and Jensen (1970) simply calls it an alphabet. Gelb (1956) calls it a syllabary. James Deese calls it "alphabetic-feature syllabary" (in personal communication 1981). Martin (1972: 83) observes, "Thus the modern Korean orthography incorporates representation of phoneme components [articulatory features?], phonemes, morphophonemes, syllables, and ... morphemes." Miller (1967: 93) calls it an "alphabet on syllabic principles" and later (1986: 40) "the Korean syllabic-phonetic script."

Among Koreans, a booklet on Han'gŭl put out by the Korean Overseas Information Service calls it an alphabet (Hahn 1981). A concise Korean–English dictionary defines it as an "alphabet [syllabary]." Sin (1992: 92) describes, "Han'gŭl is originally an alphabet, ... but in writing it is a syllabary." Most importantly, the *Explanations and Examples of Hunmin Chŏng'ŭm* (1446) points out that the Chŏng'ŭm is an alphabet but has the characteristic of a syllabary.

Let us first consider Han'gŭl as a featural system. Han'gŭl letters were created taking articulatory features into consideration, as described in "Han'gŭl as an Alphabet" and illustrated in Table 13-1. For example, for the articulatory feature of strong aspiration, a stroke is added inside the *k*-letter to create the *k'*-letter. Yet, I hesitate to call Han'gŭl a featural script, for reasons such as: only some but not all letters were created based on articulatory features; "articulatory feature" or "distinctive feature" is a technical term unfamiliar to people not trained in linguistics; and Han'gŭl's featural characteristics have only minor relevance to its learning and use.

Let us now consider Han'gŭl as an alphabet or a syllabary. Han'gŭl is indeed an alphabet in that each letter codes a phoneme. Yet to call it simply an alphabet will mislead the readers to think that Han'gŭl is written like an ordinary alphabet in a linear string of letters. Han'gŭl is used in reading and writing like a syllabary in that two or more letters are packaged into a syllable block. The packaging method generates about 12,800 syllable blocks using only 24 alphabetic letters, of which 2,000 blocks are actually used. In learning, too, Han'gŭl is learned more as a set of syllable blocks than as alphabetic letters, as shown in the next chapter.

For Han'gŭl, but not necessarily for other phonetic scripts used for other languages, its likeness to a syllabary has many advantages, some mentioned already and some to be mentioned in the next chapter. To mention one advantage here, the Korean language uses 2,000 different syllables requiring that many syllable blocks; yet these many blocks are not a collection of unrelated graphs but form a systematically interrelated set. As someone interested in the question of how a script is learned and used, I consider this advantage of Han'gŭl as most unique and useful.

The two or more Han'gŭl letters packaged into a syllable block can be analyzed individually. In *ka, ke, ta,* 가, 게, 다, note that the first and second blocks share the initial consonant /k/, and the first and third blocks share the vowel /a/, which are reflected in the the shapes of the syllable blocks. In this characteristic, Han'gŭl is not like a typical syllabary, such as Japanese Kana, in which each sign as an unanalyzed whole represents one syllable, such as *ka, ke, ta* か,け,た;   note the lack of relations among the shapes of Kana signs that represent the same consonant or vowel. For Japanese, which uses only about 110 different syllables, the collection of 46 unrelated Kana signs does not pose a big problem for learning and using. (The 46 basic Kana signs are re-used in modified shapes to produce 25 secondary and 35 compound signs to represent the 110 different syllables or moras; chap. 19.)

Considering all these characteristics, I have called Han'gŭl an "alphabetic syllabary" (Taylor 1980). The label captures the prominent, useful, and unique characteristics of Han'gŭl; at the same time it is neither long nor unfamiliar. The label has received more support than objection. A unique kind of script calls for a unique label.

14

Learning Han'gŭl and Hancha

Because of its simplicity and rationality, Han'gŭl can be learned painlessly and rapidly. In his postface to the *Explanations and Examples of Hunmin Chŏng'ŭm*, Chŏng In-ji (1446) observed, "The bright can learn the system in a single morning, and even the not-so-bright can do so within ten days." In his book *A Guide to Korean Characters*, Grant (1979: 12) spends a mere half page on Han'gŭl, claiming, "The Korean alphabet is so simple that its sixteen totally distinct letters can be learned in **minutes** with the aid of the hangul-in-a-hurry chart." (Emphasis added; Grant devotes the rest of his book to explaining Hancha.) Learning simple Han'gŭl syllable blocks may require more than minutes or a single morning but not much more. According to one report, Han'gŭl was learned in mere 100 hours — 8 hours per week for a few months — by adult illiterates in 1947 in N. Korea (Yi Yun-p'yo 1991).

Teaching Han'gŭl as an Alphabet or a Syllabary

Han'gŭl, being an alphabetic syllabary, can be taught as an alphabet or as a syllabary. Let us survey how it has been taught throughout its 500-year history.

In the 16th century, some years after its creation, Han'gŭl was seldom taught directly but was indirectly acquired while learning Hancha, as it was used to give the sounds and meanings of Hancha. In the 19th century, women, children, and laborers picked up Han'gŭl, or acquired it without much teaching, from a Han'gŭl syllable chart (table 13-4) that might be hung on a wall. After the educational and cultural reform of 1894 proper primary schools were established to teach reading and writing. Textbooks, which were written in a mixture of Han'gŭl and Hancha, included the Han'gŭl syllable chart.

In the later years of the Japanese rule, between 1938 and 1945, the Korean language was not allowed in schools. Right after the end of World War II and of the Japanese rule, when Han'gŭl began to be taught once more in schools, it was taught more as an alphabet than as a syllabary, no doubt emulating the teaching of the Roman alphabet in the West: Children learned individual alphabet letters and their phonemes, and then learned to package them into syllable blocks. The alphabetic method does not appeal to young children, as it deals with small meaningless sound units, phonemes. It also requires some ability to analyze and synthesize sounds, which young children find difficult. In 1948 the teaching unit jumped from phoneme–letters to sentences, bypassing syllables, syllable blocks, and words. Both methods produced a few primary school graduates who failed to master Han'gŭl (Ch'oe 1986). In the 1960s the noted educator Yi Ung-baek (1988) advocated the use of syllables and syllable blocks as teaching units. He proposed displaying the Han'gŭl syllable chart prominently at the beginning of a textbook, in front of a classroom, and over a desk at home.

Lately the syllable block has been the primary teaching unit, which has many advantages over an alphabetic letter. A Korean syllable is far more likely to be meaningful than is a phoneme, in that a syllable often by itself represents a morpheme or a word. And a meaningful item is easier to learn than a meaningless one. For example, each of two phonemes and their letters, (*k'*) ㅋ and (*o*) ㅗ, is meaningless, but when the two are joined, the resulting syllable block *k'o* ㅋ ('nose') is meaningful. The syllable block is the actual, and familiar, reading unit.

A syllable is a larger, more concrete and stable phonetic unit than is a phoneme, and so is easier for readers to become aware of, to "manipulate," and to learn, than is a phoneme. About phoneme manipulation, in the United States, 46% of 4-year olds tested could segment an English word into syllables, but none of them could segment a word into phonemes (Liberman et al. 1974). In the same study, 70% of 6-year olds who began to read could do the phoneme-segmentation task. In China, even literate adults could not easily add or delete individual consonants to or from spoken Chinese words (Read et al. 1986). Chinese speakers would have no difficulty segmenting a word or phrase into syllables, because a Chinese syllable is a concrete, prominent, and familiar unit, which represents one Chinese morpheme and is written in one Chinese character.

These studies, besides showing that syllables are easier to manipulate than phonemes, show that people can proficiently manipulate phonemes usually after, but not before, they become literate in an alphabet. (Some educators in the West believe that phoneme awareness is a prerequisite to learning to read in an alphabet.) Further, they tend not to become aware of phonemes, if they become literate in logographs or syllabaries. Finally, because a syllable is easier to isolate as a unit than a phoneme, in the development of writing systems a syllabary begat an alphabet, not the other way around (chap. 1).

The beauty and ingenuity of Han'gŭl is that people do not have to learn 2,000 unrelated graphs for 2,000 syllables; they merely have to learn the 24 letters and the systematic way they package into syllable blocks. They learn easily—through deduction, instruction, and practice—all the syllable blocks in the basic chart. Once people learn these systematically constructed syllable blocks, they should have little trouble pronouncing any syllable string, whether familiar, unfamiliar, or nonsense. There is no need to consult a dictionary for either pronouncing or spelling.

Han'gŭl Teaching in School

Modern primary and secondary education in Korea puts great emphasis on teaching the Korean language, i.e., reading and writing Han'gŭl and some Hancha. In primary school the national language takes up the largest proportion of the class periods, about one-quarter (more than one-quarter in the first three grades and less in the second three grades), compared to more than one-third in China and Japan. The children learn Han'gŭl in primary school and Hancha in middle school and high school. The same is true in N. Korea, except that middle school there starts at grade 5 rather than the usual 7. Described below is the way Han'gŭl and Hancha are taught in S. Korea.

Children enter primary school at age 6 or 7, almost all of them already reading some words in Han'gŭl. In one survey, close to 90% of preschoolers had been given lessons in Han'gŭl at home by their parents (Ch'oe 1986).

Between 1982 and 1989, the textbook series used in primary school was *Correct Living,* which aimed to give children a moral education by way of lessons in reading. Even in the very first text, words were included if they were needed for moral education, regardless of their familiarity or complexity. Consequently, as many as 600 new words, some in complex syllable blocks, were introduced in the beginning text, which most teachers considered too difficult for the children. In a survey of over 2,000 children only one-third of first graders mastered Han'gŭl, the rest showing varying deficiencies (Ch'oe 1986). Only by the second semester of the third grade did children fully master Han'gŭl.

Since 1989 a three-pronged approach to teaching the Korean language has been adopted, using a standard series of textbooks with two volumes in each grade for each of the three language skills: reading, writing, and speaking–listening. Each week the teacher focuses on speaking–listening skills in the first two language class periods, on reading in the next three periods (two periods in the 4th–6th grades), and on writing in the last two periods. The three language skills are unified by a common topic so that the children learn to speak about, listen to, read about, and write about, the same topic, a new topic each week. The topics — e.g., tree planting, family life, greeting, letter writing — are chosen for their relevance to the children's daily living.

Volume I-1 (Grade I, volume 1) of the textbook for speaking–listening contains many pictures around which children and a teacher can make up stories. Textbooks on reading are centered around teaching Han'gŭl syllable blocks. At its very beginning, volume I-1 displays the basic Han'gŭl syllable chart: 14 basic consonant letters are arranged in columns and the 10 basic vowel letters in rows to generate 140 CV syllable blocks (table 13-4). But actual learning of the chart — reading aloud the syllable blocks in the chart after their teacher — does not begin until page 39. On the same page, the children are asked to read and find in the chart the CV blocks that make up words, such as 두부, 노루 *tubu, noru* ('beancurd', 'deer'). For the syllable block *tu,* children find the consonant letter *t* on the leftmost column and the vowel letter *u* on the top row; in the cell where the two intersect they hit the target. The same syllable chart is repeated on page 47, but this time it contains eleven blanks, which children have to fill in. The basic chart teaches only CVs, but the accompanying texts contain some CVCs and compound vowel letters as well as a few CVCCs. The teaching of these complex syllable blocks is delayed to later volumes.

Along with the Han'gŭl chart, volume I-1 teaches individual words (e.g., "mother," "tree"), followed by brief phrases ("our mother," "big tree"), and then short sentences, such as:

Let's plant trees. Let's plant trees on mountains and in villages. Let's take care of the trees. Let's all take care of the trees.

The idea here is to teach Han'gŭl words for familiar objects and use them in sentences, repeating them in different but linked sets of sentences. Volume I-1 for reading is accompanied by volume I-1 for writing, which teaches penmanship, dictation, and sentence composition.

Volume I-2, too, begins with the basic Han'gŭl chart. It also displays on its later pages advanced charts, one with the 14 basic consonant letters by 5 compound vowel letters and another with 5 doubled consonant letters by 10 basic vowel letters. In addition, volume I-2 contains stories and poems, along with comprehension questions on them. Presumably these charts are used to teach CVCs and CVCCs as well. If so, within the first grade, children should have mastered fully how to read all the 2,000 Han'gŭl syllable blocks in the language, simple ones perhaps better than complex ones.

Later volumes include longer and more complex stories, including Aesop's fables such as "Ant and dove" and "Hare and tortoise." Many "wh-" and "how" comprehension questions are asked about them: e.g., "What did the ant fall into?" and "How did the dove know that the hunter came?" In subsequent years the children should keep practising reading and spelling Han'gŭl, as well as improving their skills in comprehending complex reading materials and in composing prose and poetry.

Instruction in Han'gŭl Spelling

Words are spelled in Han'gŭl as they sound, usually but not always. This is why spelling has to be taught in primary school. Before considering Han'gŭl spelling, let us consider the familiar English spelling.

In English some words are spelled as they sound (e.g., *pet, desk, tenet*), but many common words are spelled irregularly, not as they sound (e.g., *should, enough, bough*). How did such irregularities come about? Some came about through the whims of individual writers and printers. For example, when printing came to England around the middle of the 15th century, pioneer printers such as William Caxton, who worked many years on the Continent, would spell words in Continental ways when in doubt. The *gh* in *ghost* and many other words are perhaps inherited from Flemish. Printers also justified lines (straightened the right hand margin) by adding extra letters rather than spaces. Some lawyers' clerks lengthened spellings, because they were paid by the inch for their writing. At any rate, in the past several hundred years, changes in spelling have lagged behind changes in speech sounds, and as a result, many words, especially common words, are not spelled as they sound.

There appears to be no way to test which of several possible spellings is correct. Take *should:* why does it contain an unpronounced *l*, and why is its vowel spelled the same as in *enough* and *bough,* even though all three vowel sequences are pronounced differently? Why do words contain the same *gh* when it is unpronounced, as in *bough,* pronounced as /f/, as in *enough,* and as /g/, as in *ghost?* Why does *toe* have the final *-e*, while the same sounding *-to* in *potato* does not? One simply has to memorize irregular spellings by rote. Who says that learning to read and write in English means simply learning the 26 letters of the alphabet?

Korean words are spelled more or less the way they sound, and written words are read as they are spelled. But speech sounds change over time and across dialects, and even within one dialect, they change in different phonetic contexts. How should words be spelled in such cases? To answer this and other questions on spelling, a comprehensive set of spelling rules was set down in 1933 by the Society of Han'gŭl Studies. This set has been adopted by both S. and N. Korea, with occasional and slight modifications that may differ between the two Koreas. The rules are sensible and comprehensive but not complicated; they, along with the names and order of Han'gŭl letters, as well as other information on writing, are set down in a thin volume, one in S. Korea (Ministry of Education 1988), and another in N. Korea (Social Science Publication 1988).

One cannot over-emphasize the importance of using one standard spelling for each word on all occasions. If you were to encounter an "English" word such as "innuff" or "eenaf" you probably would not recognize it instantly as *enough,* even though the misspelled words represent the sound of the word more closely. Why? It is because as a skilled reader you recognize a common short word by its familiar shape rather than by translating it into a sequence of sounds ("Logographs vs Phonetic Graphs: Research" in chap. 6).

The Han'gŭl spelling rules ensure that each word has one standard spelling, which eventually becomes a familiar shape to help its recognition. According to the 1988 spelling rules promulgated by the Ministry of Education in S. Korea, the general rule includes three items.

Rule 1. Spell words as they sound in standard Korean, ensuring that they follow word-formation rules. For example, the standard native word for "sky" is *ha'nŭl,* which is *ha'nal* in a certain dialect. Use the standard. And spell *ha'nŭl* as 하 늘 (CV CVC), and not as "han'ŭl" 한 을 (CVC VC), for there is no reason to attach *n* to the first syllable.

What are the word-formation rules? Divide a phrase between a noun and its postposition or between a verb stem and its ending, and spell each of these items consistently, even when a noun or verb stem sounds different with a different postposition or ending (grammatical morpheme). For example, the verb stem *mŏk* ('to eat') takes various endings, some beginning with consonants and some with vowels, as in *mŏkda, mŏkko, mŏk'ŏ, mŏk'ŭni,* in which the stem is always spelled in the same CVC (먹), even though with the vowel endings the word sounds like "mŏgŏ" 머거 (CV CV). (In romanization, Korean words are spelled as they sound, as described shortly.)

There are some exceptions to the rule. A certain verb stem requires irregular endings in such a way that its final consonant in CVC completely drops out or changes to a quite different sound, as in *NOLta, NOnŭn, NOBnida* ('to play', 'playing', 'to play' in polite form; the verb stem is in uppercase). In such words, spell the way the words sound.

In most CVCC words, one of the -CC is silent when pronounced in isolation, but the silent -C is kept in spelling, because it is pronounced when followed by a vowel grammatical morpheme: 값 *kap(s)* ('price') by itself is pronounced as *kap* but with the postposition *i* as *kapsi.* Spelled according to rule 1, the shape of the word *kaps* in one syllable block is distinct and constant, and so is the postposition *i* (which marks the subject of a sentence). There is no other Korean word spelled as *kaps,* whereas there are many other words spelled as *kap,* such as Sino-Korean 'box', 'grade A', 'promontory', and native *kapkaphada* ('irksome'), *kapchaki* ('suddenly'), and *kapsida* ('let's go'). Furthermore, without this rule the postposition *i* will be spelled variously as *si, p'i, mi,* and so on, depending on the final C of the preceding noun. For example, *kap(s) + i* will be spelled as *kap-si* and *ip'* ('leaf') + *i* as *i-p'i.* Such unruly spelling would play havoc with rapid recognition of words from their constant and familiar shapes. Spelling rule 1 prevents such an undesirable event from happening.

Rule 1 is not arbitrary: a speller merely has to test a word with a grammatical morpheme that begins with a vowel to see that a silent consonant in -CC is pronounced. By contrast, the silent *l* in the English words *balk* and *balky* is usually not pronounced yet is kept in spelling. Worse, it is pronounced in other similarly spelled words, *bulk* and *bulky*.

As a corollary to rule 1, words that may sound the same in some contexts are spelled differently because they are different words. For example, the words for "mouth" and "leaf" sound the same when spoken in isolation but are nevertheless distinguished in spelling: *ip* ('mouth' 입) and *ip'* ('leaf' 잎), respectively. The phonetic difference between the two words becomes apparent when a vowel postposition follows them: *ibi* and *ip'i*. One particular syllable that sounds like "nat" in isolation has six different spellings according to its several different meanings: 낫 ('sickle' or 'better'), 낮 ('day time' or 'low'), 낯 ('face'), 낟 ('a grain'), 낱 ('a piece'), 날 ('be born').

The spelling of words in Han'gŭl has been standardized in such a way as to preserve, so far as possible, the logograph-like property of the syllable blocks. Almost all CVCC syllable blocks and many CVC blocks are like logographs. For example, one particular block 낯 by itself and in its invariant form means "face" and nothing else in whatever context, just as its logographic Hancha counterpart 面 does. But remember that a syllable block is a phonetic script. Because a block consists of a sequence of alphabetic letters that codes a sequence of phonemes, it can be pronounced precisely and usually only in one way. By contrast, its character counterpart is a true simple logograph, which began as a pictograph, containing no sound-indicating component, and so can be pronounced in many different ways: *mian* in Chinese; *myŏn* in Korean; and *omo, omote, tsura, -zura, men* in Japanese.

Because Han'gŭl spelling rule 1 is useful and rational, once it is learned there is hardly any need to consult a dictionary for spelling or to hold a spelling bee. In English, too, sometimes a stem and words derived from it or its inflected versions maintain the same spelling, as in *hear–heard*, in which *-ear-* is maintained even though its sound changes. However, more often a stem and its inflected form differ both in sound and spelling, as in *sing–sung–sang*. It is not obvious which English words should be of the first kind (invariant spelling) and which of the second kind (varied spelling), and in case of the second kind, how spelling should change. So, people occasionally have to consult a dictionary for correct spelling.

Rule 2 of the general rule for Han'gŭl spelling concerns spacing. Each Korean phrase consists of a noun and its postposition or a verb/adjective and its ending. In text each phrase is separated by a space, as in

aiGA mulUL masiNDA ('[A] child drink[s] water'),

in which the postpositions *ga* and *ŭl* and the verb ending *-nda* are capitalized for illustration. Spacing makes reading easy by organizing a text into phrase units; without spacing a reader has to do the organizing by him/herself. One aspect of skilled reading in any script is to organize a text into ever larger and meaningful processing units: phonemes into syllables, syllables into words, words into phrases, phrases into sentences, and so on (Taylor and Taylor 1983). Regular and consistent spacing also helps Korean readers develop, consciously or unconsciously, an efficient reading strategy: They should attend to an item following a space (an important content word) more closely than to one just before a space (less important grammatical morpheme). Korean readers can appreciate the advantage of spacing, when they try to read old texts written before the 19th century without spacing.

Rule 3 is about spelling European loan words. Only the available Han'gŭl letters should be used in writing them. (In Japanese special Katakana letters are available for writing foreign words.) Certain English consonants not available in Korean have to be replaced by other similar sounds and their letters: English /f/ by Korean *p'*, English /v/ by Korean *b*, English initial /l/ by Korean *r*, the two sounds of English *th-* by Korean *d*, *s*, *j*, and so on. The Korean *p'* for English /f/ produces some unrecognizable "English words," such as *pastput*, which turns out to be *fast food*. The two different English words, *fork* and *pork*, are spelled the same in Korean. In some words the Korean *h* might be closer to the English /f/ than is the Korean *p'*. But even certain devices that are available in Korean are not used. For example, in the Korean spelling *rejŏbum* for English *leisure boom*, a space that separates the two words is omitted and the long vowel in the second word is ignored.

North Korea has its own Han'gŭl spelling rules, which are for the most part the same as those of South Korea but differ in some details. To cite one difference, the Sino-Korean word that came from the Chinese word *laoren* is spelled *roin* in N. Korea and *noin* in S. Korea. As mentioned in "Han'gŭl as an Alphabet," the names and the order of Han'gŭl letters in N. Korea slightly differ from those in S. Korea. Typical of N. Korea, even a booklet on spelling rules contains the obligatory statement, "The great premier Comrade Kim Il Sung and the beloved leader Comrade Kim Chŏng-il (Kim Il Sung's son and heir designate) have instructed us as follows."

The N. Korean booklet on spelling includes rules on writing direction, which runs left to right horizontally, though the traditional vertical direction is allowed for special texts. The S. Korean booklet does not include rules on writing direction, which can be horizontal or vertical even within one newspaper copy ("Rational Hancha Use in the Present" in chap. 12). Punctuation marks used in N. Korea are similar to those used in S. Korea, which in turn are similar to those used in China and Japan, as described in in Chapter 7.

Han'gŭl Spelling vs Romanized Spelling

The Korean language, like the Chinese language and the Japanese language, can be written in the letters of a Roman alphabet, in particular those of the English alphabet, for the benefit of Western readers. In Korea a Roman alphabet is never suggested as a candidate to be the sole script, as is occasionally the case in China (chap. 8) or Japan (chap. 20). Thus, romanizing Korean is given only a brief description here, after "Instruction in Han'gŭl Spelling" to show how the two methods of spelling contrast.

An efficient romanization system should transcribe faithfully the sounds of a language, using only the existing letters of a Roman alphabet without extra symbols or special marks, and one standard romanization system should be adopted so that one Korean word appears always in one spelling. Unfortunately, in all these aspects, the romanization of the Korean language is at present less than satisfactory. It is not firmly standardized so that one word is seen in a variety of Roman spellings, and special marks not available on a regular keyboard are used. For example, I have seen Han'gŭl spelled as: Hangul, Han'gul, Han-gul, Hangeul, Hankul, Han-Gul, and so on.

The richness of the Korean sound system spawns many different romanizing systems, of which the better known are: the McCune and Reischauer (M-R) system published in 1939; the Yale system by Martin and Lee (1969); the S. Korean official system devised by the Ministry of Education in 1959 and revised in 1984 along the lines of the M-R system; and the N. Korean system devised by the North Korean Academy of Sciences. However, the two Koreas seem to be trying to agree on one standard system of romanization.

The five systems have identical Roman letters for only 14 of the 40 Korean letters, and differ on the remaining 26. Phonetically, the Korean stop consonants are distinguished in three ways (lax, tense aspirated, tense unaspirated), compared to two ways in English (voiced and voiceless) (table 11-1). In different systems the lax bilabial ㅂ is romanized either as *p* or *b* and its tense aspirated counterpart as *ph, p'*, or *p*. The Korean vowel system is rich, with 10 finely differentiated vowels, some of them not found in English. To write them, some romanization systems use special marks (e.g., a breve over *ŏ* and *ŭ* or a dot over *e*).

The romanization system adopted by many authors, and used in this book, is the one devised by G. M. McCune and E. O. Reischauer, abbreviated here as the M–R system. The sound values of its letters are Italian vowels and the English consonants in their most common and regular sounds, as in the Hepburn system for Japanese and the Wade–Giles system for Chinese (chap. 1). For example, the three vowels — *i, a, o* — are pronounced as in *piano* and *g* as in *get* rather than in *gem*.

In the M–R romanization system, to help foreigners pronounce Korean words, a word is spelled variously in different phonetic contexts. The Han'gŭl letter ㄱ is pronounced like the English /k/ at the initial position of a syllable, like /g/ between two vowels, and as *-ng* before a nasal sound. These euphonic changes are reflected in M–R romanizing as *kuGŏ kuNGmun haKkwa* (the letters of interest are in uppercase for illustration). By contrast, in Han'gŭl spelling, to aid word recognition, a word has one standard spelling, regardless of how its sound may change in different phonetic contexts. For the same phrase the final *k*-letter ㄱ is unchanged in different phonetic contexts, as in 국어 국문 학과 "kuK'ŏ kuKmun haKkwa" ('national language and national literature department').

Table 14-1 shows the M-R letters for Han'gŭl consonant letters. There is no one-to-one relation between the two scripts in most cases: Between one and seven Roman letters are used to represent the same Han'gŭl consonant letter. Consider the most troublesome Han'gŭl letter *siot* ㅅ : It is romanized as *s* in the initial position but as *sh, n, t, d, p, k*, in the final position of a syllable. Examples: 웃옷 *uDoT* ('outside wear') and 옛이야기 *yeNNiyagi* ('old tale'). Conversely, take the nine native CVC words that are spelled with six different final Cs in Han'gŭl, as described in the preceding section: Because the words all sound *nat* they are romanized uniformly as *nat*. In CVCC Han'gŭl syllable blocks, one of the two final Cs is usually silent when a syllable is pronounced in isolation, as in *kap(s)* ('price') and *ta(l)k* ('hen'); the unpronounced sound (enclosed in parentheses) is deleted in the M–R romanization but is included in Han'gŭl spelling.

The M–R system uses a breve over two vowel letters, *ŏ*, which sounds like *uh* or the *o* in *bottle,* and *ŭ*, whose sound is between the *oo* in *foot* and the *ee* in *queer.* The rightside parenthesis) written small is used for a strongly aspirated consonant, but such a symbol is not found in most keyboards, including mine; it is usually replaced by an inverted apostrophe, as in *k'* for the initial sound in *kick.* The normal apostrophe then is used to mark a break between a syllable that ends in *-n* or *-ng* followed by a vowel, as in *Han'gŭl* (CVC CVC) vs *Hang'ŭl* (CVC VC).

In romanized Korean text, in contrast to English text or in romanized Japanese text, the first letter at the beginning of a sentence is not capitalized, but the first letter of a title of a book or the name of a person or a place is capitalized. Punctuation marks are similar to those used for English and other languages

Table 14-1. M–R Roman Letters for Han'gŭl Consonants

Han'gŭl	M–R Romanization
ㄱ	k, g, ng
ㄴ	n, l
ㄷ	t, ch, j, d
ㄹ	l, r, n
ㅁ	m
ㅂ	p, b
ㅅ	s, sh, n, t, d, p, k
ㅇ	ng
ㅈ	ch, j
ㅊ	ch'
ㅋ	k'
ㅌ	t', ch
ㅍ	p'
ㅎ	h

(chap. 7). A postposition is separated from its noun by a space, as in 1, in contrast to Han'gŭl spelling in which it is attached to its noun, as in 2.

1. Romanized: *saram i pap ŭl mŏgŭni* ....

2. if romanized to reflect Han'gŭl spelling: *saram'i pab'ŭl mŏk'ŭni* ....

('As [a] person eat[s] rice ....') In romanized text (1), without a space between a noun and its postposition there would be ambiguity in syllable breaks; in Han'gŭl spelling (2) no space is needed, as there is no ambiguity.

In short, the M–R romanization tries to spell a Korean word as it sounds, without trying to preserve one consistent spelling for it in changing phonetic contexts. In so doing, it diverges greatly from Han'gŭl spelling, which does try to preserve one consistent spelling for each word in changing phonetic contexts.

Hancha Teaching in School

Both South and North Korea attempted for a while to abolish Hancha but now teach them in secondary schools ("Misguided Attempts to Abolish Hancha " in chap. 12). In S. Korea 1,800 Hancha are designated as educational, 900 of them to be taught in middle school and 900 more in high school. The goal of Hancha teaching, as decreed by the Ministry of Education, is teaching Hancha and Hancha words as well as comprehension and appreciation of Chinese and Korean classics written in Hancha.

Let us look at one textbook, *Introduction to Hancha*, used in the first year of middle school. Some Hancha learned in the first few lessons are the same kind of Chinese characters as are learned by first graders of primary schools in China and Japan. However, the pace of progress in the Korean textbook is more brisk.

- Lessons 1–3. Individual Hancha. Pictographs, accompanied by pictures, for such concrete objects as the sun and the moon, and indicators for such relational concepts as numerals.

- Lesson 4. Meaning composites, such as 明 ('sun + moon = bright'). This Hancha is learned as *palkŭl myŏng*: its meaning represented by its native word counterpart, *palkŭl* ('bright'), and its Sino-Korean sound *myŏng*.
- Lessons 5–6. Semantic–phonetic composites, such as 江 ('water' + *kong* = 'river' *kang*). (The phonetic component does not give the exact sound of this Hancha, as it does not in its Chinese counterpart, 'water' + *gong* = 'river' *jiang*; table 3-3).
- Lessons 7–13. Two-Hancha compound words, some of which represent abstract concepts, such as "harmony" and "recollection."
- Lessons 14–20. Four-Hancha idiomatic phrases, such as *yok sok pu dal* ('wish, speed, not, reach' or "if you try to get something in a great hurry you may end up not getting it").
- Lessons 21–27. Hancha words and phrases in brief sentences or poems, all from Chinese or Korean classics, with grammatical morphemes in Han'gŭl.

Advanced textbooks present longer texts—passages from the Confucian classics and Korean classics. To help in the oral reading of Chinese texts, a native grammatical morpheme in Han'gŭl is added to the end of each phrase or clause, within which Sino-Korean words in Hancha are arranged in a Chinese word order. See Kugyŏl (fig. 12-1b) for an example of such a text.

How well are Hancha learned in S. Korea? Not very well. In several studies, Korean college students and adults were slower to recognize words in Hancha than the same words in Han'gŭl (chap. 15). There are possible reasons. Perhaps Hancha are unnecessarily difficult when taught using Chinese and Korean classics rather than contemporary writings, because the classics use sometimes uncommon Hancha as well as Chinese word order; perhaps Hancha do not appear sufficiently often in contemporary reading materials to motivate the students and to give them opportunities for practice; and perhaps Hancha classes held once or twice per week, and only in secondary school, are not sufficient.

Hancha teaching should begin in primary school in order to help children learn properly the Korean vocabulary, which contains numerous S-K words. The meanings of many S-K words are not fully grasped when they are written in a phonetic script instead of logographic characters. In a vocabulary test, O (1973) asked 70 sixth graders to define 25 familiar S-K words. Their score was a dismal 26.5 out of 100. Consider *kugŏ*, which consists of two Hancha: *kuk* ('nation') and *ŏ* ('language'), which join to form a compound word meaning "national language," which is the most familiar and important school subject. Only 6 of the 70 children defined the word correctly, and the rest gave various plausible but wrong answers, such as "Han'gŭl book," "book on vocabulary lessons," "book containing prose and poetry," which are the kinds of books used in *kugŏ* classes, but none is the precise definition of the word *kugŏ*.

Once schoolchildren learn the Hancha for *kuk*, they can easily learn hundreds of S-K compound words containing it, such as *kukka* ('national song') and *kukkyŏng* ('national border'). Moreover, these words are shared among Korean, Japanese, and Chinese. In some experiments, Hancha lessons in primary school was a help not only in studying the national language but also in studying other school subjects (reported in Sin 1992). In some primary schools, more and more children study Hancha unofficially during self-study hours, special activity hours, and vacations. The newspaper *Chosun Ilbo* points out that Chinese characters, which are used by one quarter of the world population, form an international script. Accordingly, the 21st Century Committee advised the President of S. Korea: "To raise internationalists, Koreans must learn Chinese characters and the English language from primary school."

The question of how Hancha are treated in N. Korea interests S. Koreans, judging from the spate of publications on it, including a recent article in *Chosun Ilbo* (Feb. 7, 1994). The question should interest also students of literacy in any script. N. Korea abolished the teaching and use of Hancha in 1949, but has revived their teaching, but not their use, since the late 1960s. Why has Hancha teaching been revived? On this question, as on many other matters great or small, the late Premier Kim Il Sung issued instructions several times. In the late 1960s he re-emphasized the non-use of Hancha in N. Korea and at the same time pointed out the need to teach Hancha. How did Kim expect people to retain the Hancha learned if they did not use the Hancha?

According to Kim, N. Koreans should be able to read old Korean texts as well as those written in S. Korea. There appear to be two other unstated reasons. First, N. Koreans want to maintain contacts with, and thereby to receive funds from, Koreans living in Japan and China where Chinese characters are heavily used. Second, they want to lay a foundation for mastery of the Korean vocabulary, which still contains many S-K words even after decades of effort to reduce them. Judging from common queries sent to a journal that deals with language issues, N. Koreans have difficulty in grasping the meanings of some S-K words. The mere fact that N. Koreans get by without Hancha does not mean that they do so easily.

Hancha are not taught in the four years of primary school in N. Korea. They are taught in higher level schools: 1,500 in the six years of secondary school, typically one class period per week; 500 additional Hancha in two years of technical school; and 1,000 additional Hancha in four years of university. About 3,000 Hancha in all are taught. But N. Koreans' knowledge of Hancha does not seem to be high. A recent visitor to N. Korea reported that her official tour guide, a graduate of the most prestigious Kim Il Sung University, could not properly write his own name in Hancha. On the other hand, recent defectors from N. Korea, including a 5th grader, knew their names in Hancha, according to an article in *Chosun Ilbo*.

In a long interview granted to a Japanese visitor, the ex-president of Kim Il Sung University stated that Hancha should be valued and that there is a plan to use some Hancha in text. He also lamented young people's lack of knowledge of Confucianism (Nakajima 1991: 278). Perhaps fewer Hancha than the present 3,000 — say 1,500 — should be taught and those thoroughly. Most importantly, Hancha learned should be constantly used in textbooks and reading materials; otherwise they are easily forgotten.

Would teaching Hancha in primary school cause undue hardship to schoolchildren? Hardly. In China, Hong Kong, and Taiwan, close to 2,800 characters are taught in primary school, in addition to an auxiliary phonetic script. In Japan 1,000 Chinese characters, with their multiple readings, are taught in primary school, in addition to two forms of a syllabary. In Korea there should be ample time to teach several hundred Hancha in primary school, especially since learning Han'gŭl takes less than a year.

In both S. and N. Korea, Hancha should be taught at all levels of school, as long as Korean reading materials contain them. And some Hancha should be used in reading materials as long as the Korean vocabulary contains many S-K words.

15

Why Should Hancha be Kept?

If Han'gŭl is such an efficient script, is there any good reason to keep Chinese characters (Hancha) in Korean? Especially when learning them requires time and effort? This question has been hotly debated for decades in Korea. By way of answering it, let us consider some linguistic advantages of keeping Hancha. The preceding chapter already touched on the usefulness of Hancha for vocabulary learning and communication between N. and S. Koreans as well as among Koreans, Chinese, and Japanese. The arguments for keeping Hancha are so cogent and urgent that they are made once more in this chapter, with more supporting reasons.

Advantages of Hancha

Hancha have advantages like those described for Hanzi in Chinese (chaps. 3 and 4): quick grasp of meaning; ready creation of compound words; concise expression; handy abbreviation, and so on. Korean is unlike Chinese in having two different kinds of vocabulary, Sino-Korean and native, and it is for the former that Hancha are useful, even critical.

Hancha clarify meanings of S-K words. Each Hancha represents the meaning of a morpheme, and when it combines with other Hancha to form a compound word, it contributes its meaning to the meaning of the compound word. Consider *tongnimmun* ('independence gate'), which consists of three Hancha–morphemes: *tok* ('sole, alone'), whose -*k* is pronounced as -*ng* before *n*; *nip* ('stand, establish'), whose -*p* is pronounced *m* before *m*; and *mun* ('gate'); the first two join to form a compound word meaning "independence," to which *mun* is added to form the three-Hancha–morpheme compound word. Each of these three Hancha–morphemes, of course, can combine with others to form related compound words, such as *TOKsin* ('sole, body' or "single"), *kungNIP* ('nation, establish' or "nationally established") or *ch'ŏnanMUN* (*Tiananmen* 'heavenly peace gate' in Beijing).

All these valuable pieces of information implicit in S-K words are lost to readers, if they learn the words in a phonetic script like Han'gŭl. In S. Korea schoolchildren are not taught Hancha in regular classes. Consequently, when 6th graders were asked to define *tongnip* ('independence'), only one out of 70 answered correctly (O 1973). The rest gave definitions such as "liberation," "regaining one's nation," "effort to unify," which are activities or concepts associated with the independence movement in Korean history but are incorrect (also "Hancha Teaching in School" in chap. 14).

Consider words such as *kukki* ('nation, flag' for "national flag"), *kugŏ* ('nation, language'), and *kungmun* ('nation, writing'). Spelled in these inconsistent ways— *kuk-, kug-, kung-*—as in the McCune–Reischauer romanization, people may not see that the three words share the same initial morpheme *kuk* ('nation'). At present, in Han'gŭl spelling the morpheme is always spelled as *kuk*. But if Koreans do not see its

Hancha, eventually they will spell the words as they sound, not realizing their close relation. Without Hancha backing, some S-K words "degenerate" into native words, in which case the meanings of constituent syllables are lost, as happened in *changko* ('big, drum'), which has become *changku*, and so can no longer be analyzed into two meaningful constituents.

If children have difficulty with common S-K words, they will have even more difficulty with learned or technical words that they will encounter as they advance to higher-level schools, because most such words are S-K. Take *simnihak*, a term with which some people may not be familiar. Write the word in three Hancha ('mind, logic, study'), and the word becomes transparent. Even when *-cha* ('person') is added to the word, the four-Hancha word is still decipherable as 'psychologist'. Each of the four constituents becomes almost meaningless, and ambiguous to boot, when written in a phonetic script. The word *psychologist* is easier to understand in Hancha than in its English version, which joins three erudite Greco–Latinate morphemes.

Here are five more technical terms that are far easier to decipher in Hancha than in Han'gŭl or English:

>*sankwa* ('birth, branch') for *obstetrics*
>*paekhyŏlbyŏng* ('white, blood, disease') for *leukemia*
>*kŭnsi* ('near, sight') for *myopia*
>*tangnyobyŏng* ('sugar, urine, disease') for *diabetes*
>*mijinkye* ('tiny, quake, instrument') for *microseismograph*

A few S-K words are illogical, perhaps because in them the Hancha are assigned to native Korean words for their sounds and not for their meanings: *kakssi* ('cabinet' + 'clan' = 'bride' or 'doll'). This way of using Chinese characters is more common in Japan, where it is called Ateji (chap. 18). Also a few Hancha have two different meanings, with or without different sounds. For example, the Hancha 易 has the sound *i* and the meaning 'easy' in words such as *nan'i* ('difficulty or ease'); it has the sound *yŏk* and the meaning 'change' in words such as *Yŏkkyŏng ('Book of Changes')*. This character has these two different uses in Chinese and Japanese as well. Such exceptions to the general pattern do not detract from the overall usefulness of S-K words in Hancha.

Hancha differentiate homophones. Chinese uses a little over 400 different syllables, which can be pronounced in different tones to produce 1300 tone syllables, and still is full of homophones, as we have seen in Part I. In pronouncing S-K words Koreans approximate the Chinese sounds of the words, thus using about 430 syllables but without tones. Because S-K words use only this limited variety of syllables, there are many homophones among them. (Korean native words use 2,000 different syllables.)

The one syllable–morpheme *sa* has as many as 40 homophones listed among the 2,600 Hancha in the *New Age Korean Dictionary* (1989); there might be still more in a larger dictionary. Perhaps because of its extreme ambiguity, the morpheme *sa* is rarely used by itself but usually occurs in a compound word along with other morphemes. But *pyŏng*, which is used alone, has three homophones that are differentiated in Hancha: 'disease', 'bottle', and 'grade C'. Even a two-Hancha compound S-K word such as *tonggi* has at least seven different meanings, such as 'motivation' and 'same period'. There are countless pairs of S-K compound words that are homophonic (e.g., *kukka* which means either 'nation, house' for "nation" or 'nation, song' for "national song"). All are distinguished in Hancha. Hancha are almost indispensable in differentiating Korean names, which are full of homophones (see "Korean Personal Names").

In N. Korea where Hancha are not used, the problem of homophones has been "solved" in a typical N. Korean manner: by taking out of the vocabulary, by a decree, one or more members of a set of homophones.

Hancha words are expressive and concise. Certain abstract concepts have no ready native words. Among them are three of the Confucian virtues, *ch'ung* ('loyalty'), *hyo* ('filial piety'), and *in* ('benevolence'). Perhaps these concepts in Hancha are so handy that Koreans (and Japanese) have never created native words for them. Such monosyllabic S-K words must be written in Hancha to be distinguished from other words of the same sound. For example, there are 11 S-K morphemes with the sound *in* among the 2,600 Hancha in the *New Age Korean Dictionary*.

What can be expressed in a long native phrase can often be expressed concisely in a word or idiom of two to four Hancha. For 'hospital', the S-K word *pyŏngwon* ('disease, institution') is concise compared with its native counterpart "alnŭn'i koch'inŭn kot" ('a place where diseases are treated'). For the public sign "no smoking," S-K *kŭm'yŏn* ('prohibit, smoking') is concise. Furthermore, the Hancha 禁 ('prohibit') *kŭm* can appear in many other prohibitions, such as *kŭmchu* ('no drinking') and *kŭmjok* ('confinement'). When one sees it, its meaning almost leaps out.

By contrast, the same prohibition in native version is wordy:

1. *tambae p'iuji masio* ('Please don't smoke cigarettes') or
2. *tambae rŭl samka chusipsio* ('Please refrain from smoking').

A direct command "don't" as in (1) is considered impolite, and so an indirect request (2) is posted in a taxi. Whether 1 or 2 is used, a native sign is much longer than its S-K version, because it is a sentence with a verb at its end, and the verb has an inflectional ending to show that the sentence is a command or request and that it is in a polite form.

Idioms in Sino-Korean are concise, because each idiom is a list of content morphemes without grammatical morphemes. Take *taedongso'i* ('big, same, small, different' or "same in general but different in details"). In native Korean it is wordy: "k'ŭn kŏt ŭn katko chŏgŭn kŏt ŭn tarŭda." Many S-K idioms are expressive, concise, and have interesting origins; moreover, they are shared with Chinese and Japanese ("Compound Words and Idioms" in chap. 4).

Hancha readily produce compound words. Two or more morphemes, each written in one Hancha, readily join to form a compound word. In a Sino-Korean dictionary, 1,800 common Hancha are used in over 10,000 compound words. The three most productive S-K morphemes are *tae* ('big'), *pu-* ('un-'), and *mu-* ('non-') (Nam 1984).

Take *tae*, which can appear in words such as *taehak* ('big, learning' or "university"), *taehop'yŏng* ('big, favorable, appraisal' or "great acclaim"), and *taedongso'i* ('big, same, small, different' or "same in general but different in details"). The meaning of *tae*, its contribution to the meaning of each compound word or idiom, and the relation among the words sharing it are clear in Hancha but not necessarily in a phonetic script.

Even division into appropriate syllable–morphemes is easier in Hancha than in a phonetic script: Is *taehop'yŏng* analyzed into
1. *taeho-p'yŏng*,
2. *taehop'-yŏng*,
3. *tae-hop'yŏng*,
4. *tae-ho-p'yŏng*?
Or none of these? It should be analyzed first into (3) as "prefix + two-Hancha compound word," and then further into (4), each syllable being represented by one Hancha–morpheme. The same observation applies to the Sino-Korean prefix *mu-*, which can appear in countless words and idioms, such as *musik* ('no knowledge' or 'ignorant'), *mu'a* ('no self' or 'self-renunciation') and *musaekmuch'ui* ('no color, no odor' or 'intangible; hard to understand').

New terms needed for modern concepts are coined easily by joining existing Sino-Korean words. For example, *wonja* ('atom') and *p'okt'an* ('bomb') join to form *wonjap'okt'an* ('atom bomb'), and *paekkwa* ('hundred, branches') and *sajŏn* ('dictionary') join to form *paekkwasajŏn* ('encyclopedia'). Such modern compound words may have been coined by the Japanese and then borrowed by the Koreans and Chinese. Anyway, this handy coining process is widespread. In the *Dictionary of Terms for Current Affairs* (Tong'a 1987), most terms are S-K and European, or hybrids of the two, and only a few are native words (also chap. 11). Take the short yet meaningful S-K *tadangche* ('multi-party system'), which involves both abbreviation and compounding: *ta-* ('multi-') used here is a S-K prefix; *dang* is the second morpheme in *chŏngdang* ('political party') and *che* is the first morpheme in *chedo* ('system'). There are no handy native words for these two S-K compound words. A compound word can join as many as ten Hancha–morphemes, as in

     pangsasŏngt'ansonyŏndaech'ukchŏngbŏp

('radiation, carbon, date, measurement method'). I doubt that this word, if written in Han'gŭl, can be understood at all; I also doubt that this S-K word can be converted to a native word.

Hancha are handy for abbreviations. So, *tadangche* ('multi-party system') results from simultaneous compounding and abbreviating S-K words. Chinese characters, because each of them is meaningful, and because they are numerous, are handy for coining short yet meaningful and unambiguous abbreviations, whether in Chinese (chap. 4), Japanese (chap. 21), or Korean.

By contrast, in the West where alphabets are used, the long name of an organization is usually shortened by using acronyms. The acronym *DPRK*, for example, is utterly meaningless, and people who encounter it for the first time—or even for the second time (it was introduced at the beginning of this Part II)—have no clue whatsoever to its meaning. It stands for "Democratic People's Republic of Korea," the official name for North Korea. Try *Nasdaq*, which stands for "National Association of Securities Dealers Automated Quotations." Many acronyms are ambiguous as well, because there are so few letters in the alphabet: *AAA* can stand for American Automobile Association, Alcoholic Anonymous Association, and many others.

In Korean the long name of an institution can be abbreviated by judiciously picking a few Hancha. *Ewhayŏjadaehakkyo* ('pear, flower, women, child, big, learning' for

"Pear Flower Women's University") can be abbreviated as *Eyŏdae* ('Pear, women, big') or even *Edae* ('Pear, big'), since there is no "Pear Flower Men's University," but there is "Pear Flower Middle School." (The S-K *tae* — 'big' — is romanized as *dae* right after a vowel.)

In the following long name, the three Hancha picked for an abbreviation are put in uppercase: *KOryŏDAEhakkyoAseamunjeYONguso* ('Koryŏ University Asian Problem Research Center'). This abbreviated name *Kodae'ayŏn* is meaningless in Han'gŭl, but it retains some meaning in Hancha. The official name for S. Korea is *Taehan Minguk* ('Great Han People's Nation'), which is commonly and unambiguously abbreviated as *Hanguk* ('Han Nation'). Not only the names of institutions but also common phrases are routinely abbreviated and contracted, as *TAEhakkyoIPhakSIhŏm* ('university entrance examination') is shortened to *taeipsi* ('big, entrance, exam').

Hancha words are rapidly and accurately recognized. S-K compound words, idioms, and abbreviations can be recognized faster and more accurately in Hancha than in Han'gŭl because of the way they are composed, as described above. In addition, the meaning of an individual logographic Hancha can be directly and rapidly grasped from its whole visual form, whereas that of a word in a phonetic script might be obtained indirectly through sequencing a series of letters and converting it into a series of phonemes. On the other hand, pronunciation is faster in a phonetic script than in logographs. These contrasting recognition modes were illustrated in Figures 6-2 and 6-3 (chap. 6) for Hancha 山 and its eight-letter English equivalent *mountain*.

The Hancha for "mountain," which depicts three peaks of a mountain, is a prototypical pictograph and learned as such. It almost always maintains its meaning in compound words: e.g., *sanmek* ('mountain range'), *sanjŏng* ('mountain top' or 'mountin arbor'), and *sanhyŏp* ('mountain gorge'). In Han'gŭl too the S-K word for "mountain" *san* is written in one syllable block 산, but its meaning may not be instantly grasped, for reasons such as: It has no pictographic origin; as a simple syllable it has many meanings other than "mountain," such as "computation," "produce," "scatter," and "acid"; it can appear as a part of native words with unrelated meanings, e.g., *sanda* ('to buy' or 'to live') and *sansan'i* ('broken to pieces').

By now, you may realize that there are many S-K morphemes in simple syllable structures, and that they are so ambiguous as to be practically meaningless when spoken or written in a phonetic script: *ŏ* ('word', 'fish', etc.) and *ki* ('period', 'machine', etc). Written in Hancha each is eminently meaningful.

Because S-K words are better recognized in Hancha, newspaper headlines, whose meanings have to be grasped at a glance, tend to make heavy use of Hancha, as described in "Rational Hancha Use in the Present" (in chap. 12). Considerate authors write uncommon S-K words in Hancha, and when they write such words in Han'gŭl they provide Hancha in parentheses. The first definition provided in a Korean dictionary for a S-K word is typically its Hancha, which often reveals the word's meaning sufficiently. The meanings of some uncommon S-K words — e.g., *mu'a* and *musaekmuch'ui*, cited above — are not grasped at all, until their Hancha are found. The other day, while being shown an antique cabinet full of English silverware, a Korean dinner guest observed that the house was full of *kabo*. In spite of the situational context, I could not grasp its meaning, until I thought of its two Hancha, "house treasures."

To conclude this section, S-K words, abbreviations, and idioms are indispensable parts of the Korean language; they can, and should, be reduced in number but cannot be eradicated from the Korean language without impoverishing it. As long as they exist, Hancha are needed to write some of them so that their meanings can be accurately and speedily recognized. As a bonus, through shared Chinese characters and words, Koreans maintain cultural links with the Chinese and the Japanese. They can also access the old and rich cultural heritage of East Asia.

Korean Personal Names

The names of Korean people are intimately associated with Hancha; indeed names are chosen for the meanings of the Hancha with which they are written. A Korean name typically consists of a family name in one Hancha and a given name in two Hancha, written in that order, as in 金英順 *Kim Yŏng-sun,* a common woman's name, which is not changed after marriage. If Korean names closely resemble Chinese names, it is not by accident that this is so.

Let us first consider family names (based on Lee Sung-u 1977). In the early history of Korea, before the birth of the three kingdoms in the 1st century BC, waves of Chinese refugees came to Korea to escape turmoil in China, bringing their Chinese clan names. With the growing influence of Chinese culture, most Korean clans adopted names, usually in single Hancha. For example, the early kings of Silla were known by their clan names, such as *Pak* and *Kim.* In the 6th century AD more Chinese people came to Korea, bringing such Chinese names as *Kang, Chu,* and *Myŏng.* The use of an S-K surname, which began among royalty dealing with China, spread among aristocrats in the 7th century. In the 10th century when the civil-service exam system was instituted in the Koryŏ kingdom, candidates had to submit their names.

The Sino-Korean surnames that started among the upper class eventually spread to all classes except the lowest. The number of different names increased to around 300 in the mid-15th century. Even today, the word that refers to "all the citizens" or "all the (king's) subjects" is *paeksŏng* ('one hundred surnames'), an S-K word. Surnames were used by almost everyone near the end of the Chosŏn kingdom in 1909, when family registration began.

The most common surname in Korea is indisputably *Kim* ('gold'). If you meet a Korean and guess his or her name to be *Kim,* you will be correct one time in five. In 1995 the heads of state of both S. Korea and N. Korea are Kims. Other common names are *Yi* (variously romanized as *Lee, Li, Rhee, I, Ee), Pak (Park), Ch'oe (Ch'oi), Chŏng (Chung),* which, along with *Kim,* account for the surnames of more than half of all Koreans. Only 35 different names account for 90% of the entire population. Today there are only about 270 different family names for over 70 million Koreans, North, South, and overseas. All these observations point to the confusing situation that many Koreans share a common family name.

The confusion is ameliorated somewhat by the system whereby one family name can be differentiated into several branches, called *pon(kwan)* ('lineages'), based on the birth places of ancestors. A marriage is allowed between two persons sharing the same name as long as the two belong to two different lineages. A good thing; otherwise one fifth of the population, 14 million, would be denied as potential spouses to poor *Kims*!

Unfortunately, one particular lineage of *Kim*, Kimhae, has 4 million members. But even Koreans who share the same surname and lineage do not always share the same ancestor, in which case they can marry.

A given name consists of two Hancha, one of which might be shared among siblings. For example, from my name *Insup* or *In-sŏp*, the second Hancha *sŏp* is shared among my siblings, male and female (e.g., *I-sŏp, Chŏng-sŏp*). Also there can be constraints on the types of Hancha used from generation to generation: One Hancha or its radical has to be selected, in successive generations, out of the five Hancha for "tree, fire, earth, metal, and water," which form the Five Phases in ancient Chinese philosophy (table 10-2). The second character in my name, *sŏp*, contains the radical 'fire', while my father's name *tong* ('east') contains 'tree'.

Of the two characters that make up a given name, after one is fixed by the doctrine of the Five Phases, the other is chosen for its desirable meaning, such as *In* ('benevolence') for boys or girls, one of the Confucian virtues, or *Chŏng* ('chastity') for girls. The Hancha chosen for given names might have poignant meanings: To express disappointment at the birth of four girls in succession, the four were named as *Il-ka* ('the first is OK'), *I-hok* ('the second is tolerable'), *Sam-so* ('the third is a laughing matter'), and *Sa-chi* ('the fourth is a shame'). Like Chinese, Koreans avoid using in their names those characters found in the names of deceased ancestors and kings. Again like Chinese, Koreans might give an unflattering name to a child in order to ward off evil spirits.

Incidentally, in calling a person who is equal or inferior to you in social standing, you attach the vocative suffix *-a* or *-ya* to a given name, as in *John-a* or *Mary-ya*. To a family name or full name you attach the S-K word *ssi* ('Mr., Mrs., Miss, Ms'), as in *Kim ssi* or *Kim Yŏng-sun ssi*.

Many Koreans share the same name, even when both the family name and given name are jointly considered. For example, in the 1977 phone directory in Seoul, there were over 100 *Kim Yŏng-ja* and *Yi Pok-sun*. Some reasons for many names being shared might be: The small variety of family names; the practice of sharing one Hancha in given names among siblings; the practice, in successive generations, of selecting one out of the few prescribed Hancha or radicals for given names. Close to 3,000 different Hancha may be used for family and given names, but only 300 of them account for 90% of the names.

If Hancha names were to be written in Han'gŭl, there would be even more Koreans who share the same name, because homophonic names that are distinguished by different Hancha would share the same Han'gŭl name. For example, five different family names written in five different Hancha are no longer distinguished when all are written in Han'gŭl as *Kang*; the same applies to five names with the same sound *Pang*, and to four family names each with the sound *Yu, Chang, Chin,* or *Chŏng*. There are numerous cases in which three or two different family names share the same sound.

For given names, two Hancha with the sound *Sun* used in girls' names—one for "obedience" and the other for "pure"—can not be distinguished in Han'gŭl. There are countless such examples of homophonic Hancha used in given names. Today a phone directory lists names in Han'gŭl. Finding the right person in it is a nightmare! To be sure of the right person, one has to know something about the target's address as well as name. Korean Hancha names have the advantages described above, without the disadvantage of Japanese Kanji names whose sounds are often idiosyncratic and unpredictable (chap. 21).

There is a recent trend or fashion in Korea to use as given names native Korean words, which are normally written in Han'gŭl. There are plenty of native words that have nice sounds, good meanings, and yet are uncommon, so far: *Sŭlgi* ('intelligence'), *Hansol* ('great pine'), and *Poram* ('worthy') for both male and female names; and *Pomsine* ('spring brook') for girls. One poignant name for the fourth daughter is *Ttalkŭ'man* ('no more daughter'). There are even books that list potential Han'gŭl names.

Romanized Korean names follow the Korean order of putting a family name before a given name. Thus *Kim Il-sung* or *Kim I.-S.* (The same order is used in China, but the reverse order is used in Japan.) A hyphen separates the two Hancha/syllables in a given name. But Koreans are prone to use idiosyncratic romanizations for their names. For example, one common family name, *Yi,* which is the one sanctioned by the M-R romanization system, can appear as *Rhee, Ree, I, Lee, Li, Ee,* and so on. Some Koreans use the order "family name–given name" when romanizing, while others use the reverse. And some Koreans omit the hyphen between the two Hancha in their given names.

For the time being, all Korean surnames are Sino-Korean and are meant to be written in Hancha. Most given names were once solidly Sino-Korean, but now some are native and are written in Han'gŭl.

Hancha–Han'gŭl Mixed vs All-Han'gŭl Text

Hancha are useful for writing individual S-K words, as has been described, but they are, or should be, even more useful in text. Korean text can be written using only Han'gŭl or using Han'gŭl and Hancha together. Today in S. Korea most texts intended for adults are in mixed scripts, but they differ greatly in the proportion of Hancha, which may range from none to over 60% of the graphs. In a cursory survey I made recently of newspapers, magazines, and popular books, less than 10% of the graphs were Hancha, and those were mostly for names of people and places, abbreviated institutional names or phrases, idioms, or very uncommon S-K words ("Rational Hancha Use in the Present" in chap. 12). One might ask: For fast and accurate reading, what is the best way to write text in Korean? In pure Han'gŭl, or with some Hancha? If the latter, using what proportion of Hancha and for what kinds of words?

Before dealing with these questions, let us take a moment to consider reading in English. In silent reading, skilled readers distinguish important information from unimportant, and process the former more deeply than the latter. In English text, important information tends to be conveyed by content words (in boldface in the example below) and less important information by function words; the two types combine to produce the sentence (by P.G. Hamerton, 1834–1894):

"The **art** of **reading** is to **skip judiciously**."

The two types of word are often distinguishable by their difference in length: the four content words in the above sentence average 8 letters, whereas the four function words average 2.25 letters. The reader's eyes tend to fixate on long content words and skip over short function words. The distinction between long and short words, which can be seen in the peripheral vision, guides a reader's eye movements. In Figure 7-2, which shows how a skilled reader's eyes move during reading an English text, all content words were fixated on, whereas all function words were skipped over. It is during a fixation that the eyes extract a word's meaning, sound, class, and other information.

Content words and function words can be made even more distinguishable by printing content words in boldface, as in "The **art** of **reading** is to **skip judiciously.**" This arrangement speeded reading (Taylor and Park 1995). In Japanese, study after study shows that Kanji–Hiragana mixed texts are read much faster than all-Hiragana texts (chap. 21).

Extrapolating from studies on English and Japanese reading, one might expect that a Hancha–Han'gŭl mixture would be easier to read than all-Han'gŭl text, if familiar Hancha are used for important content words. Figure 15-1 shows three ways a Korean text can be written: (a) a mixture of two scripts, in which Hancha are used for S-K content words, while Han'gŭl are used for native content words and grammatical morphemes; (b) all kinds of words are written in only one script, Han'gŭl; and (c) all kinds of words are written in Hancha only. In which of (a), (b), and (c), would readers of any script readily distinguish between content words and grammatical morphemes so that they can attend more to the former than the latter? The answer is obviously (a).

(a) Han'gŭl–Hancha mixture: 나 는 每日 學校 에 간다
(b) All Han'gŭl: 나 는 매일 학교에 간다
(c) All Hancha (Idu): 他人矣婦 女乙犯姦 為在乙 良
(d) Kanji and Hiragana: 私 は 毎日字校 へ行く
(e) All Hiragana: わた し は まいに ち が っこうへいく

Figure 15-1. The sentence ('I every day school go') written in various scripts and manners (parts of figs. 1-4 and 12-1)

Yet, experiments that compared all-Han'gŭl texts to Han'gŭl–Hancha mixed texts have consistently shown that all-Han'gŭl texts are read faster than mixed-script texts (Kang et al. 1983; Noh et al. 1977). In one recent experiment, 15 paragraphs of similar length and difficulty were prepared with different proportions of Hancha: 0%, 10%, and 50% (Taylor and Park 1995). University students in Korea silently read each paragraph displayed on a computer screen. They all passed the simple comprehension tests, but their reading speeds differed for the three kinds of texts, from fastest to slowest: 0% Hancha, 10% Hancha, and 50% Hancha. These results are unexpected in the light of the studies on English texts. Most unexpectedly the Korean results differ from Japanese results. There are several possible explanations for these differences.

In a Korean text some important content words, if they are native, are in Han'gŭl, whereas in a Japanese text, even native content words are often in Kanji. In Figure 15-1, compare how the first word for 'I' and the last word for 'go' are written in (a) and (d). So, Japanese readers can develop the strategy, "Spot and process Kanji words at the expense of Hiragana words." Korean readers too develop "Spot and process Hancha words" but with less confidence, for they cannot ignore Han'gŭl words, which might be important content words. In a Han'gŭl-only text, Korean readers have only weak visual clues to the two types of words: Since a phrase tends to consist of one content word with one grammatical morpheme, and is surrounded by spaces, the Han'gŭl block(s) following and preceding a space may well be a content word and a grammatical morpheme, respectively.

The difference in visual complexity is smaller between Han'gŭl syllable blocks (2 to 13 strokes) and official Hancha (1 to 26 strokes) than between Japanese Hiragana (1 to 6 strokes) and official Kanji (1 to 24 strokes). Thus, content words in Hancha may stand out from grammatical items in Han'gŭl but perhaps not as prominently as do content words in Kanji from grammatical items in Hiragana. In Korean the length of the text remains more or less the same between (a) and (b), whereas in Japanese, (d) is shorter than (e).

There may also be a technical artifact affecting the results of the Taylor and Park study, working against the Hancha–Han'gŭl mixture. The reading materials were presented to the students on a computer screen. A screen has a lower resolution than a printed page, making complex Hancha, but not simple Han'gŭl, appear a little blurred. A reader who is not familiar with a written symbol must look more closely at its details in order to identify it, and this is hard to do on a low-resolution display.

Perhaps most critically, Korean students are far more practised in reading all-Han'gŭl texts than mixed texts. They learn Hancha not in primary school but only in middle and high schools, and then half-heartedly. In and out of school they are not well practised in reading Hancha, which are used sparingly in normal text. They are likely to see S-K words often in Han'gŭl and only occasionally in Hancha. By contrast, the Japanese are far more practised in reading Kanji–Hiragana mixed texts than all-Hiragana texts. They learn Kanji in every level of school, including primary school, and all texts, except those for very young children, make heavy use of Kanji. And in Japanese a particular word tends to be written consistently in one script, be it Kanji, Hiragana, or Katakana.

To find the effect of practice, in one of Taylor and Park's experiments, the students were given practice in reading aloud the Hancha words taken out of the Hancha–Han'gŭl mixed paragraphs, until they could read the Hancha words almost as fast as the Han'gŭl words. The practice involved reading the Hancha word list repeatedly several times over two to three days. After this practice, the differences in reading time among the three paragraphs (each with 0%, 10%, or 50% Hancha) either disappeared (between 0% and 10%) or decreased (between 10% and 50%), as shown in Figure 15-2

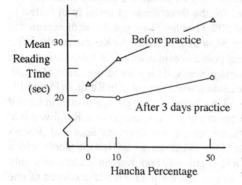

Mean Reading Time (sec)

Before practice

After 3 days practice

0   10   50

Hancha Percentage

Figure 15-2. The effect of practice in reading Hancha words on time to read texts (containing the practised words) in three different proportions of Hancha (Taylor and Park 1995; with permission of Kluwer Academic)

If a few days of practice makes this much difference, how much more difference would a few months or years of pactice make? In Park and Shon's study (1990), students who major in history or Chinese study that involves reading texts with many Hancha were faster in reading aloud Hancha words than students who major in science and engineering.

So, Koreans must answer through research the following kinds of questions. Can Han'gŭl–Hancha texts be read faster than all-Han'gŭl texts after practice? How extensive should practice be? And are the time and effort expended in learning and practising Hancha justified by the benefit of efficient text reading? These questions must be answered before deciding whether Hancha should be kept or abolished.

Conclusions: Streamline and Keep Hancha

Chinese characters, properly learned and used, help Korean reading. To be sure, learning Hancha costs time and effort, but this cost is not high; it can be further reduced by rationalizing and streamlining Hancha and Hancha use.

First, outmoded S-K words and idioms should not be used. When one looks at Hancha–Han'gŭl mixed texts of the late 19th and early 20th centuries, one is struck by the heavy proportion of Hancha. For example, in a randomly chosen paragraph from *Observations on a Journey to the West (Sŏyu Kyŏnmun)* by Yu Kil-chun published in 1895, out of 158 graphs 90 are Hancha and 68 are Han'gŭl. Some S-K words in Hancha are old-fashioned or literary and have been replaced by native or colloquial words: *yŏ* ('I') by *na* and *pinch'ŏkhada* by *mullich'ida* ('push aside'); the Hancha for *pin* is not in the list of 2,600 common Hancha.

Secondly, the number of Hancha used and learned should be judiciously limited. In S. Korea this number is at present only 1,800 (out of a possible 50,000). (For word processing, the Korean Industrial Standard specified 4,888 frequent Hancha in the base set.) In N. Korea 3,000 Hancha are taught in secondary and post-secondary schools, but as the Hancha learned do not appear in ordinary reading materials, they are easily forgotten. So, N. Koreans experience only the labor, but not the fruits, of learning a large number of complex Hancha. It would be far more sensible to learn about 1,500 Hancha and use them constantly than to learn twice as many Hancha only to forget them because of non-use.

Thirdly, overly complex Hancha—those with more than, say, 21 strokes—should be simplified, preferably in coordination with similar simplifications in Japanese and Chinese. A complex character may not be necessarily recognized more slowly than a simple one, because it is recognized not as a series of strokes but as a whole pattern ("Complex vs Simple Characters" in chap. 3). Nevertheless highly complex characters are undesirable. In such a character one has to sometimes use a magnifying glass to sort out an intricate inner detail. Also the time and effort to write characters by hand tends to increase proportionally to its number of strokes. True, in word processing, a character can be entered using a phonetic script almost instantly regardless of its complexity. But many people still have to write characters by hand.

Remember that Chinese characters have to be complex only in order to make their huge numbers discriminable from one another. When the number of Hancha is limited to only 1,500, there is no need for any of them to be exceedingly complex. So the official Hancha should not include the extremely complex characters, which tend to represent uncommon or esoteric and infrequent concepts, anyway. For the 1,800 official Hancha in S. Korea, the simplest Hancha has one stroke and the most complex one 26 strokes; the most common stroke number is 11. If some complex characters are included because of the importance of their concepts, they should be simplified judiciously in the manner outlined in "Simplifying Character Shapes" (in chap. 8), but preferably not in such a way as to make them unintelligible to Japanese and Chinese.

In a reader-friendly text, different types of word are written in their own appropriate script—Han'gŭl for native words, Hancha for some S-K items, Arabic numerals for numbers and calculations, English letters for well-known acronyms and abbreviations (e.g., *apt* for *apartment; KBS* for the Korean Broadcasting System) so that they can be visually differentiated to help silent readers allocate their mental resources efficiently. A Korean address using all these different scripts is far easier to read than one using only Han'gŭl.

Furthermore, words should be consistently written in their customary scripts to help readers become familiar with their written forms. In Japanese research, the speed and accuracy of recognizing a word depends not so much on the simplicity or complexity of its written form but on whether it is written in a customary or non-customary script ("Preschoolers Acquire Reading" in chap. 22). Reading direction, too, should be consistently in one direction, be it vertical or horizontal. Reading habit exerts a potent influence on reading efficiency, and people who read words consistently in one script and in one direction are bound to be more practised in them than readers who divide their practice between two quite different scripts and directions (chap. 7).

If Hancha are deemed to be necessary and worth learning, they must be learned early, from primary school, and thoroughly. The question is, whether learning Hancha in addition to Han'gŭl is an unbearable hardship. The answer is no: learning a limited number, say 1,500, of common Hancha is no hardship, especially when each Hancha has one reading, and when no Hancha is overly complex. Chinese schoolchildren learn close to 2,800 characters, and Japanese schoolchildren learn about 1,000 characters in multiple sounds.

The large number and the complex shapes of Hancha are apparent, and so are the time and effort needed to learn them. Thus, some Koreans advocate eliminating Hancha on intuitive grounds, not realizing their benefits, which are subtle and sometimes have to be demonstrated in research.

To conclude, Hancha are useful, even essential, for S-K words and are worth keeping. They not only should be taught at all levels of schools but also should be used widely, consistently, and judiciously in everyday reading materials. The use of Hancha, Arabic numerals, occasional English letters, and other symbols in no way implies that Han'gŭl is deficient; rather it implies that a text is easier to read when it contains a variety of scripts to differentiate different types of items. The Society of Han'gŭl Studies declared: "The assertion of restricted use of Hancha is the greatest enemy of the exclusive use of Han'gŭl." On the contrary, the exclusive use of Han'gŭl is an enemy of efficient reading, while the restricted use of Hancha is its friend.

16

History of Education and Literacy in Korea

Now that we have learned about the scripts used in Korea, let us learn about Korean education and literacy using them. We consider the two topics from a historical perspective, as we did in Part I on Chinese and will do again in Part III on Japanese. The history of education and literacy not only is interesting in its own right but also delineates factors other than scripts—political, economic, and educational policies— that affect the spread of literacy (based on Lee Ki-baik 1984; Nahm 1990).

For hundreds of years, until the early 19th century, education in Korea meant teaching the Confucian classics to a small privileged group of men who prepared for the civil service examinations. In the late 19th and the early 20th centuries, Korea attempted, without much success, to modernize education. Only some years after the liberation of Korea from Japanese rule in 1945, did both South and North Korea achieve the kind of truly universal and modern education that produces mass literacy.

Civil Service Examination

For over a millennium, state examinations for recruiting bureaucrats, open only to sons of a ruling and wealthy class, set the tone for education in Korea. Because the exams tested mainly knowledge of the difficult yet impractical Confucian classics, education meant studying them for years.

During the Unified Silla kingdom (668–935 AD), some Korean men studied in Tang China to become prominent Confucian scholars. Some of them even passed the civil service exams there. They urged the Silla government to recruit civil servants who were distinguished by learning rather than by hereditary lineage. Their urging was accepted only in part: In 788 a quasi-civil service exam was set up to recruit mid-ranking bureaucrats, while high-ranking bureaucrats continued to be recruited without the exam mainly from royalty and aristocracy.

In 958 the Koryŏ kingdom set up a full-scale, elaborate state civil service exam, which was modelled on the Chinese system, using the same or similar terminology and organization, and testing similar subject matter. The exam system was called *kwagŏ*, the Korean reading of the Chinese term *keju* ('branches, raise' for "select talents through exams in various branches"). There were no exams to select military officials until the last year of the Koryŏ kingdom. Along with the exam system there continued to be a system for sons of hereditary aristocratic families to receive certain official appointments without exams.

During the Chosŏn kingdom (1392–1910) the exam system took on central importance. Qualifying exams were conducted in two levels, licentiate and erudite. The licentiate exams were of two kinds: the classics licentiate, which tested candidates on the Confucian Five Classics and the Four Books, and the literary licentiate, which tested them for their ability to compose prose and poetry using formal Chinese literary forms.

After studying Hancha, calligraphy, and the Confucian classics for several years at various levels of school (described in the next section), the students were qualified to sit for the licentiate exams, and if they passed a first stage exam held at the provincial level, they proceeded to Seoul for a second-stage exam, which determined who would receive the degrees of classics licentiate (*saengwon*; *shengyuan* in Chinese) or literary licentiate (*chinsa*; *jinshi* in Chinese). These licentiates then might enter the National Confucian Academy *(Sŏnggyun'gwan),* and could sit for two stages of the Erudite Exams. Those who survived this series of exams could then sit a palace exam held in the presence of a king, who ranked the candidates according to their performance. After this series of gruelling exams, the successful candidates were rewarded with high-ranking official positions. The nation's top scholar was honored with the label *changwŏn* (*zhuanyuan* in Chinese; 'grand top').

As in Ming and Qing China, the exams were originally to be held once in three years, but eventually they were held more often, to mark national or royal festive occasions. As a consequence, more men passed the exams than there were available high-ranking official positions. Inevitably there arose squabbles over the positions among rival scholarly groups, not to mention bribes and the sale of official positions. And those lucky enough to have positions were kept busy amassing all the advantages they could during their short period of office.

Successful candidates at the civil service exams tended to be limited to the ruling class or gentry called *yangban* ('two branches', meaning civil and military branches of the bureaucracy), who at one time comprised less than 10% of the population. Though *yangban* status was not hereditary by law, a majority of this class were members of old and prominent lineages that descended from generations of officials. When a *yangban* lineage did not produce a successful candidate in three successive generations, it could be demoted in status.

In the Chosŏn kingdom a sequence of military exams paralleled the civil exams. There were government schools and special exams for candidates for low-ranking positions as technical officials in such fields as medicine, law, astronomy, and foreign languages. These technical exams were the hereditary preserve of the social class called "middle people" (*chungin*). The middle people ranked below the gentry class (*yangban*) but above the commoners (*sangmin*)—such as farmers, artisans, and merchants—who comprised the bulk of the population. Below the commoners were slaves and "despised class" (*ch'ŏnmin*) who did such "degrading" works as butchering, grave digging, and tanning. Candidates to become Buddhist monks were given exams of their own, but only up to the middle of the 15th century, after which they were given no exams.

The exam system had both positive and negative effects, as it did in China. It selected bureaucrats more for their scholarly ability than for their family connections, and so fostered respect for learning. In the old exam system only sons of the upper class were eligible for the most prestigious exams; even sons of the upper class, if illegitimate, were at one time barred from the exams. The men selected by the exams were scholars steeped in impractical antiquarian and historical learning rather than being equipped in practical skills; even their scholarly ability, centered around writing an essay in a prescribed format and rote memorizing the Confucian literature, was shallow. They may or may not have had the kind of personality necessary for managing diverse branches of a government. What the Korean elites studied for so long and so arduously were foreign, Chinese texts.

In short, the exam system warped, hideously, the educational system and stood in the way of modern universal education and literacy. It was finally abolished only in 1894, having lasted for a thousand years!

Traditional Education

From early in the history of Korea there were national and private schools to teach Chinese characters and Confucian classics to the sons of upper-class families. The schools increased in number over the years, but throughout dynastic history they never produced mass literacy.

In 372 AD the Koguryŏ kingdom established a national Confucian academy called *T'aehak* to teach the Confucian classics, literature, and martial arts to the sons of aristocratic families. It trained future bureaucrats. There were also many private schools, *kyŏngdang*, teaching similar subjects at a lower level.

The Paekche kingdom (18 BC–660) began Chinese study early in its history, and sent scholars to Japan as teachers of Chinese characters and texts. Since the title of savant or erudite (*paksa*, the modern term for an academic Ph.D. degree) was given to teachers of the Chinese classics, Confucian educational institutions must have existed.

The Silla kingdom (57 BC–668) had an educational system known as *Hwarang-do* ('Way of the flower of manhood') to train future leaders. Young men were recruited from the upper-class to be educated in academic and military subjects. This educational system provided the basis for Silla to unify the three kingdoms in the 7th century.

During the Unified Silla kingdom (668–935), Confucianism gradually emerged as an ideology of political reform. Thus, in 682 the National Confucian College, *Kukhak,* later renamed as the National Confucian University, *T'aehakkam,* was established to teach the Confucian classics to male members of the aristocracy aged between 15 and 30. It was a state school for training public servants. In later years some students went to Tang China to study Confucianism firsthand.

During the Koryŏ kingdom, in 992, the National University (*Kukchagam*) was established at the capital, Kaesŏng. By the 12th century it consisted of six colleges: Three of them taught Chinese studies, especially the Confucian classics, to the sons of high ranking officials, while the three other colleges taught law, calligraphy, and accounting or math to the sons of lower-ranking officials and commoners. Outside the capital, there were state-run provincial schools, *hyanggyo*, which taught the Confucian classics at a secondary level to the sons of local dignitaries. Successful students at the provincial schools were admitted to the National University at the capital.

There was a temporary decline in state education in later days of Koryŏ, and some prominent Confucian scholars founded private academies in the capital, to prepare aristocratic youths for the state exams. The first such school was founded in 1055, and soon there were twelve. Some private academies enjoyed prestige because of their high success rate at the state exams. Eventually, the sons of aristocratic families considered it a greater honor to attend one of these twelve private academies than the state schools.

During the Chosŏn kingdom (1392–1910), Neo-Confucianism was adopted as the state ideology, while Koryŏ's educational system remained more or less intact. In 1398 Koryŏ's National University *(Kukchagam)* moved from Kaesŏng to the new capital, Seoul, and its name was changed to the National Confucian Academy, *Sŏnggyun'gwan*. This highest state institution of Confucian education, complete with a shrine to honor Confucius, admitted between 100 and 200 students of 15 years of age or older. It still exists in Seoul, keeping alive the traditional Confucian rites.[1] In the early 15th century additional four universities, called *Sahak*, were established in Seoul. They were similar to the National Confucian Academy in educational policies but smaller in size and lower in educational level.

All over Korea—in Seoul, and in smaller towns, and villages—private elementary schools called *sŏdang* ('reading hall', which began in Koryŏ) proliferated, to teach basic Chinese characters to the young sons of privileged as well as ordinary families. Some promising graduates of *sŏdang* advanced to a provincial school, *hyanggyo*, and then to a university in the capital. A *sŏdang* class, held in a private house with one teacher, was small and informal, as depicted in Figure 16-1.

Figure 16-1. Sŏdang ('reading hall'), a small, informal class of boys (who wore braided hair) being taught reading during the Chŏson kingdom. One boy is crying after being physically chastized by the teacher, a customary punishment. This well-known painting by Kim Hong-do (1766–?) (the National Central Museum, Seoul) is copied on a souvenir plate sold at the Korean Folk Village near Seoul.

---

[1] In the 1980s when officials of the People's Republic of China re-instituted the ceremony to commemorate Confucius' birthday in Qufu, Shandong Province, they did not know how to put on the proper ceremony. So in 1989 they invited the Sŏnggyun'gwan to come and demonstrate it.

In the 16th century, the Neo-Confucian literati were crushed by successive purges in factional rivalries. These literati founded in rural areas several private academies (*sŏwŏn*), both as educational facilities to instruct sons of local gentry and as shrines to honor prominent Confucian scholars from the past. Such Confucian academies sprang up in many regions outside the capital, and by the beginning of the 17th century they numbered over one hundred. With these academies, the purged Neo-Confucian literati laid the foundation for a comeback. Eventually they did re-enter government service in the capital in the reign of King Sŏnjo (1567–1608), and in the end came to dominate the political processes of the Chosŏn kingdom. By the end of the 18th century, there were over 700 Confucian academies throughout Korea.

Between the 17th and 18th centuries, one of the most important intellectual movements was practical learning (*sirhak*). Scholars of this movement, who were mostly outside the government, rebelled against the Neo-Confucianists who were preoccupied with empty theorizing and incessant factional fights. They sought truth from facts, and wanted to study something that could be useful for a contemporary society. Some of them called for a new system of recruiting civil servants to replace the traditional civil service exams and for the establishment of a classless society to replace the traditional rigidly hierarchic social structure.

The tradition of practical learning was inherited in the 19th century by scholars of the "opening-up/enlightenment period" (*kaehwa ki*), those who wanted to open Korea to outside, especially Western, ideas. Korea, which had closed all its doors to foreign influences in 1801, began in 1876 to open them, with a treaty with Japan followed in 1882 by one with the United Stated. After these treaties, progressive scholars advocated educating people in Western science and technology in order to develop modern industry.

The movements of practical learning and enlightenment, though they did bring about some changes, could not radically reform the hidebound government. As recently as the middle of the 19th century, Korean education was characterized as traditional, Chinese, Confucian, civil-service exam-centered, male-dominated, and elitist. With such a backward and severely limited educational system, Korea became easy prey for the expansionist Japanese, who were not shackled by the civil service exam system and who had adopted modern education in the Meiji Restoration of the 19th century.

Modern Education

In the late 19th century, as the Chosŏn kingdom, under the grandiose name of "The Great Han Empire," was tottering to its end, it came into contact with Western culture, initially via China and Japan. To meet the new challenge, a sweeping reform called "the Kabo Reform" was carried out in many areas—e.g., social, educational, administrative, and economic—between 1894 and 1896. First of all, the government decreed, "laws and decrees shall be basically in the national writing [Han'gŭl], though Hancha translations can be added, and a Hancha–Han'gŭl mixture can be also used." Before this decree, most documents were written using only Hancha in Idu (fig. 12-1a). The reform also abolished the civil service exams, sent some 200 students to Japan, and established a new educational system.

King Kojong was aware of the importance of education, as can be seen in his 1895 edict:

> When one looks at the state of affairs in the world, one finds that in all those nations that maintain their independence through wealth and power and thus have gained ascendancy, the citizens are enlightened in their knowledge. Enlightened knowledge is attained through excellence of education, and so education truly is of fundamental importance in preserving our nation. [Lee K.-B. 1984: 331]

The new educational system consisted of primary, middle, and normal schools (for training teachers) as well as foreign language schools to teach modern subjects. But the government schools still tended to focus on training future officials and to attract the sons of gentry. To meet the growing need of the ordinary people for knowledge and education, many private schools were established by Korean patriots, who wanted to lay the foundations for an independent Korea. (At the time both Japan and China were meddling in Korean affairs.) The first modern private school was Wŏnsan Academy, founded in 1883 in Wŏnsan, a new port city in North Korea, in response to a request from the city's residents.

A few years later modern schools were built by American Protestant missionaries in Seoul, one for boys in 1885 and then another for girls in 1886. The latter, Ewha Women's School, was the first educational institution for women in Korea. It began with a single student, and even in 1897, had only 40 students, mostly orphans and girls from poor families (Fisher 1928). Today its offspring are the prestigious Ewha Women's University and Ewha Girls' Middle and High School (my own alma mater).

In 1905 the Protectorate Treaty was imposed by Japan over Korea as a first step toward annexation in 1910. The treaty deprived Korea of its control over foreign affairs and appointed a Japanese resident-general to look after them.

Meanwhile, the number of private schools for boys and girls established by the Koreans themselves kept increasing until it reached 3,000. Those most eager to establish private schools were not from the ruling class but were commoners. The schools taught the new Western learning in such social science subjects as history and geography, and such math subjects as arithmetic and algebra. Above all, the schools were hotbeds of nationalism, so much so that the Japanese resident-general enacted a law requiring that private schools be operated only with government sanction and that only authorized textbooks be used. Many of the private schools were forced to close.

After annexing Korea in 1910, Japan's educational policy emphasized vocational education that would equip the Koreans in simple manual skills so that they could perform menial tasks for the Japanese rulers. Education for Koreans was virtually limited to primary education, with some meager secondary education. There was only one university for a population of 24 million people! (But there were over 30 different types of prisons for Koreans.)

The primary schools increased in number, but many were for Japanese residents, who flocked to Korea to take up key positions in education, bureaucracy, and business. (In 1935 there were 619,000 Japanese residents among 22,208,000 Koreans; Nahm 1990. The Japanese returned to Japan in 1945 when their nation was defeated in World War II.) Only a fraction of the Korean population received any education. Even by 1936 only 25% of the school-age children—40% of the boys and 10% of the girls—

were enrolled in primary schools in Korea. (At the time, the enrollment figure for Japanese children in Korea was close to 100%.)

Furthermore, education was geared to turning Koreans into loyal Japanese subjects. In 1938 the use of the Korean language in schools was banned, and Japanese became mandatory. In 1940 a Korean surname, which typically has one Hancha in Um/Chinese reading, had to be changed into a Japanese name that typically has two Kanji in Kun/Japanese readings. For example, the most common surname, *Kim* ('gold'), might be changed to a Japanese–Korean name *Kaneoka* ('gold, hill'). But by adopting Japanese names the Koreans could neither conceal their identities nor escape Japanese discrimination against them, because their Japanese names remained "Japanized Korean names," and because they had to identify their original names in documents.

Even under the suffocating oppression of Japanese colonial rule, the surviving private schools kept up Korean national education and served as a breeding ground of nationalists. The study of the Korean language and Han'gŭl was suppressed but could not be extinguished. A handful of dedicated scholars kept it alive underground; some scholars went to prison, and two of them perished there. Thanks to the dedication and effort of these scholars, the teaching of Korean and Han'gŭl could be resumed without delay after independence in 1945.

Education Today in S. and N. Korea

In 1948 two governments were founded in Korea, one in the south and one in the north. Both have put great emphasis on improving the quantity and quality of education. Despite a temporary setback caused by the ruinous Korean War (1950–1953), education has made huge progress. Let us consider first S. Korea and then N. Korea.

Today, S. Korea, like many other nations, has adopted a school system that consists of 2–3 years of kindergarten, 6 years of primary school, 3 years of middle school, 3 years of high school, and 2–4 years of college or university. The Ministry of Education oversees the formal education, the compilation of textbooks, and the maintenance of educational facilities. It sets a yearly enrollment quota for universities, and even of science students. Above all, it sets successive 5-year programs in educational reform and expansion.

Compulsory and free education lasts 6 years; it lasts 9 years in many urban areas, and is planned to be so nation-wide by 1997. At every level of school, classes tend to be twice as large as in North America, but a movement to reduce class size is afoot. Anyway, because of the pupils' disciplined class-room behavior and the teacher's textbook-centered group teaching, the large class size does not pose a big problem. The traditional teaching has been a transfer of information from a teacher to his or her students through a lecture. Now there is a movement to encourage interactions among students as well as between them and a teacher.

At each grade of primary school, the Korean language, largely reading and writing, is given the largest time allotment, 6–7 class periods per week. The two most important subjects, the national language and mathematics, together take up 45% of class time in the two lowest grades, and 35% in the four higher grades (Kim I-jong 1992).

The 3-year middle school attracts virtually all primary-school graduates. The Korean language is still important and is alloted 4 to 5 class periods per week, but so is English. English listening is now part of the qualifying exams for high school entrance. The next two most important subjects, mathematics and science, are given 3 to 4 class periods per week. These four core subjects—Korean, math, oral English, and English text—take up 35% of the class periods. In the 6th and latest educational development plan, Hancha, computer, and environmental study have become elective subjects.

The 3-year high school attracts most of the middle-school graduates, and the dropout rate is low. English is an important subject. There are classes in Hancha as well as in classic Korean and Chinese literature. Korean language and literature are required, while Korean writing and grammar, as well as Chinese text, are elective. The four core subjects—Korean, math, English, and Chinese text—take up 30% of class periods. High school is divided into two streams: general academic and vocational. Currently, 59% take the general and 41% take the vocational stream. The government aims to increase the latter to 50%, in its drive to rapidly industrialize the nation.

Admission to a middle school, a high school, and a university used to be through an exam hell, which was caused by the differential rankings of schools, and in the case of universities, also by an enrollment limitation set by the Ministry of Education. Most students wanted to go to the best middle school that was most successful in sending its graduates to the best high school that, in turn, was most successful in sending its graduates to the best university. Graduation from the best university, Seoul National University, helps most of its graduates to obtain prestigious positions in society.

In order to alleviate, if not eliminate, the exam hell, the government implemented various bold policies. Entrance exams to middle schools were abolished in 1969. Admission to high school is by a system implemented in 1973: preliminary screening selects a certain number of applicants, who are then assigned to schools within the district of residence through a lottery. Some parents move their residence so that their children can be assigned to a district with a reputable school.

The annual quota for university entrants is set by the Ministry of Education, and it was 30.6% of high school graduates in 1993, but is planned to in crease slightly in the future. Admission to a university used to be through a nation-wide, state-run examination. Since 1994 students take a scholastic aptitude test (SAT), and high scorers are selected to be given another exam by each university. Each year one million candidates take the exam for about 250,000 places at 200 universities and colleges. Thus the exam is intensely competitive, especially for places at the most prestigious Seoul National University.

What happens to those who fail university entrance exams? Many candidates take the exam for a second or third time. There is even a word for such repeaters, *jaesuseng* ('re-learning students'). Some go to junior colleges, whose graduates do not have bright prospects for future employment. Some students choose to emigrate to North America, where doors to university entrance are open more widely.

Many Korean students, like other East Asian students, study hard, perhaps too hard. They have 222 school days a year, compared to N. American students' 180. They do many hours of home work. They go to cram schools for extra study after regular schools, as do Japanese and Taiwanese students. After-school tutoring was banned in 1980, but extra study without a tutor still goes on. And since 1989 private tutoring has been again allowed when school is not in session. Some high schools provide after school self-study hours, which can last until 10 or 11 p.m. There is a saying in Korea, as in Japan: "Sleep 4 hours and you pass the exam; sleep 5 hours and you fail it."

In S. Korea and Japan, and perhaps in Taiwan too, many middle-class mothers — who tend to be well-educated and affluent, and to live in condominiums with much free time — stay home and devote their energy and time to their children's education. In S. Korea, almost all urban parents subscribe to daily newspapers for children, such as *Children's Tong'a Daily (So'nyŏn Tong'a)*. The parents also supervise their children in completing daily worksheets, which provide children with opportunities to review and preview school lessons. The worksheets are delivered to homes, and the completed ones picked up for marking, by their publisher every day.

Thanks to the government's emphasis on, and its citizens' respect for, education, there have been spectacular quantitative improvements in education over the past few decades. Between 1980 and 1991, the rate of kindergarten enrollment increased from 7% to 61%. Between 1945 and 1989, the number of schoolchildren increased by a factor of 4, of middle school students by a factor of 29, of high school students by a factor of 58, and of university or college students by a factor of 183 (Ministry of Education 1991).

Meanwhile, in 1971 the government launched a program to raise the educational, cultural, and scientific knowledge and standards of rural communities, in a movement called "the New community." Radio and correspondence schools were made available to rural people, and vocational schools were opened to out-of-school youth.

Not only in quantity but also in quality, Korean education has made progress. Consider the results of the Second International Assessment of Educational Progress conducted by the Educational Testing Service (Princeton, New Jersey) during 1990–1991; they were widely reported in the media in February 1992. S. Korean 13 year-olds ranked first in both science and math among 15 nations compared, which included S. Korea, Taiwan, Switzerland, Hungary, the former Soviet Union, Slovenia, Italy, Israel, Canada, France, Scotland, Spain, United States, Ireland, and Jordan, in the order of scores in science, from high to low. Interestingly, another East Asian nation, Taiwan, ranked second in science and first in math in a tie with S. Korea. Japanese students did not participate in this particular contest, but they do well in other contests. Sadly the "mighty" United States of America ranking second from the bottom in math and third from the bottom in science.

At S. Korean universities and colleges a relatively large proportion of the students — 54% (1993) vs 25% in N. America — study sciences, engineering, medicine, and pharmacy, while the rest study humanities, social sciences, arts, physical education, and teaching. As a result, S. Korea, which had few research scientists and engineers four decades ago, now has many. Yet, S. Korea cannot afford to rest on its laurels; it has to produce even more research scientists and engineers if it is to catch up with advanced industrial nations. It has set an ambitious target of spending 5% of the gross domestic product on research and development by the year 2000, about triple the current Canadian level.

The educational system in N. Korea differs from that in S. Korea (based on Kim Min-su 1985; Mun 1990). After a reorganization in 1972–1976, children start one year of preschool at age 4, one year of kindergarten at age 5, four years of primary school at age 6, and six years of middle school at age 10. Altogether, they receive 11-years of compulsory education. N. Korea allows 11 years of specialized education in areas such as music, drama, and foreign languages for talented children, starting at age 6.

At the upper level, there are two or three years of either normal school (teachers' college) or higher technical school, which lead to four or six years of university or college, which in turn lead to three or six years of graduate school. At the apex of the educational system is Kim Il Sung University, named after the "Great Leader" of N. Korea, who died in 1994.

In N. Korea, as in S. Korea, primary and middle schools put great emphasis on teaching the national language. In the primary grades about one-third of the time is allocated to the Korean language, one-quarter to mathematics, and the rest of the time is allocated to eight other subjects such as history, science, and geography. Peculiar to N. Korea, there is a course titled "the early childhood of our beloved leader Kim Il Sung," which takes up about 4% of the school time. For about two decades after the establishment of the Communist government in 1948, Russian was the favored foreign language, and Hancha was not taught in schools. But since the late 1960s English and Hancha have been taught in secondary schools. N. Korean education devalues intellectual achievement for its own sake; rather it values teaching technical skills and "correct" political ideology, i.e., "Communist morality," which teaches children to be anti-American, anti-Japanese, anti-South Korean, and to adulate the great leader Kim Il Sung.

With such an educational system, N. Korea produces citizens who are literate using Han'gŭl (called Chosŏncha, 'Korean letters'), who are trained in artistic, linguistic, and technical skills, and who are thoroughly indoctrinated in the N. Korean brand of Communism. On the other hand, N. Koreans are shut out from advanced technology and science, and artistic diversity, not to mention from democracy and a market economy. As a result, they live in a totalitarian society with a dismally low living standard. The N. Koreans provide us with a prime example of mass literacy not being a sufficient condition for prosperity and happiness.

S. Korean and other East Asian students perform well in spite of being burdened with four handicaps, compared to North American students: the relatively small educational expenditure (around 4% of GNP, compared to Canada's 7%); the large class size; the time and effort spent on learning a foreign language, English; and the time and effort spent on learning supposedly complex writing systems. N. American students are "lucky" in that they do not have to spend as much time and effort learning Japanese or other East Asian language as do East Asian students in learning English. If they did, they would have less time and energy left to study math, science, and English. Yet, there will come a day, if it hasn't already dawned, when N. American students have to learn Japanese or other East Asian languages.

What sets East Asians apart from North Americans is their attitudes toward education. East Asian students, their parents, and their governments value education as the major, if not the sole, means to get ahead in society. Even in North America, students from Asia enjoy a well-founded reputation for excelling in math, science, and school achievement. Obviously, they bring their healthy respect for learning and good study habits to their adopted countries. In the 1980's an educator observed in Hawaii, one of the most multi-ethnic states of the United States of America:

> What groups are taking the greatest advantage of school opportunities in Hawaii? First, the Koreans; second, the Chinese; third, the Japanese; fourth the Caucasian-Hawaiians; fifth, the Asiatic Hawaiians; and in order after these the Portuguese, Hawaiians, Spanish, 'other' Caucasians, Puerto Ricans, and Filipinos. The Koreans, Chinese, and Japanese have great traditions favoring education. [Potter 1982, cited in R. Kim 1984]

East Asia is teeming with people, and most of its regions have few natural resources. Its most important asset is its well-trained, hard-working citizens. In East Asia, the business of school is to teach students core subjects; in N. America it is to coddle students.

Printing and Publications

As in Part I, we gauge the literacy level of a nation indirectly through books and magazines printed and published. Korea has a long and venerable tradition of printing and publishing. In particular it can boast the world's first serious use of movable metal type in printing.

The books printed before the creation of Han'gŭl in the mid-15th century were all written in Hancha; of those printed over the next few centuries some were in Hancha, some in Han'gŭl, and some in a mixture of the two; today most books are in Han'gŭl only, or have but a sprinkling of Hancha.

As early as the 4th century AD a history book was compiled in Koguryŏ and another in Paekche, and in the 6th century one in Silla, according to the later history books described below, but all three have been lost.

During the Unified Silla kingdom (668–935), woodblock printing was developed and used to reproduce a variety of material, especially Buddhist sutras and Confucian texts. In woodblock printing, one block is carved to print a whole page of a book. The world's oldest extant example of woodblock printing is believed to be the copy of the Dharani Sutra found in a pagoda at Pulguksa Temple in Kyŏngju, S. Korea. It may have been printed between AD 704 and 751, the year the pagoda was erected. In the early 8th-century several books were written on Silla history and geography, such as *Tales of Silla* and *Biographies of Eminent Monks* by Kim Tae-mun, but they have been lost.

During the Koryŏ kingdom (918–1392) woodblock printing flourished, and many kinds of books were published. There were libraries holding tens of thousands of books. The earliest surviving Korean history is the *History of Three Kingdoms (Samguk Sagi)* written by Kim Pu-sik in 1145 under the order of a Koryŏ king. Its geography section records the old native place names of the three kingdoms before they were changed to Sino-Korean names in the 8th century. Another history book, *Memorabilia of the Three Kingdoms (Samguk Yusa)*, was written by the monk Iryŏn in 1280. It preserves 14 *hyangga*, native poems, which are valuable in showing how native words were written in Hancha. These histories record the existence of the earlier history books on the individual kingdoms of Silla, Paekche, and Koguryŏ.

A mammoth collection of Buddhist scriptures, the *Tripitaka (Taejangkyŏng)* in 5,048 volumes, was completed between 1021 and 1087, only to be burned during the Mongol invasion in 1232. The second printing of the scripture, known as the *Koryŏ Tripitaka* or *Tripitaka Koreana,* was completed between 1236 and 1251. This work—in over 80,000 wood blocks—is regarded as the most complete, oldest, and finest among some twenty versions of *Tripitaka* originating in East Asia, and is preserved in Haeinsa Temple on Mt. Kaya in S. Korea as one of the world's cultural treasures. In 1236 Korea's oldest surviving medical treatise, *Emergency Remedies of Folk Medicine,* appeared.

Woodblock printing has many advantages, especially when one needs to print many copies of one particular book, in repeated editions ("Invention of Paper and Printing" in chap. 10). But when one needs to print a small number of copies of many kinds of works, printing by movable type is more efficient than by woodblock. In Koryŏ the normal run of an edition tended to be small, as books were for a small group of educated upper-class readers. So Koryŏ printers were interested in developing movable type. There is a record of the use of cast metal type in 1234 to print the 50-volume *Prescribed Texts for Rites of the Past and Present,* but no copies remain today. One extant Buddhist scripture, now kept in the library of Koryŏ University, is believed to have been printed in 1297. Another Buddhist scripture printed in 1377 is preserved in the National Library of Paris. In 1392, the last year of the Koryŏ kingdom, a national office for book publication was set up for casting type and printing books.

The use of cast metal movable type in Koryŏ in 1234 preceded by some 200 years the first use of it in Germany by Johann Gutenberg in the mid-15th century. Movable type had been invented in China in the 11th century, but it never really caught on there, where the type blocks were at first fashioned in clay or engraved on wood. Cast bronze type appeared in China only in the late 17th century or early 18th century. Cast type is essential if the characters are to be the same on each occurrence.

In 1403 the Chosŏn kingdom established a national metal printing press, improving its movable type sets four times, and printed the Confucian classics and historical literature. In the mid-15th century during King Sejong's reign, two important documents were published: *Hunmin Chŏng'ŭm (Correct Sounds to Instruct People)* and *Explanations and Examples of Hunmin Chŏng'ŭm* (see "Creation and Adoption of Han'gŭl" in chap. 13). They were originally written in Hancha, and the Hancha texts were translated into Han'gŭl. To demonstrate the efficacy of Han'gŭl, King Sejong established the Office for Publication and had it publish a number of major works that contained both Hancha and Han'gŭl. Here are a few of the important early works:

- *Songs of Flying Dragons (Yongbiŏch'ŏnka),* a eulogy of the virtues of the royal ancestors, consisting of 125 stanzas or cantos. Completed in 1447, it was the first work that used the new phonetic script, Han'gŭl.

- *Paraphrased Accounts of Buddha's Life (Sŏkbosangjŏl),* a collection of devotional verse completed in 1447 to pray for the soul of Sejong's deceased queen.

- *Dictionary of Proper Korean Pronunciations (Tongguk Chŏng'ŭm),* a Sino–Korean dictionary, in 1447.

In the late 15th century King Sejong's son, King Sejo, had numerous Buddhist texts translated into Han'gŭl with some Hancha. One queen translated into Han'gŭl a few books on moral education for women. Agricultural manuals for peasants, and military texts whose contents were to be kept secret from foreigners, were written in Han'gŭl. In 1527 Ch'oe Se-jin wrote *Explanations of Characters (Hunmong Chahoe)*, using Han'gŭl to explain 3,360 common Hancha, thus teaching Han'gŭl in the process of teaching Hancha. The book competed with the *Thousand-Character Essay* (chap. 9) as a popular textbook of Hancha for children.

Between the 17th and 18th centuries, there appeared popular stories written largely in Han'gŭl. Many of the authors as well as the readers of these stories were commoners. Let us sample two of the stories. In Hŏ Kyun's (1569–1618) *The Story of Hong Kil-tong*, the protagonist, Hong, was an illegitimate son of a high-ranking government official. In the feudal era, illegitimate sons looked forward to a bleak future: At one time they could not take a civil service exam; at other times, when they could, if they passed it they could hold only a minor position or none at all. Hong rebelled against this inequity. He organized farmers who had become bandits after losing their lands. This outlaw band, like Robin Hood's band, took ill-gotten gains from corrupt officials and distributed them among the poor and helpless commoners. Unlike Robin Hood, Hong and his followers escaped to a remote island and created a utopia there.

One of the enduring popular novels is *The Story of Ch'un-hyang*, by an anonymous author. In a small town a high-born young man, Mong-nyong ('Dream dragon'), falls in love with Ch'un-hyang ('Spring fragrance'), the daughter of a courtesan. To complicate the story, the two lovers are separated when the young man, after passing a civil service exam, goes to the capital and obtains an official position as an inspector. During the separation a corrupt and tyrannical local official tries to force Ch'un-hyang into serving him as a courtesan. Later, the inspector returns to the town disguised as a beggar, and exposes and punishes the tyrannical official. Then the two lovers are reunited to live happily ever after. So this love story has an undercurrent of social criticism.

Between the 17th and 19th centuries books on such practical subjects as medicine, agriculture, the national language, and foreign languages were published. There were also several anthologies of poems and songs, such as *Enduring Poetry of Korea, Songs of Korea,* and *Anthology of Korean Poetry,* a collection mostly of *sijo* ('songs of time').

Sijo is a form of native Korean poem in a prescribed syllable structure: It consists of three lines, each having 4 feet, and each foot containing 3 to 5 syllables. This form of poem began in the late Koryŏ period and flowered in the mid-Chosŏn period. *Sijo* were composed and read by many literate people, including courtesans. Here is one well-known sample by Yang Sa-ŏn (1517–?). Its *T'aesan* may refer to the Mount Taishan, the famous holy mountain in Shandong Province of China; it is said to have 7,000 steps. Or it may simply mean a great mountain.

t'aesan i nopta hadoe hanŭl are moe iroda [3, 4, 4, 4 syllables]
orŭgo tto orŭmyŏn modorŭri ŏpkŏnmanŭn [3, 4, 4, 4 syllables]
saram i che ani orŭgo moe man nopta hadŏra [3, 5, 4, 3 syllables]

A great mountain may be high but still lies under the sky.
If people keep climbing it, they are sure to reach the top.
But they do not keep climbing, and complain that the mountain is too high.

As noted earlier, during much of the 19th century, the Chosŏn kingdom pursued a policy of isolation and was dubbed the "hermit kingdom." However, between the late 19th and early 20th centuries, it came increasingly under the influence of, and meddling by, foreign powers. Some progressive scholars agitated for opening up Korea to foreign influence in order to modernize their outmoded, Confucian society. The period between 1876, when Korea opened one of its ports to Japan, and 1910 when it was annexed by Japanese, is called the "opening-up" or "enlightenment" period (*kaehwa ki*).

As a movement to enlighten citizens, several newspapers appeared. The first to be published was *Hansŏng Sunbo* (once in 10 days) in 1883, using only Hancha. It became *Hansŏng Weekly* in 1886, using basically a Hancha–Han'gŭl mixture. Another newspaper *The Independent (Tongnip)* was noteworthy for its use of Han'gŭl only, allowing many Koreans, regardless of their gender and social standing, to read it. It also introduced spacing between phrases to make reading easy. Its copy editor was none other than the pioneer of Han'gŭl study, Chu Si-gyŏng, who was instrumental in these innovations. The paper contained an English section as well, helping English speakers learn about Korea. It came to serve as the organ of the Independence Society. These papers, and a few others that followed them, were closed by the Japanese colonial rulers after only a few years. Short-lived as they were, these papers did much to arouse Korean people to modern ideas and nationalism.

Still on the topic of newspapers, on March 1st 1919, Koreans staged a huge anti-Japanese, pro-independence uprising with much bloodshed. After the uprising the Japanese rulers relaxed their grip on the mass media just a little and allowed two dailies, *Chosun Ilbo* and *Tong'a Ilbo*, to be published. The two are still published today as leading newspapers of S. Korea. (See fig. 12-2 showing the use of Hancha in *Chosun Ilbo* between 1920 and 1990.)

During the enlightenment period, some young scholars were sent abroad—mostly to Japan, America, and China—for obervation and study. One such scholar was Yu Kil-chun who studied both in Japan and America, and visited Europe as well. His travelogue published in 1895, *Observations on a Journey to the West*, was the first book written in a mixture of Hancha and Han'gŭl. As noted in "Conclusions: Streamline and Keep Hancha" (in chap. 15), its use of Hancha was heavy, by today's norm. At any rate, it introduced to Korea a few hundred new words—e.g., *kwahak* ('science') and *pakmulgwan* ('museum')—coined by the Chinese or Japanese for modern Western concepts and objects.

Yu also wrote *Grammar of Korean*, the first modern work on the subject, which was followed by *A Korean Grammar* and *A Phonology of Korean* by the Han'gŭl scholar Chu Si-gyŏng.

In the early 20th century, so-called "new novels" were written in a modern style that used Han'gŭl only (with occasional Hancha enclosed in parentheses) and that closely reflected contemporary speech. They could be read for pleasure by ordinary people. The first new novel is considered to be Yi In-jik's *Tears of Blood (Hyŏl ŭi Nu)* serialized in 1906 in a newspaper, and the first long novel is Yi Kwang-su's *The Heartless (Mujŏng)*, serialized in 1917 in another newspaper. They described protagonists who rebelled against feudal social order and championed nationalism and modernization. The new novels ushered in the modern Korean literature.

In the same period, some translation dictionaries such as Korean–French and Korean–English were published, and a few English books (e.g., *Pilgrim's Progress, Gulliver's Travels,* and *Robinson Crusoe*) were translated into Korean. The Bible, too, was translated into Korean, especially between 1900 and 1905, when it was translated officially and definitively by a multi-denominational committee. A few books on Korea were written in European languages. Two examples are *A Forbidden Land: Voyage to Corea* by Ernst Oppert, first in German and then in English, and *The Hermit Nation* by W. E. Griffis.

Today the publishing industry in S. Korea is thriving, printing close to 30,000 titles (first printing only) in 1994, an increase of 3,000 titles from 1993. It publishes also thousands of different periodicals. Reflecting the Korean passion for education, home study books and children's books accounted for over 70% of the copies sold. Books, often in inexpensive paperback form, and magazines are sold at numerous book stores, some located at major subway stations. Kyobo Book Center in Seoul claims to be the largest bookstore in the world. (In Toronto, Canada, one bookstore carries the name "The World's Biggest Bookstore.")

In 1992 S. Korea had over 100 dailies, including 2 English papers and 1 Chinese paper. The number of daily newspapers per 1,000 people in 1988–1990 was 280 in S. Korea, compared to 632 in Hong Kong, 587 in Japan, 250 in the United States, and 30 in China (*The Globe and Mail,* Jan. 1, 1994).

There are over 1,000 national, public, university, school, and special libraries throughout S. Korea, possessing collectively close to 49 million books. There are not yet neighborhood libraries in urban centers, such as are found in N. America. In small villages, however, there are libraries for farmers and fishermen. These village libraries, together with the "new community" movements, radio and television, newspapers, have contributed to narrowing the once vast cultural and literacy gap between the urban and rural areas.

N. Korea has its own publishing industry. Its major newspaper is the *The Labor Daily (Rodong Simmun)*, which is bought by 30% of the households. It publishes books on their "beloved" leader Kim Il Sung, as well as on diverse topics such as the Korean language and literature. Some non-political N. Korean books, especially those on the Korean language and scripts, are reproduced in S. Korea, in an effort to keep abreast with the affairs of N. Korea.

Mass Literacy

Now that we have surveyed historically Korea's progress in education and publication, let us move on to mass literacy, i.e., functional literacy for the entire population of a nation.

For hundreds of years literacy in Korea was confined to a small elite class who had the time and money needed to study the difficult Confucian classics to prepare for civil service exams. They were all male. In Korea, as in China, ignorance in women was considered virtue, and so females did not receive formal education. But some females in literate households learned to read and write Han'gŭl, if not Hancha. Some courtesans who had to entertain male literati were literate enough to read and compose poems.

Even in modern times only a few Korean children were educated in school, as described in "Modern Education." As a result, most Koreans were illiterate when Japan annexed Korea in 1910. During the Japanese rule, Korean nationalists campaigned to eradicate illiteracy and at the same time to imbue their rural brethren with nationalism and modern ideas. In 1922 Christian nationalists organized Sunday schools and Bible schools to teach reading and writing to over 540,000 children who were otherwise unable to attend school. Korean newspapers launched campaigns against illiteracy, one in 1929 with the slogan, "We must learn in order to survive," and another in 1931 with the slogan "Go among the people," sending thousands of students to villages as teachers. Thanks to these campaigns, over 80,000 men and women learned to read and write. These numbers may appear impressive but they were only a drop in the ocean, considering that the Korean population in 1935 was 22,208,000. All of these campaigns were stopped by the Japanese in 1934 (Nahm 1990).

When Korea was liberated from the Japanese rule in 1945, the rate of illiteracy was as high as 78%; in S. Korea it had decreased to 4% in 1958, and it decreased further to 0.8% in 1973, and to 0.5% in 1975 (Ministry of Education 1991). Today South Korea can claim close to 100% literacy in Han'gŭl, thanks to almost 9 years of universal compulsory education. If there are illiterates, they are likely to be found among old females in rural areas. Literacy in Hancha, however, is limited. S. Koreans with only primary school education do not know Hancha. Those with middle school education have ideally learned 900 Hancha, and those with high school education have learned an additional 900 Hancha. But the students' mastery of the 1,800 Hancha is not strong, perhaps because the students do not learn them thoroughly and do not see them often in their reading.

To attain high-level literacy, and to broaden their intellectual and commercial horizons, Koreans may need to know some English, the preeminent international language. Since most Koreans nowadays go to secondary school where English is an important school subject, there is no reason why they should not be able to attain this high-level literacy. But despite much time and effort spent on learning English, most Koreans hardly speak it, perhaps because of inadequate teaching and lack of opportunity. At most they may be able to listen to simple speech and read simple text. Worse, soon after leaving school, they quickly forget what little English they learned at school.

What about literacy in North Korea? Right after liberation in 1945, the government set up in every community literacy courses that adults could follow each evening after work, employing as teachers vacationing secondary-school and college students. As a result of the campaign, illiteracy was virtually eliminated by 1949. While some people lapsed back into illiteracy during the 3-year Korean War, a renewed campaign after the war once again wiped out adult illiteracy. By 1976 the government had improved all adults' educational achievement to the equivalent of middle-school graduation and had set a new goal of raising it to that of high-school graduation. In their knowledge of Hancha, however, N. Koreans appear to be even less competent than S.

Koreans, mainly because they do not see Hancha in ordinary reading material even after learning Hancha in secondary schools.

The Korean phonetic script, Han'gŭl, is easy to master. Mass literacy using this script is not difficult to attain in Korea, which is small in area and which is populated by a racially and culturally homogeneous people speaking one language. The Koreans value education as a means for a better life. For similar reasons, most of the two million ethnic Koreans living in the Korean Autonomous Region in Jilin Province and elsewhere in northeastern China are literate (Lee 1986). Their literacy rate is higher than that of most of the 54 other ethnic minorities, and even higher than that of Han Chinese.

Finally, Korea is an ideal case to test whether mass literacy is a prerequisite to **and** a guarantee for economic success. Compare South Korea, which has achieved both mass literacy and economic success, to North Korea, which has achieved mass literacy but not economic success. N. Korea shares a high rate of literacy with other former Communist countries, such as Hungary and Poland. Obviously for economic success, mass literacy must be accompanied by a favorable political–economic system.

Part II: Summary and Conclusions

The Korean peninsula is divided into two nations with radically different political–economic systems: S. Korea has a multi-party democracy with a market economy, while N. Korea has a Communist regime with a command economy. Yet the two Koreas share the same language, scripts, and historical culture.

The Korean language has a rich inventory of 31 phonemes, which combine to form thousands of syllables which may be of a variety of forms, such as V (vowel alone), CV (consonant–vowel), CVC, or CVCC. Its vocabulary contains native, Sino-Korean, and European loan words. Native words use all the phonemes and syllables of the Korean language, whereas S-K words, which are Chinese words that were adopted into Korean long ago, use only about 440 of the Korean syllables. Native words tend to be everyday words that represent concrete meanings, whereas S-K words tend to be learned words that represent abstract meanings. Native words are written only in the Korean phonetic script, Han'gŭl, whereas S-K words can be written in either Han'gŭl or Chinese characters, Hancha. European loan words are either translated into S-K words or transcribed phonetically in Han'gŭl.

Hancha came to Korea over 2000 years ago and began to be used seriously about 1700 years ago. Initially they were used to transcribe phonetically the Korean names of people and places. Later they were used to write content words of all kinds, S-K or native, as well as native grammatical morphemes. Hancha were ill-suited for such uses. Today, they are used rationally and sparingly, perhaps too sparingly, to represent some Sino-Korean words.

The phonetic script Han'gŭl was invented in the mid-15th century by King Sejong. It is an alphabet in that each of its letters represents a Korean phoneme. As an alphabet, it has a few unique features. For example, simple consonant and vowel letters are used as basic elements to build increasingly complex letters that code other consonants and vowels having added articulatory features. And consonant letters and vowel letters are distinctively shaped. Han'gŭl is unique also in that it is used like a syllabary: two or more alphabetic letters are packaged into a syllable block, which can be a CV, CVC, or CVCC (the final -C or -CC being written underneath the initial CV-, and a null consonant being used if the syllable starts with a vowel). The syllable block is a reading and teaching unit. By packaging its 24 alphabetic letters, Han'gŭl could generate over 12,800 syllable blocks, of which about 2,000 are actually used.

Han'gŭl can be taught efficiently using the basic syllable chart, which arranges 10 basic vowel letters in rows and 14 basic consonant letters in columns to generate 140 CV syllable blocks. The chart can be expanded to include the final consonant letter or letter cluster under some of the CV blocks. Learning simple CV syllable blocks is quick, but learning complex blocks, such as CVCCs, and spelling rules, takes additional time.

Han'gŭl is a phonetic script par excellence, and by and large a word is spelled as it sounds, and read as it is spelled. Even when Korean words change their sounds in different phonetic contexts and dialects, they are spelled in one standard way. The standardized spelling ensures that a word appears in one invariant visual shape, allowing easy recognition. It provides a contrast to romanized spelling, which spells Korean words as they sound, to help foreigners pronounce them.

Korean text can be written using Han'gŭl alone, as is done in N. Korea and sometimes in S. Korea. But text should be easier to read, if Hancha are used to write certain S-K words such as infrequent words, idioms, technical terms, abbreviations, names of people or places, and homophones, while Han'gŭl is used to write grammatical morphemes, native content words, as well as some frequent S-K words and European loan words.

In S. Korea 1,800 Hancha are designated as educational, to be taught in secondary schools. They are not too difficult to learn, because their number is relatively small, and because each of them is given only one Um/Chinese reading. In N. Korea 3,000 Hancha are taught in secondary and post-secondary schools, but are not used in everyday writing and reading. It is more efficient to learn well a small number—say, 1,500—of judiciously selected Hancha and use them constantly than to learn a large number of Hancha and use them sparingly or not at all.

For over 1000 years education and literacy in Korea were confined to a small elite class who had time and money to study for civil service exams, which tested knowledge of the Confucian classics. In a political and social reform of 1894, the all-Hancha writing system was replaced by Hancha–Han'gŭl mixed writing, the civil-service exam system was abolished, and the educational system began to be modernized. But in 1910 Korea fell under Japanese rule, and its education languished for 36 years until the end of World War II.

After the 1945 liberation, both South and North Korean governments have made concerted efforts to provide education to all their citizens, male and female, in both urban and rural areas. Today, compulsory education is universal and lasts almost 9 years in S. Korea and 11 years in N. Korea. Consequently, virtually all Koreans have received some education and are literate in Han'gŭl, if not necessarily in Hancha.

Such mass literacy has contributed to rapid industrialization and prosperity in S. Korea but has not had such a happy effect in N. Korea, where Communism and a command economy get in the way of economic success.

Bibliography for Part II

The original authors' English translations and romanized spellings are used when available.

In English

Baek Eung-jin. *Modern Korean syntax*. Seoul: Canadian Society for Korean Linguistics and Language Teaching, 1984. It describes Korean syntax for English-speakers learning Korean.

Bouwhuis, D. G. *Visual recognition of words*. Doctoral dissertation, Eindhoven, Netherlands: Institute for Perception Research, 1979.

Ch'oe Yongho. Culture. In Lee H. Peter (Ed.) *Sourcebook of Korean civilization*. New York: Columbia University Press, 1993.

Chung W. L. Hangeul and computing. In V. H. Mair and Y.-Q. Liu (Eds.) *Characters and computers*. Amsterdam: IOS Press, 1991.

Coulmas, Florian. *The writing systems of the world*. See Chapter 1.

Diringer, D. *The alphabet: A key to history of mankind*. See Chapter 1.

Eckert, Carter J., Lee Ki-baik, Lew Young Ick, Robinson, Michael, and Wagner, Edward W. *Korea old and new: A history*. Seoul: Ilchogak for the Korea Institute, Harvard University, 1990. As a Koren history from its Paleolithic beginning to 1990, it is authoritative and up-to-date. Except a few maps, it contains no pictures and graphs.

Fisher, J. E. *Democracy and mission education in Korea*. New York: Teachers' College, Columbia University, 1928.

Gelb, I. J. *A study of writing*. See Chapter 1.

Grant, Bruce. *A guide to Korean characters*. Elizabeth, N.J. and Seoul: Hollym International, 1979. It gives a scanty description of Han'gŭl but detailed description of Hancha, including a list of 1,800 official Hancha arranged according to Han'gŭl order.

Haber, L. R., Haber, R. N., and Furlin, K. R. Word length and word shape as sources of information in reading. *Reading Research Quarterly*, 1983, *18*, 165–189.

Hahn Gap-soo. *Han'gŭl*. Seoul: Korea Overseas Information Service, 1981. This thin volume, written by the director of the Korean Language Research Society, gives a quick introduction to the Koran phonetic script.

(A) *handbook of Korea*. Seoul: Korea Overseas Information Service, 1993. This handsome book with many pictures gives information on such areas as history, language, and education of S. Korea.

Hope, E. R. Letter shapes in the Korean Onmun and Mongol hP'ags-pa alphabets. *Orient*, 1957, *10*, 150-159.

Jensen, H. *Sign, symbol and script*. See Chapter 1.

Kang T.-J., Chong J.-Y., and Taylor, I. Reading in all-Hangul or Hangul–Kanji mixed scripts. In Taylor, I. and Taylor, M.M. *The psychology of reading*. See Part I.

Kim J. Ch.-u. *Pictorial Sino-Korean characters (Fun with Hancha)*. Elizabeth, New Jersey and Seoul: Hollym International, 1987. It introduces Hancha to English speakers.

Kim Jin-p'yŏng. The letterforms of Han'gŭl: Its origin and process of transformation. In Korean National Commission for UNESCO (Ed.) *The Korean language*. Arch Cape, Oregon: Pace International Research, 1983.

Kim Pyong-won. Reading and reading instruction in Korea: Past and present. In D. Feitelson (Ed.) *Mother tongue or second language?* Newark, Del.: International Reading Association, 1979.

Kim Ransoo. *Korean education in research perspective*. Seoul: Jung Gak, 1984.

Korea annual. Seoul: Yonhap News Agency, 1994. This handbook on Korea provides up-to-date information.

Korean National Commision for UNESCO (Ed.) *The Korean language*. Oregon: Arch Cape, Pace International Research, 1983. It introduces the Korean language and writing to English speakers.

Ledyard, Gari, K. *The Korean language reform of 1446: The origin, background, and early history of the Korean alphabet*. Michigan, Ann Arbor: University of Microfilms International. A Ph.D. thesis, University of California, Berkeley, 1966. An exhaustive study on Han'gŭl's origin, especially on its debt or non-debt to Paspa script.

Lee Chae-Jin. *China's Korean minority: the politics of ethnic education*. Boulder: Westview Press, 1986. It describes 2 million Koreans in China who run a full Korean educational system, with a high literacy rate.

Lee Ki-baik (translations into English by E. W. Wagner). *A new history of Korea*. Cambridge. Mass: Harvard University Press, 1984. A readable introduction to Korean history from its hazy beginning 4000 years ago to the 1960s.

Liberman, I. Y., Shankweiler, D., Fischer, F. W., and Carter, B. Explicit syllable and phoneme segmentation in the young child. *Journal of Experimental Child Psychology*, 1974, *18*, 201–212.

Martin, Samuel E. Nonalphabetic writing systems: Some observations. In J. F. Kavanagh and I. G. Mattingly (Eds.), *Language by ear and by eye*. Cambridge, Mass.: MIT Press, 1972.

Martin, Samuel E. and Lee Young-Sook C. *Beginning Korean*. New Haven: Yale University Press, 1969.

McCune, G. A. and Reischauer, E. O. The Romanization of the Korean language, based upon its phonetic structure. *Transactions of the Korean Branch of the Royal Asiatic Society*. Seoul, 1939, vol. 29.

Ministry of Education, S. Korea. *Education in Korea: 1989–1990*. Seoul: National Institute of Educational Research and Training, 1991. The booklet traces the history of Korean education up to 1990. Its many tables and figures are useful.

Nahm, Andrew C. *Korea, tradition and transformation*. Elizabeth, N.J. and Seoul: Hollym International, 1988. Korean history from its beginning to the 1980s. Its useful "Chronology" at the end of the book lists significant events and their dates.

Payne, Philip Barton. *LaserKOREAN: User's manual*. Edmonds, WA: Linguistic Software, 1991.

Rayner, Keith and Pollatsek, Alexander. *The psychology of reading*. 1989. See Part I.

Read, C., Zhang Y.-F., Nie H.-Y., and Ding B.-Q. The ability to manipulate speech sounds depends on knowing alphabetic writing. *Cognition*, 1986, *24*, 31–44.

Sampson, Geoffrey. *Wring systems*. Calif.: Stanford University Press, 1985. A linguist describes a variety of writing systems of the world.

Simpson, Greg, B. and Kang Hyewon. The flexibile use of phonological information in word recognition in Korean. *Journal of Memory and Language*, 1994, *33*, 319–331.

Taylor, Insup. The Korean writing system: An alphabet? A syllabary? A logography? In P. A. Kolers, M. E. Wrolstad, and H. Bouma (Eds.), *Visible language 2*. New York: Plenum Press, 1980.

Taylor, Insup and Park Kwonsaeng. Differential processing of content words and function words: Chinese characters and phonetic scripts. In I. Taylor and D. R. Olson (Eds.) *Scripts and literacy: Reading and learning to read in alphabets, syllabaries, and Chinese characters*. The Netherlands: Kluwer Academic, 1995.

In Korean (or Japanese, or Chinese)

Amano K. Formation of the act of analyzing phonemic structure of words and its relation to learning Japanese syllabic characters (Kanamoji). *Japanese Journal of Educational Psychology*, 1970, *18*, 76–89 (in Japanese).

An Pyŏng-hi. Policies and theories on Hancha problems. See Lee Ki-moon, An Pyŏng-hi, Kang Sin-hang, and four others.

Chang Chi-yŏng and Chang Se-kyŏng. *Idu sajŏn (A dictionary of Idu)*. Seoul: Tosŏ Publishing Co. 1991. It gives a brief history of Idu and defines grammatical morphemes in Idu.

Cho Se-yong. *Hanchaŏge kihwaŏ yŏngu (Research on Sino-Korean words nativized)*. Seoul: Kodae Minjok Munhwa Yŏnguso, 1991. Some Korean "native" words are Sino-Korean words that have undergone sound changes.

Ch'oe Hyon-sop. Letter education in the early reading stage. In *Seminar for reforming educational process of national language and Chinese study*. Seoul, 1986, 157–177.

Hangugŏ Omun Yŏnguhoe (Research Center for Spoken and Written Korean Language; compiled). *Han'gŭl kwa Hancha (Han'gŭl and Hancha)*. Seoul: Ilchogak 1985. A collection of journal articles and newspaper editorials that argue, passionately, for the use of Hancha.

Han'gŭl 2.0 kinŭng sŏlmyŏngsŏ (Han'gŭl 2.0 manual). Seoul: Han'gŭl kwa cŏmpyut'ŏ, 1992.

Hatori Reiko. History of Hancha education in North Korea. In Kim Min-su (Ed.) *Pukhan ŭi Chosŏn'ŏ yŏngusa: 1945–1990 (History of Korean language research in N. Korea)*. Seoul: Nokchin Publishing, 1991.

Hŏ Ung. *Han'gŭl kwa minjok munhwa (Han'gŭl and people's culture)*. Seoul: Commemoration of King Sejong, 1974/1985. This small volume explains the structure and history of Han'gŭl.

Kang Sin-hang. *Hunmin Chŏng'ŭm (Correct sounds)*. Seoul: Sinkumunsa, 1974. This thin volume presents the *Hunmin Chŏng'ŭm* and the *Explanations and Examples of Hunmin Chŏng'ŭm* with annotations and explanations.

Kang Sin-hang. Realities and acceptance policies of foreign words. See Lee Ki-moon, An Pyŏng-hi, Kang Sin-hang, and four others.

Kang Sin-hang. *Hunmin Chŏng'ŭm yŏngu (Research on the Correct sounds)*. Seoul: Sŏnggyun'gwan University Press, 1990. It gives a detailed account of the Hunmin Chŏng'ŭm and cultural background surrounding it.

Kim Chong-t'aek. Han'gŭl seen from a theory of writing systems. In Kim Min-su et al. (Eds.) *Kugŏ wa minjok munhwa (National language and culture)*. Seoul: Chimmundang, 1984.

Kim Chong-t'aek. *Kugŏ ŏhŭiron (Theory of the Korean vocabulary)*. Seoul: T'ab Publication, 1992. Korean vocabulary—native, Sino-Korean, and foreign—is historically described.

Kim Hwe-bo. *Han'gŭl mal ssuki (Spelling of Han'gŭl words)*. Seoul: Chongno Sŏjŏk, 1985. A useful handbook on various aspects of writing the Korean language, including Han'gŭl spelling, grammar, lists of compound words, and Hancha words that can be converted into Han'gŭl words.

Kim I-jong. *Kugŏkwa kyoyuk iron kwa silje (Education of the national language: theory and practice)*. Seoul: Kyoyuk Kwahaksa, 1992. It describes in detail education of the Korean language in the past and present.

Kim Min-su. *Pukhan ŭi kugŏ yŏngu (Research on the Korean language in North Korea)*. Seoul: Koryŏ University Press, 1985. It provides information on the educational system and teaching of the Korean language in North Korea.

Kim Min-su. Our names. In Kim Min-su et al. (Eds.) *Kugŏ wa minjok munhwa (National language and culture)*. Seoul: Chimmundang, 1984.

Kim Min-su. *Sin kugŏ haksa (New history of the Korean language)*. Seoul: Ilchogak, 1980. It gives history of the Korean language study from the ancient times to the present day. It is replete with footnotes, which in fact carry important information.

Lee Ki-moon. *Kugŏsa kaesŏl (An outline of Korean language history)*. Seoul: Minjung Sŏgwan, 1972. In tracing the history of Korean language, both spoken and written, it gives a good discussion of Hancha use in the past and of the creation of Han'gŭl.

Lee Ki-moon. Personal communication that comments on Part II of this book, Sept. 17, 1992.

Lee Ki-moon, An Pyŏng-hi, Kang Sin-hang, and four others. *Hankugŏmun ŭi chemunje (Various problems of Korean text)*. Seoul: Ilchisa, 1983. It deals with problems such as Han'gŭl spelling; education of, and policies on, Hancha; foreign words; and new words.

Lee Sung-u. *Hanguk'in ŭi sŏngmyŏng (Names of Korean people)*. Seoul: Ch'angjosa, 1977. It gives the history and variety of Korean family names and given names.

Ministry of Education. *Kugŏ sunhwa cheryŏ (Materials for purifying the national language)*. Seoul: National Language Institute, 1983. This booklet lists S-K words, European words, and Japanese words that should be, might be, or can be, replaced by native words.

Ministry of Education. *Han'gŭl matchumpŏp kyujŏng (Han'gŭl spelling rules)*. Seoul: National Language Institute, 1988. It is a thin but authoritative booklet on Han'gŭl spelling in S. Korea.

Mun Yong-rin. Educational system and policy. In Ch'oe Myŏng (Ed.) *Pukhan kaeron (Outline of North Korea)*. Seoul: Ulyu Munhwasa 1990.

Nakajima Mineo. Modern culture and Kanji culture in East Asia. In S. Nakanishi and N. Yamamoto (Eds.) *Kanji bunka o kangaeru (Thinking of Kanji culture)*. Tokyo: Taishukan, 1991. (in Japanese)

Nam Kwang-u. Theory on mixed use of the native script and Hancha. In Kim Min-su et al. (Eds.) *Kugŏ wa minjok munhwa (National language and culture)*. Seoul: Chimmundang, 1984.

New age Korean language dicationary (Sae kugŏ chajŏn). Seoul: Kyohaksa, 1989. At its end it lists 2,600 Hancha.

Noh Myeong-wan, Hwang I.-C, Park Y.-S., and Kim B.-W. A study on the development of adults' speed reading program. *Research Bulletin*, 1977, *10*, No. 97, Korean Institute for Research in the Behavioral Sciences.

Noh Myeong-wan, Park Yŏng-mok, and Kwon Kyong-ŏn. *Kugŏkwa kyoyuknon (Theory of national language education)*. Seoul: Kab'ul Ch'ulp'ansa, 1988. One of its chapters provides a background to the newly adopted primary-school textbooks for the Korean language.

O Ji-ho. Schoolchildren's knowledge of the national language. *Omun Yŏngu*, 1973, 1.

Ogina Tsunao, Kim Dong-jun, Umeda Hiroyuki, Rah Sung-sook, and Ro Hyun-song. A comparative study of Japanese and Korean honorific usage based upon the social status of the addressee. *Chōsen Gakuho*, July 1990, vol. 136. (In Japanese)

Park Pyong-ch'ae. *Kugŏ paltalsa (Developmental history of the national language)*. Seoul: Seyongsa, 1990. It traces the changes in the Korean language and its writing system from the ancient times to the present.

Park Young-mok and Shon Young-ai. *The influence of the Korean orthographic systems on the processes of reading: Han'gŭl system vs Han'gŭl with Hancha system*. Institute of Korean Educational Development, 1990.

Shim Jae-Kee. *Koyohan ach'im, nunbusin haetsal (Calm morning, blinding sun)*. Seoul: Chimmundang, 1993. A collection of delightful essays on the Korean language.

Shim Jae-Kee. Hidden compound words in Korean. *Korean Studies in Canada*, 1995, vol. 3 (Center for Korean Studies, University of Toronto).

Sim Kyŏng-ho. Education of Hancha and Chinese text in North Korea. In Ko Yŏng-kŭn (Ed.). *Pukhan ŭi mal kwa kŭl (N. Korea's language and writing)*. Seoul: Ulyu Munhwasa, 1989 and 1990. A good description of language policies and Hancha teaching in N. Korea.

Sin Ch'ang-sun. *Kugŏ chŏngsŏbŏp yŏngu (Research on orthography of the national language)*. Seoul: Chimmundang, 1992. It critically examines Han'gŭl spelling rules and advocates passionately the use of Hancha.

Sin Ch'ang-sun, Chi Ch'un-su, Yi In-sŏp, and Kim Chung-chin. *Kugŏ p'yokipŏp ŭi chŏnkae wa kŏmt'o (Development and examination of the method of writing the national language)*. Seoul: The Academy of Korean Studies, 1992. This book on Hancha use stands out among recent books for its generous use of Hancha.

Social Science Publication (of Noth Korea). *Chosŏnmal kyupŏmjip (Korean spelling rules)*, 1988. Han'gŭl spelling in N. Korea is the same as that in S. Korea in broad outline but differs in details (also Seoul: T'ap Publications, 1989).

Tong'a Ilbo Sa. *Hyŏndae yong'ŏ sajŏn (Dictionary of terms for current affairs)*. Seoul: Tong'a Daily, 1987. It defines 3,000 terms, which are mostly Sino-Korean, European, and hybrids of the two. Native Korean terms are scarce.

Wŏn Kwang-ho. *Igŏsi Han'gŭl ida (This is Han'gŭl)*. Seoul: Samchungdang, 1987. He tabulates all possible Han'gŭl syllable blocks (about 12,800) and found that 1,832 of them are actually used.

Yi Hŭi-sŭng. *Kugŏ taesajŏn (Great dictionary of the national language)*. 1961.

Yi Hyŏn-hui and Kong Yong-yŏng. *Hanguk munhwa wa yŏksa (Culture and history of Korea)*. Seoul: Yŏngsŏl Publishing Co., 1993.

Yi Sŏk-chu. The change in newspaper writing style. Han'guk Onron Yŏn'guwŏn, 1990. Cited in Sin Ch'ang-sun, et al, 1992, above.

Yi Un-jŏng. *Nam-puk Han ŏmun kyubop ŏttŏk'e tarŭnga (How do S. and N. Korean language rules differ)*. Seoul: Kugŏ Munhwasa, 1992. A mini-dictionary of words that replace S-K words in two Koreas.

Yi Ung-baek. *Sok Kugŏ kyoyuksa yŏngu (Research on history of national language education, sequel)*. Seoul: Singu Munhwasa, 1988.

Yi Yun-p'yo. History of North Korea's language purification. In Kim Min-su (Ed.) *Pukhan ŭi Chosŏn'ŏ yŏngusa 1945–1990 (History of Korean language research in North Korea)*. Seoul: Nokchin Publishing, 1991.

Zhongguo minzu guwenzi tulu (The old scripts of Chinese nationalities). Compiled by Zhongguo Minzu Guwenzi Yanjiuhui, Beijing: Zhongguo Shehuixue Cubanshe, 1990. It has an excellent description of the Mongolian Paspa script. It also shows several sample texts in the script. (in Chinese)

Part III

Japanese

The complex Japanese language and its writing system are inventions of the devil, designed to prevent the spread of Gospel.

Attributed to Francis Xavier (1506–1552), Spanish Jesuit missionary in Japan

There can be no doubt, ... that the Japanese worker, the product of the Japanese educational system, is an extraordinarily hard-working person, strongly oriented to quality work, ... and superbly educated with the [literacy and numeracy] skills he needs for his job.

former U.S. ambassador to Japan, Edwin Reischauer, in Duke (1986: xvii)

Japan and Japanese

Japan is a chain of four main islands and numerous smaller islands in the Pacific Ocean, off the eastern edge of East Asia (map fig. 1-1). The largest island is Honshu, which contains the capital Tokyo as well as other large cities such as Osaka and Kyoto. The land area of Japan, 377,835 sq km, is slightly smaller than California, one of the states of the United States. Because of its mountains and forests, only a little over one tenth of its already small land is arable, yet its population, about 125 million, is almost half of the US population, 261.6 million.

On its west Japan faces the giant land mass of China as well as a bridge to that land mass, the Korean peninsula. For many centuries Japan borrowed, initially by way of Korea, the Chinese writing system, thousands of Chinese words, Buddhism, Confucianism, and many other elements of Chinese culture. In modern times, as the influence of China has declined while that of the West has risen, Japan has been borrowing science and technology from the West, but it still keeps many Chinese cultural elements, including the use of Chinese characters and words.

Japan is populated basically by one ethnic group, Japanese, who speak a single language, the Japanese language. The largest ethnic minority are 700,000 Koreans, most of whom were born in Japan and speak Japanese as a mother tongue, occasionally along with Korean. Other notable ethnic minorities are Chinese and a tiny group of aborigines, Ainu speakers. The Ainu are confined to the northern island of Hokkaidō, and are now close to extinction as a separate group through intermarriage with the Japanese over the centuries. Ainu is described as a language-isolate, as its origin and relation to other languages are not clearly known. Outside Japan, about 250,000 ethnic Japanese live in such S. American nations as Brazil and such N. American nations as the United States, especially Hawaii. Some live outside Japan temporarily for business. Wherever they may live, ethnic Japanese tend to maintain Japanese schools and culture.

Our discussion of writing begins with the Yamato court, which consolidated its sovereign rule between AD c. 350 and 710. The period is called also Kofun ('old tomb'), because objects were buried with the dead in tomb mounds. After the Yamato court, Japanese history is divided into numerous eras or periods, each associated with a different capital city (e.g., Nara; Heian, which is now Kyoto), a part of Kyoto (Muromachi), a shōgun (Tokugawa), or an emperor (e.g., Meiji, Shōwa, or Heisei).

During the Meiji era Japan modernized itself by absorbing many Western ideas and institutions. During the Shōwa era, Japan was defeated in World War II, and was governed for 7 years, between 1945 and 1952, by the Occupation of the Allied Forces headed by General Douglas MacArthur. During these years major reforms were made in education and writing systems. Among the peoples of East Asia, the Japanese were the first in modern times to absorb Western culture and technology, and the first to become a military power and then an economic superpower.

Table Part III-1 lists some significant events in Japanese history related to writing. These events will be elaborated in the rest of Part III.

Table Part III-1. Scripts and Literacy in Some Japanese Eras

Era	Years AD	Scripts and Literacy
Yamato	c. 350–710	Chinese characters and Buddhism introduced
Nara	710–794	First surviving history and poetry books in Kanji
Heian	794–1185	Two forms of Kana develop out of Kanji; stories in Kana
Muromachi	1333–1568	Romanization of Japanese by Jesuit missionary
Edo/Tokugawa	1600–1868	Some European words; a variety of schools teach reading
Meiji	1868–1912	Many European words; new words coined on Chinese model; 4–6 year compulsory education; limit number of Kanji; Kana–Kanji mix common; Hepburn romanization
Shōwa	1926–1989	Lists of official Kanji; 9-year compulsory education; 12 -year schooling common; *manga* ('comics') and *juku* ('cram schools') become popular
Heisei	1989–	Additional Kanji for education and names; no school on one Sataurday

17

Japanese Language

Before discussing the Japanese writing system, it is necessary to learn a little about the Japanese language, sometimes in relation to Chinese, Korean, and English. Linguistically, Japanese is unrelated to Chinese; it is believed to be related to Korean, yet it is similar to Korean only in syntax, not in speech sounds and native vocabulary. Despite the linguistic differences, Japanese, like Korean, has borrowed many thousands of words and characters from Chinese.

The Japanese language is spoken by virtually all the people—regardless of their ethnic origin—living in Japan and by some of the quarter million ethnic Japanese living outside Japan. In its number of speakers, about 125 million, it ranks the 6th among languages of the world, after Chinese, English, Russian, Hindi, and Spanish. The Japanese language is now taught in some—but alas, not enough—schools around the world, particularly in the Asian nations of Korea and China. It has replaced a European language as the favored foreign language taught in schools in Australia. It is beginning to be taught in some schools in the Pacific Rim regions of the United States and Canada.

The Japanese language has many different dialects, most of which are mutually intelligible, except between those spoken in regions widely separated geographically. The dialect least intelligible to most Japanese is spoken in the Ryukyu Islands, a string of 60 tiny islands lying between Japan and Taiwan in the west Pacific Ocean. Even among these islands different dialects are spoken, as indicated in the saying,

Mijinu kawaree kutōba kawayun (Ryukyu dialect)
Mizuga kawareba kotobaga kawaru (standard)
'When water (island) changes, speech changes'.

The two main dialects of the Japanese language are the eastern dialect, Kantō, which includes the Tokyo dialect, and the western dialect, Kansai, which includes the Osaka and Kyoto dialects. The following two examples show how the two dialects differ: *katta* (east) vs *kōta* (west; 'bought'); *shinai* (east) vs *shiyahen* (west; 'not do'). The eastern dialect, especially the variety spoken by cultured Tokyo residents, is more or less the standard language, which today is understood by almost all Japanese, including those on the Ryukyu Islands, thanks to spread of education, mass communication, and transportation. Standard Japanese is discussed in this book.

Speech Sounds, Syllables, and Moras

The Japanese language uses the following inventory of speech sounds or phonemes (Shibatani 1990).

5 vowels: a, e, i, o, u
16 consonants: p, t, k, b, d, g, s, h, z, j, r, m, n, w, N, Q

The vowels are pronounced like Spanish or Italian vowels. For example, the vowels *a, i,* and *o* are pronounced like those in the Italian word *piano*. All Japanese vowels can be pronounced either short or long, sometimes affecting the meaning, as in *to* ('door') vs *tō* ('ten'), and sometimes without affecting the meaning, as in *sayo(o)nara* ('goodbye').

The first 14 consonants have sound values similar to the most common, regular forms of their English counterparts (chap. 1). For example, *g* is as in *get* rather than in *gem*. Japanese consonants can occur only at the initial positions of syllables, as in *pe* and *ta*, except for the two sounds at the end of the list, represented as N and Q.

The nasal N occurs only in the final position of a syllable, where it sounds like the English final *-n, -m, -ng* in different phonetic contexts: *-n* before *n, t, d; -m* before *m, p, b*; and *-ng* before *k* or *g*.

The sound symbolized by Q stands for a doubled consonant, technically called a geminate consonant; it can occur only at the medial position of a Japanese word, as in *gakkō* ('school'), in which *-kk-* is pronounced as in the English *bookkeeper* but not as in the Korean *kkae* ('sesame'). In the Japanese Kana syllabary, all doubled consonants are written with the same syllable sign つ written small, independently of which consonant—*k, t, s,* and *p*—is doubled; in romanization, however, four different doubled letters are used, as shown in the following four words.

がっこう　*gakkō* ('school')
いったい　*ittai* ('generally')
いっせい　*issei* ('generation')
はっぱ　*happa* ('leaf')

The 5 vowels and the 16 consonants add up to 21 phonemes, which is about half the number of phonomes used in English. The Japanese sound system lacks many sounds used in English, such as the two initial sounds in *thick* and *that*, and /v/ and /l/.

Most Japanese sounds are relatively stable, in that they tend not to change in different phonetic contexts; some do, perhaps for smooth articulation, much as the English suffix *-s* changes its sound in *dogs, houses,* and *eats* (/-z/, /-iz/, and /-s/, respectively). The Japanese word *kana* becomes *-gana* in a compound words such as *hiragana, furigana, okurigana,* but not in *katakana*. These different Kana will be the topics of discussion in Chapter 19 "Kana: Japanese Syllabary." In another example, the vowel *e* in *sake* ('wine') becomes *a* in the compound word *sakaya* ('wine store'). These changes in sound are reflected in Japanese phonetic writing, in contrast to English spelling convention.

The small inventory of Japanese sounds is used to produce a small inventory of extremely simple syllables. A syllable may consist of a vowel alone—any of *a, i, u, e, o*; a consonant and a vowel (CV)—or any of the 14 consonants (other than N or Q) followed by any of the 5 Vs, as in *pa, mi, ku, be, do*. Japanese does not use closed syllables that end in consonants, as in English *dog*, except when a syllable ends in -N. Nor does it use consonant clusters, such as the English *FRieND*, anywhere in a word.

Besides the two now familiar sound units, the phoneme and the syllable, the Japanese sound system uses a unit called a "mora," which is a short beat, the time to pronounce a short syllable, such as the vowel *e* or the consonant–vowel syllable *de*. That is, the time to pronounce one mora, be it *e* or *de*, is constant. A lengthened vowel, such as *ō*, or a sequence of two vowels, such as in *ie* (pronounced as two discrete vowels, *i* and then *e*), is counted as two moras. Whereas a syllable (e.g., *ka, ne*) normally includes at least one vowel, a mora need not. So, the final nasal N, called the moraic nasal, is counted as one mora. If you were to clap your hands at an even rate, you would clap four times to mark four moras while you pronounce each of the following words: *wa.ga.ma.ma* ('headstrong'), *ga.k.ko.o* ('school'), and *shi.n.bu.n* ('newspaper').

The mora is the important phonetic unit in Japanese because it is the unit of the Japanese phonetic script: Each mora is represented by one Japanese syllabary sign. The mora is also the unit used in two forms of Japanese poetry: *waka*, a 31-mora poem in five lines of 5-7-5-7-7 moras per line, and *haiku*, a 17-mora poem in three lines of 5-7-5, shown here.

Shi zu ka sa ya	Such quiet!
I wa ni shi mi ko mu	A cicada's cry
se mi no ko e	penetrates the rocks.
[Bashō, 1644–1694]	

In most cases, as in the above *haiku*, moras match syllables: Sounds such as *a, ka, de, ro* are one item each whether counted in syllables or moras. So I will use the familiar term syllable to refer to both the syllable and the mora, unless the distinction is important.

Japanese speakers, like Chinese speakers, are far more familiar with the syllables, which are simply structured and which are the units of writing, than with the phonemes that make up the syllables. Even preschoolers can easily segment a word into syllables (Amano 1970), on the one hand, and adults have difficulty segmenting a word into phonemes, on the other. Consider a children's riddle: "What is the reverse of *kazaguruma* ('pinwheel')?" A Japanese speaker may answer, "maruguzaka," a reversal of the word in syllables rather than in phonemes. An English speaker might be more likely to say "amurugazak," reversing the sequence of phonemes.

Altogether, there are now 110 (112 in another count) different moras or syllables in Japanese, one of the smallest inventories of any major language. By comparison, the approximate numbers of syllables used in the three other languages of our interest are: 400 (or 1,300 with tones) in Chinese; 2,000 in Korean; and several thousand in English.

The simple sound system of the Japanese language has consequences, some positive and some negative, as we shall see. It gives rise to many homophones, but it can be easily represented by a simple syllabary. The simple sound system may help foreigners in learning Japanese, but it poses problems for Japanese in learning foreign languages. More relevant to this Part III, it poses a problem in writing foreign loan words for Japanese readers.

Composition of Japanese Vocabulary

The Japanese vocabulary is made up of four types of words: Japanese native, Sino-Japanese (borrowed from Chinese long ago), foreign loan (mostly European, with some Chinese words borrowed in modern times), and hybrids (Sino-Japanese or foreign word stems with Japanese endings). Chinese words that were adopted in Japan long ago (e.g., *gakkō* 'school') are treated as Sino-Japanese words, whereas the handful that were adopted in modern times (e.g., *maajan* 'mahjong') are treated as foreign loan words. Sino-Japanese words include hundreds of words coined by the Japanese on a Chinese model between the end of the 19th and the beginning of the 20th centuries when Japan was absorbing, in a large scale, such Western concepts as democracy and psychology. Such words were then borrowed by the Chinese and the Koreans ("Foreign Loan Words" in chap. 2).

Table 17-1 lists the four types of words, along with examples of each type and their relative frequencies. The data for 1891, 1956, and 1969 are based on dictionaries, while the 1964 data are based on a survey of 90 magazines made by the National Language Research Institute, excluding grammatical morphemes and the names of people and places. (% from Hayashi 1982: 60 and 62). In the hybrid word *aisuru*, the Sino-Japanese *ai* is joined by native *-suru*, a verb 'to do' and its ending.

Table 17-1. Four Types of Japanese Words in Dictionaries and Magazines

Category	Example	Proportion %			
		1891	1956	1969	1964
Sino-Jap	gakkō ('school')	34.7	53.6	52.9	47.5
Native	kawa ('river')	55.8	36.6	37.1	36.7
Foreign	terebi ('television')	1.4	3.5	7.8	9.8
Hybrid	ai-*suru* ('to love')	8.1	6.2	2.2	6.0

The 1891 dictionary has a large proportion of native words, perhaps because it contains old words found in books such as the 8th century anthology of poems, *Man'yōshū*. Sino-Japanese words form the majority of different words in the modern Japanese vocabulary, but native words are used more frequently. This pattern was found in the survey of 90 magazines: 54% occurrences of native words to 41% Sino-Japanese words; 3% foreign loan words and 2% hybrids. The greater use of native words than Sino-Japanese words and foreign words is even more pronounced in speech, especially in casual speech.

Foreign loan words seem to be increasing at the expense of Sino-Japanese words and native words, to judge from Table 17-1 and also from two dictionaries of new words, one published in 1960 and the other in 1980, as shown in Table 17-2 (based on M. Nomura 1988: 135).

Why and how are the four types of words—native, Sino-Japanese, foreign, and hybrid—distinguished? The four tend to be written in different scripts so that schoolchildren learn them as different, and adult writers have to distinguish them. Let us consider the four types in some detail.

Table 17-2. Composition of New Words in 1960 and 1980

	Native	Sino-Japanese	Foreign	Hybrid
1960	3.6%	40.2%	43.0%	13.2%
1980	1.9	28.8	57.6	11.7

Japanese Native vs Sino-Japanese Words

Japanese native morphemes tend to be multi-syllabic, while Sino-Japanese morphemes are often monosyllabic. The Japanese one-morpheme words *hana* ('flower') and *kuruma* ('vehicle') have two syllables and three syllables, respectively, while the Chinese morphemes for these two are one-syllable long, *hua* and *che*. The Japanese one-morpheme word *sayo(o)nara* ('goodbye') has four (or five) moras or syllables. Japanese morphemes have to be multi-syllabic to reduce the number of homophones: Since Japanese uses only around 110 different syllables, the same monosyllable would have to be used again and again for many different morphemes. Only a handful of Japanese morphemes—54 in one count—are monosyllabic, and they are sometimes repeated for easy recognition, as *me* ('eye') in *omeme* (*o-* is the deferential prefix; this word tends to be spoken to young children) and *ha* ('leaf') in *happa*, with a sound change.

Table 17-3 shows examples of Japanese monosyllabic as well as multi-syllabic words. All the items in the table are listed as word entries in a concise Japanese–English dictionary. They are all Japanese native words, except *hon*, which has a CVC syllable structure, and is of Chinese origin. Here and elsewhere the hyphens are inserted between morphemes for illustration; they are not shown in Japanese writing. "Morph" refers to the number of morphemes in a word.

Two-morpheme compound words are common among both Japanese native words and Sino-Japanese words, but three- or four-morpheme compounding is rarer and less natural in Japanese words than in Sino-Japanese words, possibly because the Japanese morphemes tend to be longer. The last two multi-morpheme native words listed in Table 17-3 were found only after flipping through several pages of a concise Japanese–English dictionary. And even though they are listed as entry words, *oshimo-osaremo-senu* (9 syllables) is rarely used, and *nanakorobiyaoki* (8 syllables) is more an idiomatic phrase than a word.

Native words are most common in words dealing with things important to Japanese daily life, such verbs as *nomu* ('to drink') and *taberu* ('ro eat') and such nouns as *ame* ('rain') and *sakana* ('fish'). Incidentally, reflecting the importance of these objects in

Table 17-3. Mono- and Multi-Syllabic Japanese Words

Morph	Syllable	Example
one	V	e (a handle) or ('feed')
	VV	ie ('house')
	CV	me ('eye')
	CVC	hon ('book')
	CVCV	kawa ('river')
	CVCVCV	kuruma ('vehicle')
	CVCVCVCV	sayonara ('goodbye')
two	CVCVCVCVCV	naka-yasumi ('recess')
	CVCVCVCVCVCV	naki-kuzureru ('break down crying')
three?	VCVCVVCVCVCVCVCV	oshimo-osaremo-senu ('acknowledged')
four	CVCVCVCVCVCVCVVCV	nana-korobi-ya-oki ('seven falls and eight rises')

Japanese life, there are several native words for different types of rain and hundreds of words for different species of fish.

Some words for different types of rain are:

harusame ('spring rain')
hisame ('cold autumn rain')
konuka'ame ('drizzling rain')
mizore ('sleet')
murasame ('shower')
naga'ame ('long spell of rain')
ōame ('downpour')
samidare ('early summer rain')
shigure ('early winter shower')
tōriame ('passing rain')
tsuyu ('spring rainy season')
yūdachi ('sudden evening shower in summer').

Sino-Japanese words are most strongly represented among words dealing with institutions, such as *gakkō* ('school'), abstract concepts, such as *jin* ('benevolence'), and scholarly disciplines, such as *gengogaku* ('linguistics'). A Sino-Japanese word can express crisply in one or two words what is expressed clumsily in several native words: the Sino-Japanese *jin* ('benevolence') used to be the native *hito (w)o megumu* ('bestow benevolence on people'), and the Sino-Japanese *jūichi* ('ten-one' or eleven) used to be the native *to (w)o amari hitotsu* ('ten with one extra'). But the Sino-Japanese *myōnichi* ('next, day' for 'tomorrow') is longer than the native *asu*.

Compared to its native counterpart, a Sino-Japanese word imparts an air of formality and respectability. A barber prefers to be called by the Sino-Japanese label *rihatsushi* ('manage, hair, master') than by the native word *tokoya-san* ('barber, shop, -san*), much as a garbage collector in the North America prefers to be called a *sanitation engineer*. (The Japanese handy suffix *-san* is attached to a person's name or profession, serving a function similar to the English titles "Mr.," "Miss," "Ms," or "Mrs.")

The proportion, status, and function of Sino-Japanese words are sometimes compared to those of Greco–Latinate words in the English vocabulary. About half of English words are of Greco–Latin origin (e.g., *psychology, perspiration, masticate)*; one third are of Anglo-Saxon *(sweat, chew);* and one tenth are foreign (e.g., Arabic *algebra,* Chinese *mahjong,* and Japanese *samurai).* Greco–Latinate words tend to be longer and less familiar than Anglo-Saxon words. However, analogies between Latinate English words and Sino-Japanese words should not be carried too far: Whereas Greek, Latin, and English belong to the same language family, Chinese and Japanese belong to two different language families; whereas Latin and English words are written in the same Roman alphabet, Sino-Japanese words are written in Chinese characters, but Japanese native words are sometimes written in a Japanese phonetic script and sometimes in Chinese characters.

European and English Loan Words

The Japanese vocabulary has been enriched, or corrupted, by an influx of European words over the past few hundred years, especially in the past few decades. Some Portuguese and Dutch words — often the names of manufactured objects — were added to the Japanese vocabulary starting in the mid-16th century, when speakers of these languages came to Japan as traders or missionaries. During the Meiji era (1868–1912), many more words were borrowed from such European languages as French in fashion and fine arts, German in philosophy and medicine, and Italian in music. After World War II, still more words were borrowed from European languages, mostly from English. Close to 90% of the European words used in Japanese were adopted in the 19th and 20th centuries (Miyazima 1992). Table 17-4 shows examples of European loan words.

Table 17-4. European Loan Words in Japanese

Language	Original	Japanese	Meaning
Portuguese	carta	karuta	playing card
Dutch	bier	biiru	beer
French	atelier	atorie	artist's studio
German	Gaze	gaaze	gauze
Italian	piano	piano	piano
English	hip	hippu	hip

Essentially the same European word is sometimes used in Japanese in differentiated meanings: Portuguese *carta* (*karuta* カルタ) for a playing card, German *Karte* (*karute* カルテ) for a card on which a physician records a patient's condition, and English *card* (*kaado* カード) for a card used in a library to record information on a book.

The proportion of European loan words in the Japanese vocabulary increased from 1.4% in 1891 to 8–10% in the 1960's (table 17-1). By the 1960's many European loan words were English. Today English loan words may form an even greater proportion of European words, because words related to the ubiquitous automobile and computer are virtually all in English, and Japanese deal with or trade with Americans more than they do with Europeans. In one count, 75% of the loan words were from English (Miyazima 1992). Because of an ever-increasing influx of such words, which can number more than 20,000, there are dictionaries devoted exclusively to them.

The other day, when I was looking in a dictionary for common Japanese native words that start with *fu-* (for reasons discussed in Chapter 22 "Learning Kanji and Kana"), I was struck by the abundance of European words, which stand out because they are written in a different script from native words. On pages 484 and 485 in Sanseido's *Daily Concise Japanese–English Dictionary* (1990), I counted 69 European — all, except the French *bourgeois*, are English — against 65 native and Sino-Japanese words combined. Such English words as フルコース *furukōsu* ('full course dinner') and プロレス *puroresu* ('professional wrestling') are unlikely to be much used, whereas such native words as 振る *furu* ('to shake, to swing') and 降る *furu* ('to fall' of snow or rain) are likely to be common. Note that the English loan words are written in angular Katakana, one form of the Japanese syllabary, while the native words are written in Kanji (Chinese character) plus curvaceous Hiragana, another form of the syllabary. Sometimes English words appear to be replacing Japanese native words. Some Japanese authors complain that when they ask in a restaurant for *ichigo*, the waitress asks back, "you mean *sutoroberi* (strawberry)?" Or when they ask for *habakari*, she asks back, "you mean *o-toire* (toilet)?"

If English speakers learning Japanese think that they already know many "English words" in the Japanese vocabulary, they are in for a rude shock. Because of the large differences in the sound systems between Japanese and English, so-called English words—e.g., *kureemu, waarudo, wōru, tsūru, sekushii, beteran, sankyū, mazaa*—are sometimes unrecognizable.[1] In transcribing European words into Japanese, the nearest Japanese sound substitutes for any sound not available in Japanese: common substitutions include *r* for /l/; *b* for /v/; *ts* for /t/; *s* for the initial sound of *thin; z* for the initial sound of *this*. Further, a consonant cluster, such as *cl-* and *-ld*, is broken up by inserting a vowel within it, and the final consonant, such as *-m* and *-l*, is made into a CV syllable by attaching a vowel after it.

Even less recognizable to English speakers are longer phrases consisting of a mixture of English words and Japanese grammatical morphemes. Here are a few masterpieces of distortion taken from Shibatani (1990: 152): *mekanikku-na dezitaru kurokku* ('mechanical digital clock') (never mind that "mechanical" cannot be "digital"); *hippu o 3 senti appu-suru* ('to up the hips by 3 centimeters') seen in an advertisement for women's undergarments, and *DERAKKUSU na PURAN wa kono KOONAA o* ('please use this corner for deluxe planning') seen in an advertisement for interior decoration (with the "English" words capitalized to help you recognize them).

English speakers' non-comprehension of Japanese–English words chagrin and frustrate Japanese too. The former American ambassador to Japan, Edwin Reischauer, commented: "It is pathetic to see the frustration of Japanese finding that English speakers cannot recognize, much less understand, many of the English words they use." Such English words—e.g., *baagenseeru* ('bargain sale') and *riaru* ('real')—are not too well understood by Japanese adults themselves, who scored only between 40 and 60 percent correct in a multiple-choice test given in 1973 by the NHK (Nippon Hōsō Kyōkai or Japan Broadcasting Corporation).

European loan words appear to be of five major kinds:

1. Words that represent European objects and concepts: *banana, arufuabetto* ('alphabet')
2. Words that represent objects and concepts that have native words: *risuto* ('list'), *rūtsu* ('root')
3. European words truncated: *masukomi* ('mass communication'), *waapuro* ('word processor')
4. European words somewhat changed in meaning: *haikara* ('high collar' → 'modish'); *waishatsu* ('white shirt' → 'dress shirt of any color'); *abekku* ('avec' French 'with' → 'boy–girl dating')
5. New words coined from existing European words: *ōeru* ('OL' for 'office lady'), *ōrudomisu* ('old miss' for 'spinster').

---

[1] The words are *claim, world, wall, tool, sexy, veteran, thank you, mother*, respectively.

Only the first two types are understandable, while the remaining three types, especially truncated ones, are hard to recognize. You probably cannot decipher the following "English" words, as my colleagues and I could not: *pasokon, mazaakon, rimokon, eakon, barikon*. The original English words are: *personal computer, mother complex, remote control, air conditioner, variable condenser*. Some *kon* words are bastards, combining Japanese words and a truncated English word, as in *namakon* ('raw concrete'). Still another *kon* word *torukon* is an abbreviation of *toruku conbaataa*, which I had to look up a dictionary of foreign words to learn that its origin is *torque converter*. The "English word" that really stumped me was *sekuhara*, which turned out to be 'sexual harassment'. What makes these Japanese–English words difficult for English speakers to understand is the fact that they are not normally truncated in English, which of course truncates or compresses some other words, such as *typo* for *typographical errors* and *TV* in North America and *telly* in the UK for *television* (*terebi* in Japanese).

An interesting Japanese–English word is *karaoke* ('singing along with a recorded accompaniment'), which consists of the Japanese word *kara* ('empty') and the truncated English word *orchestra*. Now, *karaoke* or *karaoki* has been borrowed back into English and used by English speakers who are oblivious to its partial English origin!

In earlier times, European words tended to be first translated into Sino-Japanese words (e.g., *denchi* 'electricity reservoir' for battery), but later some of them were transcribed phonetically (*batteri*). Today European words tend to be transcribed phonetically, bypassing the stage of Sino-Japanese words. (This trend in Japan is opposite from that in China; chap. 2.)

Sometimes the same concept in a foreign word and a Sino-Japanese word can have subtly different meanings. For example, *pinpon* ('ping-pong') tends to be used for an amateur sport, while the same word in Sino-Japanese *takkyū* ('table ball') is used for a professional sport. They may correspond to the English contrast of *ping-pong* and *table tennis*. Other times, a foreign word, especially when truncated, is shorter and easier to write in a phonetic script than its Sino-Japanese synonym in Chinese characters: Compare *hyakkaten* 百貨店 to *depaato* (デパート) for *department store*. For whatever reasons, when words have both Sino-Japanese and European versions, Sino-Japanese versions seem to be losing out.

The same concept can be sometimes expressed in the three types of words — native, Sino-Japanese, and European — in different situations for different effects. In general, native words have broader meanings than their loan counterparts; Sino-Japanese words suggest formality; and European words impart an air of modishness and sophistication. For example, the native *torikesi* ('cancel' or 'take back') can be applied to various kinds of cancelling, including taking back one's words; the Sino-Japanese word *kaiyaku* ('dissolution') refers to the cancellation of contracts and other formal transactions; the English loan word *kyanseru* ('cancel') is used only for the cancellation of appointments or ticket reservations (Shibatani 1990: 144). A similar phenomenon occurs in English: Compare *eatery, restaurant*, and *bistro*.

One does not have to be a linguistic purist to be alarmed by such a massive influx of European words into Japanese, especially when some of these words duplicate native and/or Sino-Japanese words, and when they are often imperfectly transcribed and understood. For example, in using *rūtsu (root)*, the writer helpfully added in parentheses its Sino-Japanese counterpart *nemoto* ('root, origin'), which is not only available but also clear in its meaning. These European words, which differ markedly in sound structure from Japanese words, are bound to distort the Japanese language and complicate its learning.

Numerals and Classifiers

Two important categories of Japanese words are numerals and classifiers, both Sino-Japanese words and native. The native numerals form a limited set, going only up to ten, while the Sino-Japanese numerals form a complete set, from one to a million, billion, and so on. (The native word *hatachi*, 'twenty', is used only in referring to an age.) In Table 17-5 the Sino-Japanese numerals are used for higher numerals, except for 14, 17, and 700, which are partly native.

Table 17-5. Japanese Native and Sino-Japanese Numerals

Number	Sino-Jap.	Native	Number	Sino-Jap.
1	ichi	hitotsu	11	jūichi
2	ni	futatsu	12	jūni
3	san	mittsu	13	jūsan
4	shi	yottsu	14	jūyon
5	go	itsutsu	15	jūgo
6	roku	muttsu	16	jūroku
7	shichi	nanatsu	17	jūnana
8	hachi	yattsu	18	jūhachi
9	kyū/ku	kokonotsu	19	jūkyu
10	jū	tō	20	nijū
			700	nanahyaku

Numerals can be used with Sino-Japanese classifiers (in uppercase), using the form,

numeral + classifier + *no* ('of') + noun, as in:
ni-HON no enpitsu ('two pencils') and
ni-HIKI no inu ('two dogs').

The classifier *-hon* is used if the noun names a cylindrical and slender object, like a pencil, a piece of chalk, or a bottle of beer, whereas *-hiki* is used if the noun names relatively small animals such as dogs, insects, and fish, but not birds or large animals, which have their own classifiers. Neither the classifier nor the noun is marked for the plural number. Japanese is like Chinese and Korean in its use of classifiers (chaps. 2 and 11), but the specific classifiers used in the three languages sometimes differ. For example, the Japanese *-hon* is pronounced in Chinese as *-ben* and is used in counting books.

Content Words and Grammatical Morphemes

Japanese words, like words of other languages, can be broadly classified as content words and grammatical morphemes (chaps. 1 and 11). Japanese content words are nouns, verbs, adjectives, and some adverbs. A noun names an object or event. Nouns form an open class, by having an unspecifiably large number of members: e.g., *mizu, kodomo, daidokoro* ('water', 'child', 'kitchen'). A Japanese noun, like a Korean noun, does not inflect for number (singular vs plural), gender (feminine vs masculine), or case (e.g., subjective, objective, or possessive). Plural number, if essential, is indicated with numerals and classifiers, as described in the preceding section.

Japanese grammatical morphemes, just like Korean ones, include postpositions after nouns and verb and adjective endings. In a sentence a noun is immediately followed by a postposition (in uppercase), which indicates the syntactic role of the noun:

> *kodomo GA mizu O nomu* ('[A] child drink[s] water').

The postpositions *ga* and *o* indicate that the first noun and the second noun play the roles of the subject and the object, respectively. Table 17-6 lists some common Japanese postpositions.

Table 17-6. Some Japanese Postpositions

Postposition	Syntactic Role
ga	marks the subject
wa	marks the topic
o	marks the direct object
de	with (by means of), in, on, at
e	to (of motion)
kara	from, after (of place or time)
made	as far as, up to, until (place or time)
ni	in, on, at, to, into
to	with (together)

Differences between the first two postpositions, *ga* and *wa*, are subtle, as can be seen in the following two sentences:

Mary ga gakusei da ('It is Mary who is a student').

Mary wa gakusei da ('Speaking of Mary, she is a student').

The Japanese word classes that change endings are verbs and adjectives. A verb describes an action or state, and relates the subject noun and the object noun in a sentence. Verbs form an open class in that they have an unspecifiably large number of members, such as *nomu, taberu,* and *furu* ('to drink', 'to eat', 'to shake/fall'). The adjective class is also open.

The endings of Japanese verbs change greatly, depending on many considerations, such as: whether an action takes place at present or took place in the past; whether a sentence is a statement or a command; whether it is addressed to a superior (polite speech) or equal (plain), as shown in Table 17-7.

Table 17-7. Some Endings of the Verb nomu *('drink')*

Sentence	Tense	Speech Level	Verb Form
Statement	present	plain	nomu
Statement	past	plain	nonda
Statement	present	polite	nomimasu
Command	present	plain	nome
Command	present	polite	nominasai

Speech level will be described in the next section. Japanese adjectives change their endings like verbs, except that they do not have the command forms.

Sentences and Plain or Polite Speech

Japanese and Korean have similar syntax. The two languages have postpositions and verb or adjective endings. The two arrange words in a sentence in such a similar way that a sentence in one language can be readily converted into another simply by replacing words from one language with those from another without disturbing their positions in the sentence. (Japanese and Korean, however, differ in their sound systems and native vocabularies.)

The Korean sentence used in Chapter 11 was ('[A] child in [the] kitchen water drink[s].'),

ai ka puŏk esŏ mul ŭl masinda.

To say the same sentence in Japanese one needs the following content words: *kodomo* ('child'), *nomu* ('drink'), *mizu* ('water'), and *daidokoro* ('kitchen'). One needs also the following three postpositions: *ga* after the subject of the sentence, *o* after the direct object, and *de* after the location word. What one does not need is a Japanese equivalent for the English articles *the/a/an* or the third-person verb ending *-s*. Now, one can arrange these content words and postpositions flexibly in any of six ways, from the most natural or common order (subject–locative–object–verb) to the least (object–subject–locative–verb):

Kodomo ga daidokoro de mizu o nomu.
Kodomo ga mizu o daidokoro de nomu.
Daidokoro de kodomo ga mizu o nomu.
Mizu o daidokoro de kodomo ga nomu.
Daidokoro de mizu o kodomo ga nomu.
Mizu o kodomo ga daidokoro de nomu.

The verb invariably comes at the end of a sentence, while the subject, the object, and the location word can vary their positions in different sentence forms, changing the nuance but not the basic message of the sentences.

The sentences given above are all statements. To change a positive statement to other forms, one merely changes the ending of the verb:

Statement: *Kodomo ga daidokoro de mizu o nomu.*
Question: *Kodomo ga daidokoro de mizu o nomuka?*
Negation: *Kodomo ga daidokoro de mizu o nomanai.*
Command: *Daidokoro de mizu o nome.*

In a Japanese sentence, as in a Korean or Chinese sentence, the subject and even the object are often not mentioned in a statement. In spite of words that seem, to an English ear, to be missing, the message is unambiguously conveyed, especially in a situational context. Take, for example,

Itadakimasu ('[I] shall eat [this food]')

announced heartily by Japanese people partaking in a meal (in lieu of saying grace at a Western dinner table). Or a dialogue in which one person asks a question,

Mieru? ('Can [you] see [it]?), which is answered,

Un, mieru ('Yeah, [I] can see [it]').

Not only in informal chat but also in formal writing, the pronouns *I* and *you* may be omitted.

Every time a Japanese sentence is produced, its level of politeness must be indicated, taking into consideration the relations of age, social position, and familiarity among the speaker/writer, the listener/reader, and any person talked about. In the use of levels of speech Japanese is similar to Korean. Generally, speakers use a polite level of speech in talking to a superior (e.g., employer, teacher, parent, elder) and a plain level of speech in talking to an inferior (e.g., child) or equal (e.g., friend). The set of sentences about a child drinking water in the preceding section are in a plain level of speech, as it is not addressed to a particular listener/reader. In modern times, the set of levels of speech has been simplified to include only two—plain and polite—rather than the old three or four.

The levels of politeness are indicated most obviously in the endings of verbs. For example, to say "This is [a] flower," the present tense verb *da* ('to be') varies in three levels, from plain, polite, to very polite:

Kore wa hana da.

Kore wa hana desu.

Kore wa hana de gozaimasu.

Even words can differ according to their levels of speech (also table 11-12). For example, plain *taberu* ('eat') changes to *meshiagaru* in respectful speech in referring to eating by the addressee and to *itadaku* in humble speech, referring to the speaker's own eating. Another linguistic device used in polite and refined speech is the deferential or honorific prefix *o-* for native words or *go-* for Sino-Japanese words that is attached to nouns as in *o-mizu* ('water') and *go-han* ('cooked rice'), and sometimes to adjectives or adverbs as in *o-hayō* ('Good morning') or verbs as in *o-kaerinasaimase* ('Welcome back home').

Speech used by women and men differs somewhat. Women tend to use more polite speech than men do, and to use the deferential prefix and the polite verb endings profusely. Compare how a command to a pupil might be given by a female teacher (1) and a male teacher (2):

1. *O-mizu o nominasai* ('Please drink water').

2. *Mizu o nome* ('Drink water').

Only men use the pronouns *boku, kimi* ('I', 'you'), while both women and men might use *watashi, anata* ('I', 'you'). In 1957 the Ministry of Education suggested that such exclusively male pronouns as *boku* and *kimi* should be restricted to intimate situations among male students, and the standard words should be *watashi* and *anata*. The present emperor, in referring to himself, now uses the ordinary word *watakushi*, instead of the old special word *chin*.

Foreigners learning Japanese find the levels of speech difficult to master. For them the best strategy is to learn and use just the polite level to everyone except to a young child, to whom they should use plain speech.

Now that we have learned something about spoken Japanese, we are ready to learn how it is written and read.

18

Kanji: Chinese Characters

Even after having discussed Chinese characters in several chapters in Part I and a few more chapters in Part II, we need a few more chapters on the topic in this Part III, because characters are used in Japanese sometimes similarly and sometimes differently from Chinese and Korean. So we ask questions such as: When and how did characters come to Japan? How many are used? What sounds are they given? How do they relate to other scripts used in Japan? How are they learned and used in text? What is their future? Answers to these questions are obtained from Nagano (1990), 12 volumes edited by Satō (1988–89), and Takebe (1979; 1991), as well as from many others cited in the text.

Scripts of Japan

The Japanese language is written and read using a variety of different scripts: Chinese characters, two forms of a syllabary, Roman letters, and Arabic numerals. All these various types of scripts originated elsewhere and have been adopted and adapted by the Japanese over hundreds of years.

The earliest time Japanese used a script was in the 4th or 5th century AD, when they adopted Chinese characters. Yet, during the Tokugawa Era (1600–1868) some Japanese nationalists, feeling embarrassed about adopting and adapting scripts from other cultures, fabricated a story that the Japanese people invented in antiquity a script of their own, called *jindai moji* ('script of the age of the gods'). There are at least a dozen varieties of such presumed indigenous Japanese scripts, all of which were "discovered" in modern times, and whose creation and use are poorly documented, as can be seen in book titles such as *The Riddle of Jindai Moji (Jindai Moji no Nazo)* (Fujiyoshi 1979) and *Excavation of Japanese Graphs (Nippon Ji no Hakkutsu)* (Sakai 1967).

One variety of *jindai moji* that is often cited in books on Japanese writing is shown in Figure 18-1. This script is clearly a copy of the Korean phonetic script, Han'gŭl, which was created by King Sejong in the mid-15th century (chap. 13). Several *jindai moji*—e.g., those for *mu* and *to*—are identical in shape and sound values to their Han'gŭl models, and others are distorted versions. Packaging a consonant letter with a vowel letter into a CV block is also modelled on Han'gŭl, except that the shapes of C letters are slightly altered, and the vowel letters are placed under the consonant letters. In another version of this Japanese script, the vowel letters are placed on the right side of the consonant letters. Han'gŭl uses one or the other CV arrangement, depending on the types of vowels.

Apparently, this and other fake scripts were taught during the height of Japan's nationalism before World War II and were cited in Japanese scholarly books on the history of writing. Today, when they are mentioned, their fake origins are pointed out,

		ㅇ	ㄱ	ㅅ	ㄷ	ㄴ	ㅎ	ㅁ		ㄹ	Hañgŭl
Consonant											
Vowel		ㅇ	ㄱ	ㅅ	ㄷ	ㄴ	ㅎ	ㅁ	ㅂ	ㄹ	ㅇ
ㅏ		a	ka	sa	ta	na	ha	ma	ya	ra	wa
ㅣ		i	ki	si	chi	ni	hi	mi		yi	ri
ㅜ		u	ku	su	tsu	nu	fu	mu		yu	ru
ㅓ		e	ke	se	te	ne	he	me		ye	re
Hañgŭl ㅗ		o	ko	so	to	no	ho	mo		yo	ro	wo

Figure 18-1. One variety of scripts of the age of gods (jindai moji), illustrating its derivation from the Korean Han'gŭl alphabetic syllabary (Table 13-4), but laid out in Japanese Kana order

usually (e.g., Kindaichi et al. 1989, *An Encyclopedia of the Japanese Language*) but not always (e.g., Sakai 1967).

The Japanese need not be embarrassed about their scripts. After all, apart from Chinese characters and the Korean phonetic script, most scripts used in the world today have been borrowed from other cultures (fig. 1-3). On the contrary, the Japanese should be proud of their two forms of syllabary called Kana, which were developed basically in Japan, albeit out of Chinese characters. Kana is a syllabary unique in the world, and is well suited to represent the Japanese language. Japanese should be proud of also their efficient use of the variety of scripts for different types of words.

Of the several different scripts used in Japan, Chinese characters, called Kanji in Japan, are the most complex and at the same time the most important. *Kanji* is the Japanese pronunciation of Chinese *Hanzi* and of Korean *Hancha*: all three terms refer to 'Chinese characters'. The term "Kanji" will be used to refer to both the singular and the plural.

Introduction and Spread of Kanji

Between the AD 4th and 7th centuries, waves of Koreans and Chinese emigrated to Japan and helped the Japanese to develop a Chinese-based culture. Many of them tutored the Japanese in arts, crafts, technology, Confucianism, Buddhism, and writing.

In early history the Koreans and the Chinese gave the Japanese some objects bearing characters. A gold seal, made in AD 57 in China and discovered in the 18th century in Japan, was inscribed with five Chinese characters, meaning "the king of the state Na of Wa [Japan], [vassal] of Han [dynasty]"(Figure 18–2). It was believed to have been given by a Chinese emperor to a Japanese envoy.

Figure 18–2. An old (AD 57) Chinese seal, bearing characters, found in Japan

Between the 2nd and 4th centuries, some bronze mirrors and swords, inscribed with several characters, were given to Japanese envoys by the Chinese. A seven-branched sword bearing a brief text written in characters was sent to Japan from the Korean Paekche kingdom in the late 4th century. It is still preserved in a shrine in Japan. From these objects the Japanese may have learned of the existence of characters, without necessarily realizing their function.

When did the Japanese begin to learn and use Chinese characters? The two earliest surviving Japanese history books — *Record of Ancient Matters (Kojiki)* (AD 712) and *Chronicle of Japan (Nihon Shoki)* (720) — record the introduction of Chinese characters to Japan by Paekche scholars, though the two books disagree on details. A Korean envoy by the name of Achiki came to Japan, accompanying two gift horses. Impressed by his knowledge of Chinese characters the Japanese emperor sent for another scholar, Wani, who arrived in Japan the following year, bearing ten volumes of the Confucian *Analects* and one volume of the *Thousand-Character Essay* (for description of these volumes, see chaps. 9 and 10).

Although the years when the two Korean tutors arrived in Japan are recorded as AD 284 and 285, scholars today consider the late 4th or early 5th century to be more likely, for various reasons. On the one hand, only in the 3rd century had the Koreans themselves begun to use Chinese characters, and on the other, in the late 4th century the Japanese were unified and became politically and socially ready to accept Chinese culture. In the early 6th century, more Paekche scholars in the Confucian classics, medicine, and calendar came to Japan as teachers for royal and aristocratic families. In the mid-6th century, a Paekche king sent to a Japanese emperor images of Buddha as well as Buddhist texts written in Chinese characters, thus introducing Buddhism into Japan.

In Japan, objects bearing characters began to be made in the 5th or early 6th century. For example, a sword excavated from an old tomb and a bronze mirror found in a temple, were made around that time, probably by a Korean immigrant. Among the Japanese, Prince Shōtoku (574–622), called the "Father of Japanese culture," studied Buddhist texts and promoted Chinese culture, including government organization and writing. In 604 he drafted a 17-article constitution in Chinese characters and Chinese text, based on the ideals of Confucianism and Buddhism. In 608 he began sending to China Japanese missions and students, who brought home many Chinese texts.

The 7th and 8th centuries were a time of assimilation of Chinese culture in Japan on a large scale, mostly among aristocrats, high-ranking officials, and Buddhist monks. To meet the state's need for a large number of literate officials, an institute called the Daigakuryō ('the University') was set up to train future officials. In the early 8th century, two history books were written in Chinese characters, and in the mid-8th century the first collection of Chinese poems in Japan appeared. A few years later, the first anthology of Japanese poems was compiled.

After their introduction to Japan, Kanji were used as the sole script until two forms of a syllabary, Kana, were created out of Kanji during the 9th century. Though Kanji are now supplemented by Kana, they still form the backbone of the Japanese writing system.

Kanji Uses in Different Times

The number of different Kanji listed in the 13-volume *Great Sino-Japanese Dictionary* is close to 50,000, including variants (Morohashi 1960). However, as in China, most are seldom used.

In modern times the use of Kanji has changed over time and across fields of inquiry. In the 90 years between 1879 and 1968, the percentage of Kanji contained in newspapers declined from over 90% to 60% of the written symbols (Kaiho and Nomura 1983). In various counts taken between 1941 and 1981, the number of different Kanji varied between 2,637 and 5,120, depending on the type of user or topic, as shown in Table 18-1 (based on Tajima 1989: 234).

Table 18-1. Number of Different Kanji in Various Uses

Use	Total Kanji (thousands)	Different Kanji	Top 2000 Account for	Year of Study
Printing Bureau	3,280	3,948		1941
Printing Bureau	45,910	5,120	99.3%	1966
90 magazines	280	3,328	98.6	1963
Newspapers	990	3,213	99.6	1976
Personal Names	2,721	2,637		1974
Japanese Literature	10,000	5,001		1981

In Table 18-1, the larger the number of total Kanji counted, the larger tends to be the number of "Different Kanji" (third column), as one might expect. The fourth column, "Top (the most frequent) 2,000 Kanji Account for" about 99% of the Kanji used in the data (only three percentages were given in Tajima's table), and between 1,000 and 3,000 different Kanji account for the remaining 1%. These Japanese numbers are somewhat smaller than the Chinese numbers, in which 2,400 characters account for 99% and 4,876 characters for the remaining 1% (see "Number of Characters" in chap. 3).

Fewer than 3,000 Kanji are used in newspapers and magazines, and of these, 2,000 account for about 99% of the uses of Kanji. These 2,000 most frequently used Kanji must be identified for children to learn, if they are to function as literate members of the Japanese society. Over the past 100 years, from the Meiji era to the present Heisei era, numerous government decrees have attempted to restrict the number and types of Kanji for common use and for school instruction. Table 18-2 shows several lists from the Shōwa and Heisei eras; of these lists, the two most prominent ones are Tōyō Kanji ('Kanji for Current/Temporary Use'; henceforth Temporary Kanji) and Jōyō Kanji ('Kanji for Common Use'; Common Kanji).

Kanji were selected for these lists if they were used frequently or were necessary for certain words. If two Kanji had the same sound and similiar meanings, only the simpler was selected. Excluded from the list were exceptionally complex Kanji, ones with limited use, and ones with Japanese readings only (with some exceptions).

The older list, Temporary Kanji, was prepared during the Occupation of the Allied Forces, and was called "temporary" because it was considered to be a temporary measure until a Roman alphabet replaced all other scripts in Japan. It severely restricted the use of Kanji: Certain types of words—e.g., pronouns, adverbs, names of

Table 18-2. Kanji Lists for Common Use and Education

Year	List (Number of Items)
1946	Temporary Kanji (1,850 Kanji)
1947	Temporary Kanji On and Kun (3,122 sounds)
1948	Kanji for primary school (881)
1951	Additional Kanji for personal names (92)
1970	Kanji for primary school (996)
1973	Temporary Kanji On and Kun, revised (3,938 sounds);
	106 Ateji and Jukujikun allowed
1976	Additional Kanji for personal names (28)
1981	Additional Kanji for personal names (54)
1981	Common Kanji (1,945; 2,187 On and 1,900 Kun sounds)
1989	Kanji for primary school (1,006)
1990	Additional Kanji for names (284)

On ('Chinese reading of Kanji'); Kun ('Japanese reading of Kanji'); Ateji ('assigned Kanji'); Jukujikun ('idiomatic Kun'). These terms will be explained shortly.

animals, plants, and household objects—were to be written not in Kanji but in Kana, the Japanese syllabary.

The later, more liberal Common Kanji list added 95 Kanji to, and subtracted 19 from, the Temporary list. People are now officially allowed to write in Kanji the names of some common animals (e.g., monkey, snake, and cat), trees (e.g., Japanese cedar), household objects (e.g., dish or plate, umbrella, and vase), idiomatic Kun (e.g., convex and concave), one male pronoun (I). In short, Common Kanji allow many content words to be written in Kanji instead of Kana.

Writers of textbooks, newspapers, and government documents tend to adhere to these lists, though not slavishily. Remember, the 2,000 most frequent Kanji account for about 99% of the Kanji used; an additional 1,000 or more Kanji are needed to account for the rest, to be used in fields such as science, technology, literature, and personal names. The JIS (The Japanese Industrial Standard) contains three levels of Kanji: the first level includes 2,965 frequent Kanji, the second level 3,388 less frequent Kanji, and the supplement includes 5,801 special and variant characters as well as the simplified forms of characters used in China. Printers and word processors normally adopt the JIS Kanji.

In voluntary tests of Kanji literacy run by a private company in Tokyo, even educated adults did not know all the official Kanji, or even all the ones taught in the early school years, but they did know some unofficial but frequently seen Kanji (see "Mass Literacy after World War II" in chap. 24). Perhaps the lists of official Kanji do not reflect the needs of everyday reading as well as they might.

Kanji Readings: On/Chinese and Kun/Japanese

In the way they use logographic Chinese characters, the Japanese, the Chinese, and the Koreans differ most clearly and dramatically in the sounds assigned to characters, as can be seen in the samples given throughout this book. The Japanese use of characters is similar to, but by no means the same as, the Korean use. For one thing, both peoples can give two quite different readings to characters, Chinese and native, but the Koreans now use only the Chinese readings ("Complicated Hancha Use in the Past" in chap. 12). By contrast, the Japanese not only use both types of readings, Chinese and native, but also use a few varieties of each type of reading, making oral reading of characters exceedingly complicated.

Consider the now familiar character for "ten" 十. It is given one sound *shi* (rising tone) in Mandarin Chinese and *sip* (no tone) in Korean but several quite different sounds: *to, tō, so, jitt-, jū, jutt-,* all without a tone, in Japanese. The first three sounds are examples of Kun readings ('Japanese native readings'), while the second three are On readings (Chinese readings). *Kun* is a Sino-Japanese word for "meaning" or "semantic gloss": The Japanese reading *tō* for "ten" is none other than the Japanese native word for "ten," so that it is akin to providing a gloss on a Sino-Japanese word. The Kun reading *tō* (no tone) sounds quite different from the Chinese *shi* (rising tone), because the two languages are unrelated. To get the flavor of the differences between Kun and On, imagine that English speakers were to adopt the Chinese character for "ten" and pronounce it either as *ten* using an English reading or as *shi* using a Chinese reading.

Besides Kun/Japanese readings, most Kanji have one or more On/Chinese readings that attempt to approximate the Kanji's Chinese sounds. On/Chinese readings are never identical to Chinese sounds because of the differences in the sound systems between Chinese and Japanese. First, Japanese syllables are without tones, whereas Chinese syllables almost always have tones. Second, the Japanese sound system uses a smaller number of phonemes and simpler syllable structures than the Chinese system. On/Chinese readings and the sounds now used in Chinese resemble each other very little for some characters, as between *jū* and *shi* ('ten'), and are very similar for some other characters, as between *san* and *shan* ('mountain').

The degree of resemblance of On/Chinese readings and Chinese sounds depends partly on when in history and from where in China particular Kanji were borrowed. Four types of On/Chinese readings can be distinguished, though an ordinary Japanese reader is not necessarily aware of them. Between the 5th and the 6th centuries the type of On reading called Go'on ('sound of Go' or the Chinese Wu state) came to Japan. It is thought to reflect a southern "dialect" of the Six dynasties period in China. Go'on came to Japan with Buddhism via Korea and tends to be used in Buddhist words.

Kan'on ('sound of Kan' or Chinese sound) was brought back to Japan in the 7th and 8th centuries by Japanese missions returning from China and was adopted by the central government. It reflects the standard language used in two great northern Chinese cities of the Tang dynasty, Xi'an (formerly Chang'an) and Luoyang. Go'on and Kan'on together account for most of the On/Chinese readings.

The third type of On reading, Tō–Sō'on ('the sounds of Chinese Tang and Song dynasties'), reflects the sound of the 14th century Hangzhou area in southern China. It is associated with Zen Buddhism. The fourth type, habitual On, is a Kanji misreading that has become entrenched by habit.

Most Kanji are given only one of the four types of On readings, but some are given as many as three in different contexts or in different words: 行 is *kō* in Kan'on, *gyō* in Go'on, and *an* in Tō–Sō'on; 名 is *myo* in Go'on, *bei* in Kan'on, and *mei* in habitual On.

The On/Chinese readings of Kanji brought about some changes in the sounds of Japanese, such as introducing the final nasal N (*-ng*) and possibly the sounds called "contracted," *ya, yu, yo* as well. In the 8th century the Japanese sound system had about 90 different syllables but now has around 110. At the same time, some On readings of Kanji changed as the Japanese sounds changed. For example, *zyau, dyau, zeu, deu, defu* are all now pronounced as *jō*. Consequently, the number of homophonic Kanji increased, that is, several Kanji with different meanings now have the same sound.

Of the 1,945 Common Kanji, 1,168 have both On/Chinese and Kun/Japanese readings, 737 have only On readings, and 40 have only Kun readings (some Kanji created in Japan, and some infrequent On readings are not in the Common Kanji list). The 1,945 Common Kanji are associated with 4,087 sounds or readings. Often one Kanji may maintain the same meaning while it is given either On or Kun reading: 池 *ike* (Kun reading) and *chi* (On reading) both mean 'pond', and 花 *hana* and *ka* both mean 'flower'. Sometimes one Kanji may be given either a Kun or On reading to go with its different meaning, such as 生 Kun *nama* ('raw') and On *sei* ('life'). Sometimes one Kanji has two different meanings in two different Kun readings: 空 *sora* ('sky') and *kara* ('empty'); other times one Kanji has two different meangs in two different On readings: 率 *ritsu* ('ratio') and *sotsu* ('lead' someone).

Once more, Chinese characters—whether called Kanji in Japanese, Hancha in Korean, or Hanzi in Chinese—are logographs (logo = word; graphs = written symbols), which represent directly the meanings and indirectly the sounds of morphemes ("Logographic Characters vs Phonetic Scripts" chap. 6). Thus, the sounds or readings of Kanji differ always from those of Hanzi and Hancha, while the meanings of Kanji remain often—by no means always—the same as those of Hanzi and Hancha.

Two-Kanji Words: Readings

Single Kanji tend to be read in Kun/Japanese, while two or more Kanji making up a compound word are more likely to be read in On/Chinese. But this pattern of reading is not a hard and fast rule. Also, two Kanji making up a compound word are usually read consistently in one way, be it On or Kun, but occasionally, one of the two Kanji is read in On and the other in Kun. Examples of mixed readings are *jūbako* ('nest of boxes') whose first Kanji is read in On and second in Kun, and *yutō* ('bath tub') whose first Kanji is read in Kun and second in On.

A multi-Kanji word with a mixed On–Kun reading can stump even expert Kanji readers. One Kanji scholar, Saiga (1978), had to ask for directions in Tokyo. When he asked for *Shiroyamaue* (the three Kanji read in Kun), the addressee was puzzled; thereupon he asked for his destination, which he knew as a three-Kanji name, as *Hakusanjo* (the three Kanji read in On), with the same puzzled reaction from the addressee, who eventually hit upon the correct name *Hakusan'ue* (On, On, Kun).

A two-Kanji word such as 生物 can have two different meanings, depending on whether it is read in On *seibutsu* ('living thing') or Kun *namamono* ('raw food'). (In English, too, *bow* has different meanings, depending on whether it is pronounced as /bou/ or /bau/.)

Multiple readings of Kanji are exploited in creating the following riddle (translated from Saiga 1978: 113).

To test the skill of a famous Kanji scholar and poet, an emperor in the Heian era challenged the scholar to read a sentence consisting of nothing but twelve repetitions of the Kanji 子. The scholar read it, without hesitation, as "Neko no ko no ko neko, shishi no ko no ko jishi" ('the child of a cat's child is a cat, the child of a lion's child is a lion').

Obviously, the scholar was aware of the Kanji's On reading *shi, ji* (also *-su, -zu*) and its Kun readings *ko* and *ne*.

A New Dictionary of Kanji Usage, which is intended for English speakers learning Japanese, presents 2,000 common Kanji divided into ten levels according to their frequency and/or importance (Kuratani et al. 1989). Most but not all of the 2,000 Kanji are from the Common Kanji list. For one particular level-1 Kanji 生 the dictionary lists six meanings, some related and some not, and most of which can be used as verbs, nouns, or adjectives: 'life', 'birth', 'growth', 'physiology', 'pupil', and 'raw'. It also lists the following 19 official and unofficial sounds:

13 (10 official) Kun/Japanese readings: *i-, iki-, ike-, u-, uma-, -umare; o-, oi-; ki-; nama; ha-, -ba-, hae-;*

4 (2 official) On/Chinese readings: *shō, -jyō; sei, -zei;* and

2 unusual Kun readings: *iku, ubu.*

Actually, this Kanji has many more unofficial and uncustomary readings, especially in place names: *yoi, nari, ai, sō, nu, gose, maru, dan, dori, sa, iko.*... It is said to have over 100 different readings!

So, the readings or sounds given to Kanji in Japanese are numerous and incredibly complex. There is a crying need to check the proliferation of these different and sometimes idiosyncratic sounds given to Kanji. In promulgating the 1,945 Common Kanji, the Japanese government did limit the readings of these Kanji to 2,187 On and 1,900 Kun, total 4,087. But the government guidelines are not slavishly observed, especially in the names of persons and places.

To complicate Kanji reading further, there are Ateji and Jukujikun. In assigning Kanji to Japanese native words, Kanji's meanings are sometimes ignored but their sounds are kept, to create Ateji ('assigned Kanji'), as in *sewa* ('care'), which ignores the two Kanji' meanings, 'world' and 'talk'. Ateji are used also to write a word with little or unknown meaning, such as a foreign word like *America,* which requires four Kanji with the meanings 'sub- or pseudo-, rice, clever, add'. (The Chinese use a similar trick to write European names; see "Foreign Loan Words" in chap. 2.) However, a handful of Ateji do reflect the meaning as well as the sound of a native word, as in *kokochi* ('mind, ground' for 'feeling'). The official Kanji allow Ateji of this kind but not ones that represent the sound without the meaning.

In Jukujikun ('idiomatic Kun') two or more Kanji are assigned to a native word, preserving their meanings but usually ignoring their customary sounds. For example, *kesa* ('this morning') is an one-morpheme native word, for which two Kanji ('now', 'morning') are assigned, disregarding the Kanji's Kun/Japanese sounds *ima'asa* and On/Chinese sounds *konchō.* Another one-morpheme native word is *miyage* ('souvenir'), for which two Kanji ('land, product') are assigned, ignoring their On/Chinese sounds *tosan.*

Ateji and Jukujikun may ensure that content words can be written in Kanji. The earlier official Kanji list, Temporary Kanji, recommended writing Ateji in Kana instead of Kanji, but the later revised list, Common Kanji, relented somewhat and sanctioned the use of 106 common Ateji and Jukujikun. Ateji that are purely sound-based are not sanctioned, and are unlikely to be recognized by either Chinese or Koreans.

Kanji, Hancha, and Hanzi Compared

Now that we have learned something about the way Chinese characters are used in each of the three languages — Chinese, Korean, and Japanese — let us pause here for a comparison.

The number of available characters — 50,000 — may be about the same in the three languages, but the number of characters designated for common use differ, partly because in Japanese and Korean, phonetic scripts are used along with characters, whereas in Chinese, characters alone are used (phonetic scripts are used only as aids to learning the sounds of characters).

- in China 3,500 Hanzi in the sounds of Putonghua ('common speech'), usually one reading per Hanzi;
- in Japan 1,945 Kanji in 2,187 On/Chinese readings and 1,900 Kun/Japanese readings, at least two quite different readings per Kanji;
- in S. Korea 1,800 Hancha in Um/Chinese readings, usually one reading per Hancha.
- in N. Korea no Hancha are used in ordinary text.

The number of common Kanji in Japan and Hancha in S. Korea may be similar, but the Kanji list and the Hancha list do not completely overlap, as each list includes a few hundred characters not found in the other. Even the shapes of characters are not always the same among Hanzi, Hancha, and Kanji. They were originally the same wherever they were used, but after about 2,000 common Hanzi have been simplified in China, some drastically, and a few hundred Kanji have been simplified in Japan, most moderately, and no Hancha have been simplified in S. Korea (or in Taiwan and Hong Kong), the shapes of the characters used in the different regions are diverging, as shown in Table 18-3

In Table 18-3, characters in the top three rows are shared among Chinese, Korean, and Japanese, with the same meanings but different, though similar sounds (On/Chinese sounds for Kanji).

Table 18-3. Hanzi, Hancha and Kanji that are the Same or that are Different

Hanzi		Hancha		Kanji		Meaning
Shape	Sound	Shape	Sound	Shape	Sound	
山	shan	山	san	山	san	mountain
学	xue	學	hak	学	gaku	learn
广	guang	廣	kwang	広	kō	wide
你	ni (you)	乏	hal	峠	tōge (mountainpass)	

Row 1. The characters have identical shapes in the three languages.

Row 2. The Hanzi and the Kanji are in the same simplified shapes, while the Hancha is in its original shape.

Row 3. The Hanzi is drastically simplified, the Kanji is moderately simplified, while the Hancha is in its original shape.

Row 4. Each of Hanzi, Hancha, and Kanji is unique. The Chinese use certain characters not used in Japanese and Korean. The Koreans have created a handful of their own Hancha, mostly by combining two characters to represent CVC syllables: *ha + (u)l = hal*, with no meaning. The Japanese have created a few hundred characters for objects and events that are important or unique in Japan. For fish names alone, numerous Kanji were created, though only a handful of them are included in the 1,945 Common Kanji. The made-in-Japan Kanji tend to be meaning composites rather than semantic–phonetic composites as most Hanzi are in China. For example, 峠 *tōge* ('mountain pass') contains three semantic components, one each for "mountain," "above," and "below."

Now let us shift our attention from individual characters to multi-character compound words. One Japanese book lists Kanji words that are used either differently or in the same way in Chinese and Japanese, considering only On/Chinese readings (Waseda 1978). Of 1,800 words examined by the Waseda team, two-thirds are used in the same way in the two languages, while one-quarter of the Kanji words are not found in Chinese. The meanings of words sometimes match and sometimes diverge, while the meanings of some other words differ markedly in the two languages. The last two categories together make up only one-tenth of the 1,800 Kanji words examined; they are ignored here. Korean Hancha words too are sometimes the same as Chinese Hanzi and/or Japanese Kanji words. Table 18-4 lists some words that are the same or different among Chinese, Korean, and Japanese.

Rows 1 and 2. The words in characters are the same in the three languages. In row 1, the Chinese word has been borrowed into Korean and Japanese, while in row 2, the Japanese word coined on a Chinese model has been borrowed into Chinese and Korean.

Row 3. The Korean word and the Japanese word are the same, but the two differ from the Chinese word. The Korean–Japanese word ('cold, stock, storage' for refrigerator) and the Chinese word ('electricity, ice, box') are synonymous and likely to be mutually intelligible.

Table 18-4. Chinese, Sino-Korean and Sino-Japanese Words

	C(hinese)	K(orean)	J(apanese)	Meaning
C=K=J	幸福	幸福	幸福	happy
	电話	電話	電話	telephone
K=J; C ≅K, J	电冰箱	冷藏庫	冷藏庫	refrigerator
C=K; C, K≠J	邮膘	郵票	切手	stamp
C≠K≠J	丈夫	男便	亭主	husband

=same, ≅ synonym, ≠ different; original vs simplified 電 ,电; 郵 ,邮

Row 4. The Korean word is the Chinese word ('mail, ticket' for stamp) borrowed, but the Japanese word ('cut, hand' for stamp) was coined by the Japanese uniquely. The Japanese word is not understandable to the Chinese and the Koreans, but the Chinese–Korean word is likely to be so to the Japanese, who use the character for 'mail' in other compound words related to mail.

Row 5. The words are coined separately in each of the three languages, and the meanings of constituent characters may not unambiguously contribute to the meaning of the compound word, "husband": the constituent characters mean 'strong, man' in the Chinese word; 'male, convenience' in the Korean word; and 'inn, host' in the Japanese word.

Because of the similarities and differences in the use of individual characters and words, as well as in syntax, speakers of Chinese, Koreans, and Japanese can make some, but not full, sense out of each other's text. The simple sentence "I go to school every day" shown in Figure 18-2 — written in Chinese characters, mixed with phonetic scripts in case of Japanese and Korean — is simple enough to be understood by Chinese, Japanese, and Koreans, because they share most content words, and because these words are written in logographic characters. Transcribed in Roman letters it is no longer mutually understandable, even when the readers of all three languages can read it aloud. Remember that even the same word shared among Chinese, Korean, and Japanese, and is written in the same character(s) is always pronounced differently in the three languages and thus becomes mutually unintelligible when read aloud.

Chinese
Hanzi: 每天 我 去学 校
Romanized: Mei tian wo qu xue xiao.

Japanese
Kanji and Hiragana: 私 は 毎日学校 へ行く
Romanized: Watashi wa mainichi gakkō e iku.

Korean
Han'gŭl with Hancha: 나 는 每日 學校 에 간다
Romanized: na nŭn maeil hakkyo e kanda.

Figure 18-2. The sentence "I go to school every day" uses some of the same characters in Chinese, Korean, and Japanese, but sounds quite different.

To conclude this chapter, Kanji and Kanji words are mostly Hanzi and Hanzi words borrowed from China, but some were created in Japan in modern times. The number of Kanji designated for common use and school teaching is fewer than that of Hanzi. Kanji also have undergone less simplification than have Hanzi. The meanings of the shared Kanji, Hancha, and Hanzi, as well as words in these scripts, are often the same, but their sounds always differ, sometimes drastically. Kanji, because of their importance in Japanese writing and reading, will be discussed again in two more chapters, after discussing the phonetic scripts used in Japan.

19

Kana: Japanese Syllabary

Besides the logographic Kanji, the Japanese use a phonetic script called Kana, a syllabary, in which one written sign represents one syllable. The word "Kana" refers to a whole syllabary as well as to individual Kana sign or signs. Let us consider the origin, form, variety, and use of Kana

Kana: Origin and Development

Kanji were the sole form of writing used in Japan for a few hundred years after their introduction in the 4th or 5th century. But the Japanese faced major problems in using only logographic characters, as did the Koreans. Chinese and Japanese differ in syntax — word order and the use of grammatical morphemes. Kanji are well suited for writing content words with meanings (nouns and stems of verbs or adjectives) but ill suited for writing Japanese grammatical morphemes, because postpositions have little meaning, and verb and adjective endings change form in different contexts. Yet, these grammatical morphemes have to be included in almost every Japanese sentence. To represent the Japanese language using Kanji, the Japanese could use the sounds of Kanji, ignoring their meanings, or vice versa. If they used the sounds of Kanji, they faced the fact that any one Japanese syllable could be represented by many different Kanji. All these problems compelled the Japanese to create Kana, not to supplant Kanji but to supplement them.

Kana developed out of the phonetic use of Kanji. In the early days of Kanji use, to write the names of people and places, the Japanese used Kanji for their sounds, ignoring their meanings. Early examples of the phonetic use of Kanji can be seen in an inscription on a 5th-century mirror and an early 8th-century registry. Such use of Chinese characters as phonetic signs was and still is practised to a limited degree by the Chinese in transcribing foreign words; it was practised at one time by the Koreans in writing their language using only Hancha, as described in "Complicated Hancha Use in the Past" (in chap. 12).

The use of Kanji for phonetic signs was widespread in the famous anthology of 4,500 poems, *Man'yōshū ('Ten Thousand Leaves')*, compiled in the late 8th century. Suppose the native Japanese word to be written was *kumo* ('cloud'). Two Kanji 久母 that have the On/Chinese reading *ku, mo* would fill the bill, if their meanings "long time, mother" were ignored. Occasionally Kun/Japanese readings were used in this manner. Also occasionally, Kanji were used as logographs for their meanings, as in 山 *yama* ('mountain'). In the phonetic use of Kanji, a Kanji with a single syllable sound was preferred to one with a two-syllable sound. The principle of one syllable for one Kanji became popular because of its simplicity and convenience. Among many Kanji that could represent each Japanese syllable, a simply shaped Kanji tended to be selected. Still, by the 8th century over 970 Kanji were used to represent the fewer than

90 syllables of the Japanese language of the day. Over 40 different Kanji were used to represent the syllable *shi* and over 30 different Kanji to represent the syllable *ka*, for example. By the 9th century, this multitude of possibilities had been reduced to one preferred Kanji for each syllable, and over time these preferred Kanji were simplified to form Kana.

Kanji used phonetically for their sounds, disregarding their meanings, are called Man'yōgana (Man'yō + kana). The term Kana could come from *karina* (*kari* 'borrowed' and *na* 'name' or 'letter') in the sense that Kana borrow the sounds of Kanji; or the term could mean 'false letter' vis-a-vis *mana* ('genuine letter'), i.e., Kanji used as logographs for their meanings. Other possible meanings suggested for *kari* are temporary, unofficial, nonregular. All these different possible meanings of the term Kana suggest that Kana is a secondary or second-class script to Kanji. *Karina* eventually became Kana via *Kanna*.

The Japanese were able to develop Kana from Kanji in this manner because of the simple sound structure of their language, which allowed them to select Kanji to fit every syllable. By contrast, the Koreans, who at one time also used Chinese characters phonetically for their sounds, were deterred from developing a Kana-like syllabary, because the sound structure of Korean is much more complex than that of Chinese and Japanese; instead they developed a phonetic script unrelated to characters.

Table 19-1 shows the Kanji origin of Kana, which comes in two forms, Katakana and Hiragana. A few Katakana signs, such as one for *mi*, developed out of cursive forms of their Kanji, while a few other signs, such as one for *chi*, are based on the full shapes of their Kanji. In the early history of Kanji use, in the Kun/Japanese reading of Chinese texts, Japanese Buddhist monks inserted Kanji for grammatical morphemes and marginal notes. These Kanji, since they had to be written between the lines and often in hurry, were sometimes merely fragments of the original Kanji, i.e., Katakana. Katakana were used mainly by men in marginal notes in Chinese texts, dictionaries, and commentaries. The practice of using fragments of Chinese characters was used at one time in Korea (fig. 12-2), but it did not develop into a separate script there.

Table 19-1. Kanji Origins of Hiragana and Katakana: Some Examples

Kanji	Hiragana	Kanji	Katakana
安	あ *(a)*	加	カ *(ka)*
乃	の *(no)*	千	チ *(chi)*
不	ふ *(fu)*	不	フ *(fu)*
天	て *(te)*	天	テ *(te)*

Each Hiragana ('plain, common, or smooth Kana') is a graceful cursive form of its original Kanji, as shown in Table 19-1. In some cases (e.g., *fu, te*) the same Kanji was the source for both Hiragana and Katakana signs. Hiragana was used mainly by female authors to write letters, poems, diaries, and eventually stories. Its existence was acknowledged publically in an anthology of Japanese poems, *Kokin Wakashū (Collection of Poems Old and New)*, that appeared in 905. One of Japan's greatest literary works, *The Tale of Genji (Genji Monogatari)* by Lady Murasaki Shikibu in the early 11th century, was written in Hiragana, with only a handful of Kanji to write Chinese loan words.

Kana developed gradually, between the 8th and 9th centuries, out of Chinese characters in the following stages:

Kanji→Kanji as phonetic signs→simplified Kanji shapes→Kana

By the beginning of the 10th century both Hiragana and Katakana were used throughout the upper levels of the Heian society. For a thousand years, there were many variant shapes of both Kana, which were finally standardized in 1900 in the Meiji era.

Kana Signs: Number and Order

So far, one Kana sign has been described as if it coded one syllable, which can be a vowel or consonant–vowel. To be more precise, one Kana codes one mora, a single beat or short syllable. As described earlier in "Speech Sounds, Syllables, and Moras"(in chap. 17), what English speakers consider to be one syllable has two moras written in two Kana signs, if the syllable has one of the following: A lengthened vowel, such as $\bar{o}$; a sequence of two vowels, such as *ie (i + e)*; a doubled consonant -*kk*- after another sound; or a nasal final N after a vowel, such as *aN*. But in most cases, a mora is a syllable: sounds such as *a, ka, de, ro* have one item whether it is a syllable or a mora. So I will continue to use the familiar term syllable instead of the unfamiliar term mora.

Table 19-2 shows the 46 basic Kana—Hiragana and Katakana—that code 5 monosyllabic vowels (*a, e, i, o, u*), 40 consonant–vowels (e.g., *ka, ha*) plus 1 nasal N, with their sounds indicated by Rōmaji or Roman letters. The Kana signs are ordered column by column starting from the left, and within each column, by five signs reading from the top down; thus, *a i u e o; ka ki ku ke ko* .... The order of the basic Kana signs is called Gojūonzu ('50-sound chart'), even though the number of basic Kana has fluctuated over the years between 50 and 46. It follows the order of listing phonemes used by Indian phoneticians for Sanskrit. Gojūonzu, like the order of letters in an alphabet, is worth remembering, because it is often used in ordering words in dictionaries and telephone directories.

In the 11th century all the basic signs of the Kana, 47 then, are used without repetition in a famous poem said to have been written by a Buddhist monk. The poem, called *Iroha uta* ('Iroha song' after the first three syllables, *i ro ha*, of the poem), provides Japanese speakers with an excellent mnemonic for learning the syllabary. It is used by children for practising Kana writing.

> *i ro ha ni ho he to chi ri nu ru [w]o*
> *wa ka yo ta re so tu ne na ra mu u*
> *[w]i no o ku ya ma ke fu ko e te*
> *a sa ki yu me mi si [w]e hi mo se su*

Here are two English translations, a modern one provided by William Skillend (for Taylor and Taylor 1983) followed by one from the last century by B. H. Chamberlain (1899).

> Its colors dazzle, even as it lies there fallen.
> Of our generation, who can be for ever?
> Today I will cross the far hills of creation,
> Waking from the shallow dream—and sober too!

Table 19-2. Hiragana and Katakana (Japanese Syllabary) in Gojūonzu (50-Sound Chart)

Hiragana	あ	か	さ	た	な	は	ま	や	ら	わ	ん
Katakana	ア	カ	サ	タ	ナ	ハ	マ	ヤ	ラ	ワ	ン
Romaji	a	ka	sa	ta	na	ha	ma	ya	ra	wa	n
	い	き	し	ち	に	ひ	み		り		
	イ	キ	シ	チ	ニ	ヒ	ミ		リ		
	i	ki	shi	chi	ni	hi	mi		ri		
	う	く	す	つ	ぬ	ふ	む	ゆ	る		
	ウ	ク	ス	ツ	ヌ	フ	ム	ユ	ル		
	u	ku	su	tsu	nu	fu	mu	yu	ru		
	え	け	せ	て	ね	へ	め		れ		
	エ	ケ	セ	テ	ネ	ヘ	メ		レ		
	e	ke	se	te	ne	he	me		re		
	お	こ	そ	と	の	ほ	も	よ	ろ	を	
	オ	コ	ソ	ト	ノ	ホ	モ	ヨ	ロ	ヲ	
	o	ko	so	to	no	ho	mo	yo	ro	wo	

Though gay in hue, they flutter down, alas!
Who then, in this world of ours, may continue forever?
Crossing today the uttermost limits of phenomenal existence,
I shall see no more fleeting dreams, neither be any longer intoxicated.

The full Kana chart would include 25 secondary Kana that code 20 voiced and 5 semi-voiced CV versions. The secondary Kana are created by adding a two comma-like mark (e.g., *ba* ば) or a tiny circle (e.g., *pa* ぱ), to the top right of 25 of the basic Kana. The 36 compound Kana (e.g., *kya* きゃ) are created by combining 36 of the basic and and secondary Kana with any of the three small-sized Kana for *ya, yo, yu*.

The number of Hiragana signs varies, depending on which kinds are included in the count.

46 basic Hiragana signs
46 + 25 (secondary signs) = 71
46 + 25 + 3 (small size signs) = 74
46 + 25 + 36 (compound signs) = 107
46 + 25 + 36 + 1 (one small size sign for doubled consonant) = 108

Katakana, being an alternate form of Kana, has the same number of signs as Hiragana. It also has some extra signs in order to transcribe foreign words. For example, to transcribe *vi-* in the English word *violin*, the mark for voicing used for some CV Kana signs is put on the top right of the vowel sign for *u*, to which a small-sized sign for *a* is added.

How to Use Kana

Kana signs transcribe the sounds of the small number of simply structured Japanese syllables. One expects the use of Kana to be simplicity itself; yet, there are some questions and ambiguities as to which Kana should be used for which words in which context. The proper use of Kana is complex enough for the government to issue sets of guidelines.

The guidelines titled "The modern use of Kana" (issued in 1946) had five items on the use of Kana; the first three accommodate changes in the Japanese sound system, and the last two concern spelling.

1. The Kana for the sounds *(w)i, (w)e, (w)o* are replaced by Kana for the sounds *i, e, o*, except that the Hiragana for *(w)o* is retained for the postposition *o*.

2. Use Kana *ka* for *kwa* and *ga* for *gwa*.

3. Use Kana *wa, i, u, e, o* for *ha, hi, hu, he, ho*; but for the postpositions, use Hiragana *ha, he*.

4. For a lengthened vowel, add Hiragana *u* to *u*, *e* to *e*, but *u* to *o*. Katakana uses a short bar for lengthened vowel.

5. Use small Kana for *ya, yu, yo* in syllables such as *kya* and also for *-kk-* in words such as *gakkō*.

The two forms of Kana, Hiragana and Katakana, are put to different uses. Hiragana are used for grammatical morphemes, such as postpositions after nouns, and verb or adjective endings. In the following sentence, the morphemes shown in uppercase would be written in Hiragana while those in lower case would be written in Kanji.

kodomo GA tsumeTAI mizu O noMU ('[A] child drink[s] cold water').

Hiragana are used also for most pronouns, such as *watashi, kimi* ('I, you'), and some adverbs *yagate* ('eventually').

Katakana are used to write the following types of words.

- modern European and Chinese loan words: *banana, maajan* ('banana', 'mahjong')
- onomatopoea (imitations of the natural sounds produced by animals or objects) *wanwan* for a dog's barking; words, often reduplicated syllables, that describe appearance or movement, such as *hetoheto* (state of exhaution) and *noronoro* (slowly).
- names of some uncommon animals and plants, such as *kame* ('tortoise') and *yashi* ('palm') (common animals and trees are written in Kanji)
- uncommon chemical names, such as *suzu* ('tin')
- representations of On/Chinese readings of Kanji.

Most of these words are content words, and when written in the sharp-edged angular Katakana, are visually distinct from grammatical morphemes written in the curvaceous Hiragana. When Kana are used in indicating the sounds of Kanji, Hiragana give Kun/Japanese readings, while Katakana give On/Chinese readings.

A Japanese verb or adjective phrase is typically written in one or two Kanji, and its ending is written in Hiragana (transcribed in upper-case), as in 表す *arawaSU* ('express') and 行う *okonaU* ('perform'). Attached mainly to a Kanji word with a Kun/Japanese reading, Okurigana ('sending' or 'guiding' Kana) clarifies the Kanji's sound and its connection to the next phrase. The same Kanji can be read differently depending on its Okurigana, as 上 being read either as 上る *noboRU* ('climb up') or as 上げる *aGERU* ('raise').

The trouble is, it is not always clear how much of a verb or adjective is considered to be an ending to be written in Hiragana. For the word *akirakani* ('clearly'), the Okurigana to follow the Kanji stem for "clear" can consist of one, two, three, or four Kana: *-ni, -kani, -rakani, -kirakani*, of which the third is the most common. Also the same Kanji stem with the Okurigana *-rui* will change the sound of the Kanji stem from *aki* to *aka*. (In English the sound of *-i-* in *pin* changes with the addition of *-e* in *pine*.)

On the use of Okurigana, the government issues from time to time sets of guidelines, as it does for Hiragana and Katakana. These guidelines are complex, consisting of four categories: principal guidelines, exceptions, allowed uses, and use with caution. I will not attempt to explain these categories, which would as thoroughly confuse you as they do me.

The main consideration is to use as short Okurigana as will not lead to ambiguities of reading. Table 19-3 shows the use of Okurigana according to two sets of guidelines, one issued in 1959 and the other in 1973. The 1973 Okurigana are usually shorter than the 1959 ones. In romanization, Okurigana are shown in upper-case letters and Kanji stems in lower-case letters, for illustration.

Table 19-3. Guidelines for Okurigana or Hiragana Endings: 1959 vs 1973

1959		1973		Meaning
araWASU	表わす	arawaSU	表す	express
okoNAU	行なう	okonaU	行う	perform
kaKARI	掛かり	kakari	掛	person in charge
toraERU	捕える	toRAERU	捕らえる	catch

Furigana or Annotating Kana

In addition to the uses already discussed, Kana can indicate the pronunciations of Kanji that have unfamiliar or unusual sounds; when used in this way they are called Furigana ('annotating Kana'). Furigana are written as tiny Kana, Katakana for On readings and Hiragana for Kun readings, as shown in Figures 19-1 and 19-2. A Japanese text can be written either vertically, as in these figures, or horizontally (chap. 7). In horizontal writing Furigana tends to be put above the Kanji and in vertical writing on the right side of the Kanji.

Beside giving the sound of unfamiliar Kanji (Figures 19-1 and 19-2a), Furigana has been put to several other, perhaps questionable, uses (19-2b–f), which I have come across in various Japanese texts.

In (a), in the first example, Furigana gives the Kun reading of a two-Kanji word, *marubashira* ('circular pillar'). In the second example, one two-Kanji word ('true') is read first as *hontō* in standard Japanese and then as *honma* in a dialect.

In (b) a foreign word, in this case, the French word *sentimentalisme*, is annotated with Furigana to give its pronunciation. (This notation is hardly helpful, since a reader who knows the meaning of this French word is likely to know its sound.)

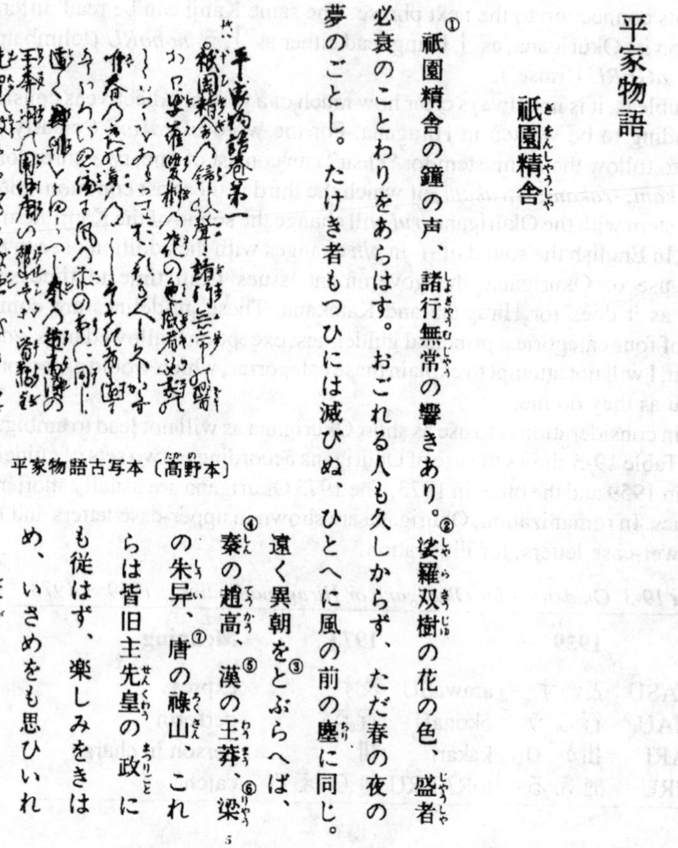
七 古典(一)
平家物語
祇園精舎
①祇園精舎の鐘の声、諸行無常の響きあり。②娑羅双樹の花の色、盛者必衰のことわりをあらはす。おごれる人も久しからず、ただ春の夜の夢のごとし。たけき者もつひには滅びぬ、ひとへに風の前の塵に同じ。
遠く異朝をとぶらへば、③④秦の趙高、⑤漢の王莽、⑥梁の朱异、⑦唐の禄山、これらは皆旧主先皇の政にも従はず、楽しみをきはめ、いさめをも思ひいれず、天下の乱れんことを
平家物語古写本〔高野本〕

Figure 19-1. A page from a textbook on the national language used in a secondary school. It shows the beginning of the 13th-century Heike Monogatari *(The Story of the Taira Clan); the inset is an old version. Both versions use furigana in several places.*

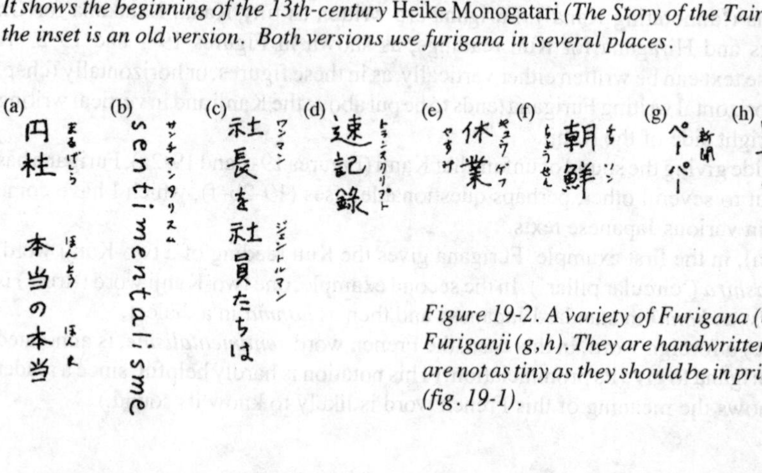
(a) 円柱 まるばしら
本当の本当 ほんとう ほんま
(b) sentimentalisme サンチマンタリスム
(c) 社長を社員たちは ワンマン ジェントルマン
(d) 速記録 トランスクリプト
(e) 休業 キュウギョウ やすみ
(f) 朝鮮 チョソン ちょうせん
(g) ペーパー 新聞
(h) いぜん 依然

Figure 19-2. A variety of Furigana (a–f) and Furiganji (g, h). They are handwritten, and so are not as tiny as they should be in printed text (fig. 19-1).

In (c) the Furigana annotate Kanji meaning *shachō* ('company president') and *shain* ('company workers'), but their sounds given in Furigana are Japanese transcriptions of the English words *one man* and *gentleman*, which neither sound nor mean the same as the Kanji. Conceivably the pair "one man" and "company president" and the pair "gentlemen" and "company workers" have related meanings. Its author, Kabashima (1979: 114), makes a questionable claim that a reader views Furigana and its Kanji word simultaneously, thus obtaining extra meaning.

In (d) a Kanji word is accompanied by Furigana that represent the sound of its English translation. Perhaps the concept in question, "transcript," is not familiar either as a Kanji word or as an English loan word, but the two together provide securely the intended meaning. In such cases, the extra time needed to recognize the word may be justified. But in a frivolous or perverse use of Furigana, the highly familiar Kanji word for "newspaper" is accompanied by the far less familiar (and imperfect) English translation "peepaa" as Furigana.

In (e) the Furigana in Hiragana on the left side of a Kanji word gives the words's meaning *yasumi* ('rest') and the Furigana in Katakana on the right side the word's sound *kyūgefu*. This Furigana example is from the Meiji era, and has the old sound instead of the contemporary *kyūgyō*. This double use of Furigana is rarely found in today's writings.

In (f), which is found in a Japanese book on Korean topics, the Furigana on the left side of a Kanji word gives a Japanese On reading *chōsen* ('Korea') in Hiragana and on the right side a Korean reading *choson* in Katakana.

In (g and h) the meanings of words in phonetic scripts can be ambiguous or hard to recognize until they are annotated with Kanji, i.e., with Furiganji. Furiganji annotates a foreign loan word in Katakana *peepaa* in the first example and a Sino-Japanese word *izen* ('as before') in Hiragana in the second example.

Furigana or Furiganji are tiny, as you can see in Figure 19-1. Because of its tiny print size, Furigana is sometimes called ruby (5 1/2 point type in Britain). Some educators worry that they may cause near-sightedness in readers. Many Japanese people are near sighted, for whatever reason. Though not a Japanese, I am near sighted and can read Furiganji, complex patterns, only when I bring them very close to my eyes after taking my glasses off. Furigana and Furiganji also complicate word processing, which lacks a means to write them, except by reducing the size of normal Kana and Kanji. None of my Japanese colleagues could produce Figure 19-2 on a word processor. Sir George Sansom, who was a British ambassador to Japan and scholar, observed: "One hesitates for an epithet to describe a system of writing which is so complex that it needs the aid of another system to explain it" (1928: 44).

Up to the end of World War II, Furigana was widely used in everyday reading material. After the war, its use was discouraged in the guidelines for the earlier official Kanji list, Temporary Kanji, but was allowed again in those for the later one, Common Kanji. At the very least, Furigana should be limited to its customary use, namely, to give the sound of unfamiliar Kanji, as in Figures 19-1 and 19-2a. All other uses can be either replaced by parentheses in text (as is sometimes done in Korea) or eliminated.

Furigana are indispensable for some names of people and places whose Kanji are not included among the official Kanji list and whose sounds can be uncustomary and even idiosyncratic. I have found it helpful that many recent technical books give Furigana for authors' names, as do business cards. Furigana are useful also for teaching the sounds of new Kanji or for indicating the uncommon sounds of old Kanji.

Katakana for Foreign Loan Words

About 10% of the words in the Japanese vocabulary are borrowed from foreign languages, mostly European, and especially from English (table 17-1). In order to represent the sounds of foreign words, there are more Katakana signs than there are Hiragana signs. Despite the extra signs, the Japanese rendition of foreign words is anything but faithful because the Japanese sound system is simple: It uses only a small number of different sounds, with no /v/, /l/, /f/, or the initial sounds in *thick* and *this;* it uses only open syllables that end in vowels (CVs) (except for the final nasal N and the medial doubled consonant); it does not use consonant clusters such as CCVCCs *(friend)* or CCCVCCCs *(strengths)*. Can you now recognize the Japanese transcriptions of English words you saw earlier in "European and English Loan Words" (in chap. 17)? Try three words, *kureemu, tsūru, waarudo.*

Modern loan words such as *kamera* ('camera'), and *maajan* ('mahjong') are written in Katakana, taking care to transcribe their sounds faithfully. But habitual spellings may override faithful transcription. Thus, *keeki* ('cake') rather than the more "faithful" *keeku*. Actually, the two deviate from /keik/ to the same degree. Sometimes two slightly different spellings of one word represent two different meanings: the habitual *sutoraiki* ('strike') for "work stoppage" but *sutoraiku* in baseball. Two or three European words are often made into one single compound word in Japanese, as in *kurabusaakuru* ('club circle'), *keesubaikeesu* ('case by case'), and *aabanekoro-jiibaaku* ('urban ecology park').

The Japanese seem to love English words, which sound new, sophisticated, modish, different, or erudite. In one page of a Japanese book on writing systems, I counted no fewer than 12 loan words from English (Hashimoto 1987: ii): *field work, group, team work, Europe, America, Asia, mechanism, technical report, unique, training, discipline, transcript.* The last two were in Furigana to accompany Kanji words (fig. 19-2d). One wonders whether a Japanese writer needs to use foreign loan words for such commonplace concepts as "group," "unique," "training," which have Sino-Japanese equivalents.

The indiscriminate use of European words imprecisely transcribed in Katakana is problematic even to Japanese, who often need dictionaries of Katakana words. One recent dictionary of Katakana words defined no fewer than 20,000 words. Katakana words "have become a *nekku* in the teaching of English in Japan," laments Matsui (1992: 149). But what is *nekku*? An abbreviation of *bottleneck*? Isn't *hurdle* a more appropriate word in this context? Such use of European words places an extra burden to foreigners learning the Japanese language, complains Matsui. As you have seen, I myself have puzzled over many "English" words transcribed in Katakana.

20

Rōmaji: Roman Letters

In addition to Kanji, Hiragana, and Katakana, Japanese use the letters of the Roman alphabet, called Rōmaji ('Roman letters'). Although the use of Rōmaji is not widespread in Japan, it merits a chapter, if only because some Japanese and foreigners advocate discarding Kanji and Kana in favor of its exclusive use. There are even organizations that are dedicated to this cause, unlike in China and Korea.

Rōmaji for European Words and Foreigners

The first romanization of Japanese was attempted by Jesuit missionaries from Europe, such as Francis Xavier (1506–1552), who arrived in Japan in 1549. In the 1590s the Jesuit mission set up in Japan a printing press with equipment brought from Europe, and printed Christian texts and Japanese literary works in Rōmaji as well as in Kanji and Kana. So Rōmaji has over 400-year history of use, without ever becoming a major script of Japan.

In modern Japanese writing, some European measurements, abbreviated, are written in the Roman letters, as in *cm* and *kg* for *centimeter* and *kilogram*. In technical writing, European words in Rōmaji may occur by themselves; or they may be accompanied by Kanji words for clarification. I have come across English words such as *distinctive features* and *touch type,* and acronyms such as *JIS* ('Japan Industrial Standard') and *NHK* ('Nippon Hōsō Kyōkai' or "Japan Broadcasting Corporation"). Rōmaji may be used also to write Japanese words for foreigners, as is done in this book (e.g., Kanji, Kana, *haiku*). Sometimes Rōmaji are used even for Japanese readers, for new images and other special effects: thus, *ote arai* ('hand wash' for a toilet, with the deferential prefix *o-*).

Some popular magazines and newspapers have European titles written in the Roman alphabet, such as *Focus, DRAGON BALL,* and *La Seine.* Even a magazine for retired people has the English title *Walk.* Some popular songs listed in *Young Song,* a supplement to a magazine for youth, have English titles and words. English words can be found in ads, store signs, product names, and company names. In Tokyo, I saw a toy store sign that contained nothing but English: TOY LAND; BF PARTY & ENJOY MARKET; 1F FASHION GOODS FLOOR; 2F AMUSEMENT FLOOR, and so on.

Figure 20-1 is a Japanese advertisement for *Recruit Journal*, a magazine for a job market for university graduates, found in the newspaper *Yomiuri* (January 8, 1991). It contains the variety of scripts described in this Part III: Kanji, Hiragana, Katakana, Furigana, Rōmaji, Arabic numerals, as well as a few English words. Note such English words as *SMALL WORLD* (written vertically), *HOW MUCH* (written horizontally), *LAST DECADE* (written at 90 degrees rotation); English acronyms such as *JAL, EC,* and *DEC*, and Japanese names referred to as *Y-san* and *K-san*; English loan words (e.g., simulation magazine, club circle) transcribed in Katakana; Arabic numerals for dates, prices, and house or phone numbers. The name of the journal in Japanese is *shūshoku* ('finding emplyment'), which has Furigana *rikurūto* ('recruit'). This ad for a journal is typical of ads for other Japanese magazines in listing many and varied topics in the variety of scripts (Figure 20-1).

One wonders, Have English words conquered Japan?

LAST DECADE

Rōmaji Styles: Hepburn, Japanese, and Cabinet

Transcribing Japanese in Rōmaji should be easy and straightforward because of the simple Japanese sound system. Yet there are over a dozen different Rōmaji systems, which depend partly on which European language — e.g., Portuguese, Dutch, German, English — underlies a system, and partly on how the system deals with the several tricky Japanese sounds. Let us consider a few significant or influential systems.

Some early Rōmaji were based largely on Portuguese spelling and sounds: thus, *v* for /u/ and *ca* for /ka/. These Rōmaji are said to have philogogical importance, since they indicate Japanese pronunciations of the early 16th and 17th centuries, some of which have been since lost (Shibatani 1990: 128). For example, the *s*-beginning syllables were transcribed as *sa, xi, su, xe, so*, indicating that the present *se* syllable was pronounced at that time as *she,* just like the *si* syllable, which is still pronounced as *shi*.

In 1885 a society was founded to promote the use of Rōmaji. It adopted a Rōmaji system based on English for the consonants and on Italian for the vowels in an attempt to represent the sounds of Japanese words as heard by English speakers. In 1886 this system was adopted in the third edition of American missionary James C. Hepburn's Japanese–English dictionary. In 1908 it was slightly

Figure 20-1. An advertisement for a magazine, in a Japanese newspaper, listing the titles of articles, prices, dates, etc. It uses a variety of scripts and writing directions. (Turn the figure sideways to see it as printed in the newspaper).

revised to eliminate *kwa, gwa, ye,* and *wo,* and came to be called "standard style" or "(revised) Hepburn style."

Meanwhile, in 1885 one member of the society, Tanakadate Aikitsu, developed his own Japanese-style Rōmaji to reflect the Japanese sound structure and Kana. The Japanese-style Rōmaji is the forerunner of the Cabinet (ordinance)-style Rōmaji, which was declared the official Japanese standard by cabinet order in 1937. But the official standard could not entirely replace the popular Hepburn style. So in 1954 the cabinet order approved two lists of Rōmaji: list 1 is the Cabinet style, which was to be taught in school and to represent the Japanese language, and list 2 is the (revised) Hepburn style for international and other uses.

Table 20-1 shows the three styles in one chart. The basic list is the Cabinet style. The 18 letters in boldface are the Hepburn style, while the 8 in italics — including two with asterisks, used for special words — are the Japanese style. The table is divided into four blocks, within each the Rōmaji are read row by row. Above a horizontal line are Rōmaji that represent the basic Kana (*a i u e o; ka ki ku ke ko; ...*) and the compound Kana (e.g., *kya, kyu, kyo; mya, myu, myo; ...*). Below the line are Rōmaji that represent secondary Kana, which in turn represent voiced consonants (e.g., *ga, gi, gu, ge, go*) and semi-voiced ones (*pa, pi, pu, pe, po*).

Table 20-1. Rōmaji in Three Styles: Cabinet, Hepburn, Japanese

a	i	u	e	o			
ka	ki	ku	ke	ko	kya	kyu	kyo
*kwa**							
sa	si	su	se	so	sya	syu	syo
	shi				**sha**	**shu**	**sho**
ta	ti	tu	te	to	tya	tyu	tyo
	chi	**tsu**			**cha**	**chu**	**cho**
na	ni	nu	ne	no	nya	nyu	nyo
ha	hi	hu	he	ho	hya	hyu	hyo
		fu					
ma	mi	mu	me	mo	mya	myu	myo
ya		yu		yo			
ra	ri	ru	re	ro	rya	ryu	ryo
wa				*wo**			
ga	gi	gu	ge	go	gya	gyu	gyo
*gwa**							
za	zi	zu	ze	zo	zya	zyu	zyo
	ji				**ja**	**ju**	**jo**
da	zi	zu	de	do	zya	zyu	zyo
	di	*du*			*dya*	*dyu*	*dyo*
	ji				**ja**	**ju**	**jo**
ba	bi	bu	be	bo	bya	byu	byo
pa	pi	pu	pe	po	pya	pyu	pyo

The basic list is in Cabinet style; differing Hepburn items are in boldface; differing Japanese-style ones in italics.

In Table 20-1 all three styles have the same Rōmaji for most but not all Japanese syllables. Look at the row for voiced *da, di, du, de, do*: the same initial consonant letter, *d-*, is used in the Japanese style; *ji* is used for the second item in the row in the Hepburn style; *zi* and *zu* are used for the second item and the third item, respectively, in the Cabinet style. Each different Kana sign has its own unique Rōmaji in the Japanese style, but not in the two other styles: each of *ji, ja, ju,* and *jo* in the Hepburn style, and each of *zi, zu, zya, zyu,* and *zyo* in the Cabinet style, is used for two different Kana signs.

The ultimate goal of the Japanese style is to replace Kanji and Kana with Rōmaji as the sole script to represent the Japanese language, and the Japanese style suits this goal. By contrast, the goal of the Hepburn style is to help foreigners pronounce the Japanese language as closely as possible, and the Hepburn style suits this goal.

This book for English readers uses Hepburn Rōmaji, which represents the English sounds more closely than do other Rōmaji styles. For example, for the Japanese word "earth," an English reader is more likely to approximate the required sound with the Hepburn Rōmaji *tsuchi* (as in *caTS* and *CHip*) than with the Cabinet Rōmaji *tuti*. In Japan it is the Hepburn system that is used in writing the names of railroad stations and the names of people on passports, for the benefit of foreigners. The Japanese software I use, *SweetJAM* (1986–1992), uses a romanization that mixes different styles. Thus to output 十 I have to type in *jyuu*, which is a mixture of the Cabinet system (*zyuu*) and the Hepburn system (*juu*). Very confusing.

Today an educated Japanese has to be familiar with the Rōmaji presented in Table 20-1.

Guidelines for Rōmaji Use

Here are guidelines for using Rōmaji.

- (a) For a long vowel, put a ^ or overbar over it, as in *Rōmaji;* (b) But for a long /i/, write *ii*; (c) In capital letters, a vowel letter can be doubled for a long vowel, as in ROOMAJI.
- For the nasal final N, which may sound like -*m*, -*n*, -*ng* in different contexts, use one letter *n*, as in *pinpon* ('ping-pong'). (But *m* is often used, as in *shimbun* 'newspaper'.)
- To separate the nasal N from the following vowel or *y*, use the apostrophe ', as in *Man'yōshū*.
- For a doubled (geminate) consonant, double its letters, as in *gakkō*.
- Capitalize the first letter of a sentence or of a proper noun.
- For special sounds, use any Rōmaji.

In Rōmaji writing, words in a sentence are separated as they are in European writing; furthermore, the linking verb ('to be') *da* and the postpositions—such as *no* and *wa*—are separated from the content words. Without extra spaces the boundaries between words and phrases would be difficult to recognize in a Rōmaji text, unlike in a Kanji–Kana mixed text where the alternations between the two types of scripts partly serve as separators. But in romanizing, a verb ending is not separated from its stem: *kaku; kakeru; kakanai* ('write; can write; don't write'). Here is how a Japanese sentence, which leaves no space between words, looks in Rōmaji with spaces between words (also fig. 20-2 below).

Ima no rōmaji no jugyō wa mōshiwake bakari no mono de hotondo mono no yaku ni tatte inai.
(Today's rōmaji instruction is in lip service only, fulfilling almost no useful purpose.)
This Japanese sentence is taken from *Rōmazi no Nippon* (*Rōmaji's Japan*, 1994, No. 494) published by the Nippon-no-Rōmazi-Sya, a society that promotes the exclusive use of Rōmaji (see next section).

Should Rōmaji Replace the Japanese Scripts?

Since the first romanization of the Japanese language by Jesuit missionaries in the 16th century, from time to time some Japanese and foreigners have advocated the exclusive use of Rōmaji. The romanization movement gained a momentum in the late 19th century when the Japanese were exposed to European culture. One of the early Japanese pioneers was Nanbu Yoshikazu, who wrote — not in Rōmaji but in Kanji — an article in 1869 and a book in 1879 advocating the use of Rōmaji to replace Kanji and Kana.

As mentioned earlier, in 1885 the Rōmaji Society adopted one Rōmaji style and published the first periodical in it, *Rōmaji Journal (ROMAJI ZASSHI)*, which lasted for 7 years. In 1905 Rōmaji Spreading Society (Rōmaji Hirome Kai) was formed, and in 1907 it adopted the revised Hepburn style of Rōmaji.

In 1886 Tanakadate Aikitsu proposed his own Japanese style Rōmaji to the Rōmaji Society. As his proposal was rejected, in 1909 he formed his own society, Nippon-no-Rōmazi-Sya ('Japan's Rōmaji Company'), which is still active. The first publication of the society was *Learning Rōmazi by Oneself (Rōmazi Hitori Geiko)*, which has been reprinted many times. The society has published over 30 other books in science and literature as well as periodicals. In 1992, in answer to a letter inquiring about the current activities of the society, Kitta, one of its members, was kind enough to send me a booklet he had authored, *Nippon no Rōmazi-undō 1582–1990 (Japan's Rōmaji Movement)*. He still sends me the society's newsletters, *Rōmazi no Nippon*. The newsletters carry some articles in Rōmaji (a torture for me to read!) and some in Kanji and Kana (a breeze to read!).

Perhaps the strongest push for the adoption of Rōmaji as the sole script came from the U.S. Education Mission to Japan in 1946 during the Occupation by the Allied Forces. The mission believed that Kanji were difficult and that the Japanese had to be rescued from the difficult Kanji. In their well-meaning but misguided view, the small minority who could read difficult Kanji texts formed a privileged elite class, and thus Kanji stood in the way of Japan's progress toward democracy and world peace. The mission recommended the speedy adoption of Rōmaji. Accordingly, the Rōmaji Education Council was formed in the Ministry of Education, and by early 1947 Rōmaji began to be taught in primary school and middle school. By 1950 it was taught along with Kanji and Kana in the majority of primary schools and half of the middle schools throughout Japan. It was used to write and read the Japanese language.

In 1950 the second American Educational Mission visited Japan, to be greeted with a report from the Ministry of Education that the general public did not accept the adoption of Rōmaji. At present, schoolchildren learn only briefly in the 4th grade how to write and read some simple common Japanese words in Rōmaji.

It is true that a Japanese text can be written entirely in Rōmaji, and that the adoption of Rōmaji would make it easier for the Japanese to harmonize with the Western culture. It is also true that the 30 or so letters of the Roman alphabet are infinitely easier to learn than the 2,000 Kanji of complex shapes with multiple readings plus 110 signs each of Hiragana and Katakana. Rōmaji is easier than Kana and Kanji for typing, typesetting, and word processing.

Why then don't the Japanese jettison their traditional cumbersome writing system and adopt the simple Rōmaji? If they do not, it is not simply because of their inertia or fear of change. After all, throughout their history the Japanese have adopted radical changes when necessary. For example, while rejecting the U.S. Education Mission's recommendation for the adoption of Rōmaji, the Japanese readily implemented the Mission's recommendation for the adoption of the U.S. system of education, including co-education.

The most likely answer is that a text written entirely in Rōmaji is hard to read silently for comprehension. This answer should be obtained through an experiment that compares reading efficiency in different scripts. But it may be difficult to find enough Japanese people who are equally practised in reading texts written in four ways: Rōmaji, Hiragana alone, Katakana alone, and a Kanji–Kana mixture. Meanwhile one can conjecture what the outcome of such a comparison might be. Besides the reading habit, there are at least three reasons why a Rōmaji text is harder to read than a Kanji–Kana or Kana text: it is long; its words lack distintinctive shapes; and the meanings of its words are extracted slowly. For another disadvantage of both Rōmaji and Kana texts, see "Kanji Stand Out in Mixed Scripts"(in chap. 21).

Consider two Kanji, one for 'light' and the other for 'aspiration'. In Kun/Japanese reading, the first Kanji requires 3 Kana (Hiragana or Katakana) and 6 Rōmaji, while the second one requires 5 Kana and 11 Rōmaji, as shown. Which is more likely to be processed as one unit, one Kanji or 6–11 Rōmaji? Not only the length but also the monotony of alternations between single consonants and single vowels in Japanese words rob them of visual distinctiveness. Compare *hikari* to *light*.

Kanji	光	志
Hiragana	ひかり	こころざし
Rōmaji	h i k a r i	k o k o r o z a s h i

With much practice a group of Rōmaji may come to be recognized as one syllable or morpheme, but it is unlikely that it will ever attain the distinctly structured shape of a Kana, or more surely of a single Kanji.

The length of visual material differs in the three scripts not only for individual words but also for texts. A Rōmaji text needs more spaces between words than does a Kana text, especially more than does a Kana–Kanji mixed text, in which alternations between the two scripts serve as separators of phrases. In one count the numbers of graphs required for the same paragraph from a newspaper editorial were: 283 Rōmaji (including the necessary spaces); 180 Kana signs (with uncustomary spaces) or 140 signs (without spaces); and 106 Kanji and Kana (no need of spaces) (Hayashi 1982: 263).

A similar pattern in the relative lengths of the three kinds of text is seen in Figure 20-2, which illustrates three brief texts, written in the customary mixture of Kanji and Hiragana, in Hiragana alone, and in Rōmaji. Texts (a, b) were selected because they are hard to read in Hiragana, while text (c) might be found in a typical cookbook.

A text is always longest in Rōmaji, intermediate in Hiragana, and shortest in mixed scripts. The longer the text, the more visual material there is to read. More critically, while reading a Rōmaji text, a reader must group a series of letters into useful linguistic and processing units, such as syllables. The task of syllable grouping is not needed in a Kana text, in which one Kana sign represents one syllable. The task of grouping a series of graphs into a meaningful morpheme is easy in a Kanji–Hiragana mixed text, since one Kanji conveniently represents this unit. One or two Kanji accompanied by a few Hiragana often represent a phrase as well.

Rōmaji are letters of a phonetic script, while Kanji are logographs. The meaning of a morpheme is directly and instantly extracted from one distinctively shaped Kanji, but it is indirectly and slowly extracted, perhaps through letter-to-sound conversion, from a sequence of 2–5 Kana or of 4–11 Rōmaji (fig. 6-3).

If the Japanese wish to adopt a phonetic script, the syllabic Kana might be better than the Roman alphabet, for reasons already given. Furthermore, learning to read is easier with a syllabary than with an alphabet (chaps. 9 and 14). Luckily, a syllabary is practicable for Japanese, which uses only about 110 simple syllables; it is not so for English, which has several thousand different syllables, some complex. In the 19th century there was a short-lived movement to use only Hiragana. The fact that the English alphabet is widely used in the world is not a good enough reason for the

No. of Graphs

(a)	K-H	母 は 歯 は 大丈夫だ	8
	H	は は は は は だ い じょ う ぶ だ	12
	Rōm	H a h a w a h a w a d a i z y ō b u d a	20
	Gloss	Mother's teeth are OK.	

(b)	K-H	我 々 は 我 々 自身の 声を	10
	H	われわれは われわれじ し ん の こ え を	16
	Rōm	W a r e w a r e w a w a r e w a r e j i s h i n n o k o e o	30
	Gloss	We write [in order to create our] own voice	

(c)	All	鶏肉と ベ−コ ンは 1.5cm の 角に 切る	17
	Rōm	K e i n i k u t o b e e k o n w a 1.5 c m n o k a k u n i k i r u	33
	Gloss	Cut chicken and bacon into 1.5cm cubes.	

Figure 20-2. Japanese texts in a variety of scripts: K = Kanji; H = Hiragana; Rōm = Rōmaji; All = these scripts plus Katakana and Arabic numerals. In (b) the symbol 々 stands for any repeated Kanji. Extra spaces needed in the Rōmaji texts are not counted.

Japanese to adopt it instead of Kana. (Incidentally, the number of users of Chinese characters is larger than that of the English alphabet.) The users of the English alphabet may be able to read aloud a Japanese text written in Rōmaji but cannot understand it, until they study the language. While they study it, they can painlessly learn simple Kana.

A text in phonetic scripts of Kana and Rōmaji might be read aloud faster, and more accurately, than that in logographic Kanji. But then, the main objective of reading a text is to obtain its meaning rather than its sound. For this main objective, a Kanji–Kana mixed text is ideal, as the next chapter will show.

The exclusive use of Rōmaji, and also of Kana, has never gained wide support among the Japanese, because it has many disadvantages for reading, on the one hand, and because Kanji has many advantages, on the other.

21

Why Keep Kanji?

Now that we have learned something about the few different scripts used in Japan, we are driven to ask, Why should the Japanese keep the complex logographic Kanji when they have three simple phonetic scripts, Katakana, Hiragana, and Rōmaji? We have already answered this question partly. To answer it fully we must consider Sino-Japanese words, which not only are numerous but also are deeply entrenched in the Japanese vocabulary; without them the Japanese vocabulary would be impoverished, if it did not collapse. Sino-Japanese words are typically written in Kanji.

Kanji Differentiate Homophones

Homophones, words with the same sound, are abundant in the Japanese language, because it uses only about 110 different syllables. By comparison, Chinese, which is also noted for its abundant homophones, uses about 1,300 different tone syllables.

Kanji differentiate homophones. For example, the native word *hana* has four different meanings: 花 ('flower'), 端 ('edge'), 鼻 ('nose'), and 洟 ('snivel'), which are clearly differentiated when written in four different Kanji. Sometimes one member of a pair of homophones, such as *kame* ('vase' or 'tortoise') is written in Kanji for one meaning ('vase', a name for a common household object), and in Katakana for another meaning ('tortoise', a name for an uncommon animal).

Kanji are even more useful, almost indispensable, in differentiating Sino-Japanese morphemes and words. Single Kanji pronounced in monosyllabic On/Chinese reading tend to have many homophones. Even though the Common Kanji list limits the On readings to 2,187, the number of homophones per syllable must still average around 20. In *A New Dictionary of Kanji Usage*, which defines 2,000 Kanji, the syllable with the largest number of homophones, 68, is *shō*, and the next largest number, 67, is *kō*. In a larger dictionary, these numbers would be larger. Even when these two Kanji are joined in *kōshō*, the compound word has 20 homophones in this small dictionary, and many more in a larger dictionary. (Recall that, in Chinese, joining two morphemes into a compound word is one way to reduce the probability that the result is homophonic; chap. 2.) All these numerous homophones will be written in different Kanji for different meanings.

Other words in a phrase or sentence are supposed to help a reader select one of the many different meanings of homophones, but they are not always adequate. Kindaichi (1978: 111) heard on the radio the phrase,

> *shikaishikaishikai.*

Write the phrase in Kanji, and its meaning ('chairmanship of the dentists' conference') will leap out. Because the compound word *kōkai* can have at least four different meanings, the sentence

> *Kōkai o kōkai suru*

can mean either "Sail an open sea" or "Regret a public disclosure." Further context would clearly distinguish the two meanings, but even within the sentence, one or other meaning becomes clear when it is written with appropriate Kanji. Or, consider the sentence,

Kisha no kisha ga kisha de kishashita.

Each of the four *kisha* is written in a different Kanji to convey the meaning "Your company's reporter returned to the office by train."

Some homophones can be used in similar contexts, thus causing various misunderstandings in daily life. Kindaichi (1978: 145–146) recounts two anecdotes. The distribution of *jun* ('semi-' 準) home-grown rice disappointed housewives who had anticipated getting *jun* ('pure, genuine' 純) home-grown rice. Or, consider the following dialogue.

B: What business are you engaged in in Tokyo?

A: I am publishing a magazine called *Nōgaku* ('*Nō* plays').

B: What? *Nōgaku* ('Science of Agriculture')? ... I would like my sons to read it, too .... "*Nō*" ('agriculture') is Japan's treasure.

A: Thank you. I am not a specialist in the field, but I would like to help this art develop and work with *nōgakushi* ('Nō players').

B: Indeed! .... It would be nice to work with the *nōgakushi* ('those holding degrees in agriculture').

The dialogue continues with more misunderstandings. There is no room for such misunderstandings when the critical words are written in Kanji: *Nōgaku* for 'Nō play' is 能 楽 and for 'science of agriculture' is 農学 . Elsewhere Kindaichi describes a scene in which an interviewer asked a man "What's your trade?," to which the man answered "It is *seika*." The question is, which of the four trades—candy maker, shoe maker, vegetable and fruit store, flower arrangement—all called *seika*, does he mean?

Morioka (1987: 70) advises his readers to look through any Japanese dictionary to be impressed with abundance of homophones. I took up his advice: In Sanseido's *Daily Concise Dictionary* (1990), in pages 118 and 119, most entry words have homophones. The sound *kisei* is shared by nine words, such as 'vigor', 'ready-made', and 'regulate', all of which are differentiated in Kanji. In speech, when listeners try to infer the meaning of an ambiguous word using context, they may visualize its Kanji. If visualization does not help, they have to ask the speaker to clarify the word's meaning.

In an experiment a homophonic target word in a sentence was better recalled when it was shown in Kanji rather than in Hiragana (Hatano and Kuhara 1981). The first of four sentences contained a homophonic target word, *hishyo*, that can mean either "secretary" or "escape from summer heat." Sentence 1 was followed by two more sentences containing the same target word in a context that did not differentiate the two meanings. Sentence 4 contained a context that could differentiate which of the two meanings was intended. As students listened to this sequence of sentences, half of them (Kanji group) were shown sentences 1 and 4 with the target in Kanji, while the other half (Kana group) were shown them in Hiragana. In a test, the target words recalled by the Kanji group were almost all correct, whereas those recalled by the Kana group contained many homophonic errors. What happened? The Kanji group could assign the correct meaning (that matched the context of sentence 4) to the target when they saw its Kanji in sentences 1 and 4, whereas the Kana group, without the help of meaning-differentiating Kanji, could initially have assigned the wrong meaning.

Meanings of Kanji Words are Grasped Well

Apart from differentiating homophones, Kanji express subtle or not so subtle differences in meanings that can be expressed in a native word. For example, the Japanese verb *toru* can be written in five different official Kanji, one each for 取る 'take', 採る 'pick', 捕る 'catch', 執 る 'execute (a duty)', and 撮 る 'take (pictures)'. The Japanese verb *naku* ('cry') is used indiscriminately for the cry of all kinds of animals. It can be written in two different official Kanji, one for 'a person cries', and another for 'a bird chirps or sings', and in several unofficial Kanji, one each for 'a child cries', 'a cat meows', 'a lamb bleats', and so on. In these examples, what is expressed with two or more native words can be expressed economically and unambiguously with one Kanji. Each of these individual Kanji contributes its specific meaning to a compound word.

On the other hand, some distinctions of meanings made by Kanji can be too subtle, or almost non-existent, for ordinary people to use consistently. Examples are: *shigeru* ('flourish'), which can be written either with 茂 or繁 ; the second Kanji of *uki* ('rainy season') can be written either as 雨季 ('season') or as 雨期('time' or 'period'). In each case, the use of the simpler and/or commoner of the two Kanji is recommended.

About half the words in the Japanese vocabulary are Sino-Japanese (table 17-1). Some Sino-Japanese words such as *gakkō* ('school') are frequently used and have few homophones, and their meanings may be grasped readily whether they are written in Kanji or Hiragana. But the same cannot be said about many other words. This section focuses on uncommon or unfamiliar Sino-Japanese words.

Typically, a Japanese dictionary or Japanese-to-foreign language dictionary lists words according to their sounds, in the order given either in the 50-sound chart (Gojūonzu, table 19-2) or the English alphabet, and defines words first by giving their Kanji. Quite often, Kanji alone provide the meanings of words. The other day when I looked up *geshi* in a Japanese–English dictionary, its Kanji 夏至('summer depart') immediately gave me its rough meaning; in fact 'summer depart' was more understandable to me than its translation "the summer solstice." The same observation extends to *geshisen* ('summer depart line') or "the tropic of Cancer."

In Japanese texts Kanji are used for most Sino-Japanese words as well as for many Japanese native content words. Kanji tend to be heavily used in road signs and newspaper headlines that have to be written in limited space and yet have to impart their messages instantly. Even in comic books intended for lower-grade schoolchildren, Kanji are used for such words, because they impart meanings faster and better than the same words written in Kana. When Sino-Japanese words are written in Kana, for whatever reason, they may be accompanied by Furiganji (fig. 19-2g, h).

A reader can grasp the meaning of a Kanji word even when she cannot pronounce it correctly. For example, for some time I used to mispronounce the two-Kanji word ('white hair') in Kun/Japanese as *shirogami*, but it turned out to be *shiraga,* another

Kun reading. The word can also be pronounced as *hakuhatsu* in On/Chinese, *baifa* in Mandarin Chinese, and *paekpal* in Korean. My understanding of the word, of course, was correct all along. In a test, when given Japanese and Sino-Japanese words in Kanji to read aloud, some testees responded with European translations, demonstrating that they knew the meanings but not the sounds of the Kanji test words ("Mass Literacy After World War II" in chap. 24).

The meaning of a logograph can be extracted directly from its visual whole pattern, whereas the meaning of a phonetically written word, especially an infrequent word, tends to be extracted indirectly, by translating the sequence of letters into a sequence of sounds, through which the meaning is obtained (figs. 6-2 and 6-3). But even in an alphabetic script familiar short words can sometimes be understood from their visual forms directly.

What do experiments show us about differences in meaning extraction between logographic Kanji and phonetic Kana? Saito (1981) gave Japanese students a short sentence containing a blank. After a brief pause, students were provided with a two-morpheme compound word written in one of four ways:

1. Kanji–Kanji
2. Kanji–Kana
3. Kana–Kanji
4. Kana–Kana.

Each compound word could complete a sentence either meaningfully or nonsensically. (To give an example from English, the sentence "The baby drinks —" is meaningful if the word inserted is *milk*, but not if it is *book*.) The students had to answer "yes" or "no" as to whether a sentence made sense. The time to respond to the four types of words was, from the fastest to the slowest: 1, 2, 3, and 4. (When the task was to read the words aloud, the order was reversed, the Kana–Kana version being fastest; chap. 6.) Customarily a compound word is written in one script, be it Kanji or Kana, rather than in a Kanji–Kana mixture. But even so, if one of the parts of the compound was in Kanji, it was understood faster than if both were in Kana. And when Kanji came before Kana in a mixed-script word, meaning extraction was faster than when Kana came before Kanji.

Several observations and experiments described here and also in Chapter 6 all provide convincing evidence that meanings are obtained faster from logographic Kanji than from the phonetic Kana.

Kanji for Compound Words

Words and morphemes are said to be productive, if they combine readily to create new compound words. For example, the English morpheme *man* is productive, as it appears in many words, such as *policeman, chairman, superman, salesman*. Japanese native morphemes and words can be joined to create compound words, but not as readily as can Sino-Japanese words written in Kanji. Let us see how productive Japanese native morphemes are:

     1. iki-mono ('living thing')
     2. iki-mono-nara-i ('living-thing study')
     3. iki-mono (O) naraU hito ('biologist')

Up to four morphemes may be joined, if tenuously, in a compound word, as in (2). But if *hito* ('person') is to be added, one or two grammatical morphemes (shown in uppercase for illustration) have to be included for naturalness, as in (3). And "narau hito" ('person who studies'), unlike its Sino-Japanese equivalent *gakusha* ('learned person' or 'scholar'), does not become one compound word but remains a two-word construction of "verb/adjective + noun."

Of the above list a dictionary lists as entry words the first word *(ikimono)* but not the second and the third. Because a Japanese morpheme can have two or more syllables, a native compound word can be long: *nakikuzureru* ('cry' and 'to collapse' for 'to break down crying') has six syllables. The process of joining native morphemes and words breaks down when used to create technical terms, because the Japanese native vocabulary lacks the morphemes for "logic" and other abstract concepts.

By contrast, the Kanji for Sino-Japanese morphemes are highly productive and readily combine to create compound words, all the while maintaining their individual meanings. In a 1980 dictionary of new words, close to 30% were Kanji compound words, but only 2% were native compound words; the rest were foreign loan words and hybrids (Nomura 1988). Here are examples of recently coined Kanji compound words.

two-Kanji word: 1 Kanji 'brain' + 1 Kanji 'death' = ('brain death')
three-Kanji word: 1 Kanji 'nuclear' + 2 Kanji 'family' = ('nuclear family')
four-Kanji word: 2 Kanji 'universe' + 2 Kanji 'science' = ('cosmology')

The third kind, which combines two two-Kanji words into one four-Kanji word, is the most common form among newly coined compound words.

Particularly productive and useful are Kanji Sino-Japanese prefixes, suffixes and abstract morphemes, such as the following:

- prefix *fu-* ('un-', negation of a state or action), as in *fu-kō, fu-chūi* ('unhappy', 'careless')
- prefix *mu-* ('non-', negation of existence), as in *mu-gaku, mu-ri* ('uneducated', 'unreasonable')
- suffix *-teki* ('-like, -al, -istic'), as in *riron-teki, sofuto-teki* ('reason, opinion, -al' = 'theoretical', 'soft')
- abstract concept *ri* ('logic, reason'), as in *ri-ron* ('reason, opinion' = 'theory').

Some Kanji are versatile and can be used as the first, second, third, or fourth constituent of a compound word. Consider the Kanji for "learn(ing)" in Figure 3-5, which is used as a constituent in countless compound words, such as 'school', 'middle school', 'student', 'scholar', 'psychology', and 'psychologist'. Once you learn the shape, sound, and meaning of the Kanji for "learning," you can learn easily numerous other words containing it.

Such suffix-like use of Kanji occurs in many words, as shown in Table 21-1 for the Kanji "vehicle, cart" whose On/Chinese reading is *sha* and whose Kun/Japanese reading is *kuruma* or *-guruma* (as the second item in a compound word). The last word in the table, *dashi*, is an example of Jukujikun (two Kanji assigned to a one-morpheme native word). One two-Kanji word has two sounds and two meanings: in On/Chinese reading *fūsha* ('windmill') and in Kun/Japanese reading *kazaguruma* ('pinwheel').

Table 21-1. Words with *Kanji* Sha (*On*) or -Guruma (*Kun*) ('*Vehicle, Car*')

Word	Morpheme	Meaning
basha	horse vehicle	horse carriage
densha	electricity vehicle	street car, tramcar
fūsha	wind wheel	windmill
guriinsha	green car	1st class on Japan Railways
jidōsha	self move vehicle	automobile
jikayōsha	private house use vehicle	private car
jinrikisha	man power vehicle	rickshaw
jitensha	self rotate wheel	bicycle
kikansha	engine car	locomotive
kōyōsha	public use vehicle	official vehicle
kūsha	empty car	vacant (of a taxi)
mansha	full vehicle	parking lot full
nibasha	load horse vehicle	horse-drawn cart, wagon
sanrinsha	three wheel vehicle	tricycle
shokudōsha	eat hall car	dining car
suisha	water wheel	water wheel
haguruma	teeth wheel	gear, cogwheel
itoguruma	thread wheel	spinning wheel
kazaguruma	wind wheel	pinwheel
mizuguruma	water wheel	water wheel
ubaguruma	nursemaid vehicle	baby carriage
dashi	mountain vehicle	float or festival car

But another two-Kanji word has the same meaning "water wheel" whether in its On reading *suisha* or its Kun reading *mizuguruma*. The point of Table 21-1 is to show that individual Kanji make reasonable contributions to the meaning of the compound words.

Table 21-1 notwithstanding, individual Kanji do not always maintain their meanings in a compound word. We encountered a few Chinese examples of illogical compound words, such as *(luo)huasheng* ('to fall, flower, live/raw' for 'peanut') ("Compound Words and Idioms" in chap. 4). The Japanese borrowed this word (The alternative Japanese words for peanut are the English loan word *piinatsu,*and *nankinmame,* which means 'Nanjing peas'.) Among hundreds of new Sino-Japanese words coined in Japan, I spotted one that puzzled me: *kōshinjyo* ('inquiry agency') consists of three Kanji: the first Kanji means ('emerge', 'arise', or 'fun'), the second means ('trust', 'believe', or 'message'), and the third means ('place'). Linguistic matters are not always logical; occasionally they can be downright arbitrary.

Some compound words apear puzzling because they are truncated versions of classic phrases. The word *bōmei* consists of two Kanji, one for 'lose' and the other for 'life', yet the word means not "loss of life" but "flight from one's native place." According to one explanation, the word comes from a Chinese classic phrase, *tōBOjikyuMEI* ('to escape to save one's life'). The meanings of some Kanji words make sense, if we use a bit of imagination: *ginkō* ('silver row' for 'bank') and *jihaku* ('self, white/blank' for 'confession'). These Kanji words still hint at their meanings far more than their English counterparts do. Most of these "illogical" words are shared among Chinese, Japanese, and Korean.

Sometimes the same Kanji has one meaning in one compound word and another meaning in another, due to the fact that some single Kanji represent two or more different meanings. The Kanji 和 *wa* has the meaning "peace, concord" in such compound words as *wakai, heiwa* ('reconciliation', 'peace'). The same Kanji has a quite different meaning "Japanese" in such Kanji words as *wago, washoku* ('Japanese native word', 'Japanese food').

Productive Kanji enrich the Japanese vocabulary, which is deficient in some useful morphemes and in the mechanism for combining them into compound words.

Kanji for Technical Terms and Abbreviations

Japanese technical terms consist of familiar morphemes in Kanji, perhaps because they are not merely translations but also explanations of the concepts. Consider the Sino-Japanese term for "biologist" 生物学者 ('living, thing, study, person'). The English word *biologist,* too, is decomposable into *bio-logy-ist,* but each of these morphemes is a learned item, a bound morpheme into the bargain. This and many other technical terms in English are composed of Latin and Greek morphemes, with which few ordinary English speakers are familiar. Compare in Table 21-2 several technical terms in English and in Japanese Kanji. Most technical terms in Kanji are shared with Chinese and Korean.

To be fair to English, the meanings of some technical terms are more transparent in English than in Kanji. *Metaphysics* is hard enough to understand, but its Kanji counterpart, *keijijyōgaku,* is even harder; it consists of four Kanji "form, and, above, learning," and the Kanji for *ji,* a conjunction, can be translated variously as 'and (so/ yet)', 'but', 'thus', 'that is', etc. This Kanji term is a truncated version of the two Chinese clauses, "Principle is the way that is above form; matter is the receptacle that is beneath form," which derives from a teaching of the prominent Neo-Confucian, Zhu Xi, of the Chinese Song Dynasty. It is one of the terms coined by the Japanese and adopted by the Chinese and the Koreans.

Some technical terms are familiar, everyday words in English but unfamiliar, technical words in Kanji. The English word in dentistry, *bridge,* is a familiar everyday word, whereas its four-Kanji Japanese equivalent, "manufactured false teeth," is an unfamiliar and technical term. But then *bridge* by itself has several meanings and is ambiguous out of context, whereas its Kanji equivalent has one unambiguous meaning.

Table 21-2. Technical Terms in English and Japanese

English	Sino-Japanese in Kanji
hermaphrodite	both, sex, animal/flower/person
hexahedron	six, sided, shape
leukemia	white, blood, disease
ophthalmoscope	exam, eye, mirror
otorhinology	ear, nose, branch/section
psychology	mind, logic, study
schizophrenia	mind, divided, disease
seismograph	earth, shake, instrument
urethritis	urine, passage, inflame

Anyway, in one study that compared ordinary words and scholarly words in ten fields such as mathematics, physics, chemistry, dentistry, the distance in meaning between the two kinds of words was smaller in English than in Japanese in all the ten fields (Hayashi 1982). Having not seen the Japanese and English technical terms compared in the study, I cannot tell how objectively and fairly they were selected.

Many names of frequently mentioned institutions and places in Japanese have abbreviated versions, as in Chinese and Korean. In English, words are often abbreviated to acronyms by using the initial letters of the component words, as in USA = United States of America, and YMCA = Young Men's Christian Association. These two acronyms are familiar. But what about less familiar acronyms such as AFDC and WHAM, or the ever-changing alphabetic soup of the civil-service bureaucracy, which provide no clues to their meanings? (AFDC = Assisted Families with Dependent Children; WHAM = Women's Health Action and Mobilization) And then there are ambiguous acronyms such as AAA that can stand for many organizations, such as Amateur Athletic Association, American Automobile Association, Agricultural Adjustment Administration, as pointed out in Chapter 4.

By contrast, abbreviated Kanji words tend to contain clues to their meanings, as in *Tōdai* ('east, large') for *Tōkyo Daigaku* ('east-capital large-learning' or 'Tōkyo University'). If this university name were to be abbreviated as TD, like an English acronym, it would be meaningless, and furthermore ambiguous, because it could stand for many other institutions, such as "Tokyo District," "Tokyo Dome," "Toronto Daycare," and "Toronto Dominion."

In Japanese abbreviations, as in Chinese and Korean ones, key characters are selected in such a way that the resulting words are distinct. Thus, if there were a university called "Tōhon Daigaku," it would probably be abbreviated as "Hondai," to distinguish it from "Tōdai." It is more important that the chosen Kanji be unambiguous than that it be the initial one in a compound word. And it is the familiarity of Kanji shape and not its sound that matters. Thus, the first Kanji of *Waseda University* is retained in the abbreviation *Sōdai* but with its sound changed from *wa* to *sō*.

Not only the names of institutions but also common phrases or sentences are abbreviated. For example, *kokuishinan* ('national, easy, private, difficult') is an abbreviation of "Entrance exams to national universities are easy, whereas those to private universities are difficult." The long name *Kokuritsukokugokenkyūsho* ('The National [Japanese] Language Research Institute') is drastically but unambiguously abbreviated into the two-Kanji word *Kokken* 国研 ('national, research').

Kanji Stand out in Mixed-Script Text

A Japanese text, as shown in countless examples in this book, is written in a mixture of Kanji, Hiragana, Katakana, Rōmaji, and Arabic numerals. The proportions of graphs in different scripts varies in different types of texts, as shown in Table 21-3. In the samples listed in the table, some texts contain more Hiragana than Kanji while other texts show the reverse pattern. In either case the two most important Japanese scripts are Kanji and Hiragana, which make up between 58 and 87% of a text. The texts examined in Table 21-3, which are intended for Japanese readers, contain only a few words in Rōmaji. Unlike most texts, sentences from a software manual for Japanese

Table 21-3. Proportions of Kanji, Hiragana, and Others in Text

Script	Paper A 1971	Paper B 1982	Software 1991
Hiragana	35.3%	47.1%	41.5%
Kanji	46.1	40.2	16.1
Katakana	6.1	3.9	28.8
English	0.0	0.0	6.8
Arabic Numeral	1.4	1.4	4.2
Rōmaji	0.4	0.0	0.0
Special Symbol	10.7	8.6	2.5

Under "Script," Special Symbols mean such items as a short bar for a long vowel in Katakana words and the symbol for a repeated graph (as in Figure 21-1b).
Paper A = 1 million graphs in newspapers, examined from the types used for 21 days in July 1971 by Kyodo Press (Hayashi 1982: 206)
Paper B = several articles from newspapers and magazines (Nakano 1989: 120)
Software = four sentences from a software manual (A & A Co. 1991)

and English word processing contains a high proportion of Katakana, reflecting the fact that many words related to computers are English loan words.

Figure 21-1 shows three brief texts written in various ways: a Kanji–Hiragana mixture, all Hiragana, all Rōmaji, and a Kanji–Hiragana–Katakana–Rōmaji–Arabic numerals mixture. Of these, only the first and the last are customary forms.

All-Hiragana texts are longer than their Kanji–Hiragana mixed versions, in part because they may need extra spaces between phrases, as opposed to a Kanji–Kana text in which alternations between the two scripts mark phrase boundaries, and in part because between two and five Kana are needed to write one Kanji. An all-Hiragana sentence is hard to read because its Kana signs have to be grouped into words and

No. of Graphs

(a) K-H	母 は 歯 は 大丈夫だ	8
H	は は は は は だ い じょ う ぶだ	12
Rōm	Haha wa ha wa daizyōbu da	20
Gloss	Mother's teeth are OK.	
(b) K-H	我 々は我 々自身の声を	10
H	われわれは われわれじ しん の こえを	16
Rōm	Wareware wa wareware jishin no koe o	30
Gloss	We write [in order to create our] own voice	
(c) All	鶏肉と ベーコンは 1.5cmの角に 切る	17
Rōm	Keiniku to beekon wa 1.5cm no kaku ni kiru	33
Gloss	Cut chicken and bacon into 1.5cm cubes.	

Figure 21-1. Japanese texts in a variety of scripts: K = Kanji; H = Hiragana; Rōm = Rōmaji; All = these scripts plus Katakana and Arabic numerals. In (b) the symbol 々 stands for any repeated Kanji. (fig. 20-2 reproduced)

phrases by the reader. Even when its phrases are separated, the sentence may still be difficult because it may consist of a string of homophones, as in texts (a) and (b). Text (a) was created, and text (b) selected, deliberately to demonstrate how difficult it is to read an all-Hiragana text, especially without spaces to mark phrase boundaries. Typical or not, they illustrate the point. Text (c) is quite ordinary, without repeating same-sounding words.

If the only function of Kanji in text were to separate words and phrases, the Japanese could simply adopt the Western practice of separating words, as is done in Rōmaji writing. Kanji do shorten a text, but the more important use of Kanji in text is to write content words. The complex and dark Kanji, with an average of ten strokes, mostly straight lines, stand out in text against a background of grammatical morphemes written in simple and light Hiragana that have an average of three strokes, mostly curved. Consider text (a): Kanji are used for the three content words—'mother', 'teeth', and 'OK'—from which readers should be able to grasp the meaning of the sentence, 'Mother's teeth are OK'; if they have difficulty in relating the three content words, they can then use the grammatical morphemes in Hiragana.

For helping readers differentiate different types of words, text (c) is ideal: Content words—two Japanese (cut, cube) and one Sino-Japanese (chicken meat)—are in Kanji; other content words—one English loan word (*bacon*) is in Katakana while the other loan word (*cm*) is in Rōmaji; still another content word describing the length of a cube is in Arabic numerals (*1.5*), and grammatical morphemes are in Hiragana.

In English a similar effect can be achieved by varying font and script as in 1 rather than in 2.

1. **Chicken meat** and **bacon** are **cut** into **1.5 cm cubes.**

2. chicken meat and bacon are cut into one-and-a-half centimeter cubes.

In an experiment, an English text in which content words were written in boldface was read faster than a regular text (Taylor and Park 1995).

Returning to Japanese reading, an experienced reader develops, consciously or unconsciously, a strategy of paying more attention to the visually dark and semantically important Kanji (and to the Arabic numerals, Rōmaji, and Katakana) than to the visually light and semantically less important Hiragana. When required to read all-Hiragana text, readers no longer can use this efficient processing strategy, and their reading is slowed considerably. Reading time is slowed also because an all-Hiragana text tends to be visually longer than a mixed text. In one experiment, college students' reading times were fastest for a Kanji–Hiragana mixed text, next for an all-Hiragana text, and slowest for an all-Katakana text (Nakano 1958). The faster reading of the all-Hiragana text than the all-Katakana text suggests that the familiarity of graphs also affects reading speed. Katakana and Hiragana equally represent the sounds of the syllables, but Katakana are normally used for special words—loan words and onomatopoeia—that do not necessarily appear in every page of a text, whereas Hiragana for grammatical morphemes appear in every sentence.

By writing in a Kanji–Hiragana mixture, a writer saves paper space but expends more time and effort, since the average stroke number is three for Hiragana but is ten for Kanji. In one experiment, the time to copy a text was fastest for Hiragana (1 min 23 sec per 100 graphs), next Katakana (1 min 37 sec), and last Kanji–Kana mixed text

23 sec per 100 graphs), next Katakana (1 min 37 sec), and last Kanji–Kana mixed text (1 min 44 sec) (Nakano 1958). Kanji, in spite of their complexity, were written almost as fast as Katakana and only slightly slower than Hiragana. Hiragana, which are as simply shaped as Katakana, were written faster than Katakana. Obviously, copying speed is affected not only by the complexity of the letter shapes but also by practice. Nakano's results suggest that it would actually be much faster to copy the same content in a Kanji–Hiragana mixture than in pure Hiragana, since the mixture uses only about 2/3 the number of graphs.

In writing a text, in contrast to copying it, a writer must recall the shapes of graphs. This recalling is likely to be more difficult for the shapes of 2,000 complex Kanji than for the 110 simple Hiragana or Katakana. But then these difficulties are minimized in word processing ("Typing and Word Processing," later in this chapter).

Kanji for Personal Names

Japanese personal names are almost always written in Kanji. The Common Kanji list limits the number of Kanji for personal names to 2,229 (1,945 Common Kanji + 284 extra), but these Kanji can be given any Kun/Japanese and On/Chinese readings. Writing Japanese names in Kanji has some advantages as well as disadvantages.

Japanese has many different family names, unlike Chinese or Korean. A typical Japanese name consists of four Kanji, two for the family name and two for the given name, in that order, as in *Satō Tarō* (for a boy) or *Suzuki Hanako* (for a girl; remember that Kun readings can have more than one syllable for each Kanji). Many boys' given names end in *-rō* ('young man') and girl's names in *-ko* ('child' or 'little one'). *Satō* is the most common Japanese family name, followed by *Suzuki*. To address a Japanese person by name, whether family or given, one typically attaches *-san* that can stand for Mr., Mrs., Ms, and Miss, as in *Suzuki-san* and *Hanako-san*. Its honorific form is *-sama*, while its familiar or diminutive form is *-chan*.

The Japanese order of "family name–given name" is the same as in Chinese and Korean, but in publications for Westerners this order may or may not be used. In this book the Japanese order is used.

For a boy's given name English-speaking parents rarely invent a name; instead they tend to choose popular and often Biblical names, such as *John* and *David*. In Japan parents may sometimes make up a name, often a native word, and then choose typically two, but occasionally one or three, Kanji to represent the meaning and/or sound of the chosen name. Apparently, the choice of Kanji is sometimes made on the basis of advice from a fortune-teller.

Suppose parents choose *Hajime* ('beginning') as a given name for their first son. To represent it, they choose one Kanji with the meaning not of "beginning" but of "spring," with the lame justification that the spring is the first of the four seasons. The customary readings of Kanji for "spring" is *shun* in On/Chinese and *haru* in Kun/Japanese, and not *hajime*. If this name were written in Kana either as *haru* or *hajime*, it would miss one of the two meanings expressed in one Kanji with an uncustomary sound. Needless to say, boys' names chosen in such a capricious way pose problems to readers, who have no way of knowing that the Kanji for "spring" is to be read in an uncustomary sound, and if so what the sound may be. This Kanji for "spring" has another unusual sound when used in a family name with another Kanji for 'sun' or 'day', as *Kasuga*. So, Kanji for boy's names may be pregnant with meaning and significance but provide inadequate or misleading clues to their sounds.

To complicate the matter further, people who have a single-Kanji given name normally use a Kun reading, but when they become famous they sometimes want to use an On reading, which has Buddhist overtones. As Prof. F. Pitts writes me, his geographer friend Ishida Hiroshi wanted to be called Ishida Kan, but his American friends hooted at the idea, and he gave up.

Miller (1986) goes as far as to suggest that Japanese given names for males are not meant to be pronounced except by their parents. The Japanese themselves are resigned to the fact that they do not know how to pronounce some given names. Mercifully, Furigana (annotating Kana) often accompany Kanji names on Japanese business cards and publications, though they are not used in a telephone directory, which is already crowded with Kanji, Kana, and Arabic numerals.

Japanese parents appear to be less choosy and fussy about girls' names; they are even content to give only Kana names to girls, such as *Banana, Midori* ('green') (a name shared by an internationally known violinist and a champion figure skater) and *Hibari* ('lark'). But one father, at the end of World War II, chose two Kanji for his daughter's name *Mutsuyo* ('harmonious world') to express his abhorrence to wars and his longing for peace. If this name were written in Kana, its felicitous meaning would not be so obvious. *Mutsu* with *ki* can mean "diaper," and *yo* can mean "night," "above," "predict/prepare," "four," or "era."

If Kanji names are written in Kana, they are bound to lose some significant meaning and/or become hard to distinguish from other names that sound the same. Several names that are differentiated in Kanji share the same sound, such as *Yasuji* (for men) and *Keiko* (for women). On the other hand, when names are written only in Kanji there is a problem of uncustomary sounds of some Kanji. So the solution to this dilemma is to use Kanji names that have customary sounds or to add Furigana if the Kanji have unusual sounds. Kana names are possible when they are native words with few homophones.

Disadvantages of Kanji

Kanji have several good features, as we have seen, but they also have a few bad features, which we now consider.

The readings or sounds of Kanji are complex not only for personal names but also for ordinary words, as described earlier, especially in "Kanji Readings: On/Chinese and Kun/Japanese" (in chap. 18). Kanji are read in two very different systems, one based on Chinese and the another on Japanese; each of On/Chinese reading and Kun/Japanese reading has a few varieties; and there is some arbitrariness as to how a Kanji is to be read in any given word.

Kanji have complex shapes, which adversely affect writing. The average stroke number is 10 for official Kanji and is 3 for Hiragana or Katakana. Kanji is more complex than Kana even allowing for the fact that one Kanji often requires two Kana signs. The more complex a shape, the more time and effort it takes to write. And a complex shape with many details is harder to recall accurately than a simple shape with few details. This is why people often make errors in writing Kanji, as described in "Learning Kanji and Kana" (in chap. 22).

Kanji are numerous; even counting only those in the Common Kanji list plus those for personal names, there are 2,229 (table 18-2). But it is not the sheer number that makes Kanji learning difficult; rather it is the lack of systematic relations among them. True, the pictographic or symbolic nature of some Kanji has mnemonic value, and the majority of Kanji are related by sharing either sound-cuing phonetics or meaning-cuing semantic components ("Six Categories of Characters" in chap. 3). But these mnemonic values and cues do not amount to a tight system. All in all, mastering a large number of complex Kanji involves much rote memorizing, takes time and effort, and is seldom perfect.

There is no one simple and consistent way to list Kanji in a dictionary. Consider *A New Dictionary of Kanji Usage* for English speakers. It lists 2,000 Kanji by the order of their frequency of use and/or importance, which is not the kind of information that people carry in their heads. Fortunately, and by necessity, the dictionary provides as indices three kinds of lists of all 2,000 Kanji (each with its entry number): the first according to the 50-sound chart, the second according to stroke number, and the third by English meanings alphabetically ordered. So, one can look up a Kanji in this dictionary whether one knows only its frequency/importance, sound, visual shape, or meaning. But at a cost of time and effort.

Looking up Kanji by sound or stroke number involves selecting the target out of several items that share the same sound or stroke number. For example, in the above dictionary, under the On/Chinese reading *shō* (which has the largest number of homophonic Kanji) 68 Kanji are listed, and under the stroke number 11 (the most common stroke number), as many as 227 Kanji are listed. And the stroke number of a Kanji, unless it is extremely small, say under 5, is not apparent by looking at the Kanji; you have to write the target Kanji yourself, carefully counting its stroke number and remembering it until you look it up in a dictionary.

For telephone directories and other large name lists, each of the individual symbols that make up Kana, Kanji, or Rōmaji names is treated like a separate word. If the initial words of two names are pronounced differently, the name whose sound comes earlier in the 50-sound chart goes first; if the words sound alike but are written with different Kanji, the name with the simpler Kanji goes first; if both the reading and Kanji are the same, the next words of the two names are compared, and so on.

In the West, by contrast, whenever we have to list a large number of words—be they words in a dictionary, books in a library, names in a phone book, topics in an index or file—we list them in a simple, and almost universal, alphabetic order. Millions of books in libraries are sorted both by authors and titles, and always in alphabetic order. Interestingly, even in Japan the alphabetic order is used sometimes for catalogue cards in the National Diet Library or seats in an auditorium.

Typing and Word Processing

Writing on a typewriter in Japanese, with its complex writing system, is awkward and time consuming. A typewriter for English (or for any other languages that use an alphabet) requires keys for 52 upper- and lower-case letters plus about ten extra symbols (e.g., * and &) and the ten Arabic numerals. But a Japanese typewriter requires keys for Hiragana and Katakana signs plus a few special symbols (e.g., a bar for the long vowel sign), and about 3,000 Kanji divided in batches according to frequency of use. A typist searches for a target Kanji, replacing a Kanji tray if necessary, and punches it on paper. Such a search is time consuming. Not surprisingly, typewriters, if they were still around, are used only in some offices by highly trained typists and not in ordinary houses.

Word processing on a computer makes Japanese writing a lot easier and faster than mechanical typewriting, though not as easy as writing in English. It is becoming popular. I now receive from Japan personal as well as business letters written on a word processor. There are even toy word processors for young children! A good, serious word processor stores a large number of Kanji: the 2,965 of the JIS (Japan Industrial Standard) level I, the 3,388 level II, and the 5,801 supplementary Kanji, and so writers have at their disposal over 12,000 Kanji. It stores also Hiragana signs and Katakana signs, as well as Rōmaji, Arabic numerals, and other kinds of letters and symbols.

A writer can input a whole sentence phonetically, either in Kana or Rōmaji, and then by using a function key, converts certain words into other scripts, such as Kanji. Since there are some patterns in the types of words customarily written in Kanji, Hiragana, Katakana, or Rōmaji, these patterns can be incorporated in software. In principle, a writer can type in a whole paragraph, even a whole passage, and then press a function key to trigger a script conversion, but this procedure is not practical, because the conversion from one script into another is error prone and needs human editing. The writer has to watch out for wrong Kanji output, which may occur because some homophonic Kanji words can be used in the same context (see "Kanji Differentiate Homophones" in this chapter). She also has to ensure that the right proportion of words is converted to scripts appropriate for the audience. This kind of adjustment and correction is easier to make sentence by sentence than passage by passage.

Recently, a Japanese graduate student in my comparative literacy class, Mariko Haneda, copied on her word processor two paragraphs on the topic of teaching the Japanese language to foreigners. She input the text in the Roman letters, and a comma or period triggered a conversion of scripts. In spite of ample context, the computer often produced "dumb" errors. For example, in the sentence, "However, since Kanji are created in China, their shapes are based on China's nature and culture, custom and habit," the phrase *shizen ya bunka* ('nature and culture') was produced as a semi-nonsensical phrase, because the native grammatical morpheme *ya* ('and') wrongly combined with the next syllable to form *yabun* ('night'), leaving behind the meaningless or ambiguous *ka*, which was converted to a Hiragana sign. This kind of error is too dumb for a human writer to make. For the phrase *fūzoku ya shūkan* ('custom and habit'), the computer produced the correct two Kanji for the first word but a homophonic wrong two Kanji that meant 'week' for the second word. Spaces provided between phrases and words might eliminate some errors, but they are not a normal feature of Japanese writing (figs. 7-1b and 20-2). A sentence can contain a long stretch of over 30 Hiragana (about 10 words) without any space or punctuation.

The users of a Japanese word processor must have considerable knowledge of many aspects of Japanese text: What words are customarily written in which scripts;

many aspects of Kanji, such as frequency of use, stroke number, Kanji for special use, On and Kun readings and relative frequency between the two. In particular, they must be able to choose the right one among many homophonic Kanji. In addition, they must have good knowledge about punctuation and spacing.

On a Japanese word processor, writers no longer have to recall the shapes of Kanji, since they merely call out the stored Kanji using its sound in one of its readings. The complexity of Kanji shape no longer causes difficulty in writing, since a computer takes the same time to output a complex or simple Kanji, unlike a person who writes each Kanji stroke by stroke. Users of a word processor may be tempted to convert more words into Kanji than they normally use in writing by hand. Someday, when people write only on computers, they may be able to read a text containing many Kanji without being able to write these Kanji by hand.

Kanji, because of their large number and multiple readings, are not as efficient as Rōmaji or Kana for mechanical typing and typesetting, but computers can greatly improve their efficiency.

Is Kanji Use Declining?

In the early history of writing, only a small group of upper class people wrote texts, and they used only Kanji, sometimes using them as logographs and sometimes as phonetic signs. Such a process must have been tortuous for a writer, and its product must have presented a reader with a formidable task, considering the fact that Japanese and Chinese are unrelated languages requiring a different set of words, grammatical morphemes, and word order in sentences.

The Japanese were compelled to create the simple phonetic script, Kana, and once created, Kana eased Japanese writing. A handful of women writers wrote mainly in Hiragana, but most writers mixed Kanji and Kana, using Kanji to write content words and Kana to write grammatical morphemes. Initially, the proportion of Kanji in a text tended to be as high as 90%, but over time it decreased. As shown in Figure 21-2, the use of Kanji declined in the hundred years between 1880 and 1980.

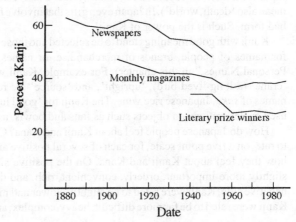

Figure 21-2. The decline in the use of Kanji, 1880—1980 (Data from Nomura 1988)

There are several possible reasons for the decline of Kanji use: Hiragana can replace Ateji ('assigned Kanji'); Katakana can replace some Sino-Japanese words, such as names of uncommon trees and animals; new words tend to be European loan words which are written in Katakana; and above all, in modern times the government has limited the number of Kanji for common use.

Will Kanji use decline further in the future? Now there is evidence that the modern trend of declining use of Kanji has halted. Even in Figure 21-2, the decline halted around 1960, after which it appears to have increased ever so slightly in two of the three sets of data. Recall that the Common Kanji list currently in use has added more Kanji to the earlier Temporary Kanji list of 1973. Since 1990, a few hundred additional Kanji have been allowed for people's names (table 18-2). In one survey, the proportion of Kanji in text, sampled every 10 years between 1906 and 1976, steadily declined from 46.8% in 1906 to 36.2% in 1956, but it remained stable thereafter—37.8% in 1966 and 38.0% in 1976. Indeed, appearance of Kanji in text may have increased recently, thanks to word processing that can readily convert words in Kana into Kanji. In the leading newspaper *Asahi*, some words (e.g., *wakaru* 'understand') that were always or usually written in Hiragana in 1969 were often written in a Kanji–Hiragana mixture in 1989 (Numamoto 1992). The use of Kanji is no longer declining; it may even rise.

What do Japanese people think about Kanji? They have favorite Kanji. Shoppers in a department store were asked to select one favorite Kanji among 100 randomly arranged in a list (Saiga 1978). Over 3,400 shoppers participated, showing their interest in Kanji. And the five Kanji with the largest votes were 愛 'love' *ai*, 愁 'pensive' *shū*, 誠 'sincere' *sei*, 夢 'dream' *yume*, and 心 'mind, heart' *kokoro*. Three of the five Kanji contain the semantic component for *kokoro* ('mind, heart'). Obviously, these five Kanji were selected for their meanings, all of which have something to do with psychological states, rather than for their sounds or shapes, which do not show any obvious pattern.

Are there disliked Kanji? Japanese people shun the number "four," because the sound of its Kanji *shi* (On reading) is homophonic to the Kanji for "death." The fourth floor in a building should be *shikai*, following *sankai* ('third floor'; *san* is a Sino-Japanese numeral), but is called *yonkai* (*yon* is a native numeral), because *shikai* can mean also 'death, world'). In Japan even gifts that involve four of anything are horribly bad form. Such is the power of Kanji!

Kanji with good meanings tend to be selected and those with bad meanings avoided for names of people, brands of merchandise, or names of stores (also "Kanji for Personal Names," in this chapter). For example, Kanji with such nice meanings as 'crane' (a long-lived bird), 'upright', and 'source' are routinely selected for brand names of *sake*, Japanese rice wine. The Kanji for 'good luck' and 'long life' are often used as decorations on objects such as fans and bowls, as in China and Korea.

How do Japanese people feel about Kanji and Kana? College students were asked to rate, on a five point scale, for each of several positive and negative adjective pairs, how they feel about Kanji and Kana. On the positive side, Kanji were rated to be slightly more important, orderly, convenient, rich, and deep than Kana. But on the negative side, Kanji were rated to be slightly slower and more constrained than Kana; Kanji were rated to be far more difficult, heavy, complex, and hard than Kana. This and the following studies were conducted by two psychologists, Kaiho and Nomura (1983).

What do the Japanese predict about the future of Kanji? Freshmen and sophomores responded to the question as follows:

- The use of Kanji will increase in the future — 5.3%
- The use of Kanji will remain the same as now — 44.0%
- The use of Kanji will decrease — 49.3%
- Kanji will disappear and Kana alone will be used — 1.3%

So, the vast majority of the college students think that the use of Kanji will in the future either remain the same as now or decrease but not disappear.

What are the attitudes of Japanese people toward the question of keeping or abolishing Kanji? Primary and secondary school students who are struggling to master Kanji may wish Kanji to be abolished, whereas adults who have already mastered the official Kanji and are enjoying their benefits may wish to keep them. Most Japanese authors of books on the Japanese language seem to be in favor of, or resigned to, keeping Kanji.

Conclusions: Keep Kanji but Streamline Them

On the positive side, Kanji, because they represent the meanings of morphemes, serve many useful functions in the Japanese language: they differentiate the abundant homophones of Japanese native and Sino-Japanese morphemes; they enrich the Japanese vocabulary with their high productivity; they provide a convenient means for creating technical terms and abbreviations; they mark content words in text for efficient reading, and so on. On the negative side, Kanji, because they are numerous and complex in shape and sound, are difficult to master; and they are inconvenient for looking up in a dictionary, for word processing, and for typesetting.

The crucial question is, Are the benefits of Kanji great enough to justify the time and effort needed to learn them? Or, can Kanji be streamlined so as to minimize their difficulty without sacrificing their usefulness? Over the years Japanese have tried to streamline, reform, and standardize their scripts, especially Kanji. The impetus for reform seems to be particularly strong when Japan comes in contact with an outside culture: the advanced European culture, including the Roman alphabet, during the Meiji era in the late 19th century, the Allied Occupation of Japan after World War II in the 1940s, and the use of computers in recent times.

In 1866 one Japanese thinker, Maejima Hisoka, advocated the abolition of Kanji in favor of the exclusive use of Hiragana. He published an all-Hiragana newspaper *Mainichi Hiragana Shimbunshi* in 1873 and 1874. Since then a few societies have sprung up to promote the exclusive use of either Hiragana or Katakana. As described in Chapter 20, a few societies exist also to promote the exclusive use of Rōmaji. In particular in 1946 the U.S. Education Mission to Japan recommended the exclusive use of Rōmaji. Despite all these movements to get rid of Kanji in favor of the exclusive use of either Kana or Rōmaji, the Japanese stubbornly cling to Kanji. Why? Let me give possible reasons by using my own experience to summarize what has been discussed so far on this topic.

If I want to write a text in Japanese, I have to practise writing Kanji, whose complex shapes are easily forgotten unless used often. And writing Kanji, even familiar ones, takes more time and effort than writing Kana. I would also have to learn by heart all the rules on how to use Kanji, Hiragana, Katakana, and Rōmaji. However, writing on a word processor alleviates, but by no means eliminate, these problems.

If I want to read aloud a Japanese text, I sometimes come across Kanji whose sounds I do not know or know insecurely, either because I have never learned them or because I once learned them but have forgotten; sometimes I know their sounds only in On, Kun, Chinese, or Korean. Yet I have little trouble in obtaining the meanings of these unpronounced or mispronounced Kanji, partly because meanings tend to be better remembered than sounds and partly because meanings can be cued by context better than sounds, especially if the Kanji has a relevant semantic component. Best of all, the meanings of logographic characters are often the same in Chinese, Korean, and Japanese.

Earlier I mentioned the two-Kanji compound word for "white hair," which I used to misread as *shirogami* in Kun when in fact it should be read as *shiraga*, another Kun reading. But my understanding of its meaning was correct all along. Oral reading of Kanji is especially troublesome in Japanese, because Kanji often have multiple readings. Moreover, there are no systematic relations among the different readings given to one Kanji. Even without the complications caused by multiple readings, oral reading of logographic Kanji is not simple, because the sound is poorly indicated by the phonetic components of the Kanji.

Kanji may be troublesome for a writer and an oral reader, but they are helpful for a silent reader. By paying attention mostly to Kanji, which represent content words, at the expense of Hiragana, which represent grammatical morphemes, I seem to read a Japanese book faster than an English book, even though I am far, far more practised in reading English than Japanese. Even without extra attention, I seem to obtain meanings from Kanji words faster than the same words in phonetic scripts. The parts of text that slow me down are long stretches of Hiragana or European words imprecisely transcribed in Katakana. On this question let me quote a Japanese expert on the Japanese writing system.

> Quite often one can get the meanings of logographic Kanji without being able to read them aloud.... Japanese people read newspapers silently; ask university students to read newspapers aloud, and they make sound errors. Only specially trained people, such as announcers, can read aloud Kanji with few errors.... It is better to get the meanings of graphs without knowing their sounds, as with Kanji, than to get the sounds of graphs without knowing their meanings, as with Rōmaji. [Takebe 1991: 94; my translation, with slight paraphrasing]

Most likely, there will be more revisions of the rules for using both Kanji and Kana. So far, since the 1946 promulgation of the Temporary Kanji, revisions have generally relaxed the restrictions on the number and use of Kanji, perhaps reflecting the fact that linguistic matters are hard to control and tame by official decree. This trend of expansion cannot be allowed forever, lest the writing system revert to its former complexity and chaos. Among the nations that use Chinese characters, Japan is unique in having to rein in a proliferation of readings given to Kanji. The official Kanji must be selected with great care, based on large-scale surveys and research. The list should be revised occasionally, and then only to add Kanji for new concepts and to eliminate rarely used ones. This kind of procedure is in fact used in Japan. If you experience déjà vu, it is because the same recommendation has been made for Chinese and Korean (Parts I and II).

Kanji are not only a tool of daily communication but also a repository of the long and rich cultural heritage of Japan. When the Japanese throw away Kanji, they will lose access to this vast and valuable cultural heritage. They also lose a certain relation with Chinese and Koreans with whom they share a culture based on Chinese words and characters. One big question is whether all educated Japanese people should be exposed to Kanji classics, which use some rare and complex Kanji as well as a Chinese word order that differs from Japanese order, or whether the classics should be read only by a handful of Kanji scholars. Currently, Chinese and Japanese classics written entirely or mostly in Kanji are introduced in secondary schools, which are attended by virtually all Japanese teenagers. The burden of learning Kanji will be considerably lightened if the classics are not imposed on secondary school students but are reserved for scholars.

So the best strategy is to keep Kanji but reduce their complexity by streamlining them. And Kanji can be used efficiently only when they are supplemented by Kana.

All these [movements to abolish Kanji], however, have so far failed, and it is safe to say that the Chinese characters are here to stay. [Shibatani 1990: 130–131]

The [Japanese writing] system has shown itself to be almost incredibly durable.... there is little reason to suspect that it will be any more vulnerable to whatever the future may have in store for the country and its people. [Miller 1967: 138]

22

Learning
Kanji and Kana

Japanese children learn a complex writing system: about 2,000 Kanji in 4,000 readings, 110 Hiragana and Katakana signs, Rōmaji, and Arabic numerals, as well as the proper uses of all these various scripts. The most important task of primary and secondary education in Japan, as in any other nation, is to equip all students with functional literacy. Accordingly, the national language, namely Japanese reading and writing, is by far the most important school subject and is given the largest number of class periods in both primary and secondary school.

Before considering schoolchildren, let us consider preschoolers, many of whom pick up at home rudimentary reading, especially Hiragana.

Preschoolers Acquire Reading

Preschoolers spend all their waking hours acquiring speech along with knowledge about the world. The word *acquire* is used to suggest that preschoolers pick up speech and knowledge informally, without specific instruction, by growing up in an environment filled with speech. They can acquire rudimentary reading in the same manner. In Japan almost all preschoolers pick up, with little or no instruction, some Hiragana at home and in kindergarten by being exposed to TV and printed materials such as comic strips, story books, letter blocks, and labels on objects. Once they pick up most of the 71 basic and secondary Hiragana, they should be able to negotiate simple stories for young children.

Between 1967 and 1970 the National Language Research Institute carried out a large-scale survey of preschoolers' reading and writing abilities (Muraishi and Amano 1972). By age 4, one-third of the preschoolers could identify the sounds of 60 Hiragana, and only one-tenth of them failed to identify any. By age 5, two-thirds of the children could read 60 or more Hiragana, and only one in a hundred could not read any Hiragana. The majority of the 5-year-olds could also write 21 or more Hiragana. A month before entering school, almost all 5-year-olds could identify the sounds of most Hiragana. As for Kanji, a month before entering school, 5-year-olds could read on average 53 of the 240 Kanji that are taught in Grades I and II. They could recognize the meanings of the Kanji and gave each Kanji at least one reading.

A decade earlier, the level achieved in the 1967–1970 survey at age 4 had been attained at age 6; but a decade later, all preschoolers could read most Hiragana and write 50 of them just before entering school. So, preschoolers' knowledge of Hiragana is high, and furthermore is steadily improving over the years.

Preschoolers can be taught to read, although some parents and educators oppose such early teaching. If parents take on the task of teaching preschoolers, what method should they use? Any reasonable method will succeed, if the children are eager to learn, and if their parents shower them with attention and encouragement. In Chapter 9, two sections were devoted to teaching preschoolers to read Chinese characters; this section applies some information from them to the Japanese situation.

The two major scripts in Japan are Kanji and Kana. It is generally assumed that Kanji, because of their large number and complex shapes, are more difficult to learn than Kana, and so Kanji are taught to children after Kana. Is the assumption justified? This question has been tackled in several studies.

In one study, 3- and 4-year olds learned to read aloud individual Hiragana or Katakana signs, e.g., く , ク *ku* and Kanji words 川 *kawa* ('river') and 軽い *karui* ('light') (Steinberg and Oka 1978). They learned the meaningful Kanji words better than the meaningless Kana signs. In another study, when tested one week later, 3- and 4-year olds also remembered the Kanji words better than the Kana signs (Oka et al. 1979). In these studies, individual Kanji were meaningful, but Kana signs were meaningless.

When individual Kanji and Kana signs were equated in meaningfulness, then the learning of the two types was similar (Haryu 1989). Imai (1979) used test materials that were monosyllabic words written either in Kanji or Katakana. His test words were *ki* ('tree'), *to* ('door'), *me* ('eye'), *ha* ('teeth'), and *su* ('bird nest'), which in Katakana were キ,ト,メ,ハ,ス and in Kanji were 木,戸,目,歯,巣. The words in the two scripts were learned almost with equal ease. In another experiment with kindergarteners, the highly pictographic oracle-bone characters (table 3-1) were learned faster than their stylized (far less pictographic) modern counterparts (Ozawa and Nomura 1981).

How should Kanji be taught to preschoolers? In the systematic or concentrated teaching method, several Kanji sharing a radical or phonetic are learned as a group. This method, sometimes called the Ishii method after the educator Ishii who championed it, is practised in some nursery schools and kindergartens in Japan (Ishii 1988). In another method, object-labelling, Kanji or Kana labels are attached to common objects in a child's environment (Steinberg and Tanaka 1989). After one year of instruction toddlers aged two and three have been able to learn a few hundred words in Kanji, Hiragana, and Katakana. They grow up reading many books, and reading at higher grade levels than their age mates in primary school. The same method can be used in teaching a group of children in nursery school.

One might propose a third, eclectic method that combines the good points from Steinberg's method and Ishii's method. That is, teach preschoolers Kanji labels for familiar objects, but in doing so, group the objects in such a way that their Kanji labels share a radical, phonetic, or even individual Kanji. For example, in one lesson, objects whose Kanji contain the radical "bamboo"—e.g., 箱, 筆 , 箸 ('box', 'pen', 'chopsticks')—would be taught, while in another lesson, objects whose Kanji contain the radical "tree" would be taught. It wouldn't hurt to point out the pictorial origins of these two radicals and many others. Words that are written in Kana for children might be also grouped, albeit with some effort, as in *furo* ('bath'), *fusuma* ('sliding screen door'), *furoshiki* ('square wrapping cloth'), and *futon*.

Both Ishii and Steinberg insist that written words should be learned in their customary scripts. Customarily, *yakyu* ('baseball') is written in Kanji, *isu* ('chair') in

Hiragana, and *ragubi* ('rugby') in Katakana. In experiments, Japanese words are recognized faster in their customary scripts than in non-customary scripts, be they Katakana, Hiragana, or Kanji (e.g., Hirose 1984; Kawakami 1993). The moderately complex shapes of some Kanji words do not pose a problem to young children. In Steinberg and Oka's (1978) study, 3- and 4-year olds could learn the sound of even a complex Kanji with 16 strokes 薬 ('medicine') on the first trial, and they learned complex Kanji as easily as simple Kanji having 3 strokes, such as 川 ('river'; see also "Complex vs Simple Characters" in chap. 3).

So preschoolers can easily learn Kanji, as long as the number of Kanji is not large, and the reading of each Kanji is limited to one type, preferably Kun/Japanese. The few hundred Kanji words learned by preschoolers, impressive though they are, provide only an opening to the long road toward full literacy. There are many more Kanji to be learned, with their multiple sounds and their sequences of strokes in writing.

Kana and Kanji Teaching in School

In the 6 years of primary school, the national (Japanese) language, which is the most important subject, is given 1,601 class periods (compared to 1,298 in S. Korea), each of which lasts 45 minutes. It takes up about one-third of the total class periods in the first two grades: 306 of 850 periods in Grade I and 315 of 910 in Grade II. It takes up about one-fifth of the class periods in the last two primary grades: 210 out of 1015 in both Grades V and VI (Ellington 1992). In the first year, learning Kana is the main task, but in later years learning Kanji takes up most class periods.

On the assumption that children have already picked up most Hiragana at home before starting school, the primary reader volume I-1 (volume 1 of Grade I) uses all the Hiragana signs. Katakana is taught in the first three grades in accordance with the guidelines set in 1977 by the Ministry of Education.

- Grade I: Read and write most Katakana; pay attention to Katakana words.
- Grade II: Read and write all Katakana; understand how Katakana is used in sentences and texts.
- Grade III: Learn the kinds of words written in Katakana and use them appropriately in sentences and text.

True, Japanese children learn individual Kana signs and Kanji, if both are meaningful, with about equal ease, as described in "Preschoolers Acquire Reading." But ultimately they master Kana faster and more securely than Kanji, for the following reasons. The Hiragana set and the Katakana set each includes only about 110 signs, about half of which are the basic signs and the other half the basic signs modified; each sign has only one consistent sound; each sign is simply shaped, having between 1 and 6 strokes. So learning to read and write the two Kana sets is relatively fast and painless. The same cannot be said about learning 2,000 Kanji, each of which is complex in shape and can have multiple readings.

Kanji teaching in Japan follows the general principles described in Chapter 9 for teaching Hanzi in China. Like Hanzi, Kanji are taught batch by batch, starting with the most common, useful, and simple ones, which tend to be pictographs and indicators. Each Kanji is taught as a whole pattern; the pictographic origins of some

Kanji are pointed out; writing, which involves analysis of each Kanji into a series of strokes, is taught along with reading. But in detail, Kanji teaching in Japan differs from Hanzi teaching in China, and also from Hancha teaching in Korea.

Because of the importance of Kanji teaching, the Ministry of Education designates a set of educational Kanji to be taught in primary and middle schools. According to the guidelines issued in 1977 and revised in 1981, in the six years of primary school, children should be able to read all the 1,006 designated Kanji (about half of the 1,945 Common Kanji) and write most of them. In the three years of middle school, children learn to read and write the rest of the Common Kanji. Table 22-1 shows the approximate numbers of Kanji learned in each grade of primary and middle schools.

In each grade of primary and middle school, children are supposed to learn to read all the designated Kanji for that grade and to write most of them. Kanji assigned for the lower grades of primary school tend to be simply shaped, while those for the higher grades tend to be complex, though research shows that simple Kanji were not necessarily easier to learn than complex Kanji, and that the Kanji for the first four grades were about the same in difficulty (Steinberg and Oka 1978).

Children are supposed to learn all 1,945 Common Kanji in the nine years of compulsory education. However, in textbooks for middle schools published by five companies in 1984, between 24 and 69 of the Common Kanji did not appear, though they were listed in appendices. Also, even for those Kanji that appeared, not all of their On/Chinese readings and Kun/Japanese readings were given. For example, Kanji 女 ('woman') is learned in Grade I with an On reading *jo* and a Kun reading *onna;* it is learned in middle school again with another On reading *nyo* and another Kun reading *me;* then it is learned in high school with yet another On reading *nyō* in compound words such as *nyōbo* ('wife') and a Kun reading *ma* in compound words such as *ama* ('woman diver'). There are several other Kanji whose various On and Kun readings are learned at different levels of school.

In secondary school, the national language, along with a foreign language, is still an important subject. Kanji are learned not only in their modern uses but also in classic Japanese and Chinese uses. Chinese classics might be poems from the 8th century Tang period, or passages from the 2500 year-old Confucian *Analects*, as in China (fig. 4-2a,b). The students learn to read aloud a Chinese text written only in characters and in Chinese syntax. There are two styles in which such a text may be read aloud. In the style called *bōyomi* ('read in a straight line like a stick') the basic Chinese word order (subject–verb–object) is read as is, without being changed into the Japanese order (subject–object–verb) and without inserting Japanese glosses. In the style called Kundoku ('Japanese reading'), a Chinese text is simultaneously punctuated, shifted in word order, analyzed, and translated into classical Japanese, to be read as if it were

Table 22-1. Educational Kanji by School Grade

School Grade		Number of Kanji
Primary	I	80
	II	160
	III	200
	IV	200
	V	185
	VI	181
Total		1006
Middle	I	250–300
	II	300–350
	III	300–400
Total		about 950

Japanese. To guide Kundoku, *kunten* ('translation marks') and Okurigana are set down next to the characters of the Chinese text.

Japanese classics might be the 11th century *Genji Monogatari* or the 13th century *Heike Monogatari* (chap. 23), heavily annotated with Furigana (fig. 19-1). They may be easier to read than Chinese classics but are much harder to read than contemporary writings, because they use old, literary expressions and because they contain many uncommon Kanji.

Let us now discuss Kanji writing, which is a regular part of language instruction. Because Kanji are numerous and complex, children spend considerable time and effort learning to write them properly. Each Kanji must be written with a specified order of strokes, basically from top to bottom and from left to right ("Shapes of Characters," in chap. 3). As in China, Kanji writing is done with the right hand; writing with the left hand is discouraged.

Kanji writing skills tend to lag behind reading skills in most tests, as we shall see. More and more Japanese people have difficulty writing even those Kanji commonly used in everyday life, for several reasons. Kanji writing requires constant practice, which is in short supply nowadays. As telephones become widely available, more and more Japanese people, like people in other wealthy industrial nations, resort to telephoning rather than letter writing. When they do write, they may use a word processor, which produces Kanji in response to Kana or Rōmaji input so that a writer no longer needs to recall the shape of the intended Kanji and to reproduce it stroke by stroke. If Japanese writers cannot recall the correct Kanji, or if they want save the time and effort of looking it up, they can always substitute Kana.

Another aspect of writing is calligraphy, which is a venerable art form in Japan as it is in China and Korea (see fig. 3-4a, a cup bearing a calligraphy work by the former Japanese Prime Minister, Nakasone). Calligraphy is taught in Japanese school. In the first grade, children are told to pay attention to the shapes of Kanji and Kana and to follow the correct stroke orders. In the third grade they write with brush and ink. In the sixth grade, children attend to the shape, size, and arrangement of Kanji and Kana on a sheet of paper. In a Japanese high school, calligraphy is offered as one of four elective art courses along with music, fine arts, and crafts. Students learn expression, appreciation, and the theory of calligraphy.

On New Year's day, or more precisely on the second day of January, in a ritual called *kakizome* ('the first writing' of the New Year with a brush), many Japanese, from the prime minister down to first graders, write some auspicious phrases in calligraphy.

Textbooks for Reading Instruction

In Japan, there is no single standard textbook for the national language; rather, there are several textbooks published by different companies, all of which, however, must follow the guidelines of the Ministry of Education and must be approved by it. A textbook for each grade consists of two volumes. Generally, Hiragana, because of their usefulness, are learned before Katakana, and Kanji are gradually introduced as part of sentences and stories.

Let us look closely at one company's introductory textbook, volume I-1, the popular *Kazaguruma* ('Pinwheel' 1988).

- pages 1–17: only basic Hiragana, in simple phrases
- pages 18–67: secondary and small-size Hiragana, in simple sentences and stories
- pages 68–81: a handful of Kanji
- pages 82–87 (end): a few Katakana words

The volume ends with a list of all Hiragana and Katakana, and the 24 Kanji learned. The Kanji are the Sino-Japanese numerals 1 to 10, and names for objects in nature such as the sun and mountain. These Kanji are either pictographs or indicators having one to seven strokes, the majority with two to four. For most of them only a Kun/Japanese reading is taught. For example, 山 ('mountain') has normally at least three different On readings, *san, -zan, -sen,* and one Kun reading *yama*; only the Kun reading, which is a native word that children already know, is taught. More than the simplicity of shapes, it is the single reading, usually Kun, associated with a Kanji that eases initial learning. But even in volume I-1, for the Sino-Japanese numerals and the Kanji for "person," both Kun and On readings are taught. Only one other Kanji ('wheel') is shown with an On/Chinese reading (though it has a Kun reading *-guruma* in the title of the textbook).

Figure 22-1, which is page 76 of volume I-1, introduces in the context of sentences four Kanji (in uppercase letters, below); it also shows the pictorial origins of these Kanji. Note the vertical writing.

i climbed [a] MOUNTAIN with [my] father.

[the] leaves of [a] TREE fell like butterflies.

in [a] RIVER flows WATER.

In volume I-1, Kanji appear only in single-Kanji words, and in volume I-2 they begin to appear in two-Kanji compound words, such as *gakkō* ('school'; On reading), *itoguruma* ('spinning wheel'; Kun reading), and three-Kanji words such

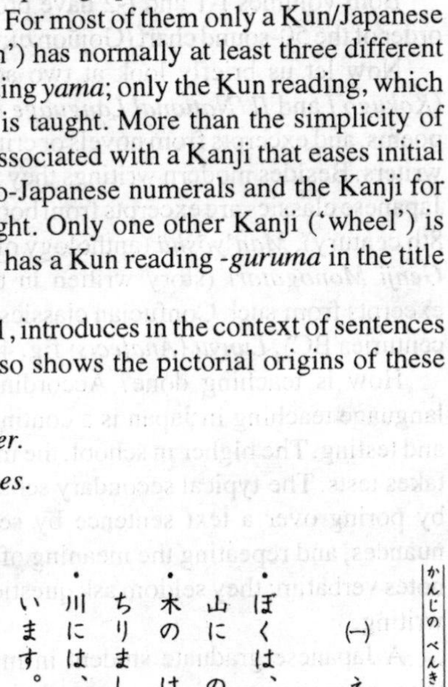

かんじの べんきょう

（一） え と かんじ

ぼくは、おとうさんと
山に のぼりました。
木の はが、ひらひらと
ちりました。
川には、水が ながれて
います。

山 やま
木 き
川 かわ
水 みず

〔木・川〕

Figure 22-1. A page from a textbook for Japanese reading, Kokugo: Kazaguruma, *Volume I-1: the top half shows three sentences written vertically in Hiragana, with four Kanji; the bottom half shows the Kun/Japanese readings and the pictographic origins of the four Kanji for 'mountain', 'tree', 'river', and 'water'.*

as *go-hyaku-en* ('five hundred yen'; On reading). Multi-Kanji words may be selected either because they use the single Kanji already learned or because they represent familiar, useful concepts. The second principle seems to apply to most multi-Kanji words in volume I-2, though both the first and second principles may apply to the numerals. The word *ningen* ('human being'), which can be written with two Kanji already learned, is written in Hiragana, perhaps because the Kanji for -*gen* was learned earlier in the Kun reading *ma* ('space, room'). To introduce too soon the same Kanji with another sound and meaning might confuse beginners.

Both volumes I-1 and I-2 have provisions for writing drill, practice in the Kana order of the 50-sound chart (Gojūonzu; table 19-2), and a list of the vocabulary learned.

Now let us briefly look at two advanced textbooks used in secondary school (*Kokugo I* and *II* '*National Language I* and *II*' 1984). The volumes consist of essays, poems, and excerpts from novels or criticisms, written mostly by established Japanese writers. Besides modern writings they introduce classics, both Japanese and Chinese. Japanese classics are excerpts from books such as *Kojiki* (history compiled in the early 8th century), *Man'yōshū* (anthology of poems compiled in the late 8th century), and *Genji Monogatari* (story written in the early 11th century). Chinese classics are excerpts from such Confucian classics (chap. 10) as *Shijing* (*Book of Poetry*, 10–8th centuries BC), *Lunyu* (*Analects*; fig. 4-2b), and Tang poems (fig. 4-2a, Du Fu).

How is teaching done? According to Duke (1986) and many other authors, language teaching in Japan is a continual process of memorization, repetition, drill, and testing. The higher in school, the more the student memorizes, repeats, drills, and takes tests. The typical secondary school teacher faithfully follows a teacher's guide by poring over a text sentence by sentence, dissecting it for meaning, analyzing nuances, and repeating the meaning of new characters. Students in turn take copious notes verbatim; they seldom ask questions, conduct discussions, or engage in creative writing.

A Japanese graduate student in my comparative literacy class, Kubota Ryuko, takes exception to this stereotyped views of Japanese language teaching. In school, especially in primary and middle schools, Ryuko had many opportunities to discuss the authors' intentions behind, as well as her own reactions to, the stories in textbooks. She also had to do a lot of writing, such as writing about her experiences and her reactions to a book.

To judge from the guides, quizzes, and drills provided in the textbooks *Kokugo I* and *II* used in secondary schools, lessons are not as mechanical and dry as described by Duke. For example, at the end of a lesson on Chinese classics, one guide asks students to discuss what the original Chinese stories are trying to say, and one drill requires them to use a dictionary to look up the meaning of *gojippohyappo* and then produce a sentence using the idiom. (The idiom is the Japanese reading of the Chinese *wu shi bu (xiao) bai bu* ('fifty steps hundred steps' or an insignificant difference; "Compound Words and Idioms" in chap. 4).

Still, teaching in Japan, as in other East Asian nations, tends to be centered around a teacher delivering a lecture to a whole class based on textbooks, far more than it is in the West.

How Well are Kanji Read and Written?

Japanese readers and writers have a good, but by no means perfect, knowledge of Kanji, as shown in several assessments of reading and writing skills. They make reading and writing errors, which are revealing.

A test involving 17 schools between 1953 and 1962 (when there were 881 educational Kanji) found the following results (Hondō 1988: 50).

- Kanji reading skills improve from Grade I (61.4% correct of the 50 grade-I Kanji) through Grade VI (91.5% of the 881 educational Kanji).
- Kanji reading skills develop fast, especially between the end of Grade III and the beginning of Grade IV, when Hiragana and Katakana have been mastered.
- Reading skills outpace writing skills; at the end of Grade VI, the ratio of difference between reading and writing skills is 10 to 7.
- In Grade VI, children can score 80% correct on Kanji that appear in popular newspapers and magazines even though they may not be in their textbooks.
- The Kanji learned can easily be forgotten, if they are exceptionally difficult or seldom used in daily life.

More recently the National Language Research Institute (1988) found the results shown in Table 22-2 on mastery of the primary-school Kanji in primary school and later high school. Reading is better than writing in every case; reading only in one of either On/Chinese or Kun/Japanese is better than reading in both On and Kun; and the primary-school Kanji are read well, but not perfectly, four years later in high school.

What kinds of errors do schoolchildren make in reading and writing Kanji? In Yamada's (1995) experiment, when 4th, 5th, and 6th graders were asked to give the sounds of 48 of the Grades III and IV Kanji, even 6th graders averaged only 61% correct on Grade III Kanji. The experimental procedures perhaps were hard for the children: the test Kanji were shown in isolation without context and had to be read only in On. Not surprisingly, the most common errors were Kun readings given when On readings were required.

In a writing test of the same Kanji, the children scored higher (68%) than in the reading test. This reversal from the typical finding—better reading than writing scores—may be due to the facts that, for writing but not for reading, context (phrases and sentences) was provided, and that, in reading, correct Kun readings were scored as errors when On readings were asked for. After "no response," the most common writing errors were homophone substitutions, i.e., correct Kanji were replaced by incorrect ones whose sounds were the same as the targets but whose shapes and meanings differed. The next most common type of error was invented Kanji that

Table 22-2. Mastery of Primary-School Kanji

	In Primary School		In High School	
	Read	Write	Read	Write
On or Kun	92.7	66.2	98.6	86.0
On and Kun	76.0	53.5	93.7	79.5

differed from the correct ones in minor details. The patterns of errors remained similar across Grades IV, V, and VI, while both reading and writing scores improved.

What kinds of errors do middle school students make? Yoshida and his colleagues (1975) asked middle school students to fill with Kanji the blanks left in phrases. The complexity of Kanji was a weak predictor of shape-based errors, which were caused not so much by dropping or adding a stroke or a dot, but more by confusing components, such as a radical or phonetic. Some writing errors were homophone substitutions. Here are two frequently confused Kanji, 鋼 and 鑛, which share the radical "metal" and the sound *kō* (the right component in each Kanji is a phonetic for *kō*, but the two have different shapes). Both Kanji mean "hard metal" and can be used in a similar context.

Homophone substitution errors are made by adults as well. For some Sino-Japanese compound words and idioms, wrong Kanji have the same sounds as the correct Kanji and have plausible meanings to boot. For example, the correct Kanji for *senmon* ('exclusive, gate' or 'specialization') is 専門, but people often write the second Kanji as 問('inquire'). The Chinese idiom *ryōsaikenbo* 良妻賢母 ('good wife, wise mother' the virtues of a woman) may be written as 料裁健母 ('cook', 'sew', 'healthy', 'mother'). Sometimes a homophone substitution error is unintentionally comical: for *seiki no kessen* ('the decisive battle of the century') 世紀の決戦 the first two Kanji might be written in error as 性器, to produce the homophonic (*seiki no kessen*—'the decisive battle of the sex organs').

Horodeck (1987), too, studied errors in reading and writing Kanji. In manuscripts written by adults he found 495 errors, 93 of which were shape based. Some of these errors were legitimate Kanji, and some were not. The remainder, 402, were homophone substitutions, 59 on Kun readings and the remainder, 343, on On readings. Horodeck interprets the results as refuting the hypothesis that meanings "trigger" Kanji when the Japanese write. In a reading test, Horodeck asked subjects to detect Kanji errors inserted in newspaper headlines. In each of the On-compound words, one Kanji had the same sound as the correct one as well as a similar but wrong shape. Examples of correct (given first) and wrong Kanji words: 妨 害 ; 防害 *bōgai* ('obstruction') and 制裁 ; 制栽 *seisai* ('sanction' or 'punishment'). Close to 52% of the subjects detected every error they saw, but 48%, missed one or more errors. Horodeck interprets this result as refuting the hypothesis that Kanji "trigger" only meanings when the Japanese read. Based on his findings on writing and reading errors, he concludes that "Kanji, however, are not 'ideographic' writing at all, but perhaps best characterized as a syllabary ..." (1987: 5).

Contrary to Horodeck's conclusions, Kanji errors can be explained as both meaning- and sound-based. Let us analyze one example of the errors in his data. Consider the word for 'obstruction': the two Kanji for the correct word are 'obstruct' and 'damage' and for the wrong word 'defend' and 'damage'. The second Kanji is identical in the correct and wrong words. The first Kanji in the two words share the same-shaped phonetic 方 *bō* but differ in their semantic components, which are 'woman' in the correct word and 'town' in the wrong word. Now, 'woman' does not contribute to its Kanji's meaning 'obstruct' in any obvious way, while 'town' contributes to its Kanji's meaning 'defend', but its shape is in an abbreviated form so that its meaning is obscured. If writers do not notice these subtle points they will fail to fully grasp the meanings of the two critical Kanji and may well confuse the two. And they are likely to substitute the more common wrong Kanji for the less common correct one.

An experiment can be designed to show directly that Kanji words are structured in memory and retrieved from it based on the meanings rather than the sounds of their first Kanji. Subjects were asked to do lexical decision, i.e., given a two-Kanji compound word, they decided whether or not it was a word (Hirose 1992). They were provided with "primes," which they had to read aloud. Of the five conditions tested, let us consider only two. (1) A prime and the first Kanji of a compound word was the same in meaning as well as in shape and sound: 会 → 会社. (2) A prime and the first Kanji was the same in sound but not in shape and meaning. The decision time was much faster in (1) where the prime had the same meaning as the target than in (2) where the prime had the same sound as the target. In the second experiment, (1) a prime and the first Kanji shared the same sound and shape, or (2) a prime shared the shape (and meaning) but not the sound, *yokogao* ('side, face' or 'profile') 横顔 → 横断 *ōdan* ('crosscut' or 'traverse'). If the sound factor were critical, condition (1) should have produced faster decisions than condition (2), but the two were about the same in decision time.

These studies show that the meanings, shapes, and sounds of some Kanji are complex and confusing, and so are error prone. The sounds of Kanji are particularly confusing because each Kanji has multiple sounds, and many Kanji share one sound. To make the matter even more confusing, several Kanji that share a sound can have similar shapes if they share a phonetic. And a semantic component may not always or obviously contribute to a Kanji's meaning.

Should Kanji be characterized as a syllabary, as Horodeck asserts? Kanji is not a syllabary by several direct and critical tests, such as: There should be only as many Kanji as there are syllables—around 110—in Japanese, and each Kanji should code one particular syllable consistently. A Japanese reader should be able to pronounce any Kanji, on the one hand, and need not attend to its meanings, on the other. Kanji fail these tests. Even Man'yōgana, in which Kanji were used mainly to represent the Japanese syllables disregarding their meanings, fail these tests, as it used many different Kanji to represent one syllable ("Kana: Origin and Development" in chap. 19). But modern Kana, of course, passes the tests and so is a proper syllabary. If Kanji were a syllabary, why was Kana created, and why are the sounds of unfamiliar Kanji annotated with Furigana? Why are Kanji selected for their meanings rather than sounds in forming compound words?

Reading Difficulties

Inevitably, in any script, there are some children who either fail to learn to read or have difficulty in learning to read. In the United States, nation-wide 4.6% of schoolchildren suffer from "learning disabilities," defined as a significant discrepancy between ability and achievement that is caused not by severe physical handicap or mental retardation (Gearheart and Gearheart 1989). Children with learning disabilities have trouble learning to read and write, and thus learning other academic subjects. They are likely to be referred to remedial teachers.

The Japanese school system does not have remedial schools or special teachers for children with learning disabilities. Does this mean that no Japanese children suffer from some kind of learning difficulties? Not necessarily. Every year a certain percentage of children fall further and further behind their peers in schoolwork. These children, called *ochikobore* ('those who have fallen to the bottom') are often responsible for incidents of violence in middle schools (Ellington 1992).

In one survey of 9,195 schoolchildren, 0.98% of them were found to have learning difficulty. In a detailed examination of eleven such children, aged between 7 years and 11 and a half, the following profile emerged (Saito et al. 1974). They were all males; four of them were left-handed; performance IQ (intelligence quotient) was higher than verbal IQ, but full IQ was within a normal range. This profile is similar to that found in the United States.

What kinds of errors do Japanese children with learning difficulty make? In writing a Kanji composed of a semantic component on the left and a phonetic on the right, they might reverse the positions of the two. In reading aloud one Kanji, they might give the sound of another Kanji related to the target in meaning: *hi* ('sun') is read aloud as *getsu* ('moon'). (Another example of the primacy of the meaning of Kanji.) They tend to experience more difficulty with On/Chinese than with Kun/Japanese readings of Kanji. In writing Kana, they might write *tonbo* ('dragonfly') as *tonmo* (no meaning) or *kippu* ('ticket') as *kipu* (no meaning). Young children could not write the four small-sized Kana signs. On the whole, they learn individual logographic Kanji better than phonetic Kana. As children advance in grades, some show improvement, while others do not.

Some authors define reading difficulty or poor reading as reading 2 or more years below grade. By this definition, the proportion of 5th graders who read at Grade III level was 21% for the Japanese, compared to 31% for the Americans and 12% for the Chinese (Stevenson and Stigler 1992). By Grade V, Japanese children are well past the stage of learning to read with Kana, and so their difficulty must come from insufficient knowledge of Kanji. The reported study does not clarify whether the Japanese children's difficulty is mainly in reading Kanji aloud or in obtaining the meanings of Kanji words.

Among Japanese students in night technical schools, reading achievement can be low, according to Rohlen (1983: 29). For example, one student assigned to read an essay aloud stumbled over three or four Kanji per sentence. The low reading skills of students at night technical schools must be viewed in perspective. In Japan, high schools are ranked in a hierarchy according to their success rates at entrance exams to good universities, and students, willy-nilly, go to appropriately ranked schools, according to their scholastic abilities. Night technical schools enroll the lowest 2% of the students in any 9th-grade graduating class; very few students from such schools go on to higher education; many — about half — drop out; and many of the students hold jobs during the day.

Even these night-school students of low reading skills presumably read Hiragana, Katakana, and hundreds of Kanji, if not all 2,000 Common Kanji. And they may experience most difficulty with mastering the over 4,000 On/Chinese and Kun/ Japanese readings of Kanji. If so, they may still be able to read popular magazines and newspapers with sufficient comprehension, for one can often obtain the meanings of some Kanji without being able to read them correctly aloud.

So, the mastery of Kanji by Japanese students and adults is far from perfect, despite the effort and time expended on it. Kanji are extraordinarily complex and confusing, in shape, meaning, and especially in sound. All the same, Kanji are learned and used because they are useful.

23

The Japanese
Educational System

The Japanese educational system equips almost every student with the functional literacy and numeracy skills needed to become a useful worker in an industrial society. Japanese primary and secondary education is touted as the foundation on which Japan's spectacular economic success has been built. As Japan has a large population in a small territory with few natural resources, how else could she have achieved economic superpower status?

Reflecting the importance of Japanese education, especially compared with American education, a spate of books, both in Japanese and English, have recently appeared on the topic. To name a few, *Tasks of Japanese and American Education* by Amashiro (1987), *The Japanese School: Lessons for Industrial America* by Duke (1986), *Education in the Japanese Life-Cycle: Implications for the United States* by Ellington (1992), *Japan's High Schools* by Rohlen (1983), and *The Learning Gap: Why our Schools are Failing and What we can Learn from Japanese and Chinese Education* by Stevenson and Stigler (1992).

Let us look into various levels of Japanese schools, especially primary and secondary schools, considering their educational philosophy, classrooms, teaching methods, achievements, and problems.

Primary and Secondary School: Overview

The success of Japanese primary and secondary education evokes much praise and perhaps envy in Western observers. The former U.S. ambassador to Japan, Edwin Reischauer, wrote in his introduction to Duke's book:

> There can be no doubt,...that the Japanese worker, the product of the Japanese educational system, is an extraordinarily hard-working person, strongly oriented to quality work, deeply loyal to his working groups and his company, and superbly educated with the skills he needs for his job. [Duke 1986: xvii]

> Japan has undoubtedly outpaced all the other major nations of the world in what should be the fundamental task of schooling, imparting to virtually all students adequately high levels of basic skills, such as literacy and high competence in mathematics, needed for life in the modern world. [xviii]

Duke himself wrote:

> No one can deny that every employer in Japan, down to the smallest and most rural level, can hire new employees with the conviction that virtually all can, at the minimum, read the newspaper and, moreover, are capable of reading with understanding fairly complex instructions on the care and operation of a new machine. [51]

The entire school is involved in the process of reading and writing. The teachers take it very seriously. The PTA stresses it. The parents expect it. The older brothers and sisters reinforce it. The Ministry of Education decrees it. Industry depends on it. There is, if you like, a perpetual and self-propelling national campaign for literacy in Japan,... [62]

Rohlen praises Japanese system for its high standard of mass education.

Japanese education, like the nation's overall industrial system, has been made into an extraordinarily efficient engine for economic advancement. Today, Japan sets the world standards in mass education. [Rohlen 1983: 25–26]

Cummings (1980) praises Japanese primary education for many reasons, including the high standards achieved, its success in teaching orderly behavior and social sensitivity, and the equality of opportunity achieved by the 9-year compulsory school system.

Does Japanese education deserve the praise heaped on it by these and other authors? What lessons can it teach us in the West?

Japanese education is a 6–3–3–4 system, i.e., 6 years of primary school, 3 years of middle school, 3 years of high school, and 4 years of university. This system, which was modelled on the U.S. system, was adopted in 1947 during the Allied Occupation following the end of World War II. The 6 years of primary school and the 3 years of middle school have been compulsory and free since then. As far as the years of schooling are concerned, Japan is no different from other developed and developing nations such as the United States, South Korea, and Taiwan. It is what goes on inside the system that distinguishes Japan from most other nations.

The Japanese educational philosophy can be summarized as follows. All children have the ability to learn what is taught at school, but they vary in levels of achievement mainly because they exert different amounts of effort, perseverance, and discipline. Any student can overcome his or her poor achievement by dint of effort, without the help of remedial teachers and counsellors. Reflecting this philosophy, the children advance to higher school grades automatically.

The physical setting of, and life in, a typical classroom in a Japanese school is Spartan with few frills: A stove with a chimney heats a room; children themselves clean their own classroom, scrubbing the floor on hands and knees. Lunch, provided by the school and paid for by the parents, is served by the children themselves and is eaten in the classroom, in the presence of their class teacher. Virtually everything about a classroom, except that lunch is now provided instead of being brought from home, is traditional and has not changed for some decades. The classroom has few frills, not because of lack of funds but because it is deliberately kept Spartan so that the children can concentrate on studying and developing character.

By contrast, in the United States, a classroom is centrally heated, and cleaning is left to a janitor. A teacher can call on remedial teachers and counsellors to deal with problem children. Computers are found in many classrooms. In short, the classroom setting in a middle- or upper-class neighborhood is luxurious. However, a classroom in a poor inner-city neighborhood tends to be in a sorry state because of insufficient funds.

In contrast to the Spartan classroom setting, the educational facilities in Japanese schools are excellent. A typical primary school has a library, a science lab, a physical education room, an arts-and-crafts room, and a music room equipped with a piano and other musical instruments. Most public primary schools have swimming pools. Computers are easily available. Both primary and secondary schools take advantage of educational TV programs.

A class in a Japanese school is well disciplined, and such daily routines as clearing the desk top, assembly, and dispersal are speedily and orderly executed. Secondary school students wear a uniform, cut their hair in a prescribed way, and carry only authorized objects on their person. The objects not allowed to be carried include watches, candies, and cash for boys; and hand mirrors, lipsticks and combs or hair brushes for girls. If the forbidden objects do not include drugs and weapons, it is because they are seldom carried anyway. In spite of the rigid regimentation, violence does occur at school, but as yet it remains at a manageable level.

Japanese primary and secondary education is centrally directed by the Ministry of Education and is uniform throughout Japan. Every Japanese child begins school on more or less the same day, stays in schools for about the same length of time, and uses similar textbooks. The date, the length of the school day, the textbooks, and the teacher's guides are all set and approved by the Ministry of Education. The Ministry sets nation-wide standards for reading and writing, down to the number and type of Kanji to be taught in each grade ("Kana and Kanji Teaching in School" in chap. 22).

By contrast, in the United States, education is under the control of the individual state or local authority, and there are 50 states. (Hawaii has no local boards but has an elected board of education). There is no central authority overseeing textbook publication. Thus the content, vocabulary, and difficulty of primary readers vary widely, depending partly on the authors' approach to reading instruction (e.g., the whole-language method vs phonics method).

In Japan classes tend to be large: the law prescribes that the class size should be 40 children in primary and middle school, reduced from 45 in the 1980s. But a class of 45 students in both levels of schools is not exceptional. In primary school, even in the first grade, a teacher keeps a large reading class together using the same book and teaching the same lesson to all at the same time. In secondary school, a teacher lectures to a whole class rather than breaking it up into discussion groups. The large class size is not detrimental in Japan and other East Asian nations where students are disciplined. In fact, a large class size is beneficial, according to Stevenson and Stigler (1992): it lowers the teaching load so that teachers can spend some time outside classrooms, preparing lessons, working with individual children, and consulting other teachers.

By contrast, in a typical American classroom, which contains 20–30 children, a teacher divides the children into reading groups with graded readers assigned according to each group's level of ability. When teachers work in a classroom with individual children or small groups, they must leave the rest of the class unattended, which means that the instructional time for the remaining children is reduced.

Japanese education is examination-driven. Children are perpetually preparing for highly competitive examinations. Frequent and standardized tests maintain a high standard of school achievement. To secure a good job with a good company or the government, a person must have graduated from a good university; to get into a good university, he must have graduated from a good high school; to get into a good high school, he must have graduated from a good middle school, and so on, down to a good kindergarten, especially in big cities like Tokyo. The better kindergartens have entrance exams for 3-year-olds! Success at the entrance exams, especially for high schools and universities, will affect, indeed determine, a Japanese student's career prospects. No wonder Japan is gripped by "examination mania" and its students go through "examination hell."

The intensely competitive entrance exams give rise to flourishing commercial cram schools, called *juku*. Cram schools are where children go after regular school for extra lessons in core school subjects, such as the Japanese language, English, and mathematics. They are patronized by some primary schoolchildren and by many secondary school students. There are cram schools for slow students, for average students, and for bright students. Typical cram schools hold classes two hours a day, a few days a week, but fast-paced ones may hold classes almost every day, even on weekends and during vacations. The fee for a child's attendance at a cram school is high; it is estimated to be about the same as the tuition at a public university.

In the next three sections, we consider the different levels of school: "Preschool and primary school," "middle and high school," and "university and its entrance examination."

Preschool and Primary School

Japanese children start institutionalized education early: some 3-year-olds and most 4–5-year-olds attend kindergarten. Over 96% of preschoolers attend either kindergartens or nursery schools (which take care of toddlers aged 6 months to 2 years, as well as children aged 3 to 5, often of working mothers). Two-thirds of the 4-year-olds in Japan attend kindergarten, compared with one-third in the United States. Though not given formal instruction in reading and writing, kindergarteners informally learn to read simple written signs or instructions and write their own names.

All Japanese children at age six start primary school. (Children with severe physical and mental handicaps have their own schools.) Schoolchildren study long and hard. On weekdays they attend primary school from 8:30 to 3:30 with a lunch break. They may stay until 4:00 or 4:30 for after-school activities. On Saturdays Japanese children used to be at school from 8:30 to 12:30. The Ministry of Education experimented with a 5-day week in some schools, and in September 1992 introduced in all primary and secondary schools one free Saturday in each month, without reducing the total number of class hours. But parents are not enthusiastic about the change, fearing that children will end up going to commercial cram schools on "free" Saturdays. Local governments offer an array of events to soak up "so much" free time. A professor at Nihon University, Ohashi Miyuki, sounded an alarm: "I almost tend to think this is some kind of a plot to weaken Japan's economic prowess by attacking the final fortress—education" (*The Globe and Mail*, Sept 12, 1992).

The number of school days a year is about 230 in Japan, compared with about 180 in the United States. A Japanese primary school not only has more school days but also devotes a higher proportion of the time to academic activities and assigns more hours of homework than a U.S. school (Table 23-1, which includes data on Taiwan).

Table 23-1. *Time Spent in Study by Schoolchildren in Japan, U.S., and Taiwan*

Country	Academic Activity		Homework		Days of School
	Grade I	Grade V	Grade I	Grade V	
Taiwan	85%	92%	77 min	114 min	240
Japan	79	87	37	57	240
U.S.	70	65	14	46	178

(based on data by Stevenson et al. 1986) The number of school days in Japan should be reduced to about 230, now that one Saturday a month is free. S. Korea has 222 school days.

However, the number of hours spent actually on academic instruction does not differ greatly among the three nations, because Japanese and Chinese children spend more time on recess, lunch, and after-school extracurricular activitities than do American children. Incidentally, one recess after each 45- or 50-minute class period may help keep the Asian children alert in the class. American children are allowed only one or two recesses in a school day.

As though the 230 days in school are not long enough, Japanese children go to the cram schools a few hours a week for extra study. According to Amashiro (1987), 6.2% of the first graders and 30% of the 6th graders nation-wide attend them. In cram schools most children study the Japanese language and math, but some take English, which is not taught in the regular primary school. Some take lessons in a non-academic subject like piano, violin, or tennis.

A Japanese teacher develops and maintains a close relation with her charges. She stays with the same class of 40–45 children for one or two years so that she gets to know them. At the beginning of a new school year, a teacher visits the home of every child in her class to meet the parents and see the home environment. The parents in turn visit the child's classroom and consult the teacher on specified days. In 1993, team teaching was introduced, assigning two teachers to each class of primary and middle school.

The two most important school subjects are the national language and arithmetic, which together take up half of the class periods: 306 and 136 periods out of total 850 in Grade I and 315 and 175 out of 910 in Grade II (Ellington 1992: 66). Three other important subjects are social studies and science, which are now combined into "life environment," and physical education. Science classes include laboratory experiments.

Middle and High School

Along with the six years of primary school the three years of middle school are compulsory and free. Middle school students have to take an entrance exam to get into high school. Accordingly the third and last year at the middle school is devoted to preparing for the exam. Though there are enough high schools, they are ranked according to their success rates in sending their graduates to good universities. The students of low-ranking high schools look forward to dimmer prospects, and need more school expenses to boot, than those of high-ranking schools.

The entrance exam tests such core subjects as the national language, English, and math, and sometimes science and social science as well. The exam score plus a report from the middle school (on a student's personality, attitude, study habits, etc.) determine admission to high school. Because the students tend to select a high school that is appropriate to their level of competence, competition at the exam is not intense. The Japanese middle school graduates who do not go to regular high school mostly go to a special high school or take a job. Only a few have no job and no school.

Extra study at commercial cram schools is normal among middle and high school students. Across the nation, half the middle school students, and in Tokyo and other large cities, two-thirds of them, are either attending cram schools or being tutored at home.

The three-year high school, described as semi-compulsory, attracts virtually all—96% in 1992—of the middle school graduates. In high schools some students join a vocational stream that prepares them for jobs, while the majority join an academic stream that prepares them for university entrance. The most important subjects in high school are the national language, English, and math, as in middle schools. English is an elective course, but a school principal invariably elects it. Japanese students do not enjoy, or suffer from, a wide (or wild!) selection of elective courses. By contrast, in the United States the proportion of students who choose such "demanding" elective courses as "preparation for marriage," "relaxation," and "driver education" increased from 12% in 1964 to 42% in 1979.

According to many authors, teaching in Japan, especially in secondary schools, emphasizes acquisition of knowledge through repeated practice and memorization rather than through analysis and critical thinking (e.g., Amashiro 1987; Duke 1986; Ellington 1992). Teaching is overwhelmingly done through lectures, which faithfully follow the textbooks and guidelines of the Ministry of Education. This teaching method is supplemented by study in labs, use of educational TV programs, and site visits to educational places.

To Westerners, Asian students are tense youngsters driven by relentless pressures for academic excellence. However, in a survey by Stevenson et al. (1993) of 11th graders in Japan, Taiwan, and the United States, unexpectedly Japanese students reported the least, and American students the most, frequent feelings of stress, academic anxiety, and aggression.

A quarter million ethnic Japanese live outside Japan, some temporarily for business reasons. They send their schoolage children—about 51,000 in 1992—either to full-time, regular Japanese schools or to supplementary schools that provide Japanese education on weekends or after regular schools. According to Namie (1991), Japanese children in Britain experience culture schock twice, once at the time of starting schooling in Britain and again on return to Japan. Apparently, the second shock is greater than the first: Children who spend some years overseas often fail to reach the level of competence in school subjects set by the Japanese Ministry of Education.

Rohlen (1983: 25) concludes that in many respects the average high school graduate in Japan is equal or superior to the average American college graduate in science, math, geography, history, music, art, and foreign language skills [at least in reading]. Anyway, the greatest achievement of the Japanese educational system is that almost all students graduate from high school, compared to 75% in North America.

University and its Entrance Examination

In North America, half of the high school graduates, male and female, aspire to go to universities and colleges, and most of them succeed. Acceptance to good universities depends not on entrance exams but on grades in high school, scores on the scholastic aptitude test (SAT), teachers' recommendations, and even athletic prowess. Once in a university, serious students can get a solid education. True, some universities have high prestige and some low, but graduates of undistinguished colleges are never doomed, and some can make their way to top positions without the cachet of a good degree.

By contrast, in Japan many high school graduates would take post-secondary education, if places were available, but only one-third of them can enter a variety of post-secondary schools, most of them 4-year universities and some, often women, 2- or 3-year junior colleges. The name of the university a student has attended matters a great deal in securing a good job with business, academia, and government. The most coveted name is Tokyo University, especially its law faculty, whose graduates have been well represented for many decades among intellectuals, company presidents, legislators, and the top positions of the national bureaucracy. "Japan does not have a class system based on birth, but a class system is born with the entrance exam to a university at age 18" (1971 report of the OECD Educational Investigative Team).

Acceptance to a good university is determined through an entrance exam, which is legendary for the intensity of its competition. All university applicants take a common, standard two-day-long entrance exam on five core subjects: national language, math, English, social science, and science. Those who make above the cut-off score on the common exam then take a second 1-day exam to enter prestigious public, and a few private, universities. Typical questions at both the common and the second exams require detailed factual answers rather than analysis and critical thinking. No wonder secondary schools and cram schools put a premium on memorization of detailed facts. Students, parents, and teachers are all obsessed with preparing for the common exam. "Schooling is geared to it, jobs are based on it, and families are preoccupied with it" (Rohlen 1983: 26). High schools themselves are ranked according to their success rates at the university entrance exam, and a few high-ranking ones produce nearly half of the successful applicants to Tokyo University.

Those students who fail to get into a good university on their first attempt will re-try the entrance exam year after year, for as many as six or seven years! Among the successful applicants at Tokyo University, one-third to one-half may be taking the test for at least the second time. Unsuccessful candidates study hard at cram schools and advanced-level cram schools called *yobikō* ('preparatory school'), whose sole purpose is to prepare students for the university entrance exam (or sometimes the high school entrance exams). There is even a name for high-school graduates whose main occupation is preparing for the university entrance exam: *rōnin* ('floating people'). (In early Japan, *rōnin* were peasants who left their land to work elsewhere. In feudal Japan *rōnin* were masterless samurai.) Incidentally, today there are far more male than female *rōnin*, reflecting the fact that in Japan life-long careers are crucial for males but not for females.

In contrast to the rigor and stress of primary and secondary education, Japanese university education is anti-climactic. The four years at a university are treated like a holiday between the rigor of the 12 years of schooling, on one side, and of the responsibility of many years of holding down a job, on the other. It is dubbed "a university playground," "four years of vacation," or "four years' liberated zone." Simply put, university students tend to be indifferent to studying, since they face no more entrance examinations, and since they obtain employment based not on their performance in university but on the name of the university they attended. If they want to receive a rigorous post-secondary education they flock to the United States. In 1983, there were 13,610 Japanese students who did so, up from only 2,168 in the 1960s (Marshall 1986).

A few university graduates continue into post-graduate education. Graduate school is not popular, partly because a B.A. degree alone can lead to a well-paying job, and partly because companies prefer to recruit individuals with a general education so that they can train the recruits in their own company ways. Many university graduates are opting for high-paying financial industry jobs over graduate schools. The Science and Technology Agency of Japan predicts that Japan will face a shortage of researchers by the year 2005.

Japanese Education: Problems

The Japanese educational system has its problems. In Japan there is a single prescribed route to success, which, moreover, starts at an early age. At university, if students want to switch their faculty, they have to take all over again the tough university entrance exam for a new faculty. There is less room for late bloomers in Japan than in North America. Those who do not go to a sequence of the "right" schools, from kindergarten to university, may have to face poor career prospects for life.

Except for *rōnin*, the Japanese educational system does not allow mature adults, those older than 25, a new beginning or re-entry into the educational system for career-oriented development. In the Japanese mind, university is for youth, not for mature students. Anyway, the tough entrance exams discourage older adults from going to university. Now, the aging population and student shortages make adult education attractive. To promote lifelong learning, the Ministry of Education has set up the University of the Air, which is directed at adult students, especially housewives and the elderly, and has expanded evening courses and correspondence education. But this kind of education, laudable though it is, is largely for personal enjoyment and enrichment rather than career development.

Long hours of study at regular school, at cram school, and at home, as well as long hours spent commuting among all these places of study, leave precious little time for children to be just children, playing and having fun with other children. The large class size, the uniform teaching, the rote memorization of information, and the indifferent standard of university education do not foster creative, original, or innovative thinking.

As one consequence of this sort of education, Japan has not produced many Nobel prize winners. Between 1948 and 1990, Japan counted seven winners, two of whom lived in the United States, whereas the United States, with twice the population of

Japan, counted 202. But perhaps it is unfair to compare Japan with the United States, which, partly thanks to immigrant scientists, stands head and shoulder above other nations in garnering Nobel prizes. Compare Japan then with nations smaller than itself such as the United Kingdom (87 winners) and France (45 winners), whose combined population is smaller than Japan's 125 million. In this area Japan's achievement is not commensurate with her mass literacy and economic superpower status. The Japanese educational policies result in people who can do correctly and well what they have been told but not in people who break new trails.

The pressure to get high scores on an exam is so intense that some students are driven to suicide. Every year as exam time arrives, the media reports student suicides, though problems with study in general rather than exams *per se* may be the cause. The rate of juvenile suicides, though high, slipped from first place in the international rankings in 1955 to fourth place in 1973. Near the time of the final examination, a few students, usually low-achieving middle-school students, turn to unruly behavior such as attacking teachers, bullying, and vandalism. Bullying is severe enough to drive several children in a year to suicide. Truancy is increasing, though not yet at an alarming rate: In 1988 over 40,000 primary and middle school students (5 per 1,000) were hard-core truants, missing more than 50 days of school, a four-fold increase since the late 1970s.

Japanese parents, students, teachers, and the media all agree that the exam hell must end.

> Time and again one reads how examinations are ruining the schools, the young, and Japanese society; how cramming produces warped personalities, crushes enthusiasm, and nips creativity in the bud. One would think education had reached a crisis point, that either the exam system must be scrapped or Japan will lose its humanity and vitality. [Rohlen 1983: 81]

As his final verdict, Rohlen observes

> Japan's high schools represent but a small part of that country's humanistic tradition, a tradition rich in beauty, sensitivity, and spirit.... The well-intended teachers and well-behaved students put their efforts to purposes that are ultimately shallow and uninspired.... It is a system without much heart [p. 320].

The Japanese themselves appear to be dissatisfied with their educational system, for whatever reasons. According to a newspaper poll, the percentage of adults who were dissatisfied with primary and middle school education rose from 22% in 1977 to 55% in 1984, while those who were satisfied fell from 49% in 1977 to 24% in 1984 (Amashiro 1987). When over 1,000 Japanese high school students who studied or are studying in the United States were polled, 53% preferred US education while only 9% preferred Japanese education; and 48% preferred US teachers while only 8% preferred Japanese teachers.

The question comes down to a choice between a highly regimented classroom where everybody learns at least basic literacy and numeracy skills, as in Japan, and a relatively free and open classroom where some students excel while many fall behind in achievement, as in North America.

How Well are Children Educated?

What are the fruits of the time and effort devoted to primary and secondary education in Japan? Japanese education provides almost all students with functional literacy, i.e., a level of reading, writing, and math skills adequate to allow them to function in an industrial society. It shapes "a whole population, workers as well as managers, to a standard inconceivable in the United States, where we are still trying to implement high school graduation competency tests that measure only minimal reading and computing skills" (Rohlen 1983: 322).

The psychologist Stevenson and his associates (1993) have carried out a cross-cultural comparison of the mathematical abilities and reading skills of children in Taipei in Taiwan, Sendai in Japan, and Minneapolis in the United States. The number of the children studied in each city was 240. The same children were tested three times: in 1980 when they were in Grade I; in 1984 when they were in Grade V; and in 1990 when they were in Grade XI. At Grade XI, 4,000 additional children who were not in the original study were included. In mathematics achievement, the Taiwanese children were at the top in each test, followed closely by the Japanese children; and the American children were far below the East Asian children. On the reading vocabulary test, the rank order from high to low scores was: Taiwanese, American, and Japanese in 1980 but Japanese, Taiwanese, and American in 1990. The achievement gap between East Asian children and American children is real and persistent.

The Second International Test of Mathematics Achievement (1980–1982) attracted students from over 20 countries as participants. Japanese 5th graders ranked first in all branches of math (such as algebra, geometry, and statistics), followed by South Korean 5th graders. The Japanese middle-school students also ranked first, while Japanese high-school students ranked second, after Hong Kong students. The degree of variation in ability among Japanese students tended to be small as compared with students from other countries.

So, if Japanese students spend a great deal of time and effort in learning to read and write complex Kanji, they do so not at the expense of other important school subjects. Also in Japanese secondary schools English, a foreign language, is an important subject. It can take up three class periods per week in middle school, and as many as six to eight class periods in high school. It is one of the three core subjects included in the entrance exams to high schools and universities. If American students were to study Japanese as long and hard as Japanese students study English, they might fall even further behind the Japanese students in math, science, and their native language.

Let us end the chapter with the highest accolade that the Japanese educational system can receive.

It should not be an exaggeration to say that in many respects the average high school graduate in Japan is equal or superior to the average American college graduate in science, math, geography, history, music, art, and foreign language skills.... Japanese education, like the nation's overall industrial system, has been made into an extraordinarily efficient engine for economic advancement. Today, Japan sets the world standards in mass education. [Rohlen 1983: 25–26]

24

History of Mass Literacy in Japan

Functional literacy has been defined in this book as follows:

People can read such everyday reading materials as newspapers and manuals, and also can fill in forms and write memos or simple letters. In addition, they have basic numeracy skills; and some can use a computer. They are likely to have finished at least middle school education ("Scripts and Literacy" in chap. 1).

A literate Japanese should know the official Kanji, Hiragana, Katakana, Rōmaji, Arabic numerals, and their proper uses. By this definition, virtually all Japanese are said to be literate, thanks to their rigorous primary and secondary education. Some Japanese writers and scholars who have university education are likely to have high-level literacy as well. Such people, in addition to possessing functional literacy, know about 1,000 extra Kanji beyond the official Kanji; they can read specialized or technical materials; some can write manuals and articles; some have knowledge of English, the preeminent international language.

Let us trace the history of literacy and traditional education in Japan.

Early Limited Literacy

When Chinese characters were introduced to Japan by Korean scholars in the 4th or 5th century, there arose a need to learn them along with Chinese culture. Initially only a small circle of Korean and Chinese immigrants, imperial family members, and aristocrats were literate in the newly introduced script. By 604 Prince Shōtoku (572/4–622) was literate enough to draft the 17-article constitution in Chinese characters and text, and in 608 he began to send to Sui and Tang China Japanese missions and students, who came home bringing Chinese learning and texts. The Prince also built the Hōryūji temple in Nara, the capital, as a place of learning as well as worship. Emperor Shōmu (701–756) built the Tōdaiji temple in Nara as well as other temples in various provinces. In time, Buddhist monks or priests joined the small elite class of literates, teaching reading at these temples.

In the Taika Reform of 645–649 Japan adopted a Chinese-style centralised, bureaucratic state. To meet the state's need for many literate bureaucrats, an institute called the Daigakuryō ('the University') was set up in Nara during the reign of Emperor Tenji (r. 661–772). It educated about 430 sons of nobility in the Confucian literature, using the texts such as *Analects* and the *Book of Filial Piety*. Those who finished the course were required to pass an examination, which included essay writing. The University saw its heyday in the early Heian period (794–1185), after which its influence waned, as many offices became the hereditary prerogative of certain ranks. There was also a *kokugaku* ('national learning') in each province to educate the sons of the provincial nobility.

To run the centralized bureaucratic government effectively, the Japanese state increasingly relied on written documents. It compiled a law code based on the Chinese Tang codes and promulgated it in 689, and conducted nation-wide censuses in 670 and 690. These have not survived. On the other hand, many pieces of written tablets of the 7th and 8th centuries have survived. A small piece of wood was planed, and on it a brief text in Chinese characters was written. The piece was then sent to an addressee, who after reading it often discarded it in a refuse dump or well, to be unearthed in the 20th century. Over 20,000 pieces of wooden tablets have been unearthed at various sites, and there is now a scholarly discipline called "wooden tablet study." Most commonly, the written tablets were used among bureaucrats in requesting goods or personnel and in reporting events or budgets. Sometimes written tablets accompanied the goods sent to an official. Occasionally, the wooden tablets were used for writing practice.

In the early 8th century, two history books—*Record of Ancient Matters (Kojiki)* (AD 712) and *Chronicle of Japan (Nihon Shoki)* (720)—were written in Chinese characters, and in the late 8th century, an anthology of Japanese poems was compiled. The use of characters in these books was too complicated to have attracted many readers. (A scholar in the 18th century spent many years to decipher *Kojiki*.)

In 828 the renowned monk Kūkai set up a private school in Kyoto for the children of commoners. It taught a broad range of subjects, including the canons of Confucianism, Daoism, and Buddhism. But the school was open only for a few years until Kūkai's death in 835. As you can see, during the Nara (710–794) and Heian (794–1185) periods monks played a considerable role in spreading education among commoners as well as aristocrats.

In the 9th century the sheer difficulty of writing and reading in Chinese characters impelled the Japanese to create two forms of Kana—Katakana and Hiragana—out of characters, as described in Chapter 19. Initially Katakana was used mostly by monks and scholars, whereas Hiragana was used by women to write letters, diaries, and eventually stories.

In the 12th century, near the end of the Heian period, the University (Daigakuryō) built in the 7th century burned down and was not re-built, and *kokugaku* ('national learning') disappeared. In the 15th century the most representative educational institution was the *Ashikaga Gakkō*, which could have been a remnant of a local *kokugaku* or perhaps founded by the warrior Ashikaga Yoshikane (d. 1199). Its enrollment reached 3,000 during the latter part of the 1500s. Its teachers and students were Buddhist priests and monks, who studied Confucianism and divination as well. (It continued to operate until 1872.) In this period, the foundation was laid for *terakoya*, to be described in the next section.

In the 16th century Christian missionaries from Europe founded schools in Japan, especially in the southwestern island, Kyūshū. The Portuguese Jesuit Luis de Almeida (c. 1525–1583) established primary schools in 200 churches and taught religion as well as reading, writing, arithmatic, manners, and songs.

Dawn of Mass Literacy

At the beginning of the feudal Edo/Tokugawa period (1600–1868), literacy was still found among a small group of special people, such as priests who kept up the traditions of scholarship in Buddhism and Confucianism in a few monastaries, and who tutored the children of noble families. Later in the period various types of schools sprang up to serve the needs of different social classes—from high to low: samurai, farmers, artisans, and merchants—thus ushering in the dawn of mass literacy in Japan.

Before official schools were established, and later along with official schools, there were private academies called *(shi)juku*, each of which was founded by a teacher— a samurai or *rōnin* (masterless samurai)—who was often a pioneer scholar in a particular field. These private academies provided a kind of middle school education for the children of samurai and better-off commoners. (Today, *juku* refers to a commercial cram school.) As a group the academies covered a wide range of learning, but each individual academy tended to specialize in a single branch of learning (e.g., Confucian, national, and Western) or of the martial arts.

The sons of samurai received a sort of compulsory education in official schools called fief or domain schools *(hankō)*. (*Han* refers to a *daimyō* domain; there were over 260 *daimyō*, feudal lords who controlled local regions, under a shōgun who was the central authority.) By the end of the Tokugawa period in 1868, all but a few small domains had created official schools. Lords of larger domains were eager to show their respect for learning, and each employed an eminent scholar as a Confucian adviser to him and as a tutor to his heir.

Typically, children entered a domain school at age around 8, having learned basic reading and writing at home or in simple schools. Some started at age 15 or older after studying at a private academy. At school the students learned Chinese studies, martial arts, and personal conduct over a period of several years. Their main task was to learn to read aloud the Chinest text of the Confucian Four Books in Kundoku ('Kun reading'), as though it were a Japanese text ("Kana and Kanji Teaching in School" in chap. 22).

Most domain schools had groups of advanced students, some well into their 20s or older. The students would spend most of their time in private study, and the remainder in regular study in groups that worked their way steadily through difficult classical texts—historical, philosophical, sometimes mathematical. There were formal examinations, often in the presence of the lord or his proxy. A man wishing to enter the lord's service had to attain a certain level of satisfactory performance in these examinations. In some schools the examinations determined promotion.

After the mid-Edo period, the children of commoners as well as of the lowest-grade samurai in urban areas attended private community schools called *terakoya* ('temple, child, facilities'), where they learned to use the abacus, to read and write in Kana and some Kanji. Pupils learned also other practical skills, such as letter writing and bookkeeping, so that they could run a small business or farm. The word *terakoya* reflects the fact that sometimes Buddhist priests provided education at temples, but non-priests such as samurai and doctors also did so at private homes. In contrast to other types of schools, about one-third of the teachers and pupils of community schools in big cities were women. Each school had between 30 to 60 pupils under a single teacher. Pupils entered community schools at age around 8 and stayed there for several years in case of boys and a few years in case of girls. By the first half of the 19th century, there were more than 15,000 community schools scattered throughout the country, and in the prosperous regions half of all children attended them.

The quality of literacy acquired in the various schools may not have been high: Upper-class children, in spite of years of arduous study, often merely learned to recite passages of the Confucian classics by heart without much understanding, whereas lower-class children learned Kana and some Kanji, which were just sufficient for the small concerns of everyday life and the perusal of popular fiction. At the time all sorts of books abounded— technical books, novels, poetry books, pornography, children's books, and so on. Most popular books were printed in Kana only or Kana with some Furigana-annotated Kanji.

Between the mid-17th and mid-19th centuries, Japan closed her doors to foreigners, except to a few Chinese and Dutch traders. It was the Dutch who introduced modern, Western science and medicine to Japan, attracting individual Japanese doctors and low-ranking samurai as students. In the 1850s, through "Dutch learning" (*rangaku*) and books translated from Dutch, the Japanese became aware of Western superiority in military science and so established a number of special schools for Western studies.

By the last part of the Tokugawa period virtually all samurai, most townsmen, and well-off peasants were literate. By the mid-19th century, 45% of the men and 15% of the women could read and write (Dore 1965). This rate of literacy is considered high for a feudal society; it must have laid a foundation for rapid industrialization in the next, Meiji period.

In the latter half of the 19th century, when Japan awoke from its 300 years of self-imposed isolation, she found herself hopelessly behind the West in matters of science, technology, and industry. The enlightened emperor, Meiji, was convinced that Japan had to build a modern system of education if it was to catch up with the West. In 1871 the Ministry of Education was established, and the following year the modern national educational system was introduced. Private community schools such as *terakoya* turned into primary schools; many official domain schools, *hankō*, became public secondary schools, some of which eventually developed into universities; the shōgunate-controlled elite schools formed the nucleus for Tōkyō University. Most of the schools of Western learning became professional schools or schools for specialized learning.

"By the last decade of the 19th century, the Japanese government managed to combine a new Western curriculum with an older [Confucian] moral underpinning designed to produce a citizenry subservient to the larger interests of the new empire" (Ellington 1992: 23).

Mass Literacy After World War II

Two years after the end of World War II, in 1947, compulsory and free education was extended to nine years—6 years of primary school and 3 years of middle school. One year later, in 1948, the first nation-wide survey of reading and writing skills was carried out by the U.S. Military Command, in cooperation with the Ministry of Education and the National Institute of Educational Research. The survey involved

21,008 people aged between 15 and 64. A few testees, 1.6%, were "complete illiterates," who could not read even a single Kana sign, while 2.1% were "partial illiterates," who could read Kana though not Kanji. Among young people aged between 15 and 24, the rate of complete illiteracy was only 0.2%.

To be functionally literate, a Japanese should be able to read and write Hiragana, Katakana, Arabic numerals, Rōmaji, and about 2,000 official Kanji in 4,000 On/Chinese and Kun/Japanese readings. Because of the 9 years of free and compulsory education since 1947, most Japanese today should have fully mastered the first three scripts and have adequate knowledge of the last two scripts.

Since 1973, one printing company in Tokyo has been conducting annual tests of Kanji reading and writing skill, involving students from 5th grade to university, as well as non-student adults. The test is conducted in giant rooms, one in Tokyo and another in Osaka. Even though no prize or reward is given out, the tests are popular enough to draw 2,000 to 3,000 volunteer testees annually. People who take such tests must be interested in learning Kanji, and so they are assumed to know Kanji better than do those who do not take the tests. Be that as it may, the test results reveal interesting patterns. Table 24-1 (based on Saiga, 1978: 214) summarizes the correct Kanji scores (out of 100) in the 6th (1977) test, which produced slightly higher scores than the 5th test (1976).

Table 24-1. Volunteer Testees' Scores of Reading and Writing Kanji

Education	Educational Kanji Read	Educational Kanji Write	Temporary Kanji Read	Temporary Kanji Write	Unofficial Kanji Read	Unofficial Kanji Write
Primary	37	26	26	2	26	18
Middle	62	33	59	20	54	41
High	79	63	84	48	72	59
Adult	92	66	95	65	89	49

As Table 24-1 shows, Kanji skills increase with educational level and the age of the testee, from primary school to middle school to high school to college/adults. On the one hand, children know some Kanji not taught in primary and middle schools; on the other, adults do not know all the Kanji taught in primary schools. Both children and adults know some unofficial Kanji found in everyday reading materials. This result suggests that the lists of official Kanji and educational Kanji do not fully reflect the use of Kanji in daily life.

One might expect adults to score 100 on the official Kanji, at least in reading if not in writing, but their score was 95. The result once again shows that it is not difficult to learn tens, even hundreds, of Kanji, but it is difficult to **master** perfectly the sounds, shapes, and meanings of all 1,950 official Kanji in over 4,000 readings. The critical question is, what Kanji score—80, 90, 100—is needed to read comfortably, looking up a dictionary only occasionally, newspapers and popular magazines? In my daily reading of English-language newspapers, I do use a dictionary, if infrequently. This frequency, or rather infrequency, is certainly comfortable.

Back to the 6th Kanji test, some of the misreadings are revealing. Given Japanese and Sino-Japanese words in Kanji to read aloud, some testees responded with

European translations. This result is not surprising in that some writers give European words as Furigana to Kanji phrases (fig. 19-2c, d). It is another piece of evidence that European words are driving out native and Sino-Japanese words. Finally, it shows dramatically that readers can retain the meanings of logographic Kanji even if they forget their sounds.

To be highly literate, or even to be functionally literate, a Japanese may have to know some English. All Japanese can read a Japanese text containing a few English words, and some Japanese can read English text. After all, almost all Japanese have received hours and hours of lessons in English in secondary schools as well as at cram schools. Even some primary school children take English at cram schools, though not at their regular schools. English, along with the Japanese language and math, is tested at the entrance exams to high school and to university. In spite of extensive study, the Japanese speakers' skill in English tends to be limited to reading simple English text; it does not extend to speaking English because the teaching method concentrates on translating short English text into Japanese.

There are bound to be some Japanese who may know Kana but not enough official Kanji to read ordinary reading materials comfortably. A few schoolchildren have difficulty in learning to read, as described in "Reading Difficulties" (in chap. 22). A few Japanese do not receive adequate secondary school education. Hereditary social outcasts, called *burakumin* ('hamlet people'), are ruthlessly discriminated against in education, and are engaged in such despised trades as butchering. Among ethnic Koreans (the largest group of "aliens" in Japan) and ethnic Chinese (the second largest group) in Kanagawa Prefecture of Japan, 8% had no schooling in 1984 (Kinbara et al. 1988). The unschooled were old, first-generation immigrants, who came to Japan as conscripted laborers, and who by now — 11 years after the survey — have substantially dwindled in number. In the same survey, the percentages of 2nd- and 3rd-generation ethnic Koreans and Chinese who received secondary or tertiary education were as high as the Japanese.

To conclude, almost all people in Japan have functional literacy to become useful workers of a highly industrialized society.

Books and Publications

A nation's literacy activities can be indirectly gauged from the books held in public libraries, published and sold in bookstores, as well as the newspapers and magazines subscribed.

The Japanese had first to learn Chinese characters before they could write books, so their books appeared relatively late, compared with Chinese books. Prince Shōtoku wrote the 17-article constitution in AD 604, and also compiled the earliest, but now lost, national histories. The first extant history book, *Record of Ancient Matters (Kojiki)*, appeared in AD 712, tracing Japanese history from its nebulous beginning to AD 628. Another history book, *Chronicles of Japan (Nihon Shoki)*, appeared in 720; it also starts at the beginning but ends at AD 697. The two were written entirely in Chinese characters, which were sometimes used to express the sounds of the Japanese language.

In the 8th century, two anthologies of verse were compiled, one of Chinese verses and the other of Japanese verses. The latter, *Man'yōshū (Ten Thousand Leaves)*, contains about 4,500 poems by about 450 poets, who could be emperors, aristocrats, monks, bureaucrats, commoners, and even beggars. The poems were written in Chinese characters, most of which were used phonetically—for their sounds rather than meanings—to represent the Japanese language. Chinese characters used like phonetic signs, Man'yōgana, eventually developed into Kana ("Kana: Japanese Syllabary" chap. 19).

The first mature Japanese novel is *The Tale of Genji* written by Lady Murasaki Shikibu in the early 11th century. It revolves around the life and loves of the handsome and talented Prince Genji and a gallery of other personages. It describes the elegance of a court society where beauty and love were constant preoccupations. Most importantly for our purpose, though it included occasional Kanji for Chinese words, it was written in Hiragana, which had been developing since the 8th century.

In the 13th century a great war tale *Heike Monogatari* or *The Tale of the Taira Clan* was written by an unknown author. The tale is about the rise, the splendor, and the eventual fall of the famous Taira clan together with other individuals caught in the tragic destiny of the Taira. The theme of the tale is the Buddhist impermanence of all things, expressed at the very beginning of the tale with a temple bell ringing.

> The hue of the flowers of the teak tree declares that they who flourish must be brought low. Yea, the proud ones are but for a moment, like an evening dream in springtime. The mighty are destroyed at the last, they are but as dust before the wind. [trans. by Sadler 1918: 1]

The story was written in a mixture of native Japanese words and words of Chinese origin, some of which were annotated with Furigana (fig. 19-1).

In the late 16th century, the Jesuit missions in the Far East set up a press in Japan with metal movable type. The press printed secular Japanese literature, such as an abridged *Feiqe no Monogatari (Heike no Monogatari)* as well as Christian literature translated into Japanese and printed in Rōmaji. The press had 25 years of activity.

During the Tokugawa period (1600–1868) the *haiku* form of poetry, a terse verse in 17 syllables or moras, reached the height of its development. The great master in this poetic form was Matsuo Bashō (1644–94), whose work was cited in "Speech Sounds, Syllables, and Moras" (in chap. 17). His work *The Narrow Road to the Deep North (Oku no Hosomichi)* became one of the great classics of Japanese literature. It is a record of the journey he took from Edo (Tokyo) to northern Japan, and contains numerous *haiku* accompanied by descriptions of the settings in which they were composed. As a Zen Buddhist Bashō strove to discover a vision of eternity in the transient world around him.

In the same period, the Japanese publishing industry, and along with it the number of book stores, grew. Many books on Buddhism, Confucianism, and Japan were published. As well, a torrent of "frivolous" works—jokes, ghost stories, guidebooks, pornography, historical novels, etc.—written mostly in Kana were mass-produced for a large merchant class that was searching for literary distraction. The merchant class, though they stood below the three other classes (samurai, peasant, and artisan) in social rank, accumulated great wealth and sometimes employed *rōnin* ('masterless samurai') to tutor their children in various subjects, especially in reading and writing.

In the latter part of the 19th century, after the Meiji Restoration, there appeared books that opened the eyes of the Japanese to the West. For example, Fukuzawa Yukichi wrote *Conditions in the Western World* describing parliaments, railways, banks, and so on, and his *Outline of Civilization* interpreted the meaning of modern civilization for the Japanese.

Today, a prodigious number of books, magazines, and newspapers is published annually in Japan, reflecting a great demand, according to sources such as *Shuppan Nenkan* (*Publication Yearbook* 1994). The number of book titles published reached 48,053 in 1993, compared to 31,297 titles in 1983. By contrast, in 1992 the United States, whose population is twice as large as that of Japan, published 48,146 titles, and the United Kingdom, whose population is half of Japan, published 78,835 titles. In terms of the number of copies of a book title printed and sold, Japan may rank high. A popular novel has a much larger print run than the 5,000 copies of a successful British novel, in spite of the fact that a novel in English has a much wider potential world audience than does one in Japanese. However, in Japan over the past few decades, the sales of books, especially on serious topics, have fallen, while the sales of magazines and comics (see the next section) have risen.

The Japanese are the world's second largest subscribers and readers of daily newspapers: 590 papers per 1,000 persons, compared to 632 in Hong Kong (highest), 250 in the United States, and 30 in China. The average Japanese household subscribes to two newspapers. The number one paper is *Yomiuri*, whose morning and evening editions combined have the world's biggest circulation, with close to 14.5 million copies daily. There are over 158 daily newspapers, including national, local, sport, and English language, with an aggregate circulation of 71 million. A survey by the Newspaper Association shows that 70% of Japanese adults read a newspaper for about 45 minutes per day. Schoolchildren read daily newspapers for children published by several national newspapers and delivered to homes throughout Japan.

As for public libraries, one of the pleasures of living in North America is that one can visit local libraries in one's own neighborhood. This pleasure is denied to most Japanese (and to Koreans, and Chinese, for that matter), though mobile libraries visit small communities. Japanese readers seem to prefer purchasing books to borrowing them from public libraries. Still, there has been progress in this area in the past few decades. For example, between 1987 and 1992, there was an increase in the number of libraries of all kinds (excluding university libraries), from 1,804 to 2,038; in the number of books held in the libraries, from 142.6 million to 185.2 million copies; and in the number of copies of books loaned out, from 249.9 million to 292 million. During the same period, university libraries too increased in number, from 930 to 1,037 and in the copies of books stored, from 56.5 million to 66.0 million.

If Japan is relatively poor in public libraries, it is rich in bookstores. In the Kanda area of Tokyo, near many of the city's colleges and universities, hundreds of bookstores, large and small, line the streets for blocks. Different stores specialize in art, history, law, medicine, foreign publications, secondhand books, and so on. One giant bookstore I visited in Tokyo had several floors, each specializing in different subjects. Near any major urban subway station, there is at least one large general-purpose bookstore. About half of all books published are paperbacks.

If the quantity of reading matter is impressive, its quality may not be. A prominent American journalist noted:

> The dedicated literacy of Japan is yet another cause of admiration, but the content of the reading matter—especially on the trains, where no one knows his neighbor and in principle everyone is unobserved—is not. Some of the men are reading books, but more are reading either 'sports papers' or thick volumes of comics, the size of telephone books. [Fallows 1986: 36]

Perhaps it is unfair to judge the quality of Japanese literacy by looking at the type of material read on trains, which are usually crowded. The mere fact that many Japanese are reading on trains is commendable; in North America only a handful do so, even though trains are not as crowded as in Japan.

Manga! Manga!

The most spectacular change in contemporary Japanese reading habits is the boom in *manga* ('random sketch' or 'comics'). There is even an English book on the subject, *Manga! Manga! The World of Japanese Comics* (Schodt 1983). Of the huge number of copies of books and magazines produced in Japan, nearly one-third are *manga*, generating a multi-billion dollar business. Japanese comic weeklies and monthlies, with such weird title as *MAGAZINE Wooooo!*, sell in the millions of copies. The *manga* readers numbered 54.8 million in 1980 and 70.8 million in 1990; they are projected to number 84 million in the year 2000.

Manga are nothing to be looked down upon: they contain much reading material in Kanji, Kana, Rōmaji, and even English words, along with drawings. Let us examine the Kanji appearing in one comic series, *Candy, Candy* (1975–1979), intended for lower-grade schoolchildren (Kinoshita 1989). It used 749 educational Kanji (74.5% of the 1,006 Educational Kanji), 927 Common Kanji (47.7% of 1,945), 3 Kanji for personal names, and 13 Kanji outside the Common Kanji. So, children are in fact reading Kanji that are above their grade levels. Many Kanji have Furigana ('annotating Kana') to aid oral reading and at the same time to teach the children Kanji sounds. Many Kanji are used instead of Kana, because the meaning of phrases can be grasped better in Kanji than in Kana, and because Kanji words use less paper space than Kana words (in a comic, words are enclosed in a balloon or written in a limited space).

In *manga* the appearances of printed Kanji, Kana, and other scripts are no different from those in regular reading materials. By contrast, in English comic strips all letters appear in uppercase, which looks quite different from regular reading material. All upper-case text is hard to read and discourages me, at least, from reading comics.

In a cross-cultural comparison, middle school students in Japan, United States, and China were asked to say *yes* or *no* to the question "I read comics yesterday." The proportion of *Yes* answers was 40% in Japan, 10% in United States, and 40% in China, which has no comics but has picture news (Sengoku 1988). Why are Japanese children, teenagers, and adults such avid consumers of comics?

> To be sure, the small child in Japan reads comics for the same reason children everywhere do—they are immediately accessible when still learning to read, and fun. But for older children, teenagers, and adults, comics are faster and easier to read than a novel, more portable than a television set, and provide an

important source of entertainment and relaxation in a highly disciplined society. [Schodt 1983: 25]

Comics that are filled with extraordinary, weird, deviant, and obscene people and events seem to provide teenagers with relief from their highly regimented everyday conduct and narrowly focused studies.

Some *manga* do deal with weighty economic or political topics, even mathematics, and are educational. Some are up-to-date as well. For example, *Introduction to the Japanese Economy in Manga* became a best seller when it was published in 1991. As the Gulf War was about to break out in January 1991, a 300-page comic entitled *Iraq vs the U.S.-led Multinational Forces* appeared in February, 1991, explaining the high-tech weapons and combat sequences that might be used. Its first printing, 50,000 copies, sold out in no time. In February 1991, an all-comics newspaper, *Comic Sankei*, was launched. It reports on news events in full-color cartoon strips, to lure the millions of Japanese readers addicted to *manga*. It has already attracted a huge following.

Contemporary serious comic artists call their works *gekiga* ('drama comics' or 'dramatic pictures'). This kind of comic depicts the real world in a straightforward manner, without aiming for comic effects. The textual material in such a comic is not necessarily contained in a balloon, as in a regular comic.

The quality of literacy in Japan may be less than exalted, but it is still better than the state of literacy in the U.S. Japanese schoolchildren spend more time reading for pleasure than do American children — 5.7 vs 3.8 hours per week (Stevenson and Stigler 1992). In his book *The Death of Literature*, Alvin Kernan (1990) points out that about 60 percent of adult Americans never read a book, and most of the rest read only one book a year on average. Canadians seem to read slightly more than Americans. In a poll conducted by a Quebec firm, 15% of Canadians (37% in French-speaking Quebec Province) had not read a book in the last 6 months (*The Toronto Star*, April 18, 1992). A thick comic book is better than no book!

Part III: Summary and Conclusions

Japan, a chain of small islands, is populated by 125 million Japanese speakers. The Japanese language has a simple sound system with around 20 phonemes that are used in about 110 different V or CV (consonant–vowel) syllables. Its vocabulary consists of native words, Sino-Japanese words, and foreign—mostly English—loan words. A Japanese sentence has a relatively free word order, as postpositions sort out the grammatical roles of nouns. The sentence usually ends in a verb or adjective, which changes its ending according to tense, type of sentence, and level of politeness. Japanese speech changes according to who is speaking to whom about whom. There are a few different levels of speech, but plain and polite are the two levels that remain in everyday use.

The Japanese language is written and read using a variety of scripts: Chinese characters called Kanji, two forms of a syllabary called Hiragana and Katakana, Rōmaji, or letters of the Roman alphabet, and Arabic numerals.

Of these, Kanji, which were introduced in the 4th or 5th century, are the oldest, most important, and at the same time the most complex. To ease learning and using them, about 2,000 Kanji (out of a possible 50,000) have been designated as official. To learn a handful of Kanji is easy, even for preschoolers. But to master all the official Kanji is another matter. What makes Kanji difficult to master is not just their complex shapes and large number but also their varied sounds. One Kanji may be pronounced in either an On/Chinese sound or a Kun/Japanese sound, or in both. And there may be varieties of On or Kun. The 2,000 official Kanji are pronounced in about 4,000 official On and Kun readings, and there are unofficial readings even of the official Kanji.

To supplement Kanji, Kana, a syllabary, was created out of Kanji in the 9th century. It has 46 basic signs plus over 50 modified signs, each of which represents one syllable (or mora), which is either a vowel or a consonant followed by a vowel. Kana come in two forms, the curvaceous Hiragana and the angular Katakana, which are put to different uses in a text. Kanji are customarily used to write content words and morphemes, such as nouns and verb stems, while Hiragana are used to write such frequent grammatical morphemes as postpositions after nouns, and the endings of verbs or adjectives. Katakana are used to write such less frequent items as foreign loan words and onomatopoetic words. Rōmaji are used for European words and Japanese acronyms. They may be used also to write the Japanese language, mainly for the benefit of foreigners.

The Japanese writing system, especially its Kanji, is legendary for its complexity. Kanji are most complex for writing and reading aloud. Yet they are kept because they are useful. Kanji differentiate homophones and convey meanings quickly. Their presence in a text makes silent reading efficient: A skilled reader develops a strategy of attending to complex shapes, which are normally Kanji that represent important content words, at the expense of simple shapes, usually Hiragana representing less important grammatical morphemes.

Most Japanese children informally learn to read Hiragana at home. Then they learn to read and write Katakana in primary school, and Kanji in both primary and secondary school. Their education is centrally directed by the Ministry of Education, with emphasis on teaching such core subjects as the national language and math, and in secondary school, English. Students are well disciplined and study hard at school, home, and commercial cram schools. Japanese students make extraordinary effort to get into good universities, but once they get there they take it easy. Nor are they keen to get into graduate schools.

Turning to the history of literacy, for a few hundred years after the introduction of Chinese characters in the 4th or 5th century, literacy was a monopoly of a small class of aristocrats and Buddhist priests. The creation of Kana in the 9th century enabled upperclass females to write diaries and stories in Hiragana.

During the feudal Tokugawa period (1600–1868) there were a variety of schools to educate the children from different social classes, such as domain schools for the sons of samurai and community schools (*terakoya*) for the sons and daughters of commoners. Some "frivolous" works written in Kana were mass produced for growing number of people who could read.

During the Meiji period (1868–1912) a modern school system was introduced, and by 1910, when schooling extended to six years, over 90% of boys and girls attended school. During this period the Japanese adopted many Western ideas and institutions, for which they coined Sino-Japanese words. (These words were then borrowed by the Chinese and the Koreans.)

In 1947, after World War II, 9-year compulsory and free education was introduced. Almost all students not only finish the 9 years of compulsory education but also take 3 additional years of high school.

Japanese are readers of newspapers and magazines. Recently, they have become avid readers of comics called *manga* that deal with diverse subjects, from pornography to economics.

Thanks to a rigorous primary and secondary education, almost all Japanese are equipped with the basic reading and writing skills needed to become effective workers and managers in an industrial society. Japan, being poor in natural resources, can count only on its human resources to become an economic superpower.

Bibliography for Part III

In English

Bowring, Richard and Kornicki, Peter. *The Cambridge encyclopedia of Japan.* Cambridge University Press, 1993. It covers many topics in one volume, with many illustrations.

Chamberlain, B. H. *A practical introduction to the study of Japanese writing.* London: Crosby Lockwood & Sons, 1905.

Cummings, William, K. *Education and equality in Japan.* Princeton, N.J.: Princeton University Press, 1980.

Dore, R. P. *Education in Tokugawa Japan.* Berkeley, CA: University of California Press, 1965.

Duke, Benjamin. *The Japanese school: Lessons for industrial America.* New York: Praeger, 1986. It describes the Japanese primary and secondary schools in intimate detail. It points out many factors that make the Japanese education a success; it also points out a few weak areas that need to be corrected.

Ellington, Lucien. *Education in the Japanese Life-Cycle: Implications for the United States.* New York: Edwin Mellen Press, 1992. It gives an up-to-date information on the Japanese educational system, from kindergartens to schools for the elderly.

Fallows, James. The Japanese are different from you and me. *The Atlantic,* 1986, September, 35–41.

Gearheart, B. R. and Gearheart, C. J. *Learning disabilities: Educational strategies.* Columbus, Ohio: Merrill Publishing, 1989.

Habein, Yaeko Sato. *The history of the Japanese writing.* Tokyo: University of Tokyo Press 1984. It traces the history of Japanese writing up to the Meiji era.

Horodeck, Richard Alan. *The role of sound in reading and writing Kanji.* Cornell University Ph.D. thesis, 1987.

Kernan, Alvin. *The death of literature.* New Haven: Yale University Press, 1990.

Kindaichi Haruhiko (translated into English from Japanese by Umeyo Hirano). *The Japanese language.* Tokyo: Tuttle, 1978 (The Japanese original in 1957). This book by a noted Japanese linguist is full of anecdotes, and is a pleasure to read.

Kodansha encyclopedia of Japan. Tokyo: Kodansha, 1983. This 9-volume, informative encyclopedia covers many topics, including Japanese language, education, history, and Japanese relations with China and Korea.

Kuratani N., Kobayashi A., and Okunishi S. (Eds), *A new dictionary of Kanji usage.* Tokyo: Gakken, 1982–1989, 12th impression. It explains 2,000 common Kanji, and is indispensable to English speakers learning Kanji and the Japanese language.

Marshall, E. School reforms aim at creativity. *Science,* 1986, *233,* 267–270.

Miller, Roy Andrew. *The Japanese language.* Chicago: University of Chicago Press, 1967. This comprehensive and useful book deals with the genetic relationship, dialects, phonology, grammar, vocabulary, and the writing system of the Japanese language.

Miller, Roy Andrew. *Nihongo: In defence of Japanese.* London: Athlone Press, 1986. A set of essays that defend the Japanese language against misconceptions.

Namie Yoshiko. The Japanese speech community. In S. Alladina and V. Edwards (Eds.) *Multilingualism in British Isles 2: Africa, the Middle East and Asia.* London: Longman 1991.

Rohlen, Thomas P. *Japan's high schools.* Berkeley, CA: University of California Press, 1983. It gives an intimate look at five high schools in Kobe that represent different standings in a hierarchy established based on success rates in passing entrance exams to universities and colleges. It frequently compares Japanese schools to American schools.

Sadler, A. L. (translator) The Heike monogatari. *Transactions of the Asiatic Scociety of Japan.* 1918, XLVI, Part II.

Sansom, [Sir] George Bailey. *An historical grammar of Japanese.* Oxford: Clarendon Press, 1928.

Schodt, Frederik. *Manga! manga! The world of Japanese comics.* Tokyo: Kodansha International, 1983.

Seeley, Christopher. *A history of writing in Japan.* Leiden: E. J. Brill, 1991. It covers in detail the introduction of Kanji into Japan, development of Kana, and the use of these scripts in modern times.

Shibatani Masayoshi. *The languages of Japan.* New York: Cambridge University Press, 1990. It describes the sounds, words, sentences, and writing system of Ainu and Japanese.

Stephens, Michael D. *Education and the future of Japan.* Tokyo: Japan Library Ltd, 1991.

Stevenson, Harold W., Chen Chuansheng, and Lee Shinying. Mathematics achievement of Chinese, Japanese, and American children: ten years later. *Science*, 1993, *259*, 53–58.

Stevenson, Harold W. and Stigler, James W. *The learning gap: Why our schools are failing and what we can learn from Japanese and Chinese education.* 1992. See Part I.

Stevenson, H. W., Stigler, J. W., Lucker, G. W., Lee S.-Y., Hsu Ch.-Chu., and Kitamara S. Reading disabilities: The case of Chinese, Japanese, and English. *Child Development*, 1982, *53*, 1164–1181.

Taylor, Insup and Park Kwonsaeng. Differential processing of content words and function words: Chinese characters vs phonetic scripts. In I. Taylor and D.R. Olson (Eds.) *Scripts and literacy: Reading and learning to read alphabets, syllabaries and characters.* The Nertherlands: Kluwer Academic Press, 1995.

Taylor, Insup and Taylor, M. M. *The psychology of reading.* 1983. See Part 1.

Twine, Nanette. Toward simplicity: Script reform movements in the Meiji period. *Monumenta Nipponica*, 1983, *38:2*, 115–32.

Unger, J. Marshall. *The fifth generation fallacy: Why Japan is betting its future on artificial intelligence.* New York: Oxford University.1987.

Yamada Jun. Asymmetries of reading and writing in Japanese children. In I. Taylor and D.R. Olson (Eds.) *Scripts and literacy: Reading and learning to read alphabets, syllabaries and characters.* The Netherlands: Kluwer Academic, 1995.

World factbook. 1993. See Chapter 1.

In Japanese

Most journal articles have English titles, figure captions, and abstracts or summaries.

Amano K. Formation of the act of analyzing phonemic structure of words and its relation to learning Japanese syllabic characters (Kanamoji). *Japanese Journal of Educational Psychology*, 1970, *18*, 76–89.

Amashiro Isao. *Sōgo ni mita nichibeikyōiku no kadai (Tasks of Japanese and American education mutually seen).* Tokyo: Daiichi Hōki, 1987. It describes primary, secondary, and post-secondary education in Japan and compares it with American education.

Asahi Nenkan (Asahi Yearbook). Tokyo: Asahi Shinbun, 1993.

Daily concise dictionary: English–Japanese (5th edition) *and Japanese–English* (4th edition). Tokyo: Sanseido, 1990.

Fujiyoshi Yoshio. *Jindai moji no nazo (The puzzle of jindai moji)* Tokyo: Tōgensha, 1978.

Haryu Etsuko. What facilitates learning to read characters by children? *Japanese Journal of Educational Psychology*, 1989, *37*, 264–269.

Hatano Giyoo and Kuhara Keiko. Recognition function of Kanji in sentence comprension. *Report on the U.S.–Japan Symposium on Cognitive Science*, 1981, 180–187.

Hayashi Ooki (chief Ed.). *Tōsetsu nihongo (The Japanese language in graphs).* Tokyo: Kadokawa, 1982. Many pieces of interesting and useful information on the Japanese language, spoken and written, are concisely and clearly presented in graphs.

Hirose Hitoshi. An investigation of the recognition process for *jukugo* by use of priming paradigms. *The Japanese Journal of Psychology*, 1992, *63*, 303–309.

Hirose Takehiko. The effect of script frequency on semantic processing of Kanji and Kana words. *The Japanese Journal of Psychology*, 1984, *55*, 173–176.

Hirose Takehiko. The effect of orthographic familiarity on word recognition. *The Japanese Journal of Psychology*, 1985, *56*, 44–47.

Hondō Hiroshi. Kanji education in primary school. In vol 12 of *Kanji kōza*. See Satō Kiyoji, below.

Imai Seishin. Examination of how Kanji are taught to young children. *Dokusho Kagaku (Science of Reading)*, 1979, *23*, 97–104.

Ishii Isao. *Nihongo no zaihakken (Re-discovery of the Japanese language)*. Tokyo: Nippon Kyōmun, 1988.

Ishikawa Matsutaro. *Hankō to terakoya (Domain schools and community schools)*. Tokyo: Kyōyukusha, 1985. This slim volume tells you a lot about the domain schools and the community schools during the feudal Tokugawa period.

Kabashima Tadao. *Nihon no moji (Written signs of Japan)*. Tokyo: Iwanami, 1979.

Kaiho Hiroyuki and Nomura Yukimasa. *Kanji jyōhoshori no shinrigaku (Psychology of Kanji information processing)*. Tokyo: Kyōyuku Shuppansha, 1983. See Part I.

Kawakami Masahiro. Script familiarity and processing unit in lexical decision with Japanese *Kana* words. *The Japanese Journal of Psychology*, 1993, *64*, 235–39.

Kinbara Samon, Ishida Reiko, Ozawa Yusaku, Kajimura Hideki, and 2 others. *Nihon no naka no Kankokujin, Chūgokujin (Koreans and Chinese among Japanese)*. Tokyo: Meiseki Shoten, 1988.

Kindaichi Haruhiko et al. *Nihongo hyakka daijiten (An encyclopedia of the Japanese language)*. Tokyo: Daishūkan, 1989. A big volume that deals with many aspects of the Japanese language, both spoken and written.

Kinoshita Tetsuo. Kanji in the comic book Candy, Candy. In vol. 10, *Kanji kōza*. See Satō Kiyoji, below.

Kitta Hirokuni. *Nippon no Rōmazi-undō 1582–1990 (Japan's Rōmaji movement)*. Tokyo: Nippon Rōmazi Educational Research, 1992.

Kobayashi Kazuhito. History of Kanji education. See vol. 12, Satō Kiyoji, below.

Kokken (The National Language Institute), report 95 *Adō, seitō no jōyō Kanji shutoku (Mastery of common Kanji by children)*. Tokyo: Tokyo Shoseki, 1988.

Matsui Yoshikazu. *Gaigokujin kara mita nihongo (The Japanese language seen by foreigners)*. Tokyo: Nihon Kyomunsha, 1992. It points out that English words transcribed in Katakana pose a problem for foreigners learning Japanese.

Morioka Kenji. *Gohi no keisei (Composition of vocabulary)*. Tokyo: Meiji Shoten, 1987.

Morohashi Tetsuji. *Daikanwa jiten (The great Chinese–Japanese dictionary)*. Tokyo: Daishūkan 1960. This mammoth 13-volume dictionary defines close to 50,000 Kanji, including variants.

Muraishi S. and Amano K. *Reading and writing abilities of preschoolers: A summary*. Tokyo: The National Language Research Institute, 1972.

Nagano Tadashi. *Nihongo no chishiki (Knowledge of the Japanese language)*. Tokyo: Tamagawa University Press, 1990. It is a handbook on the use of Japanese writing as well as laws on education.

Nakano Sukezō and Nagano Masaru. Problems with national writing. *Kotoba no kōgaku (Language engineering)* (vol. 6) in Endō Yoshimoto et al. (Eds.) *Kotoba no kagaku (Science of language)*. Tokyo: Nakayama Shoten, 1958.

Nippon nenkan (Japan statistical yearbook). Tokyo: Statistical Bureau, 1993/94.

Nomoto Kikuo. Future society and Kanji. See vol. 11 of Satō Kiyoji (Ed.).

Nomura Masa'aki. *Kanji no mirai (The future of Kanji)*. Tokyo: Tsukushima, 1988.

Numamoto Katsuaki. Writing the Japanese language. In Nagao Syōso (Ed.) *Nihongo gaku (The study of th Japanese language)*. Osaka: Izumi Shoten, 1992.

Oka Naoki, Mori Toshiaki, and Kakigi Shoji. Learning of reading Kanji and Kana moji in young children. *The Japanese Journal of Psychology*, 1979, *50*, 49–52.

Ozawa Atsuo and Nomura Yukimasu. The effects of discrimination and decoding process on the reading of Kanji and Kana script in young children. *Japanese Journal of Educational Psychology*, 1981, *29*, 199–206.

Saiga Hideo. *Kanji to asobu (Fun with Kanji)*. Tokyo: Mainichi Shinbunsha, 1978. The author has many interesting observations to recount about the uses and misuses of Kanji.

Saito Hirofumi. Use of graphemic and phonemic encoding in reading Kanji and Kana. *The Japanese Journal of Psychology*, 1981, *52*, 266–273.

Saito Hisako, Mizuyama Shingo, and Kamiya Ikuji. Learning disability. *Psychology and Neurology of Children*, 1974, *4*, 177–185.

Sakai Yoshio. *Nihonji no hakkutsu (Excavation of Japanese graphs)*. Tokyo: Yamanaka Geiki, 1967.

Satō Kiyoji (Ed.). *Kanji kōza (Lectures on Kanji)*. Tokyo: Meiji Shoten, 1988–1989. In 12 edited volumes, this work covers many aspects of Kanji, such as *What is Kanji?* (vol. 1), *Kanji and Kana* (vol. 4), *Modern living and Kanji* (vol. 10), *Kanji and problems of the national language* (vol. 11), and *Kanji education* (vol. 12).

Satō Yasumasa. Character form and printing, in *Kotoba no kōgaku (Language engineering)* (vol. 6) of Endō Yoshimoto et al. (Eds.) *Kotoba no kagaku (Science of language)*. Tokyo: Nakayama Shoten, 1958.

Sengoku Tamotsu, Kawagae Haruhito, and Satō Gunei. *Nihon no chūgakusei (Japan's middle school students)*. Tokyo: NHK Books, 1987/1988.

Shuppan nenkan (Publication yearbook). In two volumes. Tokyo: Shuppan Nyūshu Sha, 1994.

Steinberg, Danny D. and Oka Naoki. Learning to read Kanji is easier than learning individual Kana. *The Japanese Journal of Psychology*, 1978, *49*, 15–21.

Steinberg, Danny D. and Tanaka Miho. *Nisai kara dōwa ga yomeru (A child can read stories from age two)*. Tokyo: Goma Books, 1989. It explains a whole-word/phrase/sentence method for teaching toddlers to read Kanji and Kana.

SweetJAM Manual: Macintosh family Japanese output/input front-end processor. Tokyo: A & A Co., 1992.

Tajima Kazuo. Computer and Kanji. In Satō Kiyoji (Ed.) *Lectures on Kanji (Kanji Kōza), vol. 11, Kanji and the problems of the national language*. Tokyo: Meiji Shoten, 1989.

Takebe Yoshiaki. *Nihongo no hyōki (Writing the Japanese language)*. Tokyo: Kadokawa Shoten, 1979.

Takebe Yoshiaki. *Moji hyōki to nihongo kyōiku (Writing and Japanese language education)*. Tokyo: Heibonsha, 1991.

Waseda University Language Education Research Center. *Chūgokugo to taiōsuru kango (Sino-Japanese words vis-a-vis Chinese words)*. Tokyo: Bunkacho 1978.

Yoshida A., Matsuda Y. and Shimura M. *A study on instruction of Chinese characters*. Tokyo University Education Department Report 14, 1975.

Postface

Having written much on a wide range of topics, I will be brief in this postface, taking just a page to drive home the core message of the book.

Chinese, Koreans, and Japanese share logographic Chinese characters, which differ in some ways from phonetic scripts, i.e., alphabets and syllabaries. Each logographic character represents primarily the meaning of a morpheme, and secondarily the syllable of the morpheme. By contrast, a letter of a phonetic script represents directly a speech sound, and through a sequence of sounds, the meaning of a morpheme.

Chinese characters have obvious disadvantages, such as their large number, complex shapes, inconvenience in typing and dictionary use. Yet, characters have been continuously used for a few thousand years by a huge number of Chinese, Korean, and Japanese peoples. Why? For the Chinese, characters transcend the speech differences among "dialects," and they suit writing the Chinese monosyllabic morphemes, which do not inflect. For the Koreans and the Japanese, characters can represent unambiguously their Sino-Korean and Sino-Japanese words, which make up more than half the vocabularies of their languages. Through characters, these three peoples can access a vast amount of written material accumulated over thousands of years, and can communicate, to some degree, with speakers of the two other languages. Characters bind people across space, time, and language.

Chinese characters are useful to the Koreans and the Japanese only if they are supplemented by phonetic scripts. When streamlined, they are not very difficult to learn and to use. Characters are suited to writing content words, but not the Korean and Japanese grammatical morphemes, which either have little meaning or change form in different contexts. In the mid-15th century the Koreans created Han'gŭl, a unique and efficient alphabetic syllabary. It is used not only for the Korean grammatical morphemes but also for many content words, native or Sino-Korean. In the 9th century the Japanese created Kana out of Chinese characters. Kana is a syllabary and has two forms: curvaceous Hiragana used for grammatical morphemes, and angular Katakana used for European loan words and onomatopoea. Chinese characters then are used for content words, Sino-Japanese or native. Different scripts used for different types of words help silent reading for comprehension.

The four "little dragons"—S. Korea, Hong Kong, Taiwan, and Singapore—as well as the economic superpower Japan put a premium on equipping their citizens with functional literacy. Their literate human resources are their best assets, as their citizens live in densely populated lands with few natural resources. Obviously, their writing systems, described as "complex" are no impediment to the achievement of mass literacy. What about China? Its economy is growing at a breakneck pace, and its illiteracy rate has been decreasing over the past few decades, if slowly. Watch out, the big dragon is breathing fire!

The 21st century may well belong to the East Asians, who value education and hard work.

Glossary

This glossary includes most of the technical and semi-technical terms appearing in this book. In order to define these terms concisely I have used other technical or semi-technical terms (enclosed in quotation marks), which are themselves items of the glossary.

For concise information on Chinese dynasties and republics, Korean kingdoms and republics, and Japanese eras, see Tables Part I-1, Part II-1, and Part III-1 respectively.

alphabet   A writing system in which one letter, in principle, represents one "phoneme," in the way that the letters of *d, o, t* represent the three phonemes in *dot*. There are a variety of alphabets, such as "Roman alphabet" and "Greek alphabet."

Altaic language family   A family that includes languages spoken in central Asia (e.g., Mongolia) to far west to Turkey. Its language have complex word formation and polysyllabic words. Some linguists include Korean and Japanese in this family.

alveolar   In articulating alveolar "consonants" such as /t/ and /d/ the tongue tip touches the alveolar ridge of the mouth above the front teeth.

aspiration   A puff of breath is produced in articulating an aspirated speech sound, such as /p/ in *pit* but not in *spit*.

Ateji (assigned Kanji)   "Kanji" assigned to Japanese native words, keeping the sound of the Kanji but ignoring their meanings, as in *sewa* ('world, talk' for 'care').

bilabial   In articulating bilabial "consonants" such as /b/ and /m/ the two lips are brought together.

Book of Changes (Yijing, I Ching)   A diviner's handbook of ancient origin. It supplied many concepts and terms to Chinese philosophical and cosmological thought for a few thousand years.

bound morpheme   See "morpheme."

bronze script (jinwen)   "Chinese characters" were cast on ceremonial bronze vessels in China over 3000 years ago. Early clan-name bronze characters were highly "pictographic," while later bronze characters used in text were less so.

calligraphy in East Asia   Traditionally "Chinese characters" (and also "Kana" and "Han'gŭl") are written on rice paper using a brush dipped in black ink. Calligraphy is an ancient and venerated art, and is practised not only by artists but also by any literate person.

Cantonese   The major Yue dialect spoken in southeastern China, around Guangzhou (Canton) as well as in Hong Kong and North America. Unlike "Mandarin," it retains the final "consonants" *-k, -t, -p,* and *-m,* and has 9 tones.

Chinese characters   Chinese characters, called "Hanzi" in Chinese, are "logographs," each of which represents a "morpheme" and its "(tone) syllable. There are as many as 50,000 characters in a large dictionary, whose shapes have to be complex for mutual discrimination. About 3,500 common characters are sufficient for "functional literacy," as two or more of them can be combined in countless ways to form compound words. Chinese characters originated in China several thousand years ago and are still used, with some modification and simplification, not only by the Chinese but also by the Japanese ("Kanji") and the Koreans ("Hancha").

Chinese language   The Chinese language is spoken by over 1 billion Chinese speakers not only in mainland China but also in Taiwan, Hong Kong, and other parts of the world. It has seven major dialects that can be mutually unintelligible (e.g., "Mandarin" and "Cantonese"). The most widely spoken dialect is standard Chinese, known as "Putonghua," "Mandarin", or "*guoyu*." A Chinese "morpheme" is spoken in one syllable with a tone, and does not inflect. Each morpheme is written in one "Chinese character."

Chinese names   A Chinese name typically consists of three "Chinese characters," the first one for the family name and the next two for the given name. About 400 different family names, including common Wang (Wong in Cantonese), Zhang, and Li.

Chosŏncha   The letters of Chosŏn or Korea. The term North Koreans use for the Korean phonetic script, "Han'gŭl."

civil service examination (keju)   In imperial China, for 1300 years, bureaucrats were recruited through civil service examinations that tested mainly written knowledge of the "Confucian classics." The examination system developed into a multi-level affair, ending with a palace exam. The preparation for the exam was long and arduous, but successful candidates were amply rewarded. The system was copied by the Koreans for 1000 years.

classifier   A word that indicates the type of object counted. It comes between a numeral and an object counted, as in *shi-BEI jiu* ('ten-CUP wine') in Chinese. Classifiers are used also in Korean and Japanese.

clerical script (lishu)   During the Qin dynasty the simple and stylized clerical script was used by official clerks. Its modified form became the official form of writing during the Han dynasty. It is the watershed that divides the archaic, mainly "pictographic" characters from the modern, stylized ones.

Confucianism   Ethical–social–political philosophy based on Confucius's teachings. It preached cultivating moral virtues (e.g., benevolence, filial piety, loyalty) in individuals and maintaining a stable society by stressing harmonious, if hierarchical, human relations. People attain this ideal state by studying the "Confucian classics" and observing Confucian rites. It was often embraced as the state ideology in imperial China. See also "Neo-Confucianism."

Confucian classics   The Confucian classics—Five Classics and Four Books—and the voluminous commentaries on them were studied by generations of candidates for the "civil service examinations." The Five Classics include *Book of Poetry, Book of Documents, "Book of Changes," Spring and Autumn Annals,* and *Record of Rites,* which "Confucius" is said to have edited, taught, or commented on. The Four Books include *Great Learning, Analects, Mencius,* and *Doctrine of Mean,* which were added in the 11th century AD.

Confucius   Confucius or Kong Fuzi (551–479 BC) was born in Qufu, Shandong Province. He held minor official positions, but mostly was shunned by various principalities. He devoted his time to educating his disciples, and his teachings are found in "Confucianism" and "Confucian classics."

consonants   Speech sounds such as /p/, /g/, and /s/ that are produced by obstructing the air flow through the throat and mouth; contrast to "vowels."

content words   Nouns, verbs, adjectives, and some adverbs that carry meanings. They form an open class in that their number is large and unspecifiable. They contrast to "grammatical morphemes."

Correct sounds (Chŏng'ŭm) See "Hunmin Chŏng'ŭm" and "Han'gŭl." North Koreans use this term or "Chosŏncha" for "Han'gŭl."

cuneiform A writing system developed in antiquity in Sumeria. A scribe used a blunt instrument that could simply be pressed on a clay tablet, producing wedge-shaped impressions.

cursive script (caoshu) This script style was developed as a shorthand version of the "clerical script" and the "standard script." Because of the drastic simplifications and distortions, cursive "Chinese characters" are not easy for untrained readers to decipher.

Daoism A Chinese philosophy of ancient origin that preaches simplicity, spontaneity, tranquility, and above all, non-action contrary to nature. Daoist practitioners of the occult searched for immortality through divination and magic.

Dawenkou culture A neolithic culture that lasted between c. 4500 and 2300 BC in China. A few of its pottery signs are considered by some scholars as ancestors of "oracle bone" characters.

diphthong A sequence of two vowels pronounced as one continuous unit, as in *boy*.

distinctive feature Articulatory (or acoustic) features such as "aspiration" and "voicing" that are present in some "phonemes" and absent in others.

empty words Chinese "grammatical morphemes," such as *le*, which indicates different states of action, and *de*, which is added to a noun to make it function like an adjective. They contrast to "full words."

eye movements As one reads, the eyes jump to a target word, on which they fixate for about a quarter of a second to obtain information. About 90% of reading time is spent on fixations. A record of eye movements is used to compare reading efficiency between vertical and horizontal reading, between Chinese and English, and so on.

Fanqie (cut and join) The sound of one "Chinese character" is indicated by using the sounds of two other characters: 老 = 里 + 好 *laŏ* = *l(i)* + *(h)aŏ*.

Five Phases (wuxing) The ancient and influential Chinese doctrine of the Five Phases elaborates the "Yin–Yang" doctrine and at the same time adds the concept of rotation, i.e., that things succeed one another as the Five Phases take their turns: wood produces fire, fire earth, earth metal, metal water, and water wood.

frequency effect People learn, recognize, and remember frequently occurring words (e.g., *cat*) faster and better than infrequent words (e.g., *cam*). The effect is found with spoken or written words of any language.

full words Chinese words are traditionally classified into "empty words," and full words, which are comparable to "content words" in other languages.

function words In English and other related languages "grammatical morphemes" include a small number of frequent and short words, such as *the, of,* and *at,* which relate, substitute for, or modify "content words" in a sentence.

functional literacy The level of reading, writing, and computing ability required to function in an industrialized society. A person may need several years of schooling to achieve it.

Furigana (annotating Kana) Tiny "Kana" that accompany "Kanji" to indicate their sounds, "Katakana" for "On/Chinese readings" and "Hiragana" for "Kun/Japanese readings."

grammatical morphemes Words or "morphemes" whose main functions in a sentence are syntactic—e.g., to relate, modify, or substitute for "content words"—rather than semantic. They form a closed class in that their number is small and fixed.

Grammatical morphemes can be "function words" in English, "postpositions" in Japanese and Korean, and "empty words" in Chinese.

Greek alphabet The Greeks added vowel letters to the "Phoenician script." The Greek alphabet is the ancestor of most modern alphabets used in the world.

guoyu (national language) "Mandarin" or standard Chinese is sometimes referred to as *guoyu* in the Republic of China or Taiwan.

haiku A form of Japanese verse consisting of three lines of 5, 7, and 5 "syllables" or "moras."

Han people The Chinese distinguish themselves from other ethnic minorities in China (e.g., Tibetans, Mongols) by calling themselves the sons and daughters of Han. The Han dynasty created a stable and unified empire over 2000 years ago. Some 92% of 1.2 billion in China itself as well as 54 millions more outside China are Han.

Hancha The Korean translation of "Hanzi," "Chinese characters." The Koreans began to use Hancha about 1700 years ago and introduced them to Japan a century later. Today Hancha are used sparingly in S. Korea for certain "Sino-Korean words." 1,800 Hancha are designated for education and common use. They are not used at all in N. Korea, where, however, 3,000 Hancha are taught in secondary and post-secondary schools. For the use of Hancha in the past, see "Idu."

Han'gŭl The word means 'great letters' and refers to the Korean "alphabet" that is used like a "syllabary." The script, created in the mid-15th century by King Sejong, is now the dominant script in both South and North Korea. Two or more of its 24 letters are packaged into a syllable block, which is the reading unit. Of the possible 12,768 blocks that can be generated, only about 2,000 are used in the language.

Han'gŭl chart By placing the 10 basic vowel letters in rows and the 14 basic consonant letters in columns, 140 CV syllable blocks can be generated. The basic chart can be expanded to include more letters, especially the final -Cs and -CCs. It is a handy teaching tool.

Hanzi The Chinese word for graphs of "Han people" or "Chinese character(s)."

Hepburn style A romanization system for Japanese, based on English for the consonants and on Italian for the vowels, in an attempt to represent the sounds of words as heard by English speakers. In 1886 this system was adopted in the third edition of American missionary James C. Hepburn's Japanese–English dictionary. It is the system preferred by international communities. See also "Rōmaji."

Hiragana See "Kana."

homophone Words, such as *rite* and *write*, that have the same sound but differ in meaning and spelling. The "Chinese language" has many homophones, which can be differentiated when written in "Chinese characters."

honorific A linguistic form used to show respect to an addressee or a person talked about.

Hun/Korean reading Hun is a "Sino-Korean word" for 'semantic gloss'. Example: 春 ('spring') is *pom* in native Korean and thus in Hun reading. The same Hancha is read *ch'un* in "Um/Chinese reading," which approximates its Chinese sound, *chun*. Today, only Um reading, but not Hun reading, is used. See also "Kun/Japanese reading" and "On/Chinese" reading.

Hunmin Chŏng'ŭm The 'Correct Sounds to Instruct People'. It is the phonetic script created by King Sejong of the Chosŏn kingdom in the mid-15th century, and also the name of the document that promulgated the script. The script is now called "Han'gŭl."

ideograph A writing system in which one graph represents one idea, which does not refer to any linguistic unit. The term is used, inappropriately, by some people to describe "Chinese characters" or "indicators."

idiom in Chinese Called *chengyu* in Chinese, an idiom typically consists of four "morphemes"–"syllables"–"Chinese characters," as in *ku jin gan lai* ('When bitterness exhausts, sweetness comes'). Chinese idioms are popular in Korean and Japanese as well.

Idu (clerical writing/reading) One old way to write the Korean language in Korean word order using only "Hancha." It included Korean "grammatical morphemes," for which Hancha were used either for their sounds or for their meanings. It was used to write documents until the late 19th century.

illiterate People of certain age—say, 15 or older—who cannot read everyday reading materials.

indicators (zhishi) One of the "six categories of characters." Indicators express relational concepts that cannot easily be drawn as pictures; e.g., the characters for 'above' and 'below' use a horizontal line with a short bar above or below it, respectively.

Indo-European language family A large group of historically related languages that includes Persian, many languages of northern India, and most languages of Europe such as English and Russian. Their words inflect for tense (e.g., *go, went*), number, etc.

Japanese language The language spoken by 125 million people, mainly in ,and some outside, Japan. It uses a small inventory of phonemes in simple "syllable" or "mora" structures (V, CV). Its basic sentence structure is "subject"–object–verb. In a sentence, nouns are followed by "postpositions," and a verb changes its ending for different sentence types (e.g., statement, question) as well as "speech levels" (polite and plain). The Japanese language is written in "Kanji," "Kana," and "Rōmaji."

Japanese names A typical Japanese name consists of four "Kanji," two for the family name and two for the given name, in that order, as in Satō Hanako. Satō is the most common family name. Kanji used in names can have unusual sounds.

Jōyō Kanji (Common Kanji) 1,945 "Kanji," in 2,187 "On/Chinese" and 1,900 "Kun/ Japanese" sounds, designated for common use and school teaching in 1981. Since 1990, 284 Kanji for personal names have been added to the list.

juku (private academy) In the Tokugawa period,*(shi) juku* educated the children of samurai and better-off commoners. Today, *juku* is a commercial cram school where Japanese children go after regular school for extra lessons in core school subjects or arts and sports.

Jukujikun (idiomatic Kun) Two or more "Kanji" are assigned to a native Japanese word, preserving their meanings but usually ignoring their sounds, as in *miyage* (souvenir), for which two Kanji 'land' and 'product' are assigned, ignoring their On/Chinese sounds, *tosan*.

Kana Kana signs ('borrowed letters') borrow the sounds but not the meanings of "Kanji." Kana is a "syllabary" in which one sign represents one syllable. Created in the 9th century by simplifying certain "Kanji," it has 46 basic signs and 60 modified ones to represent about 110 different "syllables" or "moras" of the "Japanese language." Kana comes in two forms: curvaceous Hiragana used for "grammatical morphemes," and angular Katakana used for European loan words and onomatopoea.

Kangxi Dictionary In the early 18th century, under the Qing emperor Kangxi, scholars classified 47,035 "Chinese characters" using 214 "radicals," and defined them.

Kanji The Japanese word for "Hanzi" or "Chinese characters," which began to be used in the 4th or 5th century AD. A few hundred Kanji have been simplified, sometimes differently from the characters used in China. Some Kanji were created in Japan. Unlike characters used in China and Korea, each Kanji typically has at least two readings, "On/Chinese" and "Kun/Japanese." Kanji are used for "content words," mostly "Sino-Japanese but some native. See also "Jōyō Kanji."

Korean language The language spoken by 67 million Koreans, mainly in N. and S. Korea but also by some of 5 million ethnic Koreans in nations such as China, United States, and Japan. It uses about 30 phonemes in five syllable structures (V, CV, VC, CVC, CVCC). Its basic word order is "subject"–object–verb. In a sentence, nouns are followed by "postpositions" and a verb changes its ending for different sentence types (e.g., statement, question) and "speech levels" (polite and plain).

Korean names A name typically consists of three "Hancha," the first one for the family name and the next two for the given name. About 270 different surnames are commonly used, but the most common Kim is possessed by one-fifth of Koreans. Native words are now fashionable for children's given names.

Kugyŏl A method once used by Koreans to ease oral reading and understanding of Chinese texts. It involved inserting native "grammatical morphemes" into Chinese text, typically between clauses. The "Hancha" for frequent grammatical morphemes were eventually simplified.

Kun/Japanese reading Typically each "Kanji" has two readings, Kun and On. For example, the Japanese native word for 'mountain' is *yama*, so the Kanji for it is read as *yama* in a Kun/Japanese reading. The same Kanji in an On/Chinese reading is *san*, which approximates the character's Chinese sound *shan*. Each of Kun and On readings tends to have a few varieties.

Kundoku A Japanese reads a Chinese text by simultaneously punctuating, shifting word order, analyzing, and translating it into classical Japanese.

left hemisphere The left half of the cerebral cortex tends to control language functions, especially speech sounds and "syntax."

lexical decision To find out the effect of a word's familiarity, length, pronunciability, etc. on its recognition, experimenters give people a set of letter strings (e.g., *net*, *ent*, or *tne*) and ask them to decide whether each string is a word or not.

literacy See "functional literacy" and "illiterate."

literary language (wenyan) In China the literary language was used for over 2000 years to write the classical literature and official documents up to the early 20th century. It is terse and elliptic, by using mostly one morpheme words and by dispensing with "empty words." Now it is largely replaced by "vernacular language."

logograph A logograph represents directly the meaning of a morpheme and indirectly its sound; it contrasts to a letter of an "alphabet" or a graph of a "syllabary" that directly represents the sound of a language and through a sequence of the sounds, a meaning. The meaning of a logograph tends to remain constant, even as its sound varies in different dialects and languages: the Arabic numeral 10 is *ten* in English, *Zehn* in German, *dix* in French; the "Chinese character" 十 is *shi* in Chinese, *jū* or *tō* in Japanese, and *sip* in Korean.

Mandarin The major Chinese dialect, the one with the greatest number of speakers, two-thirds of the "Han people." In imperial China it was the language spoken by central government officials, *mandarins*. It is the standard language not only in China, where it is called "Putonghua," but also in Taiwan, where it is called "guoyu."

manga (comics) Comics, called *manga*, are hugely popular in Japan. Of the large number of copies of books and magazines produced in Japan, nearly one-third are comics. Manga texts use "Kanji," "Kana," and "Rōmaji," like any non-comics text.

Man'yōgana In the 8th century anthology of Japanese poems, *Man'yōshū (Ten Thousand Leaves)*, "Kanji" were often used phonetically for their sounds, ignoring their meanings, thus starting the process of creating the phonetic script "Kana." About 970 different Kanji were used to represent about the 90 different Japanese syllables of the day.

McCune–Reischauer (M–R) romanization The standard system of romanizing the "Korean language" devised by G.M. McCune and E.O. Reischauer. It aims to help non-Koreans pronounce Korean, and does not reflect the way Korean is spelled in "Han'gŭl." The sound values of its letters are Italian vowels and English consonants in their most common and regular sounds. Because of the complexity of the Korean sounds, the M–R system uses a breve over two vowels—*ŏ* and *ŭ*—and also doubled letters (e.g., *kk*) for "tense consonants."

meaning composite It is one of the "six categories of characters." A meaning composite combines two or more simple characters for their meanings, as in 日 (sun) + 月 (moon) = 明 (bright).

mora A short beat, or the time to pronounce a short syllable, such as the vowel *e* or the CV *de*. Unlike a syllable, a mora (-*n*, -*ng*) need not contain a vowel. The mora is the unit of the Japanese "Kana."

morpheme The smallest meaningful unit of a language. A free morpheme can stand alone as a word, whereas a bound morpheme—"prefix" or "suffix"—exists only as a part of a word. The English word *un-kind-ly* consists of three morphemes: prefix + free morpheme + suffix. The linguistic unit represented by a "Chinese character" is a morpheme.

nasal To articulate the nasal consonants *n, m, -ng*, the nasal cavity is open while the air flow through the mouth is blocked.

Neo-Confucianism It developed in the Song dynasty in the 11th century and became the dominant ideology in the Ming and Qing dynasties in China, in the Chosŏn kingdom in Korea, and Tokugawa period in Japan. It retains the basic "Confucian" ethics, while incorporating some ideas from Buddhism and Daoism to develop a theory of the universe.

Okurigana (guiding Kana) Attached usually to a "Kanji" word with a "Kun/Japanese reading," Okurigana clarifies the Kanji's sound and its connection to the next phrase.

On/Chinese reading See "Kun/Japanese reading."

oracle-bone script (jiaguwen) "Chinese characters," many of them "pictographs," were inscribed on turtle shells and oxen bones used in divination 3400 years ago during the Shang/Yin dynasty. Of 4,500 different characters found, one-third have been deciphered.

Paspa script Also 'Phags-pa or hPhagspa. The Mongolian "alphabet" created in the 13th century by the Tibetan monk hPhagspa as a variation on the Tibetan alphabet. Some scholars hypothesized that Paspa served as a model for the Korean "Han'gŭl."

Phoenician script This ancient script used a handful of simple linear symbols to represent the consonants of a Semitic language. It begat the "Greek alphabet."

phoneme In a given language similar speech sounds are regarded as belonging to the same phoneme as long as they do not cause changes in word meaning. The number of phonemes varies across languages but is usually around 30. Some phonemes are "consonants," and some are "vowels." A phoneme is conventionally written between slashes, as in /p/. It is the unit of an alphabet.

phonetic component See "semantic–phonetic composite."

phonetic loan One "Chinese character" may be used for another one with a different meaning, if the two share the same or similar sound. Example: the "pictograph" for 'scorpion' is used for the unpicturable character for 'ten thousand', as the two share the sound *wan*.

phonics A method of teaching reading that teaches children letter–sound relations so that they can sound out any printed words, be they familiar, unfamiliar, or nonsense. The method is possible with a phonetic script but not with "logographic" "Chinese characters."

pictograph A written symbol is a drawing of the object it represents. Many "Chinese characters" began as pictographs. Some modern, stylized characters betray their pictographic origins, as 山 shows the three peaks of a mountain.

Pinyin An official romanization system for "Putonghua" or the standard "Chinese language." It uses the 26 letters of the English alphabet plus *u*. It was adopted in the People's Republic of China in 1979, and is used in teaching the sounds of "logographic" "Chinese characters."

postposition In some languages, a postposition follows each noun in a sentence to indicate its "syntactic" role. The postpositions—*ga* and *o* in Japanese, and *ka* and *ŭl* in Korean—follow the "subject" and the object.

predicate A linguistic item such as a verb that in a sentence follows a "subject," a noun, and says something about it. In *Cats / eat cheese*, the first part is the subject and the second the predicate.

prefix A bound "morpheme" that is attached to the beginning of a word to modify its meaning. Example: *un-* in *unkind*.

pronunciation latency In a word-recognition experiment, a "subject" views a word flashed on a screen, and starts pronouncing it as quickly as possible. The latency is the time between the presentation and the start of pronunciation. The latency is shorter for words in phonetic scripts than for those in logographs.

Putonghua (common speech) The standard "Chinese language" in the People's Republic of China. It is based on the northern dialect or "Mandarin" but incorporates some elements from other dialects. It is promoted by the government through the school system and the mass media.

radical A section head or classifier of characters based on their shapes. There were 540 radicals in the AD 121 work on characters, "Shuowen Jiezi," 214 in the 18th century "Kangxi Dictionary," and are around 200 in the simplified characters used today. A radical often, but not always, matches a "semantic component."

Roman alphabet An alphabet derived from the Latin alphabet, which in turn was derived from the "Greek alphabet." Most contemporary alphabets used in Europe, including English and Spanish, are Roman alphabets. Chinese, Korean, and Japanese can be written in the Roman alphabet, usually for the benefit of readers of this script. See "Hepburn style," "McCune–Reischauer," "Pinyin," and "Rōmaji."

Rōmaji The Japanese word for "Roman letters." For Japanese readers, Rōmaji tend to be used in ads, magazine titles, and certain European words, but not in writing an entire text. Their main use is in writing the Japanese language for foreigners.

rōnin (floating people) In early Japan, *rōnin* were peasants who left their land to work elsewhere. In feudal Japan *rōnin* were masterless samurai or warriors. Today, they are high-school graduates whose sole occupation is preparing for university entrance exams after failing them at the first, second... attempts. S. Korea also has such students, who are called *jaesuseng* (re-learning students).

semantic component See "semantic–phonetic composite."

semantic–phonetic composite One of the "six categories of characters." Between 80 and 90% of modern "Chinese characters" belong to this category. A composite consists of a phonetic component, which indicates, if unreliably, the tone syllable of the composite, and a semantic component, which cues, broadly, the semantic field to which the composite belongs.

semi-cursive script (xingshu) It developed alongside the "standard script" for hand-writing. Its graceful characters do not deviate too much from those of the regular script and are legible.

Shuowen Jiezi *'Explanations of Simple Characters and Analysis of Composite Characters'*. It is the work of the lexicographer Xu Shen, who in AD 121, classified 9,353 "small-seal" characters into "six categories of characters."

sijo A form of Korean verse consisting of three lines, each having 4 feet, and each foot containing 3 to 5 syllables.

Sino-Japanese words Thousands of Chinese words borrowed by Japanese over the centuries. Sino-Japanese words include the hundreds of words coined by Japanese on a Chinese model to represent modern, Western concepts. Such words have been often borrowed by the Chinese and the Koreans. Sino-Japanese words tend to be learned words, and are normally written in "Kanji."

Sino-Korean words In their early history, Koreans borrowed thousands of words—mostly for learned concepts—from Chinese, until such words formed the majority of their vocabulary. Now there is a movement to replace some Sino-Korean words with native words, and to write many Sino-Korean words in "Han'gŭl" instead of "Hancha."

Sino-Tibetan language family All the historical stages and dialectal variations of Chinese belong to the Sinitic branch of this family. Morphemes in many Sino-Tibetan languages, including Chinese, are monosyllabic and tonal.

six categories of characters "Chinese characters" are not simply a collection of unrelated arbitrary symbols, but are classifiable into six categories, based on their uses and structures. The six are: "pictographs," "indicators," "meaning composites," mutually defining (insignificant), "phonetic loans," and "semantic–phonetic composites." See also "Shuowen Jiezi."

small-seal script (xiaozhuan) The first emperor of the Qin dynasty (221–206 BC) had his minister standardize as small-seal characters the varied shapes of characters that were in use in different principalities during the Warring States. The script represents the last stage of archaic Chinese writing. It is used today only on seals.

sŏdang (reading hall) In the Chosŏn kingdoms of Korea, informal, private schools, called sŏdang, taught basic Chinese characters to young children.

speech levels In languages such as Korean and Japanese, speech changes its levels, depending on the social relations between a speaker, a listener, and a person talked about. The changes are most pronounced in verb endings. A speaker tends to use polite speech to a superior and plain one to an equal or inferior.

standard script (kaishu) This script style of "Chinese characters" began in the latter part of the Han dynasty and became dominant with the advent of printing technology in the late Tang and early Song dynaties. It is the one prevalent today.

stop consonant Speech sounds such as /p/ and /d/ are produced by closing the vocal tract completely, allowing air pressure to build up behind the closure, which is then abruptly opened.

strokes Strokes are dots, vertical, diagonal, and horizontal lines that are assembled to form a structured written symbol. A stroke by itself neither codes a sound nor represents a meaning. The number of strokes is a conventional index of the complexity of "Chinese characters": the simplest characters has one stroke, while the most complex one in a large dictionary has 64 strokes.

subject See "predicate."

subject In a psychological experiment a person who performs a task as instructed by an experimenter.

suffix A bound "morpheme" attached to the end of a word to modify the word's "syntactic" status and meaning, as in -*al* in *national*. In the "Chinese language," a suffix such as -*zi* is attached to some morphemes to indicate that they are names of common objects, as in *maozi* ('hat').

syllabary A writing system, such as "Kana," in which one graph represents one "syllable."

syllable Loosely, one syllable contains one and only one "vowel," as do CV ("consonant–vowel") *go*, CVC *dot*, and CCVCC *blend*. Languages differ greatly in the number and types of syllables they use.

syntax In each language a set of syntactic rules specifies how and in what order "content words" and "grammatical morphemes" are put together in a sentence.

Temporary Kanji (Tōyō Kanji) 1,850 "Kanji," in 3,122 sounds, designated in 1946 for daily use and education in Japan. The list was called temporary because it was considered to be a temporary measure until a "Roman alphabet" replaced all other scripts. Instead, it was replaced later by "Jōyō Kanji."

tense consonants The five Korean tense "consonants"—*pp, tt, ss, tch,* and *kk*—are produced with great muscle tension, by tightening up the throat.

terakoya (temple, child, facilities) Private community schools that taught, often in temples, rudimentary literacy and practical skills to children of commoners during the Tokugawa period.

Thousand Character Essay The essay was composed by a scholar in the 5th or 6th century AD on topics such as nature and morality, ingeniously using one thousand "Chinese characters" supplied to him, never repeating any. It was a popular primer for teaching characters in China, Korea, and Japan in traditional education.

tones Pitch variations for distinguishing words having the same sound pattern. In "Mandarin" Chinese *mai* with a fall–rise tone means 'buy', while the same syllable with a falling tone means 'sell'. Mandarin uses four tones, while "Cantonese" uses nine.

tone syllable A Chinese syllable including its tone. Several "morphemes" can share the same tone syllable, creating "homophones."

Um/Chinese reading See "Hun/Korean reading."

vernacular language (baihua) In Chinese the vernacular style of writing reflects contemporary everyday speech. It contains many two-morpheme words and "empty words," reducing the chance of being misunderstood. Since the early 20th century it has largely replaced classic "literary language."

whole-word method A method of teaching reading that relates a whole, unanalyzed word to its sound and meaning. Contrasted to "phonics."

voiced/voiceless The vocal folds vibrate in producing voiced /b/ and /d/ but not voiceless /p/ and /t/.

vowels Speech sounds produced by letting the air flow through the oral cavity without interruption. Different vowels, such as /a/ and /o/, are produced by changing the shapes of the oral cavities.

Wade–Giles system A romanization system for Chinese developed by Sir Thomas F. Wade in 1867 and modified by Herbert A. Giles in 1912. It was intended for international use, and was based largely on English. It has been supplanted by "Pinyin" in China but not in Taiwan and some library systems in the West.

Yin–Yang According to this ancient and influential Chinese worldview, in all natural phenomena and human affairs, the two forces of Yin and Yang complement each other, as a male does a female, or grow one out of the other, as day does out of night and vice versa.

Zhuyinfuhao The National/"Mandarin" Phonetic Symbols now used in Taiwan to annotate the sounds of "Chinese characters." There are 37 simply shaped symbols, each representing either the initial or the final of the Chinese "syllables."

Subject Index

Author Index

In the STUDIES IN WRITTEN LANGUAGE AND LITERACY series the following titles have been published thus far:

1. VERHOEVEN, Ludo (ed.): Functional Literacy. Theoretical issues and educational implications. 1993.

2. KAPITZKE, Cushla: Literacy and Religion. The textual politics and practice of Seventh-day Adventism. 1995.

3. TAYLOR, Insup and M. Martin Taylor: Writing and literacy in Chinese, Korean and Japanese. 1995.